Diaspora Language Contact

Language Contact and Bilingualism

Editor
Yaron Matras

Volume 17

Diaspora Language Contact

The Speech of Croatian Speakers Abroad

Edited by Jim Hlavac and Diana Stolac
With a foreword by Sarah Thomason

DE GRUYTER
MOUTON

ISBN 978-1-5015-2142-3
e-ISBN (PDF) 978-1-5015-0391-7
e-ISBN (EPUB) 978-1-5015-0381-8
ISSN 2190-698X

Library of Congress Control Number: 2021932205

Bibliographic information published by the Deutsche Nationalbibliothek
The Deutsche Nationalbibliothek lists this publication in the Deutsche Nationalbibliografie;
detailed bibliographic data are available on the Internet at http://dnb.dnb.de.

© 2023 Walter de Gruyter Inc., Boston/Berlin
This volume is text- and page-identical with the hardback published in 2021.
Cover image: Anette L innea Rasmus/Fotolia
Typesetting: Integra Software Services Pvt. Ltd.
Printing and binding: CPI books GmbH, Leck

www.degruyter.com

Foreword for *Diaspora Language Contact: The Speech of Croatian Speakers Abroad*

Books and articles about language contact have been pouring from the presses in great numbers for several decades now, which makes it hard for yet another book on the subject to stand out. This book, given its specialized focus, might seem at first glance to fall into the yet-another-book category. It does not. Its appeal to an audience of Slavic linguists is obvious, but it will also appeal to a much broader audience, because it addresses core issues in language contact research in novel and particularly effective ways. First, the editors provided the authors of the ten case studies – which focus on diasporic Croatian communities in nine countries – with detailed guidelines for their chapters, thus ensuring parallel organization and therefore ease of comparability across all ten of those chapters. Second, following an introduction and three other stage-setting chapters, chapter 5, co-written by authors of the case studies, provides an overview of the ten communities and their sociolinguistic settings. This chapter highlights the similarities and differences among the ten contact situations. Third, chapter 2, written by the first editor, discusses theoretical approaches to the study of language contact and situates the Croatian diaspora within the research area; the authors of the case studies have generally followed his lead, adopting his terminology and framing their analyses in ways that work well with his approach.

The result of these three editorial choices is a book which, while encompassing considerable diversity, forms a coherent whole. Readers will learn a great deal from any one chapter, and they will also be able to follow particular sociolinguistic and linguistic features through the ten case studies. The fact that the case studies fit together makes the book especially valuable. All of them contain detailed sociolinguistic information about the community as well as spoken data elicited by various means from community members. Several topics appear in most or all of the case studies. Among them are the analysis of socioeconomic dominance, language shift, and other sociolinguistic factors, code-switching, lexical transference (a term preferred by these authors to 'borrowing' and 'interference'), loan translations, word order features, syntactic calques, case morphology (a frequent partial casualty in these contact situations), gender, and discourse markers. Readers interested in attrition, or degree of nativization of loanwords, or the maintenance (or not) of immigrant languages, or any number of other topics that recur in the book will find rich material for study here.

Reading these chapters gave me a strong feeling of nostalgia, together with regret for a long-ago missed opportunity. In 1965–66 I spent a year in the old Yugoslavia doing library research and fieldwork for a dissertation project on word formation in dialects of the language then known as Serbo-Croatian (or Croato-Serbian), primarily Croatian, Serbian, and Montenegrin dialects. I had no particular interest in language contact back then, and it wasn't until I read this book that I fully realized how much I had overlooked. For instance, I knew nothing about code-switching at the time; and yet it arose as an issue in my research, because to collect dialect features in villages I had to try to avoid having consultants codeswitch to the standard dialect I spoke. And I remember being fascinated by Rešetar's 1911 monograph on Molise Croatian (*Die serbokroatischen Kolonien Süditaliens*), but though my dissertation notes the loss of the neuter gender in Molise Croatian noun declension, I don't think I even mentioned the probable influence of Italian on that development. Now that it's many decades too late, I wish I had been able to predict my future passion for contact phenomena; it would have improved the dissertation.

Thanks to publications like this book and other work on language contact, language contact is on so many linguists' agendas that young scholars are of course much less likely nowadays to overlook opportunities to study it. The book makes a major contribution to the field: I am confident that it will both educate readers and inspire further research in the areas it covers, especially (but not only) language contacts in diasporic communities. I recommend it wholeheartedly to everyone with an interest in language contact.

Sarah Thomason
University of Michigan, April 2020

Acknowledgements

We are grateful to Assoc. Prof. Peter Houtzagers (University of Groningen) for kindly permitting the re-production of Map 1 and Map 2 relating to the settlement areas of speakers of Burgenland Croatian discussed in Chapter 3.

We are also grateful to Dr Máté Kitanics (University of Pécs) for kindly permitting the re-production of Map 4 relating to the settlement areas of Croatian-speakers across southern Hungary also discussed in Chapter 3.

We would like to thank Dr Angela Tiziana Tarantini (Monash University) for providing detailed and illuminating explanation of aspects of Italian morphosyntax relevant to examples of data presented in Chapter 15.

Prof. Victor Friedman would like to thank the staff and colleagues at the Department of Languages and Linguistics and its Centre for Research on Language Diversity (CRLD) of La Trobe University for their support while he was either a visitor or on the faculty, during which time the research and drafting of chapter 4 was completed.

We extend our great appreciation and thanks to the reviewers of the chapters contained in this volume and we are grateful for their observations and suggestions offered.

Lastly, we would like to thank all the Croatian-speakers who allowed their speech to be recorded, who completed sociolinguistic questionnaires and who otherwise have provided rich descriptions of their lives as bi- or multi-linguals and rich descriptions of Croatian as a diaspora language.

Contents

Foreword for *Diaspora Language Contact: The Speech of Croatian Speakers Abroad* —— V

Acknowledgements —— VII

Abbreviations, acronyms and contractions —— XIII

Jim Hlavac and Diana Stolac
Introduction —— 1

Background and theoretical concepts

Jim Hlavac
Research on languages in contact: Locating Croatian as a diaspora language within the field of contact linguistics —— 29

Aleksandra Ščukanec, Walter Breu and Dora Vuk
Diachronic perspectives on change in spoken Croatian amongst Croatian indigenous minorities in Austria, Italy and Hungary —— 101

Victor A. Friedman
Diaspora vs sprachbund: Shift, drift, and convergence —— 187

Croatian in Western Europe

Germany

Marijana Kresić Vukosav and Lucija Šimičić
Some aspects of language contact among Croatian-speakers in Lower Saxony, Germany —— 217

Austria

Aleksandra Ščukanec
Post-WWII Croatian migrants in Austria and Croatian-German language contacts —— 251

Norway

Hanne Skaaden
Tu i tamo se gađam padežima – 'Here and there I struggle with my cases'.
Croatian migrant speakers in Norway and their use of the dative —— 285

Italy

Nada Županović Filipin, Jim Hlavac and Vesna Piasevoli
Features of the speech of Croatian-speakers in Italy —— 319

Vesna Piasevoli
The Croatian speech of first- and second-generation Croats in Trieste —— 361

Croatian in North America

USA

Dunja Jutronić
The Croatian language in the USA: Changes in Croatian syntax as a result of contact with English —— 405

Canada

Ivana Petrović
Features in the speech of Croatian-speakers in the greater Toronto area —— 447

Croatian in the southern hemisphere

Australia

Jim Hlavac and Diana Stolac
Features in the Croatian speech of three generations of Croatian-Australians —— 493

New Zealand

Hans-Peter Stoffel and Jim Hlavac
Croatian dialect speakers from Dalmatia and their linguistic contact with English and Māori in New Zealand —— 553

Argentina

Anita Skelin Horvat, Maša Musulin and Ana Gabrijela Blažević
Croatian in Argentina: Lexical transfers in the speech of bilingual Croatian-Spanish speakers —— 595

Conclusion

Jim Hlavac and Carol Myers-Scotton
Intra-clausal code-switching and possessive constructions in heritage varieties of Croatian: An MLF-based examination —— 627

Subject index —— 661

Author index —— 683

Abbreviations, acronyms and contractions

1	first person
2	second person
3	third person
α	alpha (significance level)
ACC	accusative case
ACT	active
ADJ	adjective
ADV	adverb(ial)
ANIM	animate
AOR	aorist
ARG.Cro	speech recorded of Croatian-speakers in Argentina
ART	article
ATTRIB	attributive
AUS.Cro	speech recorded of Croatian-speakers in Australia
AUT.Cro	speech recorded of Croatian-speakers in Austria
AUX	auxiliary
BGLD.Cro	speech recorded of Croatian-speakers in Burgenland (Austria)
CAN.Cro	speech recorded of Croatian-speakers in Canada
CL	clitic
COLL	collective or mass noun
COMP	complementizer
COND	conditional
CONJ	conjunction
COP	copula
Cro	Croatian
DAT	dative case
DEF	definite
DEM	demonstrative
DET	determiner
DIMIN	diminutive
DIR	direct
ED.PTC	editing particle
Eng.	English
F	feminine gender
FEM.1	feminine nouns of the first class (mostly ending in –*a*)
FEM.2	feminine nouns of the second class (ending in a consonant)
FNRJ	*Federativna Narodna Republika Jugoslavija* 'Federal People's Republic of Yugoslavia' (1945–1963)
FUT	future tense
GEN	genitive case
Gen.1	first-generation Croatian speakers (i.e. those born in the homeland)
Gen.1A	first-generation Croatian speakers who emigrated in late adolescence or as adults

Gen.1B	first-generation Croatian speakers who emigrated as children or before the onset of adolescence.
Gen.2	second-generation Croatian speakers, i.e. those born in the diaspora to the children of Gen.1 parents.
Gen.3	third-generation Croatian speakers born in the diaspora as the grandchildren of Gen.1 speakers
Gen.4	fourth-generation Croatian speakers born in the diaspora as the great-grandchildren of Gen.1 speakers (and as grandchildren of Gen.2 speakers, and as the children of Gen.3 speakers)
Ger.	German
GER.Cro	speech recorded of Croatian-speakers in Germany
HMLD.Cro	homeland Croatian, i.e. any speech variety (standard or non-standard) used in Croatia, or any variety (standard or non-standard) used in the speech of Croatian-speakers resident in Bosnia-Herzegovina, the province of Vojvodina in Serbia, or in the Bay of Cattaro area of Montenegro.
HUN.Cro	speech recorded of Croatian-speakers in Hungary
HUN-Bar.Cro	speech recorded of Croatian Štokavian-speaking Bošnjaks and Šokacs from Baranya (Hungary)
HUN-Pom.	Croatian speech recorded of Croatian Kajkavian-speakers from Pomurje (Hungary)
IMP	imperative
INANIM	inanimate
INDF	indefinite
INF	infinitive
INS	instrumental case
INT	interrogative
INTR	intransitive
IPRF	imperfect
IPFV	imperfective
Ital.	Italian
ITAL.Cro	speech recorded of Croatian-speakers in Italy
L_{maj}	majority language
L_{min}	minority language
L1	first language defined by dominance
LM	language maintenance
LOC	locative case
LS	language shift
M	masculine gender; statistical mean score
MOL.Cro	speech recorded of Croatian-speakers in Molise (Italy)
N	neuter gender
NDH	*Nezavisna Država Hrvatska* 'Independent State of Croatia' (1941–1945)
NEG	negation, negative
NOM	nominative case
Nor.	Norwegian
NOR.Cro	speech recorded of Croatian-speakers in Norway
NP	noun phrase
NUM	numeral

NZ.Cro	speech recorded of Croatian-speakers in New Zealand
NZ.Eng	New Zealand English
OBJ	object
OBL	oblique
p	p-value
PART	participle
PASS	passive
PRF	perfect
PFV	perfective
PL	plural
PLUR	*pluralia tantum*
POSS	possessive
PREP	preposition
PRS	present tense
PRON	pronoun
PST	past
PST.PTCP	past tense participle
PTC	polysemous particle (e.g., "da")
PTCP	participle
QP	question particle
REL	relative
REFL	reflexive (particle or pronoun)
Russ.	Russian
SBJ	subject
sd	standard deviation
SFRY	Socialist Federal Republic of Yugoslavia (1963–1991)
SG	singular
Span.	Spanish
SVO	subject, verb, object
TR	transitive
TRS.Cro	speech recorded of Croatian-speakers in Trieste, Italy
USA.Cro	speech recorded of Croatian-speakers in the USA
VOC	vocative case
VP	verb phrase
WWI	World War 1
WWII	World War 2

Jim Hlavac and Diana Stolac
Introduction

We commence this volume with some brief accounts from Croatian-speakers about themselves and about living abroad:

Voices from the Croatian diaspora

Applying to migrate and fulfilling the requirements of the destination country – Canada

> ... i treći puta su nas primili, dobili smo sve dokumente, **legal** dokumente, prošli smo kroz cijeli **procedure** da bi se došlo ovdje kao **landed immigrants** i tu smo došli ...

> '... and the third time we were accepted, we got all the documents, **legal** documents, we went through the whole **procedure** to come here as **landed immigrants** and we arrived here ...' (Female, first-generation speaker), (Data corpus: Ivana Petrović 2007–2013)

Having children and being pragmatic about one's circumstances – Argentina

> Već kad mi se rodila prva kćer, kao da sam ja rekla, **se acabó**, tu živim, to moram prihvatiti.

> 'Already when my first daughter was born, like I said, **se acabó** ('that's it, it's over'), I live here, I have to accept that.' (Female, first-generation speaker), (Data corpus: Anita Skelin Horvat 2016)

Living in a society that has feelings of ambivalence towards those from the eastern shores of the Adriatic – Italy

> Malo sam znala talijanski; moj svekar je govorio da sam kao jedna izgubljena ptica. Hrvatski mi je služio za posao. Zapravo, kad su moja djeca bila malena, onda nije bilo hrvatske škole, čak nije bilo poželjno ni čuti ni govoriti hrvatski na ulici ili u autobusu.

> 'I spoke very little Italian. My father in-law used to say that I was like a lost bird. I used Croatian for work. To tell you the truth, when my children were little there was no Croatian school. In fact, speaking Croatian in the street or on the bus was something frowned upon.' (Female, first-generation speaker), (Data corpus: Vesna Piasevoli 2016)

The joys of learning another language – Germany

> Taj – **Rumpelstilzchen**. To ne može ni jedan strani čovjek izgovoriti ... dobite jednu.. čvor u jeziku.

> 'That word – **Rumpelstiltskin**. No foreigner can pronounce that ... you get a.. your tongue gets tied.' (Female, first-generation speaker) (Data corpus: Marijana Kresić Vukosav & Lucija Šimičić 2016)

Jim Hlavac, Monash University
Diana Stolac, University of Rijeka

Dealing with the reality of a competitive labour market – Austria

> ... *što je još frustrirajuće kod tih ljudi jest činjenica devedesetipet posto njih je* **überqualifiziert**.

> '... what is even more frustrating for these people is the fact that ninety-five percent of them are **überqualifiziert** ('overqualified'). (Male, first-generation speaker) (Data corpus: Aleksandra Ščukanec 2016)

Promising to catch up with a time-poor friend – New Zealand

> *Pipica ja ću ti* **ringat lejta** *kad nisi* **bizi**, *adio!*

> 'Pipitsa, I'll **ring** you **later** when you aren't **busy**. Bye for now.' (Stoffel 2011: 415)

Growing up in a small town in Pennsylvania, getting married, moving out and then visiting mum and dad at their place – America

> *O, čekaj, prva* **dženeracija**, *posli pustiju kuću kad su ženjeni i žena je engleški, govori engleški. Doma onda dojedu na mat ili otac kuču, pustiju sve engleški vonka, kad dojedu nutra, brojiš po rvaski, govoriš po rvaski sa svojima. Onda kad ideš vonka vrata odma onda sve natrag engleški, pustiš rvaski doma.*

> 'Oh, wait, the first **generation**, after they leave home when they're married and the wife is English, they speak English. Then they go to their mother or father's house, they leave all English outside, as soon as they enter inside, you count in Croatian, speak Croatian with your family. Then when you go out the door, then immediately everything is back in English, you leave Croatian at home.' (Jutronić-Tihomirović 1985: 101)

These short episodes provided by seven people living in different countries across four continents probably relate to anyone who has migrated and may also be familiar to anyone who has family members or friends who have migrated. They tell of the red-tape and administrative obstacles in applying to immigrate to another country (and in getting settled in that country), momentous moments such as the birth of a child that 'decide one's fate', and of the unease of knowing that one's nationality and language may not always be well received in the country that one ends up in. They tell of the effort in having to learn and speak another language and of those memorable moments when one comes across an impossibly difficult word to pronounce. They show people's belief and investment in their own education, only to discover that their qualifications still do not match those required of the labour market that they so desperately want to be a part of. They also tell of the pressures of modern life, people's lack of time and of the oft-used phrase "I'll call you later". And they tell of being in one setting and speaking one language, and then moving to another setting and speaking another language.

They are short descriptions that recount administrative-procedural, personal, socio-political, linguistic, occupational, lifestyle-related and contextualised events in these speakers' lives. These are most likely well known and common to lots of migrants (and non-migrants). But there is something particular about these events, and that is that they all traverse multiple places, multiple ways of doing things, multiple societies, multiple languages, multiple ways of life or multiple speech communities. When interacting with others who share a similar background, it is no coincidence that people who are migrants or who are the products of migration recount things by often drawing on two (or more) languages. This happens in six of the seven accounts given above and the occurrence of words from another language in otherwise Croatian speech appears to be unremarkable to both speaker and listener. These words are shown above in bold and to a great extent these words relate to realia or the situation of their lives in the diaspora and are supplied by the societally dominant language: *legal dokumente*, *procedure* and *landed immigrants* from Canadian English, *se acabó* 'that's it, it's over' from Argentinian Spanish, *Rumpelstilzchen* 'Rumpelstiltskin' and *überqualifiziert* 'over-qualified' from German, *ringat* 'to ring', *lejta* 'later' and *bizi* 'busy' from New Zealand English, and *dženeracija* from USA English.

This is a book that does not really give a voice to Croatian-speaking immigrants and their descendants as such, although the many excerpts that are presented here taken from interviews with people living in the Croatian diaspora offer us an insight into many things about their lives, and not just the way they speak Croatian. Instead, this book gives a voice to their *speech*, their *vernacular*, their *communicative repertoires* and their *linguistic* (and *non-linguistic*) *behaviour* when interacting with others using their first or heritage language, Croatian. We have foregrounded events related by diaspora speakers about their lives at the beginning of this book to emphasise that in looking at people's speech, we do not lose sight of *speakers*, of *communicative networks*, of *speech communities* and of *speakers' consumption of texts* (*verbal, written* and *visual*) that are the pre-requisites for any examination of spoken language, how it is used and what form it takes.

This book also presents data from areas in three countries neighbouring Croatia that have long-standing communities of speakers that are, at least locally, considered autochthonous: Burgenland in eastern Austria (with smaller numbers of speakers in far-western Hungary and south-west Slovakia); Molise in south-central Italy; clusters of villages in south-west and southern Hungary. The data from these three situations in neighbouring countries informs us historically of the developments that can occur in the speech of Croatian-speakers living in communities dislocated from the homeland. The diachronic perspective that data from these situations provides foregrounds the focus of this book which is a presentation of the linguistic features, i.e. spoken language of the speech of Croatian-speakers residing in the following nine countries, listed here by continent: Austria, Germany,

Italy and Norway (Europe); Canada and the United States of America (North America); Australia and New Zealand (Oceania); and Argentina (South America). One chapter each is devoted to eight of the nine countries, with one country – Italy – represented by two chapters according to the areas of residence of speakers. All ten chapters provide synchronically-based descriptions of Croatian-speakers' speech preceded by a sociolinguistic outline that relates to Croatian-speakers as well as Croatian as a transposed or immigrant language in that country.

We aimed at the commencement of this multi-site investigation to look at Croatian-origin immigrants living abroad, to look at who (still) speaks Croatian, to look at where and with whom they speak it (via sociolinguistic data-gathering tools), to look at how they speak it (via recorded interviews that were transcribed and subjected to analysis mostly for lexical and structural features) and to examine and to describe the form of their language from a contact linguistics approach. We endeavoured to have as many countries represented as possible to enable a cross-national comparison of data from the various samples, and we are very pleased that this volume encompasses ten data samples from nine different countries across four continents. We also endeavoured to have speakers from different vintages of migration included in the data samples, as well as speakers belonging to different generations. All data samples feature speakers from two or more migration waves and speakers belonging to at least two different generational groups. As such, this volume encompasses a heterogeneous group of speakers and this, as we anticipated, has resulted in variation and diversity in the linguistic data presented here. There is only a relatively small number of studies on Croatian spoken in migrant and transposed settings and this volume enables contact linguists and those interested in language contact phenomena to gain an insight into the form and outcomes of language contact involving Croatian-speakers.

This volume looks at speakers of Croatian in immigrant settings referred to as the Croatian diaspora. The notion of *diaspora* is not new, nor is the activity that it refers to, i.e. 'people dispersing'. The movement of people and their linguistic repertoires is one of the main premises of language contact research and this volume focuses solely on groups of speakers residing outside Croatia or outside other adjoining countries in south-east Europe. Our aim is to look at the situation of Croatian emigrants and their descendants in not one country or continent, but at a cross-section of their countries of residence from North America (Canada and the USA) to South America (Argentina), and from Western Europe (Austria, Germany, Italy and Norway) to Oceania (Australia and New Zealand).

1 Croatian in language contact settings

Croatian is a small to mid-sized language. Ethnologue (2018) lists the total number of speakers as 6,670,820. Approximately 5 million of them are what we term 'homeland speakers'. These are speakers who speak Croatian typically as their first-acquired and dominant language, and who are resident in Croatia, Bosnia-Herzegovina, the province of Vojvodina in Serbia, or in the Bay of Cattaro area of Montenegro. The term 'homeland Croatian' employed in this book refers to any speech variety (standard or non-standard) used in Croatia, or any variety (standard or non-standard) used in the speech of Croatian-speakers resident in Bosnia-Herzegovina, the Serbian province of Vojvodina, or in the Bay of Cattaro area of Montenegro. Thus, speakers of homeland Croatian are residents of the above countries, province or region and, they are also autochthonous to them. They use Croatian typically as their primary and dominant language in most if not all interactions with fellow 'homeland speakers'. The term 'homeland Croatian' is broader than the term 'Croatian as used in Croatia' as speakers of Croatian, as has been shown, are domiciled in areas beyond the borders of modern-day Croatia. Further, Croatian-speaking immigrants in the diaspora originate not only from Croatia, but also from Bosnia-Herzegovina (west Herzegovina, central Bosnia, the Bosnian Posavina region in northern Bosnia, as well as areas in north-west Bosnia around the city of Banja Luka), Vojvodina (regions of Bačka and eastern Syrmia) in Serbia and the Bay of Cattaro in Montenegro. In all these areas Croatian has official status: it is the official language in Croatia; it is the co-official language in Bosnia-Herzegovina (along with Bosnian and Serbian); it is a recognised minority language in Serbia and Montenegro.

Looking at the development of Croatian historically, we see that it is a language that has been in long-standing contact with a number of other languages, many of them genealogically quite different. As such, Croatian is a contact language *par excellence* as it has had substantial contact with non Indo-European languages such as Hungarian and Turkish, with other language families within the larger Indo-European group of languages, namely Romance and Germanic, with smaller other ones such as Albanian and Greek, and with other Slavic languages as well. Remembering that the sociolinguistic situation is strongly co-determinant of linguistic outcomes, the socio-politically subordinate relationship that Croatian-speakers had to speakers of most of these other languages means that input from these languages into varieties of Croatian was often substantial and extensive.

In order of chronological contact, these contributing languages have been varieties of Romance, firstly Latin (since the seventh century), Finno-Ugric Hungarian (since the eleventh century), Ottoman Turkish (since the fifteenth century), Venetian Italian (since the fifteenth century), German (since the sixteenth century – including both Habsburg Austrian German and varieties of German such as Bavarian, Swabian, Alemannic, Alsatian, Franconian and Hessian spoken by German settlers in northern and eastern Croatia) and Standard Italian (from the late nineteenth century). Contact has occurred with further languages such as Istrian Italian, Romany, Czech, Slovak, Ukrainian, Ruthenian, Istro-Romanian and Arbanasi Albanian spoken by ethnic minorities within Croatia. The two latter languages, Romanian and Albanian are also languages that Croatian is in contact with via Croatian linguistic exclaves i.e. the Krashovani Croats in the Caraş-Severin and Timiş counties of Romanian Banat, and the Janjevo Croats living in Kosovo. There are no remaining Greek linguistic exclaves in Croatia, or Croatian ones in Greece, but lexical input from (Ancient) Greek has occurred, usually via Latin, German or Italian as intermediaries, and in some cases via Serbian in relation to some cultural-religious terms. French has had some lexical input too, usually via German or Italian as intermediary languages, but also in a direct way during the period of 1809 to 1814 when the 'Illyrian Provinces' were under Napoleonic Rule. Croatian-speakers have been co-habiting with Roms and Jews for centuries. However, due to the socio-economically subordinate status of the first group, and the relatively small population of the second group, their languages, namely Romany, Sephardic Judaeo-Spanish (Ladino) spoken in Dubrovnik and Sarajevo and Ashkenazi Yiddish spoken in northern and central Croatia, have had relatively little influence on Croatian.

Of course, contact has been intense with speakers of other South Slavic languages. In particular, varieties of Serbian spoken amongst Serbs in various areas of Croatia, Bosnia-Herzegovina and Vojvodina with whom Croats in those areas have co-habited for centuries have had an influence on local varieties of Croatian, while from the early twentieth century onwards, Belgrade-based Standard Serbian has also had an influence on Croatian. The same applies to ethnically Bosniak speakers of Bosnian with whom Croats living in various areas of Bosnia-Herzegovina have been co-habiting in for centuries, and with speakers of Montenegrin in the Bay of Cattaro area in Montenegro.

Standardisation of Croatian occurred in the mid-nineteenth century with the adoption of a Roman-script alphabet with diacritics marking certain graphemes as proposed by Ljudevit Gaj in 1830, and by the decision in favour of Štokavian as the basis of the standard ahead of Čakavian and Kajkavian, both of which were varieties that had substantial literary traditions until this time. The choice for Štokavian was made chiefly because this was the variety spoken by the single largest number of Croatians, but also because the native languages of other South Slavs – namely Serbs, Montenegrins and Bosniaks – were based also on Štokavian. Linguistic (and political) union with other South Slavs was a goal of the Illyrian Movement, a group of pan-Slavist intellectuals at the time based mainly in Croatian-speaking areas of the Habsburg Empire. One of the achievements of this movement was the

Bečki književni dogovor 'Vienna Literary Agreement' of 1850, an unofficial and non-binding declaration signed by eight philologists that recommended the use of some orthographic conventions to be applied across all languages, and for the level of mutual comprehensibility of varieties spoken by all groups to be increased through a process of (more or less) voluntary convergence. The agreement was supported by some but opposed by many others in Croatia (Moguš 1995).

The desire for greater commonality with others' linguistic and literary traditions was but one of the factors that lexicographers in the different 'philological schools' of the time (i.e. those in Zadar, Rijeka and Zagreb) kept in mind as Croatian went through the final stages of its codification and standardisation in the last decades of the nineteenth century (Vince 1990). By the end of that century, Standard Croatian was a code based on the Štokavian dialect with substantial input from both Čakavian and Kajkavian varieties. Most of the codified lexical, syntactic, morphological and phonetic features were common to or similar to those used by other groups of South Slavs, while a certain number were distinct (Lisac, Pranjković, Samardžija & Bičanić 2015). It was not until 1918 that almost all speakers of these languages lived together in a common state, and Croatian as a distinct standard pre-dated the creation of hypernyms such as 'Serbian-Croatian-Slovenian', the initial official language of the inter-war Kingdom of Serbs, Croats and Slovenes, or the terms 'Serbo-Croatian', 'Croato-Serbian' or 'Croatian or Serbian' as post-WWII terms used in the Federal People's Republic of Yugoslavia, known later as the Socialist Federal Republic of Yugoslavia (SFRY). By the mid-1950s, a policy that foresaw the union of Croatian with Serbian was in place, i.e. the 'one language with two variants' policy. It was a policy pursued not only for political purposes as a homogenising or nation-building exercise, but as a linguistic one that premised widespread mutual comprehensibility as a basis for the four codified standards. The strong version of the convergence position in post-WWII Yugoslavia until 1989 was that descriptions of the standard language in each of the four constituent Socialist Republics of Bosnia-Herzegovina, Croatia, Montenegro and Serbia were to be aligned with each other with the intention to maximise similarity and to reduce differences by classifying many of these as non-standard or regional.

Notwithstanding the policy of centralism and actively enforced linguistic convergence that had been pursued in the SFRY in the 1950s and 1960s, in 1967 a group representing almost all Croatian linguists of the time issued the 'Declaration on the Name and Status of the Croatian Literary Language' that advocated the reinstatement of 'Croatian' as a recognised and distinct standard language (as it had been in the immediate post-WWII years in the newly re-formed Yugoslavia). After the Declaration, in 1971, the designation given for the official language of the Socialist Republic of Croatia within SFRY was a rather cumbersome compromise: 'the

Croatian literary language, the standard form of the national language known as Croatian or Serbian'. As stated above, since 1990, the designation of the native language of Croatians in Croatia, Bosnia-Herzegovina and also as minorities in Montenegro and Serbia is 'Croatian'. A comprehensive description of the Croatian language itself, its standard and non-standard forms, and the designations within which Croatian-speakers have been encompassed goes beyond the bounds of this chapter (see Greenberg 2004; Brozović 2006; Langston & Peti-Stantić 2014). The common language project of 'Serbo-Croatian', 'Croato-Serbian' or 'Croatian or Serbian' did have two effects in terms of language contact that are relevant to this book's focus. First, there were fewer barriers for forms from these languages (Serbian in particular, less so Bosnian and Montenegrin) to enter Croatian and input was substantial. Second, forms from other languages (e.g. Russian, Bulgarian, French, Italian, Turkish, Arabic, Romany) that had entered Serbian, Bosnian and Montenegrin as 'intermediary languages' could sometimes then be more easily adopted in Croatian.

Contact with other Slavic languages has also been substantial: with Slovene to the immediate north-west; with Czech and Slovak via the Czech- and Slovak-speaking linguistic minorities in Croatia; and with Russian and again with Czech as source languages whose lexical stock was sometimes drawn on in the codification of Croatian. Last but not least, since the middle of the twentieth century, English is now the most conspicuous language that Croatian is in contact with. The adoption of English-origin lexical items is now widespread in many fields, contexts and thematic areas. We note that what can occur in English-speaking countries in the diaspora may occur later on in the homeland. In the early 1970s, the Croatian-American historian, George Jure Prpić identified "a new word" in American-Croatian speech, namely *lajkati* 'to like' (Prpić 1971: 226). Since the emergence of Facebook and other social media in the early 2000s, the same word *lajkati* has become a widely-used new word in the homeland too. More recently we observe the adoption of pragmatic forms (in their original form or via loan translation) and the influence of English structure (perhaps via translated texts) in word order, the frequency of gerunds and even in the feature marking of some NPs, e.g. *Zagreb film festival*.

2 The Croatian(-speaking) diaspora

This brings us to the remaining 1.67 million speakers that are not in the 'homeland', but in the diaspora. As a proportion of the total number of Croatian-speakers, those in the diaspora account for about 25% of speakers world-wide. The word *diaspora* is of Greek origin, meaning 'disperse'. In English the term gained currency in reference to Jews who lived outside an established or ancestral homeland. The defining characteristic of the term *diaspora* is that people who are otherwise geographically dislocated from one another have a shared form of identification that their origins lie in a common homeland in which they (currently) do not reside. In the case of the *Jewish diaspora*, acquisition of the languages of others with whom Jews lived usually occurred, while the continued use of group-specific languages such as Yiddish and that of Hebrew (for specific religious purposes) is shown to be variable (Fishman 2002; 2008). The term is one used by in-group members about themselves and/or out-group members who define others as belonging to a group whose origins lie outside their current country of residence. The term is used widely in sociolinguistics to refer to non-indigenous groups consisting of emigrants and their descendants (Mills 2005; Isurin 2011; Newlin-Łukowicz 2015). In the context of this book, diaspora is employed here as a hypernym referring to that collective group of Croatian-origin emigrants, and their descendants. More specifically, this book focuses on those emigrants and their descendants, who *use* Croatian or who *have some proficiency* in it.

Although Croatian is a European language spoken by a sizeable number of immigrants in countries such as the USA, Canada, Australia, and Germany, it has remained comparatively under-studied as a diaspora language in comparison to other (European) languages spoken by emigrants in similar situations. This is based perhaps on a number of factors. First, speakers of other languages such as Spanish, German, Italian, Russian, Chinese and Arabic typically outnumber Croatian-speakers, and Croatian is but one of the two dozen or so 'mid-range' ethnic languages used across these countries. Second, Croatian does not often feature in the repertoires of contact linguists for the language to be a focus of study in language contact studies. Third, there have been data collection obstacles in the identification of Croatian-speakers where over the last 125 years or so, Croatian-speaking emigres were often classified as 'Austrians' (as citizens of the Habsburg Empire), citizens of the 'Kingdom of Serbs, Croats and Slovenes', and later as the 'Kingdom of Yugoslavia', and then after the short-lived 'Independent State of Croatia' (1941–1945), as citizens of the 'Federal People's Republic of Yugoslavia', then the 'Socialist Federal Republic of Yugoslavia' until Croatian independence in 1991. For these, and for other reasons, it has often been difficult to track and record numbers of Croatian-speakers in emigrant settings, and for their language to be clearly identified as Croatian.

The notion of a *Croatian diaspora* itself is a comparatively recent one that has existed only since the beginning of the twentieth century, or in its contemporary sense, since the 1960s when organised and sanctioned mass-emigration from (what was then) Yugoslavia commenced (Nejašmić 1991). The following socio-economic and demographic features characterise contemporary Croatian diaspora communities: urban-dwelling; availability of employment as the chief determinant of place of residence; lower socio-economic profile with lower income/fewer assets compared to other, 'mainstream' co-residents of their societies due to three conspicuous groups – old age pensioners, variable emergence of cohorts of 'upwardly mobile' second-generation and third-generation members, recently-arrived skilled migrants yet to establish themselves; variable level of education and occupational skills – from those with rudimentary education from rural areas to the highly-educated. In general, there has been a shift from, in a stereotypical sense, lowly-educated and unskilled (male) migrants from rural or less developed areas who emigrated in the 1960s and 1970s to highly-educated and skilled migrants from urban areas who left in the twenty-first century, particularly since Croatia's accession to the European Union in mid-2013.

The relative 'recency' of the immigrant settings studied in chapters 5–14 means that the approach taken in these chapters is synchronic only. There are relatively few long-standing institutions or notions of 'continuing presence' acknowledged by the host society or by groups of Croatian-speakers themselves. This, combined with a low level of density within the localities in which they reside, relatively high levels of mobility, and variable levels of endogamy mean most Croatian-speakers live in settings that do not have the levels of sociolinguistic stability that characterise(d) the long-standing 'indigenous' Croatian-speaking minorities in Burgenland (Austria, Hungary and Slovakia), Molise (Italy) or the linguistic exclaves across southern Hungary.

Below is an overview of migration waves of Croatian-speakers with details of events that acted as catalysts for emigration and the destination countries that emigrants settled in.

Late nineteenth century – Outbreak of phylloxera and a failure of grape and other crops leading to mass emigration from Dalmatia to South America, New Zealand and the United States of America.

Late nineteenth century – Chain migration from the Croatian Littoral and Kvarner islands and central Croatia (Karlovac area, Banija, Kordun) to the United States of America.

Early twentieth century – Chain migration from rural areas due to over-population/ lack of arable land from all Croatian-speaking areas to the United States of America, South America, New Zealand.

Inter-war years – Chain migration from rural areas due to over-population/ lack of arable land from all Croatian-speaking areas to North and South America, New Zealand, Australia; political migration of members of the Ustaša movement to Italy.

WWII – deportation of captured/arrested Anti-Fascist Partisans to labour or POW camps in Nazi-held areas elsewhere in Europe.

Immediate post-WWII period (1945–1955) – Departure or emigration of office-bearers, supporters and military personnel of the Independent State of Croatia to Western Europe, North and South America; Departure or emigration of supporters of other parties (e.g. HSS – Croatian Peasant Party) and others who opposed the establishment of a Communist form of government and society; expulsion of ethnic Germans from Slavonia, Syrmia, Baranya to Germany and Austria; departure of ethnic Italians and others from Istria, Rijeka and the Croatian Littoral to Italy, often followed by their re-migration to North or South America, or Australia.

1960s – tacitly encouraged economic and/or political emigration from rural areas of central Bosnia and from west Hercegovina, economic emigration from Croatia to Canada, Australia, United States; organised economic emigration of blue-collar guest workers 'Gastarbeiter' from all regions of Bosnia-Herzegovina and Croatia to Germany.

1970s – political emigration to Canada, United States, Australia, Germany after the crush of the 'Croatian Spring' in 1971.

1980s – skilled migration (economic) due to economic stagnation and political instability in the Socialist Federal Republic of Yugoslavia.

1990s – wars in Croatia and Bosnia-Herzegovina; refugees seeking protection in Germany, Austria and Switzerland; re-settlement of refugees from Croatia and Bosnia-Herzegovina in Canada, Australia and the United States of America

2000s – emigration of skilled migrants to Germany, Austria, Canada, the United States of America, Australia, New Zealand.

2013 to present – Croatia's accession to the European Union and the removal of obstacles for Croatian citizens to work in most other EU countries – emigration of skilled or service-industry workers (and their families) to Germany, Austria, Ireland.

The data samples of informants presented in chapters 5–14 encompass nearly all of the above waves of emigrants with each chapter typically featuring informants from a number of waves, whether as first-generation speakers or as speakers from subsequent generations whose parents, grandparents or even great-grandparents arrived in waves going further back in time. Table 1 below provides estimated numbers of Croatian-origin persons residing in 14 other European countries, two countries in North America, nine in South America, two in Oceania and one in Africa. It is important to note that these figures relate to the estimated numbers of persons of Croatian origin, and not to the estimated numbers of Croatian-speakers in these countries.

Table 1: Estimated numbers of Croatian-origin persons domiciled in 28 countries that are destination countries of settlement for Croatian emigrants and their descendants. Source: Central State Office for Croats Abroad (2019).

Continent	Number	Continent	Number
Europe			
Germany	350,000	**North America**	
Austria	90,000	USA	1,200,000
Switzerland	80,000	Canada	250,000
Italy	60,000		
France	40,000	**South America**	
Sweden	35,000	Argentina	250,000
Netherlands	10,000	Chile	200,000
Belgium	6,000	Brazil	20,000
United Kingdom	5,000	Peru	6,000
Ireland	4,000	Bolivia	5,000
Russia	3,000	Paraguay	5,000
Luxembourg	2,000	Uruguay	5,000
Norway	2,000	Venezuela	5,000
Denmark	1,000	Ecuador	4,000
		Oceania	
Africa		Australia	250,000
South Africa	8,000	New Zealand	40,000
		Total	**2,900,000**

The total number of Croatian-origin emigrants shown in Table 1 above is 2,900,000. This figure of nearly 3 million people residing in countries across the Croatian diaspora is larger than the above-mentioned figure of approx. 1.67 million Croatian-speakers. This indicates that of all Croatian-origin persons in the diaspora, approx. 57% have proficiency in the language.

The top five countries with the largest number of Croatian-origin persons – the United States of America, Germany, Argentina, Australia and Canada – are each represented with a chapter in this volume. Three further countries – Austria, Italy and New Zealand – that are amongst the top ten countries of settlement are also represented in this volume. Norway is the only country represented in this volume that has a relatively small Croatian immigrant population. This volume can therefore claim to be representative of the cross-national distribution of Croatian-origin emigrants according to their country of residence. We, however, make no claim that the data presented is statistically representative of all varieties of Croatian spoken across the diaspora.

3 Multi-site studies of the same heritage language in diaspora or transposed settings

Most studies focusing on migrant languages examine one setting and the use and form of one migrant language in contact with the societally dominant language of the host country. However, there are a number of studies or projects that have looked at one particular language and groups of speakers in multiple settings. All of these studies are synchronic in their approach. We outline here the main characteristics of these studies.

The oldest and most comprehensive project of this kind was the *Deutsche Sprache in Europa und Übersee* 'German in Europe and Abroad' project which consisted of 15 volumes, each of which was usually devoted to a particular country that itself was home to a sizeable German-speaking population. Volumes in the project were published from 1977 to 1993, and each volume consisted of information on the local sociolinguistic situation of German-speakers and the German-speaking community in general, followed by a description of the forms characteristic of speakers residing in transposed or minority settings in Europe (Belgium, Eastern Lorraine, Luxembourg, Hungary and Great Britain), North America (Canada and the United States of America), Africa (Namibia, South Africa) and Australia (Leibnitz-Institut für deutsche Sprache, n.d.).

A volume with 14 contributions on Spanish in bi- and multi-lingual settings entitled *Spanish in Contact: Issues in Bilingualism*, edited by Roca and Jensen (1996) contains two papers on English-Spanish code-switching and three further ones looking at structural change and calques. The remaining papers examine trilingualism, language acquisition, language forms, phonology and language planning issues. In the following year *Dutch Overseas: Studies in maintenance and loss of Dutch as an immigrant language* edited by Jetske Klatter-Folmer and Sjaak Kroon (1997) was published. Although the focus is on language maintenance of Dutch as well as shift from it, the volume features numerous examples of lexical innovation and morphosyntactic change in émigré Dutch.

More recently, Anna Fenyvesi's (2005) edited volume entitled *Hungarian Language Contact outside Hungary* contains sociolinguistic data and linguistic descriptions (borrowing, code-switching and structural changes) of the speech of Hungarian-speakers living elsewhere in Europe, and in the United States of America and Australia. A contribution that focuses exclusively on immigrant settings is *Germanic Heritage Languages in North America. Acquisition, attrition and change* edited by Bondi Johannessen and Salmons (2015). The volume spans five main areas: acquisition, phonetic and phonological change, morphosyntactic and pragmatic change, lexical change, and variation and real-time change, with data from Dutch, German, Icelandic, Norwegian, Pennsylvania Dutch, Swedish, West Frisian and Yiddish. Each contribution adopts a chiefly descriptive approach that is anchored in the linguistic field of the phenomena being studied.

The *Encyclopedia of Arabic Language and Linguistics*, a five-volume series published from 2005 to 2009, has sporadic chapters that look at lexical transference into (and less so from) Arabic, mainly in the spoken or written versions in predominantly Arabic-speaking countries rather than in diaspora settings. In that series, Sarah Thomason's (2006) chapter, entitled *Arabic in contact with other languages*, is the only contribution that systematically examines contact phenomena from a contact linguistics perspective. Diachronic and synchronic approaches to contact situations are found in a recently published volume of papers *Arabic in Contact* edited by Manfredi and Tosco (2018) that focuses on contact in predominantly Arabic-speaking countries and not immigrant settings. A mostly synchronic approach is followed in *Biculturalism and Spanish in Contact* edited by Núñez Méndez (2018) that contains three studies of Spanish in immigrant settings (all in the USA) and three further studies in borderland areas in and adjacent to Spanish-speaking countries in Latin America. A converse approach to that adopted in this book is Clyne and Kipp's (1999) volume on speakers of three immigrant languages in Australia, Spanish, Arabic and Chinese. That volume featured one destination country of immigration only, but examined regional and national varieties of each of these languages, depending on the source country of migrants (e.g. Arabic-speakers from Lebanon, Egypt and Iraq).

We are informed by these multi-site or multi-faceted studies in the approach that they adopt to speakers, speech communities and the form and structure of migrant or minority languages. In particular, Fenyvesi's (2005) volume *Hungarian Language Contact outside Hungary* has provided us with a model for the study of sociolinguistic and linguistic features amongst speakers of a minority or migrant language, and the current volume sees itself as a contribution to the growing body of work on heritage languages within the discipline of contact linguistics. Further, we are informed by Kim Potowski's (2018) edited volume *The Routledge Handbook of Spanish as a Heritage Language* that has 14 chapters that present linguistic data on the Spanish of heritage speakers. Of interest to us are the chapters focusing on lexicon (Fairclough and Garza 2018) and morphology, syntax and semantics (Montrul 2018).

4 Aims of this volume and its theoretical framework

We have two main areas of focus: firstly, the general sociolinguistic situation of Croatian-speakers in these countries and the sociolinguistic situation of groups of Croatian-speaking informants in particular; secondly, a description of the Croatian speech of multiple generations of speakers in nine different contact situations. Language contact research now, or at least since Thomason and Kaufman's (1988) seminal work and Myers-Scotton's complementary studies on social factors (1993a) and grammatical structure of bilingual speech (1993b), typically addresses the sociolinguistic situations of transposed speech communities as strong, co-determining factors of linguistic outcomes.

Of interest in an examination of diaspora speakers is to see what has been recorded about the speech of long-standing communities who have, over centuries, continued to use Croatian as a means of communication. We are informed by research on speakers of Burgenland Croatian (Austria, Hungary and Slovakia) and Molise Croatian (Italy) from communities whose ancestors migrated approx. 500 years ago, as well as from data from two of the nine Croatian-speaking ethnic minority communities in Hungary living in regions adjacent to Croatia. These are presented in Chapter 3. Further, a diachronically-focused overview with reference to areal linguistic features is provided in Chapter 4.

Thus, this volume has a diachronic component that sets the scene, while the approach taken for the greater part is mostly synchronic, i.e. most chapters that make up the central part of this volume from chapters 5–14 examine spoken data that has been recorded over the last five years, with only three chapters also featuring data older than this. The approach taken in these chapters is descriptive, analytical and evaluative in presenting data and contextualising it within the existing body of knowledge on immigrant languages and within contemporary frameworks widely employed in contact linguistics.

We are informed by Muysken (2000), Thomason (2001), Field (2002), Myers-Scotton (2002) and Winford (2003) in the selection of features that the authors of chapters 5–14 present and focus on. Phenomena that are characteristic of language contact situations of recent vintage (but not only recent vintage ones) and which are comparatively extrinsic such as the transference of lexemes are presented as well as those that are instances of change at a more intrinsic level such as phraseological calques to the possibility of significant structural change. This volume therefore represents contemporary research on diaspora speakers and the linguistic forms present in their speech that reflect their transposed situation. Two large groupings of linguistics categories are distinguished: phonology, lexicon, pragmatics and semantics; structure – morphosyntax.

The focus of analysis of the contributors in this volume is transference (lexical and/or structural) from the societally-dominant language in the host societies into speakers' repertoires and other innovations or phenomena that differ from those found in any variety, standard or non-standard, of what we term 'homeland Croatian'. Thus, the focus is comparative, i.e. looking at the lexical and/or structural features of the societally-dominant language and how these may (or may not) be transferred or replicated in diaspora varieties. These areas are all represented as well-known contact scenarios and are central themes in contemporary research on heritage languages such as Polinsky's (2018) *Heritage Languages and Their Speakers* and *Heritage Languages. A language contact approach* by Aalberse, Backus and Muysken (2019).

5 The studies in this volume

This volume contains 15 chapters which are grouped into three parts. The first part (chapters 1–4) consists of the book's 'preliminaries' – these background research on languages in contact and diaspora languages and provide an overview of the languages of three sets of Croatian *sprachinseln* and of languages in the Balkan *sprachbund*. The second part of the book (chapters 5–14) presents data on Croatian-speakers in the diaspora in the following four continents and nine countries: Europe (Austria, Germany, Italy and Norway), North America (Canada and the USA), South America (Argentina) and Oceania (Australia and New Zealand). The third part of the book is the concluding chapter 15.

Chapter 2, entitled *Research in languages in contact: locating Croatian as a diaspora language within the field of contact linguistics*, gives a re-cap of the term *languages in contact* before moving to discuss the contributions that diachronic and synchronic studies have made to research on languages in contact in general. This chapter introduces and defines the concept of *contact linguistics* which has emerged as a more concise term to describe what has now become an established sub-discipline of linguistics. This chapter gives brief outlines of key studies, terms and frameworks that are used within the field. The terms *heritage languages* and *heritage language speakers* are defined followed by a discussion how these terms to relate to Croatian-speakers of various vintages of migration belonging to different generational groups. The terms used in this book are outlined also in this chapter, and examples of diaspora Croatian speech are presented and explained to show how these terms are applied in the descriptions provided in this volume. The chapter concludes with an overview of the findings from previous studies on the language and linguistic profiles of Croatian-speakers in migrant or transposed settings.

Chapter 3 focuses on the situation and linguistic outcomes of Croatian-speakers residing in *sprachinseln* in neighbouring countries and is entitled, *Diachronic perspectives on change in spoken Croatian amongst Croatian indigenous minorities in Austria, Italy and Hungary*. The chapter has three authors. Each is a specialist for a particular Croatian-speaking minority: Aleksandra Ščukanec (University of Zagreb) for Burgenland Croatian spoken in eastern Austria, western Hungary and southern Slovakia; Walter Breu (University of Konstanz) for Molise Croatian spoken in central Italy; and Dora Vuk (University of Regensburg) for two groups of Croatian-speakers indigenous to Hungary – Kajkavian-speakers living in the Mura River Valley in south-west Hungary and ethnically Croatian Bošnjaks and Šokacs (*Bošnjaci i Šokci*) who are Štokavian-speakers living in the south-central Hungarian region of Baranya. The value of the chapter is that it sets out those phenomena that are reported to have occurred in communities that have continued to speak Croatian while being geographically dislocated from the original homeland for centuries. This diachronic focus informs of phenomena that can and have happened over time in settings where Croatian has been in contact with languages of other genealogical groups: Germanic, Romance and Finno-Ugric.

Chapter 4 from Victor Friedman (University of Chicago and La Trobe University) is entitled *Diaspora vs Sprachbund: Shift, Drift and Convergence*. This chapter outlines language contact phenomena that have occurred uni- and multi-laterally between the languages that make up the Balkan *sprachbund*. The chapter underlines how transference of lexical forms and grammatical structures can occur between typologically different languages. In the case of grammatical structures, this can lead to outcomes such as convergence, usually asymmetrical and other forms of change. The relevance of this to the other studies in this volume is that one of the languages 'central' to the Balkan *sprachbund* is Macedonian, a South Slavic language like Croatian. Friedman compares changes in one of the *sprachinseln* communities, Molise Croatian, with those that have occurred in Macedonian and Balkan Slavic in general. Friedman evaluates the processes and mechanics of these changes in discussing how these could also occur in the repertoires of speakers in the diaspora.

The second part of this volume focuses on linguistic data from the ten studies across diaspora communities in nine countries. In line with the tradition of contact linguistics research that includes a description of sociolinguistic features that contextualise the situation of bi- or multilingual speakers, each of the chapters 5–8 and 10–14 is prefaced by a sociolinguistic overview that contains the following: history of contact, vintages of emigration; (*de jure* or other) status of the Croatian language; number of residents with Croatian heritage, number of Croatian-speakers; geographic distribution, socio-economic profile; infrastructure (including provision for school instruction in Croatian); domain use, language maintenance and shift; contacts with Croatia, host society attitudes towards Croats. The sociolinguistic overviews thus provide information relating to demographic, socio-political, sociolinguistic and socio-psychological (attitudinal) features of Croatian communities in the nine countries. These features are instrumental in helping us understand if, how and how much diaspora community members can use Croatian in interactions with others, or as a medium in other, self-directed activities. Table 2 contains an overview of the size of the sociolinguistic samples presented in the introductory sections of chapters 5–8 and 10–14 respectively.

Table 2: Number and generational membership of informants of sociolinguistic corpora presented in chapters 5–14.

	USA	Canada	Argentina	Australia	NZ	Austria	Germany	Italy (incl. Trieste)	Norway	Total
Data collection period / Generation	1985	2014	2016	1996–1997, 2010	1970–1990	2016	2016	2015, 2016	2016	
Gen.1A	8	110	1	40	41	15	18	18	6	257
Gen.1B				26	0	5		2	1	34
Gen.2	12	110	177	117	60	9	21	12	3	521
Gen.3&4			156	10	19		4			189
Total	**20**	**220**	**337**	**193**	**120**	**29**	**43**	**32**	**10**	**1,004**

Chapter 5 focuses on the country with the largest Croatian-speaking diaspora in Europe, Germany. Marijana Kresić Vukosav and Lucija Šimičić, both based at the University of Zadar, are the authors of the chapter entitled *Some aspects of language contact among Croatian-speakers in Lower Saxony, Germany*. Their chapter's sample has two corpora: a larger sociolinguistic one based on survey responses from 44 informants across three generations; a smaller one based on recorded interviews with 12 first- and second-generation speakers. The sociolinguistic sample contains data on acquisition of macro-skills, self-reported language competence, domain-based language use, ethnic self-identification and language attitudes. Semi-formal interviews yield a 6.5 hour sample that is analysed for the following: intra-clausal code-switching; inter-clausal code-switching; covert cross-linguistic influence / convergence (morphosyntactic calques); and semantic transfers and loan translations.

Aleksandra Ščukanec from the University of Zagreb is the author of Chapter 6 entitled *Post WWII Croatian migrants in Austria and Croatian-German language contacts*. The context examined is a post-migration one of Croatian migrants residing in Austria. There are two corpora presented: a sociolinguistic one based on questionnaires completed by 29 informants; a corpus of linguistic data based on recorded interviews with 21 informants. From the sociolinguistic corpus, data are presented on the following: contacts with the homeland; domain-based use of Croatian; data on acquisition of Croatian and German; (family) language policies; designations for the language of Croatian migrants in Austria; attitudes towards language and language maintenance; and reported attitudes to code-switching or bilingual speech. Analysis of the linguistic data focuses on the following: lexical transfers, including their morphological (non-)integration; code-switching; loan translations; and structural transference.

In Chapter 7 the focus is on the relatively small Croatian-speaking community in Norway. Hanne Skaaden from Oslo Metropolitan University addresses what is often regarded as a conspicuous characteristic of speakers of Croatian as a heritage language: their case endings. The title of the chapter contains a quote that directly mentions this: *Tu i tamo se gađam padežima* – *'Here and there I struggle with my cases'. Croatian migrant speakers in Norway and their use of the dative.* Using visual stimuli in the form of an animated narrative, 'The Pear Story', which features protagonists doing things to or for each other, the focus of the chapter is on speakers' verbal production of forms relating to actions that are readily described via dative constructions. The visual stimuli contain numerous examples of protagonists giving, taking and losing things, and of them helping and approaching each other. The frequency of dative constructions, number of dative tokens and a quantification of pronominal vs. nominal forms are also presented. Similar corpora from other speakers of comparable heritage languages, as well as corpora from homeland speakers are employed as points of comparison. Analysis then focuses on the different sub-types of dative use, e.g. as a directional, indirect object, possession and their frequency amongst the 10 heritage speaker informants. Findings gained relate to inter-generational variation amongst the heritage language informants, and between them as a group compared to homeland-based speakers.

Chapter 8 takes us to Italy and the title of this chapter is *Features of the speech of Croatian-speakers in Italy* by Nada Županović Filipin (University of Zagreb), Jim Hlavac (Monash University) and Vesna Piasevoli (University of Trieste). The chapter features three corpora: nine sociolinguistics-focused interviews with first- and second-generation speakers collected in Croatia including speech recordings; thirteen sociolinguistics-focused recorded interviews conducted with second-generation speakers together with their responses from a detailed sociolinguistics written questionnaire; recordings featuring 34 different speakers from the first, second and third generations when interacting with each other in family or intra-group settings. Linguistic data is examined according to the following features: phonology: lexical transference and code-switching; semantic transference and loan translations; the possessive adjectives *svoj* (Cro.) and *suo* (Ital.); structural change.

Chapter 9 also features Croatian-Italian informants, all of whom are residents of Trieste, a city which is only 40km from the Croatian border. Trieste has been a city to which Croatians have gravitated for centuries – as seafarers, merchants, labourers, university students and shopping tourists, to name but a few. Vesna Piasevoli (University of Trieste) commences this chapter, entitled *The Croatian speech of first- and second-generation Croats in Trieste*, with a historical overview of Trieste's rich and varied linguistic profile. The author is a long-term resident of Trieste and she employs an ethnographic approach which yields a large number of biographical accounts that are fascinating and at times very moving. Trieste's geographical location and socio-political relations in the northern Adriatic have meant that, at times, it has been advantageous to have a Croatian-Italian bi-cultural and bilingual identity, and at other times less so. The presentation of linguistic data gained from recorded and transcribed interviews is given with the following categorisations: lexical transference; loan translations; structural innovations including employment of *jedan* 'one' as a nascent indefinite article, personal pronouns and pro-drop, numerals and case-marking, case-marking in NPs, possessive constructions, word order, dependent clause conjunctions, syntactic calques and verbal aspect; and code-switching.

Dunja Jutronić (University of Maribor, University of Split) has been studying Croatian-English bilingualism amongst Croatian-Americans for roughly 50 years and has published a book *Hrvatski jezik u SAD* 'The Croatian Language in the USA' and numerous articles on this topic. She is the author of Chapter 10, entitled *The Croatian Language in the USA: Changes in Croatian Syntax as a Result of Contact with English*. The United States of America is a rich environment for research on heritage languages and their speakers, and it is the country that boasts the largest number of people of Croatian-origin residing outside Croatia: 1,200,000. This large group is itself heterogeneous and encompasses sub-groups that range from recently-arrived, first-generation migrants to fifth- or even sixth-generation Croatian-Americans, most of whom express their ethnic affiliation not via proficiency in the language but in other ways, such as associations with their extended family, food (e.g. *sarma* 'cabbage rolls'), music (e.g. stringed instruments such as *tambura* or *mandolina*), religion, or by making sure that they "spend some time in Croatia" when they go on a European vacation. In her previous publications, Jutronić has looked at lexical, semantic and morphosyntactic features of first- and second-generation speakers. As the title suggests, this chapter focuses on morphosyntactic features only, in the speech of 11 second-generation speakers. The features examined are: overt possessive adjectives; personal pronouns and pro-drop; word order and clitics; overt (non-subject) personal pronouns; use of AUX and COP verbs; possessive constructions; passive constructions; and numerals and dates.

The other major destination country for Croatians migrating to North America has been Canada. In comparison to the USA, emigration to Canada is of a more recent vintage and sizeable numbers of Croatian emigrants started settling there only from the 1960s onwards, particularly in Toronto. Croatian-speakers living in that city and its surrounds are the focus of Chapter 11, *Features in the speech of Croatian-speakers in the Greater Toronto area*. The author is Ivana Petrović based at the University of Split. Her chapter draws on two corpora, the first being a sociolinguistic one based on 220 informants (110 first-generation, 110 second-generation) that contains data on the following: socio-economic status; educational level; self-reported proficiency in both languages; domain-based language use; language attitudes. Analysis of the second corpus, that of linguistic data, is structured according to the following categories: lexical change; structural change encompassing case-marking, subject pronouns and pro-drop, forms of non-subject personal pronouns, reflexive pronouns, possessive pronouns, word order (clitics), prepositions and semantic transference, loan translations, and *jedan* 'one' as a nascent indefinite article.

Similar to Canada, Australia has witnessed the arrival of sizeable numbers of Croatian immigrants only since the 1960s. Chapter 12 is entitled *Features in the speech of three generations of Croatian-Australians* and comes from the two editors of this volume, Jim Hlavac (Monash University) and Diana Stolac (University of Rijeka). As the title indicates, this chapter presents data from three generations with two sets of corpora: a smaller one which is based on responses to a sociolinguistic questionnaire that elicited responses on the following: domain-based language use including intra-family interactions, social and free-time activities, the religious domain, media consumption, the workplaces, transactional domain and attendance at formal instruction in Croatian. The larger part of this chapter focuses on linguistic data, supplied by all 100 informants of the sociolinguistic sample, and a further 98 informants from a number of generations. Analysis of linguistic data is structured according to the following categories: lexicon and pragmatics (gender allocation of nouns, integration of verbs, affirmatives and discourse markers); semantic transfers, loan translations and de-semanticised verbs; code-switching; and morphology and syntax (case-, gender- and number-marking in NPs, *jedan* 'one' as a nascent indefinite article, verbs and valence, word order, syntactic transference).

Chapter 13 is from Hans-Peter Stoffel (University of Auckland) and Jim Hlavac (Monash University) and is entitled *Croatian dialect speakers from Dalmatia and their linguistic contact with English and Māori in New Zealand*. As the title indicates, this is the only chapter that includes, alongside English, input from an indigenous language into the speech of Croatian immigrants. Although New Zealand as a destination country is the one located furthest from Croatia, sizeable number of emigrants from central Dalmatia began settling there at the end of the nineteenth century. Most of them were young men, and for many, their first form of employment was digging up fossilized resin from *kauri* trees, a back-breaking task. Some sent for or went back to find wives, while others married local women, many of them Māori. In some cases, this led to tri-lingual Croatian-Māori-English households. The effect of education and occupational advancement has led to the upward mobility of those in the second and third generations, and this along with relocation to urban areas has led to shift to English amongst younger Croatian-origin New Zealanders. The first author, Hans-Peter Stoffel, has been studying Croatian-English bilingualism for nearly fifty years, and has published numerous studies focussing on all aspects of Croatian spoken (and written) in New Zealand, including detailed description of its phonological, lexical, semantic, pragmatic, morphological, syntactic and prosodic features. The larger part of the chapter is devoted to a description of the form of speakers' Croatian speech. Analysis of this is structured according to the following categories: lexical transference (including phonological and/or morphological integration of transferred nouns and verbs, and co-occurrence with equivalent Croatian forms); discourse markers; semantic transference and loan translations; code-switching; morphosyntactic features – change and convergence (including feature-marking in NPs, agreement within NPs and subject-verb agreement).

The chapter that concludes the second part of this volume is Chapter 14 from three researchers, all from the University of Zagreb, Anita Skelin Horvat, Maša Musulin and Ana Gabrijela Blažević. The chapter is entitled *Croatian in Argentina: lexical transfers in the speech of bilingual Croatian-Spanish speakers*. Argentina has the largest number of Croatian-origin immigrants in Latin America. This chapter contains data from two corpora. The first consists of 337 responses from first-, second- and third-generation speakers. The main part of the chapter presents data from the second corpus that consists of recordings with 12 informants: 5 from the first generation; 5 from the second generation; and one each from the third and fourth generations. The analysis of linguistic data is organised according to the following categories: lexical transfers and loan translations (with sub-sections each devoted to nouns, adjectives, verbs, adverbs and discourse markers); and morphosyntactic change. Table 3 shows the total number of informants from whom recordings were gained that form the corpora of linguistic data presented in Chapters 5–14.

The third part of this edited volume is Chapter 15. It is a concluding chapter that re-visits select examples of similar phenomena. Due to the large number of

Table 3: Number of informants who provided spoken recordings for the linguistic data in each of the nine diaspora countries and the collection period of these.

	USA	Canada	Argentina	Australia	NZ	Austria	Germany	Italy (incl. Trieste)	Norway	Total
Collection period	1980	2007	2016	1996–1997, 2010	1970–1990	2016	2016	2015, 2016	2016	
Gen. 1A		11	5	5	19	11	3	23	6	83
Gen. 1B				5		3		2	1	11
Gen. 2	11	11	5	100	25	7	9	17	3	188
Gen. 3&4			2	3	10			2		17
Total	11	22	12	113	54	21	12	44	10	299

different phenomena and the even larger number of individual examples presented in this volume, only two of the most recurring ones are addressed in this last chapter that is entitled *Intra-clausal code-switching and possessive constructions in heritage varieties of Croatian: an MLF-based examination*. It is authored by one of the editors, Jim Hlavac (Monash University) and Carol Myers-Scotton (Michigan State University). Myers-Scotton (1993, 2002) developed the *Matrix Language Frame* (hereafter *MLF*) *model* and as a progression of this, a theoretical framework of categorising morphemes according to their conceptual or structural role, known as the *4-M model*. One aim of Chapter 15 is to examine phenomena that are reported in at least three or more settings. Recurrence is an indicator that a particular phenomenon is occurring not only on the basis of a specific setting or due to contact with a particular other language; rather, it points to that phenomenon being one that we can view as being not only possible, but perhaps even likely in contact settings. A second aim of Chapter 15 is to apply the principles of the MLF model and the 4-M model to see how the models have the explanatory power to account for particular phenomena.

The MLF model and the 4-M model contain principles that predict which types of morphemes can be supplied by the 'matrix' or morphosyntactically dominant language and what types of morphemes are likely to be supplied by the incurring or embedded language (EL). The examples taken from chapters 5–14 that are re-presented in Chapter 15, namely those of intra-clausal code-switching and possessive constructions, are examined and discussed to show how predictions from the 4-M model apply to EL items. In most cases, particular types of morphemes from the ML perform the function of integrating EL items into the morphosyntactic frame of an otherwise ML clause. Attention is drawn to those instances where this appears not to be the case. Chapter 15 also outlines the characteristics of a *Composite Matrix Language*, and how this is a theoretical construct that can account for particularly conspicuous examples of structural innovation or change.

This volume incorporates both diachronic and synchronic approaches, and encompasses studies of long-standing Croatian *sprachinseln* as well as comparatively young communities. It features material from four continents, nine countries, up to four generations of speakers, immigrants (or their descendants) of different vintages of migration, and hundreds of examples as evidence of how people speak. Notwithstanding this, we are very aware that the data presented in this volume are still narrower in scope and frequency than the range of linguistic forms that are found in the speech of Croatian-speakers across the diaspora. We are conscious that speakers from the first-generation and the second-generation are better represented compared to those from the third or the fourth generation. In part, this is a consequence of the numbers of younger generation members who have shifted to the societally dominant languages, which excluded them from being informants in the studies of this volume. We are conscious that this volume does not contain data from the sizeable communities in Chile, Switzerland, France, Sweden, Brazil and the Netherlands, nor are there data from the only country in Africa in which a significant number of Croatian immigrants live, South Africa. We are also conscious that those who have left Croatia since the country's accession to the European Union on 1 July 2013 are under-represented in the studies of this volume. Media reports of 189,000 people leaving since mid-2013 (Poslovni Dnevnik 2019) are evidence that very recent migrants make up a significant proportion of the total number of Croatian-speakers abroad. Their level of mobility, their level of proficiency in the language of their host society, and their level of contact with other Croatian-speakers (whether via networks with others in countries with a sizeable Croatian diaspora community or through communication channels with those back home) are factors that are likely to have an effect on their use of Croatian and its form that may be different from speakers from older vintages of migration. The feature of contemporary communication tools, social media, and consumption of electronic-based texts is not widely examined in the studies of this volume and it is likely that these may be key means for those recently departed and their children to maintain or establish communicative networks with other Croatian-speakers.

Notwithstanding these shortcomings, we hope that this volume will inform readers through its descriptive, interpretive and integrative framework and that it can serve as an instructive contribution to contact linguistics as a cross-national examination of speakers of the same heritage language.

References

Aalberse, Suzanne, Ad Backus & Pieter Muysken. 2019. *Heritage Languages. A language contact approach.* Amsterdam: John Benjamins.
Bondi Johannessen, Janne & Joseph Salmons. (eds.) 2015. *Germanic Heritage Languages in North America. Acquisition, attrition and change.* Amsterdam: John Benjamins.
Brozović, Dalibor. 2006. *Neka bitna pitanja hrvatskoga jezičnog standarda.* [Some substantial questions concerning Standard Croatian] Zagreb: Školska knjiga.
Central State Office for Croats Abroad. 2019. *Hrvatski iseljenici u prekomorskim i europskim državama i njihovi potomci.* [Croatian emigrants in overseas countries and in other European countries and their descendants] https://hrvatiizvanrh.gov.hr/hrvati-izvan-rh/hrvatsko-iseljenistvo/hrvatski-iseljenici-u-prekomorskim-i-europskim-drzavama-i-njihovi-potomci/749 (accessed 11 December 2019)
Clyne, Michael & Sandra Kipp. 1999. *Pluricentric Languages in an Immigrant Context.* Berlin: Mouton de Gruyter.
Ethnologue. 2018. *Languages of the World: Croatian.* Retrieved from: https://www.ethnologue.com/language/hrv (accessed 10 November 2018)
Fairclough, Marta & Anel Garza. 2018. The lexicon of Spanish heritage language speakers. In Kim Potowski (ed.). *The Routledge Handbook of Spanish as a Heritage Language.* 178–189. Abingdon, Oxon: Routledge.
Fenyvesi, Anna. (ed.) 2005. *Hungarian Language Contact outside Hungary.* Amsterdam: John Benjamins.
Field, Frederic. 2002. *Linguistic borrowing in bilingual contexts.* Amsterdam: John Benjamins.
Fishman, Joshua A. 2002. The holiness of Yiddish: Who says Yiddish is holy and why? *Language Policy*, 1(2). 123.
Fishman, Joshua A. 2008. Language Maintenance, Language Shift, and Reversing Language Shift. In Tej K. Bhatia & William C. Ritchie (eds.) *The handbook of bilingualism.* 406–436. Malden, MA: Blackwell.
Greenberg, Robert. 2004. *Language and Identity in the Balkans.* Oxford: Oxford University Press.
Isurin, Ludmila. 2011. *Russian Diaspora. Culture, Identity, and Language Change.* Berlin: De Gruyter Mouton.
Jutronić-Tihomirović, Dunja. 1985. *Hrvatski jezik u SAD* [The Croatian Language in the USA]. Split: Logos.
Klatter-Folmer, Jetske & Sjaak Kroon. (eds.) 1997. *Dutch Overseas: Studies in maintenance and loss of Dutch as an immigrant language.* Tilburg: Tilburg University Press.
Langston, Keith & Anita Peti-Stantić. 2014. *Language Planning and National Identity in Croatia.* Basingstoke, Hampshire: Palgrave.
Leibnitz-Institut für deutsche Sprache. (n.d.) *Deutsche Sprache in Europa und Übersee Berichte und Forschungen.* https://pub.ids-mannheim.de/abgeschlossen/dseu/ (accessed 15 July 2019)
Lisac, Josip, Ivo Pranjković, Marko Samardžija & Ante Bičanić. 2015. (eds.) *Povijest hrvatskoga jezika. 4. knjiga: 19. stoljeće.* [The History of the Croatian Language. Vol. 4: 19th Century]. Zagreb: Društvo za promicanje hrvatske kulture i znanosti CROATICA.
Manfredi, Stefano & Mauro Tosco. (eds.) 2018. *Arabic in Contact.* Amsterdam: John Benjamins.
Mills, Jean. (2005). Connecting Communities: Identity, Language and Diaspora. *International Journal of Bilingual Education and Bilingualism*, 8(4). 253–274.

Moguš, Milan. 1995. *A History of the Croatian Language: Toward a Common Standard*. Zagreb: Nakladni zavod Globus.
Montrul, Silvina. 2018. Morphology, syntax and semantics in Spanish as a heritage language. In Kim Potowski (ed.) *The Routledge Handbook of Spanish as a Heritage Language*. 145–163. Abingdon, Oxon: Routledge.
Muysken, Pieter. 2000. *Bilingual speech. A typology of code-mixing*. Cambridge, UK: Cambridge University Press.
Myers-Scotton, Carol. 1993a. *Duelling languages. Grammatical structure in codeswitching*. Oxford: Clarendon Press.
Myers-Scotton, Carol. 1993b. *Social Motivations for Codeswitching: Evidence from Africa*. Oxford: Clarendon Press.
Myers-Scotton, Carol. 2002. *Contact linguistics. Bilingual encounters and grammatical outcomes*. Oxford: Oxford University Press.
Nejašmić, Ivica. 1991. *Depopulacija u Hrvatskoj. Korijeni, stanje, izgledi*. [De-population in Croatia: roots, current situation, prospects]. Zagreb: Globus Nakladni zavod / Institut za migracije i narodnosti Sveučilišta u Zagrebu.
Newlin-Łukowicz, Luiza. 2015. Language Variation in the Diaspora: Polish Immigrant Communities in the U.S. and the U.K. *Language and Linguistics Compass*, 9(8). 332–346.
Núñez Méndez, Eva. (ed.) 2018. *Biculturalism and Spanish in Contact*. London: Routledge.
Polinsky, Maria. 2018. *Heritage Languages and Their Speakers*. Cambridge, UK: Cambridge University Press.
Poslovni Dnevnik. [The Business Daily] 2019. (1 Oct.) *Objavljen porazni podatak koliko je ljudi napustilo Hrvatsku u posljednjih 5 godina*. [Devastating figures just published reveal how many people have left Croatia in the last 5 years] http://www.poslovni.hr/hrvatska/od-2013-do-2018-iz-hrvatske-otislo-189000-ljudi-358026 (accessed 13 December 2019)
Potowski, Kim. (ed.) 2018. *The Routledge Handbook of Spanish as a Heritage Language*. Abingdon, Oxon: Routledge.
Prpić, George Jure. 1971. *The Croatian Immigrants in America*. New York: Philosophical Library.
Roca, Ana & John Jensen. (eds.) 1996. *Spanish in Contact: Issues in Bilingualism*. Somerville, MA: Cascadilla Press.
Stoffel, Hans-Peter. 2011. The Joy of "Migranto". Dalmatian Skits as a Source for the Study of Croatian-English Language Contact in New Zealand. In Wolfgang Pöckl, Ingeborg Ohnheiser & Peter Sandrini (eds.) *Translation – Sprachvariation – Mehrsprachigkeit. Festschrift für Lew Zybatow zum 60. Geburtstag*, 407–422. Frankfurt a.M.: Peter Lang.
Thomason, Sarah. 2001. *Language Contact. An Introduction*. Edinburgh: Edinburgh University Press.
Thomason, Sarah. 2006. Arabic in contact with other languages. In Kees Versteegh, Mushira Eid, Alaa Elgibali, Manfred Woidich and Andrzej Zaborski (eds.) *Encyclopedia of Arabic Language and Linguistics*. 664–674. Leiden: Brill.
Thomason, Sarah & Terrence Kaufman. 1988. *Language contact, creolization, and genetic linguistics*. Berkeley: University of California Press.
Vince, Zlatko. 1990. *Putovima hrvatskoga književnog jezika*. [The paths by which the Croatian Literary Language developed] Zagreb: Nakladni zavod Matice hrvatske.
Winford, Donald. 2003. *An introduction to contact linguistics*. Malden, MA: Blackwell.

Background and theoretical concepts

Jim Hlavac
Research on languages in contact: Locating Croatian as a diaspora language within the field of contact linguistics

1 Languages in contact

Since the middle of the twentieth century and Weinreich's (1953) seminal book, the study of languages in contact has become an established sub-field of linguistics. Of course, it is *speakers* of different languages that are in contact with each other, rather than the languages themselves. The foregrounding of *languages* rather than *speakers* in the designation of the sub-field reflects the fact it has been *linguistic forms* perhaps more so than the *sociolinguistic situation* of the speakers that was the focus of many early studies. The field of languages in contact thus boasts a large number of studies that focus on linguistic outcomes such as borrowing, code-switching, morpho-syntactic change, calques, mixed languages as well as pidgins and creoles. At the same time, sociolinguistic data about speakers and speech communities are now a feature of many studies in the field – as the focus in their own right e.g. Gal (1979), Fishman (2008). In others, sociolinguistic features such as bi- or multi-lingual settings and domain-based language use are studied as key determinants of linguistic outcomes e.g. Thomason and Kaufman (1988), Myers-Scotton (1993), Li (1994), Backus (1996), Field (2002). A description of the social context of the language contact setting and sociolinguistic data on informants is now a regular feature of linguistically-focused studies.

As stated, the focus of this volume is on linguistic forms, and this chapter will focus mainly on features relevant to their description. This chapter does not provide a comprehensive overview of the many strands of language contact research and of the many developments that have occurred in recent years, but instead sets out concepts, models and terms that foreground the presentation of studies from the respective language contact situations.

Jim Hlavac, Monash University

https://doi.org/10.1515/9781501503917-002

2 Diachronic and synchronic perspectives

The focus of this book is on the linguistic repertoires of Croatian-speakers in diaspora settings. The linguistic data presented in this volume are from samples that are relatively contemporary, i.e. collected over the last 35 years. At the same time, language contact situations have a historical dimension, and researchers studying present-day communities may ask themselves a number of questions about what is already known of contact situations. Some of these questions may be:

What is known about contact between Croatian with these same other languages in the homeland?

What is known about the speech of previous generations of Croatian-speakers who resided outside their homeland?

Which forms or structures in their speech (or written texts) are reported to have changed, to have been augmented or to have even been replaced by others?

Are there patterns from historically-based contact situations that can inform our understanding of contemporary ones?

It may be instructive to briefly look first at language contact in the homeland and to see what studies there record about the influences of surrounding languages on Croatian itself.

A number of these studies focus on lexical items as the most conspicuous manifestations of language contact. For example, there are general dictionaries listing words from other languages (e.g. Klaić 1982; Anić and Goldstein 1999), transfers and calques that have entered Croatian (Turk 2013) as well as dictionaries of words or studies of lexical contribution supplied from specific languages that have entered Croatian such as German (Striedter-Temps 1958; Grotzky 1978; Glovacki-Bernardi 1998; Golubović 2007), Turkish (Škaljić 2004), (Venetian) Italian (Sočanac 2004; Ljubičić 2011), Hungarian (Hadrovics 1985; Žagar-Szentesi 2005) as well as English (Filipović 1990). A finding from most of these dictionaries or lexically-based studies is that long-standing contact usually results in lexical contributions that are phonologically and morphologically (and graphemically) fully adapted into Croatian. There is perhaps one exception to this, and this is English-Croatian contact. English-Croatian contact is comparatively recent, i.e. widespread teaching of English as a foreign language did not commence in Croatia until the 1960s; around the world, English started to become popular on a major scale only in the 1960s, and it was not until about this time that sizeable numbers of Croatian-speakers started to emigrate to predominately Anglophone countries. The comparative recency of English-Croatian contact in comparison to German-Croatian or Italian-Croatian contact means that it is possible to locate variation in the degree of integration of English-origin items that have entered Croatian. These range from fully adapted ones, e.g. *vikendom* weekend-INS.M.SG 'on the weekends', to ones that are of very recent vintage and are not adapted, e.g. *catering* [keɪtəɹɪŋ], 'semi-adapted', e.g. [keɪterɪng], or more or less fully adapted, e.g. [keterɪng], sometimes now spelt as *ketering*. The overall pattern is that a longer period of use usually results in adaptation, and with the passage of time, it is likely that *catering* will become phonologically and morphologically integrated in the same way that *weekend* already has. Although the homeland situation differs from that abroad, patterns of adaptation found amongst Croatia-based speakers offer a point of comparison when looking at the vernaculars of those speakers located elsewhere.

Beyond the lexis, historical grammars of Croatian tend to be structured in a way that provides a chronological account of historic events and key protagonists and their contributions to the development of what would later become the standard language (Moguš 1995; Lisac et al. 2015). This approach to diachrony is somewhat different to that taken by researchers of language contact who typically adopt a typologically based narrative of changes that have occurred in a language. One book that does provide a description of the main typological features of Croatian (and Serbian) is Brozović and Ivić's (1988) succinct but insightful overview that sets out examples of internal (i.e. 'inter-dialectal') influences and external influences in relation to forms that have been adopted in the standard as well as forms that are considered non-standard. Case inflection forms are one example that Brozović and Ivić (1988: 20–22) focus on. Historically, DAT and LOC case inflection forms of nouns, adjectives and determiners were distinct, but these, at least in the standard language, have given way to converged forms due chiefly to inter-dialectal influence and syncretism. Thus, in standard Croatian, the DAT and LOC forms for the phrase 'this tall man' are the same – *ovom visokom čovjeku*. Forms that still distinguish the two cases are stylistically marked as upper register, e.g. DAT *ovomu visokom čovjeku* vs. LOC *ovome visokom čovjeku*. In other instances, syncretism of ACC and LOC forms remains a feature of non-standard varieties only and is not part of the standard. Jutronić-Tihomirović (1988/1989) shows how the collapsing of the movement vs. position distinction in the urban dialect of Split and some central Dalmatian dialects is a salient feature of these non-standard varieties that distinguishes them from standard Croatian.

Historically, changes have occurred in the verb system as well. An analytic tense consisting of 'to be' *biti* and a past participle that is inflected for gender and number – the perfect tense – has become the default past tense to express events in the past. It is not evident that internal or inter-dialectal influence is responsible for the expansion of the perfect tense. Certainly, the spread of the perfect tense has led to a reduction of the aorist and imperfect tenses: in the case of the aorist to the disappearance of its use with imperfective verbs, and in the case of the imperfect, to the disappearance of its use with perfective verbs. What is likely is that the attributing factor for the popularisation of the perfect has been 'typological drift', i.e. a possible pre-disposition towards a single (albeit compound) past tense as a language-internal feature, combined with external influence that records a similar pattern of the popularisation of compound perfect tenses in surrounding languages identified by Heine and Kuteva (2006: 37). The argument for the 'economy' of one past tense form can also be advanced where one form then obviates the need to distinguish morphological suffixes of the aorist from those of the imperfect. In another verbal construction, the mediopassive, change has occurred. Croatian like all Slavic languages has mediopassive constructions with a REFL particle, such as *vidi se kuća* 'see-3SG REFL house-NOM.F.SG' 'the house is seen' = 'the house is visible'. Alongside this is a more recent non-standard construction with the same meaning in which 'house' is marked with the accusative: *vidi se kuću* 'see-3SG REFL house-ACC.F.SG.'. In regard to the accusative construction, Brozović and Ivić (1988: 37) attribute unspecified "foreign influences" for its occurrence.

In regard to the development of other constructions foreign influence is uncontroversial. Brozović and Ivić (1988: 39) locate influence from German and Italian for structures in (non-standard) Croatian such as the preposition *za* 'for' with an infinitive, e.g. *dobro za jesti* 'good-ADV for eat-INF', based on models from German (*gut zum Essen*) and/or Italian (*buono da mangiare*). External influence accounts for forms such as *idem dolje* go-1SG down 'I'm going down(stairs)' (cf. German *ich gehe runter*) instead of a verb with a prefix indicating direction of movement, e.g. *silazim* 'I am descending'. German influence also accounts for the occurrence of DAT REFL in constructions such as *kupio sam si knjigu* 'buy-PST.M.SG AUX-1SG REFL.DAT book-ACC.F.SG' (cf. German *ich kaufte mir ein Buch.* 'I bought myself a book.') where standard varieties would not have a REFL or would have it as an optional adverbial phrase: *kupio sam knjigu (za sebe)* 'buy-PST.M.SG AUX.1SG book-ACC.F.SG (for+ACC self-ACC)'.

Bound morphemes are also borrowed. These are usually verbal or nominal prefixes or suffixes, e.g. the verbal suffix *–irati* from German. Brozović and Ivić (1988: 42) list German as the intermediary language responsible for the adoption of other suffixes of Latin of Greek origin, such as *–ant, -ator, -acija, -ancija, -izam, -ist, -aža,* that occur not only in 'internationalisms', but also as suffixes on indigenous roots: *zabušant* 'shirker', *drmator* 'head honcho', *uživacija* 'pleasure/enjoyment' *žderancija* 'over-eating', *kajkavizam* 'Kajkavian word', *vezist* 'signalman' and *gnjavaža* 'hassle'. The following suffixes were borrowed from Turkish, *-ana, -džija, -lija, -luk,* and all can be productively affixed to domestic roots: *teretana* 'exercise gym', *račundžija* 'thrifty person', *režimlija* 'supporter of a regime', *bezobrazluk* 'impudence'. The nominal suffix *–ov* from Hungarian that can be affixed to domestic adjectives, e.g. *šarov* 'multi-coloured dog' is less obvious to most, due to the indigenous homophonous possessive suffix *-ov*.

Historically, language contact has not stopped at lexical and morphological incursions. In the late nineteenth and early twentieth century, most residents of cities in eastern Croatia such as Osijek (Ger. Esseg, Hung. Eszék) were bi- or multilingual. This led to conventionalised mixed codes such as *Essekerisch* or *esekerski govor* 'Esseker speech' a predominatly German vernacular based on Bavarian-Austrian dialects. Alongside this, the Slavonian dialect of Croatian spoken in the city itself also contained numerous German and Hungarian transfers. In addition, standard and regional varieties of Hungarian were used as well (Petrović 2001, 2008; Binder 2006). The same can be said about the residents of cities along the Adriatic Sea at that time (and up to WWII) where varieties of Italian were spoken alongside varieties of Croatian, e.g. *Fiumano* in Rijeka (Spicijarić Paškvan & Crnić Novosel 2014) and *Zaratino* in Zadar (Škevin and Jazidžija 2017), while in Zagreb and across northern Croatia, German supplied much lexical stock or was a contributing code to conventionalised bilingual speech (Novak and Piškorec 2006). This latter variety was sometimes pejoratively referred to as *švapčarenje* 'speaking Swabian'.

The transfer of forms and constructions was not restricted to urban areas; nearly all rural dialects bear considerable stock from other languages, and the degree of influence is commensurate to the length of time and geographical spread that German, Turkish, Italian and Hungarian were used across south-east Europe. The sociolinguistic situation of the lands in which Croats lived accounts for the super-stratum influence that these languages exerted onto Croatian. In languages in contact research, the link between social conditions and linguistic outcomes is something that has become irrefutable, at least since the publication of Thomason and Kaufman's (1988) book.

There are two Croatian varieties outside the homeland spoken in minority settings which have been well studied from a diachronic perspective: Burgenland Croatian spoken in eastern Austria, far-western Hungary and south-west Slovakia (Brabec 1983; Weilguni 1983; Nyomárkay 1996; Neweklowsky 2010); Molise Croatian spoken in central Italy (Rešetar 1911; Breu 1998; Breu and Piccoli 2000; Sammartino 2004; Scotti 2006). Both are minority languages that have existed for approx. 500 years in relative isolation from the Croatian-speaking homeland. The development of Burgenland Croatian has been particularly well studied, not least due to the codification of a supra-regional standard (Benčić 1972) that has resulted in the publication of trilingual dictionaries (Bencsics et al. 1982; 1991), a grammar (Benčić et al. 2003) and textbooks for adult L2-learners (Karall 2000). Molise Croatian, spoken by a smaller number of speakers, is now endangered, although extensive dictionaries (Breu and Piccoli 2000) and a grammar (Sammartino 2004) exist to record its forms.

As stated in chapter 1, a feature of this volume is the presentation of diachronically based research contained in chapters 3 and 4 that foregrounds and informs the presentation of data in chapters 5 to 14. The matching of synchronic data with that of diachronic studies is something that has been often called for, but not always realised. Some researchers conceptualise the connection between synchrony to diachrony in a very direct sense. According to a usage-based approach (Bybee 2010) where usage is seen to co-determine competency, "instances of interference or grammatical deviation [can be seen] as synchronically manifesting, and furthering structural change" (Backus, Demirçay and Sevinç 2013: 5), where "structural change" is understood as an occurrence uncovered through diachronic analysis. Further, while single instances of unusual forms of bilingual speech grab the attention of contact linguists, I am reminded of Backus's (2015) call for analyses of data sets to focus firstly on recurrent contact phenomena, and to identify how frequent and widespread the linguistic forms are that are found. He made this appeal in relation to the examination of both diachronically and synchronically-focused data sets.

3 Contact linguistics

The title of this section shows a progression in terminology: the number of studies on languages in contact has increased to the extent that a tighter designation is now used for this sub-discipline – contact linguistics, also the title of Carol Myers-Scotton's book, published in 2002. Much of the ground work for the establishment of contact linguistics as a distinct sub-discipline was achieved with Thomason and Kaufman's (1988) seminal work which encompassed both diachronic and synchronic perspectives. Their book brought together key areas of language contact research – lexical and morpho-syntactic borrowing, typological comparison, instances of mixed speech and code-switching, the development of pidgins and creoles, and settings of language maintenance and shift – that established the parameters of research now known as contact linguistics. The most prominent strand of contact linguistics is that which focuses on structural linguistic features. Thus, contact linguistics encompasses all traditional sub-fields of linguistics, with the more widely-studied ones being: lexis – the study of single lexical items or groups of lexical items transferred from one language into another; morphology and syntax – the study of the transfer or replication of morphological forms and/or syntactic features from one language into another. This volume also focuses mostly on these sub-fields. The sub-field of semantics is addressed here in the form of calques, loan translations and instances of semantic transference. The other sub-fields of phonology and pragmatics are touched on only in a small number of chapters.

As the name suggests, 'contact linguistics' looks at linguistic forms that result from a language (or rather its speakers) coming into contact with another, i.e. with an external entity. Thus, in the first instance, contact linguistics deals with externally-induced change. But, change may occur without or independent of external influence. To delineate the type of change that is attributable to external factors, I adopt Thomason's (2003: 688) definition of contact-induced language change: "contact between languages (or dialects) [as] a source of linguistic change whenever a change occurs that would have been unlikely, or at least less likely, to occur outside a specific contact situation" (Thomason 2003: 688), with the provisos suggested by Heine and Kuteva (2005: 22) that the degree of this likelihood cannot always be clearly established, and that contact-induced language change need not be restricted only to those changes that are otherwise thought to be unlikely to happen in non-contact situations. In other words, contact-induced language change can result in innovations that are known to occur in non-contact situations – a point that Thomason (2001) herself emphasises in several places. Dual- or multiple causation for change is a possibility that contact linguists always need to always consider (Verschik 2008).

While change cannot always be attributed to one source only, the susceptibility of certain items or forms to change has been reasonably well studied, as well as the directionality of change in a typological sense. For example, it has long been known that analytic constructions are more likely to be borrowed than inflectional categories. Weinreich (1953: 41) wrote: "Significantly, in the interference of two grammatical patterns it is ordinarily the one which uses relatively free and invariant morphemes in its paradigm – one might say, the more explicit pattern – which serves as the model of imitation". Thomason (2001: 69) writes that "less tightly structured features are easier to borrow than features that fit into tightly integrated closed structures", inflectional morphology being an example of the latter. According to Dahl (2004: 127–128), "what is borrowed, or calqued (i.e. translated), in grammar will most frequently be periphrastic constructions or free markers, and less often affixes, although the latter is also observed to happen". Mono-morphemic forms are more likely to be transferred than multi-morphemic ones. This suggests that analytic constructions rather than synthetic constructions (or rather synthetic forms) are prone to borrowing. In south-east Europe, contact linguistics studies have identified this, e.g.

> Changes that made the languages of the Balkan linguistic area converge structurally were neither clearly simplifying nor clearly complexifying. These changes represent a tendency towards a certain syntactic type, that is, explicit analytic marking. (Lindstedt 2019: 70)

Haspelmath and Michaelis (2017: 14) also come to a similar conclusion, that "analyticization is generally favoured by language-contact situations". Interestingly, Lindstedt (2019: 81) notes that "grammatical borrowing that favours change towards analytism may occur both when L1 speakers use another language and also when L2 speakers transfer features from the native languages."

It therefore appears that borrowing increases analytism and that the 'transparency' of categories in a donor language means that such 'transparent' forms are amenable candidates for transfer. Looking at contact linguistic outcomes in a broader and comparative perspective, taxonomies of borrowability have been developed which match linguistic outcomes with the type and length of contact. Of course, the likelihood of movement of forms across languages depends on the social mores of groups and the proficiency levels of the speakers, as well as linguistic attributes of the forms themselves. But across many samples patterns are recognisable. The following scales of borrowability are posited by Field (2002) and Winford (2003) according to grammatical category or morphosyntactic function. Their scales contain a hierarchical ordering of most borrowed forms to least likely borrowed forms from left to right:

> nouns > verbs > adjectives > adverbs, prepositions, interjections
> content item > function word > agglutinating affix > fusional affix   (Field 2002: 35, 38)

> nouns > adjectives > verbs > prepositions > co-ordinating conjunctions > quantifiers > determiners > free pronouns > clitic pronouns > subordinating conjunctions.   (Winford 2003: 51)

Winford (2009) also mentions Van Coetsem (1988: 25) who earlier had observed a "stability gradient", i.e., certain components of language, such as phonology, morphology and syntax, tend to be more stable and hence resistant to change. Others, particularly the lexicon, are less stable, and thus more prone to change. Thomason (2001) gives a more fine-grained description of borrowability and distinguishes four general stages of contact:

1. Casual contact [...] only non-basic vocabulary borrowed.

   Lexicon: Content words – most often nouns, but also verbs, adjectives, and adverbs

   Structure: None.

2. Slightly more intense contact [...]

   Lexicon: Function words ... content words, non-based vocabulary.

Structure: Only minor structural borrowing . . . Phonological features realised by new phones but in loanwords only; syntactic features such as new functions or functional restrictions for previously existing syntactic structures, or functional restrictions for previously existing syntactic structures, or increased usage of previously rare word order

3. More intense contact [. . .] basic as well as non-basic vocabulary borrowed, moderate structural borrowing:

    Lexicon: More function words borrowed; basic vocabulary [. . .] may also be borrowed including such closed-class items as pronouns and low numerals, as well as nouns and verbs and adjectives; derivational affixes may be borrowed too.

    Structure: More significant structural features are borrowed, though usually without resulting major typological change in the borrowing language [. . .] In syntax, such features as word order (e.g. SVO beginning to replace SOV or vice versa) [. . .] In morphology, borrowed inflectional affixes and categories may be added to native words especially if they fit well typologically with previously existing patterns

4. Intense contact (very extensive bilingualism among borrowing-language speakers, social factors strongly favouring borrowing); continuing heavy lexical borrowing in all sections of the lexicon, heavy structural borrowing.

    Lexicon: Heavy borrowing.

    Structure: Anything goes, including structural borrowing that results in major typological changes in the borrowing language [...] In syntax, sweeping changes in such features as word order, relative clauses, negation, co-ordination, subordination, comparison and quantification. In morphology, typologically disruptive changes such as the replacement of flexional by agglutinative morphology or vice versa, the addition or loss of morphological categories that do not match in source and borrowing languages, and the wholesale loss or addition of agreement patterns. (Thomason: 2001: 70–71)

In regard to the fourth and last stage on Thomason's (2001) borrowing scale, examples of this type of intense contact are found in diachronic studies of language contact in south-east Europe, most notably amongst the languages of the Balkan sprachbund. Lindstedt (2019: 74, 77, original punctuation) notes that "explicit analytic marking can be typologically opposed to inflectional (synthetic) marking, as well as to implicit analytic marking with word order alone and to the absence of marking" and that for two of the Slavic languages in the area, Macedonian and Bulgarian, this resulted in a "decrease of case distinctions, and the increased use of prepositions". Changes recorded in other South Slavic languages inform our understanding of what can occur in Croatian in analogous contact situations.

Thomason's (2001) four stages of contact represent the degrees to which one language can be influenced by another. The linguistic forms that characterise each stage can also be labelled according to other, congruent descriptions such as those set out in Myers-Scotton's (1993, 2002) Matrix Language Framework (hereafter MLF). The basis of the MLF is the categorisation of morphemes according to the role that they play. The first type of morpheme is content morphemes (roughly congruent to 'free morphemes' in other grammatical descriptions) which assign or receive a thematic role and which are conceptually activated as lexemes or items with pragmatic inference. The other type of morpheme is system morphemes which do not assign or receive a thematic role, and which occur depending on information from their syntactic head or across a whole clause (or CP – projection of complimentizer). There are three groups of system morphemes. Those system morphemes that occur on the basis of information from their syntactic head (such as a noun) are "early system morphemes" and examples include determiners or plural forms. Those system morphemes that occur "without reference to the properties of a head" but due to "the grammatical configuration of a maximal projection" are termed "bridge system morphemes" (Myers-Scotton 2002: 75). Examples of these include possessive *of* and *'s* in English. The last group are the "outsider system morphemes" which occur on the basis of features across the morphosyntactic grid of the clause (or CP). Examples of outsider system morphemes are subject-verb markers and case affixes.

Using the MLF 4-way distinction of morphemes, Myers-Scotton (2002: 242–245) matches degree of contact with the type of morphemes that are likely to be imported from the contributing language. (Myers-Scotton's [2002] description is matched against Thomason and Kaufman's [1988: 74–75] borrowing scale that has five stages, but these are congruent to the four described above in Thomason [2001].) Stages 1 and 2 relate to the transfer of content morphemes only, with stage 3 including also "inflectional suffixes" that are system morphemes, including late ones. In stage 4 all types of morphemes are possible, including outsider system morphemes that are generated at the level of grammatical relations across the clause. In relation to the types of forms that occur in stages 3 and 4, Myers-Scotton (2002) suggests that structural input from the contributing language is not an accidental or arbitrary phenomenon and where this occurs, it is evidence that the frame of the matrix language itself has changed so that it is supplied by structural information from not only the original language but also the contributing one alongside it. This is termed a "Matrix Language Turnover" (Myers-Scotton 2002: 247) where the term "turnover" is not meant to suggest that the old Matrix Language has been displaced by another one; rather, that it is being augmented by input from another language the effect of which can be partial replacement or co-occurrence of forms, or outcomes that reflect an amalgamation of structure from two sources. The splitting and combining of abstract structure supplied by two codes that result in a changed Matrix Language is described in terms of it being a "Composite Matrix Language" (Myers-Scotton 2002: 228) which is further described in Section 4 and 5.3.3.

4 Heritage languages and speakers of heritage languages

Language is passed on from one generation to the next, from parent to child, but the language of a child is rarely identical to that of its parent(s) due to input received from others, from older-generation, but also same-generation interlocutors, in particular peer groups. The notion of input is important here, as parental input (along with input from a range of other speakers and sources) is seen as an enabler for the full acquisition of a linguistic variety, i.e. a command of the target ('felicitous' or 'correct') forms used in the various sub-fields of a language. This language, to be sure, need not be a standard variety of a language, although those acquiring a standard variety can be advantaged by the greater number of speakers and resources that are acquisitional models for that variety. In the case of speakers of minority languages – whether they reside in long-standing linguistic enclaves or in diaspora communities of recent vintage – volume and variety of input from parents (and other speakers of the minority language) play a decisive role in a child's acquisition of the target forms of the minority language. Reduced input through it being supplied from only a small number of interlocutors (e.g. parents, older-generational family members), and the functional restrictedness of acquisition have consequences on heritage speakers' use of the minority language. Restricted acquisition and reduced use, in turn, have consequences on both the form of the minority language used by younger speakers (Montrul 2016), as well as the likelihood that they will shift from it (Myers-Scotton 1996).

These features pertain to *heritage languages*, a term that has been used since the 1970s in North America, but which are often referred to as *minority languages* (particularly in Europe), *ethnic languages* (North America, Australia) or *community languages* (Australia). A heritage language is a person's first acquired language (in chronological terms) or acquired contemporaneously with another language, usually the socio-politically dominant language. The socio-politically dominant language then becomes, with the passage of time and often with entry into the formal schooling system, that person's dominant language (Rothman 2009). This opens up the following questions in regard to the heritage language:

> What level of acquisition has the person reached in the heritage language at the point when the language of the society in which they live has started to become their dominant one?
>
> Is their acquisition of the heritage language frozen, i.e. arrested or even liable to attrition, or does acquisition continue to progress at a rate and in ways that are just different from those of monolinguals?
>
> Do the proficiency levels (*competence* in Chomsky's terms) of heritage language speakers differ from those of monolingual speakers of the same language?
>
> Do the linguistic forms (*performance* in Chomsky's terms) of heritage language speakers differ from those of monolingual speakers of the same language?

Forty years of contact linguistics and sociolinguistic research tells us that both the competence and performance of heritage language speakers are different than those of homeland speakers (Haugen 1973; Clyne 1991; Brinton, Kagan & Bauckus 2008). Speakers acquire varieties based on the input and the situation of their setting; when these are different, the linguistic outcomes are also different. This is a necessarily vague implication, as in reality, there are heritage language speakers who are seemingly indistinguishable from homeland speakers (e.g. the only obvious difference may be a narrower repertoire of registers of which they have active command) and there are heritage language speakers whose active or passive command is severely limited (Polinsky 2006, 2007).

The definition of heritage language speaker used throughout this volume is a functional-linguistic one: a person residing outside a predominantly Croatian-speaking environment who has aural and oral proficiency in Croatian and whose speech bears forms recognisably attributable to *any* variety of vernacular Croatian, whether standard or non-standard (Valdés 2000). In this volume, heritage language varieties of Croatian are contrasted with *Homeland Croatian* which is defined here as *any* variety of vernacular Croatian, whether standard or non-standard, that is spoken or used in Croatia, or the areas of origin of Croatian-speakers from Bosnia-Herzegovina, Serbia or Montenegro. The term *Homeland Croatian* (hereafter HMLD.Cro) is therefore not synonymous with *Standard Croatian*. It is, as stated, a hypernym encompassing all varieties used in the homeland, where 'homeland' is understood here as a geographically based label. Geography is, in the first instance, the characteristic that distinguishes the speakers whose speech is presented in this book. In linguistic terms, HMLD.Cro is a point of contrast or "baseline" against which data from speakers of heritage Croatian is compared. As discussed below, a monolingual variety of HMLD.Cro is not always the model or the form of input that younger generation heritage speakers receive. Equivalent forms or constructions from HMLD.Cro are provided only for the purpose of linguistic comparison, and it is not suggested that they are forms or constructions available to heritage language speakers.

To return to the question of describing the acquisitional pathway of the heritage language speaker and to account for how heritage language competence relates to heritage language speakers' performance, I posit that the following phenomena can occur which account for speakers' active command of the formal properties of the language. (Morphological and syntactic forms are the most conspicuous amongst these, but in principle these relate to the lexicon, phonology, semantics and pragmatics in analogous ways.) Depending on the number of years that a speaker was exposed to and developed a proficiency in the heritage language (sequentially preceding or simultaneously acquired with the socio-politically dominant language), a (child) speaker's acquisition may encompass many, most or nearly all of the forms recorded in the acquisition of the same language by same-age (child) homeland speakers. Entry into the school system is, as stated, an event that 'punctuates' the acquisition of the heritage language. Studies that track the acquisition and forms used in the speech of young heritage language speakers (Bolonyai 2002; Montrul 2002; Silva-Corvalán 2003) record that

> [i]ncomplete bilingual L1 [heritage language] acquisition may precede or co-occur with attrition, the erosion or restructuring of the L1 in extensive contact with the L2 [. . .]. When this happens, linguistic outcomes of incomplete acquisition and those of incipient attrition may be rather difficult to distinguish. (Bolonyai 2007: 4. Square brackets added.)

The term "incomplete acquisition" has been commonly used to describe heritage language speakers' level of competence (Levine 2000; Montrul 2008; Pires and Rothman 2009). This term lacks precision as it does not capture, for example, instances where children appear to successfully acquire many features, but at a later stage they cease using them, or it can be the case that acquisition of features occurs at a different rate, i.e. where speakers have very varied trajectories of acquisition. Putnam and Sánchez (2013) and Kupisch and Rothman (2018) suggest that complete acquisition of reduced input may be a more accurate description of some heritage speakers' level of competence. Aalberse, Backus and Muysken (2019: 146–149, original puncutation) also problematise the term 'incomplete acquisition' and remind us of a finding, well known in FLA and SLA, that *volume* and *type* of input have predictable consequences: ". . . heritage speakers receive less input than the baseline (quantitatively different) and they receive different input (qualitatively different) in the sense that it is often limited to the informal, domestic register". It is also unclear whether incomplete acquisition refers to things that are known to occur amongst heritage speakers at various stages of their formative years, i.e. where their competence in the heritage language is modified, re-conceptualised or subject to "U-shaped learning" (Polinsky 2007: 162). I therefore adopt Polinsky and Scontras's term "divergent attainment" to refer to a description of competence that is a "[...] system different from the baseline [homeland variety]. Heritage speakers encounter input that is different both qualitatively and quantitatively from the monolingual learner; as a result, they could arrive at a different mental representation of their linguistic knowledge" (Polinsky and Scontras 2019: 4. Square brackets added). The notion of 'divergent attainment' closely matches descriptions of 'individual variation' or language change at the level of an individual who

> has acquired a grammar that differs in at least this respect from the grammars of other individuals in the speech community; and the reason that this individual has acquired a grammar that is innovative in this sense is that s/he has been exposed to primary linguistic data that is significantly different to that which previous acquirers were exposed to.
> (Lucas 2015: 520)

Both Polinsky and Scontras's (2019) and Lucas's (2015) descriptions refer to a situation that can give rise to some bilingual speakers having a composite matrix language (Myers-Scotton 2002: 99–105), a concept mentioned in Section 3. What this means is that their 'competence' (in Chomskyan terms) in the heritage language can consist of structural categories and forms supplied from their dominant language, as well as from the heritage language. To be sure, a composite matrix language is not an automatic consequence of the situation described above by Lucas (2015). But it is one that can develop amongst, for example, some speakers of the second or third generation.

The term 'divergent attainment' is also a more precise term to use for second- and third-generation speakers than the term 'attrition'. It is often hard to discern which forms might have once been acquired and then subsequently abandoned in the acquisition trajectories of second- and third-generation speakers. For this reason, the term 'attrition' is used in this volume only in reference to linguistic forms of reduction occurring in the speech of those who migrated as older adolescents or adults (i.e. Gen.1A speakers – see below section 4.1) and who had fully acquired Croatian before emigration. Such speakers are labelled "forgetters" by Polinsky (2007: 189). This notion of forgetting or (momentary) non-access to forms is a reminder that novel or conspicuous forms used in diaspora vernaculars occur not only in the speech of younger-generation speakers, but in the speech of first-generation, i.e. 'homeland-born' speakers as well.

The linguistic forms used by first-generation speakers who are the parents, grandparents or older generation 'homeland-born' speakers of second- and third-generation speakers are the key input that heritage-language speakers receive. Sociolinguistic and domain-based data (Otheguy and Zentella 2012; Pauwels 2016) are instructive sources to check

> whether the input that heritage speakers get from the older immigrant generation is already different from the baseline – that is, whether any of the properties attested in the heritage language spoken by the second generation may be derived from the first generation grammar itself. (Benmamoun, Montrul and Polinsky 2013: 170)

The point made above by Benmamoun, Montrul and Polinsky (2013) cannot be made strongly enough. Not many studies track the source input that is provided to Gen.2 speakers and those of subsequent generations. One that does is Otheguy, Zentella and Livert (2007) who show how overt subject pronoun use amongst Gen.1A speakers is a model accounting for commensurately higher use amongst younger speakers.

The term 'L1' is referred to above by Bolonyai (2007) as the first acquired language that is also the heritage language of a younger speaker, but one that is no longer the child's dominant language. In the chapters of this volume, the term 'L1' is used to refer to the language in which a speaker has dominance, i.e. the language in which a speaker has relatively higher proficiency in (Silva-Corvalán & Treffers-Daller 2015). Thus, this definition is not related to chronology of acquisition. This means that for Gen.2 speakers who acquired Croatian before another language, Croatian may be their L2 if their self-reported dominance is in another language, typically the socio-politically dominant language of the country they reside in. The socio-politically dominant language, in this case, is their L1, and not Croatian. Dominance and higher proficiency typically result from greater exposure and input, and ability to display greater lexical richness, fluency (Daller et al., 2011), discourse patterns (Flecken, 2011) and a greater command of different registers (Köpke and Genevska-Hanke, 2018). I acknowledge that in certain settings, in regard to certain thematic topics and with certain interlocutors, the dominant language may not be the most readily available language in psycholinguistic terms, and that dominance is not always an issue of relative proficiency (Gertken et al, 2014). But, as a general yardstick, identification of L1 is based on proficiency level. Further, some speakers, e.g. many Gen.1B and some Gen.2, ones may have acquisitional profiles that show that their proficiency level in Croatian and the other language is comparable. In these instances, I describe these speakers as having two L1s. (See below Table 1.)

Focusing on those speakers who have Croatian as their L2, is is possible to identify four causative factors that determine outcomes in the speech of heritage language speakers: divergent attainment, attrition, transference and (structural) change. (The last three factors can certainly relate also to speakers with Croatian as their L1, but my focus is here mainly on those with it as their L2.) The third term, transference, will be discussed in greater detail in section 5.3.1, and structural changes will be outlined in 5.3.3. I focus here briefly on the first two factors. Some of the effects of divergent attainment and/or attrition can be the following: attrition in the lexicon and structural attrition (e.g. syncretism of case forms) (Polinsky 2006: 252); changes in a speaker's grammatical system that appear to be non-random and related to an increased redundancy in expression (Polinsky 2006: 252). For languages such as Hungarian and Russian, that are highly inflective ones like Croatian, morphological change, where it occurs, is "more pronounced and pervasive in nominal morphology than in verbal morphology", and in regard to different types of morphemes being prone to change, it is found that "[l]ow-proficiency heritage speakers of Russian have an error rate of about 40% in the nominal morphology, but less than 20% in their verbal agreement morphology" (Benmamoun, Montrul and Polinsky 2013: 142).

Much but by no means all of the data collected by Polinsky and her collaborators is gained through prompted description of pictures, acceptability ratings of model sentences and translation tasks (Polinsky 2006, 2008, 2016; Dubinina and Polinsky 2013). This has enabled a degree of comparability of output from heritage language speakers in relation to specific linguistic features to show how different speakers use similar or dissimilar forms based on the same visual or other stimuli. Most chapters of this volume do not feature data gathered from informants in a systematic or elicited way such as prompted description via visual stimuli, and they therefore do not give a fine-grained description of variation compared across their respective samples. No chapter contains longitudinal data on the same speaker or groups of speakers, so a trajectory of acquisition, including attrition, or 'forgetting' or a reconfiguration of previously acquired forms is not provided. Nonetheless, linguistic data that are congruent to the findings reported in heritage language research literature are often described by the authors of chapters in the terms used within the heritage language research literature.

As stated, the common definition of a heritage language relates to a language acquired in a functionally restricted context, typically the family home, while the socio-politically dominant language outside the home is another language (Rothman 2009: 156). This definition does not readily apply to adult migrants who acquired the heritage language (usually) in a first language environment without the presence of a language that is the socio-politically dominant language of the country that they later emigrated to as adults. However, first-generation speakers are defined in this volume also as heritage-language speakers for a number of reasons: their own speech typically bears evidence of change – most prominently in the lexicon, but also in the areas of semantics, pragmatics, syntax (e.g. word order) and in some instances, even morphosyntax (Schmid 2011). Further, first generation speakers are the key models for further generations acquiring the heritage language. Extending Benmamoun, Montrul and Polinsky's (2013) comments about the linguistic form of models provided by first-generation speakers to younger speakers, Polinsky and Scontras (2019: 8) observe that first generation speakers' "input language is likely to deviate already from the [. . .] variety of the homeland, so changes present in the heritage language might already have been present in the input from which the heritage language was learned". This means that particular forms that second- and subsequent-generation speakers use may not be forms resulting from their own divergent attainment of the heritage language, but forms that they replicate verbatim from the speech of first-generation speakers. Generational membership and linguistic repertoire is discussed further in the following section.

A last point that I make here is a sociolinguistic one with psycholinguistic consequences. When using the heritage language, second-generation and subsequent-generation speakers in particular, but also first-generation speakers, are usually interacting with interlocutors who themselves are bilingual. This means that they are in a "bilingual mode" (Grosjean 1999) when using the heritage language, not a "monolingual mode". Even if they use a monolingual or strongly heritage-language dominant variety, they have the ability and freedom to draw on forms from the other language because they know that these are likely to be understood. Cross-generational and intra-group bilingualism, and the acquisition and recurrent use of a heritage language in bilingual mode are the sociolinguistic and psycholinguistic bases for bilingual speech.

4.1 Heritage language speakers and generational membership

Those born in Croatia or in regions of Bosnia-Herzegovina, Serbia and Montenegro in which Croatian is spoken and who emigrate are labelled here 'first-generation speakers'. The contraction 'Gen.1' is used in this volume to refer to speakers belonging to this generation. In contact linguistics research, a distinction is usually made between those who migrated as late adolescents or adults who are classified as first-generation A (hereafter 'Gen.1A') and those who migrated as children or young adolescents, classified as first-generation

B (hereafter 'Gen.1B') (Haugen 1953: 334; Clyne 1975: 177–180). In the case of Gen.1A speakers, their first-acquired language typically remains their dominant language and their acquisition of the language of the country of residence typically bears evidence of transference from their L1, Croatian. For older Gen.1B speakers, Croatian is likely to have been fully acquired or at least acquired to an advanced degree, and after emigration, it is unlikely that complete attrition or forgetting of Croatian will occur; the language of the country of residence will typically be fully acquired or at least to an advanced degree. But for Gen.1B speakers who migrated in their early childhood, their acquisition of Croatian may resemble that of a heritage speaker. The term divergent attainment may best describe their acquisition in which the heritage language proficiency is attained to different levels. In psycholinguistic terms, the socio-politically dominant language is the one in which these speakers have dominance, at least across a wide number of functions.

For the second generation (hereafter Gen.2), i.e. children of Gen.1A or Gen.1B parents,[1] Croatian is likely to be (but not always!) the language that they acquire in the home/family setting. This refers primarily to the macro-skills *listening* and *speaking* that are first acquired in Croatian, or Croatian is one of the languages acquired contemporaneously with another language in what is known as *bilingual first language acquisition* (De Houwer 2009). A sample of 100 informants whose speech I have written about widely, e.g. Hlavac (2003: 18–19), that consisted of 88 Gen.2 and 12 Gen.1B informants. Of these 100 informants, 75 of them first acquired listening and 76 first acquired speaking in Croatian, while the single most common self-diagnosed ratings of their Croatian ability in these same macro-skills were not 'excellent', but 'good' for listening (60%) and 'good' for speaking (46%). As stated, while Croatian is usually acquired first, after commencing mainstream schooling in which the language of instruction is the socio-politically dominant language, this latter language usually becomes their L1. Petrović (2017) also records similar findings amongst Canadian-Croatians.

In the previous section, I mentioned that Gen.2 speakers' acquisition of Croatian is characterised by restrictedness of input and the functional restrictedness of its use. For this reason, Croatian is commonly referred to by Gen.2 speakers themselves as their 'less strong language' i.e. their L2. But, some others report

---

[1] In the studies and data samples referred to in most chapters of this book, almost all data from Gen.2 and Gen.3 speakers relate to speakers who are the products of endogamous relationships where both parents were Croatian-speakers. Descriptions of speakers who are the product of exogamous relationships in which only one parent is a Croatian-speaker receive little or only passing attention in this book and we do not address the effect of exogamy in family language policy (Barron-Hauwaert 2004).

that they 'feel just as home in Croatian as [they] do in the [socio-politically dominant] language', i.e. they have two L1s. For most Gen.2 speakers, cross-linguistic influence on Croatian is from L1 to L2; for a smaller number it is from L1 to L1, i.e. from one 'co-dominant' language to another.

Third generation (hereafter 'Gen.3') speakers are those born to Gen.2 parents, and their grandparents are Gen.1A or Gen.1B immigrants. For some, the home/family domain may be predominantly or partly Croatian, according to interlocutor. But few other domains, with the exception of education in the event that the speakers attend Croatian language classes, would feature the use of Croatian. The L1 of Gen.3 speakers is the socio-politically dominant language of the host society.

For the fourth generation, (hereafter 'Gen.4'), there is often no family connection with speakers born in the original homeland, and within the home/family domain where others use Croatian with them, these speakers themselves are usually heritage speakers, i.e. L2-users of Croatian. This does not mean, however, that in other domains, Gen.4 speakers do not have interaction with 'homeland-born' speakers. But in almost all cases, they designate Croatian as their L2. Table 1 below contains proficiency-based descriptions (L1 vs. L2) of Croatian and the socio-politically dominant language of the country of residence in relation to generation membership.

Table 1: Speakers and generations: descriptions of Croatian and other languages as L1 or L2, and directionality of cross-linguistic influence.

	Self-perceived proficiency level in Croatian (as L1 or L2)	Self-perceived proficiency level in language other than Croatian (as L1 or L2)	Cross-linguistic influence from other language on Croatian is:
Gen.1A	L1	L2	L2 > L1
Gen.1B	L1	L1	L1 > L1
	L1	L2	L2 > L1
	L2	L1	L1 > L2
Gen.2	L2	L1	L1 > L2
	L1	L1	L1 > L1
Gen.3	L2	L1	L1 > L2
Gen.4	L2	L1	L1 > L2

In relation to the generation groups in the left-hand column, we can see that for Gen.1A, Gen.3 and Gen.4, a description of these speakers' L1s and L2s is clear. But for Gen.1B and Gen.2, the situation is less clear and speakers from both these generations may describe their L1 as Croatian (more likely for Gen.1B, less likely for Gen.2), Croatian as their L2 (less likely for Gen.1B, more likely for Gen.2), or that they have two L1s, one being Croatian, the other the language. The right-hand column in Table 1 shows the directionality of cross-linguistic transference into Croatian. The data sets in most chapters feature speech at least from Gen.1A, Gen.1B and Gen.2 informants. This means that instances of language contact in relation to Croatian can be both from L2 into L1, L1 into L1, as well as from L2 into L1. Identification of the generational membership of each informant informs our understanding of the linguistic data that that informant provides.

Not mentioned in Table 1 are speakers who are of 'mixed' generations. For example, a child born to a Gen.1A father and a Gen.2 mother is likely to have a linguistic profile that contains features of a Gen.2 speaker and those of a Gen.3 speaker, and could be described as having a generational membership that is Gen.2/3. As stated, some Gen.1B speakers who emigrate before school age are likely to be more similar to Gen.2 speakers than to Gen.1A ones.

Further, the above descriptions relate to speakers who *have acquired* Croatian, and where the acquisitional setting is largely non-formal, naturalistic, based on countless intra-family or social interactions. To be sure, Croatian need not be the exclusive code used in these settings, but substantial and frequent input in Croatian (even a bilingual version thereof) is a defining characteristic for acquisition so that speakers can perform a variety of functions in it. If a Gen.2 member has not acquired Croatian in the home/family domain, it is possible that they may not acquire what is known as communicative competence (Hymes 1966, Leung 2005). Here, we understand communicative competence to refer to a proficiency level in the lexicon, grammar, semantics, phonology and pragmatics (social knowledge on how to understand and use utterances) of a variety *that is characteristic of, or appropriate to the Croatian vernaculars used in the settings, domains and contexts of their locality or area of residence*. I add in italics here sociolinguistic features of the definition of communicative competence to emphasise that acquisition and functional use of Croatian is tied to specific social or interactional settings – these are likely to be the home/family, social life/friends domains, with the possibility that Croatian may be used to some degree in the workplace, education, religion, media, neighbourhood, commercial/transactional domains. Those Croatian-origin persons who do not acquire Croatian in these settings, but who may later acquire a knowledge of it via self- or formal instruction as adults are likely to have an acquisitional trajectory of Croatian and proficiency level in it that is more similar to that of speakers who are learners of Croatian as a foreign language (Cvikić 2016).

As alluded to above, it cannot be taken for granted that the code used in intra-family interactions between Gen.1B parents and their Gen.2 children, or between Gen.2 parents and their Gen.3 children, or between Gen.1A grandparents and their Gen. 3 grand-children will be Croatian (to any degree). Research on language maintenance of migrant languages in 'New World' settings indicates that language shift is common by the third generation and that language maintenance is rare beyond the third generation (Fishman 2008; Pauwels 2016). Amongst some groups or families even Gen.2 children of Gen.1A migrants may not acquire their parents' language if the 'family language policy' (Tannenbaum 2012) does not enable transmission of the heritage language.

5 Contact linguistics terminology and heritage languages

The two previous sections discussed heritage languages, speakers and generational membership. It is possible to make a few comments on the likely proficiency levels in Croatian and in the other language(s) of diaspora speakers, and how these levels may influence the type and frequency of contact linguistic phenomena. Table 1 above contains descriptions of speakers grouped according to generational membership. Table 1 uses the acronyms L1 and L2 to refer to speakers' 'dominant' and 'non-dominant' language in presenting the following three features: self-perceived level of proficiency in Croatian; self-perceived level of proficiency in the socio-politically dominant language of their country of residence; directionality of cross-linguistic influence *on* Croatian.

While the focus of this book is on Croatian as the 'recipient' of contact language phenomena, I acknowledge that the level of proficiency that a speaker has has an effect on the type of phenomena that are likely to occur. As is shown in Table 1 the direction of influence can be distinguished according to what status the language has in a speaker's linguistic repertoire. When this occurs from the L2 onto the L1, this is termed "interference" by Thomason and Kaufman (1988) and Van Coetsem (1988) or "imposition" by Johanson (1999a). When it occurs from the L1 onto the L2, it can be termed "borrowing" (Thomason and Kaufman 1988; Van Coetsem 1988) or "adoption" Johanson (1999a). Directionality of contact from L1 to L2 patterns in ways different from that of L2 into L1. Rayfield (1970: 85, cited in Thomason and Kaufman 1988: 40) describes bilinguals with Yiddish (L1) and English (L2) and the type and degree of influence from one language onto another in the following way: L2 into L1 – lexicon (very strong), phonology (weak), morphosyntax (moderate); L1 into L2 – lexicon (moderate), phonology (strong), morphosyntax (strong). Johanson (2002) locates similar patterns amongst Finno-Ugric bilinguals and the influence of their L1 into their Russian, and from Russian into their L1. Studies of the linguistic repertoires of Croatian-origin Gen.1A migrants attest to similar differences in the type and degree of cross-linguistic influence according to whether it is into their L1 or their L2, e.g. Jutronić-Tihomirović (1983, 1985), Filipović (1991, 1997).

Looking beyond Gen.1A to subsequent generations, cross-generational comparison of speakers reveals further differences. Ad Backus and his collaborators have studied Turkish-Dutch bilingualism across different groups and vintages of migrants for over 20 years. Backus (1996: 387–388) reports the following in relation to the Turkish(-Dutch) speech of four generational groups: Turkish L1 Gen.1A speakers use very little Dutch with use of it restricted to one- or two-word transfers or insertions, very often nouns that are usually morphologically integrated into Turkish; the speech of Gen.1B speakers is characterised by intra-clausal insertions and alternations, while stretches of reported speech (from Dutch) can result in inter-clausal code-switches, but overall Turkish remains the matrix language determining utterances' morphosyntactic grid; Gen.2 speakers' speech includes intra- and inter-clausal code-switching (insertions and alternations) and a higher frequency thereof compared to Gen.1B, and in some instances, Dutch is the matrix language into which Turkish insertions occur. For Gen.3 Turkish-Dutch speakers, Backus, Demirçay and Sevinç (2013) report widespread bi-directional code-switching, frequent use of loan translations, and some change in morphosyntactic feature marking in Turkish. Jake and Myers-Scotton (2002) record even greater contrasts in the linguistic forms used in the bilingual speech of first-generation Arabic-English bilinguals in Detroit compared to those used by second-generation ones. In most examples given in the chapters of this book, the generational membership of the speaker is provided and this gives the reader some information on whether the speaker is using Croatian as their dominant or non-dominant language. In some chapters, a quantification of forms found is cross-tabulated with generational membership.

5.1 Equivalence, correspondence and congruence across languages

The first term used in this section's heading, *equivalence*, refers to the notion of sameness or at least similarity of linguistic forms and/or features cross-linguistically. Bilingual discourse is a product of speakers' alignment of forms and/or features from two codes and this alignment bears witness to speakers' mental representation of forms and features, and how these supplied by two languages may be combined within a clause, utterance or stretch of discourse. Although most bilinguals are not highly knowledgeable of grammar, they typically match and align items from their languages in similar ways. Weinreich (1953: 7–8) describes this in the following way: "in situations of intense language contact, speakers tend to develop some mechanism for equating 'similar concepts and categories across languages, as equivalence relations, or in short, equivalence (or isomorphism)". This sense of the cross-linguistic equivalence of categories (or sometimes lack thereof) determines how speakers combine material from their codes (or not). Woolford (1983: 535) suggests that the regularities of alignment of items in the speech of bilinguals mean that "category labels of different grammars have a cross-linguistic identity". In regard to contact-induced change, Heine and Kuteva (2005: 4) contend that this "seems to be based on some kind of interlingual identification, in our case on some way of equating a grammatical concept or structure." What these statements from researchers mean is that examples of bilingual speech are taken as evidence that bilingual speakers align formal categories across their languages and employ forms and features in a way that reflects this. Sebba (2009: 41, original punctuation, square brackets added) observes that "the existence of CS [code-switching] is itself taken as *evidence* for such equivalence". Sebba (2009) notes at the same time that most accounts of bilingual speech pre-suppose a level of formal equivalence or *congruence* of categories between languages in the first place. While bilingual speakers can and do combine forms from two languages in patterned ways that suggest a level of congruence between categories of the participating languages, Sebba (2009) cautions that the key protagonist is the speaker and researchers cannot presume that speakers' notions of cross-linguistic congruence are identical to how formal categories may appear to correspond to each other in linguistic descriptions of the participating languages.

The term equivalence was adopted in the designation of a constraint as part of one of the first structurally-focussed models of code-switching, namely the "equivalence constraint" (Poplack 1980: 586). This constraint predicted that code-switching between languages could take place at every point within a clause if the grammars of both languages on each side of the code-switching point match in terms of the ordering of constituents. Subsequent research has shown that code-switching is a process not determined primarily by surface level congruence, and this constraint has been challenged in a number of studies, e.g. Bentahila and Davies (1983), Berg-Seligson (1986), Myers-Scotton (1993), Halmari (1997) and Hlavac (2003). Notwithstanding this, the notion of equivalence referring not only to linear congruence, but also to similarity or sameness of categories across linguistic sub-fields is observable across data sets.

Adding a frequency-based perspective to the notion of equivalence, Johanson (2002: 41–64) uses the term "attractiveness" to refer to an element's likelihood or susceptibility to be transferred (or "copied" to use his terminology). Analytic constructions and forms that have a transparency of content and expression are listed by him as being attractive candidates for transfer. Thomason (2001: 76) talks about the same thing, in slightly more abstract terms and locates markedness (where marked features are less likely to be borrowed, although this may be of lesser importance for diaspora situations), the degree of embeddedness that a form or feature has in a particular language's system, and typological distance between languages (with a lesser chance of equivalence across categories) as three factors that determine the likelihood of cross-linguistic transfer. Myers-Scotton and Jake (2015) invoke "complexity", a term akin to Thomason's first two factors, i.e. markedness and degree of embeddedness, to account for why there are different outcomes in speakers' code-switching patterns according to the languages that they are drawing on.

5.2 Hierarchical symmetry/asymmetry and explanatory models for code-switching

Discussion above on the notion of equivalence included mention of constraints to code-switching. Discussion on the hierarchical relations that pertain to bilingual speech is part of a larger, widely-debated topic in contact linguistics: the relationship between the contributing languages where code-switching or morphological change occurs. This relates to whether neither language is superordinate or subordinate to the other and both languages (or universal principles) determine the morphosyntactic grid of an utterance (e.g. Mahootian 1993; MacSwan 2000; Chan 2003), or whether the relationship between the two is asymmetrical and the morphosyntactic rules of one language predominate. In most but not all examples of bilingual speech, one language is clearly more dominant. Sociolinguistic (interlocutors, setting), psycholinguistic (mode, 'I'm speaking [mostly] language *x*') and discourse-pragmatic (topic, footing, 'I employ [mostly] language *x* to achieve *y*') features usually point to which is the more dominant language, but these features are indicative only and cannot be determinative of what is a structurally-based notion.

Explanations of bilingual speech that locate an asymmetrical relationship between the two languages go back to the early 1980s (Sridhar and Sridhar 1980), with Joshi (1984) using the term 'matrix' to refer to the dominant language. Identification of a matrix language in bilingual speech is part of the methodological approach of a number of studies on contact situations, e.g. Backus (1996), Muysken (2000) re. "base language", or Johanson (2002) re. "base code", even where the authors do not necessarily posit this as a universal feature. The notion of a matrix language not only to describe but also account for structural outcomes has been furthest developed by Myers-Scotton (2002) in the Matrix Language Frame (MLF) that distinguishes the (superordinate) matrix language from the (subordinate) embedded language. The MLF has been employed as a theoretical model in a large number of contact linguistics studies, e.g. Bolonyai (1998), Fuller

(2000), Schmitt (2000). The MLF model can be applied to a matrix language that is co-terminous with a homeland-based, largely monolingual version of a minority language – a typical example of this is the speech of Gen.1A migrants. Further, the model can be applied to a matrix language that itself has undergone change (i.e. a composite matrix language) so that the abstract structure is supplied from two systems – a typical example of this are some language structures recorded in the speech of some Gen.2 or Gen.3 speakers.

The MLF model propounds that even if there is structural contribution from two sources, it is not equal, and the outcomes in diaspora settings amongst Gen.2 and Gen.3 speakers are usually either heritage-language dominant composite matrix languages such as that described as 'American Russian' (Polinsky 2006) or majority-language dominant composite matrix languages such as that found in New York Jewish English (Tannen 1981) with lexical and pragmatic input from Yiddish. The MLF model is outlined in further detail in Chapter 15 (Hlavac and Myers-Scotton, this volume).

5.3 Terminology used in this volume

Although contact linguistics is a comparatively young discipline there is already a large number of terms that relate to the same or very similar phenomena, e.g. the presence of a single lexical item from language *x* in a clause whose remaining items are in language *y* can be termed as being any of the following: lexical transfer, borrowing, loanword, insertion, code-copy or code-switch. The presentation of linguistic data in chapters six to fifteen is sequenced according to conventional designations. These chapters present linguistic data from most if not all of the following sub-fields of linguistic description: pragmatics, lexicon, semantics and morphosyntax. In relation to the sub-fields of lexicon and morphosyntax, a variety of terms are used to refer to the same or similar phenomena. Section 5.3.1 below provides a brief outline of these terms relating to lexical items, 5.3.2 presents those relating to semantic change and loan translation, while 5.3.3 sets out terminology relating to morphosyntax.

5.3.1 Lexical transference, borrowing, insertion, alternation, code-switching and congruent lexicalisation

As this long heading suggests, there are a variety of terms to describe the same or similar phenomena, here referring to the contribution of lexical items (including discourse markers) from two languages within the same clause, utterance or turn.

The term 'transference' is from Clyne (1991, 2003) and it refers to the process of items, forms or features traversing linguistic boundaries, with the product of this being a 'transfer'. The term avoids the normative connotations of 'interference' or the connotations of 'ownership' and 'ephemerality' that 'borrowing' has. The advantage of the terms 'transference' and 'transfer' is that they are two terms that distinguish the process from the manifestation, and they can be combined with any sub-field of linguistics, e.g. 'phonological transference', 'semantic transfer'. The term 'transfer' in relation to lexical items, i.e. 'lexical transfers' is preferred to the term 'loanword', which suggests a relationship of ownership and which, in lay terms, is applied to words that are formally codified as recipient language items. For example, in Croatian, the equivalent terms for loanwords, namely *posuđenice* 'borrowed words' (Binder 2006; Glovacki-Bernardi 2013) are used to describe what is core vocabulary in non-standard varieties, while the slightly pejorative term *tuđice* meaning 'alien words' is used by purists to describe core vocabulary that is etymologically non-domestic as well as non-core vocabulary in standard and non-standard varieties of Croatian (e.g. Šimundić 1994). The neutral term *strane riječi* 'foreign words' is the designation for foreign-origin lexemes used in reference books and dictionaries, even where most of these have been phonologically, morphologically, semantically and graphemically integrated into Croatian (e.g. Klaić 1982).

The term 'borrowing' is commonly used within and outside contact linguistics. Like, 'loanword', the term suggests a relationship of ownership that cannot logically pertain as languages as non-human agents do not 'own' particular forms. In lay terms, it suggests perhaps a chance insertion, but in the contact linguistics literature, it has come to refer to a form that is a stable and habitualised 'other-language' form in bilinguals' repertoires, based on the work of Poplack (1980, 2012). A distinction using linguistic criteria such as phonological and/or morphological form or recurrence to argue that some groups of lexical transfers occupy a different conceptual role in speakers' lexicons from others has been largely rejected by many contact linguists, e.g. Field (2002), Gardner-Chloros (2009), Treffers-Daller (2005) or Winford (2009). Thus the term (nonce) *borrowing* is seldom used in this volume.

A term to refer not only to lexemes, but to any material that traverses linguistic boundaries is 'code-copying' coined by Johanson (2002). In reference to lexemes, it refers to input from two source languages within the same clause, i.e. intraclausal code-switching. Johanson (2002: 9) distinguishes degree of replication of source language features in bilingual speech such that 'global code-copying' refers to elements being copied "as a block of material, combinational, semantic and frequential structural properties" while 'selective code-copying' refers to "selected structural properties being copied". Although Johanson's terminology

is not used in this book, the notion of complete vs. partial adoption of inserted elements is one that accompanies description of many of the examples presented.

In section 3 above, the terms 'insertion' and 'alternation' are frequently used. In general terms, the first refers to (usually) lexical material, often single words or referentially simplex constructions, that are transferred from one language *within* a clause boundary, i.e. insertions are examples of intra-clausal code-switching, or code-mixing to use Muysken's (2000, 2008) terminology. In contrast, where multiple-item clusters or even clause-length sequences of transferred items occur, these are termed *alternations* by Muysken (2000, 2008). These are often, though not always, clause-length clusters. The boundary between *insertion* and *alternation* is fluid, and Backus (2003) remarks that a Cognitive Grammar application of the notion of 'lexical unit' could result in clusters which are considered insertions to be re-classified as alternations. In the chapters of this book, where the term alternation occurs, it is commonly used as a synonym for inter-clausal code-switches. A strict formal distinction between the two terms is not universally applied in the chapters of this book, and the two terms, where used, function more or less as synonyms for shorter vs. longer sequences of other-language or transferred lexical forms.

The term *code-switching* is used widely in contact linguistics. An uncontroversial definition of it is provided by Gardner-Chloros (2009: 4) ". . . use of several languages or dialects in the same conversation or sentence by bilingual people". This understanding of 'code' as a synonym for 'language' or 'dialect' reflects the perspectives of those contact linguists who focus on the structural characteristics of bilingual texts. Another strand of contact linguistics research understands 'code' and 'code-switching' in the sense of Basil Bernstein (1971) as a variety reflecting social identity that need not be synonymous with a particular language or dialect (e.g. Auer 1999). Conversational or discourse-based perspectives of code-switching are not the focus of this book, and interaction-specific features of code-switching such as discourse-internal foci that appear to account for speakers' changes in code are mentioned only in passing, if at all. The focus of this book remains on lexical and structural features.

As a term, code-switching most readily refers to lexical items, or at least the majority of studies that use the term study examples from the lexicon of one language being transferred into another language. Code-switching has, to some extent, become a hypernym for many kinds of contact linguistic phenomena that do not themselves feature the cross-linguistic transfer of lexemes, such as semantic or syntactic transference. Both Johanson (2002) and Verschik (2008) point out that 'code-switching', usually understood as a lexically-focused term where forms from more than language contribute to an utterance, does not readily encompass phenomena such as semantic transference, or grammatical change where the forms (i.e. all morphemes) of an utterance are supplied from one language only. In this book, such instances are categorised under labels that distinguish these from code-switching. The term 'code-switch' (here referring to the product of a process known as 'code-switching') as well as the term 'transfer' are the terms used most widely in this volume to refer to the presence of lexical items that originate from the donor languages of the societies in which Croatian immigrants reside. Figure 1 provides a list of features that more closely describe the attributes of each designation.

Term Feature	Transfer	Code-switch
phonological integration likely	+/−	−/(+)
morphological integration likely	+/−	−/(+)
grammatical integration likely	+/−	−/(+)
simultaneous integration on all levels likely	+/−	−
single word	+	−/(+)
multi-word cluster	−/(+)	−
higher relative frequency (by same speaker)	+(−)	−
statistically recurrent (across speech community)	+	−
use, recognition, acceptance in speech community	+	?
monolingual speakers	+	−
bilingual speakers	+	+
lexical 'need'	+/−	−
viewed as part of recipient language lexicon	+/−	−
metalinguistic awareness present	−/(+)	+/(−)
result of diachronic process	+/(−)	−

Figure 1: Features of transfers and code-switches. (The symbol given first refers to this as the dominant quality – whether present [+] or absent [−]. Round brackets refer to a lower quantification of this quality.).

Figure 1 above shows that there are general differences in the presence of integration, number of donor language items, levels of frequency and recurrence, lexical 'need' and 'membership' of the recipient language (i.e. Croatian as a heritage language) lexicon as well as speakers' level of awareness of the items as 'other-language' ones or not. Some features are shared between the two and there is a degree of overlap meaning that the boundary between the terms 'transfer' and 'code-switch' is not categorical.

One characteristic missing from Figure 1 above is a description of which parts of speech are encompassed by the terms lexical transfers and/or code-switches. The reason why this information is not given is because both categories can encompass forms belonging to any part of speech. In relation to code-switching, phrase- or clause-long alternations contain forms of all kinds of grammatical categories. Lexical transfers relate to any item with a content referential value, but in practice, single-word or lexically simplex forms that make up the bulk of lexical transfers are nouns, which appear as the most 'transferable' group, as stated in the borrowability continuums of Thomason (2001), Field (2002) and Winford (2003) in Section 3 above.

Unsurprisingly, data sets on heritage varieties of Croatian also record a high number of transferred nouns and I present here firstly instances of phonological adaptation that also contain affixation of Croatian nominal suffixes. Based on a corpus of written texts from newspapers, Surdučki's (1966) records the following transfers that attracted the following Croatian nominal suffixes: *-ac, mauntac* 'Mountie', member of the Royal Canadian Mounted Police; *-aj, butlegeraj* 'bootlegging joint'; *-ar, bizničar* 'businessman, shop owner'; *-aš, unijaš* 'union member; *-ić, bojsić* 'boy (diminutive)'; *-ist, grocerist* 'grocer'; *-ija, groserija* 'grocery'. Phonological as well as morphosyntactic integration shown via inflectional morphology is evident in example (1) from Gasiński's (1986) corpus of recorded speech:

(1) i   **polismen**   sa   **flašlajtom**   ga
     and   policeman-NOM.M.SG   with+INS   flashlight-INS.M.SG   him-ACC
     ište   a   on   na   **polismena**
     search-3SG   but   he-NOM   at-ACC policeman-ACC.M.SG
     'And when the **policeman** with a **flashlight** was looking for him, he attacked the **policeman**.' (Gasiński 1986: 37)

Both transfers, *policeman* and *flashlight*, are integrated as masculine nouns. In the case of *polisman*-M, biological gender is a likely influence for this, while for *flašlajt*-M the phonotactic form – in particular its word-final consonant – is likely to determine its allocation as a masculine gender noun (cf. HMLD.Cro *baterija*-F 'flashlight'). In Croatian-English contact situations, the word-final consonant of many English-origin lexemes (and also many German, Dutch and Norwegian-origin ones as well) results in most transfers being assigned masculine gender. Samples that examine this feature reveal the following percentages of masculine gender nouns: Surdučki (1966) 92% of 352 nouns in a written corpus; Surdučki (1978) over 90% of 2,402 nouns in recorded speech; Gasiński (1986: 36) 66% of 91 nouns; Hlavac (2003) 79% (206) of 260 nouns in recorded speech with 21% (52) feminine and only two neuter. Jutronić-Tihomirović (1985: 33) records a similar trend in her data, but also a small number of anomalous neuter transfers, e.g. *barjelo* 'barrel' and *štrudelo* 'strudel'. In general, the gender of an equivalent Croatian noun does not influence gender allocation, and it is rare for instances such as the following to be recorded, where *paint* is allocated feminine gender, apparently on the basis of its Croatian equivalent, *boja*-F:

(2) *filila   se   **pejnt**   a   požućela   jako*
    peel-PST.F.SG   REFL   paint-NOM.F.SG and turn yellow-PST.F.SG strongly
    'The **paint**-F was peeling off. It got very yellow.' (Jutronić-Tihomirović 1985: 37)

Instances of morphological integration can include the presence of English-origin bound morphemes, such as the plural marker, *-s*, but morphemes which have relations external to their head (i.e. outside the NP) are supplied by Croatian, the matrix language:

(3) *volim   Kuban**eze***
    like-1SG   Cuban-**PL(ENG)**-ACC.M.PL(CRO)
    'I like Cuban**s**.' (Albijanić 1982: 17)

Lexical transfers that are phonologically and morphologically unintegrated are recorded in many samples such as Croatian-USA English ones, e.g. *na žalost iman* **heart trouble** 'Unfortunately, I have **heart trouble**' (Albijanić 1982: 13), *naš* ***druggist**, ovaj od apoteke, od ljekarne* 'our **druggist**, that one from the drugstore, pharmacy' (Ward 1980: 11), as well as Croatian-Danish ones, e.g. *imamo veliki reol* 'We have a big **bookcase**' (Pavlinić-Wolf 1988: 163). Ablijanić quantifies the number of lexical transfers in his corpus collected from Dalmatian immigrants in California and Jutronić's data collected amongst Croats in Pennsylvannia and reports that their frequency in the speech of first-generation speakers is between 5% and 8%, while for second-generation speakers it is between 9% and 19%. Further, while 99% of English transfers were "assimilated" (i.e. phonologically and morphologically integrated) amongst first-generation speakers, the percentage amongst younger speakers varies from 50% to only 11% (Albijanić 1982: 18).

Adjectives and adverbs are generally the next most likely parts of speech to be transferred into heritage varieties of Croatian. Suffixes are also widely affixed to transferred adjectives, e.g. *-an*, *šugeran* 'sugary', *-ski*, *kaurski* 'of the Kauri tree', *-ov*, *-titrov* 'of the ti-tree', *-ast*, *-čokast* 'chalky gum' (Stoffel 1981a: 245). An example of an adjective integrated with the first mentioned suffix, *-an* is: *ni* *jena ulica nije bila **pejvena*** 'not even one street was **paved**' (Gasiński 1986: 38). Adjectives in their unintegrated forms are also reported: *već sam bila **pregnant** sa mojom curicom* 'I was already **pregnant** with my daughter' (Ward 1980: 11); *bili smo veoma **poor** tada* 'We were very **poor** then' (Albijanić 1982: 13). In Croatian, adverbs derived from adjectives have the NOM.N.SG form, while others are inflectionless content morphemes, e.g. *odmah* 'straight away', *uvijek* 'always'. This appears to lead to most transferred adverbs occurring in an unintegrated form: *idemo svi tri **together*** 'Let's all three of us go **together**' (Albijanić 1982: 13); *ja posjećujem **oft** susjede, kada radim **spät**, odma' vide da..* 'I visit **often** the neighbours, when I work **late**, straight away they see..' (Stölting 1984: 42). Conjunctions are less frequently transferred. Gasiński (1986: 40) records just two in the speech of first-generation speakers: *koz* 'cos' and *bat* 'but', while Hlavac (2003: 98) reports only three in a corpus of over 1,300 transfers.

Verbs are a part of speech that warrant some attention as they are central to the morphosyntactic grid of a clause. They are not as likely to be transferred as nouns, adjectives or adverbs, but more so than conjunctions or prepositions. A conspicuous feature of transferred verbs is that they are much more likely to be morphologically (and phonologically) integrated: amongst first-generation speakers integration is close to 100%; amongst second-generation speakers Hlavac (2003: 98) reports that 71% are morphologically integrated in comparison to an average percentage of integration for other parts of speech of around only 10%. Amongst speakers of both generations, Gasiński (1986: 39) locates 22 "assimilated" verbs, and only 2 unassimilated ones. All of Surdučki's (1966: 57) 40 verbs from a written text corpus are integrated. Integration involves allocation to one of the four main groups of verbs classified according to infinitive suffix: *-ati*; *-i-ti* and *-je-ti*; *-Ø-ti*; *-nu-ti*. Surdučki's (1966: 57) reports that the *-ati* ending is the most productive, with the following sub-groups of that suffix: *–(ov)ati*, eg. *čelandžovati* 'to challenge'; *-(ev)ati* e.g. *stokpajlevati* 'to stockpile'; *-(ir)ati* e.g. *rezidirati* 'to reside'; and *–ati*, e.g. *spatati* 'to spot'. In contrast, Gasiński (1986: 39) reports that the suffix *-it(i)* (18 examples) is more productive than the *-at(i)* suffix (4 examples). His sample is smaller than that of Surdučki (1966). Example (4) contains an instance of an English-origin verb that has attracted an *–it(i)* suffix:

(4) oni **fide**   a   goje   svinje   sa   ribom
    they feed-3PL and nourish-3PL pig-ACC.F.PL with+INS fish-INS.F.SG
    'They **feed** and raise the pigs on fish.' (Gasiński 1986: 39)

Transferred verbs can occur in impersonal constructions that do not exist in the donor language:

(5) jemu   se   **štufalo**
    him-DAT   REFL   stuff-PST.N.SG
    'He was **stuffed** up/bored.' (Gasiński 1986: 39). HMLD.Cro: njemu je dosadilo.

As stated, verbs are usually morphologically integrated by second-generation speakers even where they remain phonologically unintegrated:

(6) nisu   nikad   pitali   **challenge-ali**   tu
    NEG.AUX-3PL   never   ask-PST.M.PL   challenge-PST.M.PL   here
    ti   je
    you-DAT   be-3SG
    'They never asked, **challenged**.. "here it is for you.."' (Starčević 2014: 267)

Verbs are integrated even where this results in conjugational suffixes occurring between the two elements of a phrasal verb, such as *hold back*:

(7) pa   ja   vas   ne   **holdan**   **back**   ajte   onda   ja
    well   I   you-ACC.PL   NEG   hold-1SG   back   come on   then   I
    'Well, I am not … **holding** you **back**, come on, then I …' (Starčević 2014: 268)

Turning now to code-switching, sometimes this term is preposed with the adjective 'classic' i.e. 'classic code-switching' (Myers-Scotton 2006) referring to a variety of speech in which bilingual speakers freely avail themselves of both codes, resulting in frequent and largely unmarked intra- and/or inter-clausal code-switching. The term also implies a high level of linguistic proficiency on the part of the speaker, at least in the language that sets the structural grid of most utterances. This means that speakers who engage in classic code-switching "have full access to the morphosyntactic frame of one of the participating languages (the source of the Matrix Language)" (Myers-Scotton 2006: 105. Original round brackets). The attributive 'classic' relates more to the sociolinguistic and situational features of the communicative interaction rather than the forms of language used themselves. The notion of 'classic code-switching' matches well the heritage language situations described in this book. Among many speakers and in many contexts, bilingual speech may be the default and unmarked variety used in many situations. Below is an example of what is referred to in this volume as an intra-clausal code-switch:

(8) *Kuća je bila stara kuća, pa smo.. je nismo… je razbili.. **demolished it**. Kad smo..*
    'The house was an old house, so we.. we didn't.. we demolished it.. **demolished it**. When we …' (Stoffel 1993: 81)

In example (8), the second clause commences in Croatian with its predicate also in Croatian, but with a code-switch after it, and a repetition of it in English. Below is an example of an inter-clausal code-switch:

(9) Kao.. **I can't make the connection,** ali iman **visual picture** u glavu..
 'Like.. **I can't make the connection**, but I have a **visual picture** in my head..' (Starčević 2014: 261)

In example (9), a turn-commencing discourse marker *kao* 'like' opens the first clause which is otherwise entirely in English. A conjunction marks the shift to Croatian, the matrix language of the second clause. Within this second clause, there is a two-item lexical transfer *visual picture* or an Embedded Language island using MLF terminology. Insertions and their status as Embedded Language islands will be re-visited in chapter 15.

A further group of code-switches that are classified neither as intra- or as inter-clausal are *extra*-clausal code-switches. These typically relate to discourse markers that occur in turn-initial or turn-final position, or turn internally. They are a discourse-bound rather than syntactic category, and they therefore transcend the morphosyntactic relations that apply to all elements within a clause. Many heritage language speakers adopt many of the pragmatic norms of the donor language culture, and when they do so, they may transfer not only the pragmatic function, but also its form. Where this happens, the number of such transferred discourse markers that are extra-clausal code-switches can be considerable. For example, in the predominantly Croatian speech of a sample of 100 mostly second-generation speakers, Hlavac (2003: 51) records 2,688 extra-clausal code-switches, compared to 1,248 intra-clausal and 277 inter-clausal ones. An example of extra-clausal code-switching is given below from a second-generation Croatian-Canadian:

(10) di, što, zašto, kad će bit svadba **you know, like** uvijek te ispitaju
 '... where, what, why, when will the wedding be, **you know, like**, they always ask you...' (Starčević 2014: 268)

The distinction of discourse markers, and similar forms such as interjections, affirmatives (e.g. polyfunctional *yeah* in many varieties of English) and so on allow a separation of these items within samples of studies that otherwise focus on structural rather than discourse-level features.

A further term is used in relation to the transfer of lexemes: *congruent lexicalisation*. This term is from Muysken (2000) who uses the term to describe a situation where a speaker's languages totally or partially share processing systems, i.e. where grammatical structures are partially overlapping. This may be due to shared genealogy. For example, Hasselmo's (1961) data on Swedish-English bilinguals and Clyne's (1991) data on older Dutch-English bilinguals shows that many such speakers do not appear to clearly distinguish their languages, either in a sociolinguistic or formal sense, and Clyne (1991) describes the rather arbitrary selection of one language or another or as "marginal passages". Genealogical (and with it, typological) similarity is one circumstance that can have congruent lexicalisation as an outcome. Alternatively, it can occur between languages genealogically unrelated to each other where structural change has occurred in a speaker's *competence* (or *langue*) of one of their languages (or possibly in both). This results in general structural equivalence between both languages, and this, in turn, enables a free and apparently unrestricted selection of either language in many situations and utterances. While the term *congruent lexicalisation* is seldom used in this volume, the notion of structural change and its manifestations is further looked at in Section 5.3.3.

5.3.2 Semantic transference, calques and loan translation

Semantic transference refers to the transfer of semantic features of a lexical item or lexical items from one language into another. An example of this is use of the Croatian item *medicina* which in homeland varieties of Croatian (hereafter HMLD. Cro) refers exclusively to the 'field of medical training and practice' and not to a type of medical treatment such as 'tablets'. A 22-year-old, second-generation Croatian-Australian uttered the following in relation to consumption of tablets; the form *medicina* is shown in bold:

(11) Što   trebaš   da   uzmeš   kakvu   **medicinu**   um
     COMP   need-2SG   COMP   take-2SG   some-ACC.F.SG   medicine-ACC.F.SG   um
     'that you have to take . . . some kind of **medicine**, um . . .' (Hlavac 2000: 442)

An equivalent HMLD.Cro utterance would contain . . . *da uzmeš* **kakve lijekove** (some kinds of **medications**), or, depending on the regiolect that the speaker comes from *da uzmeš kakvu* **medecinu**. Here, the semantic features of English *medicine* have been transferred to change, in this case to broaden the semantic field of Croatian *medicina* that results in the above utterance. Broadening or expansion of an item's semantic properties due to cross-linguistic influence is perhaps the most conspicuous form of semantic transference; Winford (2002: 33) reminds us that semantic transference can also result in restriction and even meaning shift in others ways that are not readily foreseeable. A similar phenomenon to *medicina* but which involves the creation of a novel form based on aligning equivalent forms in the recipient language is the form *pričekirati* based on English 'pre-check':

(12) bremze   i   to   se   sve   mora   **pričekirati**
     brakes-NOM.F.PL and that REFL all-ACC.N.SG must-3SG pre-check-INF
     i   onda kad   si   **pričekirao**   sve   onda
     and   then when AUX-2SG pre-check-PTCP.M.SG all-ACC.N.SG then
     se   mora
     REFL must-3SG
     '... the brakes, all that needs to be **pre-checked** and then when you've **pre-checked** everything, then you have to ...' (Hlavac 2000: 431)

English *pre-check* roughly means 'checking something as a procedure that precedes another procedure'. Croatian has a productive prefix *pri* which can be affixed to both verbs and nouns which means 'adjacent to/conjoining' and which is almost a homophone to the English prefix *pre-*. In standard Croatian, *čekirati* does not exist as verb, but its meaning is likely to be understood by many speakers of HMLD.Cro due to the term 'check-in', a lexical transfer used in non-standard varieties of HMLD. Cro, and through analogy, that *čekirati* relates to a 'checking' activity. The morphemic constituents of *pre-check* are replicated through the employment of equivalent morphemes in Croatian. These single-word items are usually known as calques.

The term *loan translation*, in its conventional sense, is synonymous to a *calque* (Appel and Muysken 1987; Winford 2003). Here, I adopt Backus and Dorleijn's (2009: 82–91) broadened use of the term to refer not only to single-morpheme items but also to two- and multi-morpheme constructions. Loan translations are recorded in a number of studies, e.g. *meko piće* 'soft drink', *stranorođen* 'foreign-born' and *sezonska čestitka* 'Season's Greetings' to verb phrases such as *praviti novac* 'make money', *skakati ka zaključku* 'jump to a conclusion' or *dati nekome kredit* 'give someone credit' (=acknowledging someone) (Surdučki 1966: 131–132). Longer word-for-word replications are *to je u redu sa mnom* 'that's alright with me' (Škvorc 2006: 20) and *kuća u dvanaejs nogu dugu* 'a house twelve feet long' (Gasiński 1986: 37). Below is an example from a second-generation Croatian-Australian that contains a replication of the English phrase *take their medical histories*:

(13) i   svako   tri   mjeseca   ja   moram
     and   every-ACC.N.SG   three+GEN.SG   month-GEN.M.SG   I   must-1SG
     uzimat   njihove   medičke   historije
     take-INF   their-ACC.F.PL   medical-ACC.F.PL   history-ACC.F.PL
     '... and every three months I have to **take their medical histories**' (Hlavac 2000: 435)

In the example given above, a loan translation consisting of the noun phrase *medička* [or *medicinska*] *historija* is collocated with the verb that the English equivalent phrase has, *uzimati* 'take'. In HMLD.Cro, a loan translation based on *medical history* namely *medicinska povijest* is starting to displace the more formal and specialised term *anamneza*. But the verb+NP construction referred to above would be more likely rendered as *napraviti pregled njihovog ranijeg zdravstvenog stanja*, lit. 'conduct an overview of their earlier health state'. The speaker in example (13) is using a phrase that is a habitualised and oft-used construction in her workplace lect, and she aligns its constituents to similar-meaning ones in Croatian. She does so knowing that her interlocutor has a similar knowledge of English lexical-semantic phrases and this facilitates her employment of the construction. Loan translations offer insights into how speakers conceptualise "semantic-pragmatic theta-bundles" (Myers-Scotton 2002: 24). They show us the way that such theta-bundles are assembled in one language and how this may influence the way that they may be assembled in another. In this volume, the terms semantic transference, calque and loan translation are used. They are used in relation to forms and constructions which according to other approaches are described as "semantic code-copying" (Johanson 2002: 12–23) or "pattern replication in the area of lexical semantics" (Matras 2009: 245). Instances of semantic transference, calques and loan translation are relatively infrequent in the chapters of this volume and they are presented following instances of lexical transference and code-switching.

5.3.3 Structural transference, grammatical change, grammaticalisation and composite matrix languages

This heading also contains a number of terms, but in this section I will focus on two phenomena only. The first term used above, 'structural transference' is analogous to the term 'lexical transference' and refers to the adoption of syntactic features from one language into another. The term typically refers to forms whose structure is different from homeland varieties of Croatian and most examples given here have this characteristic. Structural transference can also refer to employment of forms that are not structurally different, but whose incidence is much less frequent. In English, the present participle is reasonably common, but the equivalent construction in Croatian is much less frequent and stylistically marked and nearly always restricted to a single head noun which succeeds it. Surdučki (1966: 135–136) locates the following multi-item NPs which would otherwise be structured as head noun + relative clause constructions in Croatian e.g. *umirući društveni system* 'dying social order', *trepteća svjetiljka* 'flickering light' and even *štrajkujući štamparski radnici* 'striking typographers'. It is unsurprising that these slightly awkward sounding constructions appeared in written texts rather than in speech. But the incidence of uncommon structures becoming more frequent can occur in spoken language as well; similar examples described as 'polysemy copying' are provided by Hansen (2018).

I now turn to an example from a Croatian-American who produced example (14). English structure requires the employment of conditionals to express particular kinds of unreal but possible actions. This conditional form is transferred via the equivalent Croatian conditional marker *bi*.

(14) to   je   jedina   njezina   želja
     that-NOM.N.SG be-3SG sole-NOM.F.SG her-NOM.F.SG wish-NOM.F.SG
     da   **bi**   ja   **došla**
     COMP COND   I   come-PST.PTCP.F.SG
     'That is her only wish that **I would come**.' (Jutronić-Tihomirović 1985: 62)

In HMLD.Cro, such a construction does not require a conditional form, and instead, a present tense 1SG form of the perfective verb *doći* 'come' is used to express the same kind of unreal but possible action, i.e. *to je jedina njezina želja da ja **dođem**-*PRES.1SG.

Syntactic transference therefore contains the replication of a syntactic structure from a donor language into the recipient language. This phenomenon is referred to as "syntactic combinational patterns of code-copying" by Johanson (2002: 105–107), as "convergence . . . [wherein] the abstract lexical structure . . . no longer comes from one language, but includes some abstract structure from another language" by Myers-Scotton (2002: 165) and as "converging structures: pattern replication" by Matras (2009: 234). Heine and Kuteva (2005: 2–3) focus almost exclusively on grammatical change and use the term "grammatical replication" to refer to the process and the term "transfer" to refer to the manifestation or result. Heine and Kuteva's (2005: 2) definition of "grammatical replication" includes both "form and meaning" which indicates that it encompasses both morphological forms as well as structural rules. Structural rules include conventions on the position of constituents in a clause. In German, those containing a compound verb form have the main verb in final position. Raecke (2006) locates examples of this in texts written by mostly Germany-born German-Croatian bilinguals:

(15) GER.Cro ti   si   o   životu   **razmišljala**
     German   du   hast über   das Leben   **nachgedacht**
              you have about   life   **thought**
     HMLD.Cro ti   si   **razmišljala** o   životu
     'you thought about life' (Raecke 2006: 153)

Here, the verb *razmišljala* 'think-PST.PTCP.F.SG' is in clause-final position as required by German syntactic rules. In Croatian, this word order pattern is stylistically marked.

Thomason and Kaufman (1988: 77–100) use the term "structural borrowing", but include within it cross-linguistic transfer of morphemes, alongside that of abstract grammatical structure only. As shown above in Section 3, Thomason (2001) uses the terms "structural interference" and "convergence" as designations for what I have described above as syntactic transference. The transference of morphemes that are conspicuous in grammatical terms, namely bound morphemes, or system morphemes (Myers-Scotton 2002: 195) is termed "morphological transference" by Clyne (2003: 77). An example given below is from a Croatian-Australian Gen.1B speaker, where the English plural marker *–s* is transferred onto to a Croatian content morpheme *auto* 'car':

(16) da   je   Australija ali   ovi   po
     COMP   be-3SG   Australia   but   this-NOM.M.PL   by+DAT
     autos   i   mnogo   yeah
     car-NOM.M.SG+PL-S   and   many   yeah
     'that it's Australia, but these.. by the **auto**s (= cars) and lots . . . yeah . . .'
     (Hlavac, 2000: 155)

An equivalent HMLD.Cro utterance would be: . . . *ovi po autima*-DAT.M.PL, or . . . *ovi po automobilima*–DAT.M.PL.

In the data samples presented in this volume, there are few examples of bound or system morphemes that are transferred cross-linguistically. Morphological transference is otherwise seldom discussed in this volume, and only where this relates to the few examples concerned.

Other examples of structural transference are the adoption of semantic or grammatical features found in donor language lexemes onto congruent lexemes in Croatian. An example below is from a German-Croatian bilingual living in Germany:

(17) sad   **pravi**   majstorsku   školu   subotom
     now   **make**-3SG vocational-ACC.F.SG   school-ACC.F.SG   Saturday-INS.F.SG
     'Now he **does** [= attends] vocational school on Saturdays' (Hansen 2018: 138)

The Croatian verb *praviti* 'to make' has a valence that is restrictive in the frames that it projects in the predicate, i.e. the types of entities that can occur as its DIR. OBJ and in HMLD.Cro the semantic features of these entities do not include educational institutions. But in German, the equivalent verb *machen* does allow such entities as its DIR.OBJ, and Hansen (2018: 142), applying Johanson's terminology, describes examples such as that above as polysemy copying, i.e. the copying of the frame elements available in a German predicate containing *machen* onto a Croatian predicate containing *praviti*. Hansen's three examples of *praviti* used in this way do not contain lexical transfers such as the 'vocational school' item being supplied from German, e.g. *sad pravi Berufsfachschule*. If and where *praviti* is employed regularly in verb $_{CRO}$ +object $_{DONOR\ LANGUAGE}$ constructions, it is possible to speak of "bilingual compound verbs" a term which Edwards and Gardner-Chloros (2007) employ to refer not only to DO-verb $_{RECIPIENT\ LANGUAGE}$ + verb $_{DONOR\ LANGUAGE}$ constructions, but also to ones where the second element is a donor language noun. *Praviti* in such constructions appears to take on the function of a DO-verb, where it is largely de-semanticised and one of a number of Croatian "light verbs" alongside *(u)činiti* 'to make/to cause' and *da(va)ti* 'to give' (Peti-Stantić, Japirko and Kežić 2016) that are 'pressed into service' in DO-constructions. If *praviti* is increasingly performing this function amongst German-Croatian bilinguals in Germany, then this can be an additive factor to account for its occurrence in the example from Hansen (2018) above.

Another example of transference of grammatical features is valence of non-canonical subjects. In the following example, the experiencer is not encoded in ACC as required in HMLD.Cro, but in DAT.

(18) **njemu**   je   još   više   sram
     him-DAT be-3SG still more   shame-NOM.M.SG
     'He is even more embarrassed.' (Hansen 2018: 145)

In HMLD.Cro the equivalent utterance has *njega*-'him-ACC' rather than *njemu*-'him-DAT' as the experiencer. Hansen (2018: 145) locates the equivalent German utterance which has a DAT experiencer as the likely influence for this, i.e. *ihm*-'him-DAT' *ist das noch peinlicher*. But he also points out the statistical infrequency of ACC as the experiencer in evaluative predicatives, as in Croatian it is the DAT that is much more frequently used, e.g. *njemu*-'him-DAT' *je neugodno* 'to him it's unpleasant' = 'he finds it unpleasant'. In general, it is the DAT that is used in most impersonal constructions where the experiencer is in non-nominative case, e.g. *njemu*-'him-DAT' *je hladno* 'to him it is cold' = 'he is cold'. Thus, it is possible to speak of contact-induced structural transference, but also possibly of overgeneralisation of the more frequent DAT-experiencer construction to displace the less frequent ACC-experiencer construction. This is in line with the descriptions of linguistic data recorded from heritage language speakers (see above 2.4), and in line with Benmamoun, Montrul and Polinsky's (2013) findings that irregular forms or less regular structures are prone to elimination.

Following on from the above example that contains the experiencer in DAT instead of ACC I come to one of the areas that has traditionally received much attention amongst language contact researchers: case marking. Croatian has seven cases and case is marked on all nouns, pronouns, determiners and adjectives, whether attributive or predicative. Case is marked in morphological inflections that bear multiple features: person and number, as well as case. In not only scholarly but also popular descriptions case marking is often invoked as a way to describe the speech of heritage speakers (and L2 learners as well), as shown in the following phrase: *dobro govori ali mu fali koji padež* 'he speaks well, but he lacks the odd case.' This is a reasonably common folk linguistic expression. Another one is contained in the title of chapter 8: *tu i tamo se gađam padežima* 'here and there, I am struggling with my cases' which is a quote from a young speaker describing how she feels like she is 'having a punt' when using a particular ending for a particular case. Looking now at instances of what this looks like, I present here an example from the Croatian speech of a young Dutch-Croatian bilingual who is recounting something that happened at home:

(19) *i*   *onda*   *otac*   *daje*   **majku**
      and   then   father-NOM.M.SG   give-3SG   **mother**-ACC.F.SG
      jedan   *poklon*
      one-NOM/ACC.M.SG   present-NOM/ACC.M.SG
      'and then father gives **mother**-ACC one present' (Gvozdanović 1993: 188)

   HMLD.Cro: i onda otac daje poklon **majci**-DAT.F.SG

In this example, there is a trivalent or bi-transitive verb *dati* 'to give' that requires marking for direct object (ACC) and indirect object (DAT). Here, *jedan poklon* is marked as the direct object (masc. inanimate nouns have the same form for ACC as NOM), while the indirect object, *majku*, attracts ACC marking, not DAT marking. There are two possible accounts for this: Dutch does not morphologically distinguish DAT from ACC for either nouns or pronouns and this example presents itself as an instance of syntactic transference of DAT and ACC non-distinction; this speaker's marking of grammatical relations is subject to change in which referents that otherwise attract oblique case-markers are now (sometimes?) being marked with less oblique marking, such as the ACC. The second account can be posited as being independent of the first as there are instances of speakers' case-marking systems changing in this way despite the fact that the model or donor language with which Croatian is in contact marks case in a way similar to Croatian, such as German (Hansen, Romić and Kolaković 2013). But it is likely that the first account leads to the second: where feature-marking is not overt in the model or donor language for a particular grammatical category, this same grammatical category in Croatian may begin to lose distinct feature-markers.

The following examples from a young adult Canadian-Croatian contain the verb *sjećati se* 'to remember', a reflexive verb that requires the patient or logical object to be in GEN.

(20) š   njon   sam   igrala   sjećam   se
     with+INS   she-INS   AUX-1SG   play-PST.F.SG   remember-1SG   REFL
     igračke   sjećam   se   **nekaku**   **veliku**
     toy-GEN.F.SG   remember-1SG   REFL   some-ACC.F.SG   big-ACC.F.SG
     lutku   sjećam   se   **drugu**   **djecu**
     doll-ACC.F.SG remember-1SG   REFL   other-ACC.F.SG children-ACC.F.SG
     'I played with her, I remember a **toy**, I remember **some sort of big doll**, I remember **other children**'. (Starčević 2015: 230).

(21) volila   sam   mačku   svoju   macu
     like-PST.F.SG   AUX-1SG   cat-ACC.F.SG   own-ACC.F.SG   kitten-ACC.F.SG
     nju   dosta   **sjećam**
     she-ACC   lot   remember-1SG
     'I loved my cat, my own kitten . . . I **remember her** a lot. . .'
     (Starčević 2015: 230).

Both examples come from the same speaker and within both turns, there are four occurrences of *sjećati se* 'remember-INF REFL'. The first one *sjećam se igračke* 'I remember a toy' has target GEN marking for the object. But the further instances of *sjećam se* in that turn have the object marked as ACC. In the last example, the REFL is omitted and the objects, *mačku* 'cat' and *macu* 'kitten', are both ACC. The examples show variation in the same verb's valence across similar narrative episodes. This variation can be accounted for by identifying the valence features of the equivalent English form *remember* and describing the non-target marking of logical objects as structural transference of the features of *remember,* a non-reflexive transitive verb. Alternatively, the examples can be interpreted as instances of variation in a process in which clause structure is tending towards a pattern of: NOM + V + ACC (not necessarily with SVO word order), with the ACC starting to function as a default oblique marker amongst some speakers. (See Section 5.3.3).

The term 'convergence', employed by many researchers as outlined above, is used in this volume less frequently. Without further information, it is not clear whether convergence refers to the process or the result, or both. Further, convergence is used as a term to refer to uni-lateral phenomena – in most studies, this is what it refers to, e.g. Myers-Scotton (2002: 175), but it can also refer to bi- or even multi-lateral phenomena, e.g. Aikhenvald and Dixon (2001) and the languages of the Balkan sprachbund (Friedman – this volume). While the notion of convergence suggests a degree of decreasing competence in the affected language, it can affect speakers who have roughly equivalent proficiency in both languages, such as many Gen.1B and some Gen.2 speakers (Ross 2007; Trudgill 2011; Lucas 2015: 531). Where the term 'convergence' is employed in this volume, with the exception of chapters 3 and 4, it refers to uni-lateral influence only, i.e. onto Croatian, and its use is accounted for in terms of only those phenomena presented.

The second phenomenon that will be outlined here is grammatical change. To be sure, syntactic transference usually results in grammatical change. However, the notion of grammatical change that I focus on here is that in which change occurs in varieties of Croatian spoken in diaspora situations and there is no clear equivalent structure in the donor language that is identifiable as a source of influence for this change. There are at least two areas to look for answers: one is that the change is 'internally motivated' and occurs due to the morphosyntactic features of Croatian wherein a propensity for particular kinds of change exists. There are developments familiar to historical linguists such as regularisations of 'uneven' paradigms that account for these kinds of changes, and these as well as others are being tracked synchronically by those studying contemporary varieties of Croatian used in the homeland (Kapović 2011; Starčević, Kapović and Sarić 2019). Such studies supply data which contributes to our understanding of change at a macro-level and allow areal linguists to track regional patterns (e.g. Heine and Kuteva 2006) and typologists to posit directions of 'drift' (e.g. Dryer 1997). In terms of such trends for change, studies on the languages of central Europe, the South Slavic region and the Balkans in general point to a gradual tendency towards analytic constructions (Sobolev 2008; Grković-Major 2011; Grošelj 2014; Lindstedt 2019), although the possible role of external influence is often hard to discount completely.

The other area to look at is the situation of the speaker and the context. Here, I refer back to the situation of many speakers of heritage languages, and Polinsky and Scontras's (2019) notion of divergent attainment outlined above (in section 2.4), that is a hypernym that encompasses a wide variety of developmental trajectories in speakers' acquisition of the heritage language. When looking to describe the types of changes that can occur in heritage languages that are apparently independent of the features of the other language, Polinsky and Scontras (2019: 13) identify changes in morphology that amount to 'overmarking', i.e. "... where a bilingual speaker does not perceive the presence of a particular morphological element, they may want to oversupply it". This can result in, for example, regular inflections for past tense added to irregular past tense forms, e.g. *wented* in English as a heritage language. Looking at a variety of contact situations, Lucas (2015: 530) uses the term "restructuring", to refer to changes that "do not involve straightforward transfer from the L1, and cannot therefore be called imposition ..." and he gives as examples of these instances where there is morphological "reduction, regularization or total elimination of verbal inflection...". Linguistic forms in the speech of informants described in this volume that are innovations that are not attributable to transference from the other language are termed in this volume 'grammatical change'.

Within the literature on grammatical change, the term 'grammaticalisation' is commonly used to refer to what is not only an alteration in a speaker's employment of a particular form to express a grammatical category, but usually a paradigmatic change that involves a re-organisation of features and feature marking. Heine and Kuteva (2005) focus on contact-induced examples of grammaticalisation. They list four parameters of this which include the following two:

> a. extension, i.e. the rise of novel grammatical meanings when linguistic expressions are extended to new contexts (context-induced reinterpretation)
>
> c. decategorialization, i.e. loss in morphosyntactic properties, characteristic of lexical or other less grammaticalized forms (Heine and Kuteva 2005: 81)

These two parameters are, in general terms, possible outcomes of the process of grammaticalisation. The mechanism for this process to take place is outlined by Heine and Kuteva (2005: 80–88) who state that this occurs when bilingual speakers notice that the model (or donor) language has a grammatical category that does not exist in the recipient language (in our case, Croatian), e.g. MODEL LANGUAGE FEATURE 'x'. A 'gap' or a 'mismatch' in the types of grammatical categories between languages alone is probably not a sufficient catalyst for cross-linguistic modelling to occur. The catalyst comes from speakers and their communicative interactions: bilingual speakers when communicating with other bilingual speakers; bilingual speakers when communicating with those who do not share the same linguistic repertoire. Friedman (2003: 110) identifies speaker-centred needs to effectively communicate with others as this parameter and observes that (bilingual) speakers' "discourse functions ... serve as entry points for the development of structural change." Although Friedman made this observation in relation to multi-lateral grammatical change occurring in languages of the Balkan sprachbund, this description that foregrounds communicative needs and discourse functions as a parameter matches well the situation of most heritage language speakers in the diaspora.

Further, bilingual speakers can create an equivalent category e.g. REPLICA LANGUAGE FEATURE 'x'. This new equivalent category can emerge where speakers assume that the emergence of this category in the model language occurred when a particular form or forms began to take on the function of that grammatical category. This is termed 'replica grammaticalisation' where the grammaticalisation process of the model language is followed in the same way as it is thought to have occurred in the model language. An example is the development of indefinite articles in German or Italian. The particular form in both languages that was 'pressed into service' to become the indefinite article was the numeral *one*, i.e. *ein* and *uno* respectively. Where German-Croatian or Italian-Croatian bilinguals interact with other Croatian-speakers (whether also speakers of German or Italian or not) and the grammatical category of indefiniteness becomes a feature of referents that are commonly used in these communicative interactions, such speakers, when speaking Croatian, may then begin to employ the Croatian numeral *one*, i.e. *jedan* in the same way as an emerging indefinite article. They do this perhaps by analogy to what they believe to have been the grammaticalisation process for the development of the indefinite article in their other language, either German or Italian. This kind of replica grammaticalisation is based on a type of isomorphism that is not uncommon in contact situations. Matras (1998: 100–1) observes that categories in model languages can result in the recipient language drawing on "a corresponding structure to initiate a corresponding processing operation". Another, but less common type of grammaticalisation is when speakers rely on "universal strategies of grammaticalization" (Heine and Kuteva 2005: 81) using material or constructions available in the recipient language to achieve REPLICA LANGUAGE FEATURE 'x' without recourse to how they assumed this was achieved in the model language.

An instance of apparent grammatical change is the use of pluperfect tense, a comparatively infrequent tense in Croatian, by Norwegian-Croatian bilinguals who employ it in Croatian in VPs in which the Norwegian pluperfect would be used:

(22) on   je   **bio**   **umro**
     he   AUX-3SG   be-PTCP.M.SG   die-PTCP.M.SG
     'He **had died**.' (past perfect) (Mønnesland 1987: 94).

   Norwegian: *han **hadde dødd**.* (pluperfect)
   HMLD.Cro: ***umro je***. 'he died' (past – here, less marked than pluperfect *bio je umro*)

Norwegian utterances referring to past events can be in the preteritum (simple past), perfect or pluperfect tense. Equivalent utterances in Croatian are almost invariably in the default past tense, consisting of the auxiliary *biti* 'be' and the active past participle marked for gender and number. The Croatian pluperfect is used to emphasise that an action occurred anterior to another action. It is not obligatory as it is in Norwegian in relation to two past actions where the pluperfect shows which one preceded the other. Where the marking of the chronologically first occurring action is a category that Norwegian-Croatian bilinguals begin to employ when speaking Croatian, they may look to Norwegian to see which forms (in this case, the preterite form of the auxiliary plus the past participle = pluperfect) perform this, and replicate a development that has occurred in Norwegian. This then functions as the Croatian marker of obligatory antecedent marking of an action in the past that precedes another. Where this category begins to become a regularly-observed feature in speakers' communicative interactions, it starts to become recurrent. This accounts for its unusually high frequency of the pluperfect that Mønnesland (1987: 84) reports amongst a group of younger speakers in Oslo.

(23) **bio   pokušao**   da   se   ubije
     AUX-PTCP.M.SG try-PTCP.M.SG   COMP REFL kill-3SG
     'He **had tried** to kill himself.' (Mønnesland 1987: 94).

   HMLD.Cro: **pokušao se** ubiti

(24) on je   **bio**   **htjeo**   da   lovi
     he AUX-3SG AUX-PTCP.M.SG   want-PTCP.M.SG   COMP catch-3SG
     ribe   ali
     fish-ACC.F.PL but
     'He **had wanted** to catch fish, but ...' (Mønnesland 1987: 94).

   HMLD.Cro: **htio je** loviti ribu, ali ...

In one instance, the pluperfect is used when it is unlikely to have preceded another action:

(25) poslije smo   **bili**   **krenuli**   za
     after   AUX-1PL   AUX-PTCT.M.PL   start off-PTCT.M.PL   for+ACC
     Slavonski Brod
     Slavonski Brod-ACC.M.SG
     'Afterwards we [had?] **made off** for Slavonski Brod.' (Mønnesland 1987: 94).

   HMLD.Cro: Poslije **smo krenuli** za Slavonski Brod.

Where a category such as chronological sequencing of actions in the past is emerging, it is possible that over-employment (or maybe a misfiring) such as the one above occur. Again, I return to the acquisitional context of heritage language speakers and the variation that can occur in their vernaculars, and with reference to Polinsky and Scontras's (2019) observation that 'over-marking' can be a feature of heritage language speakers' speech. It may be that use of the pluperfect form is also achieving something else. Haspelmath and Michaelis (2017) observe that a characteristic of heritage language speaker's language can be 'extra-transparency':

> In social situations [...] people need to make an extra effort to make themselves understood – they need to add extra transparency. This naturally leads to the overuse of content items for grammatical meanings, which may become fixed when more and more speakers adopt the innovative uses. (Haspelmath and Michaelis 2017: 15)

Here it appears that the same kind of contact-induced change is occurring amongst a number of speakers, pointing to grammaticalisation of obligatory sequence marking of past actions as a nascent process. The form of the three-part compound pluperfect tense in Croatian is 'more analytical' than the default Croatian past tense, and it is possible that this added transparency is a second causative factor. Without more data from a larger number of speakers it is not possible to talk of grammaticalisation as a fully-fledged development in the Croatian repertoires of young Norwegian-Croatian bilinguals. Heine and Kuteva (2005: 81) make the observation that "grammaticalization is a gradual process that may involve generations of speakers and extend over centuries". Data from pidgin and creole studies (eg. Vellupillai 2015) suggests that it can occur over two or three generations, while data from Light Walpiri spoken in Australia suggests that it is observable within one generation. O'Shannessy (2005: 43–44) reports that amongst other developments, speakers under 30 employ *na* derived from English *wanna* 'want to' and affix it to pronouns as an auxiliary to indicate mood for actions occurring in present and future time, something that is not attested amongst older speakers. In a heritage language context, Błaszczyk (2015) reports that Polish-German bilinguals are regularly using *ten* 'this' and *jeden* 'one' when speaking Polish as a feature of definiteness and indefiniteness modelled on German definite and indefinite articles. It appears that perhaps even within one generation, a recurrence of forms may point to the emergence of what looks to be a regularisation pattern.

The discussion above of examples from Norwegian-Croatian bilinguals points to causative sources that can be described either as 'one-off' instances of structural transference, or as phenomena that are indicative of a deeper, even paradigmatic characteristic of the speaker's competence in Croatian. This is often referred to as 'convergence', a term I outlined above, and here I use it referring to an outcome. What this means is that the matrix language that forms the morphosyntactic grid is based on input from two codes, not one. This need not mean that there are surface level morphemes supplied by both, but at different levels of abstraction, the structures of two codes, not one, are recognisable. Myers-Scotton (2006) describes this in the following terms:

> In bilingual CPs [projections of complementizer], the abstract lexical structure underlying a given element, with its surface from entirely in one language, can represent the splitting off of one or more levels from an element in one language and its combining with levels in another language... [W]hen speakers produce structures for which the source of structure is split between two or more varieties – the result is what is called a composite Matrix Language. (Myers-Scotton 2006: 99. Square brackets added.)

The notion of a composite matrix language is employed in a number of contact linguistics studies to account for extensive structural change in heritage languages with or without surface morphemes from both codes, e.g. Bolonyai (1998), Türker (2000), Jake and Myers-Scotton (2002) and Fuller (2010).

To return to examples of the Croatian speech of Dutch-Croatian bilinguals from Gvozdanović's (1993) study, I present the following excerpt as an instance of what appears to be change occurring at a paradigmatic level in this speaker's competence in Croatian. The excerpt contains no surface morphemes from Dutch:

(26) ja vidim **jedna** **žena** onda **ide**
I see-1SG one-NOM.F.SG woman-NOM.F.SG then go-3SG
plakati
cry-IPFV.INF
'I see **a woman**... then she **goes to cry** [=starts to cry].' (Gvozdanović 1993: 188)

Dutch: ik zie **een vrouw**.. dan **gaat ze huilen**.
HMLD.Cro: vidim **ženu**-ACC... onda **zaplače**-PFV.3SG / onda **počne**-PFV.3SG **plakati**-IPFV.INF.

I focus on two parts of the utterance. The object of *vidim* 'I see' is not assigned a direct object marker, i.e. ACC morphology. In Dutch, nominal objects are morphologically identical to nominal subjects. Thus, absence of overt object marking, at least in nominals, appears to underpin this speaker's Croatian competence, perhaps better expressed as *langue*. The linguistic structures that make up the speaker's Croatian *langue* include structural input from Dutch such that at the functional level of speech production, information outside the maximal projection does not call up morphological features to overtly mark nominals for features such as oblique case marking. This explains the NOM marking of *jedna žena* 'one/a woman' which is a direct object.

The second part that I focus on is the second clause *onda ide*-IPFV *plakati*-IPFV 'she goes to cry [=starts to cry]'. This second clause contains two imperfective verbs. Semantically, the second clause describes an activity wherein the subject is about to commence an action, i.e. *gaat ze* 'goes to' which is similar in form and function to English *going to*. In HMLD.Cro, the sense of 'start to cry' would be expressed via a perfective verb (in its present tense). So, this would mean the same verb *plakati* 'to cry' would attract the prefix *za-* meaning 'beginning to', yielding *zaplakati* 'to start to cry'. Addition of the prefix *za-* to *plakati* yielding *zaplakati* immediately results in a verb with perfective aspect, and the present tense form of that verb is *zaplače*-PFV.3SG. It appears that the Dutch model of *gaat ze huilen* has been replicated as an instance of transference of syntactic features of the Dutch construction to result in an equivalent isomorphic Croatian construction. To account for this in a general sense, it is possible to posit that on a 'verb-by-verb' basis, in the Croatian *langue* of this speaker, VPs may be influenced by the structure of Dutch VPs resulting in instances such as that above. But it may be that change at a deeper level of language production is occurring, as employment of a construction such as *ide plakati* 'goes to cry' is indicative of the lexical semantic properties of the verb that encode the feature of aspect.

Looking at aspect, I briefly refer to developments in Russian as spoken as a heritage language, which has a similar system of verbal aspect as Croatian. One account that is offered in relation to the occurrence of aspect marking of verbs in Russian as a heritage language spoken in the US compared to homeland Russian is that particular aspectual forms of a verb are liable to attrition in the same way as other items in the Russian lexicon are. In other words, that aspectual form of a verb that is statistically less frequent is prone to attrition in the same way that statistically infrequent lexical items are also prone to attrition, or even to them not being acquired in the first place (Maslov 1974). Returning to example (26), and considering why the speaker used *plakati*-IPFV rather than *zaplakati*-PRV, it can be hypothesised that frequency could be a key factor. The form *plakati* is much more frequently used form in present tense narratives, e.g. *zašto plačeš?* 'why are you crying?', as well as in past tense ones, e.g. *plakao sam k'o dijete* 'I cried/was crying like a child', i.e. for either present or past actions, *plakati*-IPFV occurs more often than *zaplakati*-PRV. The verb 'to cry' is probably less likely to occur in future tense narratives and where it does occur, it is perhaps more likely to occur in its PFV form *zaplakat ću* 'I'll burst into tears' than in the IPFV form *plakat ću* 'I'll cry/be crying'. Following from this, as *plakati* is more common than *zaplakati*, where *zaplakati* is replaced by *plakati* the reasoning for this according to the Frequency Theory

(Maslov 1974) is that the more common and semantically broader term is employed in place of a less common and semantically narrower term in the same way that heritage language speakers use lexical hypernyms to refer to lesser known terms.

Another interpretation of change in heritage language speakers' conceptualisation of aspect is Pereltsvaig's adaptation of the notion of telicity. Pereltsvaig (2008: 30, original punctuation, square brackets added) distinguishes between whether a verb form is commonly used to denote "events with a bounded Path ... [meaning that they imply] an action towards an end-point on a Path", in which case the PFV form of the verb is more likely to be acquired or used, or whether a verb form is commonly used to denote "no Path or with a non-bounded Path" in which case it is likely to be used in its IPFV form. The lexical-semantic features of the verb *to cry* suggest it is on a non-bounded Path, i.e. it is not clear that the act of crying is bounded semantically, nor is there a sense of completion that can be achieved by the verb. This means that *to cry* is conceptualised as a 'non-accomplishment' verb and always IPFV. What this then means when the lexical-semantic value of 'commencing to cry' is expressed, which would otherwise be expressed by the PFV verb (*zaplakati*) as the 'commencement to cry' *is* an action that can be 'achieved', the speaker does not have the PFV form to draw on. So, an analytic construction based on a Dutch model is pressed into service to achieve the 'commencement' meaning. When comparing which theory appears to have greater explanatory power to account for apparent changes in aspect marking in the speech of Russian-Americans, Pereltsvaig (2005) reports that her adapted version of telicity (the test for whether an action is conceived of having a bounded Path or a non-bounded Path) is able to explain these changes more often than the predictions of the Frequency Theory. In terms of speech production, amongst those speakers whose speech shows evidence of change in aspect marking, it is possible to posit this as a change at an abstract level of production. In terms of Myers-Scotton's (2002: 24) four-stage production process, changes in the marking of aspect as a lexical-semantic feature may be occurring at the conceptual level of speakers' speech production resulting in the non-production of content morphemes that mark aspect – at least for those verb-pairs where aspect is marked via prefix or infix.

6 An overview of studies on Croatian in diaspora settings

Section 5.3 above set out the categories and interpretative approach to the data sets that are presented in this volume. Examples were drawn from a number of studies that have been conducted over the last 50 years or so. This section provides an overview of most of these studies, focusing on the description of linguistic forms, mainly from spoken but also from written corpora. Some sociolinguistically-based studies are also included here, where they complement the situation of speakers and contexts from which linguistic data is drawn.

The earliest studies on Croatian in a diaspora setting were conducted in North America by homeland-based researchers. An example is Surdučki (1966) whose first study is based on a large corpus of 500 editions of émigré newspapers in which he identifies large numbers of lexical transfers and loan translations but few instances of code-switching and syntactic transference. The absence of the latter two categories is unsurprising for a corpus based on printed texts. Albin and Alexander (1972) collected a sample of spoken data from first- and second-generation speakers, mainly of speakers from Dalmatia in the San Pedro area of California, with follow up collections published in Albin (1976) and Albijanić (1982). In all of these, "switching", "phonological, morphological, syntactic, lexical interference", as well as "loanblends and loanshifts" are recorded (Albin 1976: 82–89).

Speech from three generations of speakers living in a formerly industrial but now semi-rural area of Pennsylvania are recorded by Jutronić (1974, 1976) later Jutronić-Tihomirović (1982), and presented in her 1985 monograph *Hrvatski jezik u SAD* 'The Croatian language in the USA'. In her many studies, Jutronić (1974/1975) Jutronić-Tihomirović (1980, 1982, 1983, 1985) generally employs the terms "phonological, lexical, and morpho-syntactic interference". In the 1985 monograph, in addition to the large number of lexical and syntactic transfers, there are also loan translations and instances of pragmatic transference. Jutronić-Tihomirović (1985) is cognisant of the speakers' dialect (non-standard) background and discusses changes in their speech with this as their 'baseline' variety.

Rudolf Filipović, who enjoyed a formidable reputation due to his work on contrastive analysis projects of Croatian and English also recorded the language of Croatian-speakers in the USA (Filipović 1979, 1980, 1981, 1982, 1985, 1991). His studies of Croatian in the USA mostly focus on lexical transfers, and the presence (or not) of phonological and morphological markers that integrate them into Croatian. While based in the homeland, the significance of Filipović's studies, as well as those of Surdučki and Jutronić(-Tihomirović) is that these researchers spent some time in diaspora communities and were acquainted with the sociolinguistic situation of diaspora speakers. They were able to compare and contextualise the influence of English on homeland varieties with that on diaspora varieties in an informed way and to record phenomena that may not have been apparent to those less acquainted with emigre settings. Some differences are predictable: in the diaspora situations, phonological integration of English-origin forms is based on their pronunciation in the host countries, and morphological integration is variable according to generational group; in the homeland, the written form of

English-origin items is more influential to its phonological integration, and morphological integration is almost always obligatory. These trends are confirmed by further studies looking at the reception of Anglicisms in homeland Croatian, e.g. Škara (1986–1987) and Muhvić-Dimanovski (1990). More recently, some have problematised the prevalence of English-origin in electronic and other media, and ask questions about viewers' and readers' comprehension of them, where the lack of phonological and graphemic integration is identified as a feature that is disadvantageous to their understanding (Balenović and Grahovac-Pražić 2016).

Other studies from North America include Gasiński (1986: 34) who examines "lexical borrowings" and subcategorises them according to word classes, while mono- and bilingual written texts are examined by Bauer (1983: 253) for "syntactic deviations". A four-member family in Toronto, consisting of two Gen.1A parents, one Gen.1B older child and one Gen.2 younger child is the focus of Starčević's (2014) PhD dissertation which is a detailed ethnographic study of bilingual speech in intra-family settings with an in-depth survey of instances of phonological, lexical, pragmatic, semantic and syntactic transference from English into Croatian.

Further studies from North America have adopted an entirely sociolinguistic approach in which language maintenance versus shift is investigated, e.g. Magner (1976), Ward (1976, 1980) and Milivojević (1984). In predominantly Francophone Montréal Ćosić (1992/1993) completed a similar survey of 59 informants. These were mainly first-generation speakers who were asked about their language proficiencies and domain-based language use. The issue of language attitudes and ethnicity amongst first- and second-generation speakers in America is touched on briefly by Živković, Šporer and Sekulić (1995). More recently, a large-scale demographic and language-maintenance focused study were undertaken by Petrović (2017) who matches Canadian census data with responses on language use and self-perceived proficiency levels from 220 informants from both the first and second generation based mainly in the Toronto metropolitan area. Petrović (2018) further reports on language use in select domains and contact with Croatia.

In the southern hemisphere, the most prolific researcher has been Hans-Peter Stoffel, based in New Zealand, who studied the speech and written texts of first-, second- and third-generation Croatian-speakers. Stoffel describes the large number of features in the bilingual speech (and written texts) in the following terms: "transfers", "loan translations" and "meaning borrowings" (Stoffel 1981a: 58–61), "morphological adaptation of loanwords" (Stoffel 1981b: 243, 1991: 418) and syntactic features of "bi-aspectual loan-verbs" (Stoffel 1988a:1). Stoffel also examines language maintenance and shift factors (Stoffel 1982) and the issue of dialect versus standard language usage in an immigrant setting (Stoffel 1994). Croatian-Māori-English trilingualism is also a topic uncovered by Stoffel (1988b) who was both observer and participant, analyst and adopted in-group-member to a very large number of Croatian-speakers in Auckland and the areas to its north. Language practices of first- and second-generation speakers in New Zealand are touched on in studies by Jakich (1987) and Dragicevich (2017), while Božić-Vrbančić's (2008) anthropological study of Croatian-Māori families and biculturalism provides further information on the use and form of Croatian alongside Māori and English.

In Australia, a number of studies have focused on code-switching (Hlavac 1999a; 2003, 2011, 2012) lexical transference (Hlavac 1999b) and discourse markers as a form of pragmatic transference (Hlavac 2006) while Hlavac (2003) examines the first two topics together with syntactic transference and grammatical change. Further outlines of aspects of bilingual speech are provided by Clissa (1996), Škvorc (2006), Stolac (2019), while Doucet (1990) focused on language maintenance patterns amongst first-generation speakers.

Moving beyond Croatian-English contact situations, it was in Sweden that the single largest research study on the acquisition and use of the heritage language was conducted: the *JUBA – jugoslaviska barn* 'Yugoslav children' project which examined multiple aspects of the language of Gen.1B and Gen.2 school-age children. The focus of the project was the children's production of Serbocroatian/Croatian, i.e. speech data gathered based on story-recounting in both languages and picture descriptions, lexical tests, directed morphological tests, phonological tests and personal interviews in the children's chronologically first learnt language.

The project was conducted in the early 1980s and yielded a number of outcomes. Perhaps the most influential was the data on children's acquisition of cases, and the finding that the use of cases patterned in a certain way, such that a system of 'case implicativity' could be posited, with the following ordering of cases: NOM, ACC, GEN, LOC, INS, DAT, VOC. (Ďurovič 1983). What this means is that the presence of any case in a system implies the presence of all other cases 'to the left', but says nothing about the cases 'to the right', i.e. if a speaker was able to produce LOC noun phrases this meant that they had full command of NOM, ACC, GEN, but not necessarily of the cases to the right. i.e. INS, DAT and VOC. Ďurovič (1983, 1984, 1987, 1988) and Stankovski, Ďurovič and Tomašević (1983) focus mainly on case systems, while an analysis of phonological features is provided by Stankovski (1987) and cross-linguistic accessing of lexical items is problematised by Friberg (1983). Usage of numerals and surrounding morphosyntactic features is reported on by Tomašević (1986) while sociolinguistic factors are discussed by Pavlinić-Wolf, Anić and Ivezić (1987).

Other research on Croatian in Western Europe has been undertaken by Stölting (1984, 1987), Stölting, Delić and Orlović (1980) and Stölting-Richert (1988) in Germany who examine intra-familial language use, children's proficiency in both languages, school progress of bilingual children and the socio-political status of a 'transposed', 'guest-worker' language in Germany. Other German-based studies include Stojanović's (1984) description of monolingualism and bilingualism amongst school-age children and their progress at school and Mihaljević's (1988) description of phonological, morphological, lexical, syntactic and semantic features in the Croatian speech of school-age children. Both Mrazović (1989) and Runje (1990) examine spoken and written texts of young Gen.1B and Gen.2 speakers as 'child migrants' in Germany. A similar approach is adopted by Ljubešić (1989, 1991) who employs diagnostic criteria in ascertaining dominance or non-dominance in Croatian on the basis of formal assessments (and self-assessments) of Gen.2 and Gen.3 speakers in Germany.

The notion of bilingual linguistic identities of Croatian-origin residents in Germany is explored by Kresić (2011). More recently, texts written in Croatian by German-born second-generation Croatian-speakers have been subjected by Raecke (2006) to an error analysis, with standard Croatian used as a point of comparison. The speech of second-generation speakers of Croatian in Germany has been examined by Hansen, Romić and Kolaković (2013) and Hansen (2018). The latter study looks closely at evidence for syntactic pattern replication occurring in heritage speakers' Croatian, with lexical entries identified as one of the catalysts for structural change. Doleschal and Mikić (2018) report on the speech of eight young adult Gen.1B speakers in Austria most of whom migrated as children. They find that in their intra-generational interactions, most turns are monolingual German while about a third are monolingual Croatian (or Bosnian) with the rest containing elements of both. Code-switching occurs most frequently at turn boundaries or within clauses as insertions. Their data is of note as it is near naturalistic and indicative of the shift in dominance towards German in the repertoires of these Gen.1B speakers.

In other parts of north-west Europe, Pavlinić-Wolf, Brčić and Jeftić (1988) discuss mother-tongue instruction for Croatian- and Serbian-speaking children in Denmark, and aspects of how their language shows evidence of lexical, syntactic and semantic influence from Danish. Magnusson (1989) conducted surveys amongst immigrants born to Yugoslavia-born parents, including Croatian-speakers that elicited data on self-rated proficiency levels, use across domains, and affective reactions to Swedish and Croatian. In Norway, Mønnesland (1987) published an overview of the types of lexical transference, bilingual polysemy, grammatical change including clitic placement and increased use of the pluperfect, and cleft sentences that represent a different organisation of theme/rheme structure in the Croatian speech of young Croatian-Norwegian bilinguals. The same kinds of changes can be found amongst first generation speakers, as discussed above in Section 5.3.3 and Skaaden (2005), in her description of the speech of mostly Gen.1A speakers, locates changes in word order within constituents of NPs.

Working in the Netherlands, Gvozdanović (1993) provides a summary of aspects of the speech (and writing) of Dutch-dominant second-generation Croatian- and Serbian-speakers, while Pavlinić (1993) reviews the situation for supplementary 'mother-tongue' instruction for both Croatian and Serbian across Western Europe. More recently, Beganović (2006) has studied grammatical and pragmatic developments under the influence of Dutch. Her study focuses on the occurrence of overt and post-verbal subjects in the speech of Gen.1 Croatian-speakers, as well as speakers of Bosnian and Serbian.

From Latin America, there are few available descriptions of either speakers or features of their language. One of the few studies is from Lasić (2009/2010) who provides a domain-based study of Croatian-speakers in Chile drawing on data on first- and second-generation speakers in the far south of the country. Isolation and a relative geographical concentration of speakers appear to have some positive effects on language maintenance efforts. A comparative and integrative description of most of these studies of immigrant varieties of Croatian is provided by Zubčić (2010) whose overview encompasses research undertaken in Europe and in other continents.

While most of the researchers were homeland-based, their experience and contact with diaspora speakers was usually extensive and they were cognisant of the situation of the speakers from whom they collected data. Other research, particularly that from defectologists, is more normative in its approach to the presentation and analysis of linguistic data. This different perspective to language contact data needs to be seen in the context of the concern that many homeland educationalists had about diaspora children's acquisition of standard Croatian, including its written form, and the ability of the children to integrate into the school system back home if their parents were to return. Re-migration or return was an avowed aim of both social and education policy at least up until 1990 that viewed Croatian emigrants, particularly those in Western Europe, as *naši građani na privremenom radu u inozemstvu* 'our citizens temporarily employed abroad' (Pavlinić and Anić 1991). In this context Švob et al.'s (1989) examination of returnee children in Croatian schools reports from most returnee informants that they have undergone a successful social but (perhaps rather ominously) an uncertain linguistic reintegration. From the perspective of a speech pathologist/defectologist, Ljubešić (1992) conducted an error analysis of written Croatian texts from nine- and ten-year-olds in Germany and came to quite negative conclusions. In a follow-up study, Ljubešić and Schöler (1995) compare the Croatian and German writing of a group of bilingual students to that of equivalent groups of monolingual Croatian and monolingual German students and come to similarly negative findings.

In the 1990s, large numbers of people left Croatia and Bosnia-Herzegovina, mostly as refugees, and this led to an increase in the number of speakers of all age groups in already existing diaspora communities in Western Europe and overseas. During this time, there were limited funds available for either the development of educational resources for children receiving instruction in Croatian in overseas countries or for studies on their language (or that of other generations). It has not been until the mid-2000s that *hrvatski kao nasljedni jezik* 'Croatian as a heritage language' has (re-)emerged as a research stream in linguistics, pedagogy and philology in general in Croatia. This development has also been advanced by the emergence of teaching and learning Croatian as a foreign language, due to the increasing numbers of foreign (and usually tertiary) students now studying in Croatia. This has led to a cross-fertilisation of research on L2-speakers compared to heritage language speakers of Croatian, e.g. Hržica (2006), Cvikić, Jelaska and Kanajet Šimić (2010).

Another development that can relate to heritage speakers' motivations to acquire (or to further their) proficiency in Croatian, whether in the homeland or in the diaspora, is language level as a prerequisite to gain Croatian citizenship. The *Croatian Citizenship Law* from 2012 sets out proficiency in Croatian as a requirement for foreign-born persons to gain citizenship. This law formalised a requirement that was a *de facto* if not *de jure* expectation of applicants for Croatian citizenship in the 1990s and 2000s. Article 8 of the 2012 law sets out three ways in which proficiency – defined in the law as a "knowledge of the Croatian language and the Roman-script alphabet"[2] – could be proven. One of these ways relates to acquisition in diaspora settings: "by way of a certificate from an overseas educational institution that confirms that instruction was carried out in Croatian or by way of a certificate showing that a course of instruction has been completed at a level of at least B1 [i.e. according to the Common European Framework of Reference for Languages]".[3] Thus, for those wishing to gain Croatian citizenship, whether they were of Croatian origin or not, linguistic proficiency was a pre-requisite. At least from mid-2013 onwards after Croatia's accession to the European Union, Croatian citizenship became a sought-after attribute for a number of foreign citizens of Croatian origin. For some schools and university-level programs teaching Croatian in Australia, proficiency in Croatian was marketed as a personal attribute that could, amongst other things, enable acquisition of Croatian citizenship and an EU passport.

However, changes made to the citizenship regulations in late 2019 meant that from 1 January 2020, proficiency in Croatian was no longer a requirement to gain Croatian citizenship. It is perhaps instructive to see how this change is viewed by non-lingusts. An interpretation of the change is given on an online legal information site in Croatia, www.iusinfo.hr which comments on these changes in the following way:

---

2 Croatian original: "poznavanje hrvatskog jezika i latiničnog pisma" (Narodne novine 2012).
3 Croatian original: "svjedodžbom inozemne obrazovne ustanove kojom se potvrđuje da je obrazovanje provedeno po programu na hrvatskom jeziku ili svjedodžbom o završenom tečaju najmanje B1 stupnja znanja hrvatskog jezika" (Narodne novine 2012).

> The procedure for emigrants, their descendants and their spouses to gain Croatian citizenship has been liberalised ... even where they do not fulfil legal requirements: [that is] knowledge of the Croatian language and Roman-script alphabet ...
>
> In order to attract Croatian emigrants back to their homeland and to make the procedure of gaining Croatian citizenship simpler, proficiency in Croatian and a knowledge of Croatian society have been removed as pre-requisites. However, it is unjustified that these same emigrants can become Croatian citizens without needing to demonstrate a basic knowledge of the Croatian language and Croatian society as components of Croatian identity. This is an elementary condition to show one's belonging to a nation – in this case the Croatian nation – and common practice in other, well-ordered European states that we like to refer to as models.
> (IUS-INFO 2019, my translation[4])

In its commentary of the changes in rules relationg to citizenhip, this source, IUS-INFO (2019), as a non-governmental, but publicly visible provider of legal information refers firstly to government policies that promote the return of Croatian emigrants and their descendants. An example of these policies is the Law on Relations of the Republic of Croatia with Croats outside the Republic of Croatia.[5] The implication of the change in the citizenship law from 2020 onwards is that it will remove a perceived obstacle for those descendants of Croatian-origin emigrants who have little or no proficiency in Croatian, and who wish to gain Croatian citizenship and to possibly return to Croatia. The IUS-INFO commentary makes two objections to the change: that those wishing to live in Croatia cannot readily demonstrate their allegiance to the country and society without knowing the language; inconsistency with similar laws in Western European countries that require proficiency in the national language for foreign-born 'returnees'. Legislative reforms and public debate on the topic are indicative of perceptions in the homeland of foreign-born people of Croatian origin, or at least of those who may be considering re-settling in Croatia. Further, they are snapshots of homeland-diaspora relations and of beliefs on the level of acquisition and use of Croatian outside Croatia.

---

4 Croatian original: "Liberalizirao se postupak stjecanja hrvatskog državljanstva prirođenjem za iseljenike, njihove potomke i njihove bračne drugove ... iako ne ispunjavaju potrebne zakonske pretpostavke: poznavanje hrvatskog jezika i latiničnog pisma..."; "Iako se ukidanjem poznavanja hrvatskog jezika i kulture želi privući hrvatske iseljenike na povrat u domovinu i pojednostaviti postupak dobivanja hrvatskog državljanstva, neopravdano je da ti isti iseljenici ne moraju dokazivati poznavanje osnova hrvatskog jezika i kulture kao dio hrvatskog identiteta kako bi postali hrvatski državljani, a što je jedan od elementarnih uvjeta za dokazivanje pripadnosti nekom narodu u ovom slučaju hrvatskom, a što je praksa i u drugim uređenim europskim državama na koju se često volimo pozivati" (IUS-INFO 2019).

5 Article 7 of this law expressly states this: "The Republic of Croatian undertakes measures that foster the return of Croatian emigrants and for the migration of their descendants to the Republic of Croatia". Croatian original: "Republika Hrvatska poduzima mjere kojima potiče povratak hrvatskih iseljenika i useljavanje njihovih potomaka u Republiku Hrvatsku" (Zakon.hr 2011).

7 Conclusion

This chapter has provided a description of Croatian as a contact language and has sought to match phenomena occurring in both homeland and transposed varieties of Croatian with categories and descriptions commonly used in contact linguistics research. These categories and descriptions most commonly focus on lexical and structural features, and these are the two main areas of attention of all chapters in this book. Further, this chapter has outlined how research on language contact situations from a diachronic perspective can inform the perspective of researchers examining synchronic situations of language contact.

Although an 'old occurrence', the presentation of contact linguistics research has been augmented here by a relatively 'young' sub-field, that of 'diaspora' or 'heritage languages'. In particular, the term "divergent attainment" (Polinsky and Scontras 2019) is welcomed as a hypernym to relate to the acquisition of a transposed language and the proficiency levels that Gen.1B, Gen.2 speakers, and those of subsequent generations have in their heritage language.

This chapter has outlined the terminology that is employed in the chapters of this book. These terms are defined and discussed in relation to the large number of terms that are currently used in contact linguistics research. Based on Clyne's (1967) pioneer research on the speech of diaspora speakers speaking their heritage language, the terms 'transference' and 'transfer' are widely employed in this volume; the first term refers to the process and the second term refers to the product. The terms 'transference' and 'transfer' can be combined with all subfields of linguistic description, e.g. lexical, semantic, phonological, syntactic, even though in this volume it is the first and last terms here that are most widely investigated. The terms 'code-switching' and 'code-switch' are also employed due to their widespread use and acceptance in the field, as well as the term 'loan translation' which refers in this volume to the sequencing of morphemes, phrasemes or select syntactic features based on patterns in a donor language.

A declared aim of this volume is to examine the speech of speakers of different vintages of migration and different generatons in different countries who have the same heritage language in common. Multi-site studies of the same heritage language remain rare and the cross-national structure of this volume may help to contribute to an understanding of language contact phenomena that is based on recurrence and spread, both geographically and across different generations of speakers. The volume builds on the existing volume of language contact research on Croatian in homeland and diaspora settings and contributes to the accessibility of data from past and contemporary corpora in this language to a contact linguistics audience.

References

Aalberse, Suzanne, Ad Backus & Pieter Muysken. 2019. *Heritage Languages. A language contact approach.* Amsterdam: John Benjamins.

Aikhenvald, Alexandra & Robert Dixon. 2002. (eds.) *Areal diffusion and genetic inheritance: problems in comparative linguistics.* Oxford University Press: Oxford.

Albijanić, Aleksandar. 1982. San Pedro revisited: Language maintenance in the San Pedro Yugoslav Community. In Roland Sussex (ed.) *The Slavic Languages in Emigre Communities.* 11–22. Edmonton: Linguistic Research Inc.

Albin, Aleksandar. 1976. A Yugoslav community in San Pedro, California. *General Linguistics* 16. 70–78.

Albin, Aleksandar & Ronelle Alexander. 1972. *The Speech of Yugoslav Immigrants in San Pedro, California.* The Hague: Martinus Nijhoff.

Anić, Vladimir & Ivo Goldstein. 1999. *Rječnik stranih riječi.* [A dictionary of foreign words] Zagreb: Novi Liber.

Appel, René & Pieter Muysken. 1987. *Language contact and bilingualism.* London: Arnold.

Auer, Peter. 1999. *Code-Switching in Conversation. Language, interaction and identity.* London: Routledge.

Bičanić, Ante, Anđela Frančić, Lana Hudeček & Milica Mihaljević. 2013. *Pregled povijesti, gramatike i pravopisa hrvatskoga jezika* [An overview of the history, grammar and orthography of the Croatian language]. Zagreb: Croatica.

Backus, Ad. 1996. *Two in one. Bilingual Speech of Turkish Immigrants in The Netherlands.* Tilburg: Tilburg University Press.

Backus, Ad. 2003. Units in codeswitching: Evidence for multimorphemic elements in the lexicon. *Linguistics* 41, 83–102.

Backus, Ad. 2015. A usage-based approach to codeswitching: The need for reconciling structure and function. In Peter Auer, Gesa von Essen & Werner Frick (eds.) *Code-switching between structural and sociolinguistic perspectives,* 19–37. Mouton de Gruyter, Berlin.

Backus, Ad & Margreet Dorleijn. 2009. Loan translation versus code-switching. In Barbara Bullock & Jacqueline Toribio (eds.) *The Cambridge Handbook of Linguistic Code-switching.* 75–94. Cambridge, UK: Cambridge University Press.

Backus, Ad, Demirçay, Derya & Yeşim Sevinç. 2013. Converging evidence on contact effects on second and third generation immigrant Turkish. *Tilburg Papers in Culture Studies* 51.

Balenović, Katica & Vesna Grahovac-Pražić. 2016. Englesko-hrvatski jezični dodiri: razumijemo li jezik televizije? [English-Croatian linguistic contacts: do we understand the language used on television?]. *Jezik* 63. 140–151.

Barron-Hauwaert, Suzanne. 2004. *Language strategies for bilingual families: The one-parent-one-language approach.* Bristol: Multilingual Matters.

Bauer, Ivan. 1983. Syntactic deviations in an American-Croatian newspaper: An approach to the phenomena of linguistic borrowing. *Folia Slavica* 6 (2). 253–263.

Beganović, Jasminka. 2006. *First language attrition and syntactic subjects. A study of Serbian, Croatian and Bosnian intermediate and advanced speakers of Dutch.* MA Thesis, University of Edinburgh.

Benčić, Nikolaus. 1972. Abriß der geschichtlichen Entwicklung der burgenländisch-kroatischen Schriftsprache [An outline of the historical development of Burgenland Croatian standard language]. *Wiener Slavistisches Jahrbuch* 17. 15-28.

Benčić, Nikola, Agnjica Csenar-Schuster, Zorka Kinda-Berlaković, Jelka Koschat, Ludvig Kuzmić, Mijo Lončarić, Gerhard Neweklowsky, Ivan Rotter, Ivo Sučić, Joško Vlašić, Sanja Vulić & Marija Znika. 2003. *Gramatika gradišćanskohrvatskoga jezika* [Grammar of the Burgenland Croatian language]. Željezno/Eisenstadt: Znanstveni institut Gradišćanskih Hrvatov.

Bencsics, Nikolaus, Božidar Finka, Antun Šojat, Josef Vlasits, Stefan Zvonarich (eds.). 1982. *Deutsch-Burgenländischkroatisches-Kroatisches Wörterbuch / Nimško-gradišćanskohrvatsko-hrvatski rječnik*. Amt der Burgenländischen Landesregierung, Landesarchiv − Landesbibliothek / Komisija za kulturne veze s inozemstvom SR Hrvatske, Zavod za jezik IFF: Eisenstadt/Zagreb.

Bencsics, Nikolaus, Božidar Finka, Ivo Szucsich Antun Šojat, Josef Vlasits, Stefan Zvonarich, Zrinka Babić, Eugenija Barić, Jasna Finka, Mijo Lončarić, Marko Lukenda, Mile Mamić, Mira Menac-Mihalić, Ante Sekulić, Ljerka Šojat & Marija Znika (eds.). 1991. *Burgenländischkroatisches-Kroatisch-Deutsches Wörterbuch / Gradišćanskohrvatsko-hrvatsko-nimški rječnik*. Komisija za kulturne veze s inozemstvom R Hrvatske, Zavod za hrvatski jezik / Amt der Burgenländischen Landesregierung, Landesarchiv − Landesbibliothek: Zagreb/Eisenstadt.

Benmamoun, Elabbas, Silvina Montrul & Maria Polinsky. 2013. Heritage languages and their speakers: Opportunities and challenges for linguistics. *Theoretical Linguistics* 39(3-4). 129-181.

Bentahila, Abdelelai & Eirlys Davies. 1983. The Syntax of Arabic-French Code-Switching. *Lingua* 59. 301-30.

Berg-Seligson, Susan. 1986. Linguistic constraints on intra-sentential code-switching: A study of Spanish/Hebrew bilingualism. *Language in Society* 15. 313-348.

Bernstein, Basil. 1971. *Class, Codes and Control. Vol 1*. London: Routledge and Kegan Paul.

Binder, Theo. 2006. *Njemačke posuđenice u hrvatskom govoru Osijeku* [German loanwords in the Croatian vernacular of Osijek]. Zagreb: FF Press.

Błaszczyk, Izabela. 2015. *Ausdruck von (In)definitheit bei polnisch-deutschen Bilingualen. Eine Analyse am Beispiel des Demonstrativums 'ten' und des Zahlworts 'jeden'*. Saarbrücken: Akademiker Verlag.

Bolonyai, Agnes. 1998. In-between languages: language shift/maintenance in childhood bilingualism. *International Journal of Bilingualism* 2(1). 21-43.

Bolonyai, Agnes. 2002. Case systems in contact: syntactic and lexical case in bilingual child language. *Southwest Journal of Linguistics* 21(2). 1-35.

Bolonyai, Agnes. 2007. (In)vulnerable agreement in incomplete bilingual L1 learners. *International Journal of Bilingualism* 11(1). 3-23.

Božić-Vrbančić, Senka. 2008. *Tarara: Croats and Maori in New Zealand. Memory, Belonging, Identity*. Dunedin: University of Otago Press.

Brabec, Ivan. (1983). Dijakronski pogled na gradišćanskohrvatski književni jezik. [A diachronic view of the Burgenland Croatian literary language] In Vitomir Belaj, Željko Besedić, Božidar Finka, Antun Šojat, Tihomir Telišman, Mirko Valentić, Božena Vranješ & Budislav Vukas (eds.), *Gradišćanski Hrvati 1533-1983* [Burgenland Croats 1533-1983], 59-70. Zagreb: Centar za istraživanje migracija i narodnosti.

Breu, Walter. 1998. Das Moliseslavische. In Peter Rehder (ed.), *Einführung in die slavischen Sprachen*, 274-278. Darmstadt: Wissenschaftliche Buchgesellschaft.

Breu, Walter & Giovanni Piccoli. 2000. *Dizionario croato molisano di Acquaviva Collecroce*. Campobasso: Naš Jezik.
Brinton, Donna, Olga Kagan & Susan Bauckus (eds.). 2008. *Heritage language education. A new field emerging*. New York: Routledge.
Brozović, Dalibor & Pavle Ivić. 1988. *Jezik, srpskohrvatski/hrvatskosrpski, hrvatski ili srpski*. [Language, Serbo-Croatian/Croato-Serbian, Croatian or Serbian] Zagreb: Jugoslavenski leksikografski zavod »Miroslav Krleža«.
Bybee, Joan. 2010. *Language, Usage and Cognition*. Cambridge, UK: Cambridge University Press.
Chan, Brian Hok-Shing. 2003 *Aspects of the syntax, the pragmatics, and the production of code-switching: Cantonese and English*. New York: Peter Lang.
Clissa. John. 1996. Language shift and diglossia among the Italo-Croatian migrants from the Molise in Western Australia. Perth: University of Western Australia. MA thesis.
Clyne, Michael. 1975 *Forschungsbericht Sprachkontakt*. Kronberg: Scriptor Verlag.
Clyne, Michael. 1991. *Community Languages. The Australian Experience*. Cambridge, UK: Cambridge University Press.
Clyne, Michael. 2003. *Dynamnics of Language Contact*. Cambridge, UK: Cambridge University Press.
Cvikić, Lidija. 2016. *Hrvatski kao ini jezik – odabrane teme* [Croatian as an L2 – selected topics]. Zagreb: Hrvatsko filološko društvo.
Cvikić, Lidija, Zrinka Jelaska & Lada Kanajet Šimić. 2010. Nasljedni govornici i njihova motivacija za učenja hrvatskoga jezika [Heritage speakers and their motivation for learning Croatian]. *Croatian Studies Review* 6. 113–127.
Ćosić, Vjekoslav. 1992/1993. Sociolingvistički status hrvatskih iseljenika u Quebecu. [The sociolinguistic status of Croatian immigrants in Quebec] *Radovi razdjela filoloških znanosti* 22(23). 27–45.
Dahl, Östen. 2004. *The growth and maintenance of linguistic complexity*. Amsterdam: John Benjamins.
Daller, Michael H., Cemal Yıldız, Nivja H. De Jong, Seda Kan & Ragıp Başbaği. 2011. Language dominance in Turkish-German bilinguals: methodological aspects of measurements in structurally different languages. *International Journal of Bilingualism* 15(2). 215–236.
De Houwer, Annick. 2009. *Bilingual First Language Acquisition*. Bristol: Multilingual Matters.
Demirçay, Derya & Ad Backus. 2014. Reassessing the typology of code-switching. *Dutch Journal of Applied Linguistics* 3(1). 30–44.
Doleschal, Ursula & Gizela Mikić. 2018. Codeswitching bei Herkunftssprecher_innen des Bosnischen oder Kroatischen. Eine Untersuchung an Material aus Kärnten. *Wiener Slawistischer Almanach* 81. 57–72.
Doucet, Jacques. 1990. First generation Serbo-Croatian speakers in Queensland: language maintenance and language shift. In Suzanne Romaine (ed.) *Language in Australia*, 270–284. Cambridge, UK: Cambridge University Press.
Dragicevich, Kaye. 2017. *Pioneer Dalmatian settlers of the Far North*. Awanui: Willow Creek Press.
Dryer, Matthew. 1997. Are grammatical relations universal? In Joan Bybee, John Haiman & Sandra Thompson (eds.) *Essays on language function and language type: dedicated to T. Givon*, 115–143. Amsterdam: John Benjamins.
Dubinina, Irina & Maria Polinsky. 2013. Russian in the U.S. In Michael Moser & Maria Polinsky (eds.) *Slavic Languages in Migration,* 130–165. Vienna: LIT Verlag.

Ďurovič, Ľubomír. 1983. The case systems in the language of diaspora children. *Slavica Lundensia* 9. 21–94.
Ďurovič, Ľubomír. 1984. The Diaspora Children's Serbo-Croatian. In: Benjamin Stolz, I. R. Titunik, & Lubomír Doležel (eds.) *Language and Literature Theory,* 19–28. Ann Arbor: University of Michigan.
Ďurovič, Ľubomír. 1987. The development of grammar systems in diaspora children's language. *Slavica Lundensia* 11. 51–85.
Ďurovič, Ľubomír. 1988. The concept of diaspora language. *Slavica Lundensia* 12. 7–9.
Edwards, Malcolm & Penelope Gardner-Chloros. 2007. Compound verbs in codeswitching: Bilinguals making do? *International Journal of Bilingualism* 11(1). 73–91.
Field, Frederic. 2002. *Linguistic borrowing in bilingual contexts.* Amsterdam: John Benjamins.
Filipović, Rudolf (ed.). 1975. *Yugoslav Serbo-Croatian-English contrastive project. Studies 6.* Zagreb: Institute of Linguistics, Faculty of Philosophy, University of Zagreb.
Filipović, Rudolf (ed.). 1976. *Yugoslav Serbo-Croatian-English contrastive project. Reports 10.* Zagreb: Institute of Linguistics, Faculty of Philosophy, University of Zagreb.
Filipović, Rudolf. 1979. Proučavanje hrvatskih dijalekata u SAD. [Studying Croatian dialects in the US]. *Bilten zavoda za lingvistiku* 3. 4–19.
Filipović, Rudolf. 1980 Croatian Dialects as Markers of Croatian Ethnicity in the United States. In Rudolf Filipović (ed.) *The Role of Ethnicity in American Society.* 99–108. Zagreb: University of Zagreb and Commission for Educational Exchanges between the USA and Yugoslavia.
Filipović, Rudolf. 1981. Hrvatski dijalekti u kontaktu s engleskim jezikom na području SAD. [Croatian dialects in contact with English in the US] *Hrvatski dijalektološki zbornik* 5. 33–37.
Filipović, Rudolf. 1982 Serbo-Croatian in the United States: Croatian Dialects in Contact with American English. In Roland Sussex (ed.) *The Slavic Languages in Emigre Communities* 23–31. Edmonton: Linguistic Research Inc.
Filipović, Rudolf (ed.) 1985. *Yugoslav Serbo-Croatian-English contrastive project. Chapters in Serbo-Croatian English contrastive grammar.* Zagreb: Institute of Linguistics, Faculty of Philosophy, University of Zagreb.
Filipović, Rudolf. (ed.) 1987. *Zagrebački kontrastivni projekt engleskog i hrvatskog ili srpskog jezika. Kontrastivna analiza engleskog i hrvatskog ili srpskog jezika III – Glagolska vremena.* Zagreb: Zavod za lingvistiku, Filozofskog fakulteta, Sveučilišta u Zagrebu.
Filipović, Rudolf. 1990 *Anglicizmi u hrvatskom ili srpskom jeziku: porijeklo – razvoj – značenje* [English-origin words in Croatian or Serbian: origin – development – meaning]. Zagreb: Jugoslavenska akademija znanosti i umjetnosti / Školska knjiga.
Filipović, Rudolf. 1991. Neposredni jezični dodiri u hrvatskim dijalektima u SAD. [Direct language contacts in Croatian dialects in the US] *Senjski zbornik* 18. 31–40.
Filipović, Rudolf (ed.). 1993. *Zagrebački kontrastivni projekt engleskog i hrvatskog jezika. Kontrastivna analiza engleskog i hrvatskog jezika IV.* [The Zagreb Croatian-English contrastive project. Contrastive analysis of English and Croatian IV] Zagreb: Zavod za lingvistiku, Filozofskog fakulteta, Sveučilišta u Zagrebu.
Filipović, Rudolf. 1997. Meaning transferred and adapted – Semantic Problems in Contact Linguistics. In Wolfgang Wölck & Annick de Houwer (eds.) *Plurilingua. Recent studies in contact linguistics,* 122–128. Bonn: Dümmler.
Fishman, Joshua A. 2008. Language maintenance, language shift, and reversing language shift. In Tej K. Bhatia & William Ritchie (eds.), *The handbook of bilingualism,* 406–436. Malden, MA: Blackwell.

Flecken, Monique. 2011. Assessing bilingual attainment: macrostructural planning in narratives. *International Journal of Bilingualism* 15(2). 164–186.
Friberg, Ann-Christin. 1983. The vocabulary test. *Slavica Lundensia* 9. 95–106.
Friedman, Victor A. 2003. Turkish in Macedonia and Beyond: Studies in Contact, Typology, and Other Phenomena in the Balkans and the Caucasus. Wiesbaden: Harrassowitz.
Fuller, Janet. 2010. Morpheme types in a matrix language turnover: the introduction of system morphemes from English into Pennsylvania German. *International Journal of Bilingualism* 4(1). 45–58.
Gal, Susan. 1979. *Language Shift. Social Determinants of Linguistic Change in Bilingual Austria*. New York: Academic Press.
Gardner-Chloros, Penelope. 2009. *Code-switching*. Cambridge: Cambridge University Press.
Gasiński, Thaddeus. 1986. English elements in the speech of the Croatian immigrant community of Santa Clara Valley, California. *Zbornik Matice Srpske za filologiju i lingvistiku* 29(2). 31–45.
Gertken, Libby, Mark Amengual & David Birdsong. 2014. Assessing language dominance with the bilingual language profile, In Pascale Leclercq, Amanda Edmonds & Heather Hilton (eds.) Measuring L2 Proficiency: Perspectives from SLA. Bristol: Multilingual Matters, 208–225.
Glovacki-Bernardi, Zrinjka. 1998. *Deutsche Lehnwörter in der Stadtsprache von Zagreb* [German loanwords in the Zagreb vernacular]. Frankfurt am Main: Peter Lang.
Glovacki-Bernardi, Zrinjka. 2013. *Agramer. Rječnik njemačkih posuđenica u zagrebačkom govoru*. [Agramer. A dictionary of German loanwords in the Zagreb urban vernacular]. Zagreb: Novi Liber.
Golubović, Biljana. 2007. *Germanismen im Serbischen und Kroatischen* [German loanwords in Serbian and Croatian]. Munich: Otto Sagner.
Grković-Major, Jasmina. 2011. The development of predicative possession in Slavic languages. In Motoki Nomachi (ed.), *The grammar of possessivity in South Slavic Languages: diachronic and synchronic perspective*, 35–54. Slavic Research Center, Hokkaido University.
Grosjean, François. 1999. The bilingual's language modes. In J. Nicol (ed.), *One mind, rwo languages: bilingual language processing*, 1–25. Oxford: Blackwell.
Grošelj, Robert. 2014. The supine and the supine clause in South Slavic languages. *Zeitschrift für Slawistik* 59(3). 301–324.
Grotzky, Johannes. 1978. Morphologische Adaption deutscher Lehnwörter im Serbokroatischen [Morphological adaption of German loanwords in Serbo-Croatian]. Munich: Dr. Rudolf Trofenik.
Gvozdanović. Jadranka. 1993. Serbian and Croatian. In Guus Extra & Ludo Verhoeven (eds.) *Community Languages in the Netherlands*, 175–192. Amsterdam: Swets and Zeitlinger.
Hadrovics, László. 1985. *Ungarische Elemente im Serbokroatischen*. Budapest: Böhlau.
Halmari, Helen. 1997. *Government and Codeswitching. Explaining American Finnish*. Amsterdam: John Benjamins.
Hansen, Björn. 2018. On the permeability of grammars: syntactic pattern replications in heritage Croatian and heritage Serbian spoken in Germany. In Jasmina Grković-Major, Björn Hansen & Barbara Sonnenhauser (eds.), *Diachronic Slavonic syntax: the interplay between internal development, language contact and metalinguistic factors*, 126–159. Berlin: De Gruyter Mouton.
Hansen, Björn, Daniel Romić & Zrinka Kolaković. 2013. Okviri za istraživanje sintaktičkih struktura govornika druge generacije bosanskoga, hrvatskoga i srpskoga jezika u

Njemačkoj [A framework for research on syntactic structures of heritage Croatian, Bosnian and Serbian as spoken by the second generation in Germany]. *Lahor* 15. 9–45.

Haspelmath, Martin & Susanne Maria Michaelis. 2017. Analytic and synthetic: typological change in varieties of European languages. In Isabelle Buchstaller & Beat Siebenhaar (eds.), *Studies in Language Variation 19,* 3–22. Language variation – European perspectives VI: Selected papers from the Eighth International Conference on Language Variation in Europe (ICLaVE 8), Leipzig, May 2015.

Hasselmo, Nils. 1961. *American Swedish.* Cambridge, USA: Harvard University. PhD thesis.

Haugen, Einar. 1953. *The Norwegian Language in America.* Philadelphia: University of Pennsylvannia Press.

Haugen, Einar. 1973. Bilingualism, Language Contact and Immigrant Languages in the US. *Current Trends in Linguistics* 10. 505–591.

Heine, Bernd & Tania Kuteva. 2005. *Language contact and grammatical change.* Cambridge, UK: Cambridge University Press.

Heine, Bernd & Tania Kuteva. 2006. *The changing languages of Europe.* Oxford: Oxford University Press.

Hlavac, Jim. 1999a. 32 years on and still triggering: Psycholinguistic processes as motivation for switching amongst Croatian-English bilinguals. *Monash University Linguistics Papers* 2(1). 11–24.

Hlavac, Jim. 1999b. Phonological integration of English transfers in Croatian: Evidence from the Croatian speech of second-generation Croatian-Australians. *Filologija* 32. 39–74.

Hlavac, Jim. 2000. Croatian in Melbourne: lexicon, switching and morphosyntactic features in the speech of second-generation bilinguals. Melbourne: Monash University. PhD thesis.

Hlavac, Jim. 2003. *Second-generation speech. Lexicon, code-switching and morpho-syntax of Croatian-English bilinguals.* Bern: Peter Lang.

Hlavac, Jim. 2006. Bilingual discourse markers: Evidence from Croatian-English code-switching. *Journal of Pragmatics* 38(11). 1870–1900.

Hlavac, Jim. 2011. Hesitation and monitoring phenomena in bilingual speech. A consequence of code-switching or a strategy to facilitates its incorporation? *Journal of Pragmatics* 43. 3793–3806.

Hlavac, Jim. 2012. Psycholinguistic, metalinguistic and socio-psychological accounts of code-switching: a comparative analysis of their incidence in a large Croatian-English sample. *Suvremena lingvisika / Contemporary Linguistics* 73. 47–71.

Hržica, Gordana. 2006. Kada je hrvatski pretežak i Hrvatima: metodologija nastave hrvatskoga kao drugog jezika. [When Croatian is too difficult for Croats: methodology for teaching Croatian as a second language] *Govor* 23(2). 163–179.

Hymes, Dell. 1966. Two types of linguistic relativity. In William Bright (ed.) Sociolinguistics, 114–158. The Hague: Mouton.

Ius-info. 2019. Zakonodavne promjene hrvatskog državljanstva. [Legislative changes to Croatian citizenship] (30.10.2019) https://www.iusinfo.hr/aktualno/u-sredistu/39645 (accessed 10 September 2020)

Jake, Janice & Carol Myers-Scotton 2002. Second generation shifts in sociopragmatic codeswitching patterns. In Aleya Rouchdy (ed.) *Language contact and language conflict in Arabic. Variations on a sociolinguistic theme.* 317–330. London: Routledge.

Jakich, Miranda. 1987. The Yugoslav Language in New Zealand. In Walter Hirsch (ed.). *Living Languages. Bilingualism and Community Languages in New Zealand,* 117–124. Auckland: Heinemann.

Johanson, Lars. 1999a. The dynamics of code-copying in language encounters. In Bernt Brendemoen, Elizabeth Lanza & Else Ryen (eds.) *Language encounters across time and space,* 37–62. Oslo: Novus.

Johanson, Lars. 1999b. Frame-changing code-copying in immigrant varieties. In Guus Extra & Ludo Verhoeven (eds.), *Bilingualism and migration*, 247–260. Berlin: Mouton de Gruyter.

Johanson, Lars. 2002. *Structural Factors in Turkic Language Contacts.* London: Routledge.

Joshi, Aravind. 1984. Processing of Sentences with Intra-Sentential Code-Switching. In: Arnold Dowty, David Karttunen and Lauri Zwicky (eds.) *Natural Language Processing: Psycholinguistic, Computational and Theoretical Perspectives,* 190–205. Cambridge, UK: Cambridge University Press.

Jutronić, Dunja. 1974. The Serbo-Croatian language in Steelton, PA. *General Linguistics* 14. 15–34.

Jutronić, Dunja. 1974/1975. Prilog proučavanju sintaktičke interferencije kod jezika u kontaktu. *Radovi razdjela filoloških znanosti* 8. 249–258.

Jutronić, Dunja. 1976. Language maintenance and language shift of the Serbo-Croatian language in Steelton, Pennsylvania. *General Linguistics* 16. 166–186.

Jutronić-Tihomirović, Dunja. 1982. The effect of dialectal variations on the adaptation of loanwords. *International Journal of Slavic Linguistics* 5. 63–73.

Jutronić-Tihomirović, Dunja. 1983. A contribution to the study of syntactic interference in language contact. *Folia Slavica* 6(2). 310–320.

Jutronić-Tihomirović, Dunja. 1985. *Hrvatski jezik u SAD* [The Croatian Language in the USA]. Split: Logos.

Jutronić-Tihomirović, Dunja. 1988/1989. Jezično prilagođavanje na sintaktičkom nivou [Linguistic adaptation on the syntactic level]. *Radovi razdjela filoloških znanosti* 18. 51–60.

Kapović, Mate. 2011. *Čiji je jezik* [Whose language is it?]. Zagreb: Algoritam.

Karall, Kristina. 2000. *Sprachkurs Burgenlandkroatisch.* Vienna: Hrvatski akademski klub / Kroatischer Akademikerklub.

Klaić, Bratoljub. 1982. *Rječnik stranih riječi* [Dictionary of foreign words]. Zagreb: Nakladni zavod Matice hrvatske.

Köpke, Barbara & Dobrinka Genevska-Hanke. 2018. First Language Attrition and Dominance: Same Same or Different? *Frontiers in Psychology* 9. 1963.

Kresić, Marijana. 2011. Deutsch-kroatische Sprachidentitäten. In Zrinjka Glovacki-Bernardi (ed.), *Deutsch in Südost- und Mitteleuropa: Kommunikationsparadigmen im Wandel* 93–104. Zagreb: FF Press.

Kupisch, Tanja & Jason Rothman. 2018. Terminology matters! Why difference is not incompleteness and how early child bilinguals are heritage speakers. *International Journal of Bilingualism* 22(5). 564–582.

Lasić, Josip. 2009/2010. Jezični identitet hrvatske iseljeničke zajednice u Čileu [Language identity of the Croatian immigrant community in Chile]. *Croatian Studies Review* 6. 163–171.

Leung, Constant. 2005. Convivial communication: Recontextualizing communicative competence. *International Journal of Applied Linguistics* 15(2). 119–144.

Labov, William. 1994. *Principles of linguistic change. Volume 1: internal change.* Oxford: Blackwell.

Levine, Glenn. 2000. *Incomplete L1 acquisition in the immigrant situation: Yiddish in the Unites States.* Tübingen: Max Niemeyer.

Li, Wei. 1994. *Three Generations, Two Languages, One Family: Language Choice and Language Shift in a Chinese Community in Britain.* Clevedon, Avon: Multilingual Matters.

Lindstedt, Jouko. 2019. Diachronic regularities explaining the tendency towards explicit analytic marking in Balkan syntax. In Iliyana Krapova & Brian Joseph (eds.), *Balkan syntax and (universal) principles of grammar,* 70–84. Berlin: De Gruyter Mouton.

Lisac, Josip, Ivo Pranjković, Marko Samardžija & Ante Bičanić. 2015. (eds.) *Povijest hrvatskoga jezika. 4. knjiga: 19. stoljeće.* [The History of the Croatian Language. Vol. 4: 19th Century]. Zagreb: Društvo za promicanje hrvatske kulture i znanosti CROATICA.

Lucas, Christopher. 2015. Contact-induced language change. In Claire Bowern & Bethwyn Evans (eds.), *The Routledge Handbook of Historical Linguistics,* 519–536.

Ljubešić, Marta. 1989. Jezični razvoj djece jugoslavenskih migranata u SR Njemačkoj. [The linguistic development of children of Yugoslav migrants in the Federal Republic of Germany] *Migracijske teme* 5(4). 353–361.

Ljubešić, Marta. 1991. Dvojezičnost i gramatičko označavanje. [Bilingualism and grammatical marking] *Primijenjena psihologija* 12(1–2). 15–20.

Ljubešić, Marta. 1992. Prilog poznavanju migracijske dvojezičnosti. [A contribution to our knowledge of migration-based bilingualism] *Migracijske teme.* 8(1). 55–67.

Ljubešić, Marta & Hermann Schöler. 1995. Sentence imitation by monolingual and bilingual children. *Logopedija* 1(2). 15–21.

Ljubičić, Maslina. 2011. *Posuđenice i lažni parovi. Hrvatski, talijanski i jezično posredovanje* [Borrowings and false friends. Croatian, Italian and linguistic mediation]. Zagreb: FF Press.

MacSwan, Jeff. 2000. The architecture of the bilingual language faculty: evidence from intrasentential code switching. *Billingualism, Language and Cognition* 3. 37–54.

Magner, Thomas. 1976. The melting pot and language maintenance in South Slavic immigrant groups. *General Linguistics* 16(2–3). 59–67.

Magnusson, Kjell. 1989. Kulturni identitet i jezik: mladi Jugoslavije u Švedskoj. *Migracijske teme* 4(4). 363–377.

Mahootian, Shahrzad. 1993. *A null theory of codeswitching.* Evanston, Ill.: Northwestern University. PhD thesis.

Maslov, Yurij. 1974. Zur Semantik der Perfektivitätsopposition. *Wiener Slavisistisches Jahrbuch* 20. 107–122.

Matras, Yaron. 1998. Convergent development, grammaticalization and the problem of 'mutual isomorphism'. In Winfried Boeder, Christoph Schroeder & Karl-Heinz Wagner (eds.) *Sprache in Raum und Zeit,* 889–103. Tübingen: Narr.

Matras, Yaron. 2009. *Language Contact.* Cambridge, UK: Cambridge University Press.

Mihaljević, Milan. 1988. Govor naše djece u dijaspori. [The speech of our children in the diaspora] *Rasprave zavoda za jezik* 14. 127–137.

Milivojević, Dragan. 1984. Language maintenance and language shift in the United Slavonian Benevolent Association of New Orleans, Louisiana. *Melbourne Slavonic Studies* 18. 46–64.

Moguš, Milan. 1995. *A history of the Croatian language: toward a common standard.* Zagreb: Nakladni zavod Globus.

Mønnesland, Svein. 1987. Norwegian interference in the language of Yugoslav children in Norway. *Slavica Lundensia* 11. 87–99.

Montrul, Silvina. 2002. Incomplete acquisition and attrition of Spanish tense / aspect distinctions in adult bilinguals. Bilingualism: language and cognition 5(1). 39–68.

Montrul, Silvina. 2008. *Incomplete acquisition in bilingualism. Re-examining the age factor.* Amsterdam: John Benjamins.

Montrul, Silvina. 2016. The acquisition of heritage languages. Cambridge: Cambridge University Press.

Mrazović, Pavica. 1989. Neke karakteristike govornog i pisanog nemačkog i srpskohrvatskog jezika dece migranata u SR Nemačkoj. [Some characteristics of spoken and written German and Serbo-Croatian of the children of migrants in the Federal Republic of Germany] In Senka Savić (ed.) *Interkulturalizam kao oblik obrazovanja dece migranata van domovine.* [Interculturalism as a form of education for the children of migrants outside their homeland] 70–77. Novi Sad: Institut za južnoslovenske jezike Filozofskog fakulteta u Novom Sadu.

Muhvić-Dimanovski, Vesna. 1990. Some recent semantic loans of English origin in Serbo-Croatian. In Rudolf Filipović & Maja Bratanić (eds.) *Languages in contact. Proceedings of the symposium of the 12th international congress of anthropological and ethnological sciences. Zagreb, July 25–27, 1988.* 151–157. Zagreb: Institute of Linguistics, University of Zagreb.

Muysken, Pieter. 2000. Bilingual speech. A typology of code-mixing. Cambridge, UK: Cambridge University Press.

Muysken, Pieter. 2008. Functional categories. Cambridge, UK: Cambridge University Press.

Myers-Scotton, Carol. 1993. Duelling languages. Grammatical structure in codeswitching. Oxford: Clarendon Press.

Myers-Scotton, Carol. 1996. One way to dusty death: The matrix language turnover hypothesis. In Lenore Grenoble & Lindsay Whaley (eds.), Language loss and community response. Cambridge & New York: Cambridge University Press,

Myers-Scotton, Carol. 2002. *Contact linguistics. Bilingual encounters and grammatical outcomes.* Oxford: Oxford University Press.

Myers-Scotton, Carol. 2006 Natural codeswitching knocks on the laboratory door *Bilingualism: language and cognition* 9(2). 203–212.

Myers-Scotton, Carol & Janice Jake. 2015. Cross-language asymmetries in code-switching patterns. In John Schwieter (ed.), *The Cambridge handbook of bilingual processing,* 416–458. Cambridge: Cambridge University Press.

Narodne novine. Službeni list Republike Hrvatske [Official Gazette of the Republic of Croatia]. 2012. *Pravilnik o načinu provjere poznavanja hrvatskog jezika i latiničnog pisma, hrvatske kulture i društvenog uređenja u postupcima stjecanja hrvatskog državljanstva.* [Regulations on the means of verifying knowledge of the Croatian language and Roman-script alphabet, and of Croatian culture and society in the procedure of acquiring Croatian citizenship.] https://narodne-novine.nn.hr/clanci/sluzbeni/2012_10_118_2563.html (accessed 14 September 2020).

Neweklowsky, Gerhard. 2010. *Die Sprache der Burgenländer Kroaten. Jezik Gradišćanskih Hrvatov* [The language of Burgenland Croats]. Trajštof/Trausdorf: Znanstveni institut Gradišćanskih Hrvatov/Wissenschaftliches Institut der Burgenländischen Kroaten.

Novak, Kristian & Velimir Piškorec. 2006. Kroatisch-deutscher Kodewechsel in Miroslav Krležas Drama 'Die Glembays'. *Zagreber Germanistische Beiträge – Beihefte* 9. 51–61.

Nyomárkay, István. 1996. Sprachhistorisches Wörterbuch des Burgenlandkroatischen. [Historical linguistic dictionary of Burgenland Croatian). Szombathely: Akadémiai Kiadó.

Otheguy, Ricardo, Ana Celia Zentella & David Livert. (2007). Language and dialect contact in Spanish in New York: Toward the formation of a speech community." *Language.* 770–802.

Otheguy, Ricardo & Ana Celia Zentella. 2012. *Spanish in New York. Language contact, dialectal levelling, and structural continuity*. New York: Oxford University Press.
O'Shannessy, Carmel. 2005. 'Light Warlpiri': A new language. *Australian Journal of Linguistics* 25(1). 31–57.
Pauwels, Anne. 2016. *Language maintenance and shift*. Cambridge, UK: Cambridge University Press.
Pavlinić, Andrina. 1993. Croatian or Serbian as a diaspora language in Western Europe. In Guus Extra & Ludo Verhoeven (eds.) *Immigrant languages in Europe*, 101–118. Clevedon, UK: Multilingual Matters.
Pavlinić, Andrina & Josip Anić. 1991. Djeca hrvatskih migranata u europskim zemljama – iseljavanje, motivacija za očuvanje i njegovanje materinskog jezika te povratak u domovinu [Children of Croatian migrants in Europe: emigration, motivation for the maintenance and preservation of the mother tongue and for return to the homeland]. *Migracijske i etničke teme* 7(3–4). 277–291.
Pavlinić-Wolf, Andrina. 1983. Considerations Concerning the Language Development of Yugoslav Migrant Children in European Host Countries. *Grazer Linguistische Studien* 19. 88–105.
Pavlinić-Wolf, Andrina. 1989. "Obrazovanje i kulturni razvitak migranata". Projekt br. 7 Savjeta za kulturnu suradnju Evropskog vijeća – kao sinteza interkulturalističke teorije i prakse. ["Education and the cultural development of migrants". Project no. 7 of the Council for cultural co-opeartion of the Council of Europe] In Senka Savić (ed.) Interkulturalizam kao oblik obrazovanja dece migranata van domovine. [Interculturalism as a form of education for the children of migrants outside their homeland]. 93–99. Novi Sad: Institut za južnoslovenske jezike Filozofskog fakulteta u Novom Sadu.
Pavlinić-Wolf, Andrina, Josip Anić & Zoran Ivezić. 1987. Jezik jugoslavenske djece koja žive u Švedskoj (Preliminarni rezultati sociolingvističkog istraživanja). [The language of Yugoslav children who live in Sweden (Preliminary results of a sociolinguistic research study)] *Slavica Lundensia* 11. 159–173.
Pavlinić-Wolf, Andrina, Karmen Brčić & Nadežda Jeftić. 1988. Supplementary mother-tongue education and the linguistic development of Yugoslav children in Denmark. *Journal of Multlingual and Multicultural Development*. 9(1–2). 151–167
Pereltsvaig, Asya. 2005. Aspect lost, aspect regained: restructuring of aspectual marking in American Russian. In Raffaella Folli, Heidi Harley, Paula Kempchinsky & Roumyana Slabakova (eds.), *Aspectual Inquiries*, 369–395. Dordrecht: Springer.
Pereltsvaig, Asya. 2008. Aspect in Russian as grammatical rather than lexical notion: evidence from Heritage Russian. *Russian Linguistics* 32(1). 27–42.
Peti-Stantić, Anita, Hrvoje Japirko & Marin Kežić. 2016. Koliko su lagani tzv. lagani glagoli u hrvatskom? [How light are so-called 'light' verbs in Croatian?] *Filološke studije* 14. 202–225.
Petrović, Ivana. 2017. Očuvanje hrvatskog jezika u Kanadi [Croatian Language Maintenance in Canada]. *Migracijske i etničke teme* 33(1). 7–36.
Petrović, Ivana. 2018. Croatian as a heritage language in Canada. *Zbornik radova Filozofskog fakulteta Sveučilišta u Splitu* 11. 59–72.
Petrović, Velimir. (2001). Essekerisch im Überblick. [An overview of Essekerisch] In Velimir Petrović (ed.), Essekerisch. Das Osijeker Deutsch [Essekerisch. The German vernacular of Osijek], 3–68. Wien: Edition Praesens.

Petrović, Velimir. 2008. Esekerski rječnik. Essekerisches Wörterbuch [A dictionary of Essekerisch – German-origin words in the urban vernacular of Osijek]. Zagreb: FF Press.

Pires, Acrisio & Jason Rothman. 2009. Disentangling sources of incomplete acquisition: An explanation for competence divergence across heritage grammars. International Journal of Bilingualism 13. 211–238.

Polinsky, Maria. 2006. Incomplete acquisition: American Russian. Journal of Slavic Linguistics 14(2). 191–262.

Polinsky, Maria. 2007. Reaching the end point and stopping midway: different scenarios in the acquisition of Russian. Russian Linguistics 31. 157–199.

Polinsky, Maria. 2008. Gender under incomplete acquisition: heritage speakers' knowledge of noun categorization. Heritage Language Journal 6(1). 40–71.

Polinsky. Maria. 2016. Structure vs. use in heritage language. *Linguistics Vanguard* 2(1). doi:10.1515/lingvan-2015-0036

Polinsky, Maria. 2018 Bilingual children and adult heritage speakers: The range of comparison. International Journal of Bilingualism 22(5). 547–563.

Polinsky, Maria & Gregory Scontras. 2019. Understanding heritage languages. Bilingualism: language and cognition. 1–17.

Poplack, Shana. 1980. Sometimes I'll start a sentence in Spanish y termino en español: towards a typology of code-switching. *Linguistics* 18. 581–618.

Poplack, Shana. 2012. What does the nonce borrowing hypothesis hypothesize? *Bilingualism: language and cognition* 15(3). 644–648.

Poplack, Shana. 2004. Code-Switching / Sprachwechsel. In Ulrich Ammon, Norbert Dittmar, Klaus J. Mattheier & Peter Trudgill (eds.), *Sociolinguistics. An international handbook of the science of language and society,* 589–596. Berlin: Walter de Gruyter.

Putnam, Michael & Liliana Sánchez. 2013. What's so incomplete about incomplete acquisition? A prolegomenon to modeling heritage language grammars. *Linguistic Approaches to Bilingualism* 3(4). 478–508.

Raecke, Jochen. 2006. Hrvatski u Njemačkoj: njemački s hrvatskim riječima? [Croatian as a second language in Germany: German with Croatian words?]. *Lahor* 2. 151–158.

Rešetar, Milan. 1911. *Die serbokroatischen Kolonien Süditaliens*. Wien: Kaiserliche Akademie der Wissenschaften.

Ross, Malcolm. 2007. Calquing and metatypy. *Journal of Language Contact* 1(1). 116–143.

Rothman, Jason. 2009. Understanding the nature and outcomes of early bilingualism: Romance languages as heritage languages. *International Journal of Bilingualism* 13, 155–163

Runje, Maja. 1990. Održavanje hrvatskog jezika u dijaspori u Njemačkoj. [Maintenace of Croatian as a diaspora language in Germany] *Marulić.Hrvatska književna revija* 23(1). 42–47.

Sebba, Mark. 2009. On the notion of congruence and convergence in code-switching. In Barbara Bullock & Almeida Toribio (eds.) *The Cambridge Handbook of Linguistics Code-switching*. 40–57. Cambridge, UK: Cambridge University Press.

Sammartino, Antonio. 2004. *S našimi riči. Con le nostre parole* [With our words]. Montemitro: Fondazione "Agostina Piccoli".

Schmid, Monika 2011. *Language attrition*. Cambridge, UK: Cambridge University Press.

Schmitt, Elena. 2000. Overt and covert codeswitching in immigrant children from Russia. *International Journal of Bilingualism* 4(1). 9–28.

Scotti, Giacomo. 2006. *Hrvatski trokut u Italiji* [A Croatian triangle in Italy]. Rijeka: Društvo hrvatskih književnika – Ogranak u Rijeci.

Silva-Corvalán, Carmen. 2003. Linguistic consequences of reduced input in bilingual first language acquisition. In Silvina Montrul & Francisco Ordóñez (eds.), Linguistic theory and language development in Hispanic languages, 375–397. Papers from the Fifth Hispanic Linguistics Symposium and the 4th Conference on the Acquisition of Spanish and Portuguese. Sommerville, MA: Cascadilla Press.

Silva-Corvalán Carmen & Jeanine Treffers-Daller. 2015. Language Dominance in Bilinguals. Issues of Measurement and Operationalization. Cambridge, MA: Cambridge University Press.

Skaaden, Hanne. 2005. First language attrition and linguistic creativity. International Journal of Bilingualism 9(3–4). 435–452.

Sobolev, Andrey. 2008. From synthetic to analytic case: variation in South Slavic Dialects. In Andrej L. Malchukov & Andrew Spencer (eds.), *The Oxford handbook of case*, 716–729. Oxford: Oxford University Press.

Sočanac, Lelija. 2004. Hrvatsko-talijanski jezični dodiri [Croatian-Italian language contacts]. Zagreb: Nakladni zavod Globus.

Spicijarić Paškvan, Nina & Mirjana Crnić Novosel. 2014. Il dialetto fiumano all'inizio del XXI secolo. *Rivista Italiana di Dialettologia* 38. 57–73.

Sridhar, Shirakipur & Kamal Sridhar. 1980. The syntax and psycholinguistics of bilingual code-switching. *Canadian Journal of Psychology* 34. 407–16.

Stankovski, Miodrag. 1987 Obstruenti u sistemima fonema i njihove destrukcije u populaciji DO7. arhiva za jezike u dijaspori. [Obstruents in the system of phonemes and their loss in the DO7 population group. Archive for languages in the diaspora] *Slavica Lundensia* 11. 7–32.

Stankovski, Miodrag, Ľubomír Ďurovič & Mijo Tomašević. 1983. Development structures in the family language of Yugoslav immigrant children in a Swedish language environment. *Slavica Lundensia* 9. 11–20.

Starčević, Anđel. 2014. *Hrvatski i engleski jezik u dodiru: hrvatska iseljenička obitelj u Kanadi* [Croatian and English in contact: an immigrant Croatian family in Canada]. Zagreb: University of Zagreb, Faculty of Humanities and Social Sciences, PhD thesis.

Starčević, Anđel, Mate Kapović & Daliborka Sarić. 2019. *Jeziku je svejedno* [Language couldn't care less]. Zagreb: Sandorf.

Striedter-Temps, Hildegard. 1958. Deutsche Lehnwörter im Serbokroatischen. Wiesbaden: Ost-Europa Institut, Free University of Berlin.

Stoffel, Hans-Peter. 1981a. The morphological adaptation of loanwords from English in New Zealand Serbo-Croatian. *Wiener Slawistischer Almanach* 7. 243–252.

Stoffel, Hans-Peter. 1981b. Observations on the Serbo-Croatian Language in New Zealand. *New Zealand Slavonic Journal* 1. 53–64.

Stoffel, Hans-Peter. 1982. Language Maintenance and Language Shift of the Serbo-Croatian Language in a New Zealand Dalmatian Community. In Roland Sussex (ed.) *The Slavic languages in emigre communities*. 121–139. Edmonton: Linguistic Research Inc.

Stoffel, Hans-Peter. 1988a. Bi-Aspectual Loan-Verbs in Migrant Serbo-Croatian. *New Zealand Slavonic Journal. Part 1. Serbo-Croatian Colloquium Papers*. 1–7.

Stoffel, Hans-Peter. 1988b. Slavisches in Polynesien. Zur Geschichte des serbokroatisch-maorisch-englischen Sprachkontakts in Neuseeland. In Bernd Christa (ed.) *Slavic themes. Papers from two hemispheres*. 349–370. Neuried: Hieronymus.

Stoffel, Hans-Peter. 1991. Common features in the morphological adaptation of English loanwords in migrant Serbo-Croatian. In Vladimir Ivir & Damir Kalogjera (eds.) *Languages in Contact and Contrast.* 417–430. Berlin: Mouton de Gruyter.

Stoffel, Hans-Peter. 1993 Slav migrant languages in the 'New World': Cases of *Migranto-before-death? Australian Slavonic and East European Studies* 7(1). 75–89.

Stoffel, Hans-Peter. 1994. Dialect and Standard Language in a Migrant Situation: The Case of New Zealand Croatian. *New Zealand Slavonic Journal. Festschrift in honour of Patrick Waddington.* 153–170.

Stojanović, Ilija. 1984. Lingvistički aspekti dvojezičnosti jugoslovenskih učenika sa srpskohrvatskog jezičkog područja u završnim razredima osnovne škole u SRNj. [Linguistic aspects of the bilingualism of Yugoslav schoolchildren from the Serbo-Croatian-spaking area in the latter years of primary school in the Federal Republic of Germany] In Andrea Nećak-Lük & Irena Štrudelj (eds.) *Dvojezičnost. Individualne in družbene razsežnosti.* [Bilingualism. Individual and societal dimensions] 221–234. Ljubljana: Društvo za uporabo jezikoslovja SR Slovenije.

Stolac, Diana. 2019. Sročnost u jeziku Hrvata u Australiji [Syntactic agreement in the language of Australian Croats]. In Ivana Vidović-Bolt (ed.), *Zbornik s međunarodnoga znanstvenog skupa Komparativnoslavističke lingvokulturalne teme (KOMPAS)* [Edited volume of KOMPAS, from an international conference on comparative Slavic and linguistic-cultural themes] 289–297. Zagreb: Srednja Europa.

Stölting, Wilfried. 1984. Serbo-Croatian in the Federal Republic of Germany. *Melbourne Slavonic Studies* 18. 27–45.

Stölting, Wilfried. 1987. Die Wanderung jugoslawischer Migrantenkinder durch die bilinguale Kompetenz. *Slavica Lundensia* 11. 113–132.

Stölting, Wilfried, Dragana Delić & Marija Orlović 1980 Die Zweisprachigkeit jugoslawischer Schüler in der Bundesrepublik Deutschland. Berlin: Balkanologische Veröffentlichungen des Osteuropa-Instituts an der Freien Universität Berlin / Harrassowitz Verlag.

Stölting-Richert, Wilfried. 1988. Linguistic, sociological and pedagogical aspects of Serbo-Croatian in West-European diaspora. *Slavica Lundensia* 12. 11–21.

Surdučki, Milan. 1966. English loanwords in the Serbo-Croatian immigrant press. *Canadian Journal of Linguistics* 12(1). 52–63; 12(2). 123–135.

Surdučki, Milan. 1978. *Srpskohrvatski i engleski u kontaktu.* [Serbo-Croatian and English in contact] Novi Sad: Matica Srpska.

Šimundić, Mate. 1994. *Rječnik suvišnih tuđica u hrvatskomu jeziku* [A Dictionary of superfluous foreign words in the Croatian language]. Zagreb: Barka.

Škaljić, Abdulah. 2004. *Turcizmi u našem jeziku* [Turkish loanwords in our language]. Sarajevo/Jastrebarsko: Karika.

Škara, Danica.1986–1987. Prilog proučavanju anglicizama u hrvatskom ili srpskom jeziku (Interferencije na razini tvorbe riječi). [A contribution to the study of Anglicisms in Croatian or Serbian (Instances of interference at the word formation level)] *Radovi razdjela filoloških znanosti.* 16, 113–122.

Škevin, Ivana & Antonia Jazidžija. 2017. Linguistic and social-identity aspects of code-switching: The case of Zadar's speakers of the Venetian dialect. In Kristina Cergol Kovacevic & Sanda Lucija Udier (eds.), *Applied linguistics research and methodology, Proceedings from the 2015 CALS conference.* 225–240. Frankfurt/M.: Peter Lang.

Škvorc, Boris. 2006. Hrvatski uokviren engleskim: jezik australskih Hrvata kao prvi i drugi jezik [Croatian framed by English: The language of Australian Croatians as s 'first' and 'second language']. *Lahor* 1. 15–26.
Švob, Melita, Sonja Podgorelec, Karmen Brčić & Vlasta Đuravonić. 1989. Uključivanje djece povratnika u škole. *Migracijske teme* 5(4). 379–391.
Tannen, Deborah. 1981. New York Jewish conversational style. *International Journal of the Sociology of Language* 30. 133–149.
Tannenbaum, Michal. 2012. Family language policy as a form of coping or defence mechanism." *Journal of Multilingual and Multicultural Development* 33(1). 57–66.
Thomason, Sarah. 2001. *Language Contact. An Introduction*. Edinburgh: Edinburgh University Press.
Thomason, Sarah. 2003. Contact as a source of language change. In Brian Joseph and Richard Janda (eds.) *Handbook of Historical Linguistics*. 686–712. Oxford; Blackwell.
Thomason, Sarah & Terrence Kaufman. 1988. *Language contact, creolization, and genetic linguistics*. Berkeley: University of California Press.
Tomašević, Mijo 1986. The usage of the numerals 2,3 and 5 in the SerboCroatian/Croatian (S-C) diaspora in Sweden. *Slavia Lundensia*. 10, 215–224.
Treffers-Daller, Jeanine. 2005. Evidence for insertional codemixing: Mixed compounds and French nominal groups in Brussels Dutch. *International Journal of Bilingualism* 9(3–4). 477–508.
Trudgill, Peter. 2001. *Sociolinguistic typology: Social determinants of linguistic complexity*. Oxford: Oxford University Press, 2011.
Turk, Marija. 2013. Jezično kalkiranje u teoriji i praksi. [Linguistic calquing in theory and practice] Zagreb: Hrvatska sveučilišna naklada i Filozofski fakultet Sveučilišta u Rijeci.
Türker, Emel. 2000. *Turkish-Norwegian codeswitching: evidence from intermediate and second generation Turkish immigrants in Norway*. PhD Dissertation. University of Oslo.
Valdés, Guadalupe. 2000. Introduction. In Lynn A. Sandstedt (ed.), Spanish for native speakers Vol. 1, 1–25. AATSP Professional Development Series Handbook for Teachers K–16. New York: Harcourt College.
Van Coetsem, Frans. 1988. *Loan phonology and the two transfer types in language contact*. Dordrecht: Foris.
Vellupillai, Viveka. 2015. Pidgins, creoles & mixed languages. An introduction. Amsterdam: John Benjamins.
Verschik, Anna. 2008. *Emerging bilingual speech. From monolingualism to code-copying*. London/New York: Continuum.
Ward, Charles. 1976. The Serbian and Croatian Communities in Milwaukee. *General Linguistics* 16(2–3). 151–165.
Ward, Charles. 1980. Intrafamilial patterns and Croatian language maintenance in America. In Charles Ward, Philip Shashko & Donald Pienkos (eds.). *Studies in Ethnicity. The East European Experience in America*. 3–14. New York: Columbia University Press.
Weilguni, Werner. 1983. Soziolinguistische Aspekte der burgenländischkroatischen Sprachsituation [Sociolinguistic aspects of the Burgenland Croatian linguistic situation]. *Wiener Slavistisches Jahrbuch* 29. 105–112.
Weinreich, Uriel. 1953. *Languages in Contact*. The Hague: Mouton.
Winford, Donald. 2003. *An introduction to contact linguistics*. Malden, MA: Blackwell.

Winford, Donald. 2009. On the unity of contact phenomena and their underlying mechanisms: The case of borrowing. In Ludmila Isurin, Donald Winford & Kees de Bot (eds.), *Multidisciplinary Approaches to Code Switching*, 279–305. https://doi.org/10.1075/sibil.41.15win

Woolford, Ellen. 1983. Bilingual Code-Switching and Syntactic Theory. Linguistic Inquiry. 14/3, 520–536.

Zakon.hr. 2011. Zakon o odnosima Republike Hrvatske s Hrvatima izvan Republike Hrvatske. [Law on relations of the Republic of Croatian with Croats outside the Republic of Croatia] https://www.zakon.hr/z/507/Zakon-o-odnosima-Republike-Hrvatske-s-Hrvatima-izvan-Republike-Hrvatske (accessed 10 September 2020.

Zubčić, Sanja. 2010. Speech of Croatian emigrants in the overseas countries and countries of Western Europe: The level of research attained. *Croatian Studies Review* 6. 141–161.

Žagar-Szentesi, Orsolya. 2005. Hrvatski u dodiru s mađarskim jezikom [Croatian in contact with Hungarian]. In Lelija Sočanac, Orsolya Žagar-Szentesi, Dragica Dragičević, Ljuba Dabo-Denegri, Antica Menac & Anja Nikolić-Hoyt (eds.), *Hrvatski jezik u dodiru s europskim jezicima* [Croatian in contact with European languages] 51–83. Zagreb: Nakladni zavod Globus.

Živković, Ilija, Željka Šporer & Duško Sekulić. 1995. Asimilacija i identitet. [Assimilation and identity] Zagreb: Školska knjiga.

Aleksandra Ščukanec, Walter Breu and Dora Vuk
Diachronic perspectives on change in spoken Croatian amongst Croatian indigenous minorities in Austria, Italy and Hungary

1 Introduction

This chapter provides a brief description of the linguistic features of the language varieties spoken by three groups of indigenous minorities located in Austria, Italy and Hungary. The respective minorities are: Burgenland Croats, 90% of whom reside in eastern Austria with smaller groups living in western Hungary and south-west Slovakia; Molise Croats, who form a *linguistic enclave* of three villages in the central Italian region of Molise;[1] two indigenous Croatian minorities living in Hungary. The first group in Hungary are the Pomurje Croats (*pomurski Hrvati*) who are Kajkavian-speakers living in the Mura River Valley in south-west Hungary and the second group are the Croatian Bošnjaks and Šokacs (*Bošnjaci i Šokci*) who are Štokavian-speakers living in the south-central Hungarian region of Baranya. This chapter features contribution from the following authors in relation to the following language groups: Aleksandra Ščukanec for Burgenland Croatian (hereafter: 'BGLD.Cro'); Walter Breu for Molise Croatian (hereafter: 'MOL.Cro'); Dora Vuk for Croatian spoken in Hungary (hereafter: 'HUN.Cro' as a hypernym relating to both groups of Croatian-speakers in Hungary, with the abbreviations 'HUN-Pom.Cro' and 'HUN-Bar.Cro' to identify data from the Kajkavian speakers from Pomurje, and the Štokavian Bošnjaks and Šokacs from Baranya respectively). All three authors have completed extensive fieldwork amongst their respective language groups and data presented here are their own, unless stated otherwise.

---

[1] The second author, Prof. Walter Breu, expresses his gratitude to the German Research Foundation (DFG) for their financial support of the field research in Molise (Italy) and more recently for their support for a project awarded to the University of Konstanz, *Der slavische Verbalaspekt in süd- und westslavischen Sprachinseln* 'Slavic verbal aspect in South and West Slavic linguistic enclaves'. Prof. Walter Breu also conveys special thanks to Prof. Giovanni Piccoli (Acquaviva) for his assistance in collecting the data.

Aleksandra Ščukanec, University of Zagreb
Walter Breu, University of Konstanz
Dora Vuk, University of Regensburg

https://doi.org/10.1515/9781501503917-003

As stated in chapter one, this edited volume contains papers that adopt a largely synchronic approach to language contact phenomena. However, and where available, linguistic data collected over a period of time are drawn on, allowing both synchronic and diachronic analysis. We are reminded that synchronic descriptions are momentary 'snap-shots' of phenomena that have developed in a particular way over time and that will continue to develop beyond that point in time at which a linguist captured a sample. To background synchronically focused presentations of the speech of Croatian diaspora communities, it is advantageous if these can be accompanied by diachronic descriptions of spoken (and written) forms of Croatian. Diachronic accounts of how Croatian has continued to be spoken (and written) over a long period of time in areas geographically distant or isolated from Croatia are instructive to us in many ways. Accounts of Croatian as a transposed, minority language continuing to be used over centuries in long-standing exclaves are of relevance to our understanding of what is happening in diaspora communities of more recent vintage. The language contact data presented in this chapter are diachronic in their description: examples of contemporary usage are discussed with reference to (historical) descriptions of the minority variety. Of particular interest are typological features – not only morphology and syntax – but features of classes of lexical items. Incidences of code-switching are also examined, along with phonology and pragmatics.

Two of the Croatian indigenous minorities that are examined here are in contact with languages – German (Burgenland Croats) and Italian (Molise Croats) – that are also the socially dominant language in the synchronic studies of Croatian-speakers in chapters 5, 6, 8 and 9. Thus a comparison of phenomena that occur in a long-standing situation of Croatian-German contact, such as Austria's Burgenland, can be made with those occurring in a much more short-lived context of Croatian-German contact, such as that amongst the post-WWII or recently departed guest workers/emigrants to Austria or Germany. Such a comparison allows us to draw implications about the possible causes of language change and the role of other languages with which Croatian is in contact. Similarly, data from MOL.Cro may be instructional to analysis of the speech of more recently arrived Croatian-speakers elsewhere in Italy. The third Croatian indigenous minority examined here is in contact with Hungarian, a Finno-Ugric language, whose typological categories contrast greatly from those of Croatian.

In sections 1.1, 1.2 and 1.3, a brief historical and sociolinguistic account of the migration and settlement of Croatian-speakers is provided together with a discussion on how Croatian as a minority language has been maintained in the three respective settings, Burgenland, Molise and Hungary. Language contact phenomena are presented in sections 2 to and 6. The lexicon, pragmatics and semantic/

phraseological features are presented in sections 2, 3 and 4 respectively with code-switching presented in section 5 and structural features in section 6.

Instances of contemporary data are mostly derived from naturalistic or elicited samples of *spoken* language from minority language speakers. Examples of written language are less often looked at, but not disregarded. The discussion focuses on the influence of the socio-politically dominant language on the Croatian minority language. That is, we foreground here language change that appears to be *externally*-motivated from the contact situation. The influence of HMLD.Cro, where relevant, is also discussed.

1.1 Burgenland Croatian (BGLD.Cro) – historical and sociolinguistic features

The Burgenland Croats (*Gradišćanski Hrvati*) are an ethnolinguistic minority located mostly in the Austrian federal state of Burgenland, with smaller numbers located in western Hungary and south-western Slovakia. Their ancestors left their homeland in the sixteenth century, fleeing the advancing Ottomans. Most originated from an area of central Croatia bounded by the rivers Sava, Kupa and Una stretching eastwards to western Slavonia, i.e. an area bounded today by Zagreb, Karlovac, Bihać and Jasenovac. Map 1 below shows the homeland areas from which the Burgenland Croats originate. Estimates of the number who left at this time vary from 60,000 (Valentić 1970) to 100,000 (Mohl 1974) to even 150,000 (Nagy 1989). As Croatia at that time was in political union with Hungary, the area that they migrated to, *zapadna Ugarska* 'western Hungary', was part of the same political entity and their migration can be seen as internal. Burgenland Croats lived in rural settlements in a region with a low population density. Geographical isolation and an agriculture-focused way of life meant that their linguistic repertoires were, over centuries, shaped by family-village networks. The communities that Burgenland Croats lived in can be considered *sprachinseln* or linguistic exclaves, but only some were monolingually Croatian, with most also containing German-speakers, less so Hungarian-speakers, and even less so Slovak-speakers.

Until the twentieth century, Hungarian was the socio-politically dominant language of the areas in which Burgenland Croats were domiciled, while German-speakers were numerically the largest contiguous group. Burgenland-Croatian-Hungarian-German trilingualism became a common feature amongst Burgenland Croats in the eighteenth and nineteenth centuries. State boundaries drawn in the twentieth century divided the area that they inhabited into three

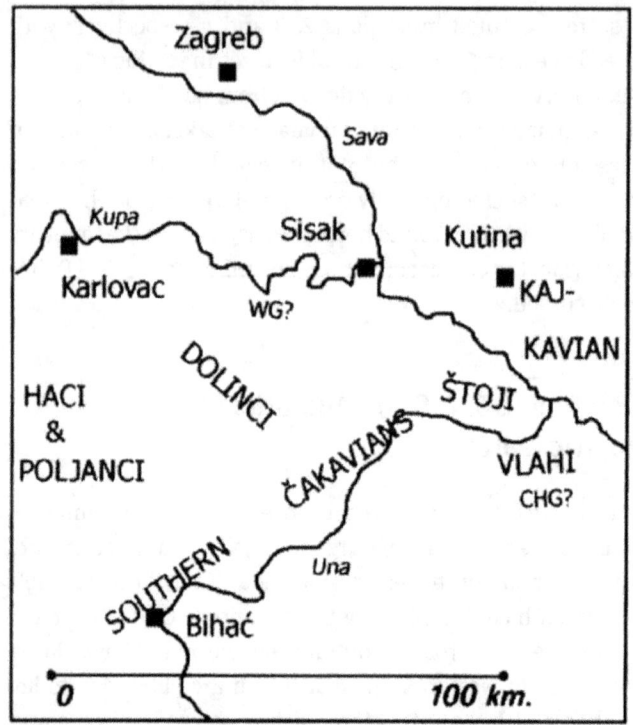

Map 1: Areas in the homeland from which Burgenland Croatians migrated in the 16th century (Houtzagers 2008: 296).

political entities: 69 of the 82 settlements are located in the Austrian federal state of Burgenland, eight in Hungary, and five are in Slovakia.

There are five clusters of the 82 settlements (all rural) along a 150 km long belt running from Hrvatski Grob/Chorvátsky Grob (Slovakia) in the north to Žamar/Reinersdorf (Austria) in the south. As most live in Austria, the Burgenland capital city, Željezno/Eisenstadt is the political, cultural and educational centre for Burgenland Croats. In general, trilingualism has been replaced by bilingualism (Burgenland Croatian + respective national language) according to speakers' country of residence. Although Hungarian was the socio-politically dominant language in the areas in which Burgenland Croats have historically lived, over the last century German has exerted a greater influence on Burgenland Croatian in Austria due to the numerical dominance of German-speakers (Benčić 1972; Neweklowsky 1975; Finka 1997).

Migration occurred in waves of different groups of speakers over a 50-year period, including speakers of all three major Croatian dialectal groups: Štokavian, Kajkavian and Čakavian. All three dialectal groups remain represented amongst today's Burgenland Croats according to the area of origin of their ancestors, with the last dialect group, Čakavian the numerically strongest, and forming the model for a standard.

In the nineteenth and twentieth centuries, dialectal variation between speakers hastened efforts to codify a common 'standard Burgenland Croatian', which now exists with trilingual, Burgenland Croatian – Standard Croatian – German dictionaries (Bencsics et al. 1982, 1991), a descriptive grammar (Sučić et al. 2003) and even textbooks for adult learners (Karall 1997) published towards the end of the twentieth century. Codification included attempted reduction in the number of German loan words and German-based calques (Benčić 1972), with efforts to replace these with domestic forms (i.e. Burgenland-based ones) and with HMLD.Cro forms.

Burgenland Croatian is a language that contains archaic forms characteristic of Croatian as it was spoken 500 years ago, e.g. palatal plosives [c], [ɟ], verbal suffix 1SG.PRES -*n*. and distinct forms for DAT, INS and LOC nouns in PL. (In homeland Croatian, syncretism has occurred across these three cases in PL.) In the case of the first two above-mentioned phenomena, these still occur in regional and non-standard varieties of homeland Croatian, while the last instance demonstrates that a 'reduction' of peculiar case forms is not unknown in homeland varieties.

Examples drawn on here are from non-normative corpora, i.e. fieldwork descriptions from Hadrovics (1974), Neweklowsky (1978, 2010), Koschat (1978), Ščukanec (2011); and also from normative descriptions such as the Burgenland Croatian grammar (Sučić et al. 2003) and the following dictionaries *Nimško-gradišćanskohrvatsko-hrvatski rječnik* ('German-Burgenland Croatian-Croatian Dictionary') (Bencsics et al. 1982), *Gradišćanskohrvatsko-hrvatsko-nimški rječnik* ('Burgenland Croatian-Croatian-German Dictionary'), (Bencsics et al. 1991). Linguistic forms presented here represent not only examples from standard Burgenland Croatian but also non-standard varieties.

Today, it is estimated that there are 25,000 to 30,000 Burgenland Croats living in Austria, the majority in Burgenland and up to 10,000 in nearby Vienna. There are up to 10,000 Burgenland Croats in Hungary. (According to the 2011 census, in two far-western counties Vas and Győr-Moson-Sopron, adjoining the Austrian border, 6,130 persons consider themselves [Burgenland] Croats, and 4,200 state their mother tongue as Croatian.) In Slovakia there are up to 2,000. (According to 2011 census results, only 1,022 persons consider themselves Burgenland Croats, and 1,234 state their mother tongue as Burgenland Croatian, Statistical Office of the Slovak Republic n.d.). Map 2 below shows the areas across Austria, Hungary, Slovakia and Czechia in which BGLD.Cro speakers live. Representatives of Burgenland Croats claim that the total number of Burgenland Croats in all three countries and abroad is around 50,000 to 55,000. In Austrian Burgenland, there are subsi-

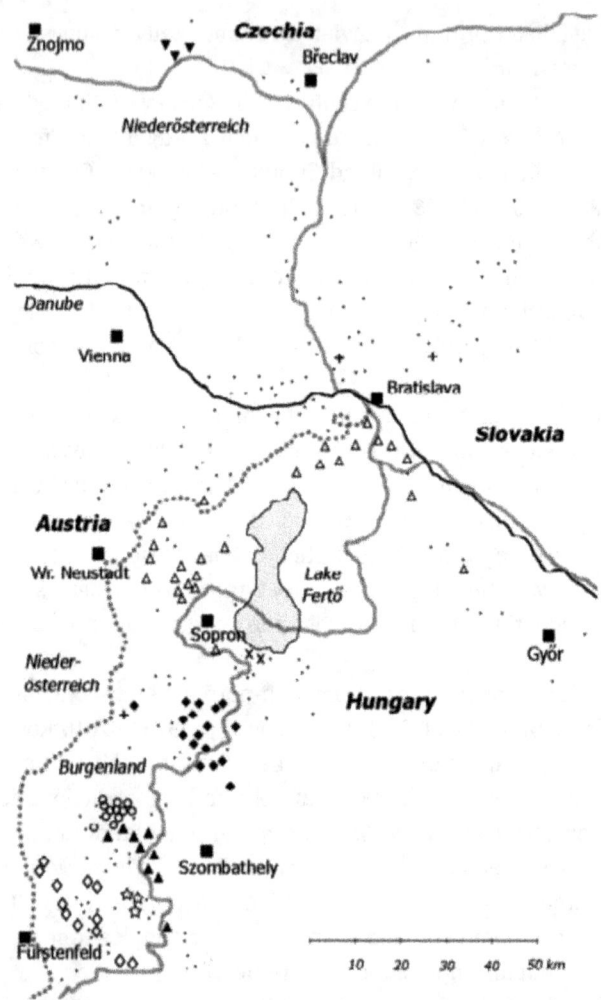

Legend to the map

▼ Moravian Croats[2] ▲ Štoji
△ Haci & Poljanci   ◊ Southern Čakavians
X Kajkavian   ☆ intermediate between Štoji and Southern Č.
◆ Dolinci   + not belonging to any of the groups
○ Vlahi   • formerly Croatian villages

Map 2: Area in which speakers of Burgenland Croatian live (Burgenland and eastern Lower Austria, Austria; far-western Hungary; south-west Slovakia; and southern Moravia, Czechia) (Houtzagers 2013: 254).

dised print and electronic resources in Burgenland Croatian, as well as regional and state support for numerous cultural activities. There are 29 bilingual primary schools and a secondary school *gimnazija/Gymnasium* in Željezno/Eisenstadt, with bilingual instruction; however, the number of hours of instruction in Burgenland Croatian has decreased over the last 50 years (Kinda-Berlaković 2005).

As in other areas of Central Europe, there have been high levels of emigration to North America over the last century. In the period from the First World War to several years after the Second World War many Burgenland Croats immigrated to the USA, Canada and South America. Some authors claim that before the First World War 33,000 Burgenland Croats had moved to the USA. Some returned around 1929 and the Great Depression, but in the interwar period and after the Second World War a further 31,000 emigrated, mainly to North America. Language maintenance of Burgenland Croatian amongst diaspora-speakers has been shown to rarely extend beyond the first generation (cf. Neweklowsky 1979; Ščukanec 2011: 161–184). Since the start of the twentieth century, internal mobility within the countries that they live in is also a feature of Burgenland Croatian life. This has intensified contact with majority-language populations, mainly German-speaking, as Burgenland Croats have moved to urban areas for study or work, in particular to Vienna, where there is a well-established Burgenland Croatian community (Rotter 1996).

1.2 Molise Croats and Molise Croatian (MOL.Cro) – historical and sociolinguistic features

Molise Croatian (MOL.Cro[2]) is still spoken in three villages adjacent to each other in the province of Campobasso in the southern Italian Region of Molise, about 35 km from the Adriatic Sea: Kruč/Acquaviva Collecroce, Mundimitar/Montemitro and Filič/San Felice del Molise. (Hereafter, only Croatian designations for the villages will be used.) The number of Slavic-speaking villages had been reduced to these three by the end of the nineteenth century. There are now only about one thousand speakers, mostly people in their forties or older who still actively use the minority language or who are at least able to understand it out of an overall

---

[2] Alternative designations for the language of the Molise Croats include *Molise Slavic* and *Našu* or *Na-našo* (Mundimitar) – the last two used by the minority speakers themselves, especially in Mundimitar/Montemitro. These terms originally refer to an adverbial, meaning "in our manner" (Breu 2008: 74, 83). The traditional ethnonym for the inhabitants was *Škavun* < Ital. *schiavone* 'Slav', while the terms 'Croat', 'Croatian' have been in use in the Croatian linguistic research literature for the last few decades. For a short overview of MOL.Cro see Breu (2011c).

number of less than two thousand people living in these villages.³ The decline of the modern Molise Croatian community commenced around 1950, when emigration to Australia and to northern parts of Italy and Europe started. The 1951 census of the ISTAT still reported an overall number of 4,883 inhabitants of the three villages, about 60–80% of whom would have been active speakers (Breu 2017a: 204–205).⁴

In regard to the general use of MOL.Cro in the three villages, there are considerable local differences, with only very few fluent speakers left in Filič, a larger number in Mundimitar, and a moderate number in Kruč. All speakers of Molise Croatian are bilingual, using the southern Italian standard variety and less so the local Molise Italian dialect as their means of communication with people from outside their language community. Most speakers also use a southern Italian standard variety with their children and intergenerational transmission of the minority variety has almost completely ceased. On the other hand, in-group speakers consistently use MOL.Cro among themselves, even in dealings with the local administration. MOL.Cro examples given in this chapter are from Kruč unless otherwise stated.

Fluent speakers predominantly resort to code-switching in the sense of spontaneously mixing in longer Italian passages. But they do use (morphologically integrated) Italian terms whenever they need them, especially with respect to technical or administrative innovations. This is not true for 'semi-speakers' who use the language only occasionally as an in-group feature and who normally mix in whole Italian sentences or whose use of MOL.Cro is restricted to the insertion of words into speech that is otherwise Italian.

The ancestors of today's Molise Croatians are thought to have migrated to Italy in the sixteenth century by sea after leaving their original homeland area of the western Neretva valley in Hercegovina. On route to Italy, their ancestors lived for some years in Dalmatia, which at that time was under the rule of the Venetian Empire. This assumption is based on the characteristics of their original dialect, with features identifying it to that part of the Štokavian-Ikavian territory where syllable-final -*l* became -*a*.⁵ Further, their speech lacks the GEN.PL ending -*ā*. This

---

3 Population totals for the three villages on 1 January 2016 were: Acquaviva 672, Mundimitar 395, Filič 634, i.e. a total of 1701 inhabitants (Guida ai Comuni, alle Province ed alle Regioni d'Italia 2018).
4 For demographic data published by the Italian Istituto Nazionale di Statistica (ISTAT) in this chapter see also Breu (2018b: 182–187), contrasting, among other things, the demographic development of MOL.Cro with the situation in the nearby Albanian enclaves of Molise.
5 Relevant linguistic examples: MOL.Cro *što* 'what' ≠ *ča* (Čakavian), *kaj* (Kajkavian); *rědъkъ > MOL.Cro *ritak* 'sparse' ≠ Jekavian *rijedak*, Ekavian *redak* (Ikavian development of Protoslavic *jat*); *nosilъ > *nosil > *nosia > MOL.Cro *nosija* 'carry (*l*-participle)' ≠ HMLD.Cro *nosio*.

is an indication that they left their original homeland before this form became widespread in Croatian in the seventeenth century.[6] Map 3 below shows the areas of origin in the homeland from which the ancestors of today's MOL.Cro speakers migrated, together with the locations of the three remaining MOL.Cro villages.

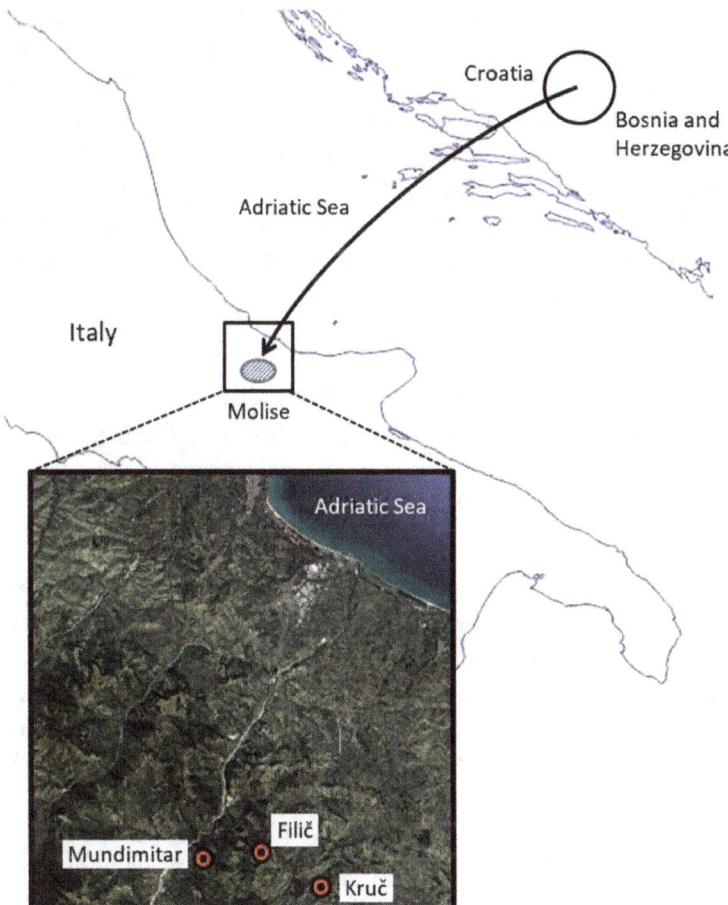

Map 3: Homeland from which speakers of MOL.Cro migrated in the 16th century.[7]

---

[6] For a description of the historical situation of the Molise Croats about a century ago, see Rešetar (1911). For an overview of the linguistic situation of several Slavic minorities in language contact situations, including Molise Croatian, see Breu (2011b).

[7] Source of black and white map: D-maps.com (2020); source of colour image: Google Earth (2020).

Contact influence comes from two sources. Initially, it was the local Italian dialect that was the model for contact-induced change. But since Italy's unification in the second half of the nineteenth century, standard Italian in its southern colloquial form has become more and more dominant and is now also a source for change and innovations.

MOL.Cro was traditionally a spoken language only. It was not until the end of the 1960s that some speakers started to write in their own vernacular. At the same time, there were others, mostly out-group members or foreigners, who began to render MOL.Cro in a written form, often employing mixed varieties that were more or less incomprehensible to in-group speakers. It was not until the twenty-first century that more elaborate examples of MOL.Cro in its written form were produced, albeit only a small number thereof. These include texts across a variety of genres, from poems to dramas, and from short stories to entire novels and even some examples of non-fiction.[8]

1.3 Croatian in Hungarian (HUN.Cro) as spoken by two indigenous communities: The Pomurje Croats and the Bošnjak- and Šokac-Croats – historical and sociolinguistic features

This section gives a brief overview on the current linguistic situation of all seven autochthonous Croatian ethnic minorities in Hungary. General sociolinguistic and demographic characteristics of the indigenous Croatian-speaking minorities in Hungary are provided, which then foreground a closer description of the two selected micro-communities. Of the available studies undertaken on Croatian in Hungary, most are dialectologically-focused, e.g. Barics, Blazsetin, Frankovics & Sokcsevits (1998), Rácz (2012), Gorjanac (2008), Tamaskó (2013) and Houtzagers (1999). More recently, sociolinguistic descriptions have been provided by Langenthal (2013) and Hergovich (2016). From a historical and linguistic point of view, the seven groups of Croatian-speakers in Hungary are descendants of Croats who left different parts of their homeland in different migration waves. Six of the seven groups live in non-conjoining areas and had little to do with each other

---

[8] See Breu (2017a, 2018a). Many poems have been published in the last two decades in Mundimitar, above all in the ongoing series *S našimi riči* ['In our own words'] by Antonio Sammartino, starting in 2004. The only Molise Croat novelist is Nicola Gliosca from Kruč. He wrote *Sep aš Mena* in 2009, and altogether completed five novels. For some of his earlier works in other genres see University of Konstanz (n.d.).

until the 1950s with improved transport and communication opportunities within Hungary (Barić 2006: 35, 100). The varieties of Croatian spoken in Hungary reflect the dialectal spectrum of the Croatian language itself (Barić 2006: 15). All three major dialects, i.e. Čakavian, Kajkavian and Štokavian, are present across the seven groups, with variation occuring across different subdialect groups as well. Map 4 shows the areas within modern-day Croatia and Bosnia-Herzegovina from which Croatian-speaking minorities in Hungary originate. The circle on the left around Velika Kaniža/Nagykanizsa shows the area where Pomurje Croats live; the circle on the right around Pečuh/Pécs and Mohač/Mohács shows the area where the Croatian Bošnjaci and Šokci communities live.

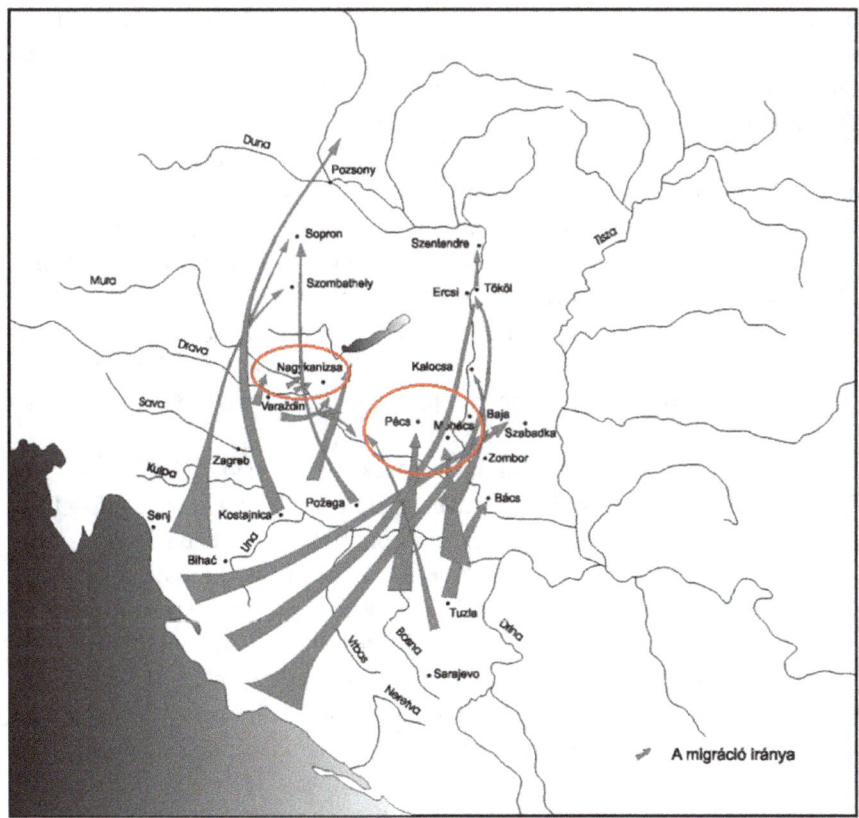

Map 4: Areas in modern-day Croatia and Bosnia-Herzegovina from which Croatian-speaking minority communities in Hungary originate. Source: Kitanics (2014).

The Burgenland Croats (*Gradišćanski Hrvati*), as outlined above in 4.1, are one of the oldest Croatian indigenous minorities living outside Croatia, with the easternmost members of this group living in western Hungary, adjoining the Austrian border (Sokcsevics 1998:3). In this part of Hungary, Kajkavian-based varieties can be found in some villages (Vedesin, Umok) around the north-west Hungarian town of Sopron (Barics, Blazsetin, Frankovics & Sokcsevits 1998; Houtzagers 1999). This section does not deal further with Burgenland Croats in Hungary, who are otherwise presented in section 1.1.

South of Burgenland along the river Mura in south-western Hungary, which forms the border between Hungary and Croatia, live the so-called Pomurje Croats (*pomurski Hrvati*) who speak a north-western sub-dialect of Kajkavian (Barić 2006: 22; Rácz 2009: 8–9, 301–302; Barics, Blazsetin, Frankovics & Sokcsevits 1998: 4). According to Kerecsényi's theory (1983: 8), the Pomurje Croats migrated in the seventeenth century from Međimurje – which is in Croatia's far north – to the other side of the Mura River. However, the most recent sociolinguistic and linguistic research conducted in the area (Rácz 2009, 2012) supports the view that they are a community autochthonous to Pomurje.

In central southern Hungary, a diversity of sub-dialects of the Štokavian dialect are spoken: several Ikavian and Ijekavian sub-dialects are used by Bošnjak-Croats (*Bošnjaci*)[9] in the villages south of Pečuh/Pécs and by Šokac-Croats (*Šokci*) in the villages east of Pečuh/Pécs, as well as in Mohač/Mohács and Santovo/Hercegszántó. These two groups, the Štokavian-speaking Bošnjak-Croats and Šokac-Croats, who live in closer proximity to each other in the Pečuh region, are grouped together as one group in the presentation of data here. This group, and the Pomurje Croats from south-west Hungary, are the groups on which our description of Croatian spoken in Hungary focuses.

The long-standing isolation of the enclaves in relation to each other and also from their original homeland led to their separate development where, to a large extent, they differed from each other and from HMLD.Cro. As Barics, Blazsetin, Frankovics and Sokcsevits (1998: 19, 2006: 35–36) point out, the dialectal diversity of the above-mentioned linguistic enclaves, together with the generally immobile and rural lifestyle of their speakers led to the formation of local identities.

According to Barić (2006), in the period between 1945 and 1947 – before the establishment of the Democratic Union of Hungarian South Slavs – an opportunity arose for the first time for the "political, cultural and linguistic" unification of all Croats in Hungary (Barić 2006: 35). The organisational unification of Hungarian Croats, Slovenes and Serbs in 1947 as an institution common to all three groups

---

[9] This name refers to the region of their origin, i.e. Western Bosnia. However, this population is not co-terminous with today's Muslim population in Bosnia-Hercegovina, who are also called *Bošnjaci*.

was not advantageous to the formation of a distinct Croatian identity in Hungary (Barić 2006: 35–37). In those three years Hungary had good relations with Yugoslavia and many educational and cultural institutions were founded, such as the minority school system in 1947. Bilateral teaching programs and cross-border cooperation flourished (Vidmarović 2008: 392, Föglein 1997: 4). However, after Tito's split with the Soviet Union in 1948, all contacts with Yugoslavia were prohibited, and Pomurje (and Podravina) Croats living in border areas adjacent to Croatia were in some cases subjected to persecution (Föglein 1997: 9). Stalin's death in 1953 brought an end to this period of non-contact, but it was not until the 1990s that the needs of minorities received measurable attention (Föglein 1997: 14).

Since the 1960s, inter-generational transmission of Croatian to younger generations has decreased substantially and native-like use of the minority language is today exclusively limited to older members of the communities (Grbić 1990: 337–338). Younger speakers often have restricted functional use of Croatian. Due to ongoing language shift, many of those speakers born in the 1960s and onwards have limited proficiency in their local Croatian dialect. For such speakers, Croatian may be used in little more than an emblematic way. For example, amongst some younger speakers, set collocations, formulaic or regularised short phrases are supplied from Croatian such as *Ajmo, dečki!* 'Come on, boys!' or *Am naj gov'riti?* 'Really?' while all other speech is in Hungarian. These insertions are usually syntactically dissociated from other elements and remain morphologically and phonologically unintegrated into Hungarian.

For those amongst whom language shift has occurred completely, we can speak of them as now being Hungarian monolinguals, while a further group is made up of Croatian-Hungarian bilinguals who speak modern Standard Croatian, a variety that they acquired through formal schooling at national minority schools in Hungary (Tamaskó 2013, Vuk research data corpus). The national minority schools were established in 1947, and until 1990, the term 'Serbo-Croatian' was employed as the designation for pupils' minority language (Vidmarović 2008: 392).

The political changes that have occurred since 1990 have allowed minorities in Hungary to organise themselves politically, and for some, this activism has increased their visibility in the general public sphere. Although language shift from Croatian dialects to Hungarian is continuing in many areas, a development since 1990 has been a more recognised presence for standard Croatian as a language of instruction or as a school subject, as the variety of language to be used in the public sphere and in bi- or multi-lingual areas.[10] It now enjoys a level of

---

10 For a detailed overview of the use of Croatian dialect, standard Croatian and Hungarian in different domains across three generations of speakers of Croatian in Hungary, see Vuk (2016).

prestige in public life in Croatian-inhabited areas of Hungary that it did not enjoy before 1990 (Vuk 2016; Dobos 2013).

On the other hand, the promotion of minority values (culture, customs etc.) and the identity formation efforts of politically active members of the communities are influencing speakers' self-perceptions: being Croat first of all means having Croatian ancestry, and being culturally active, and does not necessarily presuppose a native-like (or any) command of Croatian (Tamaskó 2013; Dobos 2013; Vuk 2016). The decreasing number of native speakers parallel with an increase in the number of those who declare themselves Croats in Hungarian censuses since 1921 is evidence of this tendency as Table 1 below demonstrates.

Table 1: Total number of Croats in Hungary according to census data 1920–2011 (Központi Statisztikai Hivatal 2014).

Years	Croatian mother tongue	Croatian nationality
1920	58,931	–
1930	47,332	–
1941*	37,885	4,711
1949	20,423	4,106
1960	33,014	14,710
1970	21,855	–
1980	20,484	13,895
1990	17,577	13,570
2001	14,326	15,597
2011	13,716	23,561

* Data from 1941 relates to the area of today's Hungary together with Međimurje and all of Bačka that were annexed in 1940–1941. See Gyurok (1998) for a detailed overview of demographic and statistical data.

A result of the long-term language contact between Croatian and Hungarian in all of the linguistic enclaves is the large repertoire of Hungarian borrowings in local Croatian varieties and the incidence of habitual (i.e. largely unmarked) code-switching amongst many, particulary older members (Tamaskó 2013; Hergovich 2016). Alternation between Hungarian and Croatian is a common, but perhaps less unmarked phenomenon in the speech of older community members when interacting amongst themselves (Tamaskó 2013; Hergovich 2016; Vuk research data corpus). Reflecting on their own mixed utterances, speakers may claim it is as part of either their own Croatian dialect or idiolect. Or they may provide a response that is well known to contact linguists researching bi-lingual groups: "It is neither Hungarian nor Croatian". The following exchange between a granddaughter and her grandmother is such an example:

(1) *Mama! Kak si ve to rekla?*   'Grandma! How did you say it?'
    Hurvatski!   'In Croatian!'
    *'**Mert**' je mađerski!*   '**Mert**' ['because'] is Hungarian!'
    Neje, i to je hurvatski.   'It's not. It is also Croatian.'

The metalinguistic comment from the grandmother about an established borrowing 'occupying a place in both languages' is understandable, given that her own home language consists of forms from both languages. Another metalinguistic observation, provided in standard Croatian by a 27-year old interviewee from Salanta, a Bošnjak-Croat village near Pečuh/Pécs, gives an insight into the 'home language' of one minority speaker:

(2) *Preformulirali smo [hrvatski jezik] onako kako nam se sviđa ... malo i mađarski pričamo, malo i hrvatski, dakle u jednoj rečenici nekad imamo i mađarske riječi.*
    We've re-formed it [Croatian] as we see fit ... we speak a little bit of Hungarian and a little bit of Croatian, so sometimes in the same sentence we have Hungarian words as well.

Descriptions of Croatian in Hungary are restricted to data from Kajkavian-speaking Pomurje-Croats and the Štokavian-speaking Bošnjak-Croats and Šokac-Croats. Linguistic analysis of HUN.Cro is taken from a corpus consisting of recorded interviews conducted with two older speakers of the Štokavian dialect spoken around Pečuh, two elder Kajkavian speaking informants (all four above 60 years), and two younger Štokavian speaking Bošnjaks (aged between 27 and 29). Data on lexical borrowings and morphological paradigms in HUN.Cro are taken from Rácz's (2012) descriptions of the Kajkavian dialect, Gorjanac's (2008) description of the Štokavian dialect of Santovo and Mandić's (2016) dictionary of the Štokavian dialect of Santovo.

2 Lexicon

The term 'lexicon' refers to lexical items that etymologically belong(ed) to languages other than Croatian that appear in the speech (or writing) of Croatian-speakers. In long-standing contact situations, these lexical items are commonly termed 'loanwords' or 'borrowings' and these are forms that are likely to have become habitualised in speakers' vernaculars. Apart from their original etymology, in a local (situational) sense, speakers otherwise perceive little or no difference between these forms and other forms in their lexicons. They are usually phonologically and morphologically integrated into Croatian, although this need not always be the case.

In BGLD.Cro, German and less often Hungarian have been source languages for loanwords and loan translations. Words with their origins from these languages can occur very commonly in most speakers' vernaculars. Pawischitz (2014: 63) goes as far as to label this "massive lexical borrowing", giving examples that "German loanwords [can be found] in everyday Burgenland Croatian communication", eg. *sojdot* ← *Soldat,* 'soldier'; *kibl* ← *Kübel* 'bin', "as well as words borrowed from Hungarian", eg. *bolt* ← *bolt,* 'shop', *jezer* ← *ezer* 'thousand', and even some Slovak loans, eg. *takaj* ← *taky* 'also'. BGLD.Cro bilingual and trilingual dictionaries that have been published bear evidence of input from German and Hungarian (Bencsics et al. 1982, 1991). While lexical borrowing was a frequent occurrence, there existed variation in the dispersal, frequency and stability of form of many borrowings. Initial attempts to develop a supra-regional code met with the challenge of codifying the large number of loanwords in use, many of which may have been specific to a cluster of villages only, and whether to draw on other means to unify the minority communities' lexical stock.

As the largest of the three groups presented in this chapter, intra-group communication, variation amongst speakers and communities, and the introduction of formal schooling in Burgenland hastened efforts towards a standardisation. These commenced in the eighteenth century when ideological movements – national romanticism and Herder's notion of language and nationality being mutually co-determinant – were in vogue, which precipitated efforts among some BGLD.Cro early lexicographers to replace loanwords with local neologisms or with models taken from HMLD.Cro. A discussion on lexicon and loanwords in BGLD.Cro therefore needs to draw attention to the standard descriptions of the language that contained fewer loanwords, and speakers' vernaculars that continued to contain these. From one of the early codifiers of BGLD.Cro, the priest Jeremijaš Šosterić, a concern for 'Croatianness' and a purist sentiment are recognisable in his description of the language, as "clumsy, awkward, with its syntax influenced by Hungarian, German and Latin" (Benčić 1972: 16. Our translation). During this period, contacts with lexicographers in Croatia, who themselves were dealing with the same questions, led to instances of harmonisation and modelling based on homeland norms that helped retain (and replenish) Croatian lexical stock and re-affirm collocational, morphological and syntactic forms. Benčić (1972: 27–28) reports that the later stages of codification such as acceptance, implementation, expansion and cultivation had been completed by the middle of the twentieth century.

The few examples of code-switching in older texts indicate to us that code-switching was relatively infrequent and/or there were normative influences that discouraged written representation of 'mixed language'. The bi- or trilingual repertoires of many speakers enabled them not only to communicate with various groups, but to employ code-switching as an intra-group speech variety, perhaps also as an inter-group one too in some cases. High-level proficiency in and frequent use of the macro-socially dominant languages German and Hungarian enabled the transfer or borrowing of forms that entered all speakers' BGLD. Cro varieties. But we do not observe major language shift, and it is likely that there were social factors that sanctioned against 'widespread use' of German or Hungarian, or 'extensive language mixing' such as code-switching. The first one was geographical isolation, already mentioned above. The second is 'social group' or the status that Burgenland Croatians had vis-à-vis German-speakers who lived in their close proximity. We posit that this is analogous to the status that Hungarian-speakers have vis-à-vis German-speakers in Burgenland as reported by Gal (1979). This relates to their social status as peasants and agricultural labourers, while the status of many German-speakers was different: that of artisans, merchants or industrial workers. Socio-occupational differences matched linguistic ones, and Burgenland Croats' continuing enactment of these socio-occupational roles enabled Croatian language maintenance. It is likely, therefore, that code-switching was negatively sanctioned due to it being a form of behaviour that transgressed social boundaries that were not readily crossed. To this, we can add the 'nationality = language' legacy of national romanticism that is present still today across central Europe. The textbook view of this ideology is that a person's language indexes his/her ethnicity and vice versa. Social behaviour that includes 'mixed language' invokes a conceptualisation of ethnic identity that is hybrid or composite. There were (and are) still many macro-level, socio-political narratives that discouraged this form of behaviour.

As stated, in BGLD.Cro there are numerous loanwords that have entered the language from both German and Hungarian and the trilingual Burgenland-Croatian/standard Croatian/German dictionary lists hundreds of such borrowings. Contact with both languages is so long-standing that for some forms there are multiple vintages of loanwards, eg. archaic *paurija* (Ger. *Bauernhof*) > contemporary *londvirtšoft* (Ger. *Landwirtschaft*) – 'farm'; archaic *fertuh* (Ger. *Vürtuch/Vortuch*) > contemporary *šiecn* (Ger. *Schürze*) – 'apron'. In other instances, a Hungarian loan (example 3) has been replaced by a more recent German-based one (example 4):

(3) okna   su   **nakinčena**   sviče
    window-NOM.PL.N   be-3PL   decorate-PPART.PL.N   candle-NOM.F.PL
    goru
    burn-3PL
    'The windows are **decorated**, candles are burning'

(4) si   grobi   su   **pešmikani**
    all-NOM.M.PL   grave-NOM.M.PL   be-3PL   decorate-PPART.M.PL
    s   kiticami
    with+INS   flower-INS.F.PL
    'All the graves are **decorated** with flowers'

The Hungarian-origin loanword *nakinčen* has over time given way to *pešmikan*, based on German *schmücken* ('decorate'). As previously mentioned, efforts to codify a supra-regional BGLD.Cro standard resulted in the creation of neologisms that referred to new terms or replaced established German (or Hungarian) borrowings. Example (5) shows two instances of such neologisms.

(5) | BGLD.Cro | Eng. | Ger. | HMLD.Cro |
    |---|---|---|---|
    | *ognjobranci* | fire-fighters | Feuerwehr | vatrogasci |
    | *jedan dijel od roditeljov* | parent | Elternteil | roditelj |

In print media, some of these forms, either neologisms or models adopted from standard Croatian, may not be well known to all speakers and German equivalents may be added, usually in brackets, e.g.:

(6) *Ovde usavršava telefonsko pojačalo – svoj prvi **izum** (**Erfindung**) . . .*
    Here he finished his work on a telephone amplifier – his first **izum** (Ger. **Erfindung**) invention . . .

While written texts may be reflective of writers' attempt to avoid German loanwords, within the corpus of German borrowings in speakers' verbal repertoires there are a large number of loans, including even separable verbs whose both parts are phonologically and morphologically integrated, eg. *ajnkafati* ← *einkaufen* 'to go shopping', *anrufati* ← *anrufen* 'to ring up'. The presence of lexical transfers from German in diaspora varieties is also recorded in GER.Cro (Kresić Vukosav and Šimičić, this volume) and AUT.Cro (Ščukanec, this volume).

In contrast to Burgenland, amongst the Molise Croats there were few social and occupational features that differentiated them from local Italian-speakers. There was little or no physical isolation of Molise Croats from Italian-speakers and bilingualism is long-standing. In exogamous marriages in which an Italian-speaker moved to a MOL.Cro village, s/he usually acquired MOL.Cro, but Italian (or rather, Molise dialect) remained a code that was understood and used by both. Widespread lexical and deep structural borrowing point to a long history of bilingualism. In contrast to Burgenland, in Molise language choice itself did not index social or economic-occupational differences between different groups.

In MOL.Cro, apart from a very small number of Čakavisms like *crikva* 'church', the lexicon is Štokavian. The MOL.Cro lexicon does not necessarily correspond directly to the forms and/or meanings of HMLD.Cro (marked here in brackets), due to its dialectal base or to semantic change, eg. *hiža* 'house' (*kuća*), *tuji* 'foreign' (*tuđi*), *kaša* 'earth, mud' (HMLD.Cro *kaša* = 'porridge'), *lastavica* 'butterfly' (HMLD.Cro *lastavica* = 'swallow'), *juha* 'noodle water' (HMLD.Cro *juha* = 'soup'). Further examples of innovations in the MOL.Cro lexicon, including semantic transfer can be found in Breu (2003: 355–363). The most prominent feature of the MOL.Cro lexicon is its extraordinarily high number of loanwords in almost all parts of speech, both in terms of word types and word tokens, with an average between 20% and 30% tokens (nouns up to almost 50%) in everyday spoken texts. Comparable corpora of other Slavic micro-languages in language contact situations have a loanword percentage of less than 5%.[11] One of the main reasons for this difference is, apart from the high percentage of borrowed nouns and verbs, the borrowing of such elementary and frequent units as the complementiser and relativiser *ke ~ ka* ← Italian *che* 'that, which', the conjunction *e* ← *e* 'and' and prepositions like *dòp* ← *dopo* 'after' and *sendza* ← *senza* 'without' and adverbs like *dža* ← *già* 'already'.[12] MOL. Cro has its own rules for the integration of inflected parts of speech. Nouns are integrated into the two gender-determined declension classes, normally with the same gender as in the dominant model variety (standard or dialectal Italian), irrespective of the ending of the equivalent Italian form (see below 4.5.1).

In spite of many borrowings common to all three villages, there are also substantial differences in the three MOL.Cro dialects (Breu 2017a: 202). A typical example is the word for 'field'. In the Kruč dialect the traditional term *njiva* continues to exist, while Mundimitar borrowed *largo*. In Filič an equivalent Italian term was borrowed: *pajiz* ← *paese* 'village, country'. Mundimitar uses *skrivit* ←

---

[11] For a comparison of oral texts from MOL.Cro with those from Upper Sorbian in Germany, Burgenland Croatian in Austria and Balkan Slavic varieties spoken in Greece, all of them glossed and with borrowings marked, see Adamou et al. (2013); for a detailed summary of lexical borrowing and code-switching in the three MOL.Cro villages, based on these texts, see Breu (2017b: 67–71). A statistical evaluation of borrowing is provided by Adamou et al. (2016).
[12] For these and other borrowings see the dictionaries published by Breu & Piccoli (2000) for Kruč, and Piccoli & Sammartino (2000) for Mundimitar.

scrivere 'to write' or *galo* ← *gallo* 'rooster', while Kruč has retained the traditional terms *pisat* and *pivac* for 'to write' and 'rooster' respectively. The presence of lexical transfers from Italian in diaspora varieties is also recorded in ITAL.Cro (Županović Filipin, Hlavac and Piasevoli, this volume) and TRS.Cro (Piasevoli, this volume).

Lexical borrowings can be found in all dialects of HUN.Cro as well. However, their number and the features of their phonological and morphological adaptation vary according to the specific features of the respective subdialect. From a semantic point of view, Hungarian loanwords denote mostly (but not exclusively) concepts that are either technical/cultural innovations or concepts, which are part of Hungarian administrative or bureaucratic jargon. Examples are given in (7). The first two are from Baranya and the last two are from Pomurje speakers:

(7) | HUN.Cro | Eng. | Hun. | HMLD.Cro |
|---|---|---|---|
| *beutalo* | referral(med.) | beutaló | uputnica |
| *sines* | actor | színész | glumac |
| *birov* | judge | bíró | sudac |
| *sinpad* | stage | színpad | pozornica |

On the other hand, there are Hungarian loanwords in HUN.Cro that are borrowings from Hungarian slang, such as *fickov* (Hun. *fickó*, 'guy') or *čičkaš* (Hun. *csicskás*, 'bellboy who does everything'). Furthermore, in both dialects analysed here, there is a considerable number of German loanwords, some of which are present in particular dialects of HMLD.Cro, as well. Examples include the following:

(8) | HUN.Cro | Eng. | Ger. | HMLD.Cro |
|---|---|---|---|
| *fertol* | quarter | Viertel | četvrt (frtalj) |
| *ajziban* | railways | Eisenbahn | željeznica (ajznban) |
| *mela* | flour | Mehl | brašno |

2.1 Gender allocation of loanwords

In BGLD.Cro, gender allocation of borrowings from German and Hungarian is usually determined by the phonotactic features of the borrowing's ending, i.e. borrowings ending in *–a* and many ending in *–e* are allocated feminine gender, while those ending in a consonant and other vowel endings, *–o* and *–i*, are allocated to masculine gender. An example of this is Hungarian origin *város* 'town', which is feminine in HMLD.Cro, ie. *varoš* F, but masculine in BGLD.Cro, i.e. *varoš* M, *glavni varoš* 'capital city', *stari varoš* 'old town', *plan varoša* 'city map'. There can be variation in the allocation of gender where the German gender of a borrowing is retained (Hlavac 1991).

The following example shows how the consonant-final feature of one borrowing, *Styling* (Ger. neuter), determines its allocation to masculine gender in BLGD. Cro, while the feminine gender of another consonant-final borrowing, *Sendung* ('radio/tv program'), is retained.

(9) ki   vrag   je   za   ti
    who   devil-NOM.M.SG be-3SG for+ACC that-DEM.ACC.M.PL
    stajling   za   **sendungu**   **zuständig**?
    styling-ACC.M.SG   for+ACC program-ACC.F.SG responsible
    'Who the hell is **responsible** for the **styling** for the **program**?'

HMLD.Cro Koji vrag je odgovoran za stajling-M u emisiji-F?

Styling is a conventionalised English-origin borrowing in German, while *Sendung*, a feminine noun in German retains its gender in BGLD.Cro and is overtly marked as ACC.F.SG. As a collocation *Styling* in German is commonly followed by the preposition *für* [+ACC]. Here, its Croatian equivalent *za* [+ACC] is employed and *Sendung* attracts the feminine accusative suffix -*u*. (The retention of its gender in German (F) is unusual, as the phonotactic structure of words with word final – *ung* from German usually renders them M. in Croatian, eg. Ger. *Kupplung*-F > Cro. *kuplung*-M 'clutch'.). Further, *zuständig* 'responsible' is the final element in the sentence, and this form is also commonly collocated with *für* in a preceding position, i.e. *für* + . . . *zuständig* ('responsible for . . .'). A tendency for German-origin nouns to be allocated masculine gender is also observable in contemporary diaspora varieties (see Kresić Vukosav and Šimičić; and Ščukanec, both this volume).

In MOL.Cro, there are only two genders for nouns. A three-gender distinction is still made in relation to adjectives (see below 6.1.2). Borrowed feminine nouns go into the only remaining feminine declension in -*a*, but with a stronger tendency to adopt the ending -*ī* (> -*i*) in the GEN/DAT/INS.PL than traditional feminine nouns, e.g. Ital. *finestra* → *funaštra* 'window', GEN.PL *funaštri*, Ital. *pace* → *pača* 'peace'. There are also exceptions, for example, when the final vowel in the Italian source is stressed. In this case, the loanwords in question either keep their feminine gender and remain uninflected, e.g. *gioventù* F → *džuvindu* F 'youth', or they change their gender and follow the alternating masculine paradigm of stems in -*l*. While the first possibility is found in all three dialects, the second one is restricted to Kruč, for example *città* F → *čita* M 'town', *čitala* GEN.SG.M (Breu 1998: 341).

As for masculine loanwords, they form their NOM/ACC.SG, as a rule, directly from the stem of the source word by replacing its original -*o*, -*e* ending with a zero ending. If it is true that there is, in principle, only one masculine declension, it is also true that several subclasses important for loanword integration exist. Again -*ī* dominates in the marginal cases of the plural, but the form of the NOM/ACC. PL depends on the suffix and varies from dialect to dialect. The most common ending, at least in Kruč, is -*a*, e.g. *ospite → ospit* 'guest', *ospita* NOM/ACC.PL, *ospiti* GEN/DAT/INS.PL. However, for nouns with the suffix -*un*- the alternative ending -*e* is used, e.g. *schiavone → Škavun* 'Slav', *Škavune* NOM/ACC.PL, *Škavuni* GEN/DAT/INS.PL.

The form of the NOM/ACC.SG depends on the stem-final consonants. Most frequent is the zero ending, e.g. *sugo → sug* 'sauce'. But when the stem ends in a consonant cluster either an alternating -*a*- is inserted into the cluster or the ending -*a* (Kruč and Filič) is chosen instead of Ø (with or without a change of M to F gender), for example *brigante* M → *brighanat*[13] 'bandit' NOM.SG.M, *brighanda* GEN.SG.M, *barile* M → *barla* 'barrel' NOM=GEN.SG.M, *apparecchio* M → *parekja* NOM.SG.F 'airplane', *parekje* GEN.SG.F. In Mundimitar the traditional -*o* ending for (now vanished) neuter nouns is not restricted to ex-neuters but may appear rather freely in borrowed masculines, e.g. *barile* M → *barilo* 'barrel' NOM.SG.M, *barila* GEN.SG.M, *largo* 'width, square' NOM.SG.M → *largo* NOM.SG.M 'field'. Stem alternations also exist, as in the case of stem-final -*l*, e.g. *ospedale → spida* NOM.SG.M 'hospital', *spidala* GEN.SG.M or *martello → martaj* NOM.SG.M 'hammer', *martaja ~ martala* GEN.SG.M. In the speech of diaspora speakers, variation in gender allocation of Italian-origin transfer is recorded. Sometimes it is phonotactic features and other times it is the gender of the transfer in Italian that determines gender allocation (see Županović Filipin, Hlavac and Piasevoli; and Piasevoli, both this volume).

Adjectives are frequently integrated with three adjectival genders, two numbers, and an additional short form in the NOM.SG, for example *giusto → jušti* M, *jušta* F, *jušto* N, *jušte* PL, short form *jušt* M etc. 'right'. As in HMLD.Cro, certain stems show alternations, e.g. *fermo → fermi* (long form), *feram* (short form) 'firm' NOM.SG.M; *debolo → debali: debuj* 'weak' NOM.SG.M. Most of the borrowed adjectives inflect for case, though there is also a certain tendency to leave borrowed adjectives altogether uninflected, even for gender and number, e.g., *speciale → spečjal* 'special', *telefonico → telefonik* 'telephone'.[14]

Hungarian nouns do not have grammatical gender and the integration of Hungarian loanwords into Croatian is determined by loanword phonotactic fea-

---

[13] The orthographical representation of *gh* [ɣ] is based on a consonant sound (velar voiceless fricative) borrowed from Molise dialect. For further details on the phonological features of MOL.Cro and orthographical representations, see Breu (1999, 2017b: 16–21).
[14] For an overview of the morphological integration of borrowed nouns and adjectives in MOL.Cro see Breu (2017b: 63–65).

tures. Although HUN.Cro dialects have a three-gender-system, the integrated loanwords are allocated either feminine or masculine gender only. Loanwords which have an -*a* ending in Hungarian are transferred in their original form and belong to the feminine declension class, e.g. *suka* ← *szuka* 'female dog'; *marha* ← *marha* 'cattle'. Loanwords with a consonant ending are integrated as masculine, eg. *parast* ← *paraszt* 'peasant'; *műhelj* ← *műhely* 'repair shop', or – by adding an –*a* ending which renders them feminine. e.g. *čonta* ← *csont* 'bone'. Loanwords that end in -*o* in Hungarian also belong to the masculine declension class, either as phonologically integrated lexemes, e.g. *fickov* ← *fickó* 'guy', or in their original form following the paradigm of the masculine declension class, e.g. *ringlo* (ACC/GEN *ringloja*) ← *ringló*, 'yellow egg plum' (cf. *kino* 'cinema' and *biro* 'office' in HMLD.Cro that are both usually masculine). Nouns ending in -*e* in Hungarian are allocated to the feminine class whereby the original -*e* ending is replaced with an -*a* ending, e.g. *fela* ← *féle* 'sort'; *figa* ← *füge* 'fig'; *bölcsöda* ← *bölcsöde* 'day-care nursery'.

As mentioned, Hungarian loanwords in their original form are genderless. However, if they denote an animate referent with biological gender, this has an effect on the morphological markers that the loanword attracts, e.g. *mafla* (Hun. *mafla*, 'stupid person') denotes both females and males in Hungarian. However, in accordance with the gender marking rules of HUN.Cro *mafla* refers only to females, and its male counterpart *mafleš* is created by adding the suffix -*eš*. The same refers to the example *ovodaš* (Hun. *óvódás*, 'children who attend preschool') and *ovodaška*, the first denoting exclusively male children, the second female ones (cf. HMLD.Cro *muško dijete u vrtiću* 'male child in a pre-school centre' and *žensko dijete u vrtiću* 'female child in a pre-school centre').

Integration of adjectives is variable. Adjectives that are morphologically integrated into HUN.Cro via overt suffixes do so according to rules common to HMLD.Cro that require marking of gender, number (and case). For example, the adjective *butasti* M.SG 'stupid' (HMLD.Cro *glup*) has the following further forms (all in NOM) to show morphological markers for gender and number: *butasta*-F.SG, *butasto*-N.SG, *butasti*-M.PL, *butaste*-F.PL, *butasta* N.PL. On the other hand, some adjectives remain morphologically unintegrated and hence indeclinable, such as the adjectives *njugot* (Hun. *nyugodt*, 'relaxed', HMLD.Cro *miran*) and *normališ* (Hun. *normális*, 'normal', HMLD.Cro *normalan*) as shown in the following examples:

(10)   bila   sem   **njugot**
       be-PTCP.F.SG   AUX-1SG   **relaxed**
       'I was **relaxed**.' (Vuk research data corpus)

(11) *Maro ti   si   ne   **normališ***
     Mary you   be-2SG NEG normal
     'Mary, you are not **normal**!' (Rácz 2012: 144).

2.2 Phonological and morphological integration of loanwords

The above section presented examples of gender allocation to loanwords, which in many instances occurs via overt morphology. This section presents data transferred items and phonological and/or morphological features that enable their integration.

In BGLD.Cro, German-origin verbs such as *merkati* ← *merken*, 'to notice' (HMLD.Cro *zapažati, primjećivati*) or *šporiti* ← *sparen*, 'to save' (HMLD.Cro *štedjeti, šparati*) are imperfective. These loans have been phonologically and morphologically integrated. When Croatian prefixes such as *za* or *pri* are affixed to these verbs, these verbs become perfective, ie. *zamerkati* 'to have just noticed' or *prišporiti* 'to save up'.

In regard to the situation of MOL.Cro, Standard Italian has four verb classes, represented by their infinitives ending in *-are, -ire* and stressed and unstressed *-ere*. In relation to the integration of Italian verbs, MOL.Cro has two productive endings only, *-at* and *-it*, with all Italian verbs in *-ere* and *-ire* allocated to the latter class. The reason for this distribution may be found in the local Italian dialects, having been the only source for integration historically (Breu 1998: 341–342; 2017b: 65). Examples are *amare* → *amat* 'to love', *servire* → *servit* 'to serve', *possedére* → *posedit* 'to possess' and *promèttere* → *primitit* 'to promise'. Verbal aspect is a feature that pertains to borrowings as well as domestic verbs, and prefixes or sufixes distinguish these. The rule is that telic source verbs become perfective, with a secondary imperfective partner formed by means of the suffix *-iva-*. Examples are: *partire* 'depart, leave' → *partit* PFV => *parčivat* IPFV, *fermare* 'to close' → *fermat* PFV => *fermivat* IPFV (Breu, Berghaus & Scholze 2017: 93–94, Breu 2017b: 65–66). In contrast to HMLD.Cro, there are no bi-aspectual loans of the type *negirati* 'to negate', i.e. MOL.Cro has *nigat* PFV and *nigivat* IPFV.

In HUN.Cro, examples of phonologically adopted loanwords are reported amongst both groups of speakers. The following borrowings are recorded by Rácz (2012) for Pomurje-Croatian, and by Gorjanac (2008) for the Štokavian-speaking Šokac-Croats:

	HUN.Cro	Eng.	Hun.	HMLD.Cro
(12)	prothetic *j* in initial position:			
	jezera	thousand	ezer	tisuća
	Jegersek	Egerszeg	Egerszeg	(Hun. toponym)
(13)	prothetic *v* in final position:			
	birov	judge	bíró	sudac
	turov	cottage cheese	túró	sir
	halov	net	háló	mreža
(14)	đ ← gy:			
	đ'ileš	meeting	gyűlés	sjednica
	f'ođlolt	ice cream	fagylalt	sladoled

The following loanwords are morphologically integrated through an added morpheme. The phonotactic structure of the Hungarian original forms is a likely cause for suffixation here – addition of the suffix morpheme obviates the difficulty of declining a loanword that ends in –*i* or –*ő*. The following examples have the suffix –*ka* for nouns, -*erati* for verbs and –*sti* for adjectives:

	HUN.Cro	Eng.	Hun.	HMLD.Cro
(15)	*čokika*	chocolcate	csoki	čokolada
	mentöka	ambulance services	mentő	hitna pomoć
	masekerati	to be self-employed	maszekolni	raditi privatno
	sirkasti	grey	szürke	siv
	butasti	unwise	buta	glup/nepametan

We also observe an instance of phonological integration of vowels where high front rounded *ű* [y:] becomes unrounded *i* (*gyűlés* → *đ'ileš*), while in another instance, the mid-front rounded vowel *ő* [ø:] remains, with only a shortening of its length to *ö* [ø], eg. *mentő* → *mentöka*. (This front rounded vowel does not exist in the vowel system of the Šokac-Croats, but the vowel of the Hungarian loanword is preserved in this example.) Palatal affricate *gy* [ɟ] is rendered as the prepalatal affricate *đ* [dʐ]. This is an example of transphonemisation to the closest available Croatian phoneme (Hlavac 1999a). The phonological and morphological integration of other-language items in contemporary diaspora varieties is usually determined by the generational membership of the speaker: first-generation speakers typically integrate lexical transfers both phonologically and morphologically; amongst second- and subsequent-generation speakers integration is more variable, dependent on the frequency of an item in communities' idiolects with higher frequency co-occurring more frequently with integration (see Jutronić; Petrović; Hlavac and Stolac; and Stoffel and Hlavac, all this volume).

3 Discourse markers and pragmatic particles

Discourse markers and other pragmatic forms that have a function at the level of discourse may more easily traverse linguistic boundaries. In a structural sense, they are usually 'extra-clausal' items, often in turn-initial or turn-final position that are not part of the morphosyntactic grid of a clause. Further, they can be a reflection of the adoption of the pragmatic norms of the socially dominant language group. This adoption can be not only the function of a pragmatic marker, but also the *form* of that pragmatic marker as it occurs in the other language. The following have been adopted from Austrian German, with little or no phonological integration into BGLD.Cro:

(16)
BGLD.Cro	Eng.	Ger.	HMLD.Cro
virklji(h)	really	wirklich	stvarno
übahaup(t)	at all	überhaupt	uopće
gonc	quite	ganz	dosta
filajht	perhaps	vielleicht	možda

MOL.Cro has pragmatic particles such as *alora* ← *allora* 'now', 'then' (HMLD.Cro *sada, tada*), and *ma* ← *ma* 'but' (HMLD.Cro *ali*). The latter particle *ma* exists in HMLD.Cro too.[15] Others, mainly conjunctions, include *pèrò* 'but' (HMLD.Cro *ali*), *e* 'and' (HMLD.Cro *i*), *o* and *ol* 'or' (HMLD.Cro *ili*), *ka* 'that' (HMLD.Cro *što, da*) and two words with the meaning 'because' *p'ke* (HMLD.Cro *zato što*) and the calque *aje-ka* (< Cro. *jer* 'because' + Mol. *ka* 'that').

In HUN.Cro, expressions from Hungarian such as *istenem* ('oh my God', HUN. Cro *ištenem*) or *nem számít* ('it doesn't matter', HUN.Cro *nem samit*) are commonly used phrases

---

15 It is listed by etymologists as an Italian borrowing (Skok, 1971: 343) or of two-fold origin as a hybrid of both Italian and Greek origin ("ukrštanjem nekoliko čestica ≈ *tal*. ma: ali, *ngrč*. má.") (Hrvatski jezični portal, n.d.), while there also remains the possibility that it is a contracted variant of Turkish-origin *ama* 'but'.

(17) ...to   da   su   jako ... **jaj ištenem** ... grubi
     ...so   that be-3PL   very ... **oh my God** ... rude-NOM.M.PL
     '... so that they are'   very ... **oh my God** ... rude.

(18) to   je   **nem**   **samit**
     it   is   **no**   **matter**-3SG
     'it does **not matter**.'

The Hungarian conjunctions *mert* ('because', HMLD.Cro *jer*) and *de* ('but', HMLD.Cro *ali*) are used as integrated conjunctions in the Pomurje dialect. The HMLD.Cro equivalent of *mert* is not present at all in the Pomurje dialect (see above example (1) in section 1.3 above). The equivalent of the second conjunction, i.e. *de* ('but', HMLD.Cro *ali*) is present, but it has — similar to some other (Croatia-based) subdialects of the Kajkavian dialect — a disjunctive meaning ('or'). There is no conjunction in Pomurje-Croatian that means 'but'.[16] Therefore the lexical gap is filled by the Hungarian equivalent *de*.[17]

(19) unda   tam   z   Mađarum   veke   mađarski,
     then   there   with+INS   Hungarian-INS.M.SG   always   Hungarian,
     de   ja   znam
     but   I   know-1SG
     'Then there with Hungarians always Hungarian, **but** I can [...].'

In the speech of Bošnjak-Croats from Pečuh, a habitual use of the unintegrated Hungarian conjunction *vagy* ('or', HMLD.Cro *ili*) can be observed. Amongst the same group of speakers, the phonologically integrated and de-semanticised particle *hát* ('so', 'now', HMLD.Cro *pa*) can also be observed:

(20) bar   sad   onim   putem   idu   **vagy**   idem
     at   least   now   that way   go-PRS.3PL   **or**   go-PRS.1SG
     'They go **or** I go at least on that way.'

(21) **hat**   znam   na   hrvatskom,   to   me   sada
     well   know-1SG   in+LOC   Croatian-LOC.M.SG   that   me-ACC   now
     '**Well** ... I know it in Croatian, that is [what is bothering me] now.'

---

16 According to Rácz (2012: 287) *ali* can have a twofold meaning, 'but' or 'or'.
17 This tendency is in accordance with Matras's (2009: 194–195, 2011: 216) findings regarding a hierarchy of borrowability for conjunctions. He reports that conjunctions with a contrastive meaning (*but*) are the most highly borrowable, followed by conjunctions with a sequential meaning (*and*, *or*) with both groups followed by those that express justification or reasoning (*so*, *because*).

These particles occur as discourse-based forms and are employed as forms reflective of the speaker's positionality, and are not, as stated above, part of a clause's morpho-syntactic grid. As such, these particles can be considered to be 'extra-clausal', occuring freely within or between clauses (Hlavac 2006). They also represent instances where speakers adopt not only a function typical of pragmatic norms of the other, socially dominant language group, but also an adoption of the *form* itself from that language group, along with its function. Examples of transferred discourse markers are found in CAN.Cro (Petrović, this volume), AUS.Cro (Hlavac and Stolac, this volume), NZ.Cro (Stoffel and Hlavac, this volume) and ARG.Cro (Skelin Horvat, Musulin and Blažević, this volume).

4 Calques – phraseological and semantic

Verb calques are common in BGLD.Cro as shown in section 6.2.1 below. Fixed expressions based on German models that consist of a verb+noun construction, where homeland Croatian typically employs a verb, are also found in the examples, with the replicated construction shown in bold in BGLD.Cro and German. HMLD.Cro equivalents are given at the end of each example.

(22) ja sam **imao moj špas.**
'I had fun'
ich **habe meinen Spaß** gehabt
dobro sam se zabavio

(23) to **mu je ležalo na srcu**
'it was close to his heart'
es hat **ihm am Herzen gelegen**
do toga mu je bilo jako stalo

(24) **spravljali su šale**
'they made jokes'
sie haben **Scherze gemacht**
šalili su se

(25) **ima s biljkami** posla
'it has to do with plants'
es **hat mit Pflanzen** zu tun
odnosi se na biljke

(26) i oni su **diozeli** na veselju familije.
'and they took part in the family celebration'
und die haben an der Familienfeier **teilgenommen.**
i oni su sudjelovali na obiteljskoj proslavi.

There are further instances in BGLD.Cro where the relationship of government between words, typically between verbs or prepositions and other words, requires morphosyntactic marking, and where German grammatical rules are transferred.

The following are further calques with longer sequences that replicate German models found in BGLD.Cro:

(27) vlak je nekoliko puti **ostao ležati na prugi**, dokle nije . . .
'The train **stopped** still many times until . . .'

    Ger.   der Zug **blieb** mehrmals **auf der Strecke liegen**, bis . . .
    HMLD.Cro vlak **se** nekoliko puta **zaustavio** sve dok nije . . .

(28) U našem selu – hvala Bogu – se nije našao ni jedan človik, ki bi ovo **bio držao za dobro**, i nije se našao, ki bi se bio ufao vanhititi Boga iz škole.
'In our village, thank God, there has never been anyone who thought **that it was a good idea**, there has never been anyone who has attempted to throw God out of school [the school curriculum]'.

    Ger.   In unserem Dorf, Gott sei Dank, hat sich keiner gefunden, **der dies für gut hält**, es hat sich keiner gefunden, der es sich vorgenommen hätte, Gott aus dem Lehrplan zu entfernen.
    HMLD.Cro U našem selu – hvala Bogu – nije se našao nijedan čovjek koji **bi smatrao da je to dobro**, nije se našao nitko tko bi pokušao izbaciti Boga iz škole (iz nastavnog plana).

(29) **Ča za ličnost** je bio Jožef Haydn i ča je dao svitu?
'**What kind of a personality** was Joseph Haydn and what did he give to the world?'

    Ger.   **Was für eine Person** war Joseph Haydn . . .
    HMLD.Cro **Kakav je čovjek bio** Joseph Haydn i što je dao svijetu?

(30) . . . kad je Martin **četernajst let star nastal** . . .
'When Martin turned fourteen years old.'

    Ger   als Martin **vierzehn Jahre alt wurde** . . .
    HMLD.Cro kad je Martin **navršio četrnaest godina** . . .

Instances of German-based calques and loan translations are found in the GER.Cro and AUT.Cro samples of contemporary diaspora speakers as well. (See Kresić Vukosav and Šimičić; and Ščukanec, both this volume). MOL.Cro has a number of calques. Below are three examples with the Italian equivalents based on Molise Italian:

	(31) *ko je sa vidija sa vidija*	(32) *si ga grem*	(33) *ga jima s njom*
	'and that was it!'	'I'm off'	'he is angry with her'
Ital	chi s'**è visto** s'**è visto**	**me ne vado**	**ce l'ha con lei**
HMLD.Cro	i to je bilo to	ja odlazim	on se ljuti na nju

Instances of Italian-based calques and loan translations are found in the ITAL.Cro and TRS.Cro samples of contemporary diaspora speakers as well. (See Županović Filipin, Hlavac and Piasevoli; and Piasevoli, both this volume).

An example of calques found in HUN.Cro is shown below (34). This example is an interesting one as it is a combination of code-switching, and at the same time, also a lexical calque. The syntactic structure of the Hungarian phrase *Mi a helyzet?* (what-N.SG the-DEF.ART situation-N.SG 'What is new with you?') is fully replicated in example (34). By inserting the obligatory copula *je*, the calqued structure is created in accordance with the syntactic rules of the replica language, Croatian. However, as the speakers do not know the Croatian equivalent of the word 'situation', they use its Hungarian counterpart, this way producing a mixed utterance, not just in terms of a covert syntactic structure, but on the overt formal level also. This phrase is commonly used by all Pomurje-Croats, even by the younger generation. Included here on the right is an equivalent construction from the speech of Bošnjak-Croats in Baranya, which itself is also a Hungarian-based calque.

(34) kaj   je   helyzet   što   je   novina?
     what   be-3SG   situation   what   be-3SG   news?
           'What is new?'   /   'What is new?'

Hun.
     mi   a   helyzet   mi   újság?
     what-N.SG   DEF.ART   situation-N.SG   what-N.SG   news-N.SG

HMLD.Cro
     što/kaj/ča   ima   novoga   što/kaj/ča je   novo
     what   have-3SG   new-GEN.N.SG   what   be-3SG new-NOM.N.SG

The similar-meaning phrase *što je novina* ('What is newspaper [= 'news']?') is a calque of an equivalent Hungarian phrase, i.e. *mi újság?* ('What is newspaper [= 'news']?'). The HUN.Cro dialects examined here are used almost exclusively in oral form only.

The (written) translation of more complex concepts, i.e. replication of compound constructions based on Hungarian models, is not a common strategy in these communities. In some instances, compound nouns from Hungarian are transferred in their original form into Croatian with varying degrees of integration. However, since the 1950s, when the first efforts were made by intellectuals and others to provide Croatian equivalents for terms used by government institutions and public services, a number of loan translations can be found that are used in schools, minority institutions and public events. The following examples are from Győrvári (2012), who analysed pedagogic terminology in HUN.Cro:

(35) *obavezna literatura* ← *kötelező irodalom* 'required reading', HMLD.Cro *lektira*

đačka samouprava ← *diákönkormányzat* 'student council', HMLD.Cro *vijeće učenika*

In the first item in example (35) above, the Hungarian NP (obligatory + literature) is replicated in Croatian, despite the existence of a one-word Croatian equivalent. In regard to the second form in example (35) above, the Hungarian compound (*diák* + *önkormányzat*) is replicated, but in a syntactially modified form, as an NP. (These examples are not frequent, as homeland HMLD.Cro equivalents and terms were usually the ones borrowed and used, thus resulting in few differences specific to HUN.Cro). The last example shows how pattern replication works in Matras and Sakel's (2007) understanding: the pivotal features of the concept are replicated in the replica language (the two elements: student + council), but at the same time, they are also modified according to the word-formation rules in Croatian, the result of which is an NP and not a compound noun as in the model language.

5 Code-switching

Code-switching is defined here as strings of words or sequences of spoken language that are transferred from one language into another, regardless of the position of the transferred items as alternations, embeddings, insertions or extra-clausal items. Our definition of code-switching includes some simplex forms and to an extent, these overlap with common discourse markers, e.g. *weißt du* (Ger. 'you know').

From BGLD.Cro we have some *written* examples of code-switching, where code-switching serves the purpose of clarification of an 'indigenous' form, *riža* through repetition of the same form with its local form, a conventionalised borrowing from German, *rajz* ('Reis'). In some written texts, German translations of lesser-known local forms are provided.

(36) *Tako uguljenu hajdu zamu u juhu i ju dinstaju na mjesto **riže (rajza)** uz meso.*
'So the buckwheat is put into the soup and they let it stew instead of with **riža (Ger. Reis.) 'rice'** with meat.

A similar instance is given below, where *dičaki* 'boys' is followed by a paraphrase in BLGD.Cro (shown here in bold) after which a single-word German equivalent is provided (shown here in brackets, as in the original):

(37) *U Beču je Haydn proživio skoro deset ljet med **dičaki, kih zadaća je u prvom redu bila da pjevaju** (Sängerknaben).*
'Haydn had been living in Vienna for almost ten years among the **boys, whose main task was to sing**' (*Sängerknaben*. Ger. 'Vienna Boys' Choir').

Sometimes analogies or phrases specific to German are transferred, and a Croatian gloss is provided that does not really function as a gloss, but as a marker that the writer otherwise wishes to apply a normative (ie. maximally Croatian) approach to lexical choices:

(38) *Kad je negdo jako bogat, mu velu, da je bogat kao **Krözus**, perzijski kralj.*
'When someone is very rich, it is said that he is as rich as **Croesus**, (Ger. *Krözus*) the king of Persia.'

These reveal some of the conventions employed by those using BGLD.Cro in its written form for a readership across all dialectal groups. Language used in written documents tended and still tends to be more normative than spoken language. This accounts for the few examples of code-switching in written texts. Code-switching is a common phenomenon amongst many speakers, occurring on the basis of situational, sociolinguistic, thematic or other constellations. For some, when in the company of other bilinguals, it may be their *unmarked* speech variety. As stated, descriptions of code-switching often distinguish between examples of insertion, i.e. the embedding of one or more forms from another language, and alternation, i.e. a shift from language to another within the same turn. An example of insertion from the BGLD.Cro corpus is the following, with the insertion from German shown in bold:

(39) *Šport **mindestens** trikrat na tjedan. To je sigurno, to držimo.*
'Sport **at least** three times a week. That's for sure. We hold to that.'

	Ger.	Sport **mindestens** dreimal die Woche. Das ist sicher, das halten wir ein.
	HMLD.Cro	Sport **barem** tri puta na tjedan. To je sigurno. Toga se držimo.

(40) *Moramo jesti* **gesünderes Brot** *... ne pit Colu i tako nešto ...*
'We should eat **healthier bread** ... not drink Coca Cola and things like that ...'

	Ger.	Wir sollen **gesünderes Brot** essen ... und keine Cola oder so was trinken ...
	HMLD.Cro	Moramo jesti **zdraviji kruh** ... ne piti Coca-Colu i tako nešto

(41) *A i zimske* **schuhe** *bi čovik mogao pravati ...*
'And one could have needed winter **shoes** ...'

	Ger.	Und Winter**schuhe** hätte man brauchen können ...
	HMLD.Cro	A i zimske **cipele** bi čovjek mogao trebati ...

German-Croatian code-switching is recorded in samples of speech from recently migrated speakers, e.g. GER.Cro (Kresić Vukosav and Šimičić, this volume) and AUT.Cro (Ščukanec, this volume). An example of alternation is given below from MOL.Cro, this as the initial code used by the speaker, followed by a long, alternated stretch in Italian, marked here in bold:

(42) *Sma čekal ka sa furnjivaša kondzilj* **per discutere [il] problem[a], fuori dal consi[glio], per non dare .. far perdere tempo, diciamo così, in consiglio.**
'We waited until the (city) council was going to finish **in order to discuss the problem, outside the council, in order not to give ... not to lose time, let's say, at the council.**'

Alternations can occur within (intra-clausal) or across (inter-clausal) clause boundaries. The example above contains intra-clausal code-switching. In some cases, lexical forms such as bilingual homophones (forms common to both languages with similar phonological forms) or established borrowings can function as 'triggers' (Clyne 1967, 2003; Hlavac 1999b) for alternational code-switching in which the speaker may be less aware or not aware at all that a change in language has occurred. In (42) above, a conventionalised borrowing *kondzilj* ('council') precedes the appeareance of its Italian equivalent, *consiglio* in the second part of the utterance. It is not clear if alternation occurred here triggered by *kondzilj* or whether this reflects this speaker's vernacular, which is characterised by unmarked code-switching. Examples (43) and (44) below are those of insertion.

The following example from MOL.Cro is taken from an account that contains an instance of insertion of an Italian adjective *russi* ('Russian' PL.M) ending instead of the MOL.Cro form *ruse* NOM.PL.M:

(43) bihu   mala   soldi   alora   bihu   ove
      be-IPRF.3PL   little   money-GEN.PL   then   be-IPRF.3PL   these-NOM
      tratora   **russi**   ke...
      tractor-NOM.PL.M   **russi-**'Russian' (NOM.PL.M) REL
      'There wasn't much money, but there were these **Russian** tractors, which...'

The next example is a case of the insertion of a technical term, for which there is no word in MOL.Cro (*ping pong*, here: 'tennis') together with the Italian prepositions *də* 'of' and *a* 'to(wards), at'. The insertion of Italian *sì* occurs rather frequently. *Sì* is a common discourse marker in some speakers' vernaculars, functioning as an affirmative alongside MOL.Cro *keja* 'yes'.

(44) je   reka: **sì,**   stoju   lipa,   one
      AUX-3SG   say-PTCP.SG.M   **sì** 'yes' be-PRS.3PL   nicely   they
      jimaju   kamba   **də ping pong**   jokaju
      have-PRS.3PL   field-ACC.M.PL   **də ping pong** [=tennis]   play-PRS.3PL
      a ping pong,   stoju   torko   lipa
      a ping pong [=tennis]   be-PRS.3PL   so much   well
      'He said: "**Yes**, they're fine. They have **tennis** courts. They play **tennis**. They're getting on really well!"'

In the following example three nouns are listed with the only (complex) abstract term supplied from Italian:

(45) su   se   frundal   tri   stvare   ke   biše
      AUX-3PL   REFL   meet-PTCP.PL   three   thing-NOM.PL.F   REL   be-IPRF.3SG
      jena   oganj   biše   voda   oš
      one-NOM.SG.M   fire-NOM.SG.M   be-IPRF.3SG   water-NOM.SG.F   and
      biše   **l'onore della persona**
      be-IPRF.3SG   **the honour of the person**
      'Three things met, which was (= were): one was fire, there was water and there was **personal honour**.'

There are four words (and five morphemes) contained in the Italian code-switch *l'onore della persona*. However, this NP is semantically simplex and could also be classified as a borrowing. In (46) below, there is insertion of an Italian (dialectal) phrase *cond delo stat* ('on behalf of the state', standard Italian: *conto dello Stato*) that could also be otherwise expressed by local MOL.Cro terms, themselves loan translations such as, *kunat do štata* or *kunat do luštat* or *za kunda do štata*:

(46) ona   kc   rabi   **cond delo stat,**   ne
     that-NOM.SG.F REL   work-PRS.3SG   **on behalf of the state**   NEG
     čini
     make-PRS.3SG
     'That one [field] that he [the Russian] works on, **on behalf of the state**, does not produce anything.'

Code-switching with repetition of a (Molise) Italian expression *tut la not* ('the whole night', standard Ital: *tutta la notte*), with an equivalent expression in MOL. Cro *tuna noču*:

(47) je   stala   **tut la not,**   tuna   noču
     AUX-3SG   stay-PTCP.SG.F   **all the night**   all   night-ACC.SG.F
     je   stala   sendza   spat.
     AUX-3SG   remain-PTCP.SG.F   without   sleep-INF
     'She spent **the whole night**, the whole night she spent without sleeping.'

The word order of (47) is the same in an equivalent Molise Italian utterance, eg. *... tutta la notte, tutta la notte è stata senza dormire*. Repetition of a phrase or construction from the other language, i.e. "bilingual couplets" (Hlavac 2011: 3795) with or without emphasis, is a frequent occurrence in diaspora vernaculars, including Italian-English ones (Kinder 1988). The following examples contain longer transferred sequences and can be considered alternations. As with larger numbers, indications of date and time in MOL.Cro are also always given in Italian (either a standard or local variety thereof):

(48) ma   biše   **la metà de la stagione**   biše
     but   be-IPRF.3SG   **alla metà della stagione** [=summer]   be-IPRF.3SG
     maša   bi   dendr   **la fine de luljo e li pringipj d'aghušt**
     must-IPRF.3SG   be-INF   between   **the end of July and the start of August**
     'Well, it was **in the middle of the season** (=summer), it was, it was probably between the **end of July and the beginning of August**'. (cf. Standard Ital.: *fra la fine di luglio e l'inizio d'agosto*).

Examples (49) and (50) are both from Kruč while (51) is from Mundimitar. The examples are from separate interactions. Some turns are commenced in Italian that coincide with expressions of indignation, although it is not clear if the code-switches alone augment their conversational implicature.

(49) *mi zbima partil* **con l'idea di fare una porcilaia,** *e zbima vrl [...] tama dol je...*
 'we had started **with the idea of making a pigsty,** and we had put [...] down there, there is...'

(50) *kaka sa ne rabi?*
 'how (= in what sense), you can't work?'

 non si può arare! Non si *... sa ne more či* ***l'aratura*** *indzom.*
 '**you can't plough! You can't** ... you can't do **the ploughing**, that's it.'

(51) *niste pol van, ste stal doma?*
 'didn't you go to the fields, did you stay at home?'

 come ti permetti *reč ke smo stal doma? Sa smo dol. Ne vidiš ke smo još* ***in tenuta militare, sporchi?***
 '**how do you take the liberty** of saying that we stayed at home? We have arrived in this moment. Don't you see that we are **still in military uniform, dirty?**'

A 'couplet', *non si* (Ital.) ... *sa ne more* (MOL.Cro) 'you can't' occurs in example (50) above. The code-switches, both intra- and inter-clausal, appear unmarked. In the following example from Filič, alternation between both languages occurs multiple times again across and within clause boundaries:

(52) *Je Dunat ...* ***conosciuto come perito,*** *ja ga zovam* ***sempr il deperitə. Tra me e lui c'è un sfottò continuo*** *ka sa ne furnjiva maj –*
 'There is Donato ... **known as the specialist,** I always call him **the emaciated** [a pun on words]. **Between me and him there is continuous joking** that never ends –'

Sociolinguistic features such as reference to another speaker can account for incidences of inter-clausal code-switching. In the following example, the (Italian) speech of another is quoted verbatim, which accounts for the clause-length code-switches into Italian.

(53) Nisa vidija re! Èo: "**Pilja sembrə!**" **Ji faccə**: "**Che coşə!**" Kaka je sa? Vamivaš ti?
'I did not see the king! Oh: "**Always take it!**" **I'll do it**. [*ji faccə*, Standard Ital.: *lo faccio io*]: "**What!**" How is it now? Are you taking it?'

In MOL.Cro, larger numbers, e.g. *kvarandòt or* 'forty-eight hours' (Standard Ital.: *quarantotto ore*) are a common group of inserted forms and have almost entirely been borrowed from Italian. For example, alongside *čjend* 'hundred' (Ital. *cento*) the original form *stotina* 'hundred' is still used, albeit much less frequently. The occurrence of a higher number here may facilitate the occurrence of the code-switched phrase *se è possibile* 'if it is possible' instead of an equivalent MOL.Cro phrase *si je posibil*:

(54) utra   **kvarandòt or,**   **se è possibile**   maša   jima
      within   **forty-eight hour**   **if is possible**   must-IPRF.2SG   must-INF
      či   ulja
      make-INF   oil-ACC.SG.M
      '[. . .] within **forty-eight hours, if possible**, you should make [=process] the oil'

Italian-Croatian code-switching is recorded in samples of speech from recently migrated speakers as well, e.g. ITAL.Cro (Županović Filipin, Hlavac and Piasevoli, this volume) and TRS.Cro (Piasevoli, this volume).

While examples of code-switching can be found in MOL.Cro speech as in the examples (43) to (54) above, what are far more common are established and fully integrated transfers (Breu 2017b: 65–72). The same applies to the HUN.Cro corpora. Here, code-switching appears to be generally less common. Instead of clause-length alternations, in HUN.Cro there is a greater frequency of single-form or simplex insertions, i.e. nouns, verbs, conjunctions or idiomatic expressions that are transferred from Hungarian. Where alternations do occur, they appear as infrequent examples of EL-islands (Myers-Scotton 2002). The facilitatating factor for some instances of code-switching into Hungarian may be an established transfer which has become part of the speaker's Croatian repertoire as in (55) below that contains the Hungarian subordinating conjunction *mert* 'because'. This subordinating form has entirely displaced the equivalent Croatian form in the Kajkavian dialect in Pomurje. In other instances, a more contemporary internationalism, such as CV in example (56) below accounts for the longer code-switch. Interestingly the 'couplet' in (56) is English and its repetition is given in Hungarian, which is likely to be more widely known than a Croatian equivalent.

(55) drugi   den   je   vunji,   **mert**   a
     other-ACC.M.SG day.ACC.M.SG be-3SG   aunt-DAT.F.SG because   DEF
     mama   v   prvi   hiži   stajela
     mother-NOM.F.SG in+LOC   first-LOC.F.SG house-LOC.F.SG   live-PTCP.F.SG
     '[...] next day from my aunty, **because my grandmother** lived in the first house'

(56) mogu   uraditi   ovaj...   **CV[sivi]**   önéletrajzot
     can-PRS.1SG create-INF   this-ACC.M.SG CV-ACC.M.SG CV-ACC.SG
     'I can create like a.....CV....CV [Hungarian].'

A further facilitating factor is the congruence of feature marking (Clyne 2003: 177–179) as shown in the examples below. In (57), the adverb *anyagilag* 'financially' is followed by its Croatian equivalent, *financijsko* 'financially' (HMLD.Cro *financijski*), which precedes *dobro* 'good'. It is not clear whether the Croatian counterpart is given due to emphasis or amplification, or due to the speaker's monitoring of their speech and the desire to 'switch back' to Croatian, or whether the speaker senses that the Hungarian adverb cannot qualify the Croatian adjective because it is perceived to be (momentarily or fundamentally) 'non-congruent' to this function. In (58), an adjective *nove* 'new-ACC.M/F.PL' commences an adjectival phrase, but its head noun is supplied from Hungarian, *dolgokat* 'things-ACC.PL', which bears only Hungarian morphological markers, including *–t* showing ACC case. In Hungarian, all nouns are marked for case, as are predicative adjectives, but attributive adjectives such as *új* 'new' in (58) below are not marked for case. In Croatian all parts of an NP bear identical case marking. As the head of the NP is from Hungarian, the speaker may feel that the case-marked adjective supplied from Croatian is not congruent to the structure of a Hungarian NP, and the counterpart adjective is inserted to immediately precede the Hungarian noun head.

(57) to   je   **anyagilag**   vagy   financijsko   dobro
     this   be-3SG   **financially** **or**   financially-ADV   good-ADJ.NOM.N.SG
     'This is **financially or** financially good/positive.'

(58) možete   kupiti   nove...   **új**   dolgokat
     can-2PL   buy-INF   new-ACC.M/F.PL   **new**   thing-ACC.PL
     'You can buy new... **new things**.'

The only example of a complete switch into Hungarian is in (59). As the speaker did not appear to know the Croatian equivalent of the word 'rails', she used the Hungarian noun *sín* and continued in Hungarian until the end of the conversation.

The Hungarian superessive case is double marked with the Croatian preposition *na* (that would otherwise require ACC 'onto') and the Hungarian superessive case suffix *–en* ('on'). The verb is repeated in the second (i.e. Hungarian) part of the utterance, this way solving the syntactic incongruence between the two parts of speech.

(59) pak   sem   se   popiknula   na   sineken
      and then   AUX-1SG   REFL   fall-PST.F.SG   on   rail-PL.SUP
      elestem,   a tojás,   a bab,   minden   elment!
      fall-PST.1SG   the egg   the bean   everything   go-PST.3SG
      'I fell on the **rails, the eggs, the beans, everything was gone**'

6 Morphosyntax

The following sections focus on structural features found in the speech of speakers in the three settings. Noun phrases and adjectives are presented first, followed by changes in verbal paradigms. Other structural phenomena such as valency of verbs, markedness of passive, word order changes and syntactic calques are presented towards the end of this section.

6.1 Paradigms – nouns and adjectives

This section presents examples of NPs that bear innovations in the marking of phi-features: gender, number and case, and the morphological features that are employed to mark these. HMLD.Cro has the following declension paradigm for nouns as shown below in Table 2:

Table 2: HMLD.Cro nominal declensions for all genders and both numbers.

	MASC.		FEM. I		NEUT.		FEM. II (-i stem)	
	SG.	PL.	SG.	PL.	SG.	PL.	SG.	PL.
NOM.	-Ø	-i, -ovi	-a	-e	-o/-e	-a	-Ø	-i
GEN.	-a	-a	-e	-a	-a	-a	-i	-i
DAT.	-u	-ima	-i	-ama	-u	-ima	-i	-ima
ACC.	=N. or G.	-e	-u	-e	=N.	-a	-Ø	-i
VOC.	=N., -e/-u	=N.	-a, -o	-e	=N.	=N.	-Ø	-i
LOC.	-u	-ima	-i	-ama	-u, -i	-ima	-i	-ima
INS.	-om/-em	-ima	-om	-ama	-om/-em	-ima	-ju, -i	-ima

As Table 3 below shows, in BGLD.Cro, declensions of nouns retain older forms, such as −ov/−ev for masculine and -Ø for feminine and neuter nouns in the GEN. PL Syncretism of DAT, LOC and INS case endings for the PL (M, N, FEM.II–*ima*., FEM.I – *ama*) has not occurred as it has in HMLD.Cro.

Table 3: BGLD.Cro nominal declensions for all genders and both numbers.

	MASC.		FEM. I		NEUT.		FEM. II (-i stem)	
	SG.	PL.	SG.	PL.	SG.	PL.	SG.	PL.
NOM.	-Ø	-i	-a	-e	-o/-e	-a	-Ø	-i
GEN.	-a	-ov/-ev, – Ø, -i	-e	-Ø	-a	- Ø, -ov/-ev	-i	-i
DAT.	-u	-om/-em	-i	-am	-u	-om/-em, -am	-i	-am
ACC.	=N.or G.	-e	-u	-e	=N.	-a	-Ø	-i
VOC.	=N., -e/-u	=N.	-a, -o	-e	=N.	=N.	-Ø	-i
LOC.	=D., -i	-i	-i	-a	-u, -i	-i	-i	-i
INS.	-om/-em	-i	-om	-ami	-om/-em	-i	-u, -ju, -om	-i

Other differences include the absence of the infix *ov-* in the plural for some monosyllabic M nouns, eg. HMLD.Cro *gradovi* NOM.M.PL 'towns', BGLD.Cro *gradi* NOM.M.PL 'towns', although it is possible that this represents an archaic form and it is HMLD.Cro that features the innovation. Distinct vocative forms are still retained much to the same degree that they are retained in HMLD.Cro, i.e. in the SG only. Loss of word-final velar fricative [-h] has led to a loss of the distinct LOC.PL suffixes as reported by Szucsich (2000):

(60a) u   *lip-ih*   *hiža-h*
       in+LOC   beautiful-LOC.F.PL   houses-LOC.F.PL

(60b) u   *lip-i*   *hiža*
       in+LOC   beautiful-SYNCRETIC SUFFIX   houses-SYNCRETIC SUFFIX

This change has occurred more recently than in HMLD.Cro. Loss of the velar fricative occurred in many varieties of HMLD.Cro and arguably its retention can be attributed to the conserving effect of the standard language. In nominal or adjectival paradigms, -*h* is found as an adjectival ending for GEN.PL only. Syncretism of the DAT/LOC/INS.PL nominal forms -*ima* (M, N), -*ama* (F), and −*im* for adjectives across all genders led to the disappearance of the −*h* suffix within the paradigm. We observe in (60) that a phonological change has led to the 'loss' of a distinct form, so that the 'remaining morphology' (-*a*) resembles that found in other forms, e.g. NOM.F.SG. This comparatively recent change may also be responsible for avoidance strategies reported amongst some speakers. For example, Szucsich (2000) observes that younger speakers often display insecurity in distinguishing or producing LOC.PL forms, and this insecurity is a catalyst for avoidance of this form and employment of alternatives, eg:

(61) *pominati   se   o   nekom*
     talk-INF   REFL   about+LOC   someone+LOC
     pominati   se   prik   koga
     talk-INF   REFL   about+ACC   someone-ACC
     'to talk about someone' > 'to talk about someone'

   Ger.
   sich   **über**   **jemanden**   unterhalten
   REFL   **about**+ACC **someone**-ACC   talk-INF

In MOL.Cro only two declension classes have been preserved, governed exclusively by the gender category. So there is a masculine declension, based on the former *o*-declension of masculines and neuters, with alternative endings in some cases, going mainly back to the older opposition of neuters and masculines, for example ∅: -*a* (-*e, -o*) in the NOM/ACC.SG and -*e*: -*ā* in the NOM/ACC.PL. The animacy opposition, with the ACC.SG being homonymous either with the NOM or with the GEN, has become optional. So, nouns referring to persons and animals are now usually declined as non-animate nouns (with variation), probably due to Italian influence, where grammatical animacy is missing, e.g. *Vidim na ljud* (ACC=NOM) as well as *vidim jenga ljudata* (ACC=GEN) 'I see a man'. Table 4 below shows MOL.Cro nominal declensions from Kruč; suprasegmentals are omitted (see Breu 2017b: 22–34).

Table 4: MOL.Cro nominal declensions for both genders and both numbers.

	MASC		FEM	
	SG.	PL.	SG.	PL.
NOM	-∅, -a	-a, -e	-a	-e
GEN	-a	-∅, -i	-e	-∅, -i
DAT	-u	-i, -ami	-u	-ami, -i
ACC	=N. or G.	-a, -e	-u	-e
INS	-am, -om	-i, -ami	-om	-ami, -i

The above paradigm does not include VOC, as the NOM form is used when addressing or calling out to others. The nominal paradigms of the dialects of Mundimitar and Filič differ somewhat from the declensions above (Breu 2017b: 22–34; Peša Matracki & Županović Filipin 2013). A distinct LOC case is also absent from the above paradigm as the movement/position opposition between ACC and LOC has been lost and peculiarly LOC morphology is found only in, for example, unanalysed adverbial phrases (Breu 2008). One of the most conspicuous features of the above paradigm is that MOL.Cro has completely lost its neuter gender in nouns. The influence of Italian seems obvious here as Italian has lost neuter gender. But neuter gender does remain in MOL.Cro as a relic form in specific contexts, namely with adjectives and pronouns in impersonal utterances (see below section 6.1.1). Breu (2013a) has shown that the contact situation accounts even for retention of neuter gender in MOL.Cro adjectives, due to the model of *Molise Italian* that itself has retained neuter gender in this case. Most frequently, former neuter nouns have become masculine, either keeping or losing their endings in the NOM/ACC.SG. In the latter case, only in Mundimitar (MM) is the original form retained, whereas otherwise -*o* and -*e* turn into -*a (akanje* or vowel reduction to -*a)*, e.g. Kruč *zlat* (≠ *zlato* MM) 'gold'; *brda* (≠*brdo* MM) 'hill'; *mor* (all dialects) (<*more*) 'sea'; *grozja* (≠*grozdje* MM) 'grapes'. In the Kruč variety, however, several former neuters have become feminine, e.g. *sreba* F (≠ *srebro* M MM) 'silver', *neba* F (≠*nebo* M MM) 'sky'. Former feminine nouns ending in a consonant (historical *i*-declension) have either kept their gender by entering the *a*-declension or they have turned into masculines retaining the original zero ending. In contrast to the formerly neuter nouns, for which the new gender distribution is arbitrary (though masculine gender is absolutely dominant), the new gender of the former FEM.II nouns depends on the gender of the Italian equivalent:[18]

(62)	MOL.Cro	Italian		HMLD.Cro
	riča F	parola F	word	riječ F.II
	stvara F	cosa F	thing	stvar F.II
	noča F	notte F	night	noć F.II
	kost M	osso M	bone	kost F.II
	krv M	sangue M	blood	krv F.II
	pamet M	giudizio M	sense	pamet F.II

---

18 Even some F.I nouns (*a*-stems) are now masculine, for example, *mbrav* M 'ant' in Montemitro, but preserved as *mbrava* F in Kruč.

In the plural, grammatical gender has been lost completely, which is *not* a feature of the local Italian contact varieties. This is a secondary result of the NOM.PL merging with the genderless ACC.PL (Breu 2013a: 94–103).

As stated, language contact is responsible for the loss of LOC in MOL.Cro, as Italian does not differentiate between expressing 'location' and 'motion towards a location'. In standard Italian *in chiesa* means both 'in the church' and '(in)to the church'. This polysemic model was copied by merging the LOC as a rule with the ACC, now expressing both concepts in MOL.Cro, too: e.g. *stojim u crikvu* (ACC.SG.F) 'I am in the church'; *su pol u crikvu* (ACC.SG.F) 'they went to the church'. But this full merger is only the final result, restricted, by now, to Kruč and Filič. In the DAT.SG.F, a characteristic difference has developed between the respective MOL.Cro varieties, with the original *-i* being preserved in Filič, but lost in Mundimitar for phonetic reasons and substituted by the accusative ending *-u* in Kruč, for example: *divojki* ≠ *divojk* ≠ *divojku* DAT.SG.F 'girl'. The merger of the DAT with the ACC in Kruč seems to be a secondary effect of the disintegration of the LOC, originally linked with the DAT by at least partial homonymy. Therefore, the dialectal differentiation in the dative could also be an indirect consequence of language contact. In the Mundimitar dialect bare (unattributed) feminine nouns still take the form of the DAT that is traditionally identical with the LOC in the *a*-declension, and again homonymous for both concepts, e.g. *stojim / su pol u crikv* (DAT.SG.F) 'I am in / they went to church'. At the same time, attributed feminines like all masculines show the accusative: *u našu crikvu* ACC.SG.F 'in / to our church'. Things become still more complicated as the Mundimitar dialect has additionally developed an adverbial form in *-o*, again polysemic for both concepts, e.g. *na-miso* 'in / to the mass'; *na-našo* 'in / into our [language]', the designation given to the MOL.Cro language in that village (Breu 2008).

As for the other case forms, the instrumental of means, originally expressed by bare nouns, merged with the comitative instrumental, resulting in an obligatory use of the preposition *s* 'with', e.g. *je otvorila vrata* **s** ('with'+INS) *ključam* 'she opened the door with a key'. This corresponds to the Italian prepositional model **con** *la chiave*, equally polysemic for both functions. In standard HMLD.Cro the comitative instrumental is expressed *without* a preposition, e.g. *otvorila je vrata ključem*, while many non-standard HMLD.Cro varieties *do* include the preposition in the same construction. In the MOL.Cro genitive, we likewise find the preposition *do* 'of', corresponding to Italian *di*, although only optionally, e.g. *hiže* GEN.SG.F ~ *do hiže* GEN.SG.F. The genitive ending itself is preserved, as it is in all other grammatical cases. The influence of Italian *di* is apparent in the incidence of *od* 'of'/'from' as a periphrastic marker of possession, together with GEN in diaspora varieties, e.g. ITAL.Cro (Županović Filipin, Hlavac and Piasevoli, this volume) and TRS.Cro (Piasevoli, this volume).

As there is no comprehensive grammatical description of the dialects of Šokac- and Bošnjak-Croats, the following table, Table 5, summarises the declension paradigms for nouns of the Pomurje-Croatian, the only systematically described Croatian dialect in Hungary, so far.

Table 5: HUN.Cro nominal declensions for both genders and both numbers.

	MASC.		FEM. I		NEUT.		FEM. II (-i stem)	
	SG.	PL.	SG.	PL.	SG.	PL.	SG.	PL.
NOM	-Ø	-i	-a	-e	-o/-e	-a	-Ø	-i
GEN	-a	-of/-ef, -i, Ø	-e	-i, Ø	-a	-Ø, -i	-i	-i
DAT	-o	-om/-am, -em	-i	-am	-i/u	-am	-i	-om, jomem, am, jam, ima
ACC	=G, N	-e	-u	-e	=N.	-a	-Ø	-i
VOC	–	–	-u, -a	–	–	–	–	–
LOC	-u	aj/-ej	-i	-aj	-i/u	-aj	-i	-ej, -aj, -joj, -ima
INS	-um	-ami/-omi, -mi	-um	-ami	-um/-em	-ami	-jom	-ami, -ima, -mi, -jami, -ijami

The declension paradigm of Pomurje-Croatian (reconstructed by Rácz 2009, 2012) are similar to those of the corresponding Kajkavian-dialects of HMLD.Cro. (For a detailed overview of the case morphology of Kajkavian dialects see Lončarić 1996). Pomurje-Croatian has a richer case morphology than HMLD.Cro, which is demonstrated by the low number of syncretic forms in the plural.

There is a syncretism of ACC and GEN in M.SG both in animate and inanimate nouns, if they have a direct object function in the sentence, or if they are combined with the preposition *po* meaning 'for', e.g. *Idi po stolca!* (go-IMP. for-PREP chair-ACC.M.SG), literally 'Go for the chair!', i.e. 'Bring the chair!'. Otherwise, NOM and ACC are syncretic in prepositional phrases, even for animate nouns. The only exception is the preposition *za*, which differentiates between animate and inanimate nouns. In prepositional phrases of *za*, the patterns are the same as in HMLD.Cro. The only vocative case marking is in F.SG, e.g. *Maru!* 'Mara!', *mamu!* 'mum!'.

All monosyllabic M.PL nouns are short, e.g. *noži* 'knives', *poži* 'snails', *rogi* 'horns'. The ending -ov/-ev (GEN.PL) from the old *u*-declension paradigm is transferred to the masculine declension paradigm (GEN.PL), whereby the voiced fricative 'v' is replaced by its voiceless counterpart 'f'. Furthermore, the old ending -eh/-ah for LOC.PL is preserved, but the velar fricative 'h' is replaced by the palatal approximant *j*. The ending -*ah* comes from feminine paradigm, but its use is now extended to the masculine and neuter paradigms as well. The extended use of the suffix -*ami* in INS.PL in all three declension classes is a similar case.

A further specific feature compared to HMLD.Cro is the use of two different endings for marking DAT and LOC in neuter SG – making a distinction between nouns with an *-o* and *-e* ending, e.g. *v seli* in village-LOC.N.SG 'in the village', *na moriju* on sea-LOC.N.SG 'at the seaside'. The ending *-i* comes from the old palatal paradigm of neuter nouns. The suffix *-u* (from the old *u*-declension) is used for marking DAT and LOC in HMLD.Cro as well.

The Ø-ending in GEN.PL in all declension classes is also a difference compared to HMLD.Cro, and it is used for certain nouns in the masculine and neuter paradigms. In GEN.M.PL it occurs for the nouns *penes* 'money' and *čas* 'time' only, while in in GEN.N.PL it occurs for *leto* 'year' and *drevo* 'wood' only. However, it is interchangable in GEN.F.PL with the other alternative ending *-i*, e.g. *žen-Ø* and *ženi* 'woman'-GEN.F.PL.

In HUN.Cro there are instances in which speakers show uncertainty in gender selection in the agreement patterns triggered by complex subjects. This variation in the marking of gender is shown in examples (63) to (65) below. Variation in the marking of gender in agreement patterns can be triggered by so-called problematic subjects (Corbett 2006), where grammatical gender is either different from the natural gender of the subject or whose gender is selected according to specific rules of agreement in Croatian. Such problematic subjects can be conjoined noun phrases, hybrid nouns and quantified nouns. It is not clear according to which criteria the gender of the subjects in the sentences below is allocated. In example (63) the target form is feminine plural; in (64) it is neuter plural, and in (65) it is neuter singular (cf. Pišković 2011; Babić 1998). (Examples (63) to (65) are from speakers of HUN.Cro who are younger than 30.) All the data in this section is from Rácz (2012) and Vuk's data corpora.

(63) *šuma*   *i*   *livada*   *su*   **bila**
      wood-NOM.F.SG and   meadow-NOM.F.SG AUX-3PL be-SG.F./PL.N
      zelena.
      green- SG.F./PL.N
      'The wood and the meadow are green.'

(64) *djeca*   **su**   **se**   **igrale**   *u*
      children.NOM.F.SG AUX-3PL   REFL.   play-PTCP.F.PL   in+LOC
      dvorištu
      courtyard-SG.M.LOC
      'Children played in the courtyard.'

(65) *pet* **knjiga**   *su*   **bila**   *na*
      five   book-GEN.F.PL   AUX-3PL   be-PTCP.F.SG./N.PL.   on+LOC
      stolu
      table.SG.M.LOC
      'There were five books on the table.'

Suffix morphemes of Croatian adjectives and past participles are multi-feature morphemes, ie. a single form indexes multiple features such as number, gender and case. Homophony of a suffix ending, eg. –*a* as the suffix morpheme for NOM.F.SG *and* NOM.N.PL, with other endings is widespread. This is a phenomenon that is likely to facilitate syncretism, which has occurred elsewhere in HMLD.Cro. We observe comparable oscilation amongst speakers of HMLD.Cro in congruent constructions where morphology marking in the predicate is variable due to other, 'problematic subjects'. In the examples given below, the legacy of number values (i.e. paucal or small groups numbering two to four) and the morphology usually required for nouns (for example animate nouns whose grammatical gender coincides with their natural gender) can lead to insecurity as to morphological marking. For HMLD. Cro speakers, such 'problematic subjects' can lead to variation in the form of predicate constructions. Three examples are given below:

(66a) *dva* *muškarca* **su**
two+GEN.SG man-PAUC AUX-3PL
došla
came-PAUC (homophonous with N.PL form)

(66b) *dva* *muškarca* **su** *došli*
two+GEN.SG man.PAUC AUX-3PL came-M.PL

(66c) *dva* *muškarca* **je** *došlo*
two+GEN.SG man.PAUC AUX-3SG came-N.SG
'Two men came.'

The first instance given above (66a) has agreement between the form of the participle and the paucal form of the subject, which is the normative and standard form. (This form is identical to the NEUT.PL ending.) This form is also arguably the most common form across non-standard varieties of HMLD.Cro. The second instance (66b) given above has a M.PL participle induced by the clearly plural and male features of the antecedent subject. This form is less frequent in non-standard varieties of HMLD.Cro, but it is also the *only* form used in BGLD. Cro (Benčić et al. 2003:164). The third instance (66c) has N.SG marking for the participle and a SG.AUX verb. The N.SG marking on the predicate verb is the required form when the subject denotes a larger number i.e. between 'five' to 'nine'. But N.SG marked predicates are less common and considered non-standard when the subject denotes a less number such as 'two'. Still, N.SG with paucal subjects is possible in many speakers' vernaculars (Franks 2009: 362). Breu (2013b: 13) remarks that the paucal, perhaps surprisingly, is retained in

MOL.Cro, eg. *dva kafèla* PC *teple* NOM.PL 'two hot coffees'. (The ADJ *teple* 'hot' is post-posed as in most attributive constructions). Instances of variable case marking after lower number paucals are recorded in TRS.Cro (Piasevoli, this volume) and USA.Cro (Jutronić, this volume).

To return to the HUN.Cro examples above, the grammatical feature of gender-marking of nouns is non-existent in Hungarian. The forms contained in examples (63) to (65) above cannot be directly linked to the influence of Hungarian. Instead, they appear as a consequence of a general language contact situation.

In other NPs, there can be features preceding a noun that reflect forms modelled on the contact situation. In the following examples, written texts in BGLD.Cro feature attributive constructions preceding a noun. In BGLD.Cro NPs can occur in attributive position describing a following noun:

(67) BGLD.Cro ... *kani postaviti **35 metri visok** jarbol*
... intends to set up a **35-metre high** flagpole

Ger. ... hat vor einen **35 Meter hohen** Fahnenmast aufzustellen
HMLD.Cro ... *kani postaviti jarbol **visok 35 metara**.*

HMLD.Cro does not allow multi-element NPs in an attributive position in the way that BLGD.Cro allows this. The usage of *participial constructions* in attributive position to form *extended attributes* (Ger. *erweiterte Attribute*) or *extended participial modifiers* (Ger. *erweiterte Partizipialbestimmungen*) is a feature of German syntax that can be transferred into BGLD. Cro, especially in written texts. (The same construction also exists in HMLD.Cro Kajkavian and this is also a result of German influence.) An example of an extended participial modifier is found below, again from a written text:

(68) BGLD.Cro *Cesar je svaki dan išao okolo podneva po njem na trg, i je onde jednu svotu pinez hitio med onde jur **na njega čekajuće** ljude.*
'Caesar walked around the square every day at midday and threw a bundle of money **at people waiting for him**.'

Ger. Caesar ging jeden Tag um Mittag auf dem Platz spazieren und warf einmal ein Bündel Geld **auf die auf ihn wartenden** Leute.
HMLD.Cro *Cesar je svaki dan oko podneva išao u šetnju na trg i jednom je bacio svotu novaca među ljude **koji su ga čekali**.*

In HUN.Cro, some adjectives are indeclinable with most of them being borrowings from Hungarian – see above examples (10) and (11) – or from German, e.g. *fest* 'strong'. Two other indeclinable adjectives *huhu* 'crazy' and *šukšuk* 'crazy' are onomathopoeic lexemes. Further to this, as in HMLD.Cro, adjectives can be functions as nominal subjects. Examples of this are *mrtef*-M.SG ('dead') meaning 'dead body, corpse'; *debeli*-M.PL ('fat') meaning 'fat people'; and *bogati*-M.PL 'rich' denoting 'rich people' (Rácz 2012: 141–146). An instance of a nominalised adjective is given in (69):

(69) **mrtef** je pre hiži.
 dead-NOM.SG.M be-3SG at+LOC home-LOC.F.SG
 'The **corpse** is in the house.'

A common phenomenon in German is nominalisation with compound nouns (Ger. *Komposita*). Relatively few are recorded amongst BGLD.Cro speakers, and the example given below is uncharacteristic of the way that denotations or concepts expressed in German via compound nouns are rendered in BGLD.Cro:

(70) *Po maši je jur na korušu počelo **željenje srićnih Vazmenih svetkov***.
 'After mass the members of the choir **started their well-wishing of Happy Easter** to each other'.

> Ger. Nach der heiligen Messe wünschten sich die Menschen im Kirchenchor **schöne Ostertage.**
> HMLD.Cro Nakon mise je na koru počelo **čestitanje uskrsnih blagdana**.
> (Sučić et al. 2003: 595)

Otherwise, BGLD.Cro equivalents of German compound nouns are expressed via NPs with multiple attributes or through extended attributes.

6.1.1 Adjectives

The nominal paradigms of BGLD.Cro and HUN.Cro have been presented above in 6.1. The adjectival paradigms in 'HUN-Pom.Cro' show a number of peculiar forms that are more numerous than that of HMLD.Cro due to its lack of syncretism of LOC/DAT/INS.PL morphological markers. Instead of marking all three cases in plural by an *-im* ending as in HMLD.Cro, 'HUN-Pom.Cro' has an *-am* ending for DAT, an *-ami* ending for INS, and an *-aj* ending for LOC in all four declension classes. A detailed overview of the adjectival paradigms in 'HUN-Pom.Cro' is provided by Rácz (2012). The adjectival paradigms feature congruent differences in relation to HMLD.Cro, especially the adjectival paradigm of MOL.Cro. MOL.Cro adjectives, in contrast to nouns, have retained their three-gender system, with the productive neuter in *-ō* (base form before its shortening) being restricted to substantivisations, e.g. *ono velko* 'the big (thing)', *jeno dobro* 'a good (thing)'. The different behaviour of the neuter with nouns and adjectives corresponds to a similar situation in Italian, especially in the central and southern dialects. The same is true for the preservation of the impersonal neuter of verbs (Breu 2013a: 105–111). A full description of MOL.Cro's adjectival paradigm is not given here; see Breu (2017b: 34–37). Instead, comparative and superlative forms are presented here from MOL.Cro.

In MOL.Cro, in the category of comparison, the comparative and the superlative have been transformed into analytic constructions like *veča lipi* 'more beautiful', *naveča lipi* 'most beautiful', different from the traditional synthetic forms in HMLD.Cro of the type *ljepši, najljepši*. These analytical constructions correspond to Italian *più bello, il più bello*. The adaptation to the Italian model goes so far as to preserve exactly the same suppletive comparatives as Italian does, for example *dobar – bolji* 'good, better', *grubi – gori* 'bad, worse', just like Italian *buono – migliore, cattivo – peggiore*. Moreover, as in the local Italian dialects, pleonastic forms like *veča bolji* 'more better' are possible. Even the frequent substitution of the adjectival comparative by the corresponding adverb has been copied. So instead of *bolji* the form *bolje* appears, just like Italians use the adverb *meglio* in the sense of the adjectival comparative *migliore* 'better' (Breu 2009).

In BGLD.Cro there are no differences in the formation of comparative and superlative forms vis-à-vis HMLD.Cro. In HUN.Pom.Cro comparative forms are either made by adding the infixes *-š/-eš*, e.g. *mefek–mekši* 'soft-softer', *lepi-lepši* 'beautiful-more beautiful'; *zdrav–zdraveši* 'healthy-healthier', *niski – nižeši* 'low-lower'. Comparative formation can occur in an analytical way, i.e. by combining the adverb *bole* 'better' with the positive form of the adjective, e.g. *pijan – bole pijan* 'drunk – more drunk'. Some adjectives have both synthetic and analytical forms, e.g. *široki – širši/bole široki* 'wide – wider'. Amongst a small number of adjectives, with both synthetic and analytical comparatives, a difference in the meanings of the two forms can be observed, e.g. *dragi – dražeši* 'expensive – more expensive' compared to *dragi – bole dragi* 'nice – nicer'.

Superlative forms are made with the prefix *naj-*, which is added to the comparative form as in HMLD.Cro, e.g. *lepi-lepši-najlepši* 'beautiful – more beautiful – the most beautiful'. On the other hand, there are analytical superlatives, which are either a combination of the adverb *najbole* 'best' (the superlative form of the adjective *dober* 'good'), and the positive of another adjective, e.g. *betežen – najbole betežen* 'sick – the most sick', or they are made by adding different verbal prefixes such as *prek* 'over' or adverbs such as *preveč or prekveč* 'too much' to the positive form of the adjectives, e.g. *pijan – preveč pijan* 'drunk – too drunk/the most drunk'. An instance of transferred comparative from English (with the suffix *-er*) is recorded in the NZ.Cro sample (see Stoffel and Hlavac, this volume) and this form occurs periphrastically with the Croatian comparative *više* 'more'.

6.2 Paradigms – verbs

BGLD.Cro, MOL.Cro and HUN.Cro feature the use of verb forms that contrast from that found in HMLD.Cro, or which are restricted to certain HMLD.Cro dialects. For example, BGLD.Cro, features an honoric 3PL form used for 3SG subjects. This construction is known in some Kajkavian folk songs in HMLD.Cro:

(71) *mamica* **su** *štrukle* **pekli** *meni*
mummy-SG.F AUX-3PL strudels.ACC.PL bake.PST.**3PL.M** me-DAT
nisu *nikaj* ***rekli***
NEG.AUX-**3PL** nothing say.PST.**3PL.M**
'Mummy (3SG) baked (3PL) strudels but [she] didn't (3PL) tell (3PL) me.'

The line from this folk song contains a SG.F. subject while all verb morphology, both AUX and PTCP, is clearly PL.M. According to Pišković (2011: 251), this construction is restricted to a small number of non-standard HMLD.Cro dialects. In BGLD.Cro this construction also occurs and it is most probably reinforced by an equivalent (but also marked) Ger. construction, eg. *der Herr Professor* **sind** *in den Ruhestand getreten* 'the professor **have** retired' (cf. Vulić and Petrović 1999: 51). Houtzagers (2012: 277) records the following example:

(72) *njeguov otadz* *už vig* ***živu***
his-SG.M father-**SG.M** already still live-**3PL**
sat ***su*** *sedamdesiet lit* ***stari***
now be-**3PL** seventy+GEN.PL year-GEN.N.PL old-**M.PL**
'His father are (= 'is') still alive. He are (= 'is') now seventy years old.'

This construction is, like its (Austrian) German counterpart, a marked one. In a comparison of 3SG verb forms found in a wide variety of speech samples Houtzagers (2012: 298) concludes that the form is used by "persons who are respected by the speaker in the affectionate way a child respects (or is by tradition bound to respect) an older relative", with further limited instances of its use restricted to those expressing closeness to others, sometimes also non-relatives. Here, the transfer of a feature carrying socio-pragmatic information (an honoric form), the 3PL verb form with a 3SG subject, in German is carried over into the BGLD.Cro varieties of some speakers. The honorific third person plural is currently not a change to the verbal paradigm of BGLD.Cro (in the same way that the same form does not represent a change to the German verbal paradigm). But forms like this may lead to other more wide-ranging innovations.

In HUN-Pom.Cro, Vuk also records similar instances of this use of a SG subject co-occuring with PL verb forms:

(73) tak   su   rekli   Štigarovi   tetec
     such   AUX-**3PL**   say-**3PL.M**   Štigar-POSS.M.**PL**   uncle-M.**SG**
     'That's what Štigar's uncle said'

This type of use of pragmatic features carried via employment of a marked verb form is not unusual. Concord between second person forms (singular and plural, formal and non-formal) and verbal forms has, over time, changed in many Romance and Germanic languages. In addition to diachronic evidence, there is synchronic evidence for more recent innovations that have occurred in different national varieties of Spanish and Portuguese. Marked forms in BGDL.Cro can become unmarked ones, depending on a range of circumstances. The influence of HMLD.Cro and the codification of a standard BGLD.Cro, however, have a conserving effect rendering this kind of further change unlikely. Grammatically singular subjects also co-occur with plural verb forms in AUS.Cro (see Hlavac and Stolac, this volume). Here external influence is clear where the equivalent English forms (e.g. *obitelj – family*, *većina – majority*) usually call for plural predicates in English.

In MOL.Cro,[19] the most important contact-induced change in its tense system is the development of a de-obligative future, formed with the auxiliary *jimat* 'to have, must'. This verb originally only had possessive meaning, but by copying the polysemic model of southern Italian *avé* 'to have, must' it acquired the additional meanings of 'must' and the function of building a future tense referring to necessary or planned states of affairs. As MOL.Cro traditionally had a volitive future tense, formed with the auxiliary *tit* 'will, to want' (HMLD.Cro *htjeti*), a modal opposition between these future forms came into being, with the volitive future being reduced to a future of probability (Breu 2011a: 156–158):

(74) ču   dokj   mam   dokj
     will-1SG   come-INF   have-1SG   come-INF
     'I will (**probably**) come.'   vs.   'I will come (**as planned**).'

---

19 For a description of the MOL.Cro verb system, including full paradigms, based on the Kruč dialect with references to the other varieties, see Breu (2017b: 46–63).

Another important contact influence did not induce a new tense, but instead prevented its disappearance. In HMLD.Cro, as in most other Slavic languages, the past perfect is not commonly used and its use is marked, indicating emphasis. But in MOL.Cro it is frequent and productive, due to transfer of concord of tenses from Italian. This means that an event occurring prior to another event in the past *must* be expressed by the past perfect. The composition of this compound tense differs both from Croatian and from Italian in having a fixed particle *bi* (with variant *ba* in Mundimitar and Filič). It fuses in most forms with the perfect, for example, *zbi doša* 'I/you had come', derived from the perfects *sa doša* 'I have come' and *si doša* 'you have come'. In the 1st and 2nd person of the plural it is even infixed, e.g. *zbima dol* 'we had come', from the perfect *sma dol* 'we have come'. This particle *bi* (or *ba*) is different from the inflected conditional marker (in Kruč: *bi* for all SG forms, *bima, bita, bi* for PL forms – see below). An example is the paradigm of the past perfect in the Kruč dialect for 'I have put' *sa bi vrga* (Mundimitar forms are different, with, for example *smo ba vrl ~ zbamo vrl* 'we had put'). The forms of the MOL.Cro past perfect are given in Table 6 (Breu 2017b: 56–57).

Table 6: Past perfect forms in MOL.Cro – AUX-*bit* + *bi* + PTCP (in part, fused).

PERS.	SINGULAR			PLURAL
	MASC.	FEM.	NEUT.	
1	sa bi vrga ~ zbi vrga	sa bi vrla ~ zbi vrla		zbima vrl
2	si bi vrga ~ zbi vrga	si bi vrla ~ zbi vrla		zbita vrl
3	je bi vrga	je bi vrla	je bi vrla	su bi vrl ~ zbi vrl

Another consequence of copying the concord of tenses is the development of analytic constructions for the future in the past, with the same modal opposition as in the normal future. These forms show the clitic imperfect of the auxiliaries from *tit* ('will', 'to want') and *jimat* ('to have, must'), e.g.:

(75) **čahu** dokj vs. **mahu** dokj
 will-IMPF.1SG come-INF **have**-IMPF.1SG come-INF
 'I would (**probably**) come.' 'I would come (**as planned**)'.

The direct model for the de-obligative future in the past of the type *mahu dokj* 'I would come (as planned)' is the dialectal construction with the imperfect of *avé* 'to have, must' + infinitive. The volitive future in the past *čahu dokj* 'I would (probably) come' is an internal analogical construction based on the modal opposition in the simple future. It exists only in the Kruč dialect. In standard Italian it is the (past) conditional that serves also as a future in the past, in the given case *sarei venuto*. Based on this model the MOL.Cro conditional *bi doša* can also be used as a third (neutral) form expressing the future in the past (Breu 2019: 403 fn. 23; 2017b: 335). Table 7 below sets out the 3SG.M verbs forms for the verb *pitati* 'to ask' found in BGLD.Cro, MOL.Cro (Kruč), HUN-Pom.Cro and HMLD.Cro.

Table 7: Verb tenses and forms in BGLD.Cro, MOL.Cro, HUN-Pom.Cro and HMLD.Cro.

	BGLD.Cro	MOL.Cro	HUN-Pom.Cro	HMLD.Cro
Infinitive	pitati	pitat	pitati	pitati
Present	pita (pitaju)	pita	pita	pita
Imperative (2SG)	pitaj	pitaj	pitaj	pitaj
Imperfect	–	pitaša	–	pitaše
Aorist	–	–	–	pita
Perfect	je pitao	je pita	je pital	je pitao
Past perfect	je bio pitao	je bi pita	bil pital	je bio pitao
Future I	pitat će	ča pitat (probability) ma pitat (de-obligative)	–	pitat će
Future II	bude pitao	–	bo pital	bude pitao
Future expressed in past	–	čaša pitat (probability) maša pitat (de-obligative)	–	–
Conditional I	bi pitao	bi pita	bi pital	bi pitao
Conditional II	bi bio imao	–	bil bi pital	bi bio imao
Present participle (present verbal adverb)	pitajući	pitajuč	pitajuč	pitajući
Past participle (past verbal adverb)	pitavši	–	–	pitavši
Passive participle	pitan	pitan	(po)pitani	pitan

Perfect formation itself resisted contact influence, as it continues to be formed exclusively by means of the auxiliary *bit* and the active *l*-participle, as in *sa doša* 'I have come', differing from the Italian way of forming the perfect by means of *avere* 'to have' (or *essere* 'to be' with intransitives) and the passive participle. MOL.Cro has a construction that is not a fully developed verb tense but a marginal construction, formed with AUX *jimat* 'have' and the passive *n/t*-participle. However, it has only resultative function referring to the present: *Jima dvi sprte pozane nazjamu*, i.e. literally 'S/he has two baskets (having been) put to the ground'.

The category of aspect has kept its traditional composition of a morphosyntactic opposition of the imperfect and the perfect on the one side, e.g. *rabahu* 'I was working' vs. *sa rabija* 'I worked', and the derivative opposition of perfective vs. imperfective on the other.[20] In view of the tendency for instances of morphosyntactic opposition to be subject to attrition, not only in Slavic languages spoken as minority ones in contact situations, but also 'homeland varieties', including HMLD.Cro where the perfect tense has almost completely replaced both the aorist and the imperfect, preservation of the imperfect in MOL.Cro may be viewed as an effect of language contact with Italian as the influencing model. The contact influence arguably goes much deeper. In all Slavic languages when at least one member of the older threefold opposition between imperfect, aorist and perfect was found to be attrited, it was always the imperfect that was lost first. This is a diachronic constant of Slavic. In Romance languages there is an opposite trend: the aorist is the first to disappear. This is exactly what has happened in the colloquial and dialectal Italian of Lower Molise: the aorist *(passato remoto)* has disappeared, while the imperfect was kept. MOL.Cro has followed this path by replacing the Slavic diachronic pattern with the Romance one (Breu 2011a: 163–169). In addition, as in Italian, the imperfect is obligatory for expressing processes and unlimited states and can never be replaced by the imperfective *l*-perfect, contrary to what has happened in HMLD.Cro. While the aorist has been lost in MOL.Cro, verbs with imperfective *and* perfective aspect can be rendered in the imperfect (Breu 2014).

Derivative aspect opposition has been preserved in MOL.Cro. There is only a slight difference with respect to other Slavic languages in that prefixation is no longer a productive means for building aspectual pairs, probably due to the fact that in Italian prefixes have no role in the semantic field of aspectuality. But traditional pairs like *krest* IPFV / *ukrest* PFV 'to steal' or *must* IPFV / *pomust* PFV 'to milk' continue to be used. In any case, the derivative aspect opposition based on suffixation like *kupit* PFV vs. *kupivat* (MM *kupiljat*) ~ *kupovat* IPFV is fully productive, even in borrowings, as mentioned above. The reason for this conservativism is probably due to the fact that in Italian there is no model for its reduction, just like in the category of case, apart from the LOC.[21]

---

[20] Both oppositions freely combine with each other, with special functions for the 'contradictory' combinations of the perfective imperfect (habituality) and the imperfective perfect (delimitation). See Breu (2014) for more details.

[21] See Breu, Berghaus & Scholze (2017) for further details about the aspectual characteristics of MOL.Cro and other Slavic micro-languages in contact situations, including BGLD.Cro.

In the category of mood the functional polysemy of the imperfect has been copied from colloquial Italian, where the imperfect has both indicative (aspecto-temporal) and counterfactual meaning. As a consequence, the MOL.Cro imperfect is competing now with the traditional *bi*-conditional and, indeed continually gaining ground, for example *dojahma* IPRF.1PL = *bihma* COND.1PL *dol* PTCP.PL 'we would have come'. A counterfactual imperfect is very unusual in other Slavic languages (Breu 2011a: 173–175).

In MOL.Cro the contact situation appears to be responsible for instances of semi-calques such as *stojima siduč* 'we are sitting' that features the MOL.Cro verb *stat* 'to stand, to be' (cf. HMLD.Cro *stati* 'to become' and *stajati* 'to stand') and a gerund. This is not an example of grammaticalisation based on Ital. PRS.PROGRESSIVE formed by means of AUX *stare* 'to be (located)' plus PRS.GERUND, but an indirect calque of Italian *siamo seduti* 'we are sitting', with the gerund (present verbal adverb) *siduč* replacing the Italian (passive) past participle *seduti*. Local Ital. Molise varieties do not contain the Italian type of PRS.PROGRESSIVE, but instead the adverb *mo* 'now' is employed as a progressive marker with a present-tense verb *mo viene* 'he is coming'. This construction is calqued in MOL.Cro as *sa gre* 'he is coming' (*sa* = *sada* 'now'). A clear case of grammaticalisation has occurred based on the Italian imminentive, formed with the help of *stare per*, lit. 'to be (located)' + 'for', meaning 'about to' + INF, eg. *sta per partire* 's/he is about to leave'. The MOL.Cro equivalent is the construction *stat za* + INF, e.g. *stoji za partit* 's/he is about to leave' (Breu 2011: 171–172).

HUN-Pom.Cro shows a simplified tense system compared with that of HMLD. Cro. From the five actively used tenses in HMLD.Cro, four are preserved: perfect and past perfect, present. The two aorist forms found in the corpus (*bi* 'be' and *reko* 'tell.AOR.1SG' 'I told/I am telling') are fossilised and have their own specific functions: the first one – in combination with an *l*-participle – marks the conditional mood as in HMLD.Cro, e.g. *bi rekel* 'be-AOR.3SG. tell.PTCP.M.SG' 'he would tell'. The second is used as a discourse marker, in this instance as a turn commencer, e.g. *Reko, pem s tobom.* 'tell'-AOR1SG, 'go'-PRS.1SG, 'with'-PREP 'you'-SG. INS. 'Actually, I will go with you'.

The verb *imati* ('to have') is exclusively used to express possessive meaning, i.e. it is not used in existential construction. That semantic gap has been filled by the special verb *jega* 'there is') and its negative form *nega* ('there is not'). Both are fossilized forms and are indeclinable occurring only in the 3SG present. The logical subject in these constructions is in GEN (Rácz 2012, Vuk research data corpus). HMLD.Cro does not have a peculiar form used for existential constructions, and instead employs *ima* ('have-PRS.3SG') and *nema* ('NEG+have-PRS.3SG') as equivalents to HUN-Pom.Cro *jega* and *nega*.

(76) **jega** tu dece
 there is here children-GEN.F.SG
 'There are children here.' (Rácz 2012: 207)

(77) **nega** tu mira
 there is.NEG here peace-GEN.M.SG
 'There is no peace here.' (Rácz 2012: 207)

An added difference compared to HMLD.Cro, is the simplified construction for marking unreal conditions in conditional sentences. The conjunctive *daj* (HMLD. Cro *da* 'if') and the indeclinable negative marker *nej* are combined with an *l*-participle. The construction is insofar simplified, as the original negative form of the verb *biti* ('be') is replaced by an indeclinable negative marker, and the main verb is always expressed by its *l*-participle form, irrespective of the temporal meaning of the construction. The tense of the main verb in HMLD.Cro changes according to the temporal reference, i.e. present unreal conditions are expressed by the present tense, past conditions by the past tense. In HUN-Pom.Cro, the main verb is always an *l*-participle, which is demonstrated in (78) and (79) below (Rácz 2012).

(78) **daj nej** tak dugo **spala,** se
 if NEG so long sleep-PST.F.SG everything
 bi mogla zgotoviti
 COND-2.SG can- PST.F.SG finish-INF
 'If you had**n't** been **sleeping** so long, you could have finished everything.'

 HMLD.Cro
 da nisi tako dugo spavala
 COMP NEG.AUX-2SG so long sleep- PST.F.SG
 mogla bi sve završiti
 can- PST.F.SG COND.2SG everything finish-INF

(79) **daj nej** vek **pil** bil bi
 if NEG always drink-PST.M.SG be-PST.M.SG COND3.SG
 trezen
 sober-NOM.M.SG
 'If he did**n't** always drink, he would be sober.'

HMLD.Cro
da	**ne**	**pije**	stalno	bio	bi	trijezan
if	NEG	drink-3SG	always	be-PST.M.SG	COND3.SG	sober- NOM.M.SG

Frequent employment of the reflexive pronoun *se* is a phenomenon typical for Kajkavian dialects. This tendency can also be observed in HUN-Pom.Cro as recorded by Rácz (2012) from whom all examples here are drawn. The reflexive pronoun is an obligatory argument in the following verbs that are non-reflexive verbs in HMLD. Cro: *plakati se* (HMLD.Cro *plakati*, 'cry'), *vučiti se* (HMLD.Cro *učiti*, 'learn'), *zmisliti se* (HMLD.Cro *izmisliti*, 'think out'), *stati se* (HMLD.Cro *ustati*, 'stand up'), *vreti se* (HMLD.Cro.Cro *vreti*, 'boil'). The reflexive pronoun *si* (self.DAT), which is a declined form of *se*, is also a frequent argument of verbs that are non-reflexive in HMLD.Cro e.g. *misliti si* (HMDL.Cro *misliti*, 'think'), *študerati si* (HMLD.Cro *razmisliti*, 'think about'), *sesti si* (HMLD.Cro *sjesti*, 'sit down'). In some particular verbs, the reflexive pronouns *se* and *si* have distinctive functions, eg. *pumoči se* (HMLD.Cro *udebljati se*, 'gain weight'), *pumoči si* (HMLD.Cro *moći*, 'to be able to do something'). In some cases, meaning differences are found with the same verb according to the presence of the reflexive marker, e.g. *prati* 'wash' (HMLD.Cro *prati*) and *prati se* 'to menstruate' (HMLD.Cro *imati menstruaciju*).

An area of interest in the contact situations is verbal aspect in which none of the other languages marks this feature in the way that Croatian, as a Slavic language, marks this. We are attentive to see if there is change occuring in this area and if there are any patterns to this. In the BGLD.Cro corpus, there are few instances of this, e.g.

(80)	ja	vam	se	**zahvalim**
	I	you-DAT	REFL	thank-PRS.**PFV**-1SG.

'I thank you'

HMLD.Cro
ja	vam	**zahvaljujem**
I	you-DAT	thank-PRS.**IPFV**-1SG

Example (80) above is from a situation in which the speaker is directly addressing the other interlocutor expressing gratitude. This requires an IPFV verb but a PFV one instead is employed. The occurrence of REFL *se* is likely to be accounted for by the German model with REFL. i.e. *ich bedanke mich* ('I thank myself' = 'I thank you'). This is of lesser interest here, more so as many non-standard varieties of HMLD.Cro feature *zahvaliti/zahvaljivati* 'to thank' also as a reflexive verb. What is of interest is that a present indicative is rendered via a PRS.PFV verb.

In the HUN.Cro corpus there are examples of change in the marking of aspect, i.e. the employment of PFV verbs in constructions that would otherwise require an IPFV verb. In example (81), the imperfective verb form is replaced by its default counterpart. The verb *dogoditi se* 'to happen' (as well as its close synonym *desiti se* 'to happen') is a telic verb, which denotes actions with an endpoint. Due to the resultative connotation of its semantic value, its default aspect is perfective. The imperfective form of the verb, *događati se* is used less frequently, i.e. when ongoing or durative telic actions are referred to. In example (81) from HUN-Bar.Cro (data from younger speakers) the two actions ('see' and 'happen') occur contemporaneously. Both have a durative meaning and the imperfective form is the expected one for both. However, for the second verb the perfective form is used.[22]

(81) oni   ne   vide   što   se   **dogodi**   na
      they   NEG   see-3PL   what.N REFL happen.**PFV-3SG** on+LOC
      dvorištu
      courtyard-LOC.M.SG
      'They do not see what is happening in the courtyard.'

Example (82) below is another instance that, at least in the vernacular of this speaker, shows fluidity in the boundary between perfective and imperfective aspect. Although there are two parallel actions in the sentence ('watching' and 'happening'), the two verbs have different aspect marking. Two imperfective verbs (*gledale* 'watch-PTCP.IPFV.F.3PL and *dešavalo* 'happen-PRS.PFV.N.3SG.') would relate to two ongoing actions in the past. However, the combination below, containing an imperfective verb *gledale* and a perfective verb *desilo* with both referring to the same contemporaneous event, contravenes the features expressed through aspect distinction. As such, this utterance appears not only 'ungrammatical' to HMLD.Cro speakers, but unclear as to whether the verbs relate to the same contemporaneous event, or to two events.

(82) i   mačke   su   **gledale**   što   **se**
      and   cat-NOM.F.PL. AUX-3PL   watch-PTCP.**IPFV**.F.3PL what   REFL
      desilo
      happen-PTCP.**PFV**.N.3SG
      '[. . .] and the cats were also watching what was happening.'

---

22 The verb *vidjeti* 'see' is biaspectual.

In a direct sense, the grammatical distinction of aspect is largely non-existent in Hungarian. (The presence of aspectual particles in Hungarian is not comparable to the typological feature of aspect that Slavic verbs possess.) This innovation cannot be directly linked to the influence of Hungarian. But the absence of a corresponding aspectual system or category in Hungarian verbs may function as an indirect influence in accounting for the above examples, i.e. aspect marking is not 'checked' as a feature of verb selection, and the 'base' form of the verb is employed as the default form. In most instances, the perfective is the 'base' form of the verb. This is the form that is used in 'generalised' meanings where information on completedness is no longer intended to be conveyed by the speaker via a particular verb form, thus the base (≈ perfective) form is used as the default. Looking further afield at contemporary diaspora language varieties, in cases where non-target aspect occurs, PFV verbs are found to be employed in constructions where otherwise IPFV verbs would be expected, e.g. ITAL.Cro (Županović Filipin, Hlavac and Piasevoli, this volume) TRS.Cro (Piasevoli, this volume) and AUS.Cro (Hlavac and Stolac, this volume).

6.2.1 Verb prefixes and verb constructions

A development in relation to verb forms is the prefixation of BGLD.Cro verbs with affixes that are Croatian equivalents of German derivational prefixes such as *her* ('to here' [towards speaker]), *hin* ('to there' [away from speaker]), *unter* ('under'), *weg* ('away') etc. In his studies of Slavic vernaculars in the Pannonian basin, Hadrovics (1958) does not discount Hungarian influence in this innovation as Hungarian has equivalent particles or adverbs that function in a way similar to German forms. Although the choice of adverbs here is clearly based on German, it is possible that a similar use of Hungarian adverbs has a reinforcing effect.

(83) *doli* ← Ger. *nieder/unter/hinunter* 'down, downwards' ← Hun. *le/alá* 'down'
gori ← Ger. *auf/hinauf/herauf* 'up, upwards' ← Hun. *fel* 'up'
kraj ← Ger. *weg* 'away' ← Hun. *elfélre* 'away';
najzad ← Ger. *zurück* 'back' ← Hun. *vissza* 'back'.

In the examples listed above, the arrows represent 'compound directionality' of influence from German, and less directly from Hungarian. Further, Szucsich (2000) observes that this innovation includes prefixes based on prepositions such as Ger. *vor* 'before, in front of' and Hun. *elő* 'forth' that yield BGLD.Cro *najpr* 'ahead', as in *si najpr zeti* 'to plan (ahead)' (Ger. *sich vornehmen*). More noticeably, this innovation can be based on *adverbs* as well, eg. Ger. *herein/hinein/ein* and Hun. *be/bele* that yield BGLD.Cro *nutar* 'inside' + verb, as in the following examples from Tornow (1992: 249):

(84) Kad se guščići izvalju, je donesemo **nutra** u toplu kuhinju
'When the goslings have hatched out, we bring them **into** the warm kitchen'

Ger. Wenn die Gänschen ausgeschlüpft sind, bringen wir sie in die warme Küche **hinein**.
HMLD.Cro Kada se guščice izlegnu, donesemo ih **u** toplu kuhinju

The following examples are from Szucsich (2000) based on Hadrovics's (1958) data:

(85) On je novine **nutar** donesao   (86) Oni su grad **nutar** zeli
'He brought **in** the newspaper.'   'They took control **of** the city.'

Ger. Er hat die Zeitung **hereingebracht**. Sie haben die Stadt **eingenommen**.
HMLD.Cro Donio je novine (**unutra**). Preuzeli su kontrolu **nad** gradom.

Verbal prefixation with an adverbial form is infrequent in most Slavic standard languages (Szucsich 2000), but is found in other Slavic languages in close contact with German, namely Upper and Lower Sorbian. Prefixes bear semantic more so than morphosyntactic features. In some cases however, there is no semantic 'addition' to the verb, as the content referential value of the Croatian stem already contains this meaning, cf. BGLD.Cro *dolidonesti* and HMLD. Croatian *donijeti* below. (The adverb *doli* means 'down', while *gori* means 'up').

(87) **doli**donesti **gori**zeti **kraj**pogledati **skroz**dojti
'bring here' 'take there' 'look away' 'come through'

Ger. **her**bringen **hin**nehmen **weg**blicken **durch**kommen
HMLD.Cro donijeti uzeti pogledati ustranu proći/prijeći

Similar constructions consisting of prefix+verb occur in HUN.Cro. These constructions, understood here as combinations of particular adverbs/prefixes + verbs, can result in new meanings that are not derivable from the original meaning of the two elements of the construction (cf. Goldberg 1995; Wasserscheidt 2015). Hungarian prefix+verb constructions are replicated in the HUN.Cro corpus. In example (88) the Hungarian construction *fent lenni* (lit. 'be up'), meaning 'being awake', is replicated through a combination of the appropriate adverb *gori*[23] and verb *biti* in Croatian.

(88)   dej   ne-j   tako   dugo   **gori**   **bila**
       if   NEG   so   long   **up**   **be**-PTCP.F.SG
       'If you **had**n't **been up** [= 'awake'] for so long [last night]!'

   HMLD.Cro
   da   nisi   **ostala**   **budna**   do   kasno
   COMP   NEG.AUX-2SG   **stay**-PTCP.F.SG **awake**-F   until   late

Example (89) below is more complex. The model construction in Hungarian *le-nézni* (literally 'down see' = 'underestimate') consists of a co-verb (*le*) and a verb (*nézni*). Similar to most co-verbs (also called verbal particles or verbal prefixes) in Hungarian, *le* has an adverbial origin, and to some extent – in combination with particular verbs – it has preserved its original spatial meaning ('down, downwards').[24] The Croatian equivalents of *le* differ from each other in their phonological form as well as in the extent of their morphological boundedness. For instance, the degree of boundedness depends on whether the prefixal *pod-* 'under-' (a bound morpheme) or adverbial *dolje* 'down' (a free morpheme) is used.

(89)   na-j   me   **dole**   **gledati**
       NEG.IMP.2SG   me-ACC   **down**-ADV   **look**-INF
       'Do not **underestimate** me!'

   HMLD.Cro
   nemoj   me   **podcjenjivati**
   NEG.IMP.2SG   me-ACC   **underestimate**-INF

Although the original Hungarian structure consists of a prefix and a verb, its replica structure in Croatian has both an adverbial *dole* 'down' and a verb *gledati* 'look'. This means that instead of a corresponding Croatian prefix, such as *pod*

---

23 A dialectal equivalent of the Standard Croatian adverb *gore* 'up'.
24 For more on aspectual function of Hungarian prefixes and their comparison with Slavic verbal prefixes, cf. Pátrovics (2002) and Hadrovics (1976).

'under' (as in the HMLD.Cro equivalent), the Hungarian construction is replicated of the adverb *dolje* being used in combination with the verb.

The replication of prefixed verbs through an adverbial construction ('adverb + verb') seems to be a common strategy not just in HUN.Cro but in BGLD.Cro, as well. There could be two reasons for this. The first one lies in the more adverbial and less aspectual character of the Hungarian and German verbal prefixes – compared with their Croatian counterparts (Pátrovics 2002; Hadrovics 1976). This facilitates the replication through an adverb + verb construction. Further, bound morphemes such as verbal prefixes, are less accessible for pattern replication (Matras 2009: 244; Romaine 1995: 64) than free lexical items (e.g. adverbs in Croatian) and this can be a further facilitator for this type of replication.[25]

In MOL.Cro, an instance of contact-induced change is the use of the *l*-participle *sta* as a variety of *bija* in the perfect of *bit* 'to be'. This use is based on the model of Ital. *essere* 'to be' and *stare* 'to be (in a place or situation)' that share a common past participle form *stato*, e.g., *Di si sta* (= *bija*) *učer?* 'Where were you yesterday?' Breu (1992: 117).

A phenomenon of 'double prefixing' verbs can be observed in HUN-Pom.Cro. The function of double prefixes is to mark added semantic value, i.e. satisfaction with the result of a particular action, or to express a higher level of intensity of the action concerned. Example (90) is an instance of double prefixing of *s-* 'around' and *po-* 'a bit' that expresses the speaker's satisfaction. In (91), the prefixes are *z-* and *ne-*. (Both examples are from Rácz 2012: 189–224).

(90) **pobral** je višne
gather-PTCP.M.SG AUX-3SG cherry-ACC.F.PL
spobral je išče i listije
gather-PTCP.M.SG AUX-3SG furthermore also leaf-ACC.N.SG
'He **gathered** the cherries and **picked** up even the leaves.' (Rácz 2012: 189)

HMLD.Cro: **pobrao** je višnje, **pokupio** je još i lišće

(91) **znebuhal** je dete kak kona
beat-PTCP.M.SG AUX3-SG child-SG.ACC like horse-ACC.SG.M
'He beat the child like a horse.'

HMLD.Cro: **istukao** je dijete kao konja

The passive exists in HMLD.Cro although its use is less frequent in spoken language compared to most Germanic languages and historically, normative authorities have

---

25 There is a Croatian [prefix + verb] construction with the same meaning, *podcijeniti*.

considered that it does not represent 'good style' in either spoken or written Croatian (Pavičić 1982). In BGLD.Cro, passive constructions occur frequently, largely under the influence of German. In Croatian, as in all Slavic languages, passive is typically marked as high register, formal and characteristic of official contexts (Pranjković 2001). In German (as in English) it is common and usually unmarked. Example (92) below is a non-active sentence featuring a reflexive construction:

(92) *imamo drugi tjedan filmski večer koji **se organizira od našeg društva**...*
 'Next week we're having a movie night **organized by our society**...'

    Ger.   Nächste Woche haben wir einen Filmabend, der **von unserem Verein organisiert wird**.
    HMLD.Cro Sljedeći tjedan imamo filmsku večer **koju organizira naše društvo**.

In MOL.Cro, besides the traditional passive, formed with the AUX *bit* 'to be', and the reflexive passive, a passive construction has developed that is based on employment of *venire* 'to come' as an AUX as in Italian, eg. *gre činjen* ('come' PRS.3SG + 'make' PASS.PTCP) 'is being made', cf. Ital. *viene fatto* ('come' PRS.3SG + 'make' PASS.PTCP). Things are complicated by the fact that in MOL.Cro, as in many other Slavic languages, *gre* does not only mean 'to come' PRS.3SG, but also 'to go'. By copying another construction of Italian, namely the andative deontic passive of the type *va fatto* ('go' PRS.3SG + 'make' PASS.PTCP) 'has to be made', a corresponding deontic passive has developed in MOL.Cro as well. As a consequence, *gre činjen* is ambiguous, in the sense that it does not only mean 'is being made', but also 'has to be made' (Breu & Makarova 2019).

6.3 Other paradigms – articles and numbers

This section presents data on the possible development of an article and forms (and agreement) of numbers. All other three contact languages, German, Italian and Hungarian, have articles. In regard to BGLD.Cro, Neweklowsky (1978) locates some incidences of an emerging *definite* article through the use of a demonstrative. But instances of such use remain comparatively rare. In Neweklowsky's (1978: 43, 231, 207) opinion, preservation of the definite vs. indefinite distinction in the adjectives of most BGLD.Cro dialects has obviated a tendency for the feature of definiteness to be expressed through means of an article, as in German. In regard to MOL.Cro an article system with the category *indefinite* article based on the form *jena* 'one' has developed and is most frequently used in its short inflected form *na*. The model for this development is the corresponding polysemy of Italian *uno*. A definite article based on demonstratives such as *ovi* 'this' or *oni* 'that' did not, however, develop in MOL.Cro. The reason for this is that there is no corresponding polysemic model: in Italian, the definite article *il* does not have any demonstrative function (Breu 2012). The development of an indefinite article before a definite one is very unusual in the languages of the world, which underlines the role of language contact in this case. Table 8 contains the declensional forms of *jena* 'one' and the indefinite pronoun *nike* 'several' (HMLD.Cro *neki*), whose use in MOL.Cro is restricted to the PL only. The plural of *jena* itself is most often used with *pluralia tantum*, for example *jene* NOM.PL. Both long forms (LF) and short forms (SF) are given, with the latter group's use restricted to attributive functions, preceding a noun. As an equivalent indefinite article, only unstressed forms are used. In order to show the exact pronunciation including vowel quantity and whispered vowels (marked by a diacritic ring underneath), this table is given with phonetic transcription (to show grammatical oppositions like *jéna* NOM.SG.M: *jé:nḁ* NOM.SG.F). The accute accent refers to rising pitch, in *nike* stress is on the first syllable with unmarked/falling pitch.

Table 8: Full paradigm of *jena* 'one' as an indefinite article in MOL.Cro.

	M.SG		F.SG		N.SG		M/F.PL	
	LF	SF	LF	SF	LF	SF	LF	PRON.
NOM	jéna	na	jé:nḁ	na	jéna	na	jé:ne̥'	nike
GEN	jén(o)ga	–	jéne	–	–	–	jén(i)hi	nikihi
DAT	jén(o)mu	–	jé:nu̥	–	–	–	jén(i)mi	nikimi
ACC	= N./G.	na	jé:nu̥	nu	jéna	na	je:ne̥	= N./G.
INS	jén(i)me	–	jéno:m	–	–	–	jén(i)mi	nikihi

Besides the existence of a short form and the total loss of the original -*d*- in the stem (cf. HMLD.Cro *jedn*-) some long forms bear unexpected suffix markers. For example, the masculine NOM.SG form is *jéna* (with a full -*a*), while the feminine NOM.SG form is *jé:nḁ* (with a whispered -*ḁ*, causing lengthening of the stressed vowel). The merger of the DAT.SG.F. and ACC.SG.F (*jé:nu̥*) occurs here as in other inflected categories in the Kruč dialect of MOL.Cro. In a similar way, the original NOM.PL forms have been substituted by ACC.PL. Despite the loss of the neuter in nouns, this gender is maintained in the singular when referring to substantivised adjectives and adverbs. Especially with substantivised adjectives, showing an original long -*o*, the neuter often preserves the original pronunciation that has not undergone phonetic change to -*a* ('akanje'), e.g. *na mala* N 'a little', *jeno dobro* N 'a good (thing)'.

Influence from Molise Italian on the MOL.Cro indefinite article is evident through the model of a short form *nu, na* (that does not exist in Standard Italian), as shown in Table 9 below. The term 'independent' used in Table 9 refers to the non-attributive, substantivised use of the number.

Table 9: Morphology of the indefinite article in Italian, Molise Italian and MOL.Cro.

	Attributive		Independent	
	MASC.	FEM.	MASC.	FEM.
Standard Italian	uno, un	una, un'	uno	una
Molise Italian	nu, n'	na, n'	unə	unə
MOL.Cro	jena, na	jena, na	jena	jena

As the MOL.Cro indefinite article exactly follows the usage of Italian *uno*, its absence is always interpreted as a definite article, for example *nu hižu* ACC.SG.F 'a house': *hižu* ACC.SG.F 'the house'. In this way a definite "zero article" Ø came into being, which in juxtaposition with the indefinite article forms a complete system, the more so as in Italian the definite article is also used in generic contexts and with mass nouns, e.g. *il latte* = MOL.Cro *mblika* NOM.SG 'milk'. Examples of the use of the MOL.Cro indef. article are given below, together with equivalent forms from Italian and HMLD.Cro (Breu 2012: 283–301):

(93) *Ja jiskam **na** mičicij.*
'I am looking for **a** friend (of mine).'
Cerco **un** amico.
Tražim Ø prijatelja.

(94) *Ja ču jimat **na** mičicij.*
'I would like to have **a** (any) friend.'
Voglio avere **un** amico.
Volio bih imati Ø prijatelja.

(95) *Si ta čuje **na** polidzjot, ta mčč pržuna.*
'If **a** (any) policeman hears you, he will lock you up.'
Se ti sente **un** poliziotto, ti mette in prigione.
Ako te čuje Ø policajac, stavit će te u zatvor.

(96) *Zov **na** medik!*
'Call **a** doctor!'
Chiama **un** medico!
Zovi Ø doktora!

Examples of the use of *jedan* performing the function of an article-like attributive are also found in other varieties of heritage Croatian, e.g. TRS.Cro (see Piasevoli, this volume), CAN.Cro (see Petrović, this volume), AUS.Cro (see Hlavac and Stolac, this volume) and ARG.Cro (see Skelin Horvat, Musulin and Blažević, this volume).

Apart from conjunctions, particles and prepositions mentioned in sections 3 and 6.2.1 above, another category of borrowings in MOL.Cro are numbers. In combination with nouns of Slavic origin and with fully integrated loanwords, the numbers from 1 to 4 are used only in their Croatian-based form, i.e. *jena, dva/dvi, tri, četar* 'one, two, three, four'. Numbers containing *jena* are declined, as are those with *dva/dvi* (*dvahi/dvihi, dvami/dvimi*) and *tri* (*trihi, trimi*). From *četar* onwards inflection does not usually occur (Breu 2013b: 16–17), with the exception of the (numeral) nouns *stotina* 'hundred' and *miljar* 'thousand'. The corresponding borrowings from the Molise Italian dialect, i.e. *nu, duj, tre, kvatr* 'one, two, three, four' only combine with morphologically non-integrated loanwords. In contrast, forms from 5 to 10 and for 100 can be drawn from either language, with integrated forms borrowed from Italian predominating, i.e. *čing, sèj, sèt, òt, nòv, dijač, čjend* 'five, six, seven, eight, nine, ten, hundred' rather than *pet, šest, sedam, osam, devet, deset, stotina*. With the exception of *stotina* 'hundred', beyond 10 only Romance-based forms are used, e.g. *unič* (cf. Ital. *undici*), *dudič, tridič* (~*tredič*), *kvatordič, kvinič, sidič* (~*sedič*), *dičasèt, dičòt* (~*dičidot*), *dičinòv, vind* (cf. Ital. *venti*), *vindòt* (cf. Ital. *ventotto*), *trendun* (cf. Ital. *trentuno*) 'eleven, twelve, thirteen, fourteen, fifteen, sixteen, seventeen, eighteen, nineteen, twenty, twenty-eight, thirty-one' (Breu 2013b).

6.4 Word order

This section examines changes in word order patterns of conjunctions, adverbials, clitics, attributive adjectives and negative forms. In contrast to Croatian, the position of the conjunction *aber* 'but' in German sentences is almost arbitrary. It can appear between the subject and predicate as a coordinating conjunction, at the beginning of a coordinative sentence, between the predicate and adverbial, as well as in other places. German *aber* can also function as an intensifier. In BGLD.Cro we locate instances in which the Croatian equivalent *ali* 'but' functions more as an intensifier than as a contrasting linking word, and where it occurs in places unknown in HMLD.Cro. In HMLD.Cro *ali* can either occur at the beginning of a main clause or at the beginning of an adversative clause, and as a coordinating conjunction only. Example (97) contains *ali* as an adverbial intensifier positioned between a modal and a main verb:

(97) *Moram **ali** priznati da me je i dobra plaća veselila.*
  'I have to admit **though** that the good salary made me happy.'
  Ich muss **aber** zugeben, dass ich mich über das gute Gehalt gefreut habe.
  Međutim moram priznati da me i dobra plaća veselila.

Verb-final influence from German is apparent in the following example where an infinitive clause with a verb in clause-final position concludes the utterance. In HMLD.Cro, these constituents are not discontinuous but adjacent to each other:

(98) *Lipo od njih, da su nas došli iz takove daljine* **pohodit**.
 'It's nice of them that they travelled so far to **visit** us.'
 Es ist schön von ihnen, dass sie von so weit gekommen sind um uns **zu besuchen**.
 Lijepo od njih što su nas došli **posjetiti** izdaleka. (Sučić et al. 2003: 595)

In German subordinate clauses, the main verb is in final position. The same word order is shown in the following example in BGLD.Cro. (The calque based on Ger. *es liegt an* 'it lies on' = 'it is attributable to' is evident here – cf. 4.4.4)

(99) *Vindar bi rado znao, kaj to* **more ležati**.
 'But I would like to know what could be the cause of that.'
 Aber ich würde gerne wissen . . . . woran das **liegen kann**.
 Ali bih rado znao **zašto** je to tako? (Sučić et al. 2003: 595)

In spoken varieties of BGLD.Cro, there are examples of numerals given in the order as they are given in German, eg:

(100) *jedanidvadeset* *petipedeset*
 'one-and-twenty' 'five-and-fifty'
 einundzwanzig fünfundfünfzig

This pre-posing of single-digit numbers in front of values between twenty and ninety-nine is adopted from German, but was not a feature included in the standardisation of BGLD.Cro. Verbal short forms or clitics, e.g. *ću* (will-FUT. AUX1SG – short form) instead of *hoću* (will-FUT.AUX.1SG – long form), or *si* (be-COP/ AUX.2SG – short form) instead of *jesi* (be-COP/AUX.2SG – long form) can appear in initial position. This is a feature shared with some Čakavian and Kajkavian dialects and its occurrence is likely to be due to this influence.

(101) **ćete** mi ga dati
 FUT.AUX-2PL me-DAT it-ACC give-INF
 '**Will** you give it to me?'

 HMLD.Cro: **hoćete** mi ga dati?

(102) **si**   i   **ti**   sporazumna
       be-2SG and   you-2SG agreed-ADJ.SG.F
       '**Are** you in agreement too?'

   HMLD.Cro: **Jesi** li i ti suglasna?

In standard Croatian, clitic forms cannot occur in initial position and their position, immediately[26] or anywhere after initial position, is determined hierarchically according to the following word order rules:

particle	AUX	DAT	ACC/GEN	REFL	3SG.AUX
1	2	3	4	5	6

This ordering of clitic is generally followed in most non-standard varieties of HMLD.Cro, as it is across most Slavic languages (Franks & King 2000). At the same time, many non-standard varieties allow clitic placement in initial position. To return to BGLD.Cro, Browne (2014) reports that while first and second person ACC and GEN clitics precede the reflexive, third person ACC and GEN clitics can *follow* the reflexive:

(103a) boju   **me**   **se**
        fear-3PL   me-GEN   REFL
        'They fear me'
        vs.

(103b) boju   **se**   **ga**[27]
        fear-3PL   REFL   him-GEN
        'They fear him.'

Browne (2014: 91) describes pronoun clitic placement *after* a reflexive as uncharacteristic of Slavic languages in general, including non-standard varieties. He addresses the possible influence of local German varieties, namely *Burgenlän-*

---

26 In sentences with clitics, the 'obligatory' placement of a clitic in second position has become a feature of high register standard Croatian. For example, the sentence *my student found him* in high register standard Croatian is *moj ga je student našao* ('my him-ACC has-3.SG student found'), while in a less marked sentence, a clitic is not placed between the initial possessive pronoun and the noun and the word order is *moj student ga je našao* ('my student him-ACC has-3SG found') (Browne 2014).

27 Browne (2014) adds that the 3SG.GEN clitic can also precede the REFL, i.e. boju ga se.

disch (the east central Bavarian/Austrian dialect spoken in Burgenland) that has clitic pronouns, as opposed to standard German. However, Browne (2014: 92) is hesitant to attribute this innovation in BGLD.Cro to the local German variety as this variety does not distinguish reflexive pronouns from non-reflexive pronouns in that way that Slavic languages do.

In MOL.Cro the position of clitics is similar to that in Italian. A prohibition of clitics in initial position does not exist, e.g. *sa mu ga da* (AUX.1SG him-DAT it-ACC give-PTCP.SG.M) 'I gave it to him'. In this sentence, there are three clitics at the very beginning that all precede the verb (Breu 2019: 417–420). Another word order innovation is the contact-induced positioning of adjectival attributes *after* the noun. Post-positioning of adjectival attributes is allowable in HMLD.Cro but is restricted to 'poetic' or stylistically marked texts. In MOL.Cro post-positioning of attributive adjectives as in the examples: *na hiža stara* 'a house old', *tartuf crni* 'the truffle black', and *na stvara velka* 'a thing big' is not marked and occurs commonly and much more frequently than pre-positioning. The different positions of the attributes lead in some cases to oppositions of the type *je na **brižna** žena* 'she is a poor woman' (pitiable, because something awful has happened to her) vs. *je na žena **brižna**.* 'she is a poor woman' (she has no money) as in Italian: *è una **povera** donna* vs. *è una donna **povera***; similarly, *na **dobri** ljud* 'a good man' (good character) vs. *na ljud **dobri*** 'a talented man' (Breu 2019: 416–417). Word order innovations can relate to the position of NEG particles in clauses. In regard to HUN.Cro, the word order rules of Hungarian negative sentences are often replicated in contact varieties. In Hungarian both focus and background negation are possible (Kiss 2011), with this rule often applying to HUN.Cro. What this means is that instead of negating the verb, which is the only option in HMLD.Cro, other elements, such as the adverb in example (104) or the sentence object in example (105) are negated. In (104) and (105), these NEG particles function as the *only* markers of negation in these sentences.

(104) **ne** **često** *koristim* *onaj* *standardni*
NEG **often** use-1SG that-ACC.M.SG standard-ACC.M.SG
jezik
language-ACC.SG
'I hardly speak the standard [...] language.'

HMLD.Cro
ne koristim **često** standardni jezik
NEG use.PRS.1SG **often** standard-ACC.M.SG language-ACC.M.SG

(105) **ne   to   pitam**
      NEG   that ask-1SG
      'I am not asking that [but something else]!'

   HMLD.Cro
   ne   pitam   to
   NEG   ask-1SG that

Instances of change in word order, including leftward fronting of clitics, are recorded in some contemporary diaspora varieties of Croatian, e.g. TRS.Cro (Piasevoli, this volume), USA.Cro (Jutronić, this volume), CAN.Cro (Petrović, this volume).

6.5 Syntactic and semantic calques

This section contains examples of syntactic constructions or semantic fields replicated in a contact variety of Croatian from other-language models. In BGLD.Cro, there are constructions that mirror German verb+preposition constructions, where a verb form is employed that matches the collocational or semantic features of German. In example (106) below, employment of *na* 'on' following *čekati* 'to wait' is based on the German model:

(106) *stalno **čeka na** svoju mamu*
      'she is always **waiting for** her mum'

   Ger.   ständig **wartet sie auf** ihre Mutti
   HMLD.Cro   stalno **čeka** svoju mamu.

The equivalent HMLD.Cro does not require a preposition. Other examples from BGLD.Cro are: *ja se veselim **na** Zagreb* 'I am looking forward **to** Zagreb', cf. Ger. ich freue mich schon **auf** Zagreb, HMLD.Cro radujem se dolasku u Zagreb; and *oduševljen sam **od** toga* 'I'm delighted **about** it', cf. Ger. ich bin **davon** begeistert, HMLD.Cro oduševljen sam time.

The following examples are instances of replications, which have a direct or indirect effect on the clause structure. Direct change is understood here as replication of complete clause templates. In contrast to this, indirect change means some kind of clause restructuring, due to a former (or parallel) contact-induced grammaticalisation of one of the clause constituents. The following examples (107b) and (108b) bear a new pattern for marking indefiniteness – *ima* ('have-PRS.3SG')

+ REL.PRON + verb – that is emerging. The sentences presented below are not comprehensible to speakers of HMLD.Cro, but they can still be frequently heard among speakers of HUN-Bar.Cro. These examples represent the replication of the corresponding, widely used Hungarian structure, *van* 'be' + REL.PRON (+ verb). Two Hungarian sentences, (107a) and (108a) taken from the Hungarian-English parallel corpus Hunglish.hu (n.d.) demonstrate this construction:

(107a) *van*   *aki*   *folytatja*   *van*   *aki*
       be-PRS.3SG   who-3SG   continue-PRS.3SG   be-3SG   who-3SG
       képtelen   *rá*
       incapable-SG   it-SUBL
       '**Some** continue [to do something]; **some** are incapable of it.'

(108a) *van*   *amikor*   *azt*   *jelenti*   *az*   *illető*   *meghalt*
       be-PRS.3SG   when   it-ACC   mean-PRS.3SG   the   person   die-PST.3SG
       '**Sometimes** it means somebody's dead.'

Replica sentences below, numbered here as (107b) and (108b), consist of the Croatian verb *imati* 'to have', which in existential constructions performs a function similar to Hungarian *van* 'to be'. However, in contrast to Hungarian *van*, the Croatian verb *imati* cannot be combined with a relative clause in HMLD.Cro without the presence of an overt subject.[28] The replica structure has a function similar to that of the indefinite pronouns: *ima + tko = netko/neki* 'somebody', *ima + kad* 'there is + when' = *katkad/ponekad/nekad* 'sometimes' etc.[29]

(107b) ***ima***   *tko*   *priča,*   ***ima***   *tko*   *ne*
       have-3SG   **who** speak-3SG   have-3SG   **who**   NEG
       '**Some of them** speak a little bit, **some of them** not at all.'

---

28 Sentences such as *Ima ljudi koji pričaju* (have-PRS.3.SG. people-GEN.M.PL who-M.PL.N. speak-PRS.3.PL.; 'There are people who speak [...]'). i.e. sentences with an overt logical (not syntactic) subject in the main clause are possible in contemporary Croatian.

29 Wasserscheidt (2015) also analyses these structures claiming that the first one has a similar corresponding structure with the additional conjunction *da* 'that' inserted between the relative pronoun and the verb. However, despite the formal similarities that structure has a different function: it refers to somebody's existence, but has no pronominal meaning. In the sentence *ima tko da priča* 'there is somebody who can speak', the speaker's existence is additionally emphasised, and not relativized, as in (107b) and (108b) above.

(108b) **ima**   **kad**   *mađarski*   **ima**   **kad**
        have-PRS.3SG when   Hungarian-ADV   have-PRS.3SG when
        hrvatski.
        Croatian-ADV
        '**Sometimes** Hungarian, **sometimes** Croatian.'

There are new use patterns for the connectors *zato* 'therefore', *onda* 'then' and *ne da* 'so that + NEG.' Examples (109) and (110) are instances of a so-called extension across categories (Heine & Kuteva 2005: 54), which refers to an extension of the grammatical function of particular words in the replica language, modelled on a corresponding multifunctional role of their counterparts in the model language. In example (109), the connector *zato*, which is a causative adverb in Croatian, serves as a connector in concessive clauses; this is a function it does not have in HMLD.Cro. Possible concessive conjunctions in standard HMLD.Cro are *opet* 'again', 'still', *ali* 'but' and *ipak* 'despite', 'still' (Silić & Pranjković 2007: 349). The corresponding Hungarian model word *azért* 'therefore' has the same adverbial function, as *zato* in contemporary HMLD.Cro, and at the same time it can serve as a connector in concessive clauses. The reason for this is that it can also be a connector in concessive sentences.[30]

(109)   **zato**   *fali*   *ova*   *sredina*
        though   miss-PRS.3SG   this-NOM.F.SG   community-NOM.F.SG
        '**Nevertheless** I miss this community.'

        HMLD.Cro
        ipak   *mi*   *nedostaje*   *ova*   *sredina*
        though   me-DAT   miss-PRS.3SG   this-NOM.F.SG   community-NOM.F.SG

A similar occurrence is found in the following example: the function of the Croatian temporal conjunction *onda* 'when', 'then' is extended. This occurs through modelling on the polyfunctional character of the corresponding Hungarian conjunction *akkor* 'then', which is also used as a conditional conjunction.[31]

---

[30] E.g. *azért szép!* (lit. 'because beautiful.') which means 'though she is beautiful!'
[31] In standard HMLD.Cro, the order of clauses in conditional sentences is the other way around: the subordinate clause is in the first place, and it is invoked by the conjunctions *ako* 'if', *ukoliko* 'in as much as', 'in so far as', *kada* 'when'. The main clause comes after the subordinate one with no conjunction between them (Silić & Pranjković 2007: 348–350).

(110) **onda** bih   imala   pozitivno   mišljenje
      then COND.1SG have.PTCP.F.SG positive-ACC.N.SG opinion-ACC.N.SG
      'I would have positive opinion about them, **if** [...]'

HMLD.Cro
imala   bih   pozitivno   mišljenje
have.PTCP.F.SG   COND.1SG positive-ACC.N.SG   opinion-ACC N.SG
ako/ukoliko
if/in as much

The function of the Hungarian conjunction *nemhogy* (lit. 'not that', meaning 'instead of') – which invokes the subordinate clause in unreal conditional sentences – is grammaticalized in HUN.Cro through a compound conjunction *ne + da/kaj* ('NEG + COMP/WHAT [INTERROG. PRONOUN]') that is modelled on the Hungarian structure as shown in example (111) below. Further, the Hungarian model structure *nemhogy* + verb_cond is completely replicated. The conjunction *ne kaj* (Hun. *nemhogy* 'instead of') invokes a counterfactual condition and is expressed via a verb in conditional mood.[32]

(111) **ne kaj**   bi   bili   pre   mene
      not that   COND.3PL   be.PTCP.M.PL   before+GEN   me-GEN
      'instead of being before me [...]'

HMLD.Cro
umjesto da   budu   prije   mene
instead   COMP   be-PRS.3PL   before+GEN   me-GEN

Elsewhere, examples of an extended use of the conjunction complementiser *da* 'that' are recorded. This occurs as the Hungarian complementizer *hogy* 'that' (HMLD.Cro *da*) can be connected with other elements – mostly adverbs and relative pronouns – in subordinate clauses in Hungarian (Kenesei, Vago & Fenyvesi 1998; Kiss 2002). Due to the high frequency of combined complementizers in Hungarian,[33] in HUN.Cro, the equivalent conjunction *da* is used and combined with relative pronouns (examples 112 and 113) in object clauses in the same way that *hogy* 'that/what' is in Hungarian.

---

[32] In standard HMLD.Cro, conterfactual conditions are invoked by the conjunction *da* 'that', and the verb is in the indicative mood in either present or in one of the past tenses.
[33] E.g. *Tudom,* **hogy mit** *csináltál.* lit. I know **that what** you have done', meaning: 'I know what have you done.'

(112) mogu   im   reći   **da**   **što**   treba
      can-PRS.1SG them-DAT tell-INF that-COMP what-SG.ACC need-PRS.3SG
      'I can tell them [**that**] **what** is needed.'

   HMLD.Cro
   mogu   im   reći   **što**   treba
   can-PRS.1SG them-DAT tell-INF what-SG.NOM need-PRS.3SG

A similar example comes from Rácz (2012: 259) from HUN-Pom.Cro-speakers:

(113) pitala   sam   ju   **da**   **de**   dela
      ask-PTC-F-SG AUX-1SG she.ACC that-COMP where work-PRS.3SG
      'I asked her [**that**] **where** she works'

   HMLD.Cro
   pitala   sam   je   **gdje**   radi
   ask-PTCP.F.SG AUX.1SG her-ACC where work-PRS.3SG

At the syntactic level there are distinctive features that illustrate the influence of German. The most obvious is the usage of commas in subordinate clauses according to the rules of German grammar and models. This is closely connected to the regular occurrence of the finite verb at the end of a clause.

(114) *što je za mene tako super **je**, da se brzo uživim i da se onda ćutim doma...*
      'it **is** great for me that I can quickly relax and that I started to feel like I'm at home...'

   Ger.:   was für mich so super **ist,** dass ich mich schnell einleben kann und mich wie zu Hause fühlen.
   HMLD.Cro meni **je** super jer se brzo uživim i počnem se osjećati kao kod kuće.

This is not only an example of a finite verb at the end of a subordinate clause, but also of the usage of a typical German structure: *Was für mich so super ist...*

We now shift our attention to semantic calques. In the following example, the German verb *leiden* 'suffer' influences selection of *trpi* 'suffer/tolerate-3SG'. German *leiden*, usually occuring with a NEG can precede objects that are human or non-human, e.g. *Ich kann ihn/das nicht leiden* 'I can't suffer him/it'; while the combination *leiden an* ('suffer from') can precede designations of illnesses, e.g. *Sie leidet an Krebs* 'She's suffering from cancer'. In HMLD.Cro, *trpjeti* 'to tolerate' is used for the first function, while *patiti* 'to suffer' is used intransitively or with a preposition *patiti od* 'suffer from' and an illness designation. We classify example (115) as both a syntactic and semantic calque as the preposition employed is also based on the German model and simultaneously there is semantic transference of the broader semantic features of German *leiden* that are transferred onto *trpjeti*.

(115) u Austriji **trpi** 800.000 ljudi **na migreni**
in Austria 800,000 people **suffer from** migraine.

in Österreich **leiden** 800.000 Menschen **an** Migräne.
HMLD.Cro U Austriji 800.000 ljudi **pati od** migrene.

Instances of syntactic calques occur in various diaspora varieties of Croatian, e.g. AUT.Cro (Ščukanec, this volume), ITAL.Cro (Županović Filipin, Hlavac and Piasevoli, this volume) TRS.Cro (Piasevoli, this volume), USA.Cro (Jutronić, this volume) and AUS.Cro (Hlavac and Stolac, this volume).

7 Conclusion

This chapter set out to provide a description of contact linguistic features present in BGLD.Cro, MOL.Cro and HUN.Cro. The first two have been physically dislocated from HMLD.Cro for approx. 500 years. In the case of MOL.Cro this has resulted in a very high percentage of borrowings and semantic calques in the lexicon and there are contact-induced structural developments in all fields of grammar. Alongside a substantial number of imported items that can be described as 'matter borrowing', we can also observe 'pattern borrowing', i.e. lexico-semantic and syntactic frames that are borrowed into minority Croatian (Matras and Sakel 2007). The transfer of polysemies present in Italian model varieties has been the most important factor for the creation of new oppositions in the replica system or, at least, new functions for existing grammatical forms. In some cases, MOL.Cro may have had a predisposition for some of these changes, as could be argued in view of initial stages of such developments in the overall history of Croatian or especially in its Dalmatian dialects. Nevertheless, it has been the situation of total language contact over the last 500 years that has made MOL.Cro in many respects behave more like a Romance than a Slavic variety. There are, however, also many areas, such as verbal aspect, the case system (except for the locative), or the formation of the perfect, in which it has remained very similar to today's HMLD.Cro.

In regard to the lexicon, archaic forms rarely used in HMLD.Cro varieties exist alongside those adopted from German, (Molise) Italian and Hungarian. The semantic fields and contexts that these relate to are varied, ranging from physical realia, designations used in public life to forms spread by various media and beyond. Transfers are almost always integrated, phonologically and/or morphologically. For nouns, this means that assignment to a Croatian gender usually occurs based on the phonotactic form of the transfer, in particular its word-final structure. Those ending in a consonant are usually allocated masculine gender and this usually overrides the influence of the gender of an equivalent Croatian form. The word-final ending -*a* of feminine transfers from Italian usually leads to these forms remaining feminine in MOL.Cro. Transfers in MOL.Cro can undergo word-final vowel -*o* deletion to facilitate integration, while in HUN.Cro this ending is retained but transfers are still allocated masculine gender. Overall, the phonotactic structure of loanwords, rather than the gender of the loanword in the donor language is likely to determine gender allocation in BGLD.Cro and HUN.Cro. In MOL.Cro the gender of Italian equivalents is influential and can lead either to addition of a suffix, -*a*, or to FEM.II nouns sometimes becoming masculine.

Verbs are less frequently borrowed but some regularities are apparent: Italian -*are* verbs are integrated as -*at* MOL.Cro verbs, while Italian -*ire* and -*ere* verbs bear the MOL.Cro -*it* verbal suffix. Conspicuous in the BGLD.Cro data are German separable verbs with particles that appear to be used inseparably in BGLD.Cro, e.g. *ajnkafati* ← *einkaufen* 'to go shopping' – *idem nešto ajnkafati* 'I'm going to go shopping'. Their use is very often restricted to verbs occurring in second position following modals or other commonly used verbs such as *ići* 'to go' and they commonly appear as infinitive forms only. In contrast, transfers based on German verb + adverb construction, e.g. *krajpogledati* ← *wegblicken* 'look away' can occur as two separate items. Discourse markers (e.g. *virklji* ← *wirklich*), high-frequency adverbs (e.g. *alora* ← *allora*) and exclamations (e.g. *jaj ištenem* ← *istenem*) are reported in all three varieties. Instances occur in which these co-occur additively to domestic (Croatian) equivalents as semantically distinct 'supplements', or even where little distinction exists between the two and idiolectal or context-specific features determine their occurrence, e.g. MOL.Cro *p'ke* ← *perché* vs. *aje-ka* 'because'.

Phraseological and semantic calques abound in the three varieties. This is unsurprising, but perhaps a feature worthy of attention as one that is present and often very widespread in long-standing contact situations. Studies of bi- or multi-lingual speech communities of a more recent vintage (e.g. Gregor 2003; Goldbach 2005) record code-switching (ie. lexical sequences of one- or multi-word insertions to longer stretches or alternations) as a statistically more prominent contact linguistic phenomenon than calques. To be sure, code-switches are recorded in corpora that describe all three varieties. But as a proportion of language contact phenomenon that occur in these long-standing, bi- or multilingual settings, code-switching is not a conspicuous or frequent feature. This is of particular note, especially where code-switching in more recent, bi- or multilingual settings appears to be reported as a frequent feature, eg. Russian-German bilinguals in Berlin (Goldbach 2005); Kinyarwanda-French bilinguals in Belgium (Gafaranga 2007), and where one may have the supposition that in longer-standing settings, the incidence of code-switching would be even greater. Habitual code-switching need not be but is commonly a precursor to language shift. The three settings studied here are long-standing contact situations in which the speech community members here have, over time, been able to withstand language shift. Therefore, code-switching does *not* figure as a common occurrence in these settings, as the presence of this would likely have led to their abandonment of the minority languages in the first place. So, the paucity of code-switching amongst these groups of 'maintainers' is evidence that code-switching often can be a precursor to shift. In a related sense, the employment of phraseological calques and loan translations may be a strategy to obviate code-switching – this was an observation made by Clyne (2003) in relation to transposed situations. Amongst the speakers of these minority languages, features other than code-switching are more prominent.

Structural comparison reveals the following: in the nominal paradigm, BGLD. Cro shows few differences compared to HMLD.Cro. In part this is due to the standardisation of a BGLD.Cro literary language in which models from HMLD.Cro were drawn on. MOL.Cro has a reduced, two-gender system for nouns and distinct forms for three or four of the cases, depending on number or case i.e. loss of LOC and VOC. (The three-gender distinction is still retained for adjectives.) The effect of this is that in MOL.Cro, the distinction between location and motion has been lost, with the ACC performing both functions. All INS forms in MOL.Cro are comitative ones requiring use of the preposition *s* 'with'. The preposition *do*+GEN 'of' (used differently from HMLD in which *do* is a spatial and temporal preposition meaning 'up to') is also used in possessive GEN constructions, although its use is not obligatory in all GEN constructions. Non-distinction of animate and inanimate masculine nouns occurs in MOL. Cro (with some exceptions involving GEN case forms). Non-distinction of animate and inanimate masculine nouns in DIR.OBJ position occurs also in HUN-Pom.Cro except after some prepositions such as *po* ('for', i.e. 'to fetch for') or *za* ('for', i.e. 'awarded to'). At the same time, HUN-Pom.Cro retains distinct forms for DAT, LOC and INS in the PL, which have undergone syncretism in HMLD.Cro.

Multi-item attributive constructions occur in BGLD.Cro, modelled on German, while in MOL.Cro, comparatives and superlatives are mostly analytic constructions with *veča* 'more' preceding the adjective or adverb, modelled on the function of

Ital. *più*. In the same way, in HUN-Pom.Cro *bole* 'better' can be employed as a comparative marker, as can the equivalent superlative *najbole* 'best' along with suffix-marked comparatives and prefix- and suffix-marked superlatives.

Non-congruence between subject and verb morphology can occur in BGLD. Cro and HUN.Cro. In the latter, non-congruence can occur between subjects with a grammatical gender that is different from the natural gender of the subject. (This phenomenon occurs in HMLD.Cro as well.) More conspicuous are SG subjects with PL predicates that occur in both BGLD.Cro and HUN.Cro, albeit in a small number of instances. These constructions occur as an equally-marked phenomenon in some non-standard varieties of HMLD.Cro spoken in northern Croatia.

A more paragidimatic change is the development of a de-obligative future in MOL.Cro that employs *jimat* 'to have, must', based on the model of southern Italian *avé* that has the function of a future referring to necessary or planned states of affairs. This has resulted in a narrowing of the meaning of conventional future constructed via *tit* 'will, to want' to denote the probability of the future action. Contact with Italian also accounts for the retention or more widespread use of the past perfect compared to HMLD.Cro. The form *bi* is combined with, and in some cases even infixed into the AUX *bit* 'to be'. The imperfect (but not the aorist) is fully retained in MOL.Cro, in contrast to HMDL.Cro. The opposite has occurred in HUN-Pom.Cro. with retention of perfect, past perfect, present and loss of the aorist as a full tense. Elsewhere in HUN-Pom.Cro, the future II is the only tense used to refer to future actions.

Instances are recorded in BGLD.Cro and HUN-Bar.Cro in which perfective verbs are used in contextual meanings that refer to ongoing or durative actions that otherwise require imperfective verbs. Where non-target use of aspectual forms occurs, it is perfective verbs that are employed in place of imperfective verbs, not vice versa.

'Double' prefixes are recorded in HUN.Cro in which two verbal prefixes mark a verb not only as perfective but with specific semantic meaning. Croatian equivalents of German and Hungarian (separable) verb particles are combined with Croatian verbs resulting in semantically 'double-marked' verb constructions, e.g. *dolidonesti* 'bring here' (Ger. *herbringen*) or *gori biti* 'stay up' (Hun. *fent lenni*). In regard to the situation of HUN.Cro, despite the fact that aspect (and gender) do not have a corresponding morphologically marked category in the dominant Hungarian language,[34] the increased insecurity in aspect (and gender) marking

---

[34] By claiming that there is no corresponding aspect in Hungarian, we mean that there is no morphologically marked aspect. However, it does not mean that perfective and imperfective aspectual meanings are non-existent in Hungarian (see Dahl 1985, Csirmaz 2003).

in the speech of younger speakers of HUN.Cro cannot be clearly attributed to the influence of Hungarian. The same tendencies can be detected in other (diaspora) contact situations with languages both overtly marking gender and/or some kind of aspect distinctions (Montrul 2002; Polinsky 2008; Benmamoun, Montrul & Polinksy 2013; Scontras, Fuchs & Polinksy 2015; Schwartz et al. 2015).

Conspicuous is the development of an indefinite article in MOL.Cro, based on the form for 'one', *jena*, usually produced in its shortened form *na*. In line with MOL.Cro adjectives, there are forms for all three genders. Word order changes occur at sentence level in BGLD.Cro with rightward movement of non-finite verbs and in the ordering of components in compound numerals such as *jedanidvadeset* 'one-and-twenty' (Ger. *einundzwanzig*). In MOL.Cro the position of the clitics has adapted to the verb-centred model of Italian. Examples of calques of syntactic structures from the respective donor languages are also recorded.

References

Adamou, Evangelia, Walter Breu, George Drettas & Lenka Scholze. 2013. Elektronische Datenbank bedrohter slavischer Varietäten in nichtslavophonen Ländern Europas (Deutschland – Italien – Österreich – Griechenland). https://pangloss.cnrs.fr/corpus?lang=en&mode=pro (accessed 03/03/2021)

Adamou, Evangelia, Walter Breu, Lenka Scholze & Rachel Xingjia Shen. 2016. Borrowing and contact intensity: a corpus-driven approach from four Slavic minority languages. *Journal of Language Contact*, 9(3). 513–542.

Babić, Stjepan. 1998. *Sročnost u hrvatskome književnome jeziku* [Agreement in the Croatian literary language] Zagreb: Matica hrvatska.

Barics, Ernő, István Blazsetin, György Frankovics & Dénes Sokcsevits. 1998. *Magyarországi horvátok* [Croats in Hungary]. Budapest: Körtánc füzetek.

Barić, Ernest. 2006. *Rode, a jezik? Radovi iz jezikoslovne kroatistike* [Brother, and what about the language? Studies from the field of Croatian linguistics]. Pečuh/Pécs: Znanstveni zavod Hrvata u Mađarskoj.

Benčić, Nikolaus. 1972. Abriß der geschichtlichen Entwicklung der burgenländisch-kroatischen Schriftsprache. *Wiener Slavistisches Jahrbuch* 17. 15–28.

Benčić, Nikola, Agnjica Csenar-Schuster, Zorka Kinda-Berlaković, Jelka Koschat, Ludvig Kuzmić, Mijo Lončarić, Gerhard Neweklowsky, Ivan Rotter, Ivo Sučić, Joško Vlašić, Sanja Vulić & Marija Znika. 2003. *Gramatika gradišćanskohrvatskoga jezika* [Grammar of the Burgenland Croatian language]. Željezno-Eisenstadt: Znanstveni institut Gradišćanskih Hrvatov.

Bencsics, Nikolaus, Božidar Finka, Antun Šojat, Josef Vlasits & Stefan Zvonarich (eds.). 1982. *Deutsch-Burgenländischkroatisches-Kroatisches Wörterbuch / Nimško-gradišćanskohrvatsko-hrvatski rječnik*. Amt der Burgenländischen Landesregierung, Landesarchiv – Landesbibliothek / Komisija za kulturne veze s inozemstvom SR Hrvatske, Zavod za jezik IFF: Željezno-Eisenstadt/Zagreb.

Bencsics, Nikolaus, Božidar Finka, Ivo Szucsich, Antun Šojat, Josef Vlasits, Stefan Zvonarich, Zrinka Babić, Eugenija Barić, Jasna Finka, Mijo Lončarić, Marko Lukenda, Mile Mamić, Mira Menac-Mihalić, Ante Sekulić, Ljerka Šojat & Marija Znika (eds.). 1991. *Burgenländischkroatisches-Kroatisch-Deutsches Wörterbuch / Gradišćanskohrvatsko-hrvatsko-nimški rječnik.* Komisija za kulturne veze s inozemstvom R Hrvatske, Zavod za hrvatski jezik / Amt der Burgenländischen Landesregierung, Landesarchiv – Landesbibliothek: Zagreb/ Željezno-Eisenstadt.

Benmamoun, Elabbas, Silvina Montrul & Maria Polinsky. 2013. Heritage languages and their speakers: opportunities and challenges for linguistics. *Theoretical Linguistics* 39. 129–181.

Breu, Walter. 1992. Das italokroatische Verbsystem zwischen slavischem Erbe und kontaktbedingter Entwicklung. In Tilmann Reuther (ed.), *Slavistische linguistik 1991,* 93–122. München: Otto Sagner.

Breu, Walter. 1998. Romanisches Adstrat im Moliseslavischen. *Die Welt der Slaven* 43. 339–354.

Breu, Walter. 1999. Phonologie und Verbkonjugation im Moliseslavischen. In Renate Rathmayr & Wolfgang Weitlaner (eds.), *Slavistische linguistik 1998,* 47–76. München: Otto Sagner.

Breu, Walter. 2003. Bilingualism and linguistic interference in the Slavic-Romance contact area of Molise (Southern Italy). In Regine Eckardt, Klaus von Heusinger & Christoph Schwarze (eds.), *Words in time,* 351–373. Berlin & New York: Mouton de Gruyter.

Breu, Walter. 2008. Der slavische Lokativ im Sprachkontakt. Ein Beitrag zur Binnendifferenzierung des Moliseslavischen. In Peter Kosta & Daniel Weiss (eds.), *Slavistische linguistik 2006/2007,* 59–102. München: Otto Sagner.

Breu, Walter. 2009. La comparazione nello slavomolisano. Un risultato tipico del contatto linguistico assoluto. In Paola Desideri, Carlo Consani, Francesca Guazzelli and Carmela Perta (eds.), *Alloglossie e comunità alloglotte nell'Italia contemporanea,* 9–36. Roma: Bulzoni.

Breu, Walter. 2011a. Il verbo slavomolisano in confronto con altre lingue minoritarie: mutamento contatto-dipendente, resistenza e sviluppo autonomo. In Walter Breu (ed.), *L'influsso dell'italiano sul sistema del verbo delle lingue minoritarie,* 149–184. Bochum: Brockmeyer.

Breu, Walter. 2011b. Language contact of minority languages in Central and Southern Europe: a comparative approach. In Bernd Kortmann & Johan van der Auwera (eds.), *The languages and linguistics of Europe. A comprehensive guide,* 429–451. Berlin & New York: De Gruyter.

Breu, Walter. 2011c. Moliškoslavenski. [Molise Slavic] In Peter Rehder (ed.), Ivan Jurčević (transl.), *Uvod u slavenske jezike,* [An introduction to the Slavic languages] 275–279. Osijek: Filozofski fakultet, Sveučilište u Osijeku

Breu, Walter. 2012. The grammaticalization of an indefinite article in Slavic micro-languages. In Björn Wiemer, Björn Hansen & Bernhard Wälchli (eds.), *Grammatical replication and borrowability in language contact,* 275–322. Berlin & Boston: De Gruyter Mouton.

Breu, Walter. 2013a. Val'ter Broj. Jazykovoj kontakt kak pričina perestrojki kategorij roda i sklonenija v molizsko-slavjanskom jazyke [Language contact as the reason for the reconstruction of the categories of gender and declension in the Molise Slavic language]. In P. M. Arkad'ev and Vjač. Vs. Ivanov (eds.), *Tipologija slavjanskix, baltijskix i balkanskix jazykov (preimuščestvenno v svete jazykovyx kontaktov),* 81–112. Sankt-Peterburg: Aletejja.

Breu, Walter. 2013b. Zahlen im totalen Sprachkontakt: Das komplexe System der Numeralia im Moliseslavischen [Numbers in total language contact: The complex system of numerals in Molise Slavic]. In Tilmann Reuther (ed.), *Slavistische Linguistik 2012,* 7–34. München: Otto Sagner.

Breu, Walter. 2014. Val'ter Broj. Funkcii nastojaščego i imperfekta soveršennogo vida i perfekta nesoveršennogo vida v molizsko-slavjanskom mikrojazyke [The functions of the perfective present and imperfect und of the imperfective perfect in the Molise Slavic micro-language]. *Scando-Slavica* 60(2). 321–350.

Breu, Walter. 2017a. Neues aus Süditalien: Das Moliseslavische auf dem Weg zur Mikroliteratursprache? In Kenneth Hanshew, Sabine Koller und Christian Prunitsch (eds.), *Texte prägen. Festschrift für Walter Koschmal* (Die Welt der Slaven, Sammelbände 61). 201–224. Wiesbaden: Harrassowitz.

Breu, Walter. 2017b. *Slavische Mikrosprachen im absoluten Sprachkontakt. Band I. Moliseslavische Texte aus Acquaviva Collecroce, Montemitro und San Felice del Molise.* (Slavistische Beiträge, 505). Wiesbaden: Harrassowitz.

Breu, Walter. 2018a. Die Moliseslaven und ihre Sprache zwischen Sprachkontakt und Verschriftlichung. In Anna Kretschmer, Gerhard Neweklowsky, Stefan Michael Newerkla & Fedor Poljakov (eds.), *Mehrheiten – Minderheiten. Sprachliche und kulturelle Identitäten der Slavia im Wandel der Zeit* (Philologica Slavia Vindobonensia 4). 37–58. Berlin: Lang.

Breu, Walter. 2018b. La situazione linguistica nei paesi arbëreshë del Molise. In Lucija Šimičić, Ivana Škevin & Nikola Vuletić (eds.), *Le isole linguistiche dell'Adriatico*. 169–197. Canterano: Aracne Editrice.

Breu, Walter. 2019. Morphosyntactic Change in Slavic Micro-languages: the Case of Molise Slavic. In Andrii Danylenko & Motoki Nomachi (eds.), *Slavic in the Language Map of Europe* (Trends in Linguistics. Studies and Monographs [TiLSM] 333). 385–432. Berlin, Boston: de Gruyter.

Breu, Walter & Anastasia Makarova. 2019. Passiv und Resultativ im Moliseslavischen: Bewahrung, Umbau und Innovation im totalen slavisch-romanischen Sprachkontakt. In Bernhard Brehmer, Aage A. Hansen-Löve & Tilmann Reuther (eds.), *Wiener Slawistischer Almanach* 83. 7–60. Berlin: Peter Lang.

Breu, Walter & Giovanni Piccoli. 2000. *Dizionario croato molisano di Acquaviva Collecroce* Campobasso: Naš Jezik.

Breu, Walter, Jasmin Berghaus & Lenka Scholze. 2016. Der Verbalaspekt im totalen Sprachkontakt. Moliseslavisch, Obersorbisch und Burgenlandkroatisch im Vergleich. In Walter Breu & Tilmann Reuther (eds.), *Slavistische Linguistik 2014. Wiener Slawistischer Almanach* 77, 55–116. Frankfurt: Lang.

Browne, Wayles. 2014. Groups of clitics in West and South Slavic languages. In Elżbieta Kaczmarska and Motoki Nomachi (eds.), *Slavic and German in contact: Studies from areal and contrastive linguistics*, 81–96. Sapparo: Slavic Research Center, Hokkaido University.

Clyne, Michael. 1967. *Transference and triggering*. The Hague: Martinus Nijhoff.

Clyne, Michael. 2003. *Dynamics of language contact*. Cambridge: Cambridge University Press.

Corbett, Greville. 2006. *Agreement*. Cambridge: Cambridge University Press.

Csirmaz, Anikó. 2003. Perfective and imperfective aspect in Hungarian. (Invisible) Differences. http://www.hum2.leidenuniv.nl/pdf/lucl/sole/console12/console12-csirmaz.pdf (accessed 25 January 2017).

Dahl, Östen. 1985. *Tense and Aspect Systems*. Oxford: Basil Blackwell Ltd.

Dobos, Balázs. 2013. Nemzetiségi nyelvhasználat Magyarországon: Jogok és tapasztalatok [Minority Language Use in Hungary: Rights and Experiences]. *Létünk* 43. 26–43.

D-maps.com (2020). Adriatic Sea, coasts (white). Available at: https://d-maps.com/carte.php?num_car=5991&lang= (visited 19 Sept 2020)

Finka, Božidar. 1997. Na gradišćanskohrvatskim jezičnim stazama [Following the path of the Burgenland Croatian language]. *Suvremena lingvistika* 43–44(1–2). 73–82.
Föglein, Gizella. 1997. A magyarországi nemzeti kisebbségek helyzetének jogi szabályozása 1945–1993 [Juridical regulation of the situation of ethnic minorities in Hungary between 1945 and 1993]. *Regio: Kisebbség, politika, társadalom* 8(1). http://epa.oszk.hu/00000/00036/00028/pdf/02.pdf (accessed 12 October 2017).
Franks, Steven & Tracy King. 2000. *A handbook of Slavic clitics*. Oxford: Oxford University Press.
Franks, Steven. 2009. Case assignment in quantified phrases. In Tilman Berger, Karl Gutschmidt, Sebastian Kempgen & Peter Kosta (eds.), *Die slavischen Sprachen: Ein internationales Handbuch zu ihrer Struktur, ihrer Geschichte und ihrer Erforschung*, 355–368. Berlin: Mouton de Gruyter.
Gafaranga, Joseph. 2007. *Talk in two languages*. Houndmills, Basingstoke: Palgrave Macmillan.
Gal, Susan. 1979. *Language shift: Social determinants of linguistic change in bilingual Austria*. San Francisco: Academic Press.
Goldbach, Alexandra. 2005. *Deutsch-russischer Sprachkontakt. Deutsche Transferenzen und Code-switching in der Rede Russischsprachiger in Berlin*. Frankfurt am Main: Peter Lang.
Goldberg, Adele. 1995. *A construction grammar approach to argument structure*. Chicago: Chicago University Press.
Google Earth (2020). Map shot of Mundimitar, Filič & Kruč. Available at: https://earth.google.com/web/ (visited 19 Sept 2020).
Gorjanac, Živko. 2008. Neke osobitosti santovačkoga šokačkog govora [Some peculiarities of the Šokac vernacular spoken in Santovo/Hercegszántó]. *Hrvatski dijalektološki zbornik* 15. 173–178.
Gradišćanskohrvatsko-hrvatsko-nimški rječnik [Burgenland Croatian-Croatian-German Dictionary]. 1991. Zagreb/Eisenstadt: Komisija za kulturne veze s inozemstvom R. Hrvatske, Zavod za hrvatski jezik, Ured Gradišćanske Zemaljske Vlade, Zemaljski arhiv – Zemaljska biblioteka.
Grbić, Jadranka. 1990. Upotreba materinjeg jezika i etnički identitet kod Hrvata u Mađarskoj [Mother tongue use and ethnic identity amongst Croats in Hungary]. *Migracijske teme* 6. 335–340.
Grbić, Jadranka.1994. Identitet, jezik i razvoj. Istraživanje o povezanosti etniciteta i jezika na primjeru hrvatske nacionalne manjine u Mađarskoj [Identity, language and development. Research on the relationship between ethnicity and language on the example of Croatian national minority in Hungary]. *Narodna umjetnost* 31. 9–143.
Gregor, Esma. 2003. *Russian-English code-switching in New York City*. Frankfurt am Main: Peter Lang.
Guida ai Comuni, alle Province ed alle Regioni d'Italia [Guide to the Municipalities, Provinces and Regions of Italy]. 2018. Statistiche demografiche Molise https://www.tuttitalia.it/molise/statistiche/. (accessed 28 December 2018)
Győrvári, Gábor. 2012. Dvojezičnost pedagoškog rada u hrvatskim školama u Mađarskoj [Bilingualism as an aspect of the pedagogical approach employed in Croatian schools in Hungary]. In Stjepan Blažetin (ed.), *X. Međunarodni kroatistički skup. Zbornik radova* [Tenth International Symposium on Croatian Studies. Conference Proceedings]. Pečuh: Znanstveni zavod Hrvata u Mađarskoj. 338–346.
Gyurok, János. 1998. A magyarországi horvátokról 1910–1990 (Szociológiai, demográfiai, történeti jellemzők a népszámlálási adatok alapján) [About Croats in Hungary 1910–1990

(Sociological, demographic and historical characteristics based on census data)]. Pécs: Gálos Nyomdász Kft.
Hadrovics, László. 1958. Adverbien als Verbalpräfixe in der Schriftsprache der burgenländischen Kroaten. *Studia Slavica Hungarica* 4, 211–249.
Hadrovics, László. 1974. *Schrifttum und Sprache der Burgenländischen Kroaten im 18. und 19. Jahrhundert.* Wien: Verlag der österreichischen Akademie der Wissenschaften.
Hadrovics László. 1976. Das System der Verbalpräfixe im Slavischen und Ungarischen. *Die Welt der Slaven* 21(1). 81–95.
Heine, Bernd & Tania Kuteva. 2005. *Language contact and grammatical change.* Cambridge: Cambridge University Press.
Hergovich, Katalin. 2016. *Višejezičnost i identitet Gradišćanskih Hrvata u Mađarskoj* [Multilingualism and identity of Burgenland Croats in Hungary]. Zagreb: Filozofski fakultet MA thesis.
Hlavac, Jim 1991. Zur Genuszuordnung von Lehnwörtern im Deutschen, Kroatischen und Serbischen. *Wiener Slawistischer Almanach* 28. 281–297.
Hlavac, Jim. 1999a. Phonological integration of English transfers in Croatian: Evidence from the Croatian speech of second-generation Croatian-Australians. *Filologija* 32. 39–74.
Hlavac, Jim. 1999b. 32 years on and *still* triggering: psyholinguistic processes as motivation for switching amongst Croatian-English bilinguals. *Monash University Linguistic Papers.* 2(1). 11–24
Hlavac, Jim. 2006. Bilingual discourse markers: Evidence from Croatian-English code-switching. *Journal of Pragmatics* 38. 1870–1900
Hlavac, Jim. 2011. Hesitation and monitoring phenomena in bilingual speech: A consequence of code-switching or a strategy to facilitate its incorporation? *Journal of Pragmatics* 43. 3973–3806.
Houtzagers, Peter. 1999. *The Kajkavian Dialect of Hidegség and Fertőhomok.* Amsterdam & Atlanta: Editions Rodopo B.V.
Houtzagers, Peter. 2008. On Burgenland Croatian Isoglosses. Studies in Slavic and General Linguistics, Vol. 34, Dutch Contributions to the Fourteenth International Congress of Slavists, Ohrid. Linguistics. (SSGL 34) Amsterdam/New York: Rodopi. 293–331.
Houtzagers, Peter. 2012. Der Herr Professor sind in den Ruhestand getreten. On the honorific third person plural in Burgenland Croatian. *Pegasus Oosteuropese Studies* 20. 277–300.
Houtzagers, Peter. 2013. Burgenland Croats and Burgenland Croatian: Some Unanswered Questions. *Rasprave. Časopis Instituta za hrvatski jezik i jezikoslovlje* 39(1): 253–269.
Hrvatski jezični portal [Croatian Language Portal]. (n.d.) *Pretraga – Homepage search* http://hjp.znanje.hr/index.php?show=main. (accessed 12 December 2018).
Hunglish.hu. n.d. *Sentence-aligned Hungarian-English parallel corpus.* http://hunglish.hu/. (accessed 12 December 2018).
Karall, Kristina. 1997. *Gradišćanskohrvatski glasi – Sprachkurs Burgenlandkroatisch* [Burgenland Croatian voices – Burgenland Croatian language course]. Wien: Hrvatski akademski klub / Kroatischer Akademikerklub.
Kenesei, Istvan, Robert M. Vago & Anna Fenyvesi. 1998. *Hungarian.* London/New York: Routledge.
Kerecsényi, Edit. 1983. *A muramenti horvátok története és anyagi kultúrája. Zalai gyűjtemény 20* [The history and material culture of Pomurje Croats. Collections from Zala vol. 20.]. The Hungarian National Archives Zala County, Zalaegerszeg. https://library.hungaricana.hu/hu/view/ZALM_zgy_20_muramenti/?pg=0&layout=s (accessed 20 October 2017).

Kinda-Berlaković, Andrea Zorka. 2005. Hrvatski nastavni jezik i dvojezično školstvo gradišćanskih Hrvata u Austriji počevši od godine 1921 [Croatian as the language of instruction and bilingual education of Burgenland Croats in Austria from 1921 onwards]. *Croatica et Slavica Iadertina* 1. 27–35.

Kinder, John. 1988. Transference markers in New Zealand Italian. Constructing context and negotiating identity. *Australian Review of Applied Linguistics* 11(1). 9–21.

Kiss, Katalin É. 2002. *The Syntax of Hungarian*. Cambridge: Cambridge University Press.

Kiss, Katalin É. 2011. Negation in Hungarian. http://www.nytud.hu/oszt/elmnyelv/mgtsz/2015/108_ekiss_neg_hungarian_in_neg_uralic.pdf (accessed 19 January 2017).

Kitanics, Máté. 2014. A Magyarországra irányuló horvát migráció a 16–18. században [Croatian Migration to Hungary between the 16th and 18th centuries]. University of Pécs/Pečuh, PhD thesis.

Koschat, Helene. 1978. *Die čakavische Mundart von Baumgarten im Burgenland*. Wien: Österreichische Akademie der Wissenschaft.

Központi Statisztikai Hivatal. [Hungarian Central Statistical Office] 2014. 2011 Évi népszámlálás. 9. Nemzetiségi adatok [Census data from 2011, Section 9. Minority data]. http://www.ksh.hu/docs/hun/xftp/idoszaki/nepsz2011/nepsz_09_2011.pdf. (accessed 12 December 2018).

Langenthal, Péter. 2013. *Hrvatski jezik u gradišćanskohrvatske mladeži* [Use of Croatian amongst Burgenland Croatian youth]. Zagreb: Filozofski fakultet, MA thesis.

Lončarić, Mijo. 1996. *Kajkavsko narječje* [Kajkavian dialect]. Zagreb: Školska knjiga.

Mandić, Živko. 2016. *Rječnik govora santovačkih Hrvata* [Dictionary of the dialects of Croats from Santovo/Hercegszántó]. Pečuh/Pécs: Znanstveni zavod Hrvata u Mađarskoj.

Matras, Yaron. 2009. *Language contact*. Cambridge: Cambridge University Press.

Matras, Yaron. 2011. Universals of structural borrowing. In Peter Siemund (ed.), *Linguistic universals and language variation*, 200–229. Berlin: Mouton.

Matras, Yaron & Jeanette Sakel. 2007. Investigating the mechanisms of pattern replication in language convergence. *Studies in Language* 31(4). 829–865.

Mohl, Adolf. 1974. Die Einwanderung der Kroaten im Jahre 1533. In Franz Palkovits (ed.), *Symposion Croaticon*. Wien.

Montrul, Silvina. 2002. Incomplete acquisition and attrition of Spanish tense/aspect distinctions in adult bilinguals. *Bilingualism: Language and Cognition* 5. 39–68.

Myers-Scotton, Carol. 2002. *Contact Linguistics*. Oxford: Oxford University Press.

Nagy, Sabine. 1989. Soziale Integration und Assimilation der Kroaten im Burgenland von der Zeit ihrer Einwanderung bis zur Gegenwart. Wien: MA thesis.

Neweklowsky, Gerhard. 1969. Die kroatischen Mundarten im Burgenland. *Wiener Slavistisches Jahrbuch* 15. 94–115.

Neweklowsky, Gerhard. 1975. Zwei kroatische Mundarten des südlichen Burgenlandes. *Wiener Slavistisches Jahrbuch* 21. 173–181.

Neweklowsky, Gerhard. 1978. *Die kroatischen Dialekte des Burgenlandes*. Wien: Verlag der österreichischen Akademie der Wissenschaften.

Neweklowsky, Gerhard. 1979. Bei Burgenländer Kroaten in Amerika. *Studia Slavica* 25. 267–272.

Neweklowsky, Gerhard. 2010. *Die Sprache der Burgenländer Kroaten. Jezik Gradišćanskih Hrvatov* [The language of Burgenland Croats]. Trajštof/Trausdorf: Znanstveni institut Gradišćanskih Hrvatov/Wissenschaftliches Institut der Burgenländischen Kroaten.

Nimško-gradišćanskohrvatsko-hrvatski rječnik [German-Burgendland Croatian-Croatian Dictionary]. 1982. Eisenstadt: Ured Gradišćanske Zemaljske Vlade, Zemaljski arhiv – Zemaljska biblioteka.

Pátrovics, Péter. 2002. Néhány gondolat a magyar igekötők eredetéről, valamint az aspektus és akciókiminőség-jelőlő funkciójuk (ki)alakulásáról [Some thoughts about the origin of Hungarian verbal prefixes and about the evolution of their aspectual and aktionsart-marking function]. *Magyar Nyelvőr* 126. 481–489.

Pawlschitz, Sabine. 2014. Burgenland-Croatian: First Signs of Language Decay. In Elżbieta Kaczmarska & Motoki Nomachi (eds.), *Slavic and German in contact: Studies from areal and contrastive Linguistics*. 59–80. Slavic Research Center, Hokkaido University.

Pavičić, Josip. 1982. *Novogovor. Sociolingvistički ogledi iz svakodnevnog života jezika* [Newspeak. Sociolinguistic perspectives from the everyday life of language]. Zagreb: Stvarnost.

Peša Matracki, Ivica & Nada Županović Filipin. 2013. Changes in the System of Oblique Cases in Molise Croatian Dialect. *Studia Romanica et Anglica Zagrabiensia* 58. 3–30.

Piccoli, Agostina & Antonio Sammartino. 2000. *Dizionario dell'idioma croato-molisano di Montemitro* [Dictionary of the Molise Croatian idiom of Montemitro]. Montemitro, Zagreb: Fondazione "Agostina Piccoli", Matica Hrvatska.

Pišković, Tanja. 2011. *Gramatika roda* [The grammar of gender]. Zagreb: Disput.

Polinsky, Maria. 2008. Gender under Incomplete Acquisition. Heritage Speakers' Knowledge of Noun Categorization. *Heritage Language Journal* 6(1). 40–71.

Pranjković, Ivo. 2001. *Druga hrvatska skladnja. Sintaktičke rasprave* [A Second Croatian Syntax. Discussions of syntactic problems] Zagreb: Hrvatska sveučilšna naklada.

Rácz, Erika. 2009. *A Mura menti kaj horvát nyelv* [The Kajkavian Croatian dialect of Pomurje]. Budapest: Eötvös Lóránd University, PhD thesis.

Rácz, Erika. 2012. *Govori pomurskih Hrvata* [The Pomurje Croatian dialects]. Pečuh/Pécs: Znanstveni zavod Hrvata u Mađarskoj.

Rešetar, Milan. 1911. *Die serbokroatischen Kolonien Süditaliens*. Wien: Kaiserliche Akademie der Wissenschaften.

Romaine, Suzanne. 1995. *Bilingualism*, 2nd edn. Oxford: Blackwell.

Rotter, Ivan. 1996. Überblick über die Literatur bei den Burgenländischen Kroaten nach dem 2. Weltkrieg. Wien: Diplomarbeit zur Erlangung des Magistergrades der Philosophie eingereicht an der Geisteswissenschaftlichen Fakultät der Universität Wien, 2. Ausgabe.

Sammartino, Antonio. 2004. *S našimi riči. Con le nostre parole* [With our words]. Montemitro.

Schwartz, Mila, Miriam Minkov, Elena Dieser, Ekaterina Protassova, Victor Moin, & Maria Polinsky. 2015. Acquisition of Russian Gender Agreement by Monolingual and Bilingual Children. *International Journal of Bilingualism* 19(6). 726–752.

Scontras, Gregory, Zuzanna Fuchs & Maria Polinsky. 2015. Heritage Language and Linguistic Theory. *Frontiers in Psychology. Language Sciences* 6(1545). 1–20.

Silić, Josip & Ivo Pranjković. 2007. *Gramatika hrvatskoga jezika za gimnazije i visoka učilišta* [Croatian grammar for secondary schools and high schools]. Zagreb: Školska knjiga.

Skok, Petar. 1971. *Etimologijski rječnik hrvatskoga ili srpskog jezika* [Etymological dictionary of Croatian or Serbian]. Zagreb: Jugoslavenska akademija znanosti i umjetnosti.

Statistical Office of the Slovak Republic. (n.d.). Demography and Social Statistics. https://slovak.statistics.sk/wps/portal/ext/home/demography (accessed 12 December 2018).

Sučić, Ivo, Nikola Benčić, Agnjica Csenar-Schuster, Zorka Kinda-Berlakovich, Jelka Koschat, Ludvig Kuzmić, Mijo Lončarić, Gerhard Neweklowsky, Ivan Rotter, Joško Vlašić, Sanja Vulić & Marija Znika. 2003. *Gramatika gradišćanskohrvatskoga jezika* [Burgenland Croatian grammar]. Željezno/Eisenstadt: Znanstveni institut Gradišćanskih Hrvatov.

Szilágyi, József. 2016. *Tukuljski Racovi. Egy rác népcsoport és rokonai múltja régi dokumentumok tükrében* [Racs from Tukulj. The past of a Rac community and of its relatives based on old documents]. Tököl.

Szucsich, Luka. 2000. Das Burgenlandkroatische: Sprachwandel, Sprachverfall, Sprachverschiebung und Sprachassimilation. In Lew Zybatow (ed.), *Sprachwandel in der Slavia. Die slavischen Sprachen an der Schwelle zum 21. Jahrhundert*, 853–875. Frankfurt: Peter Lang.

Ščukanec, Aleksandra. 2011. *Njemačko-hrvatski jezični dodiri u Gradišću* [German-Croatian language contacts in Burgenland]. Zagreb: Hrvatska matica iseljenika [Croatian Homeland Foundation].

Tamaskó, Eszter. 2013. Zamjena jezika u dvojezičnom Dušnoku [Language shift in bilingual Dušnok]. In Krešimir Bobaš (ed.), *Međunarodna studentska konferencija. Jučer, danas, sutra – slavistika* [International Student Conference. Yesterday, Today, Tomorrow – Slavic Studies], Zagreb, 9–11. XI. 2013. Zagreb: Klub studenata južne slavistike.

Tornow, Siegfried. 1992. Etappen des Sprachwechsels beim Übergang vom Kroatischen zum Deutschen im Burgenland. *Zeitschrift für Slawistik* 37. 248–251.

University of Konstanz. n.d. *Acquaviva Collecroce* http://www.uni-konstanz.de/FuF/Philo/Sprachwiss/slavistik/acqua/Gliosca_I.htm (accessed 19 September 2020).

Valentić, Mirko. 1970. *Gradišćanski Hrvati od XVI. stoljeća do danas* [Burgenland Croats from the 16th century until the present day]. Zagreb: Povijesni muzej Hrvatske, Medicinska naklada.

Vidmarović, Đuro. 2008. *Teme o Hrvatima u Mađarskoj: Studije, članci, prikazi, osvrti, pisma* [Topics about Croats in Hungary: research studies, articles, stories, reviews, letters]. Split: Naklada Bošković.

Vuk, Dora. 2016. Is it necessary for Croats to Speak Croatian in Hungary? Paper presented at First International Conference on Sociolinguistics 2016, Budapest, 1–3 September.

Vulić, Sanja & Bernadina Petrović. 1999. *Govor Hrvatskoga Groba u Slovačkoj* [Local idiom of Hrvatski Grob in Slovakia]. Zagreb: Sekcija Društva hrvatskih književnika i Hrvatskoga centra PEN-a za proučavanje književnosti u hrvatskom iseljeništvu.

Wasserscheidt, Philipp. 2015. *Bilinguales Sprechen. Ein konstruktionsgrammatischer Ansatz*. Berlin: Freie Universität dissertation.

Victor A. Friedman
Diaspora vs sprachbund: Shift, drift, and convergence

1 Introduction

In their important study of language contact and change, Thomason and Kaufman (1988: 93), declared the analytical challenges of sprachbunds "notoriously messy."[1] This messiness is due to the fact that a sprachbund arises under conditions that Friedman and Joseph (forthcoming) have called a kind of "4-M model" (pace Myers-Scotton and Jake 2000, 2016): multilateral, multidirectional, mutual, multilingualism.[2] Unlike the situation with diaspora languages, where there is always a clear, socially determined directionality, in a sprachbund, as Thomason and Kaufman point out, directionality is difficult – and sometimes even impossible – to establish. Here it is worth noting, as Ilievski (1973) observes, that in a sprachbund situation, directionality is sometimes irrelevant. In the Friedman and Joseph 4-M model, the point is the fact that there *is* convergence rather than the question of whether there is an identifiable source for that convergence. This is quite distinct from most diasporic situations, where a dominant local majority usually assimilates (at least in a linguistic sense) an in-coming minority. Still linguistic dominance of the host population is not always a given.[3]

Although the principles for identifying a sprachbund, as originally elaborated by Trubetzkoy (1923, 1930), do not rule out one consisting of only two languages, just as the language family can contain but a single language, nonetheless, the classic situations, and certainly the Balkans, are multilingual rather than bilingual.[4] Sprachbund

---

[1] Following Friedman and Joseph (forthcoming) I treat sprachbund as an adapted loanword, like *pretzel*.
[2] The diaspora situations found in New World countries are often multilateral but uni-directional, from socially dominant language into the migrant, transposed language, and multilingualism is restricted to individuals or a specific group rather than being societal.
[3] To be sure, the concept of *dominance*, is a complex issue that involves a variety of factors, as discussed later in this chapter.
[4] Trubetzkoy's classic formulation, first in Russian (1923) and then in German (1930) is the following: "Groups comprising languages that display a great similarity with respect to syntax, that show a similarity in the principles of morphological structure, and that offer a large number of common culture words, and often also other similarities in the structure of the sound system, but at the same time have no regular sound correspondences, no agreement in the phonological

Victor A. Friedman, University of Chicago, LaTrobe University

https://doi.org/10.1515/9781501503917-004

multilingualism also involves mutuality, in that speakers use each other's languages. It is multidirectional and multilateral in that it is stable across generations and is not limited by social factors such as gender, class, or profession nor by values such as prestige and intimacy. Although, to be sure, each of these social factors can play a role in a specific set of situations within the larger sprachbund, as examplified for the Balkans by Récatas (1934), Koufogiorgiou (2003), and Kahl (2011: 204–207). For example, in the case of the Balkan sprachbund, as shown by Gołąb (1976), changes in Slavic and Romance verbal systems on the territories that became Romania and Macedonia involved different types of shifts in Romanian and Macedonian, resulting from different types of power relations, such that Romanian was influenced by Bulgarian (in the use of 'be' as an auxiliary), while Macedonian was influenced by Aromanian (in a complex set of interactions involving both 'be' and 'have' as auxiliaries) (cf. Gołąb 1984: 135). As Friedman (1995, 2000) points out, in the Balkans, Romani and Judezmo generally involved unidirectional multilingualism, although, as Bunis (1982: 54–54) notes for Judezmo, and as I have observed in the course of my own field work in the Balkans over the past 45 years for Romani, even the languages of the most marginalized groups were also learned and used – albeit less frequently – by non-members of those groups. Lindstedt (2000) also made the useful observation that languages more or less in the middle of the prestige continuum – in the case of the Balkans, Slavic, Romance, and Albanian (cf. Friedman 2006a) – are sometimes more likely to show convergence than languages at either end (Greek, Turkish, Romani, Judezmo).[5] In comparing sprachbund languages to diaspora languages, a combination of temporal and sociolinguistic factors can be crucial in distinguishing the two. Županović Filipin, Hlavac and Piasevoli (this volume, and sources cited therein) makes the point that in many diaspora situations, the results of language contact are gone within three generations, i.e., the contact is unstable, and usually

---

form of morphological elements, and no common basic vocabulary – such language groups we call *Sprachbünde*. Groups consisting of languages that possess a considerable amount of common basic vocabulary, that show correspondences in the phonological expression of morphological categories, and, above all, display regular sound correspondences – such language groups we call language families. Thus, for example, Bulgarian belongs on the one hand to the Slavic language family (together with Serbo-Croatian, Polish, Russian, etc.,) and on the other hand to the Balkan Sprachbund (together with Modern Greek, Albanian, and Romanian)." To this we can add that the other languages of the Balkan Sprachbund are Macedonian, Aromanian, Meglenoromanian, Romani, and, to some extent, West Rumelian Turkish, Gagauz, Balkan Judezmo, and the Torlak dialects of the former Serbo-Croatian.

5 Even these superficially valid power relations, however, must be nuanced for the applicability at the local level. In the town of Debar, Albanian and Macedonian were privileged as urban, while Turkish – which in other towns was a prestigious urban language, was considered rural (Friedman forthcoming).

unidirectional. Such was not the case, however, for Molise Croatian (henceforth MOL.Cro). As Breu (in Šćukanec, Breu and Vuk, this volume) observes:

> There was little or no physical isolation of Molise Croats from Italian-speakers and bilingualism is long-standing. In exogamous marriages in which an Italian-speaker moved to a MOL.Cro village, s/he usually acquired MOL.Cro but Italian (or rather, Molise dialect) remained a code that was understood and used by both. Widespread lexical and deep structural borrowing point to a long history of bilingualism. In contrast to Burgenland, in Molise language choice itself did not index social or economic-occupational differences between different groups.

A crucial similarity between MOL.Cro and the Balkan languages is that marriages were contracted along religious rather than linguistic lines. A crucial difference between MOL.Cro and the languages of the Balkan sprachbund, however, is one of directionality. It seems that Molise Italian was not influenced by the Croatian diaspora; if it had been, then one could speak of a sprachbund rather than a diaspora.[6] It is this lack of multidirectionality that is crucial. Here it is worth noting that a diaspora does have the potential to influence the language into whose domain it migrates. For example, Labov (2007) has demonstrated that a diaspora of a small but economically powerful number of Brooklyn English-speakers in nineteenth-century New Orleans influenced the pronunciation of vocalic /r/ in the city's dialect and those of its environs. Similarly, the influence of Yiddish on English in New York, for example, is striking (cf. Labov 1966). In all such cases however, the populations themselves were diverse and dynamic (and basically urban, although the /r/ example did affect the surrounding countryside). Given the relative social equality among speakers of Molise Italian and MOL.Cro, it would be interesting to try to examine the Molise Italian dialect of the villages where MOL.Cro was once spoken, as well as MOL.Cro in terms of various developments (see Šćukanec, Breu and Vuk, this volume). Still, the dominance of Italian seems to have been consistent over the centuries.

What then is the difference between a diaspora and a sprachbund? In fact, sprachbunds, like diasporas, have their origins in the migration of one or more speech communities into territory occupied by another or others. However, a sprachbund is to be differentiated from the kind of bilingualism on territories where various invaders meet one another, as in the cases of Belgium or Switzerland, where (relatively) indigenous Celtic languages were replaced by competing Romance and Germanic invaders. The Balkan sprachbund, while the result of

---

6 All evidence points to MOL.Cro as having been in steady, albeit gradual, retreat since its arrival in Italy. Molise Italian itself has not received much attention, and insofar as it has, contact with Croatian is never mentioned (Iannacito 2000, Breu 2003: 353).

successive migrations over the course of millennia, nonetheless took the definitive shape that it has today precisely during the period, and in the region, where Ottoman rule lasted the longest (Friedman and Joseph forthcoming; cf. Asenova 2002: 214). It is thus the case (pace Masica 2001: 239), that politics – in its broad sense – can be a determining factor in the formation of a sprachbund. This is a type of political economy, as is poignantly expressed in the Balkan proverb 'languages are wealth' (in Croatian: *čovjek vrijedi onoliko koliko jezika govori* cf. Friedman and Joseph forthcoming). Thus, in comparing diaspora Croatian with homeland Croatian and with Balkan Slavic (henceforth BS),[7] MOL.Cro provides an exceptionally relevant example for examining the differences and similarities between a diaspora and a sprachbund, and in this contribution, I attempt to elucidate these issues.

2 Croatian in the homeland and in the diaspora

Croatian provides a unique opportunity to compare internally and externally motivated change with linguistic developments in the Balkans and even to interrogate the linguistic definitions of Balkan, sprachbund, and diaspora. Thus, for example, an important Balkan linguistic boundary, viz. the choice of 'will' (as opposed to 'be') as the auxiliary verb used for (at least some) future formation, cuts through Croatian and Croatia, just as did the maximal northwestern border of the Ottoman Empire. Diasporas are generally characterized by unidirectional power relations, while in a sprachbund, directionality is more complex. Such complexity, however, is also seen in the diasporic Croatian of New Zealand, where Māori and English were both involved (Stoffel and Hlavac, this volume).[8] In that situation, in-coming speakers of Croatian were in contact with both the indigenous but marginalized and less prestigious Māori and the dominating language of the island, English. The complexity of the situation in New Zealand can be compared to that of West Rumelian Turkish (WRT, i.e. the Turkish of Albania, Kosovo, and Macedonia [except the Yürük dialect of eastern Macedonia] and some adjacent regions). Although Turkish had the prestige of political power in the Ottoman Empire, WRT

---

[7] Balkan Slavic is roughly equivalent to East South Slavic, i.e. Macedonian and Bulgarian, but also, for many features, the Slavic dialects of southern Kosovo and southeastern Serbia. Some Balkan features (such as the use of lexical 'want' to mark the future) extend into Štokavian and Čakavian Croatian. Kajkavian Croatian, like Slovene, is mostly unaffected by Balkan features, although some items extend even that far northward, e.g. the Turkism *hajde*.
[8] Cf. Labov (1966).

shows significant influence resulting from language shift, such that WRT displays classic substratum effects, while Turkish also remains a significant contributor as a superstrate and adstrate as well (Friedman 2006b, Friedman and Joseph forthcoming). Actually, if we compare Māori to Albanian and English to Turkish, then Croatian in New Zealand is reminiscent of BS in terms of certain kinds of power relationships.[9]

In terms of diaspora Croatian dialects, that of Molise is especially interesting to the Balkanist owing to a combination of having moved out of the Balkans in the early 16th century and at the same time remaining in contact with Romance – a language group that participates in the Balkan Linguistic League. A crucial difference is that MOL.Cro emigrated, while the Balkan linguistic league was formed by successive immigration into the Balkans over the course of millenia with varying degrees of stability and shift. Questions regarding stability and shift in Mol CRO will be revisited in the sections that follow.

In comparing MOL.Cro to BS, Breu (2003: 352–353), describes Romance influence in the former as adstrate or superstrate while in the latter as substrate. The situation is somewhat more complex than that, however, as shown by Gołąb (1976). As indicated above, in comparing the developments of auxiliaries in the Macedonian/Aromanian and Bulgarian/Romanian verbal systems, Gołąb shows that Macedonian is influenced by Aromanian in its use of 'have' while Romanian is influenced by Bulgarian in its use of 'be'. Given what we know of the history of the two parts of the Balkans, it appears that Romance-speakers shifted to Slavic in Macedonia, while Slavic-speakers shifted to Romance in Romania, i.e. BS and Balkan Romance (henceforth BR) are both substrate and adstrate (or superstrate) languages depending on the local conditions in different parts of the Balkans. Here Hamp's (1989) concept of *differential bindings* is useful, i.e. both intensity and directionality of contact-induced changes can vary across space as well as time.

3 Molise Croatian and Balkan Slavic compared: Selected features

In the sections that follow, some of the most salient features of MOL.Cro and BS that are relevant for the study of contact induced change in the respective situations are examined: 3.1 clitic order, 3.2 gender, 3.3 substantival declension,

---

[9] To be sure, the analogy requires qualification and nuancing, but many of the relevant parameters are quite similar, especially up to the early twentieth century.

3.4 preposition calquing, 3.5 referentiality, 3.6 the verb (imperfect, future, and pluperfect), and 3.7, the lexicon.

3.1 Clitic order

Clitic order in MOL.Cro and BS provides a good illustration of parallel innovation, both of which are arguably contact induced. We know from Old Church Slavonic that when Slavic arrived in the Balkans, it had a more or less Wackernagelian rule for placement of clitics. Such a rule continues to this day in Croatian – including the Hercegovinian dialects that are the source of MOL.Cro – and thus must have been in the original dialect of the Croats who migrated to Molise. (In Kajkavian and Čakavian dialects, clitics can occur in clause-initial position.) In MOL.Cro however, as in Italian, clitics are tied to the verb in such a way that they can occur in absolute initial position, as seen in Table 1.

Table 1: Clitic Placement in Molise Croatian constructions and comparative constructions in Italian and Standard Croatian based on Sammartino (2004: 28–30, 163, 194–195, 315).

MOL.Cro	Italian	HMLD.Cro	English
je doša rano	è venuto presto	došao je rano	he came early
ču riva sutra	arriverò domani	stići ću sutra	I will arrive tomorrow
me gledate eš mučite	me guardate i tacete	gledate me i šutite	you watch me and are quiet
je mi ga donija jučer	me l'ha portato ieri	donio mi ga je jučer	he brought me it yesterday

Note that in the fourth example in Table 1, the pronominal clitics follow the auxiliary verb (AUX) in MOL.Cro but precede the AUX in Standard Italian. Note also that the Standard Italian AUX is 'have' (an innovation attested already in Latin), whereas in MOL.Cro it is 'be' (inherited from Slavic). In Molise Italian, however, the AUX 'be' has been generalized even for transitive verbs, although 'have' can be used facultatively in the 1sg (Iannacito 2000: 178).[10]

Turning now to BS and Croatian in Croatia the differences between 1) Western Macedonian, 2) Eastern Macedonian and Bulgarian, and 3) Croatian (as well as

---

[10] Note that 'be' is also generalized in some other South Italian dialects, although the person splits are different (Ledgeway 2016). Proclisis vs enclisis is sometime also determined by whether the AUX is 'have' vs 'be', respectively, which parallels Slavic (Pescarini in press). This same difference also applies to Macedonian, i.e. the inherited perfect in 'be' takes enclitic object pronouns while in the new 'have' prefect the object pronouns are proclitic. See Friedman and Joseph (forthcoming) for additional details.

Bosnian, Montenegrin, and Serbian) are that 1) Macedonian requires the clitic to precede the finite verb even in absolute initial position;[11] 2) Bulgarian has almost the same requirement, but if the result would put the clitic in absolute initial position, it must follow the verb; 3) the basic rule for Croatian (as well as Bosnian, Montenegrin, and Serbian) is to place the clitic after the first stressed item in the clause. These facts are illustrated in 1 (a-d)

(1) a. *Ja mu ga često dajem* (Croatian)
       I him-DAT it-ACC often give-PRS.1SG
   b. *Az često mu go davam* (Bulgarian)
       I often him-DAT it-ACC give-PRS.1SG
   c. *Davam mu go često* (Bulgarian)
       give-PRS.1SG him-DAT it-ACC often
   d. *Mu go davam često* (Macedonian)
       him-DAT it-ACC give-PRS.1SG often
       'I often give it to him/I give it to him often'[12]

(2) a. *mu go dade* (Macedonian)
   b. *i_ a dha* (Albanian)
   c. *î_ l dă* (Romanian)
   d. *tou to édhosa* (Greek)
      him-DAT it-ACC give-AOR.3SG
      'He gave it to him.'[13]

In both MOL.Cro and West Macedonian, the circumstantial evidence that sentence initial clitics developed in the context of language contact is overwhelming. In the case of MOL.Cro, the driver was Italian, while in West Macedonian the change is part of the complex convergent process involving all four language groups (cf. Ilievski 1973, cited above). Thus, for MOL.Cro, the change in clitic ordering seems to be a clear result of contact with Italian, while in BS the same change occurs in the dialects with the most complex and strongest Balkan contact (cf. Friedman 2018a). Variation in clitic position is an occurrence in many diaspora-

---

11 The imperative in this respect is non-finite, cf. the arguments in Joseph (1983). This is basically the same rule as in Italian (Pescarini 2016).
12 The adverb can be moved about to render effects much like those in English. The details are not relevant here other than the fact that the adverb cannot come between the clitics and the verb in Balkan Slavic.
13 In Romanian and Albanian, the two clitics are written as single orthographic items, indicated here by the underline.

based varieties of Croatian, e.g. ITAL.Cro (Županović Filipin, Hlavac and Piasevoli, this volume), USA.Cro (Jutronić, this volume) and CAN.Cro (Petrović, this volume).

3.2 Grammatical gender

The treatment of grammatical gender in MOL.Cro vis-à-vis BS is also instructive. The simplification from the inherited Indo-European 3-gender system (M-N-F) to a 2-gender system (M-F), is characteristic of all of Romance as well as Albanian. For Indo-Aryan, represented in the Balkans by Romani, although the confusion of M and N begins in the Old Indo-Aryan period and is well advanced in some areas in the Middle Indo-Aryan period, Modern Indo-Aryan languages show a split of gender loss and preservation separating, e.g. Punjabi (MF) vs Gujarati (MNF) and complete loss in eastern Modern Indo-Aryan (Masica 1991: 220–221).

In the variety of MOL.Cro spoken in Kruč/Acquaviva, inherited neuters become masculine, thus recapitulating the Romance development, and inherited i-stems (which all end in a surface or underlying consonant) assign gender to M or F based on the gender of the Italian equivalent (Sammartino 2004: 205–206). This development is a real difference between MOL.Cro and BS, which, like Modern Greek, has been quite conservative in maintaining its three genders.[14]

3.3 Declension

MOL.Cro preserves most of the inherited Croatian declensional distinctions (Sammartino 2004: 38–64, 204–230) despite its intense contact with the dominant Italian, which lacks them. It turns out that in this respect MOL.Cro is like many other Croatian diaspora dialects in intense contact with languages that do not have such morphology, e.g. English and Swedish (cf. Hlavac 2003 and sources cited therein). When comparing MOL.Cro with BS in this respect, it turns out that the cliché about Balkan Slavic analyticity is itself in need of greater nuancing.

First, as discussed in Friedman and Joseph (forthcoming, v. also Vidoeski 1998: 78–93) complete replacement of substantival declension in BS, i.e. the total

---

[14] To be sure, some gender reassignment has occurred, e.g., in Macedonian. In general, this change has been in the direction of changing inherited F i-stems to M, although changes in the opposite direction also occur, e.g. *pesok* 'sand' DEF *pesokta*. Note that the Aromanian F is correctly interpreted as the equivalent of the Macedonian N in the calquing of the 'have' perfect (Gołąb 1984: 134–135).

elimination of case morphology,[15] is basically limited to a stretch of territory comprising most of western Bulgaria, the southeast of the Republic of North Macedonia, and all but the western and eastern peripheries of Aegean [Greek] Macedonia, with a secondary area in eastern Thrace. The first region is defined more or less by a line running along the Danube from Lom to Somovit, then on the west it goes southward to the west of Sofia and between Kjustendil and Stanke Dimitrov (Dupnica) to Delčevo (Tsarevo Selo) and the river Bregalnica. It then follows the Bregalnica to the Crna into Aegean Macedonia, where the line runs east of Lerin (Florina), Kostur (Kastoria), and Nestram (Nestorion). On the east, the line runs southward west of Pleven and Pirdop, east of Panagjurishte and Pazardzhik, west of Plovdiv, crossing the Greek border east of Gotse Delchev (Nevrokop) and continues between Serres (Serrai) and Drama to the mouth of the river Struma (Strymon). The second area consists of the Strandzha region: starting at a point on the Black Sea north of Burgas, the line runs south of Yambol, east of Kharmanli, west of Svilengrad to Ivaylovgrad, then runs southeast across Greek Thrace and into Turkish Thrace north of Uzunköprü and Tekirdağ to the Sea of Marmara.

Outside of these two areas, all BS dialects preserve some ACC and in some areas also DAT nominal forms, albeit sometimes the preservations are associated with the definite article. Still, this means that for the most part BS does not differ as much from the non-BS Slavic languages as is usually represented. In fact, over all, the BS situation is closer to that of the Torlak (Prizren-Timok) dialects of southern Serbia and Kosovo (cf. Friedman 1977). In terms of the timing of this innovation, Wahlström (2015) has demonstrated that while the beginnings of the elimination of case morphology are indeed attested in Old Church Slavonic and therefore can be posited as occurring in Common Slavic, in fact case inflection in general continued into the 16th century, and, as just seen, well beyond that in most of BS.[16] It is thus the case that, as with many other features considered typical of the Balkan sprachbund, this one achieved its current form during the

---

[15] I am excluding the vocative here. Wahlström (2015) is right to include it in his general study, but in terms of leveling, the vocative is subject to different social pressures than the cases that indicate the relationship of items within the clause. It can be noted that while the relational case system of MOL.Cro is fairly robust, the vocative is facultative or absent and in the variety of MOL. Cro spoken in Kruč/Acquaviva, the locative has merged with (and been replaced by) the accusative, which Breu (2003: 265) attributes to contact with Italian.

[16] Note that I am using *innovation* in the sense of any type of linguistic change, including the replacement of one feature by another. Such replacements are frequently described in terms of 'attrition' or 'loss', when in fact 'replacement', i.e. a kind of innovation, is the change in question. Note also the use of *contact-induced change* rather than 'interference', which latter term implies some sort of lack of competence or some absolute value of purity as opposed to the fact

Ottoman period. Moreover, with regard to the regions where elimination of substantival case morphology was complete, it seems that this was an innovation that spread from a center outwards. It would appear that it began in an area with less linguistic diversity and spread to areas with more complex language contact, where it met with resistance, arguably owing to the congruence of case inflection in non-BS contact languages. There is however, also another possible factor. The major centers of medieval Balkan Slavic literacy (and thus, power and prestige) were in southwestern Macedonia (Ohrid) and northeastern Bulgaria (Pliska, then Preslav, then Tărnovo). While difficult if not impossible to document, it is not unreasonable to speculate that these centers of literacy exerted some influence on the preservation of case morphology.[17] It is striking that the main area of total case elimination is located between the general orbits of these two centers.[18] The explanation for the other region of total elimination – basically the Strandzha region and the part of Thrace immediately to its southeast – is not readily explicable at this time. Like the central non-inflecting region, it is relatively far from the traditional centers of Balkan Slavic literacy, but the Strandzha massif is a relatively isolated area, while the lowlands of eastern Thrace have a significant history of multilingualism. A possible factor here is migration. As Schallert (2017) has shown, there is a significant element of speakers who migrated to this region from parts of Macedonia where case has been entirely eliminated. It is possible to speculate, therefore, that this tendency was brought with these speakers, and that this might account for the discontinuous distribution of the phenomenon.

3.4 Preposition calquing

Breu (2003: 365–367) notes the use of the preposition *do* 'up to, until' as a calque on Italian *di*, etc. 'of, from, etc.', as in *hiža do one žene* '[the] house of that woman', *buk'ir do ovoga* 'his glass' (literally 'glass of this one'), *vrata do hiže* (Italian. *porta di casa*) '[the] door of [the] house' (Breu 1990: 54, Breu 2003: 365–367). As Breu (2003: 367) points out, the fact that MOL.Cro continues to use the genitive with the preposition *do*, usage he attributes to Italian influence, means that the contact-

---

that change as a linguistic phenomenon is universal, and that the effects of language contact are among the various causal elements in change.

17 Here it should be remembered that all the Slavic languages restructured the inherited case system in one way or another, recycling and reassigning endings and eliminating or creating new distinctions. The point here is that the fact of conservatism itself is significant.

18 The Rhodopian and Thracian dialects, however, could owe their relative conservatism in this respect to marginality or isolation.

induced change has resulted in a more complex structure. (See Ščukanec, Breu & Vuk, this volume.) Also worth noting in terms of comparison with BS is that BS selects ablative *od* or locative/allative *na* for genitive-possessive relationships, e.g. *kukjata na / od taa žena* 'the house of that woman'.[19] The fact of preposition calquing in and of itself is not remarkable, but MOL.Cro is noteworthy in preserving declension while also calquing preposition usage. The phonological resemblance of MOL.Cro *do* and Italian *di*, etc., is undoubtedly a contributing factor to the MOL.Cro choice, whereas in BS, the already existing multivalence of *od* and *na* (and the Balkan merger of possessor and recipient, cf. Wahlström 2015) made those choices more natural. Periphrastic use of *od* in possessive constructions is also recorded in samples of ITAL.Cro (Županović Filipin, Hlavac and Piasevoli, this volume), TRS.Cro (Piasevoli, this volume), USA.Cro (Jutronić, this volume) and AUS.Cro (see Hlavac and Stolac, this volume).

3.5 Referentiality: Definite and indefinite articles

The contrast in the realization of referentiality in MOL.Cro and BS is exemplary of the significance of Hamp's (1977) distinction between the areal and the typological, and the importance of historical linguistics for areal linguistics. While the manifestations taken out of historical context may seem typologically natural, it is the historical context that allows for an areal dimension to the explanations. As Breu (2003: 367–368 and this volume) has noted, MOL.Cro developed an indefinite article on the model of the Italian one, but unlike Croatian dialects in contact with German – at least to some extent – (but like those in contact with Hungarian), it did not develop a definite article (cf. Ščukanec, Breu & Vuk, this volume.). Breu attributes this to the opacity of the relationship between the Italian definite article and its historical precursor, the Latin demonstrative pronoun, by the time MOL.Cro came in contact with Italian. This in turn points to both the antiquity and the role of Romance in the postposed definite article of BS. As Gołąb (1997) points out, the postposed structure in Balkan Latin was transparent at the time of its earliest contacts with BS, and it was no doubt reinforced by the native possibilities in Slavic. On the other hand, MOL.Cro and BS also differ significantly in that MOL.Cro has a two-way distinction in which Ø functions like the Italian definite article, whereas BS has a 3-way distinction between indefinite article, definite article, and Ø.

---

[19] Heine and Kuteva (2006: 169) use the term 'allative' to describe *do* in citing the examples from Breu (1990), which is consistent with the use of this term for some languages.

The BS indefinite marker, which can be called an article insofar as it can be used with generics, albeit often facultatively, patterns like Greek and Balkan Romani (as opposed to Balkan Romance, Albanian, and Turkish), (Friedman 2003). In the former Serbo-Croatian, the use of *jedan* 'one' and its co-forms (*jedna*, etc.) as a marker of indefiniteness was more characteristic of the Serbian standard than the Croatian, or perhaps it was more the object of prescription in Croatian but of description in Serbian (Friedman 2000). Maretić (1963: 510) writes for Croato-Serbian: ". . . many modern writers spoil the language by using the numeral *jedan* without any need on the model of German *ein*, French *un*, Italian *uno*."[20] This contrasts with Stevanović (1986: 313) who writes for Serbo-Croatian: "The numeral *jedan* is used very often in our language not as a numeral but more as a kind of indefinite article."[21] Hinrichs and Hinrichs (1995: 55–57) write that indefinite use of *jedan* is more common in Serbian than in Croatian (or Bosnian). More recently, Belaj and Matovac (2015: 17) have argued that *jedan* can have the characteristics of an indefinite article in Croatian, albeit "not fully developed as a grammatical category on its own (in the sense of indefinite articles in e.g. English, German, Spanish or Italian)." The basic point for the purposes of this chapter, however, is that the MOL.Cro indefinite article and the BS indefinite article/marker, both arose in contexts of contact with languages with robustly grammaticalized indefinite articles, whereas in HMLD.Cro the development, while progressing on its own, presumably, still has not gone as far.

Examples of the use of *jedan* performing the function of an article-like attributive are also found in other varieties of heritage Croatian, e.g. TRS.Cro (see Piasevoli, this volume), CAN.Cro (see Petrović, this volume) and ARG.Cro (see Skelin Horvat, Musulin and Blažević, this volume).

3.6 The verb

The Balkan sprachbund is well known for shared innovations in verbal categories, e.g. the replacement of infinitives with analytic subjunctives, the harmonizing of future marking using a particle descended from lexical 'want' (although lexical 'have' also has a role to play in some of the languages), the development of new perfects and pluperfects in some of the languages, and various types of evidential categories. At the same time, there is a shared conservatism in the

---

[20] Original: "[. . .] mnogi današnji pisci kvare jezik upotrebljavajući broj *jedan* bez ikakve potrebe prema njemačkom artikulu *ein*, franc. *un*, ital. *uno* . . ." (Maretić 1963: 510)

[21] Original: "Broj *jedan* se vrlo često u našem jeziku upotrebljava – ne da se njim označi broj, nego više kao neka vrsta neodređenog člana . . ." (Stevanović 1986: 313)

preservation of inherited synthetic past tenses. In comparing MOL.Cro to BS, the influence of Italian on the former can be seen in the synthetic pasts, the future, and the pluperfect.

3.6.1 The Imperfect

In terms of verbal categories, MOL.Cro shows both innovations and conservatisms that raise the important question of diagnostics in language contact, and here, too, a comparison with BS is instructive. In non-Balkan Romance, the aorist was, for the most part, replaced by the new, analytic perfect in 'have', a replacement that also occurs to a large extent in the dialects of Romanian furthest from the Balkans, i.e. in the dialects of those territories that were Ottoman for the shortest period. As in Romance, however, the MOL.Cro imperfect remains vital. (See Ščukanec, Breu & Vuk, this volume.) As Breu (2003: 369) observes, this is contrary to the general tendency in non-Balkan Slavic, where the imperfect is lost before the aorist, which latter is still marginally alive in Croatian as well as Serbian, Montenegrin, and Bosnian in all the dialects north and west of the Torlak area. In Torlak, as in Macedonian and Bulgarian, both synthetic tenses are vital.

In general, in areal as in genealogical linguistics, it is shared innovation rather than conservatism that functions as diagnostic. Nonetheless, the fact that the respective patterns of conservation follow those of the relevant contact languages is noteworthy, and the elimination of the aorist rather than the imperfect, contrary to the general South Slavic tendency, is an innovation shared, more or less, with Western Romance.[22] Thus for MOL.Cro the fact that the relative innovations and conservations not only pattern with Italian but go counter to the rest of Slavic in general, and to Croatian in particular (cf., e.g. Maretić 1963: 616), can be taken as affected by contact with Italian. In the case of BS, the fact that the preservation occurs precisely in the region of intense Balkan linguistic contact and attenuates to the north and west argues for resistance to innovation in this area as a Balkan linguistic feature. This point shows that resistance to innovation, especially in the context where such innovation is available, is not merely a peripheral archaism but itself part of the larger complexity of language contact phenomena.

---

22 To be sure, in both Slavic and Romance outside the Balkans there has been a tendency to replace aorists with perfects – an inherited Latin innovation in the case of Romance and an inherited Common Slavic construction in the case of Slavic. Still, the very preservation of the aorist in South Slavic (except Slovene) and its complete elimination in North Slavic (except Sorbian) represents the state of affairs when MOL.Cro came into contact with Italian.

3.6.2 Future marking

Developments in future marking are also noteworthy in both MOL.Cro and BS. In the Balkans, 'have' was in competition with 'want' as the future marking auxiliary, and in fact both auxiliaries are employed there, albeit with various specifications depending on language and dialect. For BS, 'want' provided the basic future marker, which ended up as an uninflecting particle *kje*, *šte*, etc. An inflecting or uninflecting *ima* 'have -PRS.3SG' can be used as a future marker that has a sense of obligation or warning. In the negative, however, the unconjugated negative of *ima*, viz *nema/njama*, is the most common negative future marker. There are two facts here that are particularly noteworthy. First, although both 'want' and 'have' could function as future markers in Common Slavic as reflected in Old Church Slavonic, the deployment of perfective aspect, especially with 'be', was more common and ultimately won out in North Slavic. Moreover, the 'be' future continued to be favored in the northern part of South Slavic, i.e., Slovene and the Kajkavian dialects of Croatian. Second, by contrast, the selection of the 'want' future spread throughout Štokavian and Čakavian, and was clearly already in place when the speakers of what became MOL.Cro left for Italy, but the negative of 'have' for the negated future is specifically BS.

Turning now to MOL.Cro, it can be seen that future markers based on 'have' and 'want' have both developed. According to Breu (2011: 156–158, cf. Breu 2003: 370) 'have' in MOL.Cro had only possessive meaning at the time when contact with Italian began and it developed the meaning of an obligative or intentional future as a result of the southern Italian use of *avé* 'to have' to mark the meaning 'must' and its function in building a future tense referring to necessary or planned states of affairs. (See Ščukanec, Breu & Vuk, this volume.) As a result, the 'want' future is now limited to a future of probability, as seen in example (3), from Breu (2011: 156–158):[23]

(3) ču   dokj   vs.   mam   dokj
    will-1SG come-INF   have-1SG come-INF
    'I will (probably) come'   'I will come (as planned)'

---

[23] Italian, including Molise Italian, has a *futuro di probabilità* 'future of probability' using the future auxiliary and past participle, but this is more like the English anterior future in its hypothetical meaning. It is worth noting here that according to Iannacito (2000: 176 ff.), the Italian synthetic future is not used in Molise Italian, but rather the present indicative with a temporal adverb. The synthetic future only occurs in the auxiliary in the formation of the a *futuro di probabilità*, which, however, uses 'be' rather than 'have' as is the case in Standard Italian, e.g. *sar:à d:àtë* = avrà dato 'will have given'. It is also limited to the third person (Iannacito 2000: 183).

According to Sammartino (2004: 101–105, 262–265), the auxiliary (or, in his terms, 'modal') 'have' is distinct from the lexical verb denoting possession in that it lacks the initial *i*, e.g. *što imaš u žep?* 'what do you have in your pocket?' vs *Sutra maš do rano* 'tomorrow you must come early', for which he gives the Standard Croatian equivalent *Sutra moraš (morat ćeš) doći rano* and the Standard Italian *Domani devi (dovrai) venire presto*. Sammartino, however, makes no mention of the use of the 'have' future as an intentional. In Sammartino's description of MOL.Cro spoken in Mundimitar/Montemitro, there is also a distinction between the 'modal' (lexical) and auxiliary (clitic) conjugations of *tit* 'want'. Table 2, adapted from Sammartino (2004: 105, 265) is illustrative. Note that the MOL.Cro negative future has a non-conjugating particle (*nežda*) that can be used in place of the negative conjugated auxiliary.

Table 2: Lexical and clitic forms of *tit* 'want, AUX.FUT' based on (Sammartino 2004: 105, 265).

AUXILIARY				LEXICAL			
MOL. Cro	HMLD. Cro	Standard Italian	English	MOL. Cro	HMLD. Cro	Standard Italian	English
Ja ču do doma	Ja ću doći kući	Io verrò a casa	I will come home	Ja hočem do doma	Ja želim doći kući	Io voglio venire a casa	I want to come home
Ja neču do doma	Ja neću doći kući	Io non verrò a casa	I won't come home	Ja ne tijem do doma	Ja ne želim doći kući	Io no voglio venire a casa	I don't want to come home
Mi čmo izatj	Mi ćemo izaći	Noi usciremo	We'll go out	Mi hočemo izatj	Mi želimo izaći	Noi vogliamo uscire	We want to go out
Mi nečmo izatj	Mi nećemo izaći	Noi non usciremo	We won't go out	Mi ne tijemo izatj	Mi ne želimo izaći	Noi non vogliamo uscire	We don't want to go out

3.6.3 Pluperfects

Breu (2003: 369) also makes the point that the pluperfect in MOL.Cro is regularly used, and attributes this to Italian influence. Here the question is one of both history and frequency, and the current situation in BS is instructive by comparison. MOL.Cro participated in the South and West Slavic innovation of adding to or replacing the synthetic past auxiliary 'be' with the analytic perfect form. Maretić (1963: 632) cites *bijah čuvao (sačuvao), bjeh čuvao (sačuvao), bio sam čuvao (sačuvao)* 'I had preserved, etc.' stating that there is no difference at all between them. In BS and Sorbian, the inherited pluperfect with a synthetic auxiliary was retained, as were synthetic pasts. The innovative analytic perfect auxiliary (which is the only pluperfect formant in Slovene) was vigorous enough to get to Bulgarian and, to a lesser extent, eastern Macedonian, which maintained the old pluperfect and integrated the new one via evidentiality (see Friedman 2018b). Neither Sorbian nor western Macedonian, however, adopted the innovation. In Macedonian the rise of a new pluperfect using the imperfect in 'have' + neuter verbal adjective (based on the new perfect) is in competition with and gradually replacing the inherited pluperfect (see Friedman 2014: 89–100 on the differences between the pluperfects), whereas in Sorbian there was no such development. Pluperfects are obsolete in Czech, archaic in Polish, infrequent in Slovak and Sorbian. In Macedonian, the old pluperfect is uncommon and obsolescent whereas in Bulgarian it is very much still in use, on a level arguably comparable to MOL.Cro. In the case of Bulgarian, it is probably the preservation of the imperfective aorist (which is now virtually obsolete in Macedonian, Friedman 1993) combined with the lack of a new pluperfect (outside the evidential system) that accounts for the robustness of the inherited pluperfect vis-à-vis its restriction in Macedonian (Friedman 2018c). Given the absence or rarity of pluperfects in Slavic, except in Bulgarian, where they are quite vital for reasons different than the situation in MOL.Cro, it seems reasonable to conclude that the robustness of the pluperfect in Italian did contribute to its relative frequency in MOL.Cro. (See Ščukanec, Breu & Vuk, this volume)

3.7 Lexical semantics

In his original characterization of the sprachbund, Trubetzkoy (1923, 1930) made a distinction between what he called *Kulturwörter* 'culture words' for the sprachbund and *Elementarwörter* 'core vocabulary' for the language family. In the past century or so, many attempts have been made to define the difference between these two general concepts (see Tadmor, Haspelmath and Taylor 2010 and discussion therein). On an intuitive level, it seems clear that words for things like eyes and ears, for activities like sleeping and seeing, numerals, pronouns, etc. should all be 'core' as opposed to words for, e.g., 'Turkish coffee pot', which are clearly culturally determined. The boundary between the two concepts is not so clear, however, and various processes of language change can blur it even further. Recently, Friedman and Joseph (2014, forthcoming) have made the argument for a class of loanwords characteristic of sprachbunds that they call Essentially Rooted In Conversation (ERIC). Such words are closed class and generally borrowing-resistant items such as kinship terms, numerals, pronouns and bound morphology, as well as conversationally based elements such as taboo expressions, idioms, and phraseology, and also discourse elements such as connectives and interjections. Some ERIC loanwords are also typical of diaspora situations, for example, borrowed discourse markers and interjections are frequently typical of diaspora languages to the extent that such items are emblematic of diaspora speech in literature (e.g. in Krle 1967, about a man who returns to Macedonia from economic migration in America). At the same time, however, some classes of ERIC loanwords, e.g. kinship terms, can be particularly resistant in diaspora languages, as they become emblematic of the community and markers of identity, e.g. words for 'grandmother' and 'grandfather' in many diaspora ethnolects.

Breu's (2003: 356) discussion of the simplification of affinal kinship terminology in MOL.Cro is worth comparing to the situation in Macedonian. Many modern Slavic languages, including Croatian and BS, have preserved a number of inherited Indo-European affinal kinship terms that were also preserved in Latin but that became obsolete in the Romance and Germanic languages, although there have also been innovations in Slavic. Macedonian serves as a particularly useful comparison with MOL.Cro in this respect. Macedonian society remained basically patrilocal well into the second half of the twentieth century, and the terms for Hu affines of the same generation (HuSi, HuBr, HuBrWi; see Table 3)[24] – inherited from Indo-European – remained very much in active use well into the 1970s. At the same time, other Macedonian affinal terms pertaining to the spouses' generation were subject to various developments, including even borrowing from Turkish (*baldəza* WiSi and *badžanak* WiSiHu, see Table 3).

Breu (2003: 356) makes the point that the MOL.Cro affinal kinship system is undergoing simplification at present, bringing it more in line with the simpler system of Italian (and, for that matter, English). While language contact is a potential driving force, the example of Macedonian suggests that changes in the social arrangement of family structure could also be at work. In Macedonia, modernization has resulted in the transformation of the old patrilocal system into one in which married children form their own households if or when they can afford to. A visible effect of this change in social relationships is that many in the youngest adult generation of Macedonian-speakers no longer have mastery over the meaning of the various affinal kinship terms, as is apparently also the case for the younger generation of MOL.Cro-speakers. In both languages there is a tendency for one term to cover all same-generation affinal relations of a given gender, but the differences between Macedonian and MOL.Cro are striking. In MOL.Cro, one of the inherited affinal terms referring to spouse's generation has been generalized, whereas in Macedonian, terms that originally referred to the relationship of

---

24 Br=brother['s], Hu=husband['s], Si=sister['s], Wi=wife['s].

Table 3: Affinal kinship terms in Italian, MOL.Cro (based on Breu 2003: 356) and Macedonian with modifications and additions. (Terms used by the youngest generation are bolded.)

Italian	English	Relationship	MOL.Cro	Macedonian	HMLD.Cro[26]
cognato	brother-in-law	SiHu	šurjak	**zet**	šogor / svak
		WiBr		šura	šogor / šurjak
		WiSiHu		**badžanak**	svak / pašanac
		HuBr	divar	dever	šogor / djever
		HuSiHu	–	zolvin	–
cognata	sister-in-law	BrWi	nevista	**snaa/nevesta**	nevjesta / šogorica
		WiSi	šurjakica	sveska, svastika, baldəza[27]	šogorica / svastika
		WiBrWi[28]		šurnea	šogorica / šurjakinja
		HuSi	zava	zolva	šogorica / zaova
		HuBrWi	[StCr jetrva][29]	jatrva (deverica)	šogorica / jetrva

child's spouse to spouse's parent had already been generalized for SiHu and BrWi and have now expanded into the other slots. These generalizations are indicated by bolding in Table 3, while obsolescent terms are in italics.[25] Here it is worth noting that in Macedonian, the old affinal terms have a nuance of referring to an older patriarchal and patrilocal society. At the same time, the Turkism *badžanak*, is frequently used appropriately. This usage itself seems to reflect the way affinal kinship networks continue to be utilized in a variety of functions outside the traditional household.

In comparing sprachbund and diaspora lexicons, the semantic points raised by Breu (2003) are worth considering. Aside from obvious borrowings, the different types of calquing analyzed by Breu also apply to the Balkans (see especially

---

25 Note that in Macedonian literal descriptive, e.g. *brat na maž mi* 'my husband's brother' for *dever*, or *na žena mi sestrata* for *sveska* 'my wife's sister' are also used.
26 All HMLD.Cro terms are listed in Anić (1998). Those terms listed second, i.e. after the forward slash (/), are often used as a generic form for any male or female in-law.
27 These three terms are distributed geographically in different parts of Macedonia. In terms of the standard, *sveska* (western) is standard, *baldaza* (eastern) is colloquial, and *svastika* (northern) and *baldəza* are dialectal.
28 Breu (2003) has WiBrSi 'wife's brother's sister' for this line, but since WiBrSi is a relationship that is identical to WiSi 'wife's sister' I am assuming a lapsus calami on Breu's part and have corrected the entry to WiBrWi, which relationship would otherwise not be represented in his table.
29 Breu does not specify the term for this relationship in MOL.Cro. Presumably the old term is obsolete.

Asenova 2002: 51–61). However, for the Balkan lexicon, as in the grammar, directionality of calqued semantics can be problematic: the various languages have influenced one another such that directionality cannot always be determined. Or, it may be that the ultimate source of a lexical item is clear, but the exact pathway among various Balkan languages is not. Nonetheless, especially significant in this respect is the shared heritage of phrasal calques – first studied by Papahagi (1908) – and especially phrasal calques from Turkish, for which Jašar-Nasteva (1962/63) is exemplary (but cf. also Friedman 1994). Here the role of Italian vis-à-vis MOL.Cro and the role of Turkish vis-à-vis the Balkan sprachbund helps illuminate the difference between adstrate and superstrate or different types of adstrate. In much of the Balkans, Turkish was a prestigious lingua franca from the fifteenth century until well into the twentieth, but, for the most part, it did not replace local languages even when local speakers converted to Islam. At the same time, the percentage of vocabulary of Turkish origin in various Balkan languages in the nineteenth century was much larger than it is today.

By contrast, Italian has been steadily eroding MOL.Cro ever since the speakers arrived in Italy, such that in the course of roughly the same time period (16th century to present) the number of Molise Croatian speaking villages has shrunk from fifteen to three (Piccoli 1993; Perinić 2006). In this, MOL.Cro is a typical diaspora language, i.e. one that eventually assimilates to the host population, albeit one that has endured for much longer than, e.g., diaspora languages in the New World. By contrast, BS is a typical group of sprachbund languages, one that remains relatively stable over an extended period of language contact. For MOL.Cro, Italian may be described as an adstrate language for those speakers who are bilingual, but in view of the steady decline of MOL.Cro over the centuries, it is more of a superstrate.[30]

4 Conclusion: Diasporas and sprachbunds

As indicated in section 3.7, a fundamental difference between MOL.Cro as a diaspora language and BS as a sprachbund language complex is the relative stability of the latter vis-à-vis attrition in the former. Some of this difference has to do with the type of dominance, i.e. social position, of Italian for MOL.Cro versus Turkish for BS. Also relevant for BS is the 4-M model (multilateral, multidirec-

---

[30] Here it can be noted that it has been suggested that West Rumelian Turkish – which has far more Balkan sprachbund features than East Rumelian Turkish – has those features as the result of being a superstrate language (Friedman 2006b).

tional, mutual, multilingualism) alluded to in section 1. In terms of grammatical change, the comparison of MOL.Cro with BS shows both parallels and differences. In its clitic order, as discussed in section 3.1, MOL.Cro shows the same types of developments found in western Macedonian (as opposed to the rest of BS or South Slavic in general). A functional approach such as that advocated by Matras (2009) would argue that bringing clitic order into alignment with the relevant contact language(s) reduces mental burden or processing time. Similarly, Breu (2003: 372) concludes that MOL.Cro-speakers, like other bilinguals, attempt "the integration of two languages in one system." In the case of MOL.Cro, this would apply to the dominant Italian. In the case of western Macedonian, however, given the multidirectionality of the multilingualism and the relative mutability of social dominance, it is clear that the western Macedonian pattern has adapted to that of the other contact languages, this adaptation is part of a larger context in which Macedonian also contributes lexicon and structure. It is thus the case that similar outcomes can have different causes.

In the nominal system, the categories of case and gender behave quite differently in MOL.Cro and BS. As discussed in sections 3.2 and 3.3. MOL.Cro shows significant gender reassignment, whereas BS does not, but MOL.Cro – like other Croatian diaspora dialects – is remarkably conservative in its treatment of case, and, whereas BS is remarkably innovative, most BS dialects are not quite as radically innovative as usually portrayed. Given the relative situations of MOL.Cro and BS, it is striking that while MOL.Cro has expanded the use of prepositions, it has retained declension. This complicates claims that bilinguals seek to make their two linguistic systems as congruent as possible. Moreover, the pattern of the elimination of case morphology in BS actually points to regions where language contact was less intense. As a nominal category, referentiality (section 3.5) provides similar points of comparison. While both MOL.Cro and BS have elaborated marking for indefiniteness in contact with languages where such elaboration had already taken place, the manner for marking definiteness evolved differently in the two languages arguably owing to the relative transparency of the connection between definiteness and deixis at the time of contact. With regard to verbal categories (section 3.6) both MOL.Cro and BS show changes in their respective tense-mood-aspect systems that are consistent with contact induced change, although here the question of conservatism as an effect of language contact is also relevant. Finally, Preposition calquing (section 3.4) and lexicon (section 3.7) can be considered together. MOL.Cro and BS show interesting similarities and differences in their adaptation to contacts languages, a point to be returned to in the following paragraph.

As noted at the outset, MOL.Cro and BS afford the opportunity to compare diaspora Slavic with sprachbund Slavic and thus interrogate the differences between diasporas and sprachbunds. A key issue in the nature of diaspora languages is that there is always a dominant adstrate to which subsequent generations generally shift (in which case the adstrate can become a superstrate), although in the case of MOL.Cro, the process of shift has been slow. The sprachbund, on the other hand, involves a more complex kind of stratigraphy than that implied by, sub-, super-, and ad- strata, although all these distinctions are also relevant. I would suggest, therefore, a fourth term: interstrate. This describes a language in intense interaction with another where influences can be mutual. The point here is that directionality cannot always be determined and is not necessarily even relevant as long as the fact of mutual convergence can be shown. This mutuality includes Mufwene's (2001) language ecological concept of feature selection, as seen, for example, in future formation (section 3.6.2). In issues such as word order (section 3.1) it is worth emphasizing that only the western Macedonian dialects, which are at the heart of a major Balkan innovation area and the most complex Balkan multilingual situation, are precisely those that have most radically altered clitic order, as has also been the case of MOL.Cro under the influence of Italian.

In the case of Italian vis-à-vis MOL.Cro, the relationship can be called adstratal only insofar as speakers of MOL.Cro retain their Croatian linguistic system. In terms of prestige, it is superstratal, and it is the language MOL.Cro-speakers have shifted to and to which they continue to shift. On the other hand, the same phenomenon of clitic ordering in western Macedonian needs to be viewed in a different light. Here Slavic interacting the Romance, Hellenic, and what Hamp (1994) has called Albanoid (i.e. the language prior to the Geg/Tosk split) adapted to the system that developed or had developed in those other languages. Owing to the lack of necessary documentation, timing is difficult or impossible to establish, but, as indicated above, what stands out is that precisely those Slavic dialects with the most complex interstratal processes (i.e., those that became western, especially southwestern, Macedonian) are the ones that ended up with the clitic order most congruent to that of the other Balkan languages. That this order should be the one found in Italian may point to some unattested tendency in late colloquial Latin, but that would not change the possibility that Albanoid and Hellenic had their roles to play in contact with western Macedonian – and each other. As noted above, grammatical processes in MOL.Cro and BS are comparable in the verb, and the treatment of declension has more resilience and complexity than is usually described, even in BS. The treatment of gender, however, is a striking difference. While simplification from MNF to MF occurs in many Indo-European branches, Slavic has been uniformly resistant, and the MOL.Cro adaptation points to a feature that is diaspora rather than sprachbund. On the other hand, the lexicon is an area where the concept of adstrate is appropriate to both situations. The difference is that in relation to MOL.Cro, while Italian is transitioning from adstrate to superstrate to the language that speakers shift to, Turkish was an adstrate that interacted with the languages and influenced their lexicons profoundly, but was not involved in actual shift except in certain limited contexts (see section 2).

To conclude, the comparison of MOL.Cro as representative of a diaspora language and BS as representative of a related but sprachbund group of languages shows that the two situations have much in common. A key difference is the nature of directionality, and, in some diasporas and sprachbunds, differing sets of social arrangements. In terms of linguistic outcomes, the differences between unidirectional convergence and multidirectional convergence appear to have similar results in cases such as word order and the verb system, but in the nominal system distinct differences occur. Given that lexically nouns are more likely to be borrowed than verbs, it can be suggested that structurally verbs are more likely to be influenced than nouns.

References

Anić, Vladimir. 1998. *Rječnik hrvatskoga jezika*. [Dictionary of the Croatian Language]. Zagreb: Novi Liber.
Asenova, Petja. 2002. *Balkansko ezikoznanie*. [Balkan Linguistics] 2nd ed. Veliko Tărnovo: Faber.
Belaj, Branimir & Darko Matovac. 2015. On the article–like use of the indefinite determiners jedan and neki in Croatian and other Slavic languages. *Suvremena lingvistika* 41(79). 1–20.
Breu, Walter. 1990. Sprache und Sprachverhalten in den slavischen Dörfen des Molise (Süditalien). In Walter Breu (ed.), *Slavistische Linguistik 1989* (Slavistische Beiträge 260), 35–65. Munich: Otto Sagner.
Breu, Walter. 2003. Bilingualism and linguistic interference in the Slavic-Romance contact area of Molise (Southern Italy). In Regine Eckardt, Klaus von Heusinger & Christoph Schwarze (eds.), *Words in time*, 351–373. Berlin and New York: Mouton de Gruyter.
Breu, Walter. 2011. Il verbo slavomolisano in confronto con altre lingue minoritarie: muta-mento contatto-dipendente, resistenza e sviluppo autonomo. In Walter Breu (ed.), *L'influsso dell'italiano sul sistema del verbo delle lingue minoritarie. Resistenza e mutamento nella morfologia e nella sintassi. Atti del 2º Convegno Internazionale – Costanza, 10–13 dicembre 2008* (=Diversitas Linguarum 29), 149–184. Bochum: Brockmeyer.
Bunis, David. 1982. Types of nonregional variation in early modern eastern spoken Judezmo. *International Journal of the Sociology of Language* 37. 41–70.
Friedman, Victor A. 1977. The morphology of case in Southeast Serbian dialects. *Folia Slavica* 1(1). 76–88.
Friedman, Victor A. 1993. The loss of the imperfective aorist in Macedonian: structural significance and Balkan context. In Robert A. Maguire & Alan Timberlake (ed.), *American Contributions to the Eleventh International Congress of Slavists*, 285–302. Columbus: Slavica.

Friedman, Victor A. 1994. Turkisms in a comparative Balkan context. In *Septième Congrès International d'Études du Sud-Est Européen: Rapports*, 521–543. Athens: Greek National Committee for Southeast European Studies.

Friedman, Victor A. 1995. Persistence and change in Ottoman patterns of codeswitching in the Republic of Macedonia: nostalgia, duress and language shift in contemporary Southeastern Europe. In Durk Gorter (ed.), *Summer school: code-switching and language contact*, 58–67. Ljouwert/Leeuwarden: Fryske Akademy.

Friedman, Victor A. 2000. After 170 years of Balkan linguistics: whither the millennium? *Mediterranean Language Review* 12. 1–15.

Friedman, Victor A. 2003. 'One' as an indefinite marker in Balkan and Non-Balkan Slavic. *Prilozi: Oddelenie za lingvistika i literaturna nauka – Makedonska Akademija na Naukite i Umetnostite* 28(1). 109–151.

Friedman, Victor A. 2006a. The Balkans as a linguistic area. In Keith Brown (ed.), *Elsevier Encyclopedia of Language and Linguistics*, vol. 1, 657–672. Oxford: Elsevier.

Friedman, Victor A. 2006b. West Rumelian Turkish in Macedonia and adjacent areas. In H. Boeschoten & L. Johanson (eds.), *Turkic language contacts*, 27–45. Wiesbaden: Harrassowitz.

Friedman, Victor A. 2014. *The grammatical categories of the Macedonian indicative*, 2nd edn. Bloomington, IN: Slavica.

Friedman, Victor A. 2018a. Reflexes of Common Slavic nasal vowels in Southwest Macedonian dialects revisited: an areal and Balkanological account. In Christina Bethin (ed.), *American Contributions to the XVI International Congress of Slavists: Linguistics*, 85–98. Bloomington, IN: Slavica.

Friedman, Victor A. 2018b. Where do evidentials come From? In Alexandra Y. Aikhenvald (ed.), *The Oxford handbook of evidentiality*, 124–147. Oxford: Oxford University Press.

Friedman, Victor A. 2018c. The pluperfect in Bulgarian and Macedonian: from Bai Ganyo to the Bombi. In Steven Franks, Vrinda Chidambaram, Brian Joseph & Iliana Krapova (eds.), *Katerino Mome: Studies in Bulgarian morphosynta in honor of Catherine Rudin*, 121–130. Bloomington, IN: Slavica.

Friedman, Victor A. Forthcoming. The Balkans. In Salikoko S. Mufwene & Anna María Escobar (eds.), *Cambridge handbook of language contact*. Cambridge: Cambridge University Press.

Friedman, Victor A. & Brian D. Joseph. 2014. Lessons from Judezmo about the Balkan Sprachbund and contact linguistics. *International Journal of the Sociology of Language* 226. 3–23.

Friedman, Victor A. & Brian D. Joseph. Forthcoming. *The Balkan languages*. Cambridge. Cambridge University Press.

Gołąb, Zbigniew. 1976. On the mechanism of Slavic–Rumanian linguistic interference in the Balkans. In Thomas Butler (ed.), *Bulgaria, past and present: studies in history, literature, economics, music, sociology, folklore & linguistics*, 296–309. Columbus: AAASS.

Gołąb, Zbigniew. 1984. *The Arumanian Dialect of Kruševo, SR Macedonia*. Skopje: MANU.

Hamp, Eric P. 1977. On some questions of areal linguistics. In K. Whistlers et al., *Proceedings of the 3rd Annual Meeting of the Berkeley Linguistics Society*, 279–282. Berkeley: Berkeley Linguistics Society.

Hamp, Eric P. 1989. Yugoslavia – A crossroads of Sprachbünde. *Zeitschrift für Balkanologie* 25(1). 44–47.

Hamp, Eric P. 1994. Albanian. In R.E. Asher (ed.), *The encyclopedia of language and linguistics*, 65–67. Oxford: Pergamon Press.

Heine, Bernd & Tania Kuteva. 2006. *The changing languages of Europe*. Oxford: Oxford University Press.
Hinrichs, Uwe & Ljiljana Hinrichs. 1995. *Serbische Umgangsprache* (Osteuropa-Institut der Freien Universität Berlin Balkanologische Veröffentlichungen 27.) Wiesbaden: Harrassowitz.
Hlavac, Jim. 2003. *Second-generation speech: lexicon, code-switching and morpho-syntax of Croatian-English bilinguals*. Bern: Peter Lang.
Iannacito, Roberta. 2000. Il dialetto di villa San Michele (Isernia). University of Toronto dissertation.
Ilievski, Petar. 1973. Kon interpretacijata na modelot na udvoeniot objekt vo makedonskiot jazik. [Towards an interpretation of the model of the double object in Macedonian] *Godišen zbornik na Filozofski fakultet na Univerzitetot Skopje*, 205–220.
Jašar-Nasteva, Olivera. 1962/63. Makedonski kalki od turskiot jazik. [Calques in Macedonian based on Turkish] *Makedonski Jazik* 13/14.109–72.
Joseph, Brian D. 1983. *The synchrony and diachrony of the Balkan infinitive*. Cambridge: Cambridge University.
Kahl, Thede. 2011. Die letzten Wanderhirten Südosteuropas und ihre Sprache. Ein neuer Sammlungsbestand im Phonogrammarchiv der Österreichischen Akademie der Wissenschaften. In Gerda Lecheitner & Christian Liebl (eds.), *Jahrbuch des Phonogrammarchivs der Akademie der Wissenschaften in Wien* 2, 193–211. Vienna: Austrian Academy of Sciences.
Koufogiorgiou, Andromahi. 2003. Linguistic practices and gender dynamics in bilingual Metsovo (Greece). *Proceedings, 6th International Conference of Greek Linguistics*. Rethimo: Crete. www.philology.uoc.gr/conferences/6thICGL/ebook/g/kouforgiogou.pdf (accessed 19 January 2019).
Krle, Risto. 1967. *Parite se otepuvačka*. [Money is a murder] Skopje: Makedonska kniga.
Labov, William. 1966. *The social stratification of English in New York City*. Washington DC: Center for Applied Linguistics.
Labov, William. 2007. Transmission and diffusion. *Language* 83(2). 344–387.
Ledgeway, Adam. 2016. The dialects of Southern Italy. In Adam Ledgeway & Martin Maiden (eds.), *The Oxford guide to the Romance languages*, 246–269. Oxford: Oxford University Press.
Lindstedt, Jouko. 2000. Linguistic Balkanization: contact-induced change by mutual reinforcement. In Dicky Gilbers, John Nerbonne & Jos Schaeken (eds.), *Languages in contact (Studies in Slavic and General Linguistics 28)*, 231–246. Amsterdam: Rodopi.
Maretić, Tomo. 1963. *Gramatika hrvatskoga ili srpskoga jezika* [A grammar of the Croatian or Serbian language], [3rd edn.]. Zagreb: Matica Hrvatska.
Masica, Colin. 1991. *The Indo-Aryan languages*. Cambridge: Cambridge University Press.
Masica, Colin. 2001. The definition and significance of linguistic areas. In Peri Bhaskararao Bhaskararao & Karumuri Venkata Subbarao (eds.), *The Yearbook of South Asian Languages and linguistics*, 205–268. New Delhi: Sage.
Matras, Yaron. 2009. *Language contact*. Cambridge: Cambridge University Press.
Mufwene, Salikoko S. 2001. *The ecology of language evolution*. Cambridge: Cambridge University Press.
Myers-Scotton, Carol & Janet L. Jake. 2000. Testing the 4-M model: An introduction. *International Journal of Bilingualism* 4(1).1–8.

Myers-Scotton, Carol & Janet L. Jake. 2016. Revisiting the 4-M model: Codeswitching and morpheme election at the abstract level. *International Journal of Bilingualism* 21(2). 340–366.

Papahagi, Pericli N. 1908. Parallele Ausdrücke und Redensarten im Rumänischen, Albanesischen, Neugriechischen und Bulgarischen (Dissertation, University of Leipzig). *Jahresbericht des Instituts für rumänische Sprache zu Leipzig* 14. 113–170.

Perinić, Ana. 2006. Moliški Hrvati: Rekonstrukcija, kreiranja i reprezentacije jednog etničkog identiteta. [Molise Croats: The reconstruction, creation and representation of an ethnic identity], *Etnološka tribina* 36(29). 91–106.

Pescarini, Diego. 2016. Clitic pronominal systems: morphophonology. In Adam Ledgeway & Martin Maiden (eds.), *The Oxford guide to the Romance languages*, 742–757. Oxford: Oxford University Press.

Pescarini, Diego. In Press. *Pronoun systems across Romance.* Oxford Encyclopedia of Romance Linguistics. Oxford: Oxford University Press.

Piccoli, Agostina. 1993. 20 000 Molisini di origine Slava (Prilog boljem poznavanju moliških Hrvata) [20,000 inhabitants of Molise of Slav origin (Towards a better understanding of Molise Croats)]. *Studia ethnologica Croatica* 5. 175–180.

Récatas, Basile. 1934. *L'état actuel du bilinguisme chez les macédo-roumains du Pinde et le role de la femme dans le langage* [The current state of bilingualism among the Aromanians of the Pindus Mountains and the role of women in language]. Paris: Librarie Droz.

Sammartino, Antonio. 2004. *Grammatica della lingua croato-molisana/Gramatika moliškohrvatskoga jezika.* Montemitro/Zagreb: Fondazione "Agostina Piccol"/Profil.

Schallert, Joseph. 2017. Conev's Macedonians: The Aegean Macedonian emigree dialect of Derekjoj/Voden in Southeastern Bulgaria. *Balkanistixa* 30(2). 281–306.

Stevanović, Mihajlo. 1986. *Savremeni srpskohrvatski jezik* [Contemporary Serbo-Croatian], Vol. 1. 5th ed. Belgrade: Naučna Kniga.

Tadmor, Uri, Martin Haspelmath & Bradley Taylor. 2010. Borrowability and the notion of basic vocabulary. *Diachronica* 27(2). 226–246.

Thomason, Sarah G. & Terrence Kaufman. 1988. *Language contact, creolization, and genetic linguistics.* Berkeley: University of California.

Trubetzkoy, Nikolai S. 1923. Vavilonskaja bašnja i smešenie jazykov. [The Tower of Babel and the Confusion of Languages] *Evrazijskij vremennik* 3. 107–124.

Trubetzkoy, Nikolai S. 1930. Proposition 16. In Cornelis de Boer, Jacobus van Ginneken & Anton G. van Hamel (eds.), *Actes du Premier Congrès International des Linguistes à La Haye, du 10–15 Avril 1928*, 17–18. Leiden: A.W. Sijthoff.

Vidoeski, Božidar. 1998. *Dijalektite na makedonskiot jazik* I. [Dialects of the Macedonian Language I]. Skopje: MANU.

Wahlström, Max. 2015. *The loss of case inflection in Bulgarian and Macedonian.* Slavica Helsingiensia 47. Helsinki: Department of Modern Languages, University of Helsinki.

Croatian in Western Europe

Germany

Marijana Kresić Vukosav and Lucija Šimičić
Some aspects of language contact among Croatian-speakers in Lower Saxony, Germany

1 Introduction

Large-scale emigration of Croatian-speakers to Germany has occurred due to political changes, armed conflicts and the economic situation of Croats in their homeland. In the post-WWII period, West Germany, as it was known until 1990, has been the target destination for large numbers of Croats from Croatia and Bosnia-Herzegovina who sought work, at least on a temporary basis, in the West (Winland 2005). The so-called *Gastarbeiter* ('guest workers') moved from their homeland to Germany in the 1960s and early 1970s mainly for economic reasons, but partially also due to political circumstances in former Yugoslavia. In these diaspora situations, Croatian is spoken as a minority language in the dominant German-speaking host society by up to three generations of speakers. The wars in Croatia and Bosnia-Herzegovina in the 1990s and Croatia's accession to the EU in 2013 triggered new waves of migration to Germany, with the latest wave occurring mainly for economic reasons.

There has been considerable German-Croatian language contact for several centuries, and the influence of German on Croatian has been prominent, particularly in relation to the lexicon (Glovacki-Bernardi 1998, 2006; Stojić 2008). Croatian-German language contact in Germany due to the more recent immigration described above has resulted in new language contact phenomena and a situation where Croatian is used as a minority language outside Croatia. These phenomena have been studied by sociolinguists and language contact researchers from a number of perspectives. The first sociolinguistic studies on the language use and language attitudes of Croatian guest workers in Germany date back to the 1970s and 1980s and relate to descriptions of the language of Yugoslav guest workers, e.g. Stojanović (1984), Stölting (1980) and Ljubešić (1989). Muysken and Rott (2013) give an overview of more recent sociolinguistic studies on ethnolects in Germany, which include varieties spoken by speakers from former Yugoslavia. Recently, studies on Croatian-German language contact have examined lexical features (e.g. Raecke 2006), syntactic features (e.g. Hansen 2018), and aspects of bilingualism that relate to identity (e.g. Kresić 2011).

Marijana Kresić Vukosav and Lucija Šimičić, University of Zadar

https://doi.org/10.1515/9781501503917-005

This chapter is structured in the following way: The remaining parts of this section present general demographic and sociolinguistic information on Croatian-origin residents in Germany and on Croatian-speakers in that country. Section 2 presents information on the informants and the sample of spoken data which is the area of focus of this chapter. Section 3 contains sociolinguistic information on our informants, i.e. vintage of emigration, generational membership, features of intra-family language use and use of Croatian across domains, area of residence, contact with other Croatian-speakers, and language attitudes. Section 4 presents a description and analysis of linguistic data and Section 5 contains the conclusion and summary of our findings.

1.1 History of contact, vintages of emigration, and the status of Croatian-speakers in Germany

Croatian-German language contacts reach back to the Middle Ages, and from the eighteenth century onwards there was considerable migration from southern and central Germany (today's federal states of Baden-Württemberg, Bavaria, Rhineland-Palatinate, Hessen), as well as from neighbouring Alsace-Lorraine to the south-east parts of the Austro-Hungarian Empire including Croatia, Bosnia-Herzegovina and especially to Vojvodina (Serbia). Until the twentieth century, contact came about due to German-speakers migrating to areas populated by Croatian-speakers, rather than vice versa. The number of Croats who travelled or migrated to Germany before the last century was small and restricted to isolated groups of miners and seasonal workers. Larger numbers of Croatian-speakers began to arrive in Germany during WWII as political prisoners or prisoners of war, then immediately after WWII as displaced persons unable to be repatriated, evacuees from the Independent State of Croatia (NDH) and later as political exiles from the newly re-established Yugoslavia. Amongst those arriving in the immediate post-WWII era were approx. 150,000 ethnic Germans who were expelled from Croatian-speaking areas of the newly-established, then-named Federal People's Republic of Yugoslavia (FNRJ) – Slavonia, Baranya, western Srijem, central Croatia and parts of northern and central Bosnia. Most of these refugees spoke Croatian alongside their native German, although after their 'repatriation' to post-WWII West Germany, few continued to use Croatian.

Germany's post-WWII 'Economic Miracle' was based on large-scale re-industrialisation that required large numbers of workers in manufacturing and heavy industry. By 1961 there were 13,000 guest workers in West Germany from the SFRY, of whom the largest number were Croatian (Spiegel 1961). Large numbers of Croats began to arrive after West Germany signed a labour recruitment agreement

(*Anwerbeabkommen*) with the SFRY in 1968 that foresaw the organised transfer of guest workers to work in Germany. Croats were disproportionately over-represented amongst the 'guest workers' from SFRY, due partly to a higher level of dissatisfaction with the economic system and also repression within the political system in the SFRY, and due to the state's tacit policy of facilitating the emigration of Croats from Bosnia-Herzegovina (Nejašmić 2014). A cessation of all guest worker recruitment programs (*Anwerbestopp*) occurred in 1973 together with a policy of forcing or encouraging guest workers to return to their country of origin. Despite this, Germany had established itself as a popular destination for Croats and continues to remain one. The large number of guest workers who stayed on and established families in Germany or who organised for their spouses and children to join them in Germany were the 'first generation' of the now very sizeable German-Croatian immigrant community.

Although over 21% or 16,800,000 of Germany's 80 million residents were born outside Germany or have at least one parent born outside the country, Germany has been slow to acknowledge itself, both in a cultural and legal sense, as an 'immigrant country'. Legislation regulating legal immigration to Germany (*Einwanderungsgesetz*) was passed only in 2019. Official policies that recognise the cultural or linguistic profile of 'non-Germans' relate to 'indigenous' minorities only, such as the Sorbs in Lusatia and the Danes in Schleswig, with Romany also partly recognised. Germany has, as have many other European countries, ratified the European Charter on Minority or Regional Languages, which recognises and supports the languages of autochthonous groups. As a non-indigenous group in Germany, Croats and the Croatian language have no recognised minority status or status as a minority language in Germany.

1.2 Number of Croatian heritage residents, number of Croatian-speakers

One German source reports that "nearly 700,000 Serbs, Croatians or Bosnians came to West Germany between 1968 and [. . .] 1991, but many have not stayed on" (Deutsche Welle 2008). Looking back over the last 40 years at statistics from their country of origin, in the 1971 census, the Socialist Republic of Croatia (then one of the constituent republics of the SFRY) recorded 157,000 citizens resident in Germany, while in 1981, the figure was 145,000. It is, as stated, not easy to identify the number of Croats and speakers of Croatian, but more recent data (2012–2014) shows they were numerically the largest group of migrants from the SFRY and continued to be so after the breakup of the SFRY in 1991. In 2019, there were 373,360 Croatian citizens residing in Germany (Statista 2020a). There has been both return migration and re-migration to other countries amongst previous migrant cohorts. However, the continually high numbers are attributable to those who fled during the wars in Croatia and Bosnia-Herzegovina in the 1990s, and to those who have migrated for economic reasons since 2013, the year of Croatia's accession to the EU.

The current official number of 373,360 Croatian citizens residing in Germany (Statista 2020a) is not an accurate representation of the total number of Croats or Croatian-speakers in Germany. First, many Croatians have acquired German citizenship, which in most cases entails the loss of Croatian citizenship, while many other Croatian-origin residents in Germany had the opportunity to gain German citizenship by being born in Germany. Second, many Croats travel to Germany to work, residing for some time in that country without officially registering a change of address. Third, there are 182,178 residents with Bosnian-Herzegovinian citizenship living in Germany (Statista 2020b), and we assume that up to roughly a third of them are ethnic Croats, so that the estimated actual number of persons with Croatian background residing in Germany is most probably higher.

Taking into account the relative recency of immigration to Germany, dating back at the earliest to the 1960s with more recent waves of immigrants, it is likely that almost all first-generation migrants still retain proficiency in Croatian, and a very large proportion of their children, the second generation, can also speak and use Croatian. Together with the smaller number of third-generation speakers with proficiency, and the tens of thousands of ethnic Germans from Croatian-speaking areas who fled Yugoslavia in 1945 and who are still alive, we estimate that there are 425,000 to 450,000 Croatian-speakers in Germany. To this, there are further 250,000 speakers (or thereabouts) of Serbian and a similar number of Bosnian-speakers in Germany with whom Croatian-speakers can communicate in their mother tongue. This further extends the number of interlocutors with whom Croatian can be used.

1.3 Geographic distribution and socio-economic profile

The majority of Croats live in the western and southern part of Germany. In 2017, there were 126,000 living in Baden-Württemberg, 95,000 in Bavaria, 61,000 in North Rhine-Westphalia, 50,000 in Hesse, 19,000 in Rhineland-Palatinate, 13,000 in Berlin, 13,000 in Lower Saxony and 7,000 in Bremen (Statistisches Bundesamt 2016: 127–129). The same source states no figures on the numbers of Croats in eastern parts of Germany such as Mecklenburg Vorpommern or Brandenburg.

It is difficult to define the socio-economic profile of Croats in Germany, due to significant differences in migration patterns in the pre-1990 period compared to more recent migration waves. While 1960s emigration from Croatia to Germany occurred primarily due to political reasons, in the 1970s and 1980s it was primarily economic conditions that precipitated emigration (Čizmić, Sopta and Šakić 2005). The differences in push and pull factors in different periods are reflected in the socio-demographic structure of Croatian emigrants to Germany. Those who left the country as guest workers, many of whom were not highly educated and who tended to work in manual and low-wage sectors, are now retired. In contrast, their children are usually well integrated into German mainstream society in terms of their educational and employment profiles. More recent emigrants from Croatia tend to belong to a younger demographic group, i.e. 25–40 years of age, with a large number having completed a university degree with previous employment experience in Croatia (Jurić 2017). As many of them moved to Germany with the hope of career advancement, their personal and socio-economic profiles tend to be different from those of earlier vintages of emigrants.

1.4 Infrastructure

The focal point of Germany's Croatian community are the 95 Croatian Catholic Missions located mainly in the western part of Germany, serviced by 90 priests. The missions are a centre of not only religious and cultural life, but also social, educational and sporting activities (Kroatenseelsorge in Deutschland 2013). The Catholic Church's social welfare organisation *Caritas* employs Croatian-speaking social workers to provide counselling and other services to German-Croats. There are over 25 Croatian local soccer clubs in Germany, a number of branches of political parties based in Croatia, and a range of artistic and cultural associations. An umbrella association, the *Kroatischer Weltkongress in Deutschland* (Croatian World Congress in Germany), encompasses more than 45 Croatian clubs and associations in Germany. It aims to foster Croats' integration into their new host country, and to assist the maintenance of Croatian culture and heritage in Germany.

Croatian language instruction for schoolchildren of Croatian origin in Germany is co-ordinated by the Croatian Ministry of Science and Education. In the 2015/2016 school year, 48 teachers were providing Croatian instruction to approximately 3,000 pupils, mostly via supplementary classes conducted in the afternoon on weekdays, i.e. as instruction additional to their regular schooling in the German educational system. Classes are held in larger cities and towns across Germany, including Stuttgart, Ulm, Mannheim, Berlin and in the federal states of Bavaria, Hessen, Saarland and Hamburg. Croatian is taught at the following universities in Germany, often in combination with Bosnian, Montenegrin and/or Serbian: Berlin (Humboldt), Cologne, Giessen, Göttingen, Hamburg, Munich and Regensburg.

1.5 Domain use, language maintenance and shift

The geographical proximity of Germany to Croatia facilitates contacts between Croats living in Germany and their family and friends in the country of origin. However, geographical proximity alone is not a safeguard of language maintenance. It was reported as early as 30 years ago that there seems to be an overall trend of attrition of Croatian at an individual level, and towards language shift amongst younger generation members (e.g. Ljubešić 1989, 1992). However, such a generalization overlooks a number of specific local contexts where such a trend may not always be the case. It is generally true that first-generation migrants tend to use Croatian in many more domains than those who belong to the second and/or third generations, and that they are linguistically dominant in Croatian in contrast to subsequent generations. However, even the speech of first-generation speakers can undergo changes with some instances of apparent simplification, reduction and codeswitching. These phenomena are also likely to depend on the length of time spent in Germany and on other socio-demographic parameters such as level of education and age. Instances of reduction and codeswitching are reportedly apparent amongst second- and third-generation migrants, with the functional restrictedness of Croatian to a smaller number of domains being both a causative circumstance and a consequential effect of changes in communicative competence.

One of the factors that is directly related to the rate of language shift is the level of integration into various Croatian networks in the host society: the denser such networks are, the more chance the speakers have to use Croatian beyond the family / home domains which facilitate language maintenance. Such social networks are often associated with sports and/or religious activities. At the same time, it should be pointed out that only certain cohorts of Croatian emigrants are actively involved in these. On the other hand, a general trend of assimilation into German society, increasing rates of exogamy and a high level of mobility within the host country (for educational and employment reasons) have a negative impact on the use of Croatian and are conducive to language shift to German. In view of the profiles of the most recent arrivals, these latter factors may be decisive in overall levels of language maintenance rather than membership in a particular generational group.

1.6 Contacts with Croatia and host society attitudes towards Croats

Most Croats living in Germany have more or less frequent contacts with their relatives and friends in Croatia. The length and frequency of their visits and the types of interactions they have seems to depend, among other factors, on the individual's sense of belonging to Croatia and Croatian culture, as well as on their Croatian language competence. Although there are individual differences recorded amongst the informants of this sample, the maintenance of strong ties with Croatia is more pronounced amongst first-generation immigrants than amongst second or third generation German-Croats.

Travel between Croatia and Germany can be achieved by car in one or two days, while the increasing number of flights between the two countries now means that travel time can be even shorter. As a result, most German-Croats visit Croatia at least once or twice a year, with a large number of them spending their summer vacations there, often in holiday apartments or houses that they themselves own.

New communication possibilities via smartphone and computer, as well as social media have enhanced opportunities and ways to interact with those back home. In addition to this, Croats in Germany, especially those belonging to the first and second generations tend to keep abreast of political and social developments in Croatia through electronic or print media such as newspapers, social media, radio and TV.

Migratory movements do not proceed in one direction only. There is a considerable number of returnees (e.g. retired pensioners) and 're-migrants' or those now spending lengthy periods of time back in Croatia, e.g. second or third generation members who study at Croatian universities or who seek to gain employment experience working in Croatia. For many of them, this is not only an educational or occupational investment, but a fulfilment of their own dream (and very often that of their parents and/or grandparents), i.e. members of their family returning to their ancestors' homeland (cf. Čapo, Hornstein Tomić and Jurčević 2014, Kresić Vukosav and Thüne 2019).

It can be observed that members of the German 'host' society have a generally positive attitude towards migrants of Croatian origin. To some extent, these host society attitudes towards Croatian immigrants can be traced back to political developments in the early 1990s when Germany was one of the first countries to recognize Croatia's independence. Croats represent a group of immigrants who have integrated relatively well into German society, also due to their relatively good German language skills and due to many similarities between German and Croatian culture. Many second- and especially third-generation Croats are quite assimilated into German culture and amongst many of these, there can be an accompanying decrease in Croatian language proficiency and a lower degree of identification with Croatian culture and society. Individual differences are also observable with respect to psychological and social distance felt towards German host society (cf. Schumann 1978). This appears to be co-determined by speakers' educational and socio-economic profiles.

2 Participants and data collection

In this chapter, we discuss the results of an analysis of the sociolinguistic profiles, language attitudes and language use of Gen.1 and Gen.2 speakers of Croatian in the north German federal state of Lower Saxony, and present an analysis of some features of the speech of emigrants in this specific diaspora situation, particularly with regard to language contact phenomena between Croatian and German found in their speech production in Croatian.[1]

The data for our analysis consists of information gathered by means of an anonymous questionnaire and through individual and group interviews relating to speakers' language biographies, language attitudes, linguistic practices and identification patterns. The fieldwork was carried out in Hannover, the capital of Lower Saxony, in November 2016. We interviewed only speakers with proficiency in Croatian, and we do not discuss the linguistic features of those Croatian origin residents in Lower Saxony who have shifted completely to German and whose proficiency in Croatian is very low, or those who have no command of Croatian. Semi-structured interviews lasting between 25–60 minutes were conducted with 12 participants: three Gen.1 participants and nine Gen.2 participants, six males and six females. We initiated the interviews and mostly conducted them in Croatian, but in a few cases interviewees spontaneously switched to German, especially towards the end of the interviews. The total length of the corpus of spoken data is 6 hours, 23 minutes and 7 seconds. It contains a variety of forms and features relevant to the field of contact linguistics, such as codeswitching (intra-clausal insertions), inter-clausal switching or alternations, covert cross-linguistic influence (convergence), lexical transferences and loan translation, which will be analysed in section 4 of this chapter.

Our relationship to the informants that contributed the data for this chapter is the following: the first author was born in Hannover, Germany, where she spent her childhood and a part of her adulthood. She is a Croatia-based linguist who has also conducted linguistic fieldwork on multilingualism, and of language use and identity amongst German-Croatian bilinguals. The second author is a Croatia-based sociolinguist and anthropological linguist who has led qualitative-based linguistic fieldwork studies on linguistic minorities in Croatia, Germany and Italy. The language variety that we employed as interviewers and fellow interlocutors in the recorded interactions with informants was mainly Croatian, although all inform-

---

[1] We would like to express our gratitude to the participants of our study who willingly agreed to help us with the data collection, as well as to Jasna Aničić from the Croatian Ministry of Science, Education and Sport, for providing us with information material on supplementary Croatian-language instruction in Germany.

ants knew that we are Croatian-German bilinguals. This largely monolingual (Croatian) variety used by the interviewers may have had an effect on informants' readiness or frequency in codeswitching or employing forms that are characteristic of 'in-group' interactions amongst members of the Croatian diaspora in Germany. The conventions in relation to the presentation of excerpts taken from the corpus are the following: informant number, generation, sex, and age – i.e. '15, Gen.2, M, 35' relates to informant no. 15 of the second generation, male and aged 35.

In this chapter, we focus on those linguistic features that derive from language contact between German and Croatian amongst members of the Croatian diaspora resident in Lower Saxony. We disregard those German-origin derived features (e.g. established borrowings and loan translations) which themselves are found in standard or non-standard varieties of homeland Croatian (hereafter: 'HMLD.Cro'). In the analysis we thus disregard long-standing German-influenced features on the assumption that they were acquired via heritage-language acquisition, and not as the result of the language contact situation that we discuss here.

At the time when the fieldwork was conducted four of our participants were active in Croatian diaspora associations such as the Croatian Catholic Mission in Hannover or the local Croatian sports (football) club. Another six occasionally participated in events organized by the Croatian community, while two had only sporadic connections with it. The personal acquaintances of the first author were our initial point of contact with participants, the afore-mentioned ethnic-specific associations and the 'snowball effect' led to contact with further participants.

The semi-structured interviews started with an elicitation of short linguistic biographies in order for us to learn about the order in which they acquired different languages, their perceived competence, language attitudes towards and the use of both Croatian and German, with further questions relating to linguistic and cultural self-identification. All Gen.1 participants had completed compulsory education in their homeland in their first language, Croatian. About half of the Germany-born Gen.2 participants had attended supplementary formal instruction in Croatian. Two of the Gen.1 participants came to Germany in the 1960s and 1970s, while the third one migrated to Germany in 2002 after having married a Gen.2 migrant. All our Gen.2 members are also children of migrants who arrived in Germany in the 1960s and 1970s. However, most of our participants keep very close ties with Croatia, visit the country for at least several weeks a year and two Gen.1 and three Gen.2 participants claim to feel comfortable speaking both Croatian and German as they use Croatian regularly at home and in many situations that involve Croatian-speaking migrants also outside of their home.

From the recorded interviews we report that the speech of both Gen.1 and Gen.2 speakers bears influence from German. We posit that this variation can be accounted for by linguistic and extra-linguistic factors, such as the amount of formal schooling in Croatian and exposure to Croatian in general, individual motivations and language attitudes. Most of our participants in the study are keenly aware of their bilingual patterns of language use:

(1) *Da, ali jest tako, mislim ubacuješ njemačke riječi. Ali često, ovaj, kad ja osjetim da, ovaj, baš na ide dobro, kad je neka kompliciranija tema, jel, tu su Nijemci ja pribacim totalno na njemački. Zato što jednostavno lakše mi je razgovarati o tome. Znači često se možda i počne neka šala ili nešto na hrvatskom, al kad, ovaj, skreneš na neke druge teme koje su malo teže, onda ja onda brže prebacim na njemački.*

'Yes, but it is like that, I think you insert German words. But often, well, when I feel that this does not work really well, if it is some complicated topic, because there are Germans around, I totally switch to German. Because it is simply easier for me to talk about that. This means that I often perhaps even start with a joke or something in Croatian, but when I get to some other topics that are a little bit more difficult, then I quickly switch to German.'

(5,Gen.2,M,40)

(2) A: *A ovisi o ekipi, sad da ima par ljudi koji više bacaju na njemački, a ima par pričaju više hrvatski pa onda ko je u tom trenutku dominantniji onda se automatski malo pribaciš [. . .]*
B: *To kad triba nešto reć da me niko ne razumije drugi onda pričamo na hrvatski to je uvik bilo najbolje miješano.*
A: *Da baš.*
B: *Čak i u razgovoru nekad miješano . . .*

A: 'Well it depends on the group, there are a few people who tend more towards German and there are a few who speak more Croatian, and then whoever is more dominant in that moment, then you automatically switch a little bit [. . .]'
B: 'That is when I need to say something and I don't want anyone else to understand me, then we speak Croatian, that was always the best, mixed.'
A: 'Yes, indeed.'
B: 'Even in conversation sometimes it is mixed . . .'

A – (10,Gen.2,M,43); B – (9,Gen.2,M,42)

As outlined by informant 5 in example (1) above, inserting German words into Croatian speech is described as a common phenomenon in bilingual speech by one of the participants himself. Switching between Croatian and German can be attributed to a number of things: conversation topic, moves internal to the interaction that index the use of one language in comparison to another, the perceived dominance of others, and other factors, such as that of an 'exclusionary function', as outlined in (2) above. The same example also suggests that 'language mixing' is not felt by the Gen.2 participants to be a negative phenomenon, but a natural and even advantageous speech style.

3 Sociolinguistic description of participants' Croatian language use

As a backdrop to the analysis of linguistic contact phenomena we were interested in gaining a broader insight into extralinguistic aspects of the sociolinguistic situation of the speakers whose language patterns we discuss. Changes in linguistic structure never occur in a social vacuum and their analysis remains only partial if they are not contextualized and interpreted in view of a broader sociolinguistic context, language attitudes and language practices. In his theory of the factors that lead to language death (or shift), Sasse (1992) provides a holistic approach to understanding the process of language decline leading to language death. Although the contexts he was primarily concerned about are generally different from situations typical of the sociolinguistic setting in diaspora communities, the process of language shift described by him is nonetheless similar in the two cases. Namely, in multilingual contexts, including a migratory one, a range of non-linguistic factors – political, economic, cultural or sociological ones, which Sasse terms External Setting (ES), lead to a distribution of domains at the level of Speech Behaviour (SB), which causes "loss or failure of development" in those areas where a majority language (L_{maj}) is preferred at the level which Sasse terms Structural Consequences (SC). Although bilingualism in such settings is often complementary at first, further pressures from the ES lead to the reduction of domains in which the minority language (L_{min}) is used. The ensuing transference and simplification may have a negative impact on language attitudes towards L_{min}. These seem to be one of the crucial triggers for intergenerational transmission, which leads to language maintenance if it is preserved, and language shift if it is interrupted. The link between language attitudes and language shift is not as straightforward in diaspora communities as many ES and SB factors may influence the structural level. However, Sasse's (1992) model is in many ways applicable in understanding the structural aspect of contact phenomena.

This is why prior to organizing individual interviews we collected questionnaire data from three generational groups. These were collected through the distribution of questionnaires (made available in both languages) at the Croatian heritage language school in Hannover and in the local Croatian Catholic Mission, as well as to further potential participants not associated with these organizations via the 'snowball' effect. Forty-four questionnaires were collected: 18 (42%) from Gen.1 speakers; 21 (45%) from Gen.2 speakers; 4 (8%) from Gen.3 speakers, while one participant did not identify a generational affiliation. Although the sample is too small to draw any conclusions about the overall patterns of migration to Lower Saxony, the collected data indicate that the majority of the respondents, most of whom moved to Germany in their late teens or early twenties, migrated in the period of the economic crisis of the 1970s and 1980s. The aim of the questionnaire study was to get an insight into socio-demographic data of Croats living in Lower Saxony, self-reported language competence, language use across domains, including private and public ones, ethnic self-identification and linguistic identification, and language attitudes. The sociolinguistic questionnaire to elicit this information was structured loosely following the model of sociolinguistic questionnaires often used in the study of multilingual contexts, e.g. Iannaccaro and Dell'Aquila (2011), and Laakso et al. (2016), including those applied in situations where a minority language is undergoing language shift, e.g. Dorian (1981) and Šimičić and Vuletić (2016). Although the frequency and domains of language use may be indicative of language vitality within a speech community, the subjective perception of the language group by its members may be more revealing of its likelihood to be maintained in further generations.

There was an additional set of questions regarding the attitudes towards and motives for language transmission and maintenance in a version of the questionnaire for adults (regardless of the generation they belonged to). We performed an analysis by running a non-parametric Kruskal-Wallis H test in SPSS on all variables of interest.[2] The generational split of our sample proved to be the most relevant variable that can account for the different behaviour of our respondents by yielding statistically significant results for other variables analysed below. Due to the small number of Gen.3 informants, the results gained from them need to be seen in this context. Otherwise, the overall size of this sample is such that we make no claim that this sample is representative of Croatian-speakers in Lower Saxony or elsewhere in Germany.

While the three generations differ significantly in terms of their claimed nationality and citizenship, no statistically significant differences were found in the responses regarding their self-identification either as Croats or as Germans or as a mixture of the two. The *post hoc* analysis shows, however, that 94.1% of Gen.1

---

[2] We opted for the Kruskal-Wallis H as it does not require the groups to be of the same size and can be used for samples that are not characterized by normal distribution.

and 78.9% of Gen.2 respondents self-identify at least to some extent as Croatian compared to 22.3% in Gen.1 and 26.4% in Gen.2 who self-identify at least partly as German. The questionnaire offered a possibility for claiming multiple identities (*I feel as ... Croatian-German, German-Croatian, both Croatian and German*), which is the reason why cumulative percentages for each generation amount to over 100%.

No significant differences were found concerning German language competence. However, in relation to Croatian, there are conspicuous differences in self-assessment of language competence for both active (speaking) and passive (comprehension) skills in Croatian and there is a clear descending trend according to generation: $M_{GEN.1}=3.83$, $M_{GEN.2}=3.31$ for comprehension and $M_{GEN.2}=3.15$ for speaking, and $M_{GEN.3}=3.00$ for comprehension and $M_{GEN.3}=2.50$ for speaking of Croatian on a scale from 1 (not at all) to 4 (completely) (Figure 1).

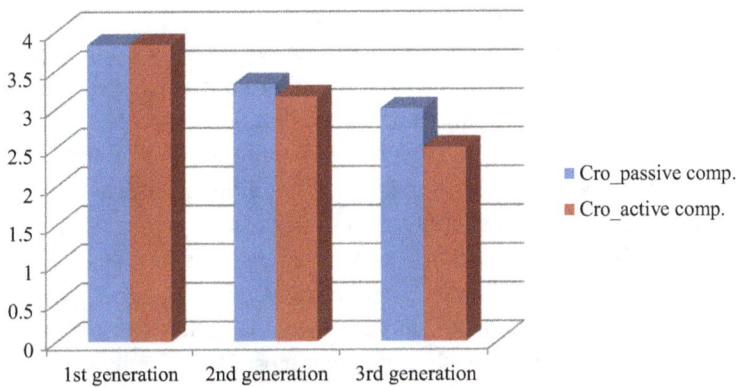

Figure 1: Level of self-reported active (productive) and passive (receptive) language competence amongst Gen.1, Gen.2 and Gen.3 Croatian-speakers. A four-value Likert scale of linguistic proficiency ranging from 1 (non-existent) to 4 (completely/fully proficient) was employed.

A similar trend is visible in the order of acquisition of macro skills; while respondents from Gen.1 acquired mostly Croatian as their L1 in both speaking and writing, Gen.2 tended to acquire spoken Croatian along with German as their L1, but due to formal schooling, acquired German first in reading and writing. The trend is even more pronounced when it comes to Gen.3, but less so in spoken language skills.

Other important sociolinguistic differences between generations concern language use in various domains, including reading books in Croatian, experiences of language normativism (whether practised by others towards them or self-directed), and finally language attitudes. There are very few domains – largely public and institutionalized ones, such as formal schooling, employment and, certain communicative situations and genres such as prayer – where the differences between generations are not statistically significant, while significant differences (p<0.05) were found in all other domains that include a variety of (semi-)private domains and communicative situations such as family, free time, contact with neighbours, activities in the Croatian Catholic Mission, in sports clubs, and a number of strictly personal and in many cases less controlled instances of language use (emotional expression, dreaming, swearing, counting, talking to pets, thinking [or self-directed 'talking'], but also joke telling, newspaper reading and language use on Facebook) (Figure 2). The overall mean scores for language use in different domains and in different genres (reliability α=0.95 on a 19-point scale) are: $M_{GEN.1}$=1.76, $M_{GEN.2}$= 2.29 and $M_{GEN.3}$=2.02 on the scale where 1 refers to Croatian and 3 to German, while 2 implies using both languages. As mentioned above, the sample of Gen.3 informants is particularly small and cannot be considered representative of all Gen.3 informants, and this partly accounts for the unexpected higher use of Croatian amongst Gen.3 informants in comparison to that of Gen.2 informants.

On a 4-point scale, 1 implies using Croatian only, 2 using both languages, 3 using German only, while 4 implies using some other language. Lower mean scores indicate, therefore, a more frequent use of the Croatian language.

Another question focused on the language of different media that our respondents consume most. There seem to be no major differences between the three generations as far as the frequency of consumption of newspapers, TV, internet portals in either German or Croatian is concerned, and the only significant difference was found in book reading in Croatian with Gen.2 and Gen.3 lagging far behind Gen.1 (M=1.82, sd=0.81 on a Likert scale from 1: regularly to 3: never). According to the results of our survey, it seems that most of the family communication (except the communication of parents to children, communication with older generations – grandparents and older relatives as well as with relatives in Croatia) is strongly affected by the length of stay in a country of immigration and there is a clear tendency amongst respondents to switch to German.

We also wanted to check to what extent the speech of Croats living in Lower Saxony was subjected to negative remarks, for example, whether informants, of any generation, had experienced being corrected or criticised by others about their language use (i.e. language normativism). That is why we introduced a questionnaire item for these dimensions although they are not commonly used in similar studies. We assume that both types of negative evaluation may be due (at least to some extent) to the perceived errors that stem from linguistic transference at any level of linguistic structure. Gen.2 speakers had significantly higher scores in both cases compared to Gen.1 (M=1.89 for language correction, and M=1.17 for mocking or criticism) when speaking Croatian in Croatia. Interestingly enough, no such differences in answers of different generations were found for using German in Germany.

Some aspects of language contact among Croatian-speakers in Lower Saxony

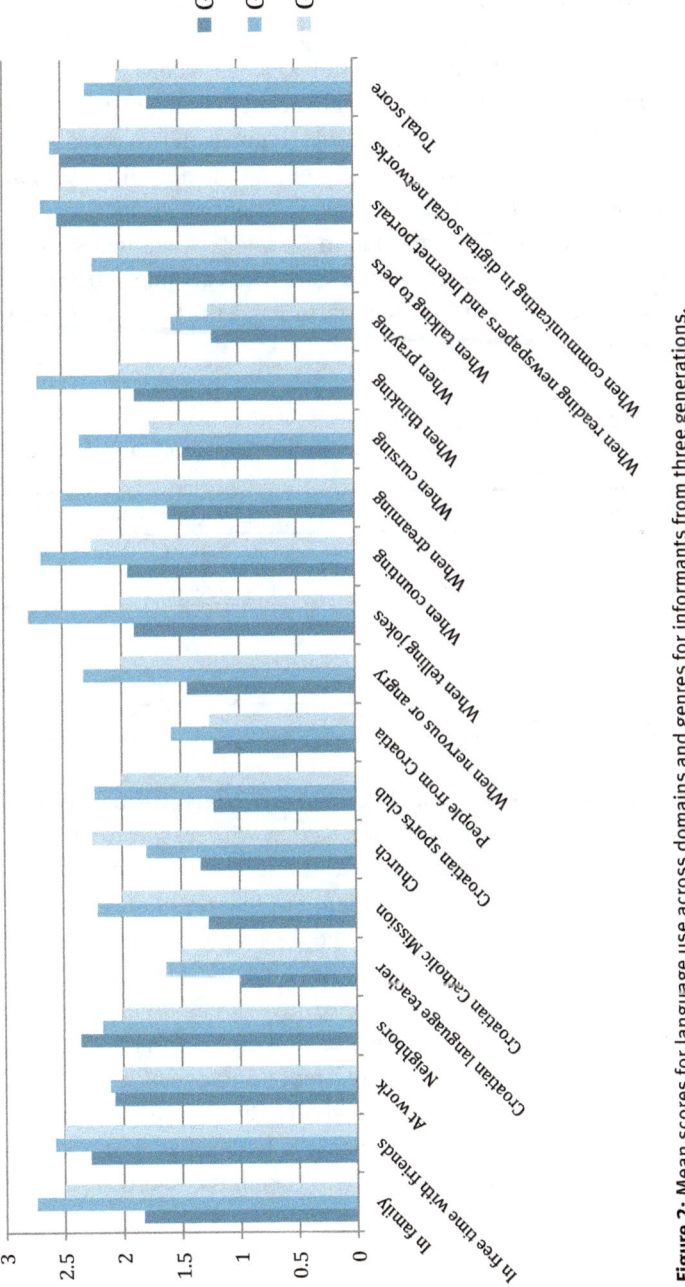

Figure 2: Mean scores for language use across domains and genres for informants from three generations.

Finally, considering the importance of language attitudes for both language transmission and language maintenance in general (e.g. Sasse 1992) it is notable that a slightly negative trend is observed in attitudes expressed towards Croatian (reliability α=0.83 on a 21-item scale) which is statistically significant: $M_{GEN.1}$=3.41, $M_{GEN.2}$=3.07 and $M_{GEN.3}$=3.06 on a 4-point Likert scale (1: not at all – 4: completely). When answers to individual questions are analysed, significant differences are found on five items as presented in Table 1 below: "I like to speak Croatian", "I express my feelings better in Croatian than in German", "Croatian is a completely useless language and there is no need to learn it", "I am interested in Croatian and would like to learn it" and "I do my best to speak the Croatian standard variety".

Table 1: Mean scores per generation for attitude statements for which statistically significant differences were found between generations on a Likert scale from 1 (not at all) to 4 (completely).

Language attitude statements (p<0.05)	Gen.1	Gen.2	Gen.3
I like speaking Croatian.	3.94	3.40	3.25
I express my feelings better in Croatian than in German.	3.44	1.83	2.00
Croatian is a completely useless language and there is no need to learn it.	1.00	1.00	1.25
I am interested in Croatian and would like to learn it.	3.92	2.83	3.5
I do my best to speak standard Croatian	3.33	2.37	2.75

One of the main results of the study was that there are differences between the three generations of Croatian migrants to Lower Saxony with respect to a number of investigated questions. The analysis showed that there are differences not only in our participants' competence in Croatian, but that Gen.1 differs significantly from Gen.2 and Gen.3 in the frequency and the domains of language use and, somewhat more surprisingly, in their attitudes towards Croatian, and more specifically towards the conative rather than cognitive or emotional aspects of language attitudes. As stated, the responses here are drawn from a sample of 44 participants only and cannot be considered representative of all Croatian-speakers in Lower Saxony or of Germany as a whole. They are, however, indicative of certain sociolinguistic and psycholinguistic tendencies that might be reflected at the structural level and that are discussed in the following section of this chapter.

4 Language contact phenomena in the spoken Croatian data

The spoken data collected in the frame of this study was transcribed and analysed with respect to language contact phenomena (cf. Kresić 2011: 98–99). More specifically, we study language contact phenomena with respect to "either (1) how the elements of two language varieties are used together in some way or (2) how the grammar of one variety affects the grammar of another" (Myers-Scotton 2006a: 234). We categorized a set of language contact phenomena into (a) intra-clausal codeswitching, (b) inter-clausal codeswitching, (c) covert cross-linguistic influence / convergence (morphosyntactic calques), and (d) semantic transfers and loan translations. Whereas categories 4.1. and 4.2. (see below) follow the Matrix Language Frame (MLF) Model (Myers-Scotton 2002, 2006a; Jake, Myers-Scotton and Gross 2002), categories 4.3–4.4 are formed on the basis of psycholinguistic approaches to language contact and bilingualism as explored in the work of one of the authors (cf. Kresić 2011; De Angelis, Jessner and Kresić 2015). The list of types of language contact and levels of linguistic description is by no means exhaustive. We are mainly interested in language contact on the morphological, lexical and syntactic, but also on the discourse-pragmatic level. It is important to point out that our analysis is restricted only to those contact-induced phenomena in the speech of Croatian diaspora members that can be traced back directly to German.

The presentation of particular contact linguistic phenomena in the examples presented in this section is, in general terms, indicative of the forms and features found in the corpus. However, an exact quantification of these features across the whole sample is not provided here since we are mainly interested in a qualitative exploration of the types of contact-linguistic phenomena occurring in the collected data.

4.1 Intra-clausal codeswitching

According to the MLF model (Myers-Scotton 1993, 2002), codeswitching is defined as the use of elements from two (or more) languages *within* one clause, i.e. the term refers to *intra-clausal* codeswitching. This phenomenon is labelled *classic codeswitching* and characterised by the dominance of the morphosyntactic structure of one of the languages, which provides the grammatical frame for the respective sentence (cf. Myers-Scotton 2006a: 239). "Morphosyntactic frame means all the abstract requirements that would make the frame well-formed in the language in question (concerning word order, morpheme order, and the necessary inflectional morphemes)". This phenomenon can be found quite frequently in the speech of the interviewed speakers across Gen.1 and Gen.2:

(3) svi   koji   su   tamo   na
    all-NOM.M.PL   REL.PRON-NOM.M.PL   AUX-3PL there at+LOC
    sajmu   radili   isto su   bili   kao
    trade-fair-LOC.M.SG   work-PST.M.PL   also AUX-3PL be-PST.3PL   like
    Nijemci   meni   isto su   svoj
    German-NOM.M.PL   me-DAT   also AUX-3PL own-ACC.M.SG
    posao   **haben**   **den**   **ernst**   **genommen**
    job-ACC.M.SG   AUX-3PL   it-ACC.M.SG   seriously   take-PST.PTCP
    'All who worked there at the trade fair, they were also like Germans to me. Also, their work, they **took it seriously**.' (12,Gen.2,F,31)

The part of the sentence that is codeswitched into German is printed in bold in all example sentences. The sentence in (3) starts in Croatian, which as the frame language supplies the morphosyntactic frame for the whole utterance. What is interesting is that the predicate is split in such a way that the auxiliary verb is supplied in the first, Croatian part of the sentence, and this auxiliary is repeated in the added part in the embedded language German, which then supplies the perfect participle plus the noun, i.e. the content word in this noun phrase (= Ger. *ernst nehmen* – Eng. *take something or someone seriously*). In other words, the Croatian AUX *su* 'be-3PL' occurs in an uncompleted Croatian phrase, and as the phrase is completed in German, the auxiliary verb is repeated in German. This suggests that in syntactic terms, the phrase *ernst nehmen* in the PRS.PRF needs to have the auxiliary verb supplied by the embedded language, in this case German. If the auxiliary in the German part of (3) had been omitted, the sentence would not be well-formed as *den*-DEF.ART.ACC.M.SG could be confused as the definite article for the noun *ernst*-ACC.M.SG. It is, in fact, a determiner functioning as a pronoun (in direct object case) referring back to the (Croatian) antecedent *posao*- 'work-ACC.M.SG'. Example (4) below contains another intra-clausal codeswitch between SBJ and PRED.

(4) ja   sam   devedeset četvrte   **Abitur**   **machen**
    I   AUX-1SG   ninety-four-GEN.F.SG   A levels   make-INF
    'I did in [19] ninety-four my *Abitur* [A-levels].' (7,Gen.2,M,41)

Similar to (3), in (4) a verb phrase in the embedded language German *Abitur machen* 'to do A-levels [to complete the last year of high school]' is added, thereby supplying the second part of the predicate. While the AUX *sam* be-1SG is supplied in Croatian, the main meaning of the predicate is expressed in German by a verb phrase consisting of the noun *Abitur* and the infinitive *machen*. The sense here is past (i.e. present perfect), but the main verb form supplied from German is not the past participle form, but the infinitive or 'baseline' form. In both (3) and (4), Croatian functions as the matrix language as it supplies the main, i.e. inflected part of the predicate and the subject form. Other instances of German-Croatian intra-clausal codeswitching are reported in AUT.Cro (see Ščukanec, this volume), as well as in studies of Croatian as a diaspora language in contact with other languages (see Ščukanec, Breu and Vuk; Županović Filipin, Hlavac and Piasevoli; Piasevoli; Petrović; Hlavac and Stolac; Stoffel and Hlavac; and Skelin Horvat, Musulin and Blažević, all this volume).

4.2 Inter- and extra-clausal codeswitching

Inter-clausal codeswitching is defined as the change to another language (here: from Croatian to German) for one or more clause(s), usually within one conversational turn, comprising full sentences in both languages (cf. Myers-Scotton 2006a: 239–240).

(5) *pa   ne   ja znam   sama*   **ich lebe zu Hause**
     well   no   I   know-1SG   self-F.SG   I   live at   home.
     'Well no . . . I know myself. **I live at home.**' (12,Gen.2,F,31)

Example (5) includes two clauses that the speaker utters within the same conversational turn, i.e. the example includes full sentences in Croatian and in German. The speaker has codeswitched to German in the second sentence. These types of inter-clausal codeswitches are common in the speech of bilinguals when conversing with other bilingual speakers, and they can be induced by the topic, the context of the conversation etc. However, from our observation, this type of codeswitching also represents a common bilingual communication strategy through which the interlocutors are drawing on their bilingual repertoires in naturalistic speech with other Croatian-Germans. The codeswitch that occurs in this example itself bears little conversational implicature and appears as an unmarked feature of speech with a peer. When in the company of other Croatian-German bilinguals, these multilingual speakers freely draw on both languages. The following exemplary turn commences in German:

(6) | *die* | *gute* | | *Frau* | *Kempel,* | *to* |
| --- | --- | --- | --- | --- | --- |
| the-NOM.F.SG | good-NOM.F.SG | | Mrs | Kempel | that-NOM.N.SG |
| *je* | *bila* | *stara* | | *njemačka* | |
| AUX.3SG | be-PST.F.SG | old-NOM.F.SG | | German-NOM.F.SG | |
| *čistačica* | | *reče* | *samo* | **"Hää?"** | *a ja* |
| cleaning lady-NOM.F.SG | | say-AOR.3SG | only | "Whaat?" | and I |
| *njoj* | **"Was stellen Sie hier dar?"** | | | | |
| her-DAT | "What do represent you here?" | | | | |

'**Good old Mrs. Kempel**, she was an old German cleaning lady, and she just said "**Whaat**?" and I replied "**What do you represent here?**"' (2,Gen.1,F,70)

Example (6) contains both, one intra-clausal codeswitch and two inter-clausal codeswitches occurring in the same conversational turn. Intra-clausal codeswitching occurs insofar as the speaker expresses the subject of the sentence in the embedded language German *Die gute Frau Kempel*... 'Good old Mrs. Kempel', and connects the rest of the sentence with this antecedent through a determiner, which is the semantically empty subject of the following copula sentence *to je bila stara njemačka čistačica* 'that was an old German cleaning lady' in the matrix language Croatian. In the following clause, the speaker introduces a passage of reported speech that is supplied in German *Hää?*, which represents an instance of inter-clausal codeswitching. Then a new introduction of reported speech in the frame language Croatian *a ja njoj* is followed by another quote of direct speech, again provided in the embedded language German *"Was stellen Sie hier dar?"*. Within the frame language Croatian, by means of the inter-clausal codeswitches, the speaker gives an account of a conversation that itself took place in Germany, thereby reproducing the reported speech segments in German as verbalised by the interlocutors themselves in the interaction. This is an example of how quoting verbatim the speech of others can be accompanied by inter-clausal codeswitching. Examples of inter-clausal codeswitches containing quotes are found also in ITAL.Cro (Županović Filipin, Hlavac and Piasevoli, this volume), CAN.Cro (Petrović, this volume), AUS.Cro (Hlavac and Stolac, this volume), NZ.Cro (Stoffel and Hlavac, this volume) and ARG.Cro (Skelin Horvat, Musulin and Blažević, this volume).

Example (7) contains an extra-clausal tag question codeswitch that functions as both a response-elicitor and turn-terminator:

(7) | *tako* | *se* | *uvijek* | *kao* | *kaže,* | **ne** *[nə]?* |
| --- | --- | --- | --- | --- | --- |
| how | REFL | always | like | say-3SG | PART |

'That's how people always, like, say it, **don't they**?' (12,Gen.2,F,31)

Again, Croatian is the matrix language in example (7), supplying the content expressed in this question, to which the tag question particle *ne* is added in the embedded language German. Following an utterance with Croatian pronunciation and intonation, this colloquial discourse particle is inserted with a clearly German pronunciation, which is indicated in phonetic transcription in square brackets at the end of the sentence. This example is classified as an extra-clausal codeswitch because the discourse particle in this case has sentence scope, i.e. by adding it to the utterance the speaker is requesting confirmation from the listener, a communicative function that is fulfilled by question tags in English (Bullock and Toribio 2009; Hlavac 2006). The use of discourse particles such as *ne* 'no' [= tag question marker] but also of interjections and modal particles or filler words such as *ja* 'yes' [= emphasis/amplification marker] is common in the speech of German-Croatian bilinguals living in a German-speaking context. This is an example of the adoption of pragmatic features from German, in both function *and* form. A discourse particle with a similar function, namely turn-final *eh* is reported as a common extra-clausal codeswitch in NZ.Cro (see Stoffel and Hlavac, this volume).

4.3 Covert cross-linguistic influence and convergence

Covert cross-linguistic influence or convergence is here understood as the shaping of morphosyntactic features of a bilingual's speech by rules from two (or more) languages, which in the analysed material is traceable to the covert morphosyntactic influence of German in the speech of our participants. Myers-Scotton (2006a) defines convergence as follows:

> sometimes speech is bilingual even though it only has surface-level words from one language (...) speech is also called bilingual if two languages are the source of the underlying structure of the clause. That is, the 'elements' making the clause bilingual that come from one of the participating languages are abstract rules, not actual words.
>
> Myers-Scotton (2006a: 234)

An alternative term for this phenomenon is *morphosyntactic calque*. Covert cross-linguistic influence, as defined in the framework of this study, differs from intra-clausal and inter-clausal codeswitching insofar as there is an adoption of (abstract) linguistic patterns, rules, principles, but no transfer of lexical material from another language (in this case German).

In the speech of our Croatian-speaking participants in Hannover, we have noticed instances of covert crosslinguistic influence or convergence in the form of morphosyntactic calques pertaining to the construction of complex subordinate clauses, especially relative clauses introduced by the question word *gdje* 'where' and subordinate clauses functioning as an object.

In the following example, the Croatian interrogative pronoun *gdje* 'where' is employed as a relative pronoun to introduce a relative clause. As in English, in German and Croatian the use of this interrogative pronoun is permissible, but only with adverbial meaning denoting a place or direction, e.g. *I went to the shop where* [= *in which*] *I met my friend*. In example (8), taken from our corpus, *gdje* is used with a *human* antecedent:

(8) *imam   prijateljice   Hrvatice   gdje*
    have-1SG   friends-ACC.F.PL   Croats-ACC.F.PL   REL.PRON
    više   pričaju   njemački   a   imam
    more   talk-3PL   German-ACC.M.SG   and   have-1SG
    Hrvatice   gdje   više   pričaju   hrvatski
    Croats-ACC.F.PL   REL.PRON   more   talk-3PL   Croatian-ACC.M.PL
    'I have Croatian girl-friends who speak more German and I have Croatian girl-friends who speak more Croatian.' (1,Gen.2,F,42)

In this example, the speaker's speech reflects covert crosslinguistic influence or convergence which consists in using *gdje* 'where' instead of *koje* 'who' REL.PRON. NOM.F.PL) as a relative pronoun introducing a relative clause. It is possible that this structural phenomenon has two possible sources, one in Croatian and one in German. The first possible origin can be traced to variation permitted in Croatian.

to   je   mjesto   na   kojem   smo   bili
that   be-3SG   place   at+LOC   which-LOC.N.SG   AUX-1PL   be-PST.1PL
jučer   to   je   mjesto   gdje   smo
yesterday   that-NOM.N.SG   be-3SG   place-NOM.N.SG   where   AUX-1PL
bili   jučer
be-PST.1PL   yesterday
'That is the place where we were yesterday.'

Both sentences are acceptable in Croatian. The first is high register to neutral; the second is neutral to low register. The second features the relative pronoun *gdje* that, although a relative pronoun, does not contain inflectional markers. As stated, this use of *gdje* is restricted to non-human antecedents. In contrast, the more high register relative pronoun *koji* can refer to both human and non-human antecedents. It appears that the incidence of *gdje* as a relative pronoun may be an emergent trend that is used in some dependent clauses for non-human antecedents as example (8) above shows, but examples such as this remain unattested in

HMLD.Cro. In order to account for this, we look at current developments in colloquial or non-standard varieties of German. Similar to its Croatian and English equivalents, the German relative pronoun *wo* ('where') can function as a relative pronoun with a non-human antecedent:

ich	*suche*	*den*	*Strand*	**wo**
I	look for-1SG	the-ACC.M.SG	beach-M.SG	REL.PRON
man	*am besten*	*baden*	*kann.*	
one	best	bathe-INF	can-3SG	

'I am looking for the beach **where** it's best to swim at.'

In non-standard varieties of German, namely southern German varieties, *wo* 'where' (or its dialectal equivalent) can function as a relative pronoun also for *human* antecedents (cf. Mösch, 2017):

der	*Mann,*	**wo**	*ich*	*gesehen*	*habe*
the-NOM.M.SG	man-M.SG	where	I	see-PST.PTCP	AUX.1SG

'The man **where** [=who(m)] I saw.'

Mösch (2017) traces the spread of *wo* as a relative pronoun for human antecedents beyond dialect corpora, and locates its use in print-media usually only where dialect-speakers are being quoted, e.g. *Der Mann, **wo** sein Publikum zum Lachen bringt* ('The man **where** makes his audience laugh'). In an internet-based corpus of over 1 million examples of relative pronouns with a human antecedent, Mösch (2017) identifies 569 uses of *wo*, with a prominent example coming from a football player from southern Germany, but who is clearly addressing a general German audience:

ich	*lerne*	*nicht*	*extra*	*Französisch*	*für*	*die*	*Spieler*
I	learn-1SG	NEG	extra	French	for+ACC	the-ACC.M.PL	players-M.PL
wo		*dieser*		*Sprache*	*nicht*	*mächtig*	*sind*
where-REL.PRON		this-GEN.F.SG		language-F.SG	NEG	capable+GEN	be-3PL

'I am not going through the trouble of learning French for players **where** [=who] can't speak this language'.

Although the speakers in this corpus are from Lower Saxony, a region where non-standard varieties of German are less frequent, the influence of non-standard German models cannot be excluded. Example (8) is an instance of covert cross-linguistic influence or convergence, i.e. of how speech can be bilingual although, on the surface level, it is made up of words from only one language. However, both German and Croatian supply the underlying structure of the clause. Dependent clause conjunctions, i.e. COMP, and their structural features in other languages are also shown to have an influence in other diaspora varieties of Croatian, e.g. ITAL.Cro (Županović Filipin, Hlavac and Piasevoli, this volume) and TRS.Cro (Piasevoli, this volume).

The second case of covert cross-linguistic influence or convergence in the construction of complex subordinate clauses pertains to subordinate clauses functioning as an object as in (9) and (10):

(9) ja mislim **je** lakše govorit njemački nego
I think-1SG be-3SG.PRS easier speak-INF German-ACC.M.SG than
hrvatski
Croatian-ACC.M.SG
'I think it is easier to speak German than Croatian.' (1,Gen.2,F,42)

HMLD.Cro
mislim **da** je lakše govoriti njemački
think-1SG COMP be-3SG easier speak-INF German-ACC.M.SG

German
Ich denke es ist leichter Deutsch zu sprechen.
I think [dummy-PRON] be-3SG easier German to speak

The omission of the dummy PRON *es* 'it', which is permissible in some varieties of spoken German, is transferred as a rule and applied to the sentence expressed in Croatian which does not allow for such a construction of a main clause plus object clause introduced without a determiner. Apart from that, in (9) the German word order rule AUX + PRED is applied within the copula verb phrase *je lakše*. Example (10) contains a similar structure at the start of a subordinate clause:

(10) ja znam **onda** će biti sve
I know-1SG then FUT.AUX-3SG be-INF all-NOM.N.SG
teže za njih
hard-COMPARATIVE for+ACC them-ACC
'I know then that it will be more and more difficult for them.' (1,Gen.2,F,42)

HMLD.Cro
ja znam da će **onda** biti sve teže za njih
I know COMP FUT.AUX-3SG then be more and more difficult for them.

German
Ich weiss, **dann wird** *es* *immer schwieriger für sie sein*
I know then FUT.AUX dummy PRON always more difficult for them be.

Example (10) above is similar through the omission of the Croatian COMP *da* based on the equivalent German construction that does not require COMP. The omission of the complementizer *dass* (Eng. 'that'), which is permissible especially in spoken German, is transferred as a rule and applied to the sentence expressed in Croatian, which does not allow for such a construction of a main clause plus object clause introduced without a determiner. Apart from that, in (9) the German word order rule AUX + PRED is applied within the copula verb phrase *je lakše* ('is easier'). Further examples of syntactic transference from German into Croatian are found in BGLD.Cro (see Ščukanec, Breu and Vuk, this volume) and in AUT.Cro (see Ščukanec, this volume).

4.4 Semantic transference and loan translations

Compensational strategies on the lexical-semantic level are used by bilingual speakers. These comprise innovations whereby the semantic features of a German equivalent are transferred onto a Croatian counterpart lexeme. An extension of the semantic field of *akceptirati* 'to accept' seems to be occurring in example (11):

(11) *i to je prvi put bilo ono da te neko* **akceptira** *sto posto.*
'and that was the first time that someone **accepts you** 100 percent.'
(7,Gen.2,M,41)

   Ger.:   Und das war das erste Mal, naja, dass dich jemand hundertprozentig akzeptiert.
   HMLD.Cro. I to je prvi put bilo ono da te netko **prihvaća** sto posto.

The meaning of the verb *akceptirati* 'to accept' has been extended according to the German model, i.e. the Ger. verb *akzeptieren*, which like Eng. *accept* can be used in the sense *to accept a person*. Croatian *akceptirati* may be used in other (financial, business etc.) contexts, but its use with reference to a person is uncommon. This example can be read as a lexical compensation strategy, but also as an extension of the semantic field of the Croatian verb *akceptirati*. In the speech contact situation the semantic field of the Croatian verb *akceptirati* seems to have been widened so that it can be assumed that in this diaspora context, under the influence of German, this verb can be used unmarked with the meaning *to accept a person*.

Another phenomenon we observe is the occurrence of loan translations (also known as calques), i.e. the translation of words or phrases from one language (either in part or in whole) to corresponding words in another language while still keeping the original meaning. Example (12) below contains such an instance:

(12) *i tamo je **radio** zanat.*
'and there he **did** vocational training' (7,Gen.2,M,41)

> Ger.: und dort hat er eine Ausbildung **gemacht**
> HMLD.Cro. i tamo je **završio** zanat.
> 'and there he **finished** vocational training'.

In (12), the German verb *machen* from the equivalent expression *eine Ausbildung machen* 'to undergo/do vocational training' has been transferred with the original meaning of Ger. *machen* 'to do' in a context in which it normally would not occur. Example (12) above is very similar to predicate constructions that Hansen (2018) reports in his German-Croatian data, mainly from Gen.2 speakers. In his data, the verb *praviti* 'to do/to make' (c.f. Ger. *machen*) is combined with direct objects relating to schooling or training in the same way that (12) above does, e.g. *sad pravi majstorsku školu* 'now do-3SG vocational school'. However, the verb *praviti* at least in HMLD.Cro, has semantic restrictions in terms of frame elements that can occur as a direct object and these frame elements are "*effected* or *affected* entit[ies]", i.e. things to which something 'has been done' (Hansen 2018: 138–139). German has fewer such frame element restrictions for the verb *machen* 'to do/to make' and this verb can co-occur with a succeeding direct object such as *educational training* with the meaning of 'undertaking' or 'completing' it, e.g. *jetzt macht er eine Ausbildung*. Hansen terms this type of transfer 'polysemy copying of a grammatical construction'. In relation to (12) above, the equivalent HMLD.Cro construction would contain the verb *završiti* 'to finish'. Example (13) contains another example of the transference of a German-based syntactic structure:

(13) *Ali opet kažem sve **leži do** roditelja.*
'And I am saying again that everything **lies up to** the parents.' (1,Gen.2,F,42)

> Ger.: Aber das sage ich nochmal, alles **liegt an** den Eltern
> HMLD.Cro. Ali opet kažem sve **je do** roditelja.
> 'And I am saying again that everything **is up to** the parents.

In (13) we have a typical example of a loan translation, which is characterized by the use of the Croatian lexeme *ležati* 'to lie' with the preposition *do* 'up to', which is a translation of the German verb *liegen an* ('lie on' = 'to be up to someone / something').

The categories of analysis employed in this study have been derived through an explorative, qualitative analysis of the collected data, which can serve as a starting-point for further, also quantitative accounts of language contact phenomena and for a further elaboration of the categories of analysis. This includes a discussion of how embedded language material, such as embedded words or borrowings and embedded language islands (cf. Myers-Scotton 2006a: 253–266), can be analysed and accounted for in bilingual speech. Further examples of loan translations based on German models are found in BGLD.Cro (see Ščukanec, Breu and Vuk, this volume) and in AUT.Cro (see Ščukanec, this volume). Loan translations in other varieties of diaspora Croatian are found in ITAL.Cro (Županović Filipin, Hlavac and Piasevoli, this volume), TRS.Cro (Piasevoli, this volume), CAN.Cro (Petrović, this volume), AUS.Cro (Hlavac and Stolac, this volume), NZ.Cro (Stoffel and Hlavac, this volume) and ARG.Cro (Skelin Horvat, Musulin and Blažević, this volume).

5 Conclusion

Among a variety of language contact phenomena found in the spoken corpus under study, we focused on the analysis of (classic) intra-clausal and inter-clausal codeswitching (Myers-Scotton 2002, 2006a, 2006b; Jake, Myers-Scotton and Gross 2002), as well as transference phenomena at the lexical-semantic level (including crosslinguistic transference and lexical compensation strategies) and the morpho-syntactic level (convergence as the effect of covert crosslinguistic influence). Although we have not carried out an exhaustive presentation of all phenomena found in the sample, we observe that the examples discussed above are typical instances of language contact phenomena that can frequently be found in bilingual Croatian-German speech. Not all types of language contact are equally represented in our data, and frequency analyses are desirable for future investigations. Intra-clausal codeswitching occurs more frequently than inter-clausal codeswitching. Both forms of codeswitching are employed by both Gen.1 and Gen.2 informants. At the same time, we make the general observation that they seem to be more used by those informants who self-reported lower proficiency in Croatian, regardless of the length of residence in Germany.

As stated above in section 2, the prevailing use of Croatian by us as the interviewers may have discouraged informants from codeswitching as much as they would have otherwise in 'in-group' interactions. What the sociolinguistic sample revealed was that participants themselves reported that codeswitching (and inter-clausal codeswitching) are the most common language strategies they employ in in-group communication. The qualitative analysis of our interview data reveals that speakers are generally more aware of codeswitching as a language contact phenomenon compared to loan translations and morpho-syntactic calques. When asked about language-contact in their speech, our informants only refer to code-switching, but never to other types of contact-induced phenomena.

The latter two strategies seem to be frequent among all speakers regardless of their self-reported linguistic proficiency in Croatian. These strategies include instances of direct translations from German into Croatian pertaining to single words, phrases or syntactic constructions. We noted several instances of an innovative introduction of a dependent clause that followed a German model, either by omitting a conjunction or by using the conjunction common in German, as well as innovations in word order in those sentences that contain a reflexive clitic in Croatian. Calquing is also visible at the lexical level in loan translations and loan innovations.

Intra-clausal alternation, inter-clausal codeswitching, covert cross-linguistic influence, semantic transfer and loan translation appear to be key aspects of language use in the bilingual participants of this study, and these phenomena call for a more detailed analysis with respect to their nature, motivation and recurrence. This chapter has offered an insight into selected linguistic contact phenomena within a diaspora community in a country which itself has one of the largest Croatian transnational communities. Due to continuing emigration to Germany, this community remains the fastest-growing of all Croatian diaspora communities. It would be useful to record further data samples from established as well as more recently arrived Croatian-speakers to study the similarity and difference of contact linguistic phenomena recorded, which may include further variation between generations, vintages of migration, and degrees to which Gen.1 speakers arrived in Germany are proficient in German. Further, as the sociolinguistic data in this chapter also indicate, the networks and settings within which speakers find themselves shape their use of both languages, which has consequences on the particular forms that speakers employ, particularly in in-group settings.

References

Bullock, Barbara & Almeida Jacqueline Toribio. 2009. Themes in the study of code-switching. In Barbara Bullock & Almeida Jacqueline Toribio (eds.), *The Cambridge Handbook of Linguistic Code-switching*, 1–18. Cambridge, UK: Cambridge University Press.

Čapo, Jasna, Caroline Hornstein Tomić & Katica Jurčević (eds.). 2014. *Didov san. Transgranična iskustva hrvatskih iseljenika* [Granddad's dream. Trans-border experiences of Croatian emigrants] Zagreb: Institut za etnologiju i folkloristiku; Institut društvenih znanosti Ivo Pilar.

Čizmić, Ivan, Marin Sopta & Vlado Šakić. 2005. *Iseljena Hrvatska*. Zagreb: Golden marketing – Tehnička knjiga.

De Angelis, Gessica, Ulrike Jessner-Schmid & Marijana Kresić (eds.). 2015. *Crosslinguistic Influence and Crosslinguistic Interaction in Multilingual Language Learning*. London: Bloomsbury.

Deutsche Welle. 2008. Yugoslav guest workers torn between Germany and home. http://www.dw.com/en/yugoslav-guest-workers-torn-between-germany-and-home/a-3847033 (accessed 25 February 2018).

Dorian, Nancy C. 1981. *Language death: The life cycle of a Scottish Gaelic dialect*. Philadelphia: University of Pennsylvania Press.

Glovacki-Bernardi, Zrinjka. 1998. *Deutsche Lehnwörter in der Stadtsprache von Zagreb*. Frankfurt a. M.: Peter Lang.

Glovacki-Bernardi, Zrinjka. 2006. Forschungsprojekte zu deutsch/österreichisch-kroatischem Sprachkontakt – theoretische Profilierung und ideologiekritische Positionen. *Zagreber Germanistische Beiträge* 9. 3–11.

Hansen, Björn. 2018. On the permeability of grammars: Syntactic pattern replications in heritage Croatian and heritage Serbian spoken in Germany. In Jasmina Grković-Major, Björn Hansen & Barbara Sonnenhauser (eds.), *The interplay between internal development, language contact and metalinguistic factors. Diachronic Slavonic Syntax*, 125–169. Berlin: De Gruyter Mouton.

Hlavac, Jim. 2006. Bilingual discourse markers: Evidence from Croatian-English code-switching. *Journal of Pragmatics* 38. 1870–1990.

Iannaccaro, Gabriele & Vittorio Dell'Aquila. 2011. Numeri soggettivi. Spunti sulla vitalità linguistica da inchieste e trattamenti quantitative. In Bruno Moretti, Elena Maria Pandolfi & Matteo Casoni (eds.), *Vitalità di una lingua minoritaria. Aspetti e proposte metodologiche*, 151–192. Bellinzona: Osservatorio Linguistico della Svizzera Italiana.

Jake, Janice L., Carol Myers-Scotton & Steven Gross. 2002. Making a minimalist approach to codeswitching work: adding the Matrix Language. *Bilingualism: Language and Cognition* 5(1). 69–91.

Jurić, Tado. 2017. Suvremeno iseljavanje Hrvata u Njemačku: karakteristike i motivi [Current emigration of Croats to Germany]. *Migracijske i etničke teme* 33(3). 337–371.

Kresić, Marijana. 2011. Deutsch-kroatische Sprachidentitäten. In Zrinjka Glovacki-Bernardi, (ed.), *Deutsch in Südost- und Mitteleuropa: Kommunikationsparadigmen im Wandel*, 93–104. Zagreb: Filozofski fakultet.

Kresić Vukosav, Marijana & Eva-Maria Thüne. 2019. Remigration as a linguistic experience: language-related aspects of "homecoming". In Ivo Fabijanić, Lidija Štrmelj, Vesna Ukic Košta & Monika Bregovic (eds.), *Migrations: Literary and Linguistic Aspects*. 297–324. Berlin: Peter Lang.

Kroatenseelsorge in Deutschland. 2013. Naslovnica [Homepage]. www.kroatenseelsorge.de/ (accessed 23 December 2016).
Laakso, Johanna, Anneli Sarhimaa, Sia Spiliopoulou Åkermark & Reetta Toivanen. 2016. *Towards openly multilingual policies and practices: Assessing minority language maintenance across Europe*. Bristol: Multilingual Matters.
Ljubešić, Marta. 1989. Jezični razvoj djece jugoslavenskih migranata u SR Njemačkoj [The linguistic development of Yugoslav migrants' children in the Federal Republic of Germany]. *Migracijske i etničke teme* 5(4). 353–361.
Ljubešić, Marta. 1992. Prilog poznavanju migrantske dvojezičnosti [A contribution to our understanding of the bilingualism of migrants]. *Migracijske i etničke teme* 8(1). 55–67.
Mösch, Matthias. 2017. *Der Mann, wo ich gesehen habe – das relative wo*. http://hypermedia.ids-mannheim.de/call/public/fragen.ansicht?v_id=129 (accessed 28 February 2018).
Muysken, Pieter & Julian Rott. 2013. Ethnolect studies in the German and the Netherlandic area. In Peter Siemund, Ingrid Gogolin, Monika Edith Schulz & Julia Davydova (eds.), *Multilingualism and language diversity in urban areas. Acquisition, identities, space, education*, 177–206. Amsterdam / Philadelphia: John Benjamins.
Myers-Scotton, Carol. 1993. *Duelling languages: Grammatical structure in codeswitching*. Oxford: Clarendon Press.
Myers-Scotton, Carol. 2002. *Contact linguistics: Bilingual encounters and grammatical outcomes*. Oxford: Oxford University Press.
Myers-Scotton, Carol. 2006a. *Multiple voices. An introduction to bilingualism*. Maiden/Oxford/Carlton: Blackwell.
Myers-Scotton, Carol. 2006b. Natural codeswitching knocks on the laboratory door. *Bilingualism: Language and Cognition* 9(2). 203–212.
Nejašmić, Ivo. 2014. Iseljavanje iz Hrvatske od 1900. do 2001.: demografske posljedice stoljetnog procesa [Emigration from Croatia from 1900 to 2001: demographic effects of a century-long process] *Migracijske i etničke teme* 30(3). 405–435.
Raecke, Jochen. 2006. Hrvatski u Njemačkoj: njemački s hrvatskim riječima? [Croatian in Germany: German with Croatian words?]. *Lahor* 2. 151–158.
Sasse, Hans-Jürgen. 1992. Language decay and contact-induced change: Similarities and differences. In Matthias Brenzinger (ed.), *Language death: Factual and theoretical explorations with special reference to East Africa*. 59–80. Berlin / New York: Mouton de Gruyter.
Schumann, John H. 1978. *The pidginization process: a model for second language acquisition*. Rowley: Newbury House Publishers.
Spiegel. 1961. *Gastarbeiter. Treck aus Titos Land*. Edition from 27.12.1961. http://www.spiegel.de/spiegel/print/d-43367882.html (accessed 28 February 2018).
Statista 2020a. *Kroatien: Anzahl der kroatischen Staatsbürger in den Mitgliedsstaaten der Europäischen Union (EU) im Jahr 2019*. https://de.statista.com/statistik/daten/studie/870670/umfrage/kroaten-in-den-laendern-der-eu/ (accessed 28 February 2018).
Statista 2020b. *Bosnien und Herzegowina: Anzahl der bosnischen Staatsbürger in den Mitgliedsstaaten der Europäischen Union (EU) im Jahr 2019*. https://de.statista.com/statistik/daten/studie/871670/umfrage/bosnier-in-den-laendern-der-eu/ (accessed 28 February 2018).
Statistisches Bundesamt. 2016. *Datenreport 2016: Sozialbericht für Deutschland*. https://www.destatis.de/DE/Publikationen/Datenreport/Datenreport.html (accessed 28 February 2018).

Stojanović, Ilija. 1984. Lingvistički aspekti dvojezičnosti jugoslovenskih učenika sa srpskohrvatskog jezičnog područja u završnim razredima osnovne škole u SRNj [Linguistic aspects of bilingualism of Yugoslav pupils from the Serbo-Croatian linguistic area in the final grades of elementary school in the Federal Republic of Germany]. *Zbornik radova Instituta za strane jezike i književnosti* 5. 413–420.

Stojić, Aneta. 2008. Njemačke posuđenice i njihovi hrvatski ekvivalenti [German loan words and their Croatian equivalents]. *Rasprave Instituta za hrvatski jezik i jezikoslovlje* 34. 357–369.

Stölting, Wilfried. 1980. *Die Zweisprachigkeit jugoslawischer Schuler in der Bundesrepublik Deutschland* Berlin: Otto Harrassowitz.

Šimičić, Lucija & Nikola Vuletić. 2016. Une langue sans futur, une identité bien vivante: représentations de la communauté arbënishtë. *Circula: revue d'idéologies linguistiques* 3. 141–162.

Winland, Daphne N. 2005. Croatian Diaspora. In Marvin Ember, Carol R. Ember & Ian Skoggard (eds.), *Encyclopedia of diasporas: Immigrant and refugee cultures around the world* 77. New York: Springer.

Austria

Aleksandra Ščukanec
Post-WWII Croatian migrants in Austria and Croatian-German language contacts

1 Introduction

The aim of this chapter is to provide insight into language usage amongst Croatian immigrants who arrived in Austria during the second half of the 20th and the early 21st centuries, mainly as so-called 'guest workers'. While there has been much sociolinguistic research on Burgenland Croatian focussing on descriptions of the Burgenland Croatian dialects and language contact (see Ščukanec, Breu and Vuk, this volume) there are very few studies on Croatian as spoken by more recent generations of Croatian immigrants in Austria, termed here AUT.Cro. This chapter provides a description of the situation, status and language usage of first- and second-generation immigrant Croatian-speakers in Austria.

Studies on Croats who have arrived in Austria in the post-WWII period mostly provide a historical, demographic and/or sociological description giving information on organisations, associations and clubs, e.g. Božić (2000), Seršić (2013), or deal with (migrant) identity, integration and assimilation issues and language policy in general, e.g. Gruber (2012) and Grbić Jakopović (2014). Croats are also often studied together with other migrant groups in Austria, and it is sometimes difficult to identify characteristics relating only or specifically to them, e.g. Busch (2006). Looking at speakers of both Croatian and Bosnian, Doleschal and Mikić (2018) provide a contact linguistics study focusing on code-switching into and from German.

This chapter presents both sociolinguistic and linguistic data. Sections 2 and 3 present some details on the research and informants, as well as a sociolinguistic description on language usage among the informants, giving a contextual framework for the analysis of the data presented in section 4. The main section of the chapter offers an interpretation of chosen examples used for illustrating morpho-syntactic features of the spoken language of Croats in Austria and contains examples of code-switching.

Note: The author would like to thank the Croatian Central State Office for Croats Abroad for providing a grant in support for this research project.

Aleksandra Ščukanec, University of Zagreb

https://doi.org/10.1515/9781501503917-006

1.1 History of contact, vintages of emigration, status

Croatian migration to Austria is long-standing. Croats first migrated to areas now in present-day Austria at the end of the fifteenth century as a result of the Ottoman advance across south-east Europe. Living in sprachinseln, the Burgenland Croats of eastern Austria have been able to retain their language and constitute an 'autochthonous' language community. Subsequent migration was steady but not large-scale. As the capital of the Austro-Hungarian Empire (1867–1916) Vienna was a focal point for Croatian students, artists and businesspeople, with many residing there temporarily or permanently (Seršić 2013: 36–88). In the latter part of the nineteenth century, movement was bi-directional: government public servants of the Habsburg administration settled in Croatia and later Bosnia-Herzegovina continuing to use German as the major official language of the Empire, and often acquiring Croatian as a subsequent language. They joined the tens of thousands of German-speakers, the *Volksdeutsche* or 'ethnic Germans', who had settled across Slavonia and Baranya in the eighteenth century.

In the twentieth century, there were multiple waves of large-scale migration from Croatia to Austria: in the immediate post-WWII years it was mainly political emigrants who sought refuge in Austria (Božić 2012: 120–121). They were outnumbered by much larger numbers of German-Croatian bilinguals, the *Volksdeutsche*, who were expelled from the newly founded FNRJ in 1945. Further waves of large-scale migration to Austria have been mostly economic: from the mid-1960s as young men coming as guest workers and subsequently bringing their families with them; from the 1980s a further small wave of skilled and tertiary-educated migrants departed Croatia for Austria; during the wars in Croatia and Bosnia-Herzegovina, at least a third of the 60,000 refugees who arrived in Austria were Croatian-speakers. In the early twenty-first century, further numbers of skilled and tertiary-educated migrants have moved from Croatia to Austria. With Croatia's mid-2013 accession to the European Union and internal freedom of movement within the EU, a further mass departure to Austria of over 13,000 people with diverse occupational backgrounds has also occurred (Kroativ 2015). Austria's geographical proximity to Croatia and the two countries' common membership in the EU now make it harder to distinguish the many Croats there as members of an 'immigrant community', or as seasonal workers or sojourners who see their permanent place of residence still within Croatia. Homeland Croatian has no *de jure* status in Austria, while Burgenland Croatian is recognised in Burgenland as an official language through national and regional legislation.

1.2 Number of Croatian-heritage residents, number of Croatian-speakers

Following an ethnographic approach that included demographic features as well, Grbić Jakopović (2014) collected data from various sources and concluded that there are currently 90,000 Croats living in Austria. One local community estimate is that there are 70,000 Croatian citizens, and in total over 100,000 people of Croatian origin in Austria, with 80% of them originally from Bosnia-Herzegovina (Stojak 2014). The total number of Austrian residents with Croatian heritage is likely to be higher, at around 120,000. According to the Austrian Central Bureau of Statistics, 94,000 Croats migrated to Austria in the 1990s (cf. Grbić Jakopović 2014). Homeland Croatian occupies the de facto status of a 'migrant language' in Austria, spoken and used by between 100,000 and 120,000 people. This higher estimation is attributed to the significant number of 'unregistered' migrants, not captured by official statistics.

1.3 Geographical distribution, socio-economic profile

The largest number of Croats in Austria, approx. 41,000, live in Vienna and surrounding Lower Austria (cf. John and Lichtblau 1990: 62, 66). Distribution elsewhere is centred on urban areas of more affluent western Austria: 29,000 live in Upper Austria, Salzburg, Tirol and Vorarlberg, with the remainder living in less affluent areas but which are geographically more proximate to Croatia, namely Styria (12,000), Carinthia (5,000) and only 1,000 in Burgenland (Božić 2000: 36, 41, 56–63; Gruber 2012: 15; Seršić 2013: 14–16). The low number of post-WWII migrants in Burgenland means that these are outnumbered by the 25,000 Burgenland Croats whose own codified variety of Croatian (Burgenland Croatian), along with German, continues to predominate in that area. Meaningful contact, including linguistic accommodation and instances of lingua receptiva, occur between Vienna-based speakers of homeland Croatian (35,000) and Burgenland Croatian (10,000). The socio-economic profile of Croats in Austria is generally considered to be lower than the Austrian average, due in part to the *Gastarbeiter* 'guest worker' generation, most of whom are now pensioners and who often financially supported family members back home. Many recent migrants are often employed in tourism, hospitality and lower-paid service industries. However, substantial numbers of recent and highly-qualified migrants work in areas congruent to their fields of specialisation and there has been a general 'upward mobility' amongst second- and third-generation Austrian-born Croats. A characterisation of the socio-economic profile of Austria-based Croats is now more difficult to make as there is great variation in the employment and financial status across the group as a whole.

1.4 Infrastructure

Notwithstanding the fact that most Austrians and Croats share the same faith, Roman Catholicism, ethnic-specific Catholic parishes or missions are perhaps the most prominent attribute of an established Croatian immigrant community in Austria. There are eight Croatian Catholic missions in the following towns and cities, Feldkirch, Graz, Innsbruck, Klagenfurt, Linz, Salzburg, St. Pölten and Vienna. The connection between religion and language cannot be overstated (Woods 2004) and the gamut of communicative settings that arise from religious-based interactions and beyond these are found to be conducive to language maintenance efforts. There are over a dozen football clubs, two students' societies in Vienna and Graz, and print-media imported from Croatia is available at major railway stations and news agencies while locally printed media is mostly restricted to bulletins for the Catholic missions. An assortment of other organisations exist that are dedicated primarily to arts, culture, folklore and economic relations (cf. Božić 2012: 122–125; Waldrauch and Sohler 2004: 201–204). Croatian immigrants are serviced by two locally produced newspapers: the Croatian community in Upper Austria publishes the monthly paper *Baština* ('Heritage') and there is also a bilingual electronic newspaper *Kroativ*. These represent initiatives from a diaspora population that perform something that 'homeland' media outlets cannot: address the specific needs and conditions of immigrants where they reside, and 'speak for' the community that they represent (Husband 2005; Kosnick 2007). Croatian-language television from Croatia is available electronically on demand, or via cable or satellite. Austrian state television transmits a 30-minute program once weekly, *Heimat, fremde Heimat* 'Homeland, foreign homeland' mostly in German, with occasional segments in 'Bosnian-Croatian-Serbian' as well as in other 'migrant languages'.

The historical position of Austria as a study destination for many university students is perhaps responsible for the number of cultural-academic organisations or Austrian branches of homeland ones, e.g. *Napredak* 'Progress', *Matica hrvatska* 'Matrix Croatica', *Hrvatski svjetski kongres* 'Croatian World Congress' and *Austrijsko društvo za kroatistiku* 'Austrian Society for Croatian Studies'.

There are approximately 15,000 school-age children with Croatian language proficiency in Austria. Mother-tongue instruction in Croatian is offered at the *Hrvatska dječja škola* 'Croatian Children's School' in Vienna at four locations and at the Catholic mission in Linz, sponsored by the Croatian Ministry of Education. Otherwise, mother-tongue instruction is provided by the Austrian Federal Ministry of Education under the designation of 'Bosnian/Croatian/Serbian' in the form of supplementary classes at mainstream public schools. There is a mixed reception to these supplementary classes on account of the linguistic models employed in the classes. Amongst some parents there is a reluctance to send children to classes taught by a teacher speaking a different language, and with a different ethno-religious identity (Batarilo 2016). Efforts to convince the Austrian authorities to offer supplementary classes in Croatian have not been successful. The consequence of this is that a small number of school-age children attend Croatian-language classes, a further small group attends classes in Bosnian/Croatian/Serbian, while most receive no instruction, due to geographical distance from available Croatian-languages schools and/or due to parental opposition to the Austrian-government sponsored supplementary classes (Batarilo 2010).

In contrast, Burgenland Croatian, as stated, enjoys a de jure status as an official minority language in the Austrian state of Burgenland, and monolingual- and bilingual school instruction in Burgenland Croatian is offered at primary and secondary school level. In addition, there are media resources and cultural activities provided in Burgenland Croatian that are subsidised by the state. At university level, Croatian is taught within the hypernym of 'Bosnian/Croatian/Serbian' at Vienna and Graz universities, with academic, teacher-training and translation/interpreting streams.

1.5 Domain use, language maintenance and shift

In general, there are high levels of support amongst first-generation speakers for their children to learn Croatian, in formal and/or naturalistic environments (Gruber 2012). Most first-generation speakers use Croatian only or predominantly Croatian with second-generation speakers. Second-generation speakers typically indicate Croatian as their mother tongue, while exhibiting greater confidence in using German. Third-generation speakers are less prominent as an identifiable group, but it is likely that many have medium to high-level proficiency in Croatian. As stated, homeland Croatian is spoken by 100,000 to 120,000 people. There are similar numbers of speakers of both Bosnian and Serbian with whom Croatian-speakers can interact in their own language. This broadening of the 'critical mass' of interlocutors with whom Croatian-speakers can use Croatian, in lingua receptiva interactions (Hlavac 2014) can both broaden the number of domains in which Croatian is used, e.g. social life, commercial transactions, friendship domain, and extend the number of interlocutors with whom Croatian is used, e.g. workmates, schoolmates, customers, service users etc. (Hlavac 2013).

1.6 Contacts with Croatia, host society attitudes towards Croats

Geographical proximity means that for many if not most Croats in Austria, contact with Croatia is frequent and extensive. Contact with relatives and exposure to different varieties of Croatian via media, travel and different social networks are invaluable resources for a child's social and linguistic development. The notion that a child need not attend formal instruction in the parents' mother tongue is held by some first-generation migrants in Austria who visit Croatia two or three times a year, with many spending their summer vacation there, and who take their children with them, immersing them in a completely Croatian-language environment.

Host society attitudes towards Croats vary greatly. There is an 'Empire-nostalgic' legacy in Austria that views Croatia and Croats as an 'allied nation' that was part of the Habsburg Empire, albeit not with the same power and prestige that were wielded by German-speaking Austrians. 'Old school, conservative' Austrians who hold such a position often view Croats as 'almost like us', especially when Croats are compared to other groups of migrants, particularly those from areas outside Europe. On the left side of the political spectrum, Croats were viewed with more mixed feelings: during the time of the SFRY, those more anti-Communist Croats were sometimes perceived as a 'disturbance' to the otherwise cordial relations between neutral Austria and non-aligned Yugoslavia; at the same time, Croatian guest-workers were sometimes wooed by the Social-Democrats as potential voters in the event that they gained Austrian citizenship. After the arrival of guest workers from the SFRY in the 1960s and 1970s, the word *Tschusch* was commonly used as a pejorative term to refer to them, as well as to all foreign guest workers (Sedlaczek 2006). The term is of interest linguistically as it is based on Austrians' perception of the Croatian words *Čuješ* [me]?! 'Do you hear [me]?!' which they often heard from the mouths of guest workers calling to each other on building sites.

In the 1990s, Austria assisted generously in the care and housing of refugees who arrived as a result of the wars in Croatia and Bosnia-Herzegovina; this included countless personal initiatives from Austrians who took in or financially assisted displaced persons. Over twenty-five years later, the image of Croats as 'political emigres from Communist eastern Europe', 'migrant guest workers' and 'war refugees' is giving way to one of fellow EU-citizens whose home country is an ever popular and highly proximate tourist destination. Younger Austrians with little or no memory of the 1990s and the preceding decades may view Croats as 'fellow Central Europeans', little different from themselves. Amongst many Gen.2 Austrian-Croatians, there is also a more relaxed and reflective view to the legacy of being Croatian in Austria: former terms of derision such as *Tschusch* and *Krowodn* (a pejorative term referring to 'Croats') are often subverted and now used playfully, or even worn as badges of pride.

2 Details of informants and research sample

Empirical data presented in this chapter are based on a corpus of questionnaires completed by 29 informants and a corpus of 21 recorded interviews. All informants were found with the help of Croatian clubs and organisations, Croatian priests working in Austria as well as through the author's social networks. The vast majority of informants were located and contacted via ethnically-affiliated organisations. In regard to the questionnaire, both Croatian and German copies were provided but all informants from both generations used the Croatian version. There were three versions of the questionnaire: one for those born in Croatia or Bosnia-Hercegovina and who migrated as older adolescents or young adults – generation 1A (hereafter: Gen.1A); one for those born in Croatia or Bosnia-Hercegovina who migrated as children – generation 1B (hereafter: Gen.1B); and one for those informants born in Austria – generation 2 (hereafter: Gen.2). The age range of informants is 14–71.

Questionnaires were sent by e-mail and an online version was also available. The data gathered from questionnaires was used primarily for obtaining a general picture of informants' reported language use as well as language attitudes. The focus of this chapter is on the second sample, based on recorded spoken interactions. The spoken data are based on semi-structured interviews in which informant narratives were elicited to gain recordings of spoken language from them (Schütze 1983; Franceschini 2001). The author is a Croatian-German bilingual, based in Croatia with long-standing ties with Croatian-speakers in Burgenland and elsewhere in Austria. Interviews with informants were conducted in Austria by the author, except for the one conducted in Zagreb. Most of the informants came to Austria in the 1990s. Most have been living there for some time, while a small number have spent only a few years there. The interviews lasted approximately an hour each with the shortest lasting 30 minutes and the longest 80 minutes, and were conducted either individually or in group settings. Key information on each informant is presented in Table 1.

Responses from the sociolinguistic sample show that as far as Gen. 1A informants are concerned, only one of them spoke German before coming to Austria. For Gen. 1B and Gen. 2 informants, Croatian was usually their chronologically first learnt language, and also the main language spoken at home. Looking at family settings cross-generationally, while younger Gen. 1B and Gen. 2 inform-

Table 1: Demographic information on three groups of informants.

	Gen. 1A	Gen. 1B	Gen. 2	Total
Number of informants who provided spoken data (no. ♀ ♂)	11	3	7	21 (10 ♀, 11 ♂)
Average age (age of youngest and oldest informant)	49.55 (40–65)	18.66 (14–25)	17.71 (15–22)	
Average length of residence in Austria in years (shortest to longest period of residence)	22.18 (13–30)	14.3 (8–22)	born in Austria	

ants reported speaking Croatian to their parents, they reported that the language of communication with their siblings was largely German. All Gen.1B and Gen.2 informants said either that both German and Croatian are their *materinski jezici* 'mother tongues' with German as their dominant language, and Croatian (in terms of chronology of acquisition) as their 'first language'.

3 Sociolinguistic description of informants' language use

This section presents a brief overview on the following: contacts with homeland; domain-based use of Croatian (including media, leisure and religious domains); data on acquisition of Croatian and German; (family) language policies; designations for the language of Croatian migrants in Austria; attitudes towards language and language maintenance; and reported attitudes to code-switching or bilingual speech.

3.1 Contact with homeland, domain-based use of Croatian

When it comes to language usage, Austria's geographical proximity to Croatia and Bosnia-Hercegovina plays an important role in enabling contacts with these two countries, and this is topicalised in many interviews. For many immigrants, Austria's geographical proximity was the reason why they moved there in the first place. Most still have family and relatives in their homeland and regularly visit them, usually twice a year – in summer and for the Christmas holidays, with many travelling more often. Some of the first-generation informants are men who live alone in Austria with the remainder of the family still in Croatia or Bosnia-Hercegovina, and they attempt to visit them every weekend, if possible. Informants from the first generation who have been living in Austria for more than two or three decades report a strong attachment to their homeland and frequently visit it. Those born in Austria or who came to Austria when they were very young usually do not feel such a strong connection to Croatia (or Bosnia-Herzegovina) or the locality that their parents are from. Still, there are a few exceptions and some younger members are even thinking about returning to their homeland, though in summer the majority of them are more attracted to the Adriatic coast than to their parents' place of birth.

As far as language maintenance is concerned, informants from the first generation said that geographical proximity should assist in the maintenance of the language amongst younger speakers, although proximity alone does not appear to have achieved this. Normative views were sometimes spontaneously expressed by four Gen.1A informants who pointed out that there are Austrian-Croats who should feel ashamed for not cherishing the culture of their homeland and their mother tongue, especially as the opportunities open to those in Austria appear more accessible than those available to Croats living in more distant countries or on other continents.

For a large number of Croats in Austria, use of Croatian language is not limited to the family domain only. Many Croats in Austria work with people who came from other regions of former Yugoslavia and they use Croatian when speaking with their co-workers. These interactions may be in Croatian, or participants may engage in lingua receptiva. However, the situation in schools is usually different. There, children mainly speak German, even to other Croats. According to Gen. 1A informants, this depends on personal preferences and inclinations, as many feel more confident in German, but it can be influenced by other factors. A Gen. 2 informant who lived in a village near Graz claims that in her school there were other students from former Yugoslavia and they were put in separate classes and discouraged from speaking Croatian so they would not cluster as a group. This possibly led to them feeling a sense of isolation from others.

3.2 Media, leisure and religious domains

Most Gen. 1A informants point out the importance of the media. All of them watch Croatian television and read Croatian newspapers, mostly electronically rather than in paper form. Some compared the current situation with the socio-political circumstances 25 or 30 years ago when they had very limited access to Croatian media and felt isolated from their homeland. The internet and social media allow them to keep informed about current affairs in their homeland. For some it is as if they were still at home and had never left. For younger generation informants, the media and leisure domain is less likely to advance language maintenance efforts (Busch 2004; Cormack 2007). Even in Austria where Croatian-language television and other media resources are readily available, some conclude that privately-owned and even government-subsided media in minority languages performs, at best, a 'restitutionary function' that offers a limited counter-balance to the mass media in large national languages (Moring and Dunbar 2008).

In Austria there are numerous Croatian clubs and organisations which are places of social gathering. The first-generation Croatian immigrants often spend their free time there, either as active members in sports clubs for instance, or for social interaction. Second-generation speakers are also highly active in many Croatian organisations, especially those to do with folklore. To an extent, intra-second-generation communication is in German rather than Croatian, but cross-generation communication is in Croatian.

3.3 Language acquisition of Croatian and German, (family) language policies, designations for the language of Croatian migrants in Austria, attitudes towards language and language maintenance

Although almost all Gen. 1A informants had no prior knowledge of German and had initial problems with the language, today they consider German their second language. Croatian remains their first language, however, and they use it whenever possible. They claim that at home they all speak Croatian and all emphasise that with their children they speak Croatian only. In their interviews two informants from the second generation recall first learning German at pre-school centres, a language then new to them as their parents spoke to them exclusively in Croatian.

One of the questions that often arises in this context is the issue of different varieties of Croatian: which variety is spoken among Croats in Austria and which variety should be taught. If the children only learn(t) Croatian at home from their parents, they speak the variety that is or was spoken in the area of Croatia or Bosnia-Hercegovina where they came from. In most cases, they acquire aural and oral conversational skills. Acquisition of reading and writing skills occurs mostly or only in German, and literary skills in Croatian are therefore variable. Three informants directed criticism towards parents who think that it is sufficient to learn the mother tongue only at home and who are oblivious to the fact that a good knowledge of the mother tongue has positive effects on learning other languages.

These informants reported that their criticism is shared not only by teachers and others involved in the educational system but also by other individuals like them who are (actively) engaged in the preservation of the Croatian language and culture. But they also said that there are still many parents who want their children to attend formal instruction in Croatian, either through language courses or at supplementary schools. However, they face one of the most complex issues regarding the Croatian language acquisition in the way formal instruction in the languages of migrants from the former SFRY is provided at Austrian schools. As outlined above in 1.4, in Austria the term *Bosnisch/Kroatisch/Serbisch* 'Bosnian/Croatian/Serbian' (hereafter 'B/C/S') is used as a designation and as a description of the language of instruction for students who were born or whose parents were born in Bosnia-Hercegovina, Croatia, Serbia or Montenegro and who wish to attend government-funded, 'mother-tongue' language classes (Bundesministerium für Bildung 2014).

Informants who are parents expect government-funded schools to provide instruction in the standard variety of the children's heritage language, but in many cases B/C/S causes confusion. B/C/S is the reason why many parents decide against enrolling their children in Croatian classes since they believe they can learn Croatian better at home and in contact with other Croats in Austria.

While teachers who the author came in contact with think one should learn both the standard variety in school and dialects or regiolects at home, it seems that the general attitude in the Croatian community in Austria is that Croatian, in whichever form it may be, regardless of the influences of Austrian German, will be preserved in the community as long as they actively use it themselves. This is a circular argument, but one that is not uncommonly heard in diaspora settings.

With regard to informants, all Gen. 1A informants are parents and mentioned the issue of B/C/S. Despite the fact that they all expressed their dissatisfaction with the designation B/C/S, only two decided against sending their children to B/C/S classes. All Gen. 1B and Gen. 2 informants attend(ed) B/C/S classes, except for one Gen. 2 informant who reported that her parents did not want her to be taught in Serbian. The informants from these two groups did not state their personal opinions regarding this subject and it could be assumed that their parents have a say in their education until they finish secondary school.

3.4 Attitudes on language use and code-switching

One section of the questionnaire included questions on code-switching in order to see whether the informants code-switch, whether they are aware of this, what kind of attitude they have and how their environment perceives it. The questions and provided responses are presented below in Table 2.

As can be seen from Table 2, almost all informants code-switch. Only in Gen.1A did two informants claim that they never code-switch, and a 45-year old female

Table 2: Reported incidence of and motivations for code-switching.

		Gen. 1A	Gen.1B	Gen.2	Total
When you speak one language (Croatian), do you sometimes insert words from other language (German)?	Yes	9	7	10	26
	No	2	0	0	2
	Sometimes	1	0	0	1
Why does it occur?	When I do not know a word from one language I use the equivalent word from the other language	3	5	4	12
	I remember a word from the other language easier	4	1	6	11
	I use code-switching because others speak like this as well	1	0	0	1
	For affect	4	1	0	5
Do your family, friends or relatives correct you when you / others code-switch?	Always	0	0	0	0
	Often	1	0	1	2
	Sometimes	2	6	6	14
	Infrequently	0	1	0	1
	Never	8	0	3	11
	No answer/other	1	0	0	1

informant stated that although she does code-switch, she does it extremely rarely. She pointed out that she is well aware of this and tries to correct herself every time since she has a negative attitude to this practice. Her points of view are shared by one Gen. 1B informant who reports code-switching but who at the same time claims to try to avoid it. The two most common reasons for code-switching were also expected prior to this study: the informants use it when they do not know a word from one language or when they remember a word from the other language more easily. Five informants use it for affect and only one informant, a 41-year-old female, uses it because those around her also use this mode of speaking. When asked whether they are corrected by others when they code-switch, only two say that this happens often; for most it happens either sometimes or never. A 28-year-old Gen.1B informant states that, although she code-switches, it is more often the case that she corrects others than her being corrected by someone else. When it comes to Gen.2 informants, only one informant (a 14-year old girl) reports being often corrected. This occurs primarily from her mother who wants her to speak both Croatian and German 'properly' and who considers code-switching an undesirable practice that she typically associates with (Croatian) guest workers.

Cross-generational comparison shows only very small differences. They are the following: Gen.1A informants report code-switching for affect more often than others and as many as eight of 12 are never corrected by others. Based on the results obtained from the questionnaires, all the informants are aware of code-switching and know exactly when they use it and why they use it, whether intentionally or spontaneously. Perhaps surprisingly even Gen. 2 informants, regardless of how young they are, have developed an awareness of this phenomenon (and clear views on it as well).

4 Presentation and analysis of spoken data

The analysis of spoken data collected in the study has shown that German influence is found at various levels. Apart from the phonological and orthographical levels, which are not discussed in this chapter, most examples illustrate German influences on the morpho-syntactic level, i.e. in the usage of both isolated lexemes and whole phrases, of certain syntactic elements and whole sentences. Since the examples were extracted from spoken material, interviews are transcribed according to phonological form: German-origin forms that are phonologically integrated into Croatian are represented here according to Croatian orthography (e.g. *šulrat* > Ger. *Schulrat* > Eng. *school council*). Only those forms that remain phonologically unintegrated are represented here according to German orthography. Details of the speaker are given after each example; thus, the following information (Gen.1A, 65, M) relates to a generation 1A speaker, aged 65 and male.

4.1 Lexical transfers

Lexical transfers are understood here as single-item or simplex code-switches, with or without phonological and/or morphological adaptation. In some examples there is a clear indication that German-origin forms are used intentionally, often shown via flagging markers such as *takozvani* 'so called' (Poplack and Sankoff 1988: 1167). In most other cases speakers did not show obvious awareness of using German expressions and these appear as instances of unmarked or 'classic' code-switching (Myers-Scotton 2006). In other instances particular German words or expressions functioned as trigger for longer code-switches (Matras 2009: 114).

In the analysed corpus most examples include nouns, either, as already mentioned, without any type of adaptation or with gender marking, mostly in the form of a demonstrative adjective. At this point, it is also important to note that some German-origin forms are excluded from analysis, as they do not represent transfers emanating from speakers' immediate situation in Austria. These relate to German loanwords that have been present for centuries in standard and non-standard varieties of Croatian spoken across northern and eastern Croatia (Žepić 2002). Thus, forms that informants are likely to have acquired and used in the homeland such as *mišung* ('mixture', Ger. *Mischung*), *šaltati* ('to switch', Ger. *schalten*) and even *bauštela* ('building site', Ger. *Baustelle*) are not included in the analysis here.

Presentation of lexical transfers will feature here those items that are phonologically and/or morphologically integrated (Hlavac 2004: 174–178). In the analysed examples, there are mostly nouns or adjectives with declension in accordance with the requirements of Croatian grammar. But before presenting examples from the corpus, it is necessary to provide a theoretical framework and to elaborate on loanwords and code-switching. In this analysis the approach proposed by Poplack and Sankoff (1988) is used, which is elaborated on by Riehl (2004). According to Riehl (2004: 20–21), code-switching may occur in whole phrases or parts of sentences but also when a single word is expressed in another language. She states that some authors like Myers-Scotton (2002: 153) would consider such examples as code-switching, while others like Poplack and Sankoff (1988: 1167) mark such instances as nonce borrowings or ad-hoc-loanwords. Such loanwords do not differ from the loanwords codified in lexicon and, as a rule, they are morphologically and syntactically integrated in the target language, which will be illustrated in examples. The following information is provided on the informant for each example: informant number, generation, age, gender. The examples of lexical transfers are classified into three categories based on the type of morphological integration: integrated, non-integrated and unclear.

4.1.1 Morphologically integrated transfers

This section presents examples in which the phonological form of German source lexemes is usually retained, regardless of the presence of Croatian morphology and inflections. Morphological integration is usually evident through inflectional suffixes. In some cases, as in (1) below, a DET-like form indicates the morphological features of case and gender:

(1) *problem   je   u   nekim   sada*
    problem-NOM.M.SG   be-3SG   in+LOC   some-LOC.M.PL   now
    segmentima   toga   jer   je   ministarstvo
    segment-LOC.M.PL   it-GEN.M.SG   because   AUX-3SG   ministry-NOM.N.SG
    uvelo   pojam   BKS
    introduce-PST.N.SG concept-ACC.M.SG 'Be-Kah-Es'

> *jedan* **_mišmaš_**
> one-ACCM.SG **mishmash**
> 'There is a problem in some segments because the Ministry introduced the term BKS [=Bosnian/Croatian/Serbian], which is a **mishmash**.' (Gen.1A,65,M)
>
> HMLD. Cro '*(neobična) mješavina / zbrka*'

The transfer *mišmaš* 'mixture' (German *Mischmasch* – itself a transfer from English) is preceded by the numeral *jedan* 'one' which marks the transfer as ACC.M.SG. The phonotactic structure of *mišmaš* – here word-final consonant – appears to account for gender allocation. The form *jedan* functions as an article or determiner in a way corresponding to the German indefinite article *ein* 'a' (and 'one'), which itself could be also seen as a transfer of feature marking (cf. section 4.4). The following example contains a flag preceding the transfer, *takozvani* 'so called'.

> (2) *konkretno to znači takozvana*
> practically this-NOM.N.SG mean-3SG so-called-NOM.F.SG
> **_Krankengeschichte_**
> **medical history**
> 'in practice this means a so-called **Krankengeschichte** ('**medical history**')' (Gen.1A,65,M)
>
> HMLD.Cro: *konkretno to znači takozvana* **povijest bolesti**. ('history of sicknesses')

As in (1) above, the preceding form in example (2), this time an adjective, indicates the morphological integration of the transfer as a NOM.F.SG noun. Here, the phonotactic structure of the loan with its –*e* [-ə] ending which characterises most feminine nouns in German is almost homophonous to the Croatian suffix –*a* [-a] that marks most feminine nouns in Croatian. The following example contains a transfer whose gender in German is also feminine:

> (3) *a dosta ih je sad kažu da je*
> and many+GEN they-GEN be-3PL.PRES now say-3PL COMP be-3SG
> *najveći* **_Einwandererzahl_** *sad u Austriji*
> biggest-NOM.M.SG **immigrant number** now in+LOC Austria-LOC.F.SG
> *su Nijemci*
> be-3PL German-NOM.M.PL
> 'There are many of them now, they say that the largest **immigrant number** [the largest group of immigrants] in Austria are Germans.' (Gen.2,22,F)

HMLD.Cro: *A dosta ih je sad, kažu da su trenutačno u Austriji Nijemci **najbrojnija skupina useljenika***. ('most numerous group of immigrants')

In (3) above, although the transfer *Einwohnerzahl* 'number of residents' is feminine in German, the preceding (superlative-form) adjective *najveći* 'biggest' is masculine. The phonotactic form of the transfer with its word-final consonant could account for this. At the same time, the direct Croatian equivalent to *Einwohnerzahl* is masculine, i.e. *broj* NOM.M.SG *stanovnika* 'number of inhabitants'. Example (4) contains another transfer whose German form is feminine:

(4) *osim   ako   nisi   taj   **Schlüsselkraft***
    unless if   be-NEG.2SG this-NOM.M.SG   **key profession**
    '... except if you don't belong to a **key profession**...' (Gen.1A,40,F)

HMLD.Cro: ... *osim ako nisi **tražena / ključna radna snaga**...* ('sought after/ key workforce')

Here, the German feminine noun *Schlüsselkraft* is used in combination with the demonstrative pronoun *taj* 'this-NOM.M.SG', which marks it as masculine. A possible Croatian equivalent would be *tražena / ključna radna snaga* 'sought after / key work staff' which is, however, feminine. As in example (3), it appears that the phonotactic structure, namely a word-final consonant determines morphological integration as a masculine noun – the vast majority of consonant-final nouns in Croatian are masculine. Further to this, three informants made side comments saying that when they use a German word when speaking Croatian, they spontaneously adapt it using a gender that seems *appropriate* in Croatian based on the ending (Hlavac 1991). It is perhaps indicative that these examples have all come from Gen.1A informants. Example (5) below comes from a Gen.2 informant:

(5) *to   je   bio   njoj   **Hindernis**   što   je*
    that AUX-3SG   be-PTCP.M.SG   she-DAT   **obstacle**   COMP   AUX-3SG
    bila   bolesna
    be-PTCP.F.SG   ill-NOM.F.SG
    'This was her **obstacle / excuse** that she was not feeling well.' (Gen.2,22,F)

HMLD.Cro: ***Izgovorila se** time da je bila bolesna.* ('She gave as an excuse')

The same tendency is apparent in example (5) above, which contains another consonant-final transfer *Hindernis*, a neuter-gender noun in German. But it is integrated morphologically as a masculine noun in Croatian, evident by the preceding

PST.PTCP and its M.SG. marking that is part of the predicate of the lexical transfer. I now move on to examine transfers occupying different syntactic roles and oblique case-marking shown in examples (6) to (9) below:

(6) *no   mislim   da   nije   upitno   kako sada*
    but   think-1SG COMP be-NEG.3SG questionable-NOM.N.SG how   now
    *vidim   njihov   **Einstellung***
    see-1SG   their-ACC.M.SG **attitude**
    'I think that is not an issue how I now view their **attitude**.' (Gen.1A,44,F)

HMLD.Cro: *No mislim da to nije upitno s obzirom na njihov sadašnji **stav**-*ACC. SG.M / *njihovo sadašnje **stajalište**-*ACC.N.SG. ('attitude/position')

In example (6) above, the German feminine noun *Einstellung* is preceded by the possessive pronoun *njihov* 'their', which bears morphology showing the integration of the transfer as masculine. Again, the influence of the consonant-final structure appears to be decisive here, although the masculine gender of its closest Croatian equivalent *stav* cannot be discounted. In example (7) below, the lexical transfer is a DIR.OBJ of the verb *imaju* have-3PL.PRES.

(7) *doduše   imaju   i   takozvane*
    admittedly   have-3PL and so-called-ACC.M.PL
    Sprachtrainere
    language coach-ACC.M.PL
    'It is true that they also have so-called **language coaches**.' (Gen.1A,61,M)

HMLD.Cro: . . . *takozvane **jezične tutore**.* ('language tutors')

The transfer *Sprachtrainere* is integrated as an ACC.M.PL form shown by multi-feature morphological markers on both the transfer itself and the preceding attributive *takozvane* 'so-called-ACC.M.PL'. The following example is preceded by a preposition *od* 'from' that requires GEN case marking:

(8) *preveo   sam   dvije   tri   brošure*
    translate-PST.M.SG AUX-1SG two+GEN.SG three+GEN.SG booklet-GEN.F.SG
    neke   od   ministarstva   neke   od
    some-ACC.F.PL from+GEN ministry-GEN.N.SG some-ACC.F.PL from+GEN
    šulrata
    school council-GEN.M.SG
    'I translated two or three booklets, some from the ministry, some from the **school council**.' (Gen.1A,65,M)

HMLD.Cro: Preveo sam dvije-tri brošure, neke (od) Ministarstva, neke (od) **prosvjetne inspekcije**.

In example (8), the German masculine transfer *Schulrat* 'school council' is integrated as a masculine Croatian transfer shown via GEN marking. The following example contains a preposition requiring LOC marking and the transfer bears morphological integration indicating this:

(9) *taj   nekakav   stav   prema*
    this-NOM.M.SG kind of-NOM.M.SG attitude-NOM.M.SG towards+LOC
    auslenderima
    foreigner-LOC.M.PL
    'This kind of attitude toward **foreigners**...' (Gen.1A,40,F)

HMLD.Cro 'Takav stav prema **strancima**...'

Looking back at examples (6) to (9), it can be observed that these are all from Gen.1A speakers and it appears that for this generational group at least, phonological and morphological integration is usually present. Examples of lexical transfers integrated into other varieties of diaspora Croatian are found in almost all other chapters of this volume.

4.1.2 Morphologically non-integrated transfers

Not all transfers are morphologically integrated. Example (10) below presents an instance of the same German-origin form *Ausländer* 'foreigners', which is not only morphologically but also phonologically unintegrated:

(10) *tamo nije   bilo   ovih*   ***Ausländer***
     there NEG.AUX-3SG   be-PST.N.SG these-GEN.M.PL **foreigners-ø**
     što   kažu
     what   say-3PL
     'There, there were no **foreigners**, as they call them.' (Gen.2,22,F)

HMLD.Cro *Tamo nije bilo **stranaca**, kako ih nazivaju.*

In the quoted example German noun *Ausländer* is used in the plural form, which is also indicated by the preceding GEN.M.PL demonstrative pronoun. In negative existential sentences with the construction *ne* NEG + *biti* 'be' the logical subject is in GEN (with the exception of singular countable nouns). In this instance, morphological markers showing integration are absent. In other examples from the corpus the form *Ausländer* was indeed used with morphological markers that integrated it into Croatian morphosyntax, e.g. *nije bilo Ausländera*-GEN.M.PL 'there were no foreigners'. The following example is one that typifies the inclusion of terms specific to the Austrian context:

(11) *i sad sam pri* **Landarbeiterkammer** *znači*
and now be-1SG in+LOC **agricultural workers' chamber** mean-3SG
Gospodarska komora k'o *Serviceleiterin*
chamber of commerce as **service manager**
'And now I work in the **Landarbeiterkammer**, that is, the **Chamber of Commerce**, as a **service manager**.' (Gen.1A,44,F)

HMLD.Cro: *I sad radim u Landarbeiterskammer, znači u Gospodarskoj komori kao* **voditeljica usluga.** ('[female] leader of services')

Neither transfer in example (11) above is phonologically integrated. The first transfer is followed by a Croatian near-equivalent, either as repetition or as a repair. The phonotactic structure and syllable length of both transfers may have been a factor in why Croatian suffix morphemes are not affixed, although this argument does perhaps seem unlikely. In general, phonologically unintegrated forms tend also to be morphologically unintegrated in this sample. The last instance presented here to illustrate this is example (12) below where a German-origin NP *mündliche Matura* 'oral school leaving exam' with a feminine noun and preceding feminine adjective is inserted as a compound-noun transfer. This is morphologically not congruent to the preceding possessive pronoun *svoj* 'my[own]-ACC.M.SG' that has masculine marking:

(12) *ja sam išla na svoj* **mündliche**
I AUX-1SG go-PST.F.SG to+ACC my-ACC.M.SG oral-F.SG
Matura otišla sa **Fieber**
school leaving exam-F.SG leave-PST.F.SG with+INS temperature-ø
'I went for my **oral school leaving exam**, left home with a **fever**...'
(Gen.2,22,F)

HMLD.Cro: *Na* **maturi** *sam na* **usmeni ispit** *došla s* **temperaturom**... ('high school leaving certificate' ... 'oral exam' ... 'temperature')

Elsewhere in example (12), phonologically unintegrated *Fieber* 'fever' does not attract morphological marking, despite the preposition *sa* 'with' preceding it, which requires instrumental case marking.

In terms of parts of speech, adverbs are the second most numerous group after nouns that occur as transfers. They are almost exclusively used in their original form without adaptation. In both German and Croatian, adverbs are non-inflecting forms. Examples include *ehrenamtlich* ('voluntarily'), *natürlich* ('naturally') or *perfekt* ('perfectly'). Another common example is a composite language phrase consisting of the Croatian pronoun *sve* 'everything' and a German ADJ. phrase *sehr gut* 'very good', i.e. *sve sehr gut* 'everything very good' usually referring to educational or occupational contexts. Lexical transfers that are morphologically unintegrated are also examined in other studies of Croatian used in diaspora contexts, e.g. ITAL.Cro (Županović Filipin, Hlavac and Piasevoli, this volume), TRS.Cro (Piasevoli, this volume), CAN.Cro (Petrović, this volume), AUS. Cro (Hlavac and Stolac, this volume), NZ.Cro (Stoffel and Hlavac, this volume) and ARG.Cro (Skelin Horvat, Musulin and Blažević, this volume).

4.2 Code-switching

As mentioned, it is not always easy to make a clear distinction between lexical transference and code-switching and different authors often have opposing views. Code-switching is commonly defined as the alternation of codes in a single speech exchange (Gumperz 1982: 59). Approaches to code-switching have varied widely but it seems that many agree that there are certain strategies when using code-switching. It can be argued whether code-switching occurs unconsciously or whether each example has some function and motivation, and speakers use it deliberately and with specific intentions. In the corpus, there are examples of code-switching that are flagged via pre-posed elements such as *takozvani* 'so-called', that are found in examples (2) and (7) above. There are also examples of post-posed forms that indicate retrospective flagging of a preceding switch. Often this takes the form of *znači* 'meaning' and a Croatian equivalent, as shown in example (11). There are other further examples of post-posed flagging in the sample, sometimes via the phrase *kako se kaže* 'how it is said' with or without a Croatian equivalent.

Many instances of code-switching are not otherwise flagged and occur unremarkably in informants' speech. The discussion below therefore focuses not on phenomena that may have a facilitative function in the production or reception of code-switching (Hlavac 2011); instead, the discussion focuses on the morpho-syntactic features of inserted or alternated items and their integration into the structural grid of the matrix language, which in almost all cases is Croatian.

(13) i   **mit**   **ausgezeichnetem Erfolg**   sam
      and with+DAT excellent-DAT.M.SG success-M.SG AUX-1SG
      maturirala
      graduate-PTCP.F.SG
      'And I graduated from high school **with excellent grades**.' (Gen.2,22,F)

   HMLD. Cro: *i maturirala sam s odličnim uspjehom.* ('with excellent success')

(14) ja se   jesam   pripremala   ali **natürlich** je
      I   REFL AUX-1SG prepare-PST.F.SG but **naturally** AUX-3SG
      to   za   mene   bilo   **eine Woche vor**
      that for+ACC me-ACC be-PTCP.N.SG   **one week before**
      'I did do some preparation, but **naturally** for me that was **one week earlier**.' (Gen.2,22,F)

   HMLD. Cro: *Pripremala sam se, ali **naravno tjedan prije**.* ('of course [a] week before')

It is also interesting to note that two informants who code-switched extensively after a while made some (meta-linguistic) comments such as *opet ja miješam* 'I'm mixing again'. To an extent they were probably motivated by a feeling that their speech was being monitored and it is possible that they would not have made such comments in an unrecorded interaction.

4.3 Loan translations

Loan translations or calques are defined here as the translation of the semantic content of donor language forms into the matrix language. In the analysed corpus there are various examples in which a German-based concept is rendered via Croatian lexical forms. It is important to note that Backus and Dorleijn (2009: 81) classify loan translations as a lexical phenomenon as well but they point out that it is both lexical and structural in its nature. The chosen examples illustrate the process of the direct translation of lexical units, both isolated and their combinations. The first example contains a translated equivalent of the German compound *Kontaktpersonen* 'contact persons':

(15) im'o   sam   telefone   i   sve
      have-PST.M.SG AUX-1SG telephone-ACC.M.PL   and all-ACC.PL.F
      kontaktne   **osobe**   i   mog'o   sam
      contact-ACC.F.PL **person**-ACC.F.PL and can-PST.M.SG   AUX-1SG

> *prvi   dan   počet*
> first-ACC.M.SG day-ACC.M.SG start-INF
> 'I had telephone numbers and names of all **contact persons** and I could have started on the first day.' (Gen.1A,52,M)

> HMLD.Cro: *imao sam telefonske brojeve i **imena svih osoba za kontakt** i mogao sam početi već prvi dan.* ('names of all people for contact')

The form *kontaktne osobe* 'contact persons' is based on a German model and is an NP with the structure ADJ+N as an equivalent of the German compound noun. HMLD.Cro employs a NP with 'names [of all persons]' as the pre-posed head. The following example contains a calqued predicate from German:

> (16) *a   tipično   je   to   da   upravo   ta*
>   and typical   be-3SG it   COMP   exactly these-NOM.F.SG
>   *djeca   koja   bi   mogla*
>   children-NOM.F.SG REL.PRON-NOM.F.SG COND can-PST.F.SG
>   **dobivat   nastavu   materinskog**
>   obtain-INF instruction-ACC.F.SG maternal-GEN.M.SG
>   **jezika**   *da   oni   sad   uče   njemački*
>   lanuage-GEN.M.SG   COMP   they-NOM now learn-3PL German-ACC.M.SG
>   'And it is typical that exactly these children that could **receive instruction in the mother tongue** that they are now learning German [in the sense of having an opportunity to attend Croatian classes].' (Gen.1A,61,M).

> HMLD. Cro: *Tipično je da upravo ta djeca koja bi mogla **dobiti mogućnost pohađanja nastave materinskog jezika**, da ona sad uče njemački.* ('receive the opportunity of attendance for instruction in the mother tongue')

In German there is a pattern of discontinuous elements that are separated from each other by one or more constituents. Compound verbs (separable prefix verbs) are typical of German. Separable prefixes usually change the meaning of the original verb, for instance *aufhören* ('to stop') as opposed to *hören* ('to hear'). In the following instance, the German verb *zurückgeben* ('to return something') with its separable prefix is rendered in Croatian via a simplex verb *vratiti* 'to return'. The separable prefix of the German verb, *zurück*, is 'carried over' into Croatian via the adverb *natrag* 'back' resulting in a tautological construction *vraćaju nazad* 'they return back':

(17) međutim   ovdje   ta   davanja   **se**   vidljivo
     however   here   these-NOM.N.PL money-NOM.N.PL   **REFL** obviously
     vraćaju   **nazad**
     return-3PL   back
     'However, the money you pay here is **returned back** to you' (Gen.1A,47,F)

   HMLD.Cro: *međutim, ovdje se ta davanja vidljivo* **vraćaju** ('charges are returned')

In HMLD. Cro, employment of *nazad* with *vratiti* stylistically marks the verb phrase as [+emphasis], e.g. *the money is really returned back to you*. However, the semantic context of the utterance does not suggest emphasis. Another similar instance given here is the example *zurückkommen* or *zurückkehren* 'to return'. These two German verbs with the same meaning are intransitive. An equivalent, 'intransitive-like' utterance in Croatian that has the reflexive particle *se* still attracts *nazad* 'back' as a pleonasm, again apparently based on the presence of *zurück* 'back' in the German equivalents:

(18) pa   **se**   onda   opet   **vratili**   iz
     then REFL   then   again   **return**-PST.3PL from+GEN
     Slavonije   **nazad**
     Slavonija-GEN.F.SG   back
     'And then they **returned** again from Slavonia.' (Gen.1B,25,M)

   HMLD. Cro: *Pa* **se** *onda opet* **vratili** *iz Slavonije.* ('returned from Slavonia')

Looking back at the loan translations contained in the sample, it is evident here that most come from Gen.1A and Gen.1B speakers. As with the incidence of integration of German-origin words transfers into Croatian, it appears that here there is a generational difference, this time in relation to the calquing of German-origin phrases or constructions. Examples of loan translation are also presented in other studies of heritage Croatian, e.g. TRS.Cro (Piasevoli, this volume), CAN.Cro (Petrović, this volume), AUS.Cro (Hlavac and Stolac, this volume), NZ.Cro (Stoffel and Hlavac, this volume) and ARG.Cro (Skelin Horvat, Musulin and Blažević, this volume).

4.4 Structural transference

At the level of syntax, the influence of German is observable in various ways: word order, syntactic structures, use of conjunctions, possessive constructions, government (valency) and verbs with (in)separable prefixes. The first four features will be examined here in this order. The influence of German on word order is common, especially in complex sentences with subordinate clauses (Raecke 2006: 153). In German declarative sentences, the finite verb is in second position in main clauses, while the word order of other elements is flexible. When the predicate contains other elements besides the finite verb, such as past participles or modal auxiliaries, these go to the end of the clause or sentence. In Croatian, unmarked word order is SVO. At the same time, noun and verb morphology enable a relatively free word order, depending on emphasis or topic structure. Utterances extracted from the corpus contain examples in which the sentence word order has a further, non-finite verb (e.g. participle, infinitive) at the end, which is characteristic of German word order that requires discontinuous constituents to be placed in clause-final position. To be sure, these word order patterns are not ungrammatical, simply marked. Such examples were found in the interviews of all informants from the second generation and two informants from Gen.1A and two informants from Gen.1B.

(19) čut   ćeš   svaki   jezik
    hear-INF FUT.AUX-2SG every-ACC.M.SG language-ACC.M.SG
    samo **nećeš**   njemački   **čut**
    only FUT.NEG.AUX-2SG German-ACC.M.SG **hear**-INF
    'You will hear all kinds of languages; only you **won't hear** German.'
    (Gen.2,17,M)

    Ger.:   Du wirst jede Sprache hören, nur Deutsch **wirst** Du nicht **hören**.
    HMLD.Cro: Čut ćeš svaki jezik, samo **nećeš čuti** njemački.

Although example (19) does not contain a one-to-one replication of the word order pattern of an equivalent German utterance, the conspicuous feature is the clause-final position of the second verb which appears to be German-influenced. Elsewhere, there are other German structures that are replicated in informants' speech, with or without the presence of transferred lexemes, for instance in relation to subordinate clauses. It is not common for Croatian compound sentences to have an interrogative adverb (or pronoun) in initial position of the sentence. This type of inversion is a common feature of compound sentences in German. The following example illustrates a modelling of this German construction:

(20) **što   je   još   frustrirajuće**   kod
    what   be-3SG also   frustrating-PRS.PTCT.N.SG   at+GEN
    tih   ljudi   jest   činjenica
    these-GEN.M.PL   people-GEN.M.PL   be-3SG   fact-NOM.F.SG
    devedeset i pet posto   njih   je   überqualifiziert
    ninety-five percent+GEN they-GEN.PL be-3SG   overqualified-ADJ

'It is also very frustrating for these people that ninety-five percent of them are overqualified.' (Gen.1A,65,M)

Ger.: *Was noch frustrierend ist für diese Leute ist der Umstand, dass...*
HMLD.Cro: **Te ljude frustrira** *činjenica da ih je devedeset i pet posto prekvalificirano [zu posao koji rade].* ('Those people are frustrated by the fact that. . .')

In contrast to German, Croatian is a pro-drop language and the subject is usually not explicitly expressed but implied in the predicate (Kunzmann-Müller 2008). In the corpus there are various examples in which the subject is expressed as in German, i.e., explicitly, whereas in Croatian a subject pronoun is typically overt, marking emphasis. In the examples given below, there was little or no rhetorical amplification or emphasis that was evident from the speaker's speech:

(21) **ja** sam to **prihvatio**
I AUX-1SG that accept-PST-M.SG
žrtvovao sam praznike
sacrifice-PTCP-M.SG AUX-1SG holiday-ACC.M.PL
'**I accepted** that, I sacrificed my holidays.' (Gen.1A,52,M)

HMLD. Cro: **Prihvatio** *sam to, žrtvovao sam praznike.*

Overt subject pronouns are a widely reported phenomenon in the speech of heritage speakers of pro-drop languages that are in contact with societally dominant languages that do not have this feature. Studies on Croatian in predominantly Anglophone countries show that this is a common feature in USA.Cro (Jutronić, this volume), CAN.Cro (Petrović, this volume), AUS.Cro (Hlavac and Stolac, this volume) and NZ.Cro (Stoffel and Hlavac, this volume).

In Croatian there are stressed and unstressed (clitic) forms of non-subject personal pronouns. Analogous to overt subjects, the full forms of object pronouns replace pronoun forms that would otherwise require a clitic form. The following example illustrates the usage of the stressed or full form *mene* ('*me*' ACC) instead of the unstressed or clitic one *me*.

(22) **ona** je mene tu podržala
she AUX-3SG me-ACC.SG here support-PST.F.SG
'**She** supported **me** here.' (Gen.1A,50,M)

HMLD.Cro: *Podržala* **me** *tu [u tome].*

Other examples of overt, full-form non-subject pronouns are found in USA.CRO (Jutronić, this volume), CAN.Cro (Petrović, this volume) and NZ.Cro (Stoffel and Hlavac voume).

The German conjunction *wenn* has two equivalents in Croatian as it does in English, *kad* ('when', in its temporal meaning) and *ako* ('if', as a conditional marker). In the following example, *ako* is employed where a temporal more so than a conditional meaning is alluded to:

(23) ali   možda   **ako** bi   tamo bila   bolja
     but   perhaps **if** COND   there be-PTCP.F.SG   better-NOM.F.SG
     budućnost   **ako** ima   boljeg   posla   i
     future-NOM.F.SG   **if** have-3SG   better-GEN.M.SG   job-GEN.M.SG   and
     to   **ako** bi   ostarjela   i   otišla   u
     that **if** COND   grow old-PST.F.SG   and go off-PST.F.SG   in+ACC
     penziju   onda bi   se   vratila   u
     pension-ACC.F.SG   then COND REFL return-PST.F.SG   in+LOC
     penziji
     pension-LOC.F.SG
     'But maybe **if** there were a better future there, **if** I have a better job and so on, **if** I grew old and retired, then I would go back as a retired person.' (Gen.2,15,F)

HMLD.Cro: *Možda **kad** bih tamo imala bolju budućnost, **kad** bih imala bolji posao i to, **kad** bih ostarila i otišla u mirovinu, onda bih se vratila, u mirovini.*

In the above example one can also observe an avoidance of conditional constructions in a way that may be common amongst Gen. 2 speakers. The informant employs the conditional marker *ako* 'if' in the first part of the sentence, and a conditional form *bi* COND *bila* PAST.F.SG accompanies it. But in the second clause *ako* is not accompanied by conditional verb, and instead the verb form is in simple present *ima* 3.SG instead of conditional *ako* 'if' *bi* COND, *imala* 'have' PST.F.SG.

In the spoken corpus there were also some examples of a possessive construction with overt use of the preposition *od* 'from', which is characteristic of German, e. g. *puno **od** njih* (Gen.2,22,F) 'lots+GEN **of**+GEN them-GEN' (= 'many of them') based on Ger. *viele von ihnen* ('many of them') whereas in the equivalent HMLD.Cro construction there is no preposition, i.e. *puno njih* 'many them'. Other examples include the following, which appears to be based on Ger.: *der Bruder **von** einem Freund von mir* 'the brother **of** a friend of mine'.

(24) brat   **od**   jednog   mog
      brother-NOM.M.SG from+GEN   one-GEN.M.SG my-GEN.M.SG
      prijatelja
      friend-GEN.M.SG
      'my friend's brother' / 'brother of a friend of mine' (Gen.1A,65,M)

   HMLD.Cro: *prijateljev brat* 'friend's brother' / *brat jednog mog prijatelja* 'brother of one of my friends'

Example (25) appears to be based on another equivalent construction from German: *die Generation meines Bruders/von meinem Bruder* ('the generation of my brother').

(25) **od**   mog   brata   generacija
      from+GEN   my-GEN.M.SG brother-GEN.M.SG   generation-NOM.F.SG
      'my brother's generation' (Gen.1B,17,F)

   HMLD. Cro: *bratova generacija/generacija mojeg brata* ('brother's generation/generation of my brother')

In example (24), use of *od* 'from' appears overt as possession is marked in most varieties of HMLD.Cro via constructions without a preposition, i.e. GEN constructions or DAT ones. In example (25) an attributive construction that preposes the head noun *generacija* featuring *od* is characteristic for some non-standard varieties of HMLD.Cro. In general, pre-posed attributive phrases in HMLD.Cro are more likely to have a DAT construction, e.g. *mom bratu njegova generacija* 'my-DAT brother-DAT his-NOM generation-NOM' (= 'my brother's generation'). In non-standard varieties of Austrian German, this DAT construction is also used, *meinem Bruder seine Generation* 'my-DAT brother-DAT his-NOM generation-NOM', but not a pre-posed GEN one as in example (25). The use of *od* as a periphrastic marker of possession together with GEN marking is recorded in other varieties of diaspora Croatian, e.g. ITAL.Cro (Županović Filipin, Hlavac and Piasevoli, this volume), TRS.Cro (Piasevoli, this volume), NZ.Cro (Stoffel and Hlavac, this volume).

5 Conclusion

This chapter presents a short description of the sociolinguistic situation of Croatian-speakers in Austria and of lexical and structural aspects of the Croatian speech of Austrian Croats. The examples from the analysed corpus illustrate many instances of German influence both at the lexical and structural level.

When it comes to lexical transfers, the phonological form of German source lexemes is mostly retained, including phonemes that do not exist in Croatian. As the consonantal inventory of German is similar to that of Croatian, those phonemes that are transferred that do not exist in Croatian are usually vowels rather than consonants, e.g. *ü, ö*. This accounts for why the phonological form of transfers in this sample patterns in a way different to that observed by Matras in other samples (2009: 232), that is, that "loanwords are more likely to introduce more new consonants than new vowels".

At the level of morphology there is a tendency for transferred items to be allocated masculine gender due to phonotactic reasons based on word-final consonant(s). It is only masculine integrated nouns that attract overt marking, i.e. inflexional suffixes, whereas marking of feminine nouns is shown through morphological marking of preceding attributes only, not on the lexical transfer itself. As far as attributives that bear part of the function of ART/DET are concerned, it is noted that most lexemes that are transferred into AUT.Cro do not 'carry over' the semantic features of person, number and gender of the German source form, at least not in terms of gender. Furthermore, lexico-grammatical features of the source forms are also not carried over, such as the occurrence of an ART/DET preceding them. However, there are two instances where there is an ART/DET as seen in examples (1) and (4): *jedan mišmaš* and *taj Schlüsselkraft*. Although the size of this corpus does not allow me to speak of a trend, there are some instances in which an indefinite article appears to be developing in AUT.Cro. The morphological adaptation of nouns (in particular) is in line with Matras's (2009: 172) observation on the morphology of donor items in other contact situations.

In the corpus some examples of flagged code-switching can also be observed, perhaps due to the circumstances of the data collection situation that led to some degree of self-monitoring. This may help account for why hesitation phenomena sometimes accompanied code-switches, such as the three examples of pre-posed and three examples of post-posed flagged code-switching. Both forms indicate informants' awareness of code-switching. Pre-posed ones might signal that code-switching is being employed as a deliberate strategy, possibly because of accessibility difficulties with Croatian forms or because they feel that German expression is more in line with what they want to say. Post-posed flagged code-switching, on the other hand, tends to be in the form of a repair. There is also a general tendency to accompany German-origin forms with hedges, translations or hesitation phenomena etc. (Hlavac 2011).

Loan translations identified in the corpus are usually one- or two-word ones. These include verb constructions whose German equivalents are compound verbs with a separable prefix with adverbial meaning. Two-word translations based on German compound nouns may be expressed as ADJ+N constructions.

As for structural changes, there is a tendency for some second or main verbs to appear in clause-final position. In compound sentences, there are instances of German-influenced inversion as well, and in general there appear to be widespread changes in many speakers' pro-drop settings as well. Subject pronouns are more frequent, but are not overt. Instead they are unmarked, contrasting to HMLD.Cro in which they are marked for emphasis or stress. Another observable tendency is the use of long forms of non-subject personal pronouns. Corpus data also illustrate the lack of distinction of *ako / kad* under the influence of the German conjunction *wenn* as well as overt use of preposition *od* 'from' to indicate possession as in German *von*. It is not possible to relate these structural phenomena to the sociolinguistic profiles of the informants. However, perhaps the most prominent feature is the occurrence of verb-final clauses.

Finally, it should be pointed out that the informants from this study share some features in their Croatian speech in Austria with those of Burgenland Croatian-speakers. These include inversion as a common feature of compound sentences in German, compound verbs together with various forms of loan translations, use of verb-final clauses which are typical of German etc. Although code-switching is widely used by Burgenland-Croats, instances of flagged code-switching are very rare. The only indication of speakers' awareness of code-switching could be found in written texts when the examples of code-switching (in some cases loan translations as well) are marked with quotation marks.

References

Backus, Ad & Margreet Dorleijn. 2009. Loan Translations versus Code-Switching. In Barbara F. Bullock & Almeida Jacqueline Toribio (eds.), *The Cambridge handbook of linguistic code-switching*, 75–93. Cambridge: Cambridge University Press.

Batarilo, Željko. 2010. *Nastava hrvatskog kao materinskog jezika u Austriji* [Instruction in Croatian as a mother tongue in Austria] http://hku.hkz-salzburg.net/pdf/novosti_obavijesti/Hrvatski_austrija_elaborat_sazetak.pdf (accessed 22 November 2018).

Batarilo, Željko. 2016. *Muke po hrvatskom jeziku. Kako nas Austrija izruguje, a Hrvatska ne mari* [A distressing situation for the Croatian language. How Austria mocks us and Croatia doesn't care] http://www.croexpress.eu/vijest.php?vijest=10383 (accessed 4 September 2018).

Božić, Saša. 2000. *Kroaten in Wien. Immigranten und Integration im Zusammenhang mehrschichtiger ethnischer Beziehungen.* Zagreb: Naklada Jesenski i Turk.

Božić Saša. 2012. Is there a Croatian diaspora in Europe? From 'Gastarbeiters' to transmigrants and ethnics. *Croatian Studies Review* 8(1). 113–129.

Bundesministerium für Bildung. 2014. Rundschreiben des BMB – Muttersprachlicher Unterricht: Information und Übermittlung der Merkblätter/Anmeldeformulare. https://www.bmb.gv.at/ministerium/rs/2004_08.html. (accessed 3 August 2019).

Busch, Brigitta. 2004. *Sprachen im Disput: Medien und Öffentlichkeit in multilingualen Gesellschaften*. Klagenfurt: Drava Diskurs.

Busch, Brigitta. 2006. Bosnisch, Kroatisch, Serbokroatisch, Jugoslawisch, Romani oder Vlachisch? Heteroglossie und 'muttersprachlicher' Unterricht in Österreich. In Peter Chichon (ed.), *Gelebte Mehrsprachigkeit*, 12–28. Wien: Praesens Verlag.

Cormack, Michael. 2007. The Media and Language Maintenance. In Mike Cormack & Niamh Hourigan (eds.), *Minority language media: Concepts, critiques and case studies*, 52–69. Clevedon, UK: Multilingual Matters.

Doleschal, Ursula & Gizela Mikić. 2018. Codeswitching bei Herkungssprecher_Innen des Bosnischen oder Kroatischen. Eine Untersuchung an Material aus Kärnten. *Wiener Slawistischer Almanach* 81. 57–72.

Franceschini, Rita. 2001. Der „Adjuvant": die Figur der Stützperson im sprachbiographischen Interview mehrsprachiger Sprecher. In Thomas Keller & Freddy Raphaël (eds.), *Biographies au pluriel / Biographien im Plural*, 227–238. Strasbourg: Presses Universitaires de Strasbourg (Collection Faustus).

Grbić Jakopović, Jadranka. 2014. *Multipliciranje zavičaja i domovina. Hrvatska dijaspora: Kronologija, destinacije i identitet* [Multiplication of homelands. Croatian diaspora: Chronology, destinations and identity]. Zagreb: FF Press.

Gruber, Barbara. 2012. Kroatische Migrant/innen in Österreich. Zahlen. Fakten. Einstellungen. In *ÖIF-Dossier n°23*. Wien.

Gumperz, John J. 1982. *Discourse Strategies*. New York: Cambridge University Press.

Hlavac, Jim. 1991. Zur Genuszuordnung von Lehnwörtern im Deutschen, Kroatischen und Serbischen. *Wiener Slawistischer Almanach* 28. 281–297.

Hlavac, Jim. 2004. Zum kroatisch-englischen Sprachkontakt: Transfers und Sprachwechselerscheinungen bei kroatischsprechenden Australiern der zweiten Generation. *Zagreber Germanistische Beiträge* Beiheft 7. 169–192.

Hlavac, Jim. 2011. Hesitation and monitoring phenomena in bilingual speech: a consequence of code-switching or a strategy to facilitate its incorporation? *Journal of Pragmatics* 43. 3793–3806.

Hlavac, Jim. 2013. Multilinguals and their sociolinguistic profiles: observations on language use amongst three vintages of migrants in Melbourne. *International Journal of Multilingualism* 10(4). 411–440.

Hlavac, Jim. 2014. Receptive multilingualism and its relevance to Translation Studies with data from interpreters of the Bosnian, Croatian and Serbian languages. *Across Languages and Cultures* 15(2). 279–301.

Husband, Charles. 2005. Minority ethnic media as communities of practice: Professionalism and identity politics in interaction. *Journal of Ethnic and Migration Studies* 31(3). 461–479.

John, Michael & Albert Lichtblau (Eds.) 1990. *Schmelztiegel Wien - einst und jetzt. Zur Geschichte und Gegenwart von Zuwanderung und Minderheiten. Aufsätze, Quellen, Kommentare*. Vienna/Cologne: Böhlau.

Kosnick, Kira. 2007. Ethnic media, transnational politics: Turkish migrant media in Germany. In Olga Bailey, Myria Georgiou & Ramaswami Harindranath (eds.), *Transnational lives and the media: Re-imagining diaspora*, 149–173. Houndmills: Palgrave-Macmillan.

Kroativ. 2015. Broj Hrvata u stalnom porastu. [Number of Croats constantly increasing] shttp://www.kroativ.at/hr/clanak/politika/broj-hrvata-u-austriji-u-stalnom-porastu-877

Kunzmann-Müller, Barbara. 2008. Problematika subjekta – opći i kontrastivni aspekti [The problematic of subject – general and contrastive aspects]. *Fluminensia* 20(2). 7–21.

Matras, Yaron. 2009. *Language Contact*. New York: Cambridge University Press.
Moring, Tom & Robert Dunbar. 2008. *The European charter for regional or minority languages and the media. Regional or minority languages No. 6*. Strasbourg: Council of Europe.
Myers-Scotton, Carol. 2002. *Contact linguistics. Bilingual encounters and grammatical outcomes*. Oxford: Oxford University Press.
Myers-Scotton, Carol. 2006. Natural codeswitching knocks on the laboratory door. *Bilingualism: Language and Cognition* 9(2). 203–212.
Poplack, Shana & Sankoff, David. 1988. Code-Switching / Sprachwechsel. In Ulrich Ammon, Dittmar, Mattheier & Peter Trudgill (eds.), *Sociolinguistics. An International Handbook of the Science of Language and Society / Soziolinguistik. Ein internationales Handbuch zur Wissenschaft von Sprache und Gesellschaft*, [2nd Edition] 1174–1180. Berlin: Mouton de Gruyter.
Raecke, Jochen. 2006. Hrvatski u Njemačkoj: njemački s hrvatskim riječima? [Croatian in Germany: German with Croatian words?]. *Lahor: časopis za hrvatski kao materinski, drugi i strani jezik* 2(2). 151–158.
Riehl, Claudia Maria. 2004. *Sprachkontaktforschung. Eine Einführung*. Tübingen: Gunter Narr Verlag.
Sedlaczek, Robert. 2006. "Tschusch!" im Wandel der Zeit. *Wiener Zeitung*. 15. Feb. 2006 https://www.wienerzeitung.at/meinung/glossen/288479-Tschusch-im-Wandel-der-Zeit.html (accessed 20 September 2018)
Seršić, Josip. 2013. *Kroatisches Wien / Hrvatski Beč* [Croatian Vienna]. Vienna: Carl Gerold's Sohn Verlagsbuchhandlung KG.
Schütze, Fritz. 1983. Biographieforschung und narratives Interview. *Neue Praxis* 13(3). 283–293.
Stojak, Marina. 2014. U Austriji živi oko 70.000 Hrvata i onih s hrvatskim korijenima [Around 70,000 Croats and those with Croatian roots live in Austria]. http://www.croexpress.eu/vijest.php?vijest=603 (accessed 20 February 2017).
Waldrauch, Harald & Karin Sohler. 2004. *Migrantenorganisationen in der Großstadt: Entstehung, Strukturen und Aktivitäten am Beispiel Wien*. Wien: Campus Verlag, Frankfurt / New York, Europäisches Zentrum.
Woods, Anya. 2004. *Medium or message? Language and faith in ethnic churches*. Clevedon, UK: Multilingual Matters.
Žepić, Stanko. 2002. Zur Geschichte der deutschen Sprache in Kroatien. *Zagreber Germanistische Beiträge* 11. 209–217.

Norway

Hanne Skaaden
Tu i tamo se gađam padežima – 'Here and there I struggle with my cases'. Croatian migrant speakers in Norway and their use of the dative

1 Introduction

This chapter investigates the Croatian spoken by diaspora speakers in Norway and their children. The first-generation speakers (Gen.1A) migrated as adults – that is, after puberty – and, thus, had Croatian as their fully developed first language (L1) at the onset of migration. The second-generation speakers (Gen.2) were born and raised in Norway and acquired Croatian in a predominantly Norwegian environment, whereas the intermediary generation (Gen.1B) experienced the onset of migration before age 12.[1] This chapter focuses on diaspora speakers' verbal commentaries of physical actions that were presented to them by way of visual stimuli, a method regularly used to elicit spoken responses from informants. In particular, the chapter concentrates on diaspora speakers' descriptions of actions that are typically expressed in Croatian via dative constructions.

The chapter is structured in the following way. The remaining parts of this section present general demographic and sociolinguistic information on Croatian-origin residents in Norway and on Croatian-speakers in that country.

---

[1] Since Einar Haugen's (1953) seminal studies of Norwegian spoken by migrants to the United States (US), the terms *first-* and *second-generation* migrant speaker have signified the observed differences in the bilingualism of adult migrants and their children. Due to the observed differences in bilingual development, research on migrant children's L1 also discerns between children born in the "New World" and the "intermediate generation", who migrated between the ages of 5 and 12 (Türker 2000: 34–35). Some use *heritage speaker* for both groups of children (Gürel & Yılmaz 2013: 39), while some speak of *early* versus *late child L2 acquisition* (Montrul 2008: 18). In terms of age of acquisition as a feature that relates to a person's ability to acquire another language to a high, near-native standard, early adolescence is often used as a chronological time-point that is likely to determine a person's potential to acquire two languages to a high level of proficiency (Skaaden 2005: 435; Schmid & Köpke 2013: 2).

Note: This study is registered with the Norwegian Centre for Research Data (NSD), Project no. 51390.

Hanne Skaaden, Oslo Metropolitan University

https://doi.org/10.1515/9781501503917-007

Section 2 presents information on the functions of the dative and semantic categories that are commonly expressed via dative constructions. Section 3 provides more detailed insights into use of the dative in Croatian and on the employment of visual stimuli as an elicitation tool. Section 4 gives details of the informants who provided the spoken data on which this chapter is based. Section 5 presents results and provides a discussion of examples presented, and section 6 contains the conclusion with findings summarized.

1.1 History of contact, vintages of emigration, status

The first Croatians arrived in Norway around 1970, albeit in small numbers. By the end of the 1980s Norway had less than 2,000 immigrants from former Yugoslavia altogether (Norwegian Government 1987–1988). The number of Croatian-speaking residents was correspondingly lower than this, and exact statistics on the number of Croatian-speakers have become available only since the turn of the century. The numbers have then increased significantly, with nearly 5,000 residents with Croatian heritage reported in 2015. With the Adriatic Coast being a popular holiday destination for Norwegians from the 1970s onwards, a significant number of Croatians have settled in Norway after meeting and marrying Norwegians on holiday in Croatia. Increases during the 1990s were due mostly to the arrival of refugees from Bosnia-Herzegovina, and the regions of Slavonia and Lika in Croatia. Further, after Croatia became a member of the European Union in 2013, Croatians have come to Norway to work on the basis of EU treaties such as the European Economic Area Agreement that allows EU citizens to work in select non-EU-member states such as Norway.

1.2 Number of Croatian-heritage residents, number of Croatian-speakers

According to official statistics, in 2016, Norway recorded nearly 5,000 residents of Croatian heritage, of which 3,747 belong to the first generation, i.e. they arrived as adults, while 754 are their children and 430 their grandchildren (Statistics Norway 2018; StatBank Norway 2019). The number of immigrants and refugees from Bosnia-Herzegovina and other parts of former Yugoslavia far outnumber the population of Croatian heritage in Norway, with 30,000 recorded. It is unclear how many of these may be Croatian. The total number of Croatian speakers in Norway is estimated at between 5,000 and 7,500.

1.3 Geographic distribution, socio-economic profile

According to Norway's official statistics, around half of all Croatians in Norway are settled in the Oslo area and surrounding counties: approximately 2,200 people. Nearly 900 are settled along the western coast, where Norway's oil industry is based. The rest are dispersed around Norway's 19 counties, with totals of between 19 to 116 residents in each, with the largest group in the Trondheim area. Most Croatians in Norway are therefore not part of close-knit Croatian linguistic communities of any considerable size.

Based on official Norwegian statistics, Croatians in Norway are well educated and well integrated into Norwegian society. Comparative data of Croatians and the national average reveal the following, calculated in percentages: completed secondary school (A-levels completion), Croats in Norway – 45%, Norwegian national average – 40%; higher education of up to and including four years, Croats in Norway – 18%, Norwegian national average – 23%; higher education of more than four years, Croats in Norway – 12%, Norwegian national average – 9%. Further, Croats are well integrated into the work force, with a very low unemployment rate of 3.5% (StatBank Norway 2019). This suggests that the educational and socio-economic profile of Croatians in Norway is congruent to or higher than Norwegian national averages.

1.4 Infrastructure

Most Croatians in the Oslo area are associated with the *Hrvatska zajednica u Norveškoj* 'Croatian community of Norway' (*Kroatisk forbund i Norge*, 2019), which was founded in 1989 and is organized around the Catholic Church in Oslo. The society organizes both cultural and sporting activities and is currently preparing a book on the history of Croatians in Norway. Between 1996 and 2013 this community association was responsible for the Croatian School in Norway (*Dopunska škola* 'Supplementary School'), which featured literacy and history classes in Croatian held fortnightly for first to fifth grades. At its most, the school had up to twenty students. The Croatian Ministry of Science, Education and Sports financed the teacher's post at the school until 2009, sending a teacher from Croatia. Between 2009 and 2013, two of the mothers settled in the Oslo area took care of teaching. Currently, there are not enough students to justify a teacher being posted from Croatia and the school is currently dormant.

1.5 Domain use, language maintenance and shift

Use of Croatian is largely restricted to the home/family and religious domain; even amongst social networks the use of Croatian is variable, due to the low numbers of Croatian-speakers in Norway and the relatively high level of integration into Norwegian society, meaning that the medium of communication with other social contacts is Norwegian. Amongst Gen.1 speakers in exogamous relationships, the 'home' language is likely to be 'predominantly Norwegian', but levels of language maintenance amongst Gen.2 speakers are medium to high, even amongst children from exogamous relationships. This points to language maintenance strategies pursued by many Croatian-speaking parents – visits to Croatia, providing visual and textual resources in and about the Croatian language for their children to acquire Croatian. Professed attitudes, particularly those of Gen.1 speakers, are highly supportive of language maintenance.

Code-switching into and from Norwegian is a feature of Gen.1 and Gen.2 Croatian-speakers' speech that is known to them, but even more conspicuous to outsiders, particularly HMLD.Cro-speakers. One of the informants taking part in this study made the following remark: "When my mother came visiting from Croatia, she could not understand what the people we met in church were saying all the time, because they blended so much Norwegian into their Croatian."

1.6 Contacts with Croatia, host society attitudes towards Croats

With relatively low airfares and frequent, direct flights between Oslo and Zagreb since 2005, Croatia and Norway are only a two-hour plane trip apart. Over the last decade, contact opportunities have increased significantly. Most Croats in Norway report visiting Croatia regularly, at least once or twice a year, usually in summer. With the internet and TV on demand or via cable, opportunities for the (passive) use of Croatian have also grown. Due to their high level of integration, as witnessed through the strong educational profile and commensurate income-level of most Croats in Norway compared to the national average, host society attitudes towards Croats are generally positive.

2 Speakers of diaspora languages and characteristics of their speech

The ease with which children learn a second language, compared to adults, is apparent. The effects of language contact on adults' L1 and their children's heritage language are perhaps less apparent. However, both generations' language skills may be affected by the limited continuous exposure to the heritage language that the migrant context offers, in combination with ample exposure to the societally dominant language (Gürel and Yılmaz 2013: 37). As an effect of this exposure Montrul, Bhatt and Bhatia (2012: 141) make the observation that "recent research has identified several vulnerable areas in heritage language grammars, among which morphosyntax is among the most affected". The effects of language contact on the L1 of adult migrants with a late onset of bilingualism are described as a psycholinguistic phenomenon under the label *attrition* (e.g., Andersen 1982; Seliger and Vago 1991; Skaaden 1999, 2005; Schmid 2002; Schmid and Köpke 2013). For the adult migrants' children who acquire their heritage language (their parents' L1) in an environment in which another language is dominant, the situation of their acquisition of Croatian may be more accurately described as "incomplete acquisition" (Montrul 2008: 20) or as "divergent attainment" (Polinsky and Scontras 2019: 4).

The specific aim of this chapter is to explore the speakers' realization of the grammatical category dative as an illustration of covert contact phenomena. More overt contact phenomena – for instance, "copies" or "calques" of Norwegian schemas that speakers apply instead of the dative – receive secondary attention. There are a number of reasons for making the dative the focus of attention. First, Croatian has morphological case markings for both nominal and pronominal constituents, whereas in contemporary Norwegian the morphological case markings are lost for nouns and are even fading for pronouns (Faarlund, Lie and Vannebo 1997: 318). Relations that may be expressed in Croatian using the dative are instead expressed in Norwegian by means of *word order, possessive pronouns*, or *prepositional phrases* (Skaaden 1999: 297). Second, previous studies have indicated that the dative is a category that is vulnerable to change for Croatian migrants in contact with Scandinavian languages. In a longitudinal study on migrant children's (Gen.2) case systems in Sweden, Đurovič (1983, 1984, 1987) shows that the dative is their last oblique case to develop and the first to undergo change. Moreover, the migrant children's case markings tended to affect the nominal constituents, while the pronominals were more resistant.[2]

---

2 Croatian has seven cases, which are traditionally referred to in the following order: nominative, genitive, dative, accusative, vocative, locative, and instrumental (e.g., Barić et al. 1990: 66).

Third, a previous study comparing the speech output of adult migrant speakers (all Gen.1A) in Norway with that of Croatian speakers who had never left their homeland showed that even for migrant speakers with a late onset of migration, the dative is vulnerable to change (Skaaden 1999). Utilizing the *Pear Story* film (Chafe 1980) as described in Section 3 below to elicit speech, the study found that, on average, when responding to the film, the homeland peers vocalized a dative twice as often as the migrants did (Skaaden 1999: 311). We return to the findings from this study and examine them in more detail below, as they serve as the backdrop for exploring the current speakers' uses of the dative.

Finally, because the dative is a grammatical category denoting the basic syntactic function of the indirect object, the findings that the dative is vulnerable in a contact situation are also interesting at the theoretical level. Schmid and Köpke (2013: 2) observe that the extent to which language contact affects the speakers' *lexicon* only, or even their *grammar*, is under debate, and that opinions vary, depending on the choice of theoretical framework. Whether language contact has an impact on the speaker's grammar is of particular importance for models that are inspired by the generative paradigm, for which a strict division between *performance* (the use of language) and *competence* (the intuitive knowledge of grammar) is vital to the basic tenets (Chomsky 1965: 3, 47–58).[3] Due to the asserted difference between lexicon and grammar, it would follow that the Gen.1A speakers' grammar remains unaffected even after extended periods of disuse (Andersen 1982: 91). Any data indicating otherwise are problematic for generative models (Sharwood-Smith and Van Buren 1991: 21, 27). Schmid and Köpke (2013: 2) accordingly hold that the effects of language contact on the L1 of late-onset bilinguals may to some degree affect "language processing during production and comprehension", but "does not change the underlying knowledge system". Within models that are inspired by the generative paradigm, accepting that language contact affects the grammar of Gen.2 and even Gen.1B speakers is less controversial, because incomplete acquisition or divergent attainment can explain the effects on grammatical structure (cf. Perpiñán 2013; Schmid and Köpke 2013; Yılmaz 2013; Polinsky and Scontras 2019).

The aim here is to demonstrate how a usage-based model of language (Langacker 1987; Janda 1993) that opposes a sharp division between lexicon and grammar may support a unified analysis of contact phenomena. Based on the

---

In longitudinal studies of migrant children's nominal case markings, however, the dative has tended to be the last of the oblique cases to appear, typically being replaced by *casus generalis* that equals the accusative form (Ďurovič 1983, 1984, 1987).

3 For criticism of Chomsky's division of *grammar/lexicon*, see Langacker (1987: 25–28) and Itkonen & Haukioja (1996: 132–138), who argue against Chomsky's dismissal of the role of *analogy* in syntax.

migrants' online speech production in a quasi-experimental design, this chapter explores the diaspora speakers' use of the grammatical category dative under the conditions of the *Pear Story* task, thus replicating a previous study (Skaaden 1999). Since the current speakers represent *first-*, *intermediate-*, and *second-* generation diaspora speakers – Gen.1A, Gen.1B, and Gen.2, respectively – the question addressed is: How do speakers of different generations realize the dative in light of a model of linguistic structure that conceptualizes it as a radial category forming around a prototype?

2.1 Some theoretical considerations in relation to transposed, diaspora languages

Due to the multitude of factors involved in bilingualism and language contact, it is difficult to pinpoint exactly which aspects of language are more vulnerable or resistant to change in a contact situation. An increasing number of studies on bilingualism and contact-induced change challenge the idea that language contact affects speakers' lexicon but not their grammar, even for speakers who migrated as adults with a fully developed L1 (Perpiñán 2013: 127). Hence, rider hypotheses, such as the interface hypothesis, occur, claiming that attrition may affect only phenomena that are "located at the interface between syntax and other external modules of grammar such as discourse and/or phonology" (Perpiñán 2013: 133). Whether the differences in data "can be located at the level of representation or the level of access" (Schmid and Köpke 2013: 2) is still a debated question, for which the answer seems to depend on the choice of theoretical model. For theoretical models of human language that challenge the sharp division between lexicon and grammar, contact data involving grammatical units are less of a problem. In a usage-based model of language, the division between symbolic (lexical) and schematic (grammatical) units is considered a matter of degree, and a basic tenet of cognitive grammar is that "lexicon, morphology, and syntax form a continuum of symbolic units serving to structure conceptual content for expressive purposes" (Langacker 1987: 35). In line with the ideas of cognitive grammar, Janda (1993: 14) holds that "grammatical elements function more to organize ideas than to specify them" but that just like lexical units, "grammatically specified notions can be seen to pattern in categories, and the categories, in turn, into integrated systems."

According to Langacker (1987: 494), a linguistic *unit* refers to a structure, whether symbolic or schematic – that is, lexical or grammatical – that is "mastered by a speaker to the point that it can be employed in a largely automatic fashion, without requiring attention to its individual parts or their arrangement." Furthermore, unit status is graded, and linguistic structures should be conceived of as "falling along a continuous scale of **entrenchment** in cognitive organization" (Langacker 1987: 59. Original emphasis). Entrenchment here implies that

> every use of a structure has a positive impact on its degree of entrenchment, whereas extended periods of disuse have a negative impact. With repeated use, a novel structure becomes progressively entrenched, to the point of becoming a unit; moreover, units are variably entrenched depending on the frequency of their occurrence [. . .]. (Langacker 1987: 59)

In speech production, then, the readiness of a linguistic unit – whether lexical or grammatical – to be activated will depend on its level of entrenchment in the individual speaker's memory. Regardless of generation, the individual speaker's exposure to the heritage language will be somewhat restricted after migration. At the same time, the impact of the societally dominant language will be massive. In terms of entrenchment, the result is a "two-way-street effect." On the one hand, frequently experienced linguistic units and schemas will be more entrenched and will, therefore, be activated more easily in a speech event. On the other hand, the units and schemas that the speaker experiences less frequently will be less entrenched. Thus, they will be less accessible in a speech event (Skaaden 1999: 149; Skaaden 2005: 442). Additionally, the human ability to reason by analogy may instigate the copying of schemas from the societally dominant language into the heritage language (Skaaden 2005: 437). This can thereby increase the use of options that are possible but marginal in the heritage language under the influence of commonly-occurring schemas from the other language, for example, in the case of NP internal word order (cf. Johanson 1993: 208; Skaaden 1999: 158; Skaaden 2005: 448). In effect, structures that are shared with the societally dominant language may activate more easily than those that are specific to the heritage language. In the current case, such an effect could, for instance, prompt the use of prepositional phrases or possessive pronouns (schemas that are shared by both languages) instead of morphological case markings (schemas that are specific to the heritage language). In accordance with a prototype model, an assumption would be that units and schemas, which are somehow *central* in the system, are relatively resistant to language contact, while those that are somehow *marginal* are more vulnerable (Skaaden 2005: 437).

3 The Croatian dative and the *Pear Story*

Denoting one of the main clause constituents in the Croatian case system, the dative is a grammatical category that "acquires the morphologic form characteristic primarily for the central type cases" (Ivić 1961: 46). Cognitive grammar, which considers even grammatical categories to have *meaning*, allows for semantic analysis of the dative (Langacker 1987; Janda 1993; Šarić 2002). Drawing on Langacker's model of linguistic structure, Janda (1993), based on Czech, describes the grammatical category *case* as a radial semantic network forming around a prototype. Janda's description of the dative's semantic network is comprehensive. Only network nodes that play a role in the *Pear Story* narratives in Croatian will receive attention here – that is, the indirect object (with semantic and syntagmatic extensions), the directly governed dative, the free dative ("affectedness by possession"), and the directional dative (with or without preposition).

3.1 The Croatian dative according to Janda's network model

The indirect object with the verb 'give' (Cro. *dati/davati*) is the prototype of the dative, as is claimed by Janda (1993: 49). From this prototype, the network unfolds through semantic and schematic or syntagmatic extensions. First, in the prototype schema of the indirect object, the dative constituent retains independent status when a "nominative acts on an accusative [the direct object] to bring it to a dative in a setting" (Janda 1993: 55). Semantic extension from the prototype typically unfolds via verbs that are synonyms, antonyms, and metonyms for 'give' – for example, *vratiti/vraćati* – 'return, give back'; *uzeti/uzimati* – 'take'; and *govoriti* – 'speak to,' respectively. Janda (1993: 64) holds that metonymic extension forms a bridge to verbs of *intransitive giving* or *taking*. Verbs for which "the meaning conveyed is 'not be available to' rather than 'take self from'" are considered to have a malfactive content (Janda 1993: 65). Examples of this category of *intransitive taking* are *ispasti/ispadati* 'fall out' and *faliti* 'be missing'. Further, the governed dative, whereby the accusative is omitted from or 'absorbed' by the verb's semantics, signifies a nominative referent acting directly on a dative through syntagmatic extension from the indirect object (Janda 1993: 55). Hence, the governed dative denotes a transitive relation of subordination "in which the nominative entity places itself in a situation controlled by the dative entity" (Janda 1993: 55, 71), for instance, *pomoći/pomagati* – 'help'. Such transitive subordination "shows the most obvious relationships to the indirect object, for when one subordinates oneself to another, one transfers oneself (or some aspect of oneself) to the other's power", according to Janda (1993: 71). In addition, a few prepositions (as well as numerous adjectives and adverbs) may govern the dative directly. At this point, Czech and Croatian grammars differ somewhat, and we return to this difference in the description of the responses to the *Pear Story*. Finally, the "free dative" of possession is a syntagmatic extension of the basic indirect object schema, wherein a "nominative acts on an accusative in a dative's sphere of control in a setting" (Janda 1993: 83). A significant difference between the prototype and free dative is that with the prototype, possession is established, while with the free dative, possession is only emphasized (Janda 1993: 53).

Šarić (2002: 19) also analyzes the Slavic dative within the framework of cognitive grammar, focusing on the dative's possessive function. She concludes that the dative of possession "is more egocentrical, more referential and more individuated than other possessive expressions." Janda (1993: 83) claims that although the dative of possession has a higher frequency in language use than the dative of the indirect object with the particular verb 'give', the latter is still the prototype, as the activity of "giving" is cognitively more fundamental. The prototype's primary status is manifested in the fact that a "true" indirect object cannot be omitted or replaced by a preposition (Janda 1993: 57, 60). Janda (1993: 83) admits that the boundaries between the dative network's nodes are sometimes subtle. She uses the analogy of the Milky Way to describe the constellations of the datives' total semantic network, as in the Milky Way, some areas are more or less densely populated, and some stars are brighter than others. Obviously, the options to utilize the dative when describing the *Pear Story* scenes amount to a fraction of the total network.

3.2 Datives as previously elicited by the *Pear Story* (Skaaden 1999)

Originally produced by Chafe (1980) to elicit narratives for psycholinguistic studies, the *Pear Story* is a 5 minute 55 second film set in grassy scenery that involves a man picking pears and several children interacting, but without dialogue. In the elicitation setting, the speakers are asked to comment on the activities throughout the film's duration as the scenes evolve simultaneously on the screen in front of them. The nature of the *Pear Story* task is such that a speaker's utilization of a certain grammatical category – for example, the dative – is a matter of individual choice. Then again, to some extent, the film's scenes restrict the speakers' choices as to what they vocalize. The actors in the *Pear Story* are typically involved in *giving, taking, stealing, losing, helping* and/or *approaching,* all of which are conceptualizations that habitually require dative constructions in Croatian. The film has, therefore, proven to be a productive means of eliciting datives (Skaaden 1999: 297).

In response to the *Pear Story* task, homeland speakers of Croatian and Serbian in Skaaden (1999) utilized the dative with nearly 40 different verbs signifying the actions commonly expressed via datives. In contrast, a group of Gen.1A migrant speakers utilized the dative with only 17 verbs. Diaspora speakers tended not to verbally describe those aspects of the visual stimuli for which homeland speakers readily used dative constructions, or if the aspects were described by the diaspora speakers they would employ prepositional phrases or pronominal constructions.

The five migrant speakers had migrated after puberty – that is, between the ages of 18 and 36. Like the current Gen.1A speakers, they all, therefore, had a fully developed L1 at the onset of migration (Skaaden 1999: 298, 313; Skaaden 2005: 439). At the time of recording, the speakers had lived in Norway for more than 20 years. The native homeland-based speakers had all grown up in predominantly monolingual environments in present-day Croatia, Bosnia–Herzegovina, or Serbia and had never lived outside their country of origin. Their ages and education levels were otherwise congruent with those of the diaspora speakers (Skaaden 1999: 86, 93; cf. Savić 1985: 131 on native Croatian-speakers' *Pear Story* narratives).

When we return to the current speakers' responses to the *Pear Story* in Section 5, the findings from the 1999 study will serve as a backdrop, and a brief overview of some of its findings is warranted here. In response to the *Pear Story*, the homeland speakers produced a dative nearly twice as frequently as the migrants (all Gen.1A) did, at 15 vs. 8 datives per 100 finite clause unit. Moreover, inter-speaker variation along this parameter was far more conspicuous among the migrants than among the homeland speakers (Skaaden 1999: 313, cf. 5.1 below). In line with the predictions of Janda's model, the migrants' most prominent dative was the indirect object with the verb *dati/davati* 'give', which is the assumed prototype (at 29.8%). In comparison, this verb yielded only a fraction (5.7%) of the datives of the homeland speakers, who instead produced datives with a wide range of synonyms for the assumed prototype, e.g. *donijeti/donositi* 'bring' and *vratiti/vraćati* 'return'. In addition, the homeland speakers used the dative with antonyms and metonyms for 'give', e.g. *uzeti/uzimati* – 'take,' *ukrasti/krasti* – 'steal,' and *uspjeti/uspijevati* 'succeed' or *zviznuti/zviždati* 'whistle at' respectively. In contrast, datives triggered by antonyms and metonyms were almost absent in these diaspora speakers' narratives. However, both homeland speakers (12.5%) and migrants (19.1%) applied datives with the verb *pomoći/pomagati* 'help'. Overall, the speakers utilized the dative in accordance with Janda's (1993) model which is based on Czech, although some differences between the Czech and Croatian dative systems came to the fore. The most striking difference was found in the *bare-case directional dative* denoting motion toward (Skaaden 1999: 307). This dative is governed by a preposition in modern Czech and other Slavic languages (Janda 1993: 98), but it is still alive as a bare case in Croatian with verbs of motion that denote direction toward an object or person (Gallis 1973: 292).[4] A considerable portion of

---

4 For instance, the expression, 'I'm going to the doctor' can be expressed without a preposition with 'doktor' in the dative case (*idem doktoru* 'go-1SG' doktoru-DAT.M.SG), with a preposition governing the dative case (*idem k doktoru* 'go-1SG' to+DAT doktoru-DAT.M.SG); or with a related preposition governing the genitive case (*idem kod doktora* 'go-1SG' at+GEN doktora-GEN.M.SG). The first

the homeland speakers' datives (27.3%) appeared with verbs denoting motion toward – that is, *prići/prilaziti* and *približiti se/približavati se* – 'approach/come closer to' (Skaaden 1999: 299–310). This dative was considerably less frequent in the narratives of the migrants (12.8%), who instead utilized prepositional phrases when narrating the same scenes (Skaaden 1999: 311, 316). Congruent data is found in USA.Cro, where less marked DAT constructions for expressing relations of possession are commonly replaced by possessive adjectives (see Jutronić, this volume).

After a brief look at the current speakers' background in Subsection 4, I will return to their *Pear Story* narratives in Subsection 5 to explore how their dative realizations accord with the previous findings and with the dative as a radial category forming around its prototype.

4 Speakers and data set

4.1 Speakers

The 10 speakers were recruited through networks within the Croatian community in Oslo. Six of them are Gen.1A speakers who grew up monolingually in Croatia and migrated to Norway in their 20s, well after puberty. At the time of recording, the Gen.1A speakers are in their 50s or early 60s and have lived in Norway for 25 to 40 years. Three of the speakers have Norwegian spouses, and three have Croatian native spouses. Three speakers (Gen.2) are children of Croatian migrants, who are born and raised in Norway in bilingual families with one Croatian and one Norwegian parent, and they have therefore acquired Croatian and Norwegian simultaneously. At the time of recording, these speakers are in their 20s and are enrolled at university in Norway. One speaker (Gen.1B_1M) had arrived in Norway with his Croatian parents at the age of 10 and is, accordingly, a speaker of the *intermediate generation*. Gen.1B_1M's bilingual biography differs from that of the Gen.2 speakers' in that contact with Croatia has been more extensive, including tertiary studies and then an extended period of employment in Croatia after completing high school in Norway. At the time of recording, the speaker, who is now in his 30s, had been living in Norway for the past five years.

All the speakers are well integrated into Norwegian society, and Norwegian is the predominant medium of communication in their daily lives. The use of Cro-

---

two examples with dative constructions are standard Croatian expressions while the last one is considered non-standard but is still commonly used and acceptable in spoken Croatian.

atian outside the home is limited to communication with family in Croatia and certain events in Oslo, such as visiting church. All Gen.1A subjects have holiday homes in Croatia and report that they visit the country several times per year. The frequency of their visits to the homeland has reportedly increased over the past couple of decades due to economic and personal factors.

In reports on their language usage patterns, all speakers report their reading of books and magazines in Croatian to be relatively limited. However, there is some variation in reported reading patterns, which seems to accord with educational level. Opportunities to stay in contact with Croatian in Norway have increased considerably in the past decades, due to greater availability of television channels, and access to texts and audio-visual contact via the internet. All subjects report having access to Croatian TV channels in Norway. However, the subjects report that they utilize this opportunity to a limited degree, which is possibly due to the extent of their immersion in Norwegian society.

In terms of usage patterns in daily life, the Gen.1A speakers with Norwegian spouses report that although both Norwegian and Croatian are spoken in their homes, Norwegian tends to dominate. Even Gen.1A speakers with Croatian spouses (Gen.1A_3F, Gen.1A_4M, and Gen.1A_6F) report that a mixture of Croatian and Norwegian is spoken at home. The reason given is that Norwegian quickly became the preferred medium of communication for their children. Characteristically, to describe his family's language usage patterns, Gen.1A_4M uses the Norwegian lexical unit *lapskaus* ('mulligan' or 'stew'): *pa, norveški i hrvatski, pravi* **lapskaus** 'well, Norwegian and Croatian, a true **mulligan**'. Extensive code-switching seems rather common when members of the Croatian community in Oslo meet. As mentioned above, one speaker reports that her mother, when visiting from Croatia, was unable to follow some of the expatriates' conversations due to their frequent code-switching to Norwegian. All the Gen.1A speakers emphasize the importance of keeping their L1 alive and passing Croatian on to their children and grandchildren, however. Overt code-switching to Norwegian was practically absent during the interactions between the speakers and the author while the data were being collected. No overt code-switches involving Norwegian lexical units occurred during the test-like *Pear Story* task except in the one instance, illustrated in (2) below.

4.2 Collection of linguistic data

Replicating the previous elicitation setting described in Section 3, the speakers were asked to describe in Croatian the *Pear Story* scenes while simultaneously watching the film, which was being played without sound. The elicitation thus captured a "snapshot" of the speakers' Croatian speech production under the specific conditions of the film's duration. All the speakers were able to respond to the task during the entire 5 minutes and 55 seconds of the film. Prior to the film sessions, the subjects had filled out a questionnaire about their language usage patterns, after which they had been asked to participate in a follow-up meeting. The speakers were thus aware that the meeting had to do with their language use and their attitudes toward Croatian. The author administered the task for each subject individually in a test room at Oslo Metropolitan University. All communication during the test situation was in Croatian. After a short welcoming brief, each subject was given the following instructions before the *Pear Story* film started and the subject was able to view the film on a laptop screen:

> Sad ću vam prikazati kratak film. Film ćete gledati bez zvuka. Zamolit ću vas, da mi – dok gledate film – ispričate sve što se događa na ekranu, neprekidno, kao da ste radijski izvjestitelj koji prenosi recimo nogometsku utakmicu, i tako da ja mogu pratiti sve što se zbiva iako sjedim okrenutih leđa tako da ne vidim ekran. Jeste li razumjeli zadatak?

> 'Now I will show you a short film. You are to watch the film without sound. And I ask you kindly – while you are watching the film – to tell me everything that is happening on the screen, live and continuously, as if you were a radio announcer giving direct commentary on a soccer game, for instance, so that I can follow everything that is going on, even though I will be sitting with my back turned so I cannot see the screen. Do you understand the task?'

The speakers had not seen the film before, but all the subjects were able to complete the task on their first attempt. The speakers' descriptions of the *Pear Story* scenes were audio-recorded, transcribed, and subsequently segmented at clause boundaries or *intonation units* – that is, a sequence of speech "verbalizing the idea of an event or state" (Chafe 1994: 66, 57) with each clause unit containing one finite verb. Once each speaker's narrative was broken down into clauses, the frequency of dative constructions could be isolated.

5 Results and discussion

With approximately six words per clause, a rate in line with normal speech production (Kess 1992: 56), the 10 speakers amongst them produced 1,019 finite clauses in their responses to the film. Because the clause count is based on the transcripts and includes false starts and repairs, longer clauses and more words may, on the one hand, indicate that the speaker needed more rephrasing to express intended conceptualizations. On the other hand, planning problems may also result in pausing or hesitation phenomena. The speakers' speech behavior differed along these lines, to some extent, as reflected in their word counts.

Table 1 shows that the speakers produced a variable number of clauses during the 355-second *Pear Story*. Notwithstanding this, all speakers were able to produce adequate responses to the scenes as they unfolded on the screen in front of them. The simultaneity of watching and commenting meant that the elicitation setting was not a "normal" speech event. However, with roughly 2.5 words per second, the Gen.1A speakers responded to the film scenes with a speech rate close to normal – that is, "about two to three words per second" (Levelt 1989: 22). A somewhat slower speech rate of 1.5 words per second may indicate increased speech-planning problems for the Gen.2 speakers.

Table 1: Number of clauses and words produced by the 10 speakers.

Speaker	No. of clauses	Words vocalized*)	Words per clause	Words per sec.
Gen.1A_1F	149	892	5.99	2.5
Gen.1A_2F	164	999	6.09	2.8
Gen.1A_3F	134	739	5.51	2.1
Gen.1A_4M	219	1217	5.56	3.4
Gen.1A_5F	105	663	6.31	1.9
Gen.1A_6F	113	707	6.26	2.0
Gen.1B_1M	109	662	6.07	1.9
Gen.2_2F	61	504	8.26	1.4
Gen.2_3F	52	312	6.00	0.9
Gen.2_4F	62	424	6.84	1.2
Mean (total)	117	712	6.3	2.0

* The count is based on the transcription, including false starts and repairs.

On average, the Gen.2 speakers produced considerably fewer clauses than adult Gen.1A speakers. This tendency confirmed the expectation that the Gen.2 speakers would have more difficulty expressing themselves in Croatian than the Gen.1A speakers, whose proficiency in Croatian was fully developed at the time of their migration. However, inter-speaker variation along this parameter cut across generation categories, and two of the Gen.1A speakers with 113 and 105 clauses were statistically more aligned with the intermediate speaker at 109.

The Gen.2 speakers explicitly confirmed that they perceived the task as difficult. Speaker Gen.2_2F's immediate comments when the film ended showed that the problem was not situated at the level of conceptualization:

(1) Gen.2_2F: *Baš je teško.*
'It is really difficult.'
Author: *A šta je teško?*
'So, what is difficult?'
Gen.2_2F: *Meni je teško . . . øm kao stić naći rijeć da objasnim šta se dešava. Mislim, ja vidim da je on/ : da je njemu nešto na koljenu ili na / . . . kad : kad padne sa bicikla, ali ne stignem objasnit.*
'For me, it's difficult... erm like to get to find (in time) the word to explain what is going on. I mean, I see that he is/: that it is something on his knee or on /. . . when : when he falls from the bike, but I don't get to explain in time'
Author: *Je'l bi bilo lakše na norveškom?*
'Would it have been easier in Norwegian?'
Gen.2_2F: *Da, puno lakše. I na engleskom isto bi bilo lakše*
'Yes, much easier. And (even) in English, it would have been easier'

Similarly, after completing the task, speakers Gen.2_3F and Gen.2_4F explicitly described their difficulties with naming certain objects – for example, the baskets that appeared in the film. In fact, speaker Gen.2_4F was the only speaker who resorted to Norwegian *kurv* ('basket') during the film session when she was unable to recall a Croatian equivalent – for example, *košara* or *korpa* 'basket'.

(2) *i onda sad kruške vadi, i stavlja u :: u øm . . ., kako se zove* **kurv**?[5]
'and now he takes out the pears and puts (them) in :: in erm . . . how does one say **basket**?' (Gen.2_4F .9–11)

Pauses and restructurings signal retrieval or planning problems and indicate that the Gen.2 speakers, in particular, needed more planning time for their Croatian speech production. As a result, the Gen.2 speakers produced fewer clauses.

Even the Gen.1A speakers admitted to having retrieval problems. For instance, after completing the task, speaker Gen.1A_2F commented on her failed attempt to name the bike's *gepek* ('bicycle back rack'). Before she resorted to calling it

---

[5] The transcriptions follow standard Croatian orthography. However, three punctuation marks (. . .) indicate a marked pause, a single punctuation mark (.) a brief pause, a slash (/) an interrupted clause, and a backslash (\) a within-word interruption (indicating that the speaker detected an error during speech planning), whereas double colons (::) indicate that the speaker's self-repair or restructuring follows. The final digit in each excerpt (e.g., 9–11 here) identifies the clause line in the speaker's transcribed response.

žica ('wire' or 'string'), her struggle during the task performance illustrates how retrieval problems may materialize in the recordings:

(3) *i diže košaru, stavlja je na . hm . na kao jedan :: jednu :: jedn\ <sigh> jednu žicu*
 'and he lifts the basket, puts it on . hm . on like a [ACC.M.SG] :a [ACC.F.SG] <sigh> a [ACC.F.SG] **wire** [ACC.F.SG].'

Due to the speaker's explicit comments on the retrieval problem upon completing the task, we know that it does not originate at the level of conceptualization. Afterward and of her own accord, Gen.1A_2F admitted to her retrieval troubles: *na primjer nisam se mogla sjetit' kako se kaže 'gepek', pa rekla žicu (smije se):* 'For instance, I could not remember how to say "gepek" ['bicycle back rack'], so I said wire (laughing).' Because she later named her target *gepek*, we also know that the retrieval problem was temporary. Other Gen.1A speakers also spontaneously described a feeling that their ability to use Croatian was no longer up to par. After completing the task, even speaker Gen.1A_1F, whose Croatian seemed quite unaffected by the migrant context, confessed, *osjećam da nisam dugo koristila hrvatski:* 'I feel that I haven't used Croatian for a long time.' Similarly, after the film, speaker Gen.1A_6F admitted that she even had problems with the grammar: *tu i tamo se gađam padežima*. This expression – which translates into 'Here and there I struggle with my cases' – is an idiomatic phrase in Croatian for 'making grammatical mistakes' or 'speaking with an accent.'

5.1 Dative occurrences during the *Pear Story* sessions

Because there is only *one* dative per finite verb, no more than one dative will normally appear in each clausal unit. As mentioned, this allows for comparison of the frequency with which the speakers produce the grammatical category once a narrative has been segmented. An exception to the pattern of one dative constituent per clause would be a self-repair (::) involving a dative. Such an occurrence is illustrated in Excerpt (4), in which the speaker corrects the pronominal form *mu* ('him-DAT') to the nominal form *dječaku* ('boy-DAT'):

(4) *a ona **mu** sada ukrala šešir*
 and she-NOM him-DAT now stole-PAST.PTC.F.SG hat-ACC.M.SG
 dječaku
 boy-DAT. M.SG
 'and she now stole **his** . . . hat . . . **the boy's** [hat]' (Gen.1B_1M .79)

In the aforementioned study involving the *Pear Story* (Skaaden 1999), the migrant speakers (all Gen.1A) produced datives with a considerably lower frequency than the homeland speakers, with a means difference of 8 versus 15 per 100 clause. Moreover, inter-speaker variation characterized the migrants' dative frequency. Their dative frequency varied from a low of 4.5 to a high of 10.9, whereas the homeland speakers showed a statistically higher but narrower range, varying from 13.1 to 16.8 datives per 100 clauses (Skaaden 1999: 313).

Inter-speaker variation is also a salient characteristic of the current speakers' dative frequency, as Table 2 shows. While Gen.1A_3F at 4.5 matches the low end of the former study's migrant speakers, Gen.1A_1F's dative frequency at 14.8 is congruent with the homeland speakers' mean (15). Dative frequency also varies considerably among the current Gen.2 speakers. At the high end, with 13.1, Gen.2_2F even matches some homeland speakers, sharply contrasting with Gen.2_3F's dative frequency at 3.8. In terms of dative frequency, inter-speaker variation cuts across the generational boundaries in the current sample, with the intermediate speaker, Gen.1B_1M, placed in the middle at 9.2.

Table 2: The speakers' dative realizations (nouns and pronouns) while commenting on the *Pear Story*.

Speaker	No. of clauses	DAT frequency	DAT tokens	Pronominal DAT (%)	Nominal DAT (%)
Gen.1A_1F	149	14.8	22	20 (91%)	2 (9%)
Gen.1A_2F	164	10.4	17	10 (59%)	7 (41%)
Gen.1A_3F	134	4.5	6	4 (67%)	2 (33%)
Gen.1A_4M	219	10.1	22	22 (100%)	0 (0%)
Gen.1A_5F	105	8.8	9	6 (67%)	3 (33%)
Gen.1A_6F	113	8.9	10	9 (90%)	1 (10%)
Gen.1B_1M	109	9.2	10	6 (60%)	4 (40%)
Gen.2_2F	61	13.1	8	6 (75%)	2 (25%)
Gen.2_3F	52	3.8	2	2 (100%)	0 (0%)
Gen.2_4F	62	8.1	5	5 (100%)	0 (0%)
Mean	117	9.2	11.1	9 (81%)	2.1 (19%)

Table 2 further illustrates that most of the informants' datives are *pronouns* at 81% (n=90). The pronoun *mu* ('him') is the most frequently occurring dative token in the data set (61%, n=68). This trend may have to do with the nature of the task. Once a speaker has identified the main actors in the film – a man and a boy – the pronoun is a natural anaphoric reference. At the same time, the pronominal case marking is known to be more resistant to change than the dative marking of nouns (e.g. Ďurovič 1984; Ivić 1985). The fact that only 19% (n=21) of the datives are nouns may, therefore, not be an entirely stylistic phenomenon. In fact, three speakers – Gen.2_3F, Gen.2_4F, and Gen.1A_4M – never produced datives with nouns. The striking detail that throughout 219 clauses, Gen.1A_4M never vocalized a nominal dative may, accordingly, relate to the contact situation rather than the narrative style.

In sum, notwithstanding the difference in the amount of speech produced by the speakers of the respective cohorts, a striking characteristic of the current data set as far as dative frequency goes, is the inter-speaker variation that cuts across the generational cohorts.

5.2 Dative subtypes

The *types* of datives that the speakers utilize are of further interest. In the previous study involving the *Pear Story*, as described in 3.2, the diaspora speakers' datives with the indirect object of 'give' (Cro. *dati/davati*) were found to stand firm. In fact, the diaspora speakers appeared to overuse this dative, as it counted for a third of their datives but only 6% of those of the homeland speakers in comparison (Skaaden 1999: 311). The finding that the assumed prototype is resistant to change while marginal network nodes suffer in a contact situation would support Janda's (1993: 56) claim that although other dative types are more frequent in the system, the prototype denotes the dative's most basic meaning. With regard to the claim that the indirect object with 'give' is the DAT prototype, worth noting here is Polinsky's observation in her study of Russian heritage speakers' dative that "multiple mapping is often eliminated in heritage language – *typically by restricting the dative form to the role of the indirect-object recipient*" (Polinsky 2018: 184–185. Emphasis added). She also notes, that "[i]n some cases, changes in the use of the dative may be observed even in the language of first-generation immigrants" (Polinsky 2018: 185). Given the similarities in Russian and Croatian case systems, comparable findings are no surprise. Interestingly, Montrul, Bhatt and Bhatia (2012: 165) also find similar trends in their study of Hindu and Urdu heritage speakers' production and acceptability judgements. They observe that while the dative is a vulnerable category, the marking of the "indirect objects is the most resilient" and note that in this regard "the crosslinguistic patterns are strikingly similar" (Montrul, Bhatt & Bhatia 2012: 181).

To explore trends in the current data set, we shall first look at the speakers' datives with 'give' before we gradually move to nodes of the dative network that are assumedly more distant from the prototype (cf. Diagram 1 in 5.3 below). All but one speaker (Gen.1B_1M) utilizes the dative as an indirect object with 'give' (*dati/davati*), as exemplified in (5–7).

(5) i   dečko   **mu**   valjda   za   nagradu
    and   boy-NOM.M.SG   him-DAT   probably   for+ACC   reward-ACC.F.SG
    daje   dvije   kruške
    give-3SG   two+GEN.SG   pear-GEN.F.SG
    'and the boy as a reward, probably, gives **him** two pears' (Gen.1A_2F .133)

(6) ...i   on   **njemu**   za   nagradu   dâ
    ...and   he-NOM   him-DAT   for+ACC   reward-ACC.F.SG   give-3SG
    dvije   kruške
    two+GEN.SG   pear-GEN.F.SG
    'and he gives **him** two pears as a reward' (Gen.1A_5F .85)

(7) da   **mu**   dâ   kapu
    to-COMP   him-DAT   give-3SG   cap-ACC.F.SG
    'to give **him** the cap' (Gen.2_4F .48)

The quantitative tendency of overemploying datives with 'give,' as found by Skaaden (1999), does not appear in the present data set. Yet, instantiations such as (8) containing "give help" appear to be Norwegian-based, and this may indicate overuse of a qualitative kind. The verb *pomoći/pomagati* ('help'), as illustrated in (22) below, would be more in line with the Croatian convention than the choice in (8):

(8) da   **mu**   dâ   pomoć
    to-COMP   him-DAT   give-3SG   help-ACC.F.SG
    'to give **him** help' (Gen.1A_4M .142)

Gen.1B_1M is the only speaker who never uses the dative with 'give' itself to describe the same scenes. However, he instead vocalizes the indirect object with near synonyms of the prototype – for example, *vratiti/vraćati* ('return'). His choices thereby match those of the aforementioned homeland speakers, who, in contrast to the migrants, used the dative with its synonyms more often than with the actual verb 'give' (Skaaden 1999: 311).

(9) i   vraća   ga   **dječaku**
    and   return-3SG   it-ACC.M   boy-DAT.M.SG
    'and returns it **to the boy**' (Gen.1B_1M .101)

Similarly, Gen.1B_1M uses *semantic extension by antonyms* twice (20%) – that is, with *ukrasti/krasti* ('steal') – as seen in (4) above. The indirect object with antonyms never occurred in the Gen.2 narratives, while the Gen.1A speakers use the indirect object with *pljačkati* ('rob') and *uzeti* ('take') four times (5%) to describe removal from a possessor, as illustrated in (10–11).

(10)   *da*   **mu**   *pljačkaju*   *kruške*
       to-COMP   him-DAT   rob-3PL   pear-ACC.F.PL
       'to rob **him** of his pears' (Gen.1A_5F .69)

(11)   *da*   *uzme*   **sebi**   *krušku*
       to-COMP   take-3SG   himself-REFL.PRON.DAT   pear-ACC.F.SG
       'to take a pear **for himself**' (Gen.1A_4M .76)

Although there is a realization of the dative in (11), Gen.1A_4M's description *uzeti sebi krušku* ('take self-REFL.PRON-DAT pear-ACC') has a Norwegian ring to it here. In fact, *ta seg en pære* ('take -REFL.PRON a pear') in the sense of "helping yourself to something" is an unmarked choice in Norwegian that denotes the activity described. In Croatian, the activity captured would normally require another verb with the instrumental instead of the dative case – for example, *poslužiti se nečim* ('serve REFL [with] something-INS'). At times, the diaspora speakers do not provide a verbal description of visual stimuli featuring the removal of objects from a possessor, or when they do, they use a pronoun, which is, once again, more in line with Norwegian conventions. In (12), we simultaneously notice that Gen.1A_4M ignores the pro-drop option, which is a trend that strengthens the impression of the influence of Norwegian in this usage event:

(12)   *da*   *li*   *su*   *stvarno*   *uzeli*
       whether   INTERR.CLITIC   AUX.3PL   really   take-PAST.3PL.M
       oni   **njegovo**   *voće?*
       they-3PL.NOM   his-POSS.PRON.ACC   fruit-ACC.COLL.
       'did they really take **his** fruit?' (Gen.1A_4M .111)

Conversely, Gen.1A_4M is one of only two Gen.1A speakers who uses datives with *metonyms* of 'give.' Extensions by metonymy from 'give' include, for instance, the "giving of verbal signals," for which the direct object is often "subsumed in the semantics of the verb and is therefore not expressed as an overt accusative" (Janda 1993: 64). Datives of metonymic extension, illustrated in (13–14), occur five times (6%) in the present Gen.1A data set. In comparison, datives of metonymic extension were utilized three times more often by homeland speakers than by the previous adult Gen.1A speakers (Skaaden 1999: 311):

(13) i   onda   ćemo   mi   **njemu**   kazat
     and   then   will-AUX.1PL we-1PL.NOM   him-DAT   tell-INF
     'and then we will tell **him**' (Gen.1A_4M .207)

(14) da   nešto   govori   **ovom**
     that-COMP something-ACC.N.SG   speak-3SG   this-DET.DAT.M.SG
     čovjeku
     man-DAT.M.SG
     'that he says something **to this man**' (Gen.1A_2F .65)

Several *Pear Story* scenes involve objects *falling out/off* – for example, pears spilling from a basket or a hat falling off someone's head – thus indicating objects "missing" or involuntarily "spilling" or "falling" from the actor's reach. These datives with a malfactive meaning, as exemplified in examples (15) to (17), are categorized by Janda (1993: 65) as *intransitive taking*.

(15) i   sve   kruške   su   **mu**   se
     and   all-NOM.F.PL   pears-NOM.F.PL AUX.3PL   him-DAT   REFL
     rasule
     spill-PAST.PART.F.PL
     'and all pears spilled out **for him**' (Gen.1A_2F .96)

(16) upravo **mu**   je   sad   pala   jedna
     just   him-DAT   AUX-3SG   now   fall-PAST.PTC.F.SG one-NOM.F.SG
     kruška   na...na   sijeno
     pear-NOM.F.SG   on...on+ACC   hay-ACC.COLL.
     'just now, a pear fell on the hay **for him**' (Gen.1B_1M .7)

(17) da   **mu**   fali   jedna   košara
     that-COMP   him-DAT   miss-3SG   one-NOM.F.SG   basket-NOM.F.SG
     sa   kruškama
     with+INS   pears-INS.F.PL
     'that there is one basket with pears missing **for him**' (Gen.2_2F .55)

Janda (1993: 63, 83) admits that subtle distinctions determine the nodes in the dative's semantic network, and the resemblance between the effects of "giving," "taking," or "losing" and the dative of possession is obvious. However, in the latter case, possession "is emphasized but not established" and "acts merely as a vehicle for affecting the dative entity" (Janda 1993: 82). The dative of possession differs in value from the relations expressed by the possessive genitive or adjectival possessives, and Šarić (2002: 19) observes that possessive datives typically involve very close relations, such as "body parts, kinship terms and other elements of the personal sphere," exactly as exemplified in (18–20):

(18) kruške   su   **mu**   bile   u
     pear-NOM.F.PL   AUX.3PL   him-DAT   be-PAST.PRT.F.PL   in+LOC
     džepu
     pocket-LOC.M.SG
     'the pears were in **his** pocket' (Gen.1B_1M .10)

(19) kakve   su   **mu**   ozljede
     what sort-NOM.F.PL   AUX.3PL   him-DAT   injury-NOM.F.PL
     'how were **his** injuries' (Gen.1B_1M .84)

(20) to   **mu**   je   valjda   sin
     that-NOM.N.SG   him-DAT   be-PRES.3SG   probably-ADV   son-NOM.M.SG
     'that is probably **his** son' (Gen.1A_1F .54)

Affectedness via possession is a frequently occurring dative in the Croatian convention (Šarić 2002: 9), but it holds a far less central position in the semantic network than the prototype, Janda (1993: 81–82) claims. This "free dative" never appears in the Gen.2's narratives. Even the Gen.1A seldom uses it (5%, n=4). Instead, they denote such relations with possessive pronouns or do not signify the relations at all. Despite it also being an option in the Croatian convention, the choice of the possessive pronoun in (21) mimics the unmarked choice in Norwegian. Its post-positioning strengthens the impression of the impact of Norwegian. The post-positioning of the pronoun is an unmarked NP internal order in Norwegian but is stylistically marked in Croatian.

(21) možda   je   to   neki
     maybe-ADV   be-PRES.3SG   it-NOM.N.SG   some-NOM.M.SG
     djed   **njegov**
     grandpa-NOM.M.SG   his-NOM.M.SG
     'maybe that is some grandpa **of his**' (Gen.1A_6F.55)

Having spilled or lost objects, the *Pear Story* actors help each other to pick them up. To describe the activity, most current speakers utilize datives with "help," as illustrated in (22), which is a schema that accords more with the Croatian convention than "to give help," with its Norwegian ring to it, as seen in (8) above.

(22) pomognu *mu*
 help-PRES.3PL him-DAT
 'they help **him**' (Gen.2_4F .39)

Representing the sub-schema of transitive subordination, the verb *pomoći/pomagati* ('help') governs the dative directly and was one of two verbs (the other being 'give') that the diaspora speakers applied notably more often than the homeland speakers in the previous study did (Skaaden 1999: 311). Interestingly, Janda (1993: 71), who annotates "help" as "GIVE help to," holds that this dative subtype "shows the most obvious relationships to the indirect object [. . .] via the intransitive giving verbs."

Finally, a striking characteristic found in Skaaden (1999) was that while richly applied by homeland speakers, the bare-case dative with verbs denoting motion toward was much less apparent in the migrants' narratives, who more frequently used prepositional phrases when describing the same scenes. This dative has been lost in other Slavic languages and is expressed by prepositional phrases (Janda 1993: 78; cf. Gallis 1973: 292; Šarić 2002: 19). The finding would, therefore, support the idea that a marginal node in the system would be vulnerable to language contact. A clear preference for prepositional phrases over bare-case forms to express motion toward does not occur with the current speakers, however. The speakers in all three generational cohorts produce bare-form datives of directedness, as examples (23) and (24) illustrate. At the same time, some speakers prefer alternatives to this dative, as examples (25) and (26) show.

(23) *približava* se **ljestvama**
 approach-PRES.3SG REFL ladder-DAT.F.PL
 'he approaches **the ladder**' (Gen.1A_1F .55)

(24) . . . hm.. *prilazi* *mu* jedna cura
 . . . hm.. approach-PRES.3SG him-DAT one-NOM.F.SG girl-NOM.F.SG
 na *drugom* *biciklu*
 on+LOC other-LOC.M.SG bike-LOC.M.SG
 '. . . hm.. a girl on another bike is approaching **him**' (Gen.2_2F. 30)

The only speaker to apply the dative with the preposition is Gen.2_4F. She uses it with the more analytic construction *dolazi prema* ('come towards +DAT'):

(25) i   sada   neka   cura   na   biciklu
     and   now-ADV some-NOM.F.SG girl-NOM.F.SG on+LOC bike-LOC.M.SG
     dolazi   **prema**   **njemu**
     comes-PRES.3SG towards+DAT   him-DAT
     'and now some girl on a bike is coming **towards him**' (Gen.2_4F.33)

To depict the scenes of approaching illustrated in (23–25), alternatives to the dative exist in Croatian, and Gen.1A_4M symptomatically chooses *dolazi* ('come') with the preposition *kod*, ('to', 'at'-Gen.):

(26) a   sad   tek   oni   **dolaze**   **kod**
     and   now   just-ADV they-NOM.3PL   come-PRES.3PL   to+GEN
     gospodina
     gentleman-GEN.M.SG
     'and just now, they **come (up) to** the gentleman' (Gen.1A_4M .198)

The Norwegian equivalent to 'approach' (*nærme seg*, 'approach-refl.') requires no preposition. More analytic than Croatian in general, Norwegian may, however, provide models for the choices made in (25–26) – for example, through schemas such as *komme imot* ('come toward') or *komme til* ('come to'), both meaning 'approach'.

6 Summary of findings and discussion

Based on data elicited from the Gen.1A, Gen.1B, and Gen.2 speakers in response to the *Pear Story*, this chapter has explored their employment of the dative and has classified their responses according to Janda's (1993) network model, portraying the dative as a radial category forming around a prototype. Diagram 1 below sums up the datives observed, categorized according to generational cohort and Janda's network with semantic and schematic or syntagmatic extensions from the prototype – that is, the indirect object with 'give' and its extensions by synonym, antonym, or metonym and intransitive taking; the governed dative; the dative of possession ('free dative'); and the dative of directedness. The types of datives utilized by the first-, intermediate-, and second-generation speakers, are presented in percentage within each cohort. The diagram displays the "space" that each dative type occupies within each generational cohort. It should be noted that due to the uneven numbers of datives produced within each cohort, the diagram indicates trends of distribution. The diagram must be read with the number of actual instantiations in mind, as well

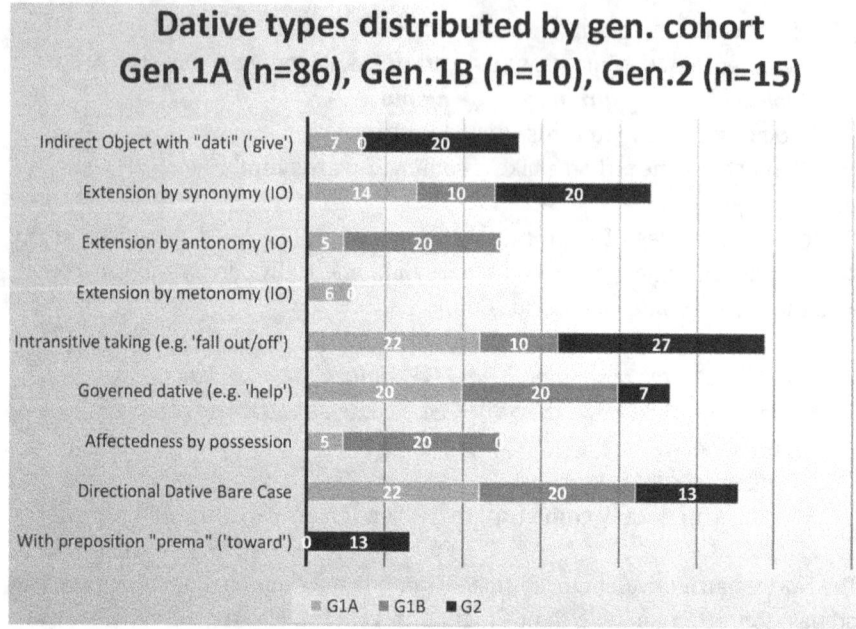

Diagram 1: Types of datives utilized by the first-, intermediate-, and second-generation speakers.

as the inter-speaker and intergenerational variations displayed in Tables 1 and 2 above. That is, within and across the cohorts, the speakers exposed varying flexibility in the number and types of datives that they used. As Table 2 above showed, three first-generation speakers (Gen.1A_1F, Gen.1A_2F, and Gen.1A_4M) accounted for 71% (n=61) of the total (n=86) datives, while speakers Gen.1A_3F, Gen.1A_5F, and Gen.1A_6F produced only 29% (n=25) between them. The intermediate speaker, Gen.1B_1M, with ten datives, showed relative flexibility in the types of datives he applied. Of the fifteen datives in the Gen.2 cohort, eight were produced by speaker Gen.2_2F and five by Gen.2_4F, while only two were produced by Gen.2_3F.

A comparison of the current speakers' responses to the *Pear Story* with those of adult migrants' (all Gen.1A) and homeland speakers' in the previous study (Skaaden 1999) indicate that the current Gen.1A align more with the latter, whereas the Gen.2 align more with the former both in terms of frequency and types of datives employed. The previous study found a clear prototype effect in that the adult migrants overused the dative prototype in comparison to homeland speakers. Conversely, these migrants' use of marginal nodes, such as the *bare-case directional dative*, withered in comparison to the homeland speakers' use, thereby supporting the assumption that marginal nodes in the radial network are more vulnerable than central nodes in a contact situation.

The present data do not replicate the prototype effect as clearly. For instance, the *bare-case directional dative* is used by speakers in all three cohorts. Even so, among the Gen.2, the assumed prototype accounts for 40% of their total datives when close synonyms for 'give' are included. Datives with verbs of *intransitive taking* and *the governed dative*, also occur in all cohorts, which would be in agreement with Janda's (1993: 65, 71) assumptions that these datives have relative prominence in the semantic network. Conversely, extensions through antonyms and metonyms, which are assumedly less central in the dative's semantic network, never occur in the Gen.2 speakers' narratives, nor does the possessive dative. In fact, extension by metonomy is rarely used, even among the present Gen.1A speakers, as Diagram 1 shows. Furthermore, when considered individually, the current Gen.1A speakers display notable differences in their dative realizations. The inter-speaker variation pertains both to the frequency (Table 2) and types of datives utilized. In terms of dative frequency, speakers at the high ends of both the Gen.1A and Gen.2 cohorts are on par with the homeland speakers in the 1999 study. For instance, Gen.2_2F, a "high achiever" among the Gen.2 at 13.1, produces datives more often than most Gen.1A speakers. At the other end of the spectrum, with a dative frequency of only 4.5, Gen.1A_3F matches the weakest migrant speakers in the previous study (Skaaden 1999: 313). In sum, inter-speaker variation both within and across generation cohorts is a striking characteristic in the current data.

The present design, which provides merely a snapshot of the speakers' dative productions in a specific setting, allows for only speculation about the factors leading to the observed inter-speaker variation. Several factors may contribute to inter-speaker variation and a single source is difficult to determine. For instance, Schmid and Köpke (2013: 4) find that for L1 attrition in the Gen.1A, extra-linguistic factors, such as length of residence, frequency of L1 use, cultural affiliation, and proficiency in the L2, "are shown not to have predicative power for individual variation." In a study of late bilingual Turkish L1 speakers in the Netherlands, Yılmaz (2013: 83–84) similarly concludes that "linguistic and cultural affiliations, length of stay or age did not play any role" in affecting inter-speaker variation. In terms of age at onset of migration and length of stay, the current Gen.1A cohort matches the 1999 adult migrants. However, there is a difference in reported visits to the homeland after migration. The present Gen.1A speakers report several and recent contacts with Croatia, while their peers in the previous study reported fewer and less recent contacts after migration (Skaaden 1999: 67; Skaaden 2005: 439). The most extensive and recent contacts with Croatia in the current sample is reported by the intermediate speaker, Gen1B_1M. In contrast, the Gen.2 speakers report limited contact with Croatia, especially in the two years prior to the recording.

Obviously, the contrasts evidenced in the fluency with which speakers of different generations utilize the dative (Table 1) support the contention that the

Gen.2's heritage language is more vulnerable to language contact than that of the Gen.1A and Gen.1B speakers. At the same time, the inter-speaker variation among the adults indicates that the migrant context may affect even the Gen.1A migrants' *organization* of their Croatian output. Challenging the sharp division between lexicon and grammar, theoretical models that view grammatical categories as radial, forming around a prototype (Langacker 1987; Janda 1993; Šarić 2002), offer a unified approach to contact phenomena that may highlight aspects of linguistic structure that are more or less vulnerable to change. The concept of *entrenchment*, as defined above, makes particular sense in terms of *the individual speaker's* usage patterns and is, thus, a factor that is difficult to capture with precision. The fact that a variable is difficult to isolate does not mean that it has no impact, however.

Here, attention was placed on the dative units in the speakers' responses to the *Pear Story* – or, rather, the lack thereof. The low frequency of datives observed in the responses of some speakers is possibly an indication of the more subtle effects of language contact. Diagram 1 does not display what the speakers do instead of employing datives. Still, some of the above excerpts reveal that schemas of linguistic structure that are more typical in Norwegian than in Croatian are employed where a dative would have readily denoted the scene or conceptualization. For instance, speakers may instead of the dative option, and seemingly by analogy to typical Norwegian schemas, choose a more analytic verb construction that does not require the dative. The result is more overt contact phenomena in terms of copies or calques as witnessed in (12) and (26). Similarly, to signify affectedness by possession, the speakers in line with prominent Norwegian schemas utilize a possessive construction instead of the dative option – for example, *njegovo voće* ('his fruit') in (12) and *djed njegov* ('grandpa [of] his') in (21). Moreover, the post-positioning of the pronoun in (21) has a particularly Norwegian ring to it. Clearly a marked choice in Croatian, the NP internal word order is the unmarked Norwegian schema and a pattern that is seen to spread in a similar contact situation (Skaaden 2005: 446–447). Also, in line with Norwegian schemas, the choice of analytic verb constructions may lead to a prepositional phrase in substitution for the directional dative, as witnessed in excerpt (25). Diagram 1 indicates that this tendency is most prominent among the Gen.2 speakers. However, the tendency also appears among Gen.1A speakers, as excerpt (26) illustrates. In the same vein, although not related to the dative, some speakers tend to ignore the pro-drop option in Croatian. Rather, in line with Norwegian, which does not allow for pro-drop, they vocalize the subject pronoun. This tendency is most strikingly present in the output of Gen.2_3F, who is also the speaker with the overall lowest dative production. She vocalizes the subject pronoun in 31% of her clauses, and three times more often than her peers. Interestingly, the tendency to ignore the pro-drop option also occurs in the output of some adult migrants, for instance, Gen.1A_4M, as illustrated in (12), (13) and (26). In concert, these instantiations indicate that the speakers' usage patterns or schemas associated with their other language, Norwegian, can impinge on their choices of expression in Croatian.

7 Conclusion

Inter-speaker variation is a salient characteristic of the Croatian diaspora speakers' utilization of the grammatical category *dative* in a Norwegian environment. As emerging in a speech elicitation setting involving the *Pear Story*, the variation cuts across generations and pertains to frequency as well as types of datives applied. In terms of dative types applied, the clear prototype effect found in the previous study is not replicated. However, in the current data set as well, the assumed prototype, the realization of the indirect object with 'give', stands firm even with speakers who produce few datives. Moreover, the structures sometimes chosen to depict scenes that a dative construction would have readily captured in Croatian, indicate that schemas that are more typical of Norwegian, may serve as substitutions for certain datives. Despite the reservations that must be made due to volume, the analysis demonstrates that usage-based models of linguistic structure may provide a window into subtle aspects of language contact that models dependent on the existence of a strict division between lexicon and grammar may overlook.

References

Andersen, Roger. 1982. Determining the linguistic attributes of language attrition. In Richard Lambert & Barbara Freed (eds.), *The loss of language skills*, 83–118. Rowley: Newbury House Publishers.

Barić, Eugenija, Mijo Lončarić, Dragica Malić, Slavko Pavešić, Mirko Peti, Vesna Zečević & Marija Znika. 1990. *Gramatika hrvatskoga književnog jezika, 2. izdanje* [Grammar of the Croatian literary language, 2nd ed.]. Zagreb: Školska knjiga.

Chafe, Wallace. 1980. *The Pear Stories: Cognitive, cultural, and linguistic aspects of narrative production*. Norwood, New Jersey: Ablex.

Chafe, Wallace. 1994. *Discourse, consciousness and time: The flow and displacement of conscious experience in speaking and writing*. Chicago: The University of Chicago Press.

Chomsky, Noam. 1965. *Aspects of the theory of syntax*. Cambridge: MIT Press.

Ďurovič, Ľubomír. 1983. The case systems in the language of diaspora children. In Ľubomír Ďurovič (ed.), *Lingua in diaspora: Studies in the language of the second generation of Yugoslav immigrant children in Sweden* (Slavica Lundensia 9), 21–95. Lund: Lund University Publications.

Ďurovič, Ľubomír. 1984. The inner consistency of a linguistic continuum. In J. J. van Baak (ed.), *Signs of friendship: To honour A.G.F. van Holk*, 89–95. Amsterdam: Rodopi.

Ďurovič, Ľubomír. 1987. The development of grammar systems in the diaspora children's language. In Ľubomír Ďurovič (ed.), *Child language in diaspora: Serbo–Croatian in West European countries* (Slavica Lundensia 11), 51–87. Lund: Lund University Publications.

Faarlund, Jan T., Svein Lie & Kjell I. Vannebo. 1997. *Norsk referansegrammatikk* [Norwegian referential grammar]. Oslo: Universitetsforlaget.

Gallis, Arne. 1973. *Beiträge zur Syntax der Richtungsverba in den slavischen Sprachen, besonders im Serbokroatischen*. Oslo: Universitetsforlaget.

Gürel, Ayşe & Gülsen Yılmaz. 2013. Restructuring in the L1 Turkish grammar: Effects of L2 English and L2 Dutch. In Monika Schmid & Barbara Köpke (eds.), *First language attrition*, 37–67. Amsterdam: John Benjamins.

Hakuta, Kenji, Ellen Bialystok & Edward Wiley. 2003. Critical evidence: The test of the critical-period hypothesis for second-language acquisition. *Psychological Science* 14(1). 31–38.

Haugen, Einar. 1953. *The Norwegian language in America: A study in bilingual behavior*. Philadelphia: University of Philadelphia Press.

Itkonen, Esa & Jussi Haukioja. 1996. A rehabilitation of analogy in syntax (and elsewhere). In András Kertész (ed.), *Metalinguistik im Wandel: Die 'kognitive Wende' in Wissenschaftstheorie und Linguistik*, 131–177. Berlin: Peter Lang.

Ivić, Milka. 1961. On the structural characteristics of the Serbocroatian case system. *International Journal of Slavic Linguistics and Poetics* (4). 38–47.

Ivić, Pavle. 1985. *Dijalektologija srpskohrvatskog jezika: uvod u štokavsko narečje*. II izdanje [Dialectology of the Serbo–Croatian language: Introduction to the Štokavian dialect. 2nd ed.]. Novi Sad: Matica Srpska.

Janda, Laura. 1993. *A geography of case semantics: The Czech dative and the Russian instrumental*. Berlin & New York: Mouton de Gruyter.

Johanson, Lars. 1993. Code-copying in immigrant Turkish. In Guus Extra & Ludo Verhoeven (eds.), *Immigrant languages in Europe*, 197–221. Clevedon: Multilingual Matters Ltd.

Kess, Joseph, F. 1992. *Psycholinguistics: Psychology, linguistics, and the study of natural language*. Amsterdam: John Benjamins.

Langacker, Ronald. 1987. *Foundations of cognitive grammar. Vol. 1. Theoretical prerequisites*. Stanford: Stanford University Press.

Levelt, Willem. 1989. *Speaking: From intention to articulation*. Cambridge: MIT Press.

Montrul, Silvina. 2008. *Incomplete acquisition in bilingualism: Re-examining the age factor*. Amsterdam: John Benjamins.

Montrul, Silvina, Rakesh Bhatt & Archna Bhatia. 2012. Erosion of case and agreement in Hindi heritage speakers. *Linguistic Approaches to Bilingualism* 2(2). 141–176. doi 10.1075/lab.2.2.02mon.

Norwegian Government (1987–1988). St.meld. nr. 39 (1987–88): *Om innvandringspolitikken*. [Norwegian White Paper about Immigration Policy].

Perpiñán, Silvia. 2013. Optionality in bilingual native grammars. In Monika Schmid & Barbara Köpke (eds.), *First language attrition*, 127–156. Amsterdam: John Benjamins.

Polinsky, Maria. 2018. *Heritage Languages and Their Speakers*. Cambridge: Cambridge University Press.

Polinsky, Maria & Gregory Scontras. 2019. Understanding heritage languages. *Bilingualism: Language and Cognition* 23(1). 4–20. doi 10.1017/S1366728919000245

Savić, Svenka. 1985. *Narativi kod dece. Serija: Usvajanje jezika* [Children's narratives. Series: Language acquisition]. Novi Sad: Filozofski fakultet. Institut za južnoslovenske jezike.

Schmid, Monika. 2002. *First language attrition, use and maintenance: The case of German Jews in Anglophone countries*. Amsterdam: John Benjamins.

Schmid, Monika & Barbara Köpke. 2013. Second language acquisition and attrition: Introduction. In Monika Schmid & Barbara Köpke (eds.), *First language attrition*, 1–5. Amsterdam: John Benjamins.

Seliger, Herbert & Robert Vago (eds.). 1991. *First language attrition*. Cambridge: Cambridge University Press.

Sharwood-Smith, Michael & Paul van Buren. 1991. First language attrition and the parameter setting model. In Herbert Seliger & Robert Vago (eds.), *First language attrition*, 17–31. Cambridge: Cambridge University Press.

Skaaden, Hanne. 1999. *In short supply of language: Signs of first language attrition in the speech of adult migrants*. Oslo: Unipub forlag.

Skaaden, Hanne. 2005. First language attrition and linguistic creativity. *International Journal of Bilingualism* 9(3–4). 435–453.

StatBank Norway. 2019. *Immigrants and migrants*. https://www.ssb.no/statistikkbanken/selectvarval/saveselections.asp

Statistics Norway. 2018. *Morsmålselevar, etter morsmål. Skoleåra 1995/96-1999/2000* [Statistics on the first language of school students, according to grade level for the years 1995–2000]. https://www.ssb.no/a/histstat/au/200004/T-44tekst.html

Šarić, Ljiljana. 2002. On the semantics of the "dative of possession" in the Slavic languages: An analysis on the basis of Russian, Polish, Croatian/Serbian and Slovenian examples. *Glossos: The Slavic and East European Language Resource Center* 3. 1–22. http://seelrc.org/glossos/ (accessed 30 January 2018).

Türker, Emel. 2000. *Turkish–Norwegian codeswitching: Evidence from intermediate and second generation Turkish immigrants in Norway*. Oslo: Unipub forlag.

Yılmaz, Gülsen. 2013. Complex embeddings in free speech production among late Turkish–Dutch bilinguals. In Monika Schmid & Barbara Köpke (eds.), *First language attrition*, 67–91. Amsterdam: John Benjamins.

Italy

Nada Županović Filipin, Jim Hlavac and Vesna Piasevoli
Features of the speech of Croatian-speakers in Italy

1 Introduction

This chapter examines some of the features of Croatian spoken by Croatian immigrants living in Italy. Italy is home to a large number of Croatian-origin residents but not all of these have active proficiency in Croatian. Contact between Croatia and Croatian-speaking areas on the east coast of the Adriatic Sea (and beyond) with Italy is long-standing and substantial. This is due to the proximity of the two countries and historical ties that record that Italy (and the Venetian Empire from the fourteenth to the eighteenth centuries) was the destination for merchants, sailors, scholars, members of the clergy and many others who settled or who would often reside there for longer or shorter periods. Permanent settlement of Croatian-speakers on the western side of the Adriatic Sea also occurred – the most conspicuous example of this are three remaining villages in Molise inhabited by migrants who left the Neretva River valley and central Dalmatia 500 years ago (see Ščukanec, Breu and Vuk, this volume). However, in general, settlement of Croatian-speakers has been across the northern and north-eastern parts of Italy, and large numbers of Croatian-origin residents still reside in these regions. Many of them have shifted to Italian, while there are others who use Croatian actively or passively. There are also large numbers of Italian-origin residents originally from Istria – the Kvarner Bay islands and Dalmatia who were evacuated to or who have resettled in Italy and who usually had proficiency in Croatian, at least at the point of their departure even if they then used Croatian infrequently after their arrival in Italy. Most members of this latter group no longer use Croatian actively, and the focus of this chapter is on more recent Croatian-origin migrants in Italy.

This chapter is structured in the following way. The remaining parts of this section present general demographic and sociolinguistic information on Croatian-origin residents in Italy and on Croatian-speakers in that country. Section 2 presents information on the informants and the sample of spoken data that is the area of focus of this chapter. Section 3 contains sociolinguistically-focused information on informants, i.e. vintage of emigration, generational membership, features of

---

Nada Županović Filipin, University of Zagreb
Jim Hlavac, Monash University
Vesna Piasevoli, University of Trieste

https://doi.org/10.1515/9781501503917-008

intra-family language use and use of Croatian across domains, area of residence and contact with other Croatian-speakers. Section 4 presents a description and analysis of linguistic data and Section 5 contains the conclusion and summary of findings.

1.1 History of contact, vintages of emigration, status

Of all countries represented in this book, Italy is the country with which Croatia has the longest-standing contacts. Croats have been travelling to and settling in Italy for centuries, forming organisations that attest to their presence on the Adriatic's western shores. For example, the *Confraternita Dalmata di San Giorgio e Trifone* 'Fraternity of St George and Triphon' was established in Venice in 1451, and the *Venerabilis Societas Confallonorum Slavorum Burghi S. Petri* 'Honourable Brotherhood of Slavs from the Roman quarter of St. Peter' in Rome was also established in the fifteenth century. It later changed its name to *Papinski hrvatski zavod sv. Jeronima* 'the Pontifical Croatian College of St. Jerome'. Both brotherhoods housed Croatian pilgrims and travellers, assisted Croatian seminarians studying in Italy and published religious and other texts in Croatian. Rome is also home to the Croatian Catholic House *Domus Croata*.

Italian-Croatian contact includes not only emigration westwards across the Adriatic Sea, but Italian-Croatian contact along the east coast of the Adriatic. Before the advent of national romanticism in the nineteenth century, language proficiency and use in Istria, the Croatian Littoral, Dalmatia and the Republic of Dubrovnik (*Ragusa*) were not so much defining characteristics of a person's nationality as attributes that could index a number of things: locality, e.g. urban vs. rural; occupation, e.g. merchant vs. craftsman; level of education; geographical mobility; social class. The ascent of the Venetian Republic led to the Adriatic Sea, in particular its eastern coastline, being seen as belonging to a single sphere. (Venetian) Italian-Croatian bilingualism was common and people and localities often bore two names, e.g. *Marin Držić/Marino Darsa, Ruđer Josip Bošković/ Ruggero Giuseppe Boscovich, Split/Spalato, Rijeka/Fiume*.

In the first half of the twentieth century, political and armed conflicts greatly changed the ethnic, demographic and linguistic landscape of the Adriatic's east coast: the mass exodus of Italian-Croatian bilinguals (mainly ethnic Italians, but also many ethnic Croats) led to a large influx of Croatian-speakers in Italy after WWII. Ethnic Italians, similar to ethnic Germans who had been expelled from Croatia, seldom maintained their second language (Croatian) in their 'repatriated' environment (cf. Kresić Vukosav and Šimičić, this volume; Ščukanec this volume). Croats who fled to Italy in the immediate post-WWII years usually sought to quickly integrate into Italian society, or to migrate again to a further country. Their Croatian names were not an obstacle to integration as many of the Italian refugees from Croatia bore Slavic surnames and their linguistic and socio-cultural profile was congruent to that of many Italian nationals.

While Croats have been a discernible group across north-east Italy, and in particular Trieste for centuries, the notion of forming an established 'immigrant community' is a more recent one that dates back only to the late twentieth century and perhaps as late as Croatian independence in 1991.

Elsewhere in Italy, in the province of Molise, a long-standing autochthonous Croatian Sprachinsel has existed for over 500 years, whose language is officially recognised as a historical minority language. It is one of the six *minoranze linguistiche storiche* 'historical linguistic minorities' as declared in law no. 482, art.2, sect. 1, on 15 December 1999. The law does not specify Molise as the area or Molise Croatian as the minority language that are recognised, i.e. *la Repubblica tutela la lingua e la cultura delle popolazioni . . . croate* 'the Italian State protects the language and the culture of the [minority] populations . . . Croatian'. In reality however, the de jure status is at present afforded to Molise Croatian only, and homeland Croatian is not afforded the same legal protection, such as instruction in mainstream schools, state-subsidised media resources etc. The possibility of 'historical minority status' being extended to the Croatian language and to Croatian-speakers in the region of Friuli-Venezia-Giulia is being explored with a submission made to the Italian Senate by Aldo Di Biagio in 2015 for this to occur (State Office for Croats Abroad 2016a).

Italy's post-WWII economic recovery and the strength of the country's many industrial centres in its north attracted economic migrants from SFRY from the 1970s onwards who came to work in Milan, Turin, Verona, Udine, Trieste, Bologna, Parma and other cities. For some, the proximity to Croatia meant that they did not view their departure from their homeland as definite or final. For others, Italy has become their home, regardless of proximity and continuing contact. Since Croatian independence and the wars in Croatia and Bosnia-Herzegovina, the existence of an immigrant or diaspora Croatian community in cities such as Trieste, Milan, Rome and Padua is a feature that is acknowledged by the immigrants themselves, as well as Italian demographers. The number of 'economic migrants' from Croatia has, since the start of the millennium, started to subside. At the same time, Italy is an increasingly popular study destination for young Croats – there are over 300 students studying in universities across northern Italy.

We conclude this section by drawing on a literary source that underlines the historical ties between Italy and Croatia. An extract from the 103rd verse of Dante Aligheri's 'The Divine Comedy' from the fourteenth century is reproduced here. It describes a Croatian pilgrim who travelled to Rome to see Veronica's veil:

> Quel è colui che forse di Croazia / viene a veder la Veronica nostra / che per l'antica fama non sazia / ...
>
> As he who from Croatia comes, perchance, / to look at our Veronica, and who, / because of its old fame, is never sated ...
>
> (Aligheri, 1321. [Vol 3, verse 369.] Trans. Courtney Langdon)

1.2 Number of Croatian-heritage residents, number of Croatian-speakers

Italian government statistics for 2018 record that there are 17,573 Croatian citizens whose registered country of residence is Italy (Tuttitalia.it 2019a). It can be assumed that these numbers reflect the 'new wave' of Croats who have not yet received Italian citizenship. There is a much larger number who either have Italian citizenship or who have dual citizenship. The number of Croats or those who acknowledge Croatian heritage is harder to estimate, but it is likely that there are around 50,000 to 60,000 across Italy, with the total number of Croatian-speakers at around 40,000.

1.3 Geographic distribution, socio-economic profile

Most of the 17,573 Croatian citizens are concentrated in Italy's north, with 26% in the Veneto region, 22% in Friuli Venezia Giulia, most of them in its largest city, Trieste (4,000), and the Lombardia region with 16%. Emilia-Romagna and Lazio have significant numbers, while in other regions the numbers are much smaller, varying from a few hundred to less than 10 (Tuttitalia.it 2019a). A proportion of the 25,034 Bosnian-Hercegovinian citizens resident in Italy are of Croatian-origin; these are also concentrated in the regions of Veneto (27%), Lombardia (16%) and Friuli Venezia Giulia (13%) (Tuttitalia.it 2019b).

While the socio-economic profile of more recent migrants is likely to be variable, due to the variety of areas that they work in, e.g. hospitality, aged care, fruit picking, construction, IT, there are more established groups of Croatian migrants whose socio-economic profile may be close to that of the overall Italian average. For example, Snježana Hefti, the president of the Croatian community in Milan reports that up to 50 firms from SFRY (during the time it still existed) had representations in cities all over the Lombardy region, many of them staffed by Croats (Personal communication to Vesna Piasevoli, 10 December 2016). After 1991, most of them stayed in Italy, finding work in Italian or international companies.

1.4 Infrastructure and schools

Over the last 25 years, particularly since Croatia's independence, associations of Croatian migrants have been established in many cities across northern and central Italy: Trieste, Milan, Veneto, Udine and Rome. Active members of these associations tend to be first-generation migrants and the activities of these associations can cover a number of areas: teaching of Croatian, charity and welfare activities for compatriots in Italy, Croatia or Bosnia-Herzegovina, furthering trade and economic ties between Italy and Croatia, organising pilgrimage tours for visitors from Croatia to shrines in Italy or for Italians to travel to holy places in Croatia and Bosnia-Herzegovina. An umbrella organisation, the nation-wide federation of Croatian associations was formed in 2001, consisting of member associations from Trieste, Milan, Rome and the Molise region, with associations from other cities, such as that in Udine formed in 2004, joining in subsequent years. The federation publishes a bilingual magazine three times yearly, *Insieme/Zajedno* 'Together'.

The organisation of musical concerts or theatre performances featuring Croatian artists visiting Italy is often taken on by individual regional associations, as well as for visits of writers or intellectuals from Croatia. Publications from these associations are less regular, e.g. *Most* 'The Bridge', a magazine produced in Trieste was launched in 1999 but ceased publication in 2001. In 2007, the Croatian community of Trieste published a comprehensive history of the Croatian presence in Trieste in Italian, entitled *Croati in Trieste*. The Croatian community in Veneto has often hosted Italy-wide get-togethers, while the smaller Croatian community in Rome has recently founded a sports club and a cultural society, *Mosaico Italo-Croato Roma*, established in 2015.

The Catholic Church is an important feature of Croatian associations across Italy. For example, in Piedmont, Croatian migrants organise activities under the auspices of Croatian Salesians living there. For those associations without their own premises, group activities typically take place in the premises of those Italian Catholic churches that host Croatian-language masses. The role of the Catholic Church in providing a venue and means to establish instruction in Croatian and the role of the Croatian Ministry of Education in financially supporting the placement and salaries of teachers in Italy working in schools with supplementary education programs is outlined in detail by Krpina (2016).

Croats do not have the status of being a recognised ethnic minority, except in the region of Molise, and so there are no regular, state-run Croatian language schools. However, in Trieste as far back as 1910 there are records of individuals trying to organise Croatian-language instruction. Examples of formal instruction known to the authors go back only as far as 1996, when the local Croatian community began organising Croatian classes for children and adults. From 1999 onwards, the Croatian Ministry of Education has financed and co-ordinated this program. The same ministry finances Croatian supplementary schooling in Rome, Udine and in nearby Manzano, with a reported total number of 160 pupils across all four schools. In 2013, Padova's local Croatian community commenced language classes for children. In 2017, this also occurred in Milan (Matica 2018). Attempts in other cities to establish similar programs have not succeeded, often due to the geographical dispersal of potential schoolchildren.

Similar to other European countries, Croatian is taught at universities often in combination with Serbian (and Bosnian), under the designation of 'Serbian and Croatian' or 'Bosnian-Croatian-Serbian'. It is taught at universities in Trieste, Udine, Padua, Venice, Torino, Bologna, Parma, Rome, Pescara, Bari and Napoli. Lecturers in Padua and Rome are funded by the Croatian Ministry of Education while those in other centres are funded by the Italian government.

1.5 Domain use, language maintenance and shift

Use of Croatian is restricted to the home/family domain, and to a lesser extent social networks, religion and media. Historically, there have been significant macro-social disincentives for Croatian-speakers to maintain the language and to pass it onto their children (see Piasevoli this volume). Levels of language maintenance vary greatly, where proximity to Croatia and frequency of contacts with (extended) family members play a role in language maintenance that local infrastructure in Italy cannot always play. Data from 2011 and 2012 show that of all groups of foreign citizens residing in Italy, Croatian citizens (along with those from Bosnia-Herzegovina, Montenegro and Serbia) have the highest average proficiency rate in Italian, with 47.6% able to use all four macro-skills in Italian with high pro ficiency (ISTAT 2014). Interestingly, a change in attitudes towards proficiency in Croatian is discernible amongst some: people of Croatian descent who otherwise do not consider themselves Croatian, often now express the desire to learn Croatian for a variety of reasons. These may be due to employment, an inheritance or an application for the return of property in Croatia. Or there can be very personal reasons, such as childhood memories, memories of their late grandparents, or because they have a Croatian partner.

1.6 Contacts with Croatia. Host country attitudes towards Croats

Similar to the situation of Austrian-Croatians, proximity to Croatia for Italian-Croatians means that contact is usually frequent, particularly in the summer months. This has consequences on children's contact with and acquisition of

Croatian in a naturalistic environment, and sometimes influences some parents in believing that trips back to Croatia are the best means for children to formally acquire Croatian. This contact is important, but not a replacement for acquisition of Croatian in a naturalistic setting within the family household.

The political and armed conflicts that occurred in the first half of the twentieth century along the east coast of the Adriatic Sea, and the departure or expulsion of tens of thousands of Italian *Esuli* 'Exiles' continues to influence popular views and opinions in Italy about Croatians. These views are predicated historically on a legacy of narratives about Croats, Slavs and Eastern Europeans in general. For these reasons, using Croatian (Slovenian or other Slavic languages) in public was sometimes not viewed favourably, particularly in Trieste (see Piasevoli, this volume).

1.7 Speakers of languages other than Italian in Italy and recent studies on Croatian-Italian language contact

Since the late 1970s Italy has witnessed the arrival of a large number of economic migrants. The social consequences of this have become the focus of research studies only in the past two decades. According to current statistics (ISTAT 2016), immigrants account for 8.3% of the country's total population today. The issue of language policy towards migrant languages has become a topic in Italian sociolinguistic literature (e.g. D'Agostino 2012: 65–69 and 221–224), often from the point of view of non-Italians' acquisition of Italian as a second language (Consani et al. 2009).

In linguistic terms, most parts of Italy can be characterised as having *dilalia* (Berruto 1987), with the exception, perhaps, of the Veneto and Campania regions (D'Agostino 2012). Dilalia refers to a sub-category of diglossia in which both the high and low variety may be used in informal speech, with a continuum of sub-varieties existing between the high and low variety. In practice, this means that in most regions, Croatian-origin residents can function communicatively by using the regional variety of Italian, which they acquired from their environment.

Descriptions of the Croatian language in Italy, apart from those focusing on the long-standing Croatian indigenous minority in Molise, are rare. One of the first was a study by Čilaš, Drpić and Lončarić (2007) that examined the speech of Croatians in Trieste. Their analysis did not find evidence of particular language features that could be described as being characteristic to the Croatian community in Trieste only. The study observed that standard Croatian alongside homeland regiolects based on speakers' place of origin were used amongst both first- and second-generation migrants. This contrasted with the authors' expectation that second-generation informants would be familiar only with the local variety of the

Croatian language used by their parents. The study noted that speakers' repertoires included both Italian and Triestino, the local variety of the Venetian dialect spoken in Trieste. Acquisition of Triestino is important as language use in Trieste and across the Veneto region shows that the regiolect is used beyond informal settings as well. Venetian dialect has a relatively high status across north-eastern Italy,

In recently published papers, Županović Filipin and Bevanda (2015) and Županović Filipin and Bevanda Tolić (2015) analyse code-switching in the families of Croatian immigrants in Italy. In the first paper, the authors describe examples of code-switching produced by first generation late adolescent Croatian-Italian bilinguals in computer mediated communication (SMS, Facebook messages). These mostly consist of single word switches, and the matrix language is routinely Croatian. In Županović Filipin and Bevanda Tolić (2015), the authors describe the generational differences in the use of code-switching: second-generation speakers use different discourse strategies compared to their parents, and the matrix language of intra-generational interactions is now shifting to Italian.

2 Informants

This chapter draws on three corpora gained via different methods. The first corpus consists of sociolinguistic interviews with first- and second-generation emigrants. Most of the informants were found with the help of Croatian-origin, Italy-born students studying Italian at the Faculty of Humanities and Social Sciences Arts at Zagreb University. The students connected the authors with members of their families and acquaintances who live in Italy. There are nine recorded interviews that make up this first corpus. Interviews were conducted during visits of students' family members and friends in Croatia. The second corpus consists of recorded interviews with Italian students whose heritage language is Croatian attending Croatian-language classes from spring 2015 to autumn 2016, as well as those attending the Croatian Language and Culture University School in 2015 and 2016.[1]

These informants were asked to fill out a questionnaire on language use, adapted from Hlavac (2003: 338–347) and modified to suit the informants' situation in Italy. The informants interviewed were asked to send the questionnaire elec-

---

[1] The first author is most grateful to all instructors of the Croaticum program at the University of Zagreb who provided intensive instruction in Croatian to heritage speakers and second-language learners. The first author is greatly indebted to professors Ines Carović and Marija Bošnjak of the Croatian Language and Culture University School for their assistance in contacting and recruiting informants for this study.

tronically to relatives and friends. In this way a further 13 questionnaires were collected by 1 December 2016. Thus the data sample encompasses a total of 22 sociolinguistic questionnaires, including nine recorded interviews. The third corpus of the data sample consists of recordings of informal and spontaneous conversations – family gatherings, shared lunches, parent-children or sibling interactions amongst members of three two-generation and two three-generation families in Italy. The conversations encompass speech recordings from a total of 34 different interlocutors. Recordings were made with the permission of the family members,[2] in the period from the summer of 2015 to summer 2016 by four students, returnee emigrants, who are related to the speakers. The students recorded situations in which members of their families engage in conversations with each other, i.e. family gatherings, shared mealtimes, and interactions across generations (e.g. parents-children) or with members of the same generation (e.g. siblings). Thus, it was possible to reduce the problem of the observer's paradox and of informants monitoring their speech. Notification of the informants of the study's research aims accompanied data collection and informants were given the chance to vet or request the deletion of the recordings.

Some informants appear in more than one of the three different corpora, and some of the informants who initially participated in an interview only, later on agreed to be recorded. The total sample of informants consists of 34 speakers. Twenty-eight of them feature in lengthy audio recordings, while for six of them there are only short excerpts included – these six were amongst the nine who filled out questionnaires as part of the first corpus. Altogether there are 26 recordings with a total duration of 8 hours and 55 minutes. The transcribed and analysed corpus encompasses approximately 45,000 tokens.

The corpus encompasses recordings of the speech of 18 Gen.1 speakers, 14 Gen.2 speakers and two Gen.3 speakers. The average age of the first-generation informants is 54 years and 4 months. These are mostly people born in 1950s and 1960s, with the exception of one man and one woman who migrated to Italy in 1999 immediately after finishing high school. The average age of second-generation informants is 23 years and 4 months, while the two third-generation informants were aged 7 and 9 at the time of recording.

All first-generation informants finished school in Croatia. Four of the 16 second-generation informants attended Croatian language instruction. These were those resident in Rome, one of the few cities in which language instruction is available. On average, these four informants attended Croatian language instruc-

---

[2] The first author is greatly indebted to four students from the Croaticum program for their assistance in the collection of spoken language recordings.

tion for 9 years. The remaining second- and third-generation informants acquired Croatian in the home/family setting only. The two informants who belong to the third generation of Croatian speakers are both growing up in linguistically favourable circumstances that promote language maintenance. Although the sample is not big enough to be able to provide more definite conclusions, their proficiency in Croatian appears comparable to that of second-generation speakers, and in some cases, it may be considered to be of a higher level, due to the sociolinguistic situation of the speakers – co-habitation with grandparents. In their speech we recorded comparatively few morphosyntactic forms that differ conspicuously from those used in homeland Croatian.

The majority of Croatian immigrants and their children live in the northern and central parts of Italy. Thus, out of nine regions included in our research only one was in the far south of Italy: Puglia with two informants. There are differences between the informants of the third corpus of the sample in regard to their social networks and contact with Croatian-speakers. The individual informants and families from Alessandria (Piedmont), Bergamo, Padua, Parma and Pescara do not know each other and are not in contact with other Croatian-speakers in Italy. In contrast, the four Croatian families from Rome and the four from Milan are closely connected to other Croatian-speakers in their locality through family, social and occupational ties.

All informants visit Croatia on average twice a year for a longer period of time, usually for Christmas holidays and summer vacations, and often also make shorter visits. Over the whole year, the combined length of these visits to Croatia amounts to approximately one and a half months.

3 Sociolinguistic description of informants' language use

Sociolinguistic analysis has shown that the informants can be grouped into two rather distinct groups based on their language use and attitudes. Emigrants whose families are part of Croatian social networks display different language habits compared to those whose families are located far from other Croatians in the surrounding area. Both groups use Croatian, to some extent, in intra-family settings. However, it appears that Croatian is the *dominant* language in intra-family communication only for informants who also use it in social interactions, i.e. those who socialize with friends and neighbours of Croatian origin, who use Croatian at the workplace, who participate in the activities of local Croatian communities, and who regularly read or view Croatian media.

There is variation amongst the informants but especially between generations in speakers' conceptualisation of their (continuing) residence in Italy. The oldest first-generation informants have more conservative attitudes in regard to language and language use compared to those who migrated to Italy more recently, usually in the 1990s. The older first-generation informants view themselves as "guest workers", even though they continue to live in Italy after retirement. Although both groups rate the importance of preserving their mother tongue very highly, older informants differ based on the fact that they communicate with their children only in Croatian and made generally negative comments on phenomena such as 'mixing languages' or code-switching. Their level of competence in Italian is lower compared to that of younger first-generation informants, and this is likely to influence their attitudes towards use of Italian in the family/home setting. This suggests perhaps that the social situation that existed in the first decades of their life in Italy was significantly different than what it has been since 2000. Since that time, the way that Croatian-speakers believe that Italians view them has changed from one of 'greater distance' – which can be conducive to language-maintenance of the minority language due to a feeling of isolationism – to one of 'lesser distance' that can enable their integration into Italian society to a greater degree, which may be a factor in hastening language shift from Croatian to Italian (Harwood, Giles and Bourhis 1994: 173–174).

Younger members of the first generation, who on average have been living in Italy for 25 years, speak both languages in communication with their children, and Italian is also present in conversations, even with their spouses. All of them say that the catalyst for this type of language use was their children. This is particularly prominent in families that are not part of Croatian social networks, i.e., who live in areas where there are few other Croatian-speakers. One noticeable aspect about intra-family communication is that there appears to be a gender-based difference to use of and attitudes towards Italian: fathers, whose competence in Italian is usually lower than that of mothers, more frequently insist on speaking Croatian when talking to their children. It is possible that those fathers who more frequently insist on using Croatian at home do so as they are conscious of their own Italian proficiency limitations. Hlavac (2003: 20–21) also recorded higher frequencies of fathers speaking Croatian to their children than mothers, and of informants more frequently speaking Croatian to their fathers than their mothers. In exogamous relationships, however, the opposite trend is to be found: children born to a Croatian-speaking mother and an Italian-speaking father are found to have higher proficiency in Croatian than children born to parents where the father is the Croatian-speaker and the mother the Italian-speaker. Greater linguistic input from mothers compared to fathers in children's formative years is likely to account for this difference. To return to the endogamous families that are the focus of this chapter, it is found that higher use of Croatian in intra-family settings frequently co-occurred with descriptions of self-identity that are 'Croatian' only. These informants, often first-generation fathers, also have a negative opinion of code-switching. But this view is a minority one; the majority of informants are indifferent towards it. In terms of how informants define themselves, around 50% of the informants identified themselves via a compound designation such as 'Italian-Croatian'.

Children born in Italy into Croatian families normally acquire Croatian as their first language with Italian also being acquired at a young age. This is often referred to as 'bilingual first language acquisition' (De Houwer 2017), i.e. acquisition of two languages either simultaneously, or in close sequence one to the other. The responses from the Gen.2 informants show that already during their primary school years Italian has become their dominant language. This is congruent to other studies that examine the bilingual repertoires of children upon commencing formal schooling that is usually monolingual in the language of the host country, e.g. Bedore et al. (2012), Curdt-Christiansen and Lanza (2018). Those Gen.2 informants who report that they never use Croatian outside the home have a lower self-reported level of all language skills. Most of these informants report using Italian with siblings, as well as with other similarly-aged Croatian-speakers. As a general observation, the overall proficiency in Croatian among the second-generation informants is variable. There are those who appear to function as almost balanced bilinguals with the only distinguishing feature between them and HMLD.Cro speakers being their lesser familiarity with different registers of standard Croatian. There are also those with more restricted proficiency, who use Croatian in intra-family situations only, and who exhibit discomfort or great effort in expressing themselves in either a monolingual or a bilingual (i.e. 'mixed') variety of Croatian.

Nevertheless, sociolinguistic data show that the Gen.2 informants all have very favourable attitudes towards Croatian, and think that it is important to preserve it and claim that they would also teach it to their children. When speaking Croatian, they code-switch frequently and do not report having negative attitudes towards it. Typically, they also self-identify via a compound designation, 'Italian-Croatians'. In contrast, second-generation speakers who grew up within social networks that feature a large number of Croatian-speakers show higher levels of language use and maintenance of Croatian in general. In general, there are highly supportive attitudes to Croatian language maintenance per se amongst *all* informants, regardless of generational membership, vintage of migration or degree of contact with other Croatian-speakers. While positive attitudes to maintenance can be conducive towards the continued use of a minority language, they are not a guarantee that this language will actually continue to be used (Garrett 2010).

A number of factors exist that are advantageous to language maintenance amongst this sample of Croatian-speakers in Italy: social networks with other Croatian-speakers; isti se tekst ponavlja na kraju paragrafa; educational facilities offering Croatian language instruction for Croatian-origin children in Trieste, Veneto, Udine, Milan and Parma – which themselves also serve as social 'focus points' for interactions that are not related to education; geographical proximity and the ability to readily travel to Croatia or Bosnia Hercegovina.

The responses also point to features that are *not* conducive to language maintenance. These include the dispersal of the informants across nine regions, resulting in a *reduced* number of possible social interactions with other Croatian-speakers than may be the case for Croatian-speakers in Italy in general. For example, the Croatian State Authority for Croats living outside Croatia estimates that of the 60,000 Croats residing in Italy, around 15,000 live in Trieste (this figure is larger than the one given in section 1.3 above, namely 4,000, which relates only to holders of Croatian citizenship), a further 20,000 live in other parts of Friuli-Venezia-Giulia and in Veneto, with the remaining 25,000 spread across other areas, including a concentration of around 4,000 in Milan. As mentioned, a paucity of opportunities to attend Catholic mass in Croatian (which is possible only in a small number of cities) and a lack of *institutional* support means that there are few resources or opportunities to actively promote the use of Croatian in public as well as private settings, and little support for the learning and acquisition of Croatian. Thus, Croatian-speakers are largely reliant on their own local resources to initiate steps such as the organisation of formal instruction in Croatian.

This lack of official status, or lack of political or economic prestige for Croatian (and for Croatian-speakers in general) has the effect that some Gen.2 speakers report seeing little or no value in their Croatian language skills as an attribute relevant to their current or future employment opportunities (Karan 2011: 139). While there is often an *expressed* affection for aspects of Croatian culture, including Croatian *linguistic* culture, these socio-political conditions in Italy may play a role in some second-generation speakers' ambivalence to *actual* participation in in-group cultural practices.

4 Presentation and analysis of data of spoken Croatian

In general terms, and as mentioned in Section 3 above, the Italian proficiency of first-generation members is a strong determiner of language choice in the households of many informants. This is not related to length of residence in Italy, as many of the older first-generation members had spent the longest periods in Italy but often held the lowest level of proficiency in Italian. Nonetheless, Italian elements – transfers and instances of code-switching and calques – occur, to various degrees, in the speech of all informants.

The following conventions are used in the excerpts to identify the speakers: generation (Gen.1, Gen.2, Gen.3); in the case of Gen.1 speakers, the number of years of residence in Italy is given in square brackets; gender ('M' or 'F'); and age. Thus, (Gen1, [41], M, 65) relates to a 65-year-old male Gen.1 informant who has resided in Italy for 41 years. Italian-origin items are shown in bold. The presentation of linguistic data in this chapter is organised in the following way. Brief comments are given in relation to phonology in 4.1, while lexical forms are presented in 4.2. Semantic transference and loan translations are examined in 4.3, and the possessive adjectives *suo / svoj* in 4.4. Instances of code-switching are presented in 4.5, while structural features are presented in 4.6.

4.1 Phonology

Italian-based intonational patterns are apparent in the speech of some Gen.2 and most Gen. 3 speakers. Certain Italian phonotactic rules are transferred, which result in epenthesis in consonant clusters characteristic of English-origin words in Italian, e.g. *sìngol* 'single' (HMLD.Cro *singl*) or the voicing of /s/ in front of a sonorant, e.g. *znijeg* 'snow'; *zlučajno* 'accidentally'; *zvugdje* 'everywhere'; *zlab* 'weak' (HMLD.Cro *snijeg, slučajno, svugdje, slab*).

Pronunciation of /l/ is more characteristic of 'Mediterranean' pronunciation and is 'softer' or 'brighter' than its Croatian counterpart. Omission of the phoneme /h/ (e. g. *aljina* 'dress'; *igijena* 'hygiene'; *onorar* 'fee') is a characteristic of many of the regiolects that the informants come from, and non-production of /h/ is likely to be reinforced by its absence in Italian. A characteristic common to all Gen.2 informants is their pronunciation of Italian toponyms and foreign anthroponyms according to Italian phonological norms. This is unsurprising as their acquisition and use of them has occurred in an exclusively Italian context, e.g. /lombar'dia/ (Lombardia), /bàtman/ (Batman), /šùmaker/ (Schumacher). These Italian toponyms remain uninflected when used in Croatian:

(1) kad idem u Hrvatsku idem preko
 when go-1SG to+ACC Croatia-ACC.F.SG go-1SG over+GEN
 Lubiana
 Lubiana-NOM.F.SG
 'When I go to Croatia, I travel via **Lubiana** [Ljubljana]'. (Gen.2,F,22)

In example (1), *Lubiana* remains in NOM despite the preceding preposition *preko* that governs GEN case. Čilaš, Drpić and Lončarić (2007: 475, 478, 481) also report that amongst Gen.2 speakers, adverbials of place that contain Italian toponyms also remain uninflected. Case-marking and inflections are examined in greater detail below in 4.6.

From the onomastic point of view, a tendency for apocopation can be observed, that is, the deletion of the final vowel or even syllable from an adjective preceding a noun. This is a common word formation process used in Italian for expressing a nickname. This is relevant to the situation of many Gen.2 members whose names may undergo a process of Italianization yielding forms such as: Mate' (Matej), Stje' (Stjepan), Ivi' (Ivica), Andre' (Andrea), Ka' (Karmen), Kri' (Kristina), Mari' (Marijana), Jele' (Jelena), Marti' (Martina) etc. Rarer is the replacement of a Croatian name with an Italian equivalent (Andrija > Andrea). In some families, an agglutinative way of nickname formation with diminutive suffixes from both languages can be heard: Marija ['mari^{j}a] (Cro.) > Mariuccia [mari'utʃa] (Ital.) > Mariuccica [mariu'tʃitsa] (Cro. + Ital. composite form).

4.2 Lexicon

The most frequent type of Italian-origin transfers in informants' speech are single-item ones, often realia from the Italian-context. Example (2) below contains three single-word items that are all phonologically and morphologically unintegrated: a conjunction, a noun and an adjective:

(2) **comunque** ako oćeš **peperoncino** imam **fresco**
however if want-2SG chilli pepper-M.SG have-1SG fresh-M.SG
'**However**, if you want **chilli pepper**, I have [a] **fresh** one.' (Gen.1,[23],F,49)

Discourse markers occur as single- or two-word items, usually unintegrated as shown in example (3), which commences with a contrastive conjunction and a negative marker.

(3) **ma no** nije ni ovdje loš **supermercato**
but no be-NEG3SG NEG here bad-NOM.M.SG supermarket-NOM.M.SG
anzi ali je godina slaba
on the contrary but be-3SG year-NOM.F.SG weak-NOM.F.SG
'**But no**, not even here is it a bad **supermarket**, **on the contrary**! But the year has been bad.' (Gen.1,[25],F,48)

Example (3) contains local realia *supermercato* which is followed by another Italian-origin discourse marker, *anzi*. In the corpus of recorded data, acronyms from Italian also occur. In example (4), an acronym used remains phonologically unintegrated, but morphologically integrated into Croatian shown via locative morphemes.

(4) *očeju   me   prevarit,   a   ja sindikatu   otišel,*
    want-3PL me-ACC deceive-INF but I union-DAT.M.SG go-PAST.SG.M
    či-dži-ele, *ja sam   u   **či-dži-eleu***
    CGIL   I   be-1SG in+LOC CGIL-LOC.M.SG
    'They want to fool me, but I went to the union, **CGIL**, I'm in the **CGIL**.' (Gen.1,[41],M,65)

In other instances, transfers occur followed by their Croatian equivalents, due either to monitoring (knowing that their speech was being recorded) or as a device to 'revert' back to what is the more unmarked code for the interaction, namely Croatian:

(5) *hrana   nije   tako **sana**   zdrava*
    food-NOM.F.SG be-NEG.3SG so   healthy-NOM.F.SG healthy-NOM.F.SG
    k'o u   Italiji
    as   in+LOC Italy-LOC.F.SG
    'The food is not as **sana**... healthy as in Italy.' (Gen.3,M,9)

Verbs are less common across the sample but are almost always morphologically and phonologically integrated. Examples (6) and (7) contain two instances of morphologically integrated verbs:

(6) ***parlam***   *ti   ja **parlam**   al   me   ne   razumiju*
    speak-1SG you-DAT I   speak-1SG but me-ACC NEG understand-3PL
    'I **talk** and **talk**, but they don't understand me.' (Gen.1,[28],F,53)

In HMLD.Cro, the stylistically marked lexical item *parlati* exists. This is itself a borrowing formed on the base or 3SG.PRES form of Ital. *parlare*, i.e. *parla-* with the verbal suffix marker *-ti*. But its use and meaning are highly marked stylistically, that is, it means 'to speak a foreign language', i.e. *parlati* – 'govoriti [stranim jezikom]' (Klaić 1982: 1011). While the modelling of HMLD.Cro *parlati* may play some role, the conversational implicature of the utterance in example (6) suggests that it is not stylistically marked, and the influence of Italian *parlare* is more likely here. In example (7), the influence of Italian *tatuarsi* 'to tattoo oneself' is apparent.

(7) još   ćeš   **se**   i   ti   **tatuirat!**
    Still   FUT-AUX.2SG REFL   and   you   tattoo-INF
    'even you'll end up **tattooing yourself** [getting a tattoo]!' (Gen.1,[27],M,55)

The equivalent form used in HMLD.Cro is *tetovirati se*, although the form *tatuirati (se)* can be found in informal narratives in electronic-based texts from HMLD.Cro speakers, most probably based on the Eng. form *to tattoo (oneself)*.

Both Italian and Croatian distinguish gender and number, while only Croatian has nominal case morphemes. In example (8) below, a lexical transfer bears gender marking different from its gender in Italian:

(8) **amore**   ti   **prego**   daj   pogledaj   je   l'
    love   you-ACC   beg-1SG   give-2SG.IMP   look-2SG.IMP   AUX-3SG   QP
    ima   vode   u   tom   **caseruolu**
    have-3SG   water-GEN.F.SG in+LOC that-LOC.M.SG saucepan-LOC.M.SG
    '**darling, please** take a look if there is water in that **saucepan**.' (Gen.1,[22],F,52)

The Italian-origin form is *casseruola* F. 'saucepan', but in example (8) it is clearly morphologically marked (LOC.M.SG) as a masculine noun, i.e. *casseruolo* 'saucepan' in its NOM form. Influence from the analogy with the Croatian noun for saucepan *lonac*, M. is possible. As can be seen, nouns and discourse markers are readily transferred from Italian. Examples of lexical transfers into other diaspora varieties of Croatian with a quantitative breakdown according to parts of speech (including gender allocation of nouns), degree of integration and thematic area are presented in other chapters of this volume: AUT.Cro (Ščukanec), GER.Cro (Kresić Vukosav and Šimičić), TRS.Cro (Piasevoli), USA.Cro (Jutronić), CAN.Cro (Petrović), AUS.Cro (Hlavac and Stolac), NZ.Cro (Stoffel and Hlavac) and ARG.Cro (Skelin Horvat, Musulin and Blažević).

4.3 Semantic transference and loan translations

Innovation can be found in examples of semantic transfers, i.e. "the transference of meanings from words in one language to words in another with some morphemic or semantic correspondence" (Clyne 2003: 77), and in loan translations that are calques involving "content, function, grammatical morphemes, and discourse patterns" (Backus and Dorleijn 2009: 82). We start by presenting an example in which the meaning of the first word, *titula* is based on Italian *titolo* 'title', and the last word *bježi* based on an equivalent *sfugge* 'escapes':

(9) **titula** te knjige mi **bježi**
    title-NOM.SG.F that-GEN.F.SG book-GEN.F.SG me-DAT run away-3SG
    'The **title** of the book **runs away from me** [= eludes me].' (Gen.2,M,18)

   Ital.: **il titolo** del libro mi **sfugge** 'the title of the book escapes me'
   HMLD.Cro.: **ne sjećam se naslova** knjige 'I don't remember the title of the book'

This example of semantic transference yields an utterance that is not comprehensible to HMLD.Cro speakers and can only be understood via 'back-translation' to Italian. Example (10) is similarly difficult to understand without recourse to the Italian equivalent, *crescere* 'to grow'.

(10) on me **porastao**
     he-NOM me-ACC grow-PAST.M.SG
     'he **grew** [= raised] me' (Gen.2,F,44)

   Ital.: mi ha **cresciuto** 'he grew me'
   HMLD.Cro: on me **odgojio** 'he reared me'

Example (10) above features a DIR.OBJ after the verb *porastao* 'grew', which in HMLD.Cro is an INTR verb only. Here, not only the semantic features of Ital. *crescere* 'to grow' have been transferred onto *porasti* 'to grow', but also its valency features that allow it to function as a TR *and* INTR verb. Loan translations are more frequent in the sample. We firstly present ones in which the elements of an NP are based on an Italian model:

(11) imate li vi kakvu **burzu**
     have-2PL QP you-2PL sort of-ACC.F.SG stock exchange-ACC.F.SG
     od studija
     of+GEN study-GEN.M.SG
     'Do you have any **stock exchanges of study** [= scholarships].' (Gen.2,F,26)

   Ital.: **borsa di studio** 'purse of study' [= scholarship]
   HMLD.Cro. **stipendija** 'scholarship'

Even more common are loan translations of VP structures from Italian, evident in examples (12) to (15):

(12) ova   blitva   ti   je   loše
     this-NOM.F.SG silverbeet-NOM.F.SG you-DAT   be-3SG bad-ADV
     začinjena   ne   mogu   je   nikako **poslat**   **doli**
     spiced-NOM.F.SG NEG can-1SG it-ACC.F no way send-INF down
     'This silver beet is not properly seasoned. I can't **send it down** [= swallow it].'
     (Gen.1,[16],F,36)

   Ital.:   **mandare giù** 'send down'
   HMLD.Cro.: **progutati** 'swallow'

(13) ja ć'   sto   puta   **promijenit**
     I + FUT-AUX.1SG hundred+GEN.PL   time-GEN.M.PL   change-INF
     ideju
     idea-ACC.F.SG
     'I'll change my **idea** [=mind] a hundred times.' (Gen.2,F,23)

   Ital.:   cambiare **idea** 'change idea'
   HMLD.Cro.   promijeniti **mišljenje** 'change opinion'

(14) teško   je   **uzet**   odluku
     difficult-ADV be-3SG take-INF   decision-ACC.F.SG
     'it's hard to **take** [= make] a decision' (Gen.2,M,22)

   Ital.:   **prendere** una decisione 'take a decision';
   HMLD.Cro.   **donijeti** odluku 'bring a decision'

(15) dogodi   se   kad   želiš   **napravit** **dobru**
     happen-3SG REFL when   wish-2SG do-INF   good-ACC.F.SG
     akciju
     action-ACC.F.SG
     'It happens when you want to **do a good action** [= good deed].' (Gen.2,M,24)

   Ital.:   fare una **buona azione** 'do a good action'
   HMLD.Cro.   učiniti **dobro djelo** 'do a good act'

In other diaspora varieties of Croatian further examples of semantic transference and loan translations are recorded, e.g. AUT.Cro (Ščukanec, this volume), TRS.Cro (Piasevoli, this volume), CAN.Cro (Petrović, this volume), AUS.Cro (Hlavac and Stolac, this volume), NZ.Cro (Stoffel and Hlavac, this volume) and ARG.Cro (Skelin Horvat, Musulin and Blažević, this volume). A change in the selection of system (or function) morphemes is evident in example (16), where the choice of preposition used in the equivalent Italian phraseme have been borrowed, which results in a construction that differs from that used in HMLD.Cro:

(16) *naljutit   ćeš   se   sa   mnom*
      anger-INF FUT.AUX-2SG REFL   with+INS me-INS
      'You'll get angry **with** [= at] me' (Gen.2,F,23)

   Ital.:   ti arrabbierai **con me** 'you'll get angry with me'
   HMLD.Cro.: naljutit ćeš se **na mene** 'you'll get angry at me'

In example (16) above, the replication of an Italian model *arrabbiarsi + con qualcuno* 'to become angry + with someone' has led to a change in the choice of preposition, from *na* 'at' (+ACC) to *s(a)* 'with' (+INS) with a subsequent change in the case-marking of the object to INS.

Another instance, this time involving the omission of morpheme structure, is example (17). The Croatian verb 'to be born', *roditi se*, is reflexive containing the particle *se* 'self' and intransitive. In Italian, 'to be born' is rendered by an intransitive verb, but which is a non-reflexive verb, *nascere*. Calquing of the syntactic features of the equivalent Italian verb results in the following example:

(17) **rodila**   sam   u   Torinu   ali   ne   živim
     born-PAST.SG.F AUX-1SG in+LOC   Torino-LOC.N.SG but NEG live-1SG
     tamo
     there
     '**I was born** in Turin, but I don't live there' (Gen.2,F,23)

   Ital.:   **sono nata** a Torino...
   HMLD.Cro: **rodila sam se** u Torinu...

Example (17) is permissible in HMLD.Cro – but it contains a different meaning, as *roditi* as a non-reflexive verb is transitive with the meaning 'to give birth', i.e. the above example in HMLD.Cro would be understood as 'I gave birth in Torino, but I don't live there'. So, in the (17), the valency of the verb *roditi* appears to have changed as the intended meaning of it here is intransitive, not transitive. In example (18), the valency of the verb has changed so that the relationship of direct object and indirect object has been swapped. In example (18), this results in a reallocation of *mama* 'mum' as an indirect object with DAT marking rather than as a direct object with ACC marking.

(18) mislim   da   će   Lea odabrat   a   onda pitat
     think-1SG COMP FUT.AUX-3SG Lea choose-INF and then ask-INF
     savjet   **mami**
     advice-ACC.M.SG. mum-DAT.F.SG
     'I think Lea will choose, and then ask advice **to mum** [= ask mum
     for advice]' (Gen.2,F,22)

   Ital.:   chiedere consiglio **alla** mamma 'ask the advice-ACC to mum-DAT'
   HMLD.Cro.   pitati **mamu za savjet** 'ask mum-ACC for+ACC advice-ACC'

Example (18) above contains an unusual but syntactically consistent (and target) application of target case marking. Changes in verb valency traverse the boundary of loan translations and syntactic transference. Further instances of changes in VP structure are given in section 4.6.3.

4.4 Possessive adjectives *suo / svoj*

Both Italian and Croatian have possessive adjectives that pattern in ways different to English possessive adjectives. In particular, we examine here possessive adjectives with 3SG antecedents. Italian has a 3SG POSS ADJ, *suo* 'his/her/its', which attracts morphological marking according to the features of the following noun. The form *suo* remains the same regardless of the gender of the possessor. Croatian distinguishes the gender of the possessor – *njegov* 'his/its', *njezin* 'her' – with morphological marking according to the features of the following noun. But, in addition to distinct forms of the POSS ADJ for each person (1. *moj*; 2. *tvoj*; 3. *njegov*) and number (singular, *tvoj* 2.SG; plural *vaš* 2.PL), Croatian has a reflexive POSS ADJ *svoj* '(one's) own' that can refer to an antecedent possessor of any person (1., 2., 3.) and number (singular, plural). Croatian *svoj* cannot occur in sentence-initial position as part of a NOM NP. But in Italian, *suo* can occur in such a position. In examples (19) and (20) below, *svoja* and *svoj* occur in sentence initial position, based on the syntactic function that its Italian equivalent *suo* can perform:

(19) **svoja**   obitelj   je   došla   prije
     own-NOM.F.SG family-NOM.F.SG AUX-3SG come-PAST.SG.F before
     svoja   mama   je   došla   prije
     own-NOM.F.SG mother-NOM.F.SG AUX-3SG come-PAST.SG.F before
     'his family came earlier, his mother came earlier' (Gen.2,F,44)

   Ital.   la **sua** famiglia... **sua** madre.
   HMLD.Cro.:   **njegova** obitelj... **njegova** majka.

(20) **svoj**   smartphone   je   skupi
     own- NOM.M.SG smartphone-NOM.M.SG   be-3SG   expensive-NOM.M.SG
     moj   nije   tako
     my-NOM.M.SG   be-NEG.3SG   such
     'His smartphone is expensive, mine's not [so]' (Gen.2,M,21)

Information from the context of the two examples enabled identification of the antecedent of *svoja* and *svoj* as a male. In HMLD.Cro, POSS ADJ forms are used that identify the gender of the possessor 3SG, i.e. *njegova obitelj* 'his family', *njegova mama* 'his mum' and *njegov smartphone* 'his smartphone'. An opposite tendency, namely the avoidance of *svoj* and non-target employment of more specific 3SG or 3PL possessive pronouns is recorded in CAN.Cro (see Petrović, this volume).

4.5 Code-switching

Code-switching in this chapter refers to multiple-word units or longer stretches of forms. Code-switching can occur at clause boundaries (here referred to as inter-clausal code-switching) or within a clause (intra-clausal code-switching). We start with two examples of inter-clausal switching, where the switch to Italian contains a quote from the speech of others:

(21) *baš mi reko jedan momak neki dan na poslu* **"Grande, Mario! Bravo, Mario! Hai fatto bene!"**.
the other day at work a guy just said to me **"Great, Mario! Well done, Mario! You did a good job!"**. (Gen.1,[43],M,64)

Example (21) contains reported speech of an utterance that was most probably produced in Italian. This is a typical example of sociolinguistically motivated code-switching where the language of the code-switch mirrors the language used by the interlocutor quoted. In example (22), the informant is quoting herself. It is possible that the expletive that she produced was *mannaggia!* 'damn!' and the code-switch reflects what she said verbatim at the time. The immediacy of the Italian expletive *mannaggia!* seems to be a catalyst or trigger (Clyne, 2003: 77–80) for the remainder of the quote, and for the rest of the turn, that are given in Italian:

(22) *kad sam kup'la, mislila sam da će bit tvrdo i da se neće moć skuvat, reko* **"*mannaggia! ho sprecato i soldi!*"** *però era buono, sai!*
when I first bought it I thought it would be tough and that it couldn't be cooked, I said, **"damn! I've wasted the money."** But it was good, you know! (Gen.1,[25],F,48)

The examples (21) and (22) came from Gen.1 speakers. In the speech of the following Gen. 2 informants, intra-clausal single-word insertions from Italian in Croatian clauses alternate with longer stretches or alternations of 3–5 word phrases from Italian. In example (23) *più di due volte alla settimana* and in example (24) *durante l'anno* occur as phrase-length code-switches, similar to inter-clausal code-switches.

(23) *čitala sam za* **tonno** *da se ne smi jest* ***più di due volte alla settimana*** *jer sadrži* **mercurio**
'I've read that **tuna** can't be eaten **more than twice a week** because it contains **mercury**' (Gen.2,F,21)

(24) ***t'immagini però****, šta će ona tamo radit, šta ima* **gente** *radit u Bosni* ***durante l'anno*** *kad nema nikog?*
'**but just imagine**, what would she do there, what can **people** do in Bosnia **during the year** when there's nobody there?' (Gen.2,F,22)

Examples (23) and (24) contain lexical forms (realia of the Italian context) such as *tonno* and *mercurio*, while time expressions are commonly reported code-switched phrases (Clyne 2003). For these Gen.2 informants, this type of speech appears to be unmarked. Awareness of it amongst some informants is low, and the above examples come from informants who report that they otherwise speak 'only Croatian' at home. It is possible that this statement is more a statement that contrasts language use at home from non-home contexts (where mostly Italian is used), but not necessarily an indication that the home variety consists of Croatian forms only. When in 'bilingual mode' (Grosjean 2013) speakers may draw on both languages with little discourse-internal meaning signified by switches between languages, i.e. 'unmarked code-switching'. There are infrequent occasions in the sample when there are metalinguistic comments or other 'flags' through which speakers draw attention to the code that they are using. These may take the form of their (usually only momentary) inability to access forms from one of their languages:

(25) *Pisao sam radove za neke druge tečajeve,* **eh, come si dice, eh, concorsi**? *Natječaje? Da, natječaje, ne tečajeve.*
'I wrote papers for some other courses, **um, what's the word, um, 'concorsi'**? Competitions? Yes, competitions, not courses.' (Gen.2,M,23)

Example (26) below contains instances of monitoring and correction, this time in a dialogue between a Gen.2 and Gen.3 speaker. The presence of a recording device may have played a role in the aunt monitoring her nephew's speech. Although fluent in Croatian, this third-generation speaker demonstrates an inability to readily access some forms in Croatian. This elicits a response of 'modelling' from his aunt:

(26) A*: *Šta ste igrali?*
'What were you playing?'
N*: *Oni su me pitali oćeš igrat nogomet? Ja reko pa naravno!*
'They asked me do you want to play football? I said of course!'
A: *Pa da! al nisi reko odma da oćeš! Prvo si šutio.*
'Well, yes! But you didn't say yes right away! Initially you remained silent.'
N: **Stavo pensando...**
'**I was thinking...**'
A: *Aha... a zašto?*
'Aha... and why?'
N: **Perché ero indeciso.**
'**Because I wasn't sure.**'
A: *Na hrvatskom, molim te, na hrvatskom!*
'In Croatian, please, in Croatian!'
N: *Pa ne znam kak se kaže! Nisam im odma reko jer* **ero indeciso.**
'Well, I don't know how to say it! I didn't tell them right away because **I wasn't sure.**'
A: *Kak se kaže* **'ero indeciso'**? *A? Pa 'bio sam neodlučan'! Tako! Ajde sada reci tako!*
'How do you say **'ero indeciso'** ['I was indecisive']? Eh? Like, 'bio sam neodlučan' ['I was indecisive']! Right! Come on, say it like that!'
N: *Bio sam neodlučan.*
'I was indecisive.'
A: *Bravo!*
'Well done!'

* Abbreviations: A: Aunt (Gen.2,F,24); N: Nephew (Gen.3,M,7)

While example (25) contained an example of a code-switch into Italian, followed by a self-correction, example (26) is one of correction coming from another interlocutor. The first code-switch by the nephew *stavo pensando* 'I was thinking' was not challenged by the aunt, but the second one was, and the aunt shifts the thematic focus of the dialogue to a meta-linguistic one, with modelling and positive feedback. But as can be seen from most of the above examples, 'unmarked' or 'classic code-switching' (Myers-Scotton 2006) is more commonly found in this corpus. This includes inter-clausal and intra-clausal code-switching within the same turn, but also across turn boundaries. To illustrate this, we present below a 10-turn excerpt featuring one Gen.1 speaker and two Gen.2 speakers:

(27) M*: ***senti che sogno ho fatto stasera!***
  'let me tell you what a dream I had last night!'
 D: ***che sogno?***
  'what dream?'
 M: *sanjala sam da sam bila na nekoj fešti, nemam pojma, uglavnom, bila sam sa Kolindom.* [smijeh]
  'I dreamt that I was at a party of some kind, I don't know, but anyway, I was with Kolinda' [The then president of Croatia: Kolinda Grabar-Kitarović] [everybody laughs]
 DB: ***eh, vabbe'...***
  'oh, well...'
 M: ***poi mi ha fatto arrabbiare papà perché non mi ha fatto la foto.*** *Ma digni se, ajde! uglavnom, stvarno baš gluposti koji puta sanjam, ništa s ničim.*
  'then dad made me angry because he didn't take the picture. Come on, get up! Anyway, sometimes I really have stupid dreams, they don't make sense.'
 DB: *evo ja baš jučer sanjao da smo ćaća i ja išli u rat*
  'just yesterday I dreamt that dad and I went to war'
 D: *a ja sam sanjala da sam išla na izlet i da sam njega našla da prodaje sladoled*
  'and I dreamt that I went on a trip and found him there selling ice cream'
 M: ***guarda che brutta fine!***
  'well, what a bad ending'
 DB: ***uno studia, studia, e alla fine va a vendere il gelato***
  'you study, study, and then you end up selling ice cream'
 M: ***eh, ma sai quanti ce ne sono... mamma mia...***
  'if you only knew how many there are like that... oh my!...'
 * Abbreviations: M: Mother (Gen.1,[25],F,48); D: daughter (Gen.2,F,21); DB: daughter's boyfriend (Gen.2,M,22);

In example (27), 59 of the lexemes in example are supplied from Croatian, while 47 are from Italian. In example (27), the exchange commences in Italian, switches to Croatian, and concludes in Italian. All three speakers use both languages and seamlessly switch between both, producing full clauses in both Italian and Croatian. This looks like an example of 'classic code-switching' (Myers-Scotton 2006), i.e. speakers avail themselves of forms from either language mostly according with micro-discourse features such as turns, changes in footing etc. accounting for why a code may change at a particular point. The first switch occurs after the form *ma* 'but', a bilingual homophone that has the same meaning and function in both languages. It may be that this bilingual homophone led to 'consequential triggering' of a switch from Italian to Croatian (Hlavac 1999; Clyne 2003). The second code-switch occurs between turns and it appears that the phrase *guarda che brutta fine* 'well, what a bad ending' was more accessible to the mother than a Croatian-language evaluation of the boyfriend's dream. This kind of bilingual talk is characterised by the relative unmarkedness of forms from either language and is now commonly described as translanguaging (Li Wei 2018).

4.6 Morphosyntax

This section presents examples in regard to the following: noun phrases (4.6.1), possessive constructions (4.6.2), verb phrases (4.6.3), word order and clitics (4.6.4), syntactic calques (4.6.5) and code-switching and structural convergence (4.6.6).

4.6.1 Noun phrases

This section focuses on the morphological marking of elements in NPs: nouns, attributive adjectives and determiners. In Croatian, all of these elements bear morphological features marking gender, number and case. As shown in example (1), some Italian toponyms do not attract case marking in NPs when this would otherwise be expected, for example, after prepositions governing a particular case. Further instances of this are given in examples (31) to (37) below. The first examples given here are those in which Croatian nouns are assigned a gender that is the gender of an Italian equivalent, but not the gender that these items have in HMLD.Cro:

(28) to   je   **pravi**   **enigma**
      that   be-3SG   real-NOM.M.SG   enigma-NOM.F.SG
      'It's a real enigma.' (Gen.2,M,26)

   Ital. enigma-M; HMLD.Cro enigma-F.

(29) **ministarstvo**   mi   je   **javio**   da
      ministry-NOM.N.SG   me-DAT AUX-3SG inform-PAST.M.SG   COMP
      su   dokumenti   gotovi
      be-3PL   document-NOM.M.PL   ready-NOM.M.PL
      'The ministry informed me that the documents are ready'. (Gen.2,M,28)

   Ital. ministero-M; HMLD.Cro ministarstvo-N.

Within NPs, some changes are also apparent in the morphological marking of number. In example (30), the number *dva* 'two' precedes a noun with plural morphology. This conforms to Italian (and English) morphological conventions. In Croatian, numbers from 2 to 4 require a paucal form, i.e. GEN.SG marking on succeeding nominals and their attributes. (See Piasevoli, this volume). Instead of paucal marking, example (30) contains an example of logical congruence between a plural number and a plural head noun:

(30) na   klupi   sjede   **dva**   **momci**
      on+LOC bench-LOC.F.SG   sit-3PL   two+GEN.SG   guy-NOM.M.PL.
      'Two guys are sitting on a bench.' (Gen.3,M,9)

   HMLD.Cro: *na klupi sjede dva **momka*** 'guy-GEN.M.SG'

We now move to examples in which case marking is the focus of analysis. The first examples are those in which non-target case marking is preceded by a preposition, i.e. items within NPs whose morphological marking is otherwise usually determined by the preceding preposition and the case that it governs. The case otherwise expected is given to the left of the arrow '>', while the case marking provided by the informant is given to the right.

We firstly present instances in which a preposition projects a particular case. Analogous to toponyms in Italian remaining uninflected as in example (1) above, some Croatian toponyms can sometimes also remain uninflected, despite prepositions requiring GEN marking.

GEN > NOM

(31) od   **Bergamo**   do   **Split**   nema
      from+GEN   Bergamo-NOM.N.SG   to+GEN   Split-NOM.M.SG   have-NEG.3SG
      let
      flight-NOM.M.SG
      'There's no flight from **Bergamo** to **Split**'. (Gen.2, F, 22)

In contrast, HMLD.Cro has GEN marking on the proper nouns *Bergamo* and *Split*, as well as the common noun *let*, which also has GEN marking as an object following the verb *imati* 'to have' in its NEG form.

HMLD.Cro:

od	**Bergama**	do	**Splita**	nema
from+GEN	Bergamo-GEN.N.SG	to+GEN	Split-GEN.M.SG	have-NEG.3SG

leta
flight-GEN.M.SG

In the following example, a Croatian chrematonym (name of a political, commercial or cultural entity) namely *Kraš* (a Zagreb-based confectionary manufacturer), remains uninflected, despite the preceding preposition requiring LOC.

LOC > NOM

(32) di se to kupi u **Kraš**
     where REFL that buy-3SG at+LOC Kraš-NOM.M.SG
     Where can that be bought? At Kraš? (Gen.2,F,26)

In HMLD.Cro, the form of *Kraš* used in the second part of the turn would be in the LOC, i.e. *U Krašu*-LOC.M.SG. In the following example, a common noun *birokracija* 'bureaucracy' appears as an uninflected form after the preposition *s* 'with' requiring LOC.

INS > NOM

(33) *imam stalno probleme s* **birokracija**
     have-1SG constantly problem-ACC.M.PL with+INS bureaucracy-NOM.F.SG
     'I keep having problems with bureaucracy' (Gen.2,F,23)

In example (33) above, the preposition *s* 'with' governs instrumental case but the noun remains as a NOM. The other noun in this clause *probleme* 'problem-ACC.M.PL' attracts target case marking. This noun is *not* preceded by a preposition. Further examples of target and non-target case marking in the same clause or turn are given below in examples (34) and (35).

ACC > ACC, ACC > NOM

In the following example, the informant produces one target ACC form as a DIR OBJ immediately following the verb, while in the following ADV phrase the components of the NP, *mala djeca* 'small children' does not attract ACC marking despite the preceding preposition *za* 'for' + ACC that requires ACC marking.

(34) kupila   sam   rječnike   za
     buy-PAST.F.SG AUX-1SG   dictionaries-ACC.M.PL   for+ACC
     mala   **djeca**
     small-NOM.F.SG children-NOM.F.SG
     'I bought dictionaries for little children.' (Gen.2,F,44)

In a similar way, example (35) below features target marking of the first ADV phrase containing a preposition *u* 'to' governing ACC with ACC marking on the following adjective and noun, while the second ADV phrase has a preposition *do* 'until/to' governing GEN with NOM morphological marking on the following adjective and noun.

ACC > ACC, GEN > NOM

(35) išao   sam   u   hrvatsku   školu
     go-PAST.M.SG AUX-1SG   in+ACC   Croatian-ACC.F.SG   school-ACC.F.SG
     do   **osmi**   **razred**
     to+GEN   eighth-NOM.M.SG   grade-ACC.M.SG
     'I went to Croatian school until eighth grade'. (Gen.2,M,24)

As example (35) shows, variation occurs in the same clause in regard to target and non-target morphological marking. This indicates that amongst some speakers, there is variation in their realisation of morphological marking. Whether this variation is an example of *free variation* in their repertoires is not clear here. We present here those examples that occurred and quantify the number of total instances to see whether there is a pattern in the type of morphological markers employed. Examples (31) to (35) above featured NPs where NOM forms are employed where otherwise oblique case marking is required. The examples given below feature instances of oblique case. Croatian prepositions such as *na* 'at'/'on' or *u* 'to'/'in' are used to express movement (ACC) or location (LOC). The corpus contains instances in which ACC marking is used in place of LOC marking. Example (36) is an instance of this:

LOC > ACC

(36) budem   u   **školu**   od   osam   do   dva
     be-PFV.1SG   in+LOC   school-ACC.F.SG   from   eight   to   two
     'I'm at school from eight to two.' (Gen.2,M,18)

The use of the verb *biti* 'to be' is clearly stative and the subsequent ADV phrase is one of position, and the preposition *u* (here 'in/at') requires LOC marking. But instead, ACC morpheme marking is used.

The above examples (31) to (36) contain NPs preceded by prepositions. The following example of non-target case marking involves an NP that is not preceded by a preposition. In the plural, NOM frequently replaces ACC, which appeared to be well retained in previous research on diaspora Croatian (Hlavac 2003: 124):

ACC > NOM

(37) *uvijek   vidim   **stari**   **prijatelji***
  always   see-1SG old-NOM.M.PL   friends-NOM.M.PL
  'I always see old friends.' (Gen.2,F,26)

In (37) after the verb, NOM forms are provided instead of ACC direct object forms *stare prijatelje* 'old friends' ACC.M.PL. The examples (31) to (35) and (37) above show a trend towards NOM as the replacement form for nouns requiring OBL markers. There are instances of the opposite, i.e. nouns that require NOM or non-overt case markers such as inanimate ACC.M.SG nouns or ACC.N.SG nouns.

Table 1 below contains a statistical representation of the non-target forms identified in the sample. The ordering of cases here is based on Ďurovič's (1983: 23) hierarchical scale of case 'implicativity' i.e. NOM < ACC < GEN < LOC < INS < DAT < VOC. Starting from a case in 'the middle' of the hierarchy, e.g. LOC, the system of implicativity means that all cases to its left, i.e. NOM, ACC and GEN are present in a speaker's active repertoire. At the same time, the system says nothing about the presence of a case 'to the right' in a speaker's repertoire, so that command of the GEN, for example, does not suggest that the same speaker has an active command of the LOC, INS, DAT or VOC.

Table 1: Quantification of non-target case forms in NPs with and without a preposition.

	Preceded by a preposition	No preposition	Preceded by a number
ACC > NOM	1	1	
GEN > NOM	3	1	1
LOC > NOM	3		
INS > NOM	1		
LOC > ACC	3		
ACC > LOC	2		
Total	13	2	1

Table 1 above provides an overview of the non-target forms. (This table does not include the 5 instances of Italian toponyms that do not attract case marking even though this would be required due to a preceding preposition.) A quantification of all NP forms found in the sample was not undertaken so it is not possible to report how frequent and representative the above examples are for all Croatian NPs, and for the marking of particular cases. What Table 1 shows is that where non-target forms occur, they are much more likely to occur in NPs preceded by a preposition than without one. This observation is congruent to the findings of NPs with non-target case marking in AUS.Cro (see Hlavac and Stolac, this volume). Other studies on diaspora Croatian have also employed Đurovič's (1983) implicativity scale as a descriptive and interpretive tool in regard to changes in case-marking, e.g. TRS.Cro (Piasevoli, this volume), CAN.Cro (Petrović, this volume) and NZ.Cro (Stoffel and Hlavac, this volume).

4.6.2 Possessive constructions and *od* 'of'/'from'

Possession in Croatian can be expressed via pre-posed attributive + nominal constructions, or via post-posed GEN constructions where the possessee precedes the possessor. The pre-posed attributive construction is more common (in both the standard and most dialects) and is considered stylistically preferable. In comparison, possessive constructions are more often expressed in Italian via post-posed constructions such as 'possessee + *di* 'of' + possessor'. Example (38) below contains an *x* of *y* construction shown by GEN marking on the post-posed possessor:

(38) živi   u   domu   studenata
     live-3SG in+LOC house-LOC.M.SG   student-GEN.M.PL
     'he lives in a **house of students** [= student dorm]' (Gen.1,[23],F,49)

   Ital.:   **casa dello studente** 'house of students'
   HMLD.Cro.: **studentski dom** 'student-ADJ house'.

The following example contains a sequence of constituents in the NP based on an Italian model. It comes from a Gen.2 speaker with post-posed *fantasy*, now an established Anglicism in Italian:

(39) to   je   jedna   priča   fantasy
     it-NOM.N be-3SG one-NOM.F.SG story-NOM.F.SG fantasy-NOM.M.SG
     'it is a **fantasy story**.' (Gen.2,M,24)

Ital.: c'è un **racconto fantasy**/fantastico
HMLD.Cro: to je **fantastična priča**/to je **priča fantazije**

In this NP, post-posed *fantasy* is the second part of a compound noun (or a noun possibly functioning as a post-posed attribute adjective). Compound noun constructions are very rare in Croatian (cf. *kamen temeljac* 'foundation stone') and instead, pre-posed possessive constructions e.g. *fantastična priča* 'fantastic story' or GEN constructions e.g. *to je priča fantazije* 'that's a story of fantasy' are more common. Employment of *jedna* 'one' here appears conspicuous. Its use is not that of a numeral; instead it appears as a "specific indefinite marker" (Belaj and Matovac 2015: 4) but not as a form which represents the development of an indefinite article as such.

Analogous to the GEN construction of example (39) above, and also to example (11) – *burzu od studija* 'scholarship' – there are other instances when the structure of Italian phrasal verb constructions has been copied onto Croatian ones. Example (40) below contains the preposition *od* 'of', based on the Italian model *parlare di* 'to tell of':

(40) *il   signore   degli   anelli   priča   **od***
     DEF.ART.M Lord-M   of-M.PL   ring-M.PL   talk-3SG   of+GEN
     ovi   obiti
     these-NOM.M.PL   hobbit-NOM.M.PL
     '"The Lord of the Rings" tells **of** these Hobbits.' (Gen.2,M,21)

Ital.: Il film 'Il Signore degli Anelli' parla **di** questi Hobbit.;
HMLD.Cro.: U filmu 'Gospodar prstenova' radi se **o** ovim Hobitima.

Semantic transference in the employment of the verb *priča* 'talk' based on Ital. *parlare* is also evident (cf. section 4.1.3). In other instances, some informants employ analytical constructions that include the preposition *od* 'of'. In HMLD. Cro, such uses of the preposition *od* are possible, but more characteristic of non-standard varieties. In the corpus two instances are recorded of the following construction: *bojati se **od*** ['of'] *nekog*-GEN 'to be afraid **of** someone', Ital. *avere paura **di*** ['of'] *qualcuno*-GEN. The standard HMLD.Cro equivalent construction lacks the preposition *od* 'of', i.e. *bojati se* [∅] *nekoga*. Further examples of the possible influence of Italian possessive constructions in accounting for the use of *od* as a possessive are found in the TRS.Cro sample (see Piasevoli, this volume), with samples of diaspora Croatian in contact with other languages also bearing this feature, e.g. USA.Cro (see Jutronić, this volume) and AUS.Cro (see Hlavac and Stolac, this volume).

4.6.3 Verbal phrases

Verbs in Croatian and Italian differ from each other in the feature of verbal aspect. In Italian, information relating to verbal aspect can be expressed via some past tenses, such as the imperfect (*l'imperfetto*), while in Croatian it is a formal feature existing in all verbs, regardless of tense. There are also a small number of 'bi-aspectual' verbs, i.e. verbs whose form is the same for both aspects. A trend amongst some speakers – all of them members of Gen. 2 – is that in some instances, for continuous or habitual events that require IPFV verbs these speakers instead sometimes employ PFV verbs, expressing these events as completed actions when the context shows that they are not:

(41) ja opet se **vratim** na ovo od prije
I again REFL return-PFV-1SG to+ACC this from before
'I'm coming back again to this from before...' (Gen.2,M,24)

HMLD.Cro. 'ja se opet **vraćam** return-IPFV-1SG na ovo od prije...'

(42) kak studiram ne **nađem** vremena za
since study-IPFV-1SG NEG find-PFV-1SG time-GEN.N.SG for+ACC
te knjige
those-ACC.F.PL books-ACC.F.PL
'As I'm studying, I can't find time for those books.' (Gen.2,F,21)

HMLD.Cro. 'kako studiram ne **nalazim** 'find-IPFV-1SG'...

(43) nisam imala puno mogućnosti
NEG.AUX-1SG have-PAST.SG.F many+GEN opportunity-GEN.F.PL
doć u Hrvatsku
come-PFV-INF to+ACC Croatia-ACC.F.SG
'I haven't had a lot of opportunities to come to Croatia.' (Gen.2,F,23)

HMLD.Cro: nisam imala puno mogućnosti **dolaziti** 'come-IPFV-INF'.

In the corpus, the number of verbs is not counted. There are seven instances of PFV forms of verbs when IPFV forms would be expected. There are no examples of IPFV forms being used where PFV would be expected. Instances of PFV verbs being used in verbal constructions where IPFV would otherwise be expected are found in TRS.Cro (see Piasevoli, this volume) and AUS.Cro (see Hlavac and Stolac, this volume). Moving from aspect to valency, example (44) contains a change in the case government rules of the verb *zavidjeti* 'to envy', which in Croatian requires DAT marking its logical object.

(44) *zavidi* **me** *zato ja imam*
 envy-3SG me-ACC because I have-1SG
 'He envies **me** because I have it'. (Gen.2,F,23)

    Ital.: invidiare **qualcuno** 'to envy someone-**ACC**'
    HMLD.Cro.: zavidjeti **nekome** 'to envy someone-**DAT**'

In (44), the object is in ACC rather than DAT. This appears to be influenced by the ACC marking of the object following the equivalent Italian verb.

4.6.4 Word order and clitics

In the data sample there are occurrences of word order that resemble Italian word order patterns. For example, sentences in Italian can start with an auxiliary or with clitic (short) pronoun forms. In the corpus there are turns and utterances that start with a short form of the auxiliary *biti* 'to be', thus resembling Italian sentence structure:

(45) **sam** *kuhala kad sam živjela sama*
 AUX-1SG cook-PAST.SG.F when AUX-1SG live-PST.SG.F alone-SG.F
 'I used to cook when I was living alone' (Gen.2,F,26)

Placement of AUX forms in clause-initial position occurs in some non-standard varieties of Croatian (e.g. many Kajkavian and Čakavian dialects) but this influence can be largely discounted for examples (45) to (47), as the speakers are from Štokavian-areas in Croatia and Bosnia-Herzegovina where this does not occur. In Italian, short forms of indirect object personal pronouns as well as the short forms of reflexive pronouns can occur in clause-initial position. (See Piasevoli, this volume.) This is a feature that is otherwise not present in the homeland variety of these speakers' Štokavian dialect:

(46) **mi je rekla** *da može*
 me-DAT AUX-3SG say-PST.SG.F COMP can-3SG
 'She told me that it's okay.' (Gen.2,M,26)

    Ital.: **mi ha detto** di sì
    HMLD.Cro: **rekla mi je** da može

(47) **ti   daju   oni   sok**
      you-DAT give-3PL they-NOM juice-ACC.M.SG
      'They will give you the juice!' (Gen.2,F,23)

   Ital.:   **ti danno** loro il succo!
   HMLD.Cro: **daju ti** sok!

It appears that the influence of Italian accounts for the appearance of short form AUX verbs, short form personal pronouns and REFL forms in clause-initial or left-posited position. In HMLD.Cro the COP (or other clitics or short forms) typically occurs in second position in such subordinate clauses (Browne 1974; Udier 2006). The position of clitics and changes in word order are examined in other studies on diaspora Croatian, e.g. TRS.Cro (Piasevoli, this volume), USA.Cro (Jutronić, this volume), CAN.Cro (Petrović, this volume) and AUS.Cro (Hlavac and Stolac, this volume).

4.6.5 Syntactic calques

In the following sentences the syntactic features reflect those that would normally be present in equivalent Italian sentences. In example (48), there is left dislocation of a direct object NP to clause-initial position. Although a DIR OBJ, this NP has NOM marking, and its syntactic function is marked via a succeeding pronoun that itself has ACC marking.

(48) *moja   najdraža   knjiga   čito*
      my-NOM.F.SG dearest-NOM.F.SG book-NOM.F.SG read-PAST.M.SG
      sam   je   kad   sam   imo   dvanaest
      AUX-1SG it-ACC.F when   AUX-1SG have-PST.M.SG twelve+GEN.PL
      godina
      year-GEN.F.PL
      'My favourite book I read it when I was twelve years old.' (Gen.2,M,18)

Example (48) is based on an Italian cleft construction that has left dislocation of the NP *il mio libro preferito* and the DIR OBJ of the main clause is a clitic pronoun (*particella pronominale*) *lo* 'it'-M which coalesces with the AUX *ho* 'have-1SG' in a portmanteau form *l'ho*. The equivalent Italian construction is: *Il mio libro preferito l'ho letto quando avevo 12 anni.* The equivalent HMLD.Cro would be:

svoju	najdražu	knjigu	sam	čit(a)o
my own-ACC.F.SG	dearest-ACC.F.SG	book-ACC.F.SG	AUX-1SG	read-PAST.M.SG

kad
when

'My-ACC favourite-ACC book-ACC I read when. . .'

Left dislocation of DIR OBJ is possible and common in HMLD.Cro. However, ACC marking is required on the DIR OBJ itself. Example (48) above appears as a calque of a syntactic construction transferred from Italian.

4.6.6 Code-switching and structural convergence

This section presents examples in which code-switching co-occurs with morphosyntactic features. In example (49), an intra-clausal code-switch occurs between an auxiliary and a main verb. A Gen.2 speaker is addressing a fellow Gen.2 speaker.

(49) Mari' jesi ti išta **decidere** kad i gdje ćeš
Mari' AUX-2SG you anything decide-INF when and where FUT.AUX-2SG
in vacanza. dimmi ti **prego** jer ni ja ne znam
on holiday give:me-DAT you please because nor I NEG know-1SG
'Mari', have you **decided** when and where to go **on holiday**? **Please tell me** because I don't know either' (Gen.2,F,21)

In the first clause of Example (49) the Croatian past tense compound verb has a Croatian AUX *jesi* that agrees with the 2SG subject. The second part of the verb is an Italian INF form *decidere* and not a PST.PTCP form *deciso* 'decided'. The equivalent Croatian PST.PTCP form would have been *odlučila* 'decide' PST.PTCP.F.SG. It is not clear why the INF form *decidere* was used. The Italian present perfect (*passato prossimo*) consists of an AUX *avere / essere* 'to have'/'to be' + PST.PTCP. This structure patterns in a way similar to the Croatian perfect (*prošlo vrijeme*) that consists of AUX *biti* 'to be' + PST.PTCP. There appear to be few obstacles in combining a Croatian AUX with an Italian PST.PTCP. Instead the INF form *decidere* occurs rather than the PST.PTCP *deciso*. The morphophonological change that occurs from INF *decidere* to the PST.PTCP form *deciso* may be an obstacle to its employment, while the –*o* ending may be perceived as morphologically not congruent to the feminine subject. The reason for this is that the equivalent Croatian PST.PTCP bears marking for the female gender of the subject, and has in this case, a feminine –*a* suffix, *odlučila*. This mismatch may account for the occurrence of the non-finite form, INF *decidere*.

In the first utterance of example (50), a code-switch occurs within an NP, between an Italian definite article *le*-F.PL 'the' and a Croatian noun *palačinke*-F.PL 'pancakes'.

(50) **mandami   la   ricetta per le   palačinke**
     send me-DAT ART-F.SG   recipe   for ART-F.PL   pancake-ACC.F.PL
     nisam   sigurna   da   stavim **tutti   gli**
     be-NEG-1SG   sure-F.SG   COMP   put-1SG all-M.PL   ART-M.PL
     ingredienti
     ingredient-M.PL
     '**Could you send me the recipe for the** pancakes? I'm not sure whether to put in **all the ingredients.**' (Gen.2,F,23)

Italian is the matrix language of the first clause and Croatian *palačinke* occurs as a clause-final insertion. The morphological marking that *palačinke* bears as a Croatian ACC.PL.F noun is morphologically integrated into the Italian NP, which also requires an –*e* ending for the (FEM) noun *palačinka*. Thus, the NP *le palačinke* is a well-formed Italian NP as it bears congruent FEM.PL –*e* for both article and noun. The morphological marking of the Italian article (F.PL) –*e* and the Croatian noun (F.PL) –*e* felicitously coincide, and the morphosyntactic integrity of the ML Italian and the EL Croatian is not compromised.

The second clause in the above example has Croatian as its matrix language, with an Italian NP occurring as a clause-final insertion. The DIR.OBJ *tutti gli ingredienti* 'all the ingredients' occurs as an Italian NP that bears the MASC.PL suffix -*i* on all constituents. This is a well-formed Italian NP, but the -*i* suffixes on all constituents are not congruent to the morphological markers of a Croatian DIR OBJ (M.PL) which are –*e*. In this instance, the grammatical well-formedness of the EL island overrides the projected morphological marking of the Croatian clause.

5 Conclusion and findings

This chapter has examined features of the Croatian-dominant speech of 25 speakers across three generations. We observe a number of language contact phenomena that are also found in other studies. On the level of phonology and as a very general observation, some informants (across generations) show evidence of the phoneme /l/ pronounced as a 'light l', i.e. with the tongue closer to the alveolar ridge, rather than the velarised 'dark l'. Voicing of /s/ in front of sonorants occurs amongst some Gen.2 and Gen.3 informants, which is another influence of Italian phonology.

On the level of the lexicon, we observe the employment of lexical transfers, discourse markers and loan translations from the other language, Italian, and also Croatian-Italian code-switching. Italian-origin lexical transfers, typically nouns, are morphologically and phonologically integrated in the speech of Gen.1 speakers, but integration is variable in the speech of Gen.2 and Gen.3 speakers, especially in relation to toponyms. Verbs, on the other hand, are universally integrated, regardless of generational membership. Loan translations, as a proportion of the overall level of Italian influence in speakers' repertoires, are reasonably conspicuous. These range from constructions that are irregular but comprehensible to HMLD.Cro speakers to incomprehensible ones. Almost all loan translations come from Gen.2 or Gen.3 speakers, with only one (also relatively transparent) loan translation recorded from a Gen.1 speaker. Changes in the valency of some verbs or in the choice of prepositions that collocate with them are observable. These occur in the speech of Gen.2 speakers only.

Code-switching occurs in intra- and inter-clausal positions as well as across changes of turn and speaker. One example (27) contains instances of different types of code-switching amongst three speakers belonging to different generational groups. There are certain sociolinguistic features (e.g. code-switching to quote others) and discourse-pragmatic ones (e.g. emphasis, augmentation, contrast), and to a lesser extent, socio-psychological ones (e.g. perceived proficiency level to express certain kinds of 'talk') that account for code-switching. However, the overall picture is that for many speakers and in many interactions when communicating with other Croatian-Italian bilinguals, code-switching is unmarked and otherwise unremarkable.

An area of interest is the occurrence of the possessive adjective *svoj* in sentence-initial position as part of a subject noun phrase. The Italian equivalent *suo* can occupy this function and the phi-features of *suo* have been transferred onto Croatian *svoj*. Some changes are recorded in the phi-features of nouns and other attributives in noun phrases, particularly in relation to gender where the gender of the equivalent Italian form is transferred onto the Croatian form, resulting in *enigma* 'enigma' and *ministarstvo* 'ministry' marked as masculine nouns.

Some changes in case marking of nouns and preceding attributives in NPs are found, again only amongst younger-generation speakers that otherwise conform to Ďurovič's (1983) implicativity scale. The only exception to the expectations of the implicativity scale is the pair LOC < > ACC, which is a well-known phenomenon in non-standard varieties of HMLD.Cro (Jutronić-Tihomirović 1988/1989). Some possessive constructions have periphrastic features, i.e. employment of *od* 'of/from' in constructions that typically feature 'possessee + possessor-GEN' in HMLD.Cro. The default equivalent construction in Italian is 'possessee + *di* 'of' + possessor'. The influence of some non-standard HMLD.Cro varieties cannot be discounted here as a co-determining factor. Verbal aspect and speakers' distinction of this feature via the formal differences in verb forms in Croatian is, amongst at least 3 of the 14 Gen.2 speakers, subject to some variation. Where non-target forms occur, perfective forms replace target imperfective ones. Congruent to Pereltsvaig's (2008) and Polinsky's (2006, 2008) studies, there are no difficulties with tense attested; aspect is the only feature of verbs that may be prone to change.

Particular types of intra-clausal code-switching, such as that occurring between an attributive and a noun in an NP or between an auxiliary verb and a main verb in a VP, yield mixed outcomes. For example, feature-marking that is target for both languages in a mixed-language NP is recorded, but perhaps only due to a coincidence in the feature marking of feminine plurals, which is the same in both languages. Further, feature marking of an Italian main verb is not congruent to the target form in the function of a past participle. Here, the feature of marking gender in Croatian past participles is a universal feature of this grammatical category, whereas in Italian, only certain past participles are marked for gender – those co-occurring with AUX *essere*. This cross-linguistic asymmetry between feature marking of past participles may account for the occurrence of an infinitive as a more 'transparent' form.

References

Aligheri, Dante 1321. *The Divine Comedy*. Vol. 3 (*Paradiso*). Trans. Courtney Langdon. Available at: https://oll.libertyfund.org/titles/alighieri-the-divine-comedy-vol-3-paradiso-english-trans (accessed 1 August 2019)

Backus, Ad & Margreet Dorleijn. 2009. Loan translations versus code-switching. In Barbara Bullock & Almeida Jacqueline Toribio (eds.), *The Cambridge Handbook of Linguistic Code-switching*, 75–94. Cambridge: Cambridge University Press.

Bedore, Lisa M., Elizabeth D. Peña, Connie L. Summers, Karin M. Boerger, Maria D. Resendiz, Kai Greene, Thomas M. Bohman & Ronald B. Glllam. 2012. The measure matters: Language dominance profiles across measures in Spanish–English bilingual children. *Bilingualism: Language and Cognition* 15(3). 616–629.

Belaj, Branimir & Darko Matovac. 2015. On the article-like use of the indefinite determiners *jedan* and *neki* in Croatian and other Slavic languages. *Suvremena lingvistika* 79. 1–20.

Berruto, Gaetano. 1987. Lingua, dialetto, diglossia, dilalia. In Günter Holtus & Johannes Kramer (eds.) *Romania et Slavia adriatica. Festschrift für Žarko Muljačić*. 57–81. Hamburg: Buske.

Browne, Wayles. 1974. Serbo-Croatian enclitics for English-speaking learners. *Journal of Slavic Linguistics* 12(1). 249–283.

Clyne, Michael. 2003. *Dynamics of Language Contact*. Cambridge: Cambridge University Press.

Consani, Carlo, Paola Desideri, Francesca Guazzelli & Carmela Perta (eds.), 2009. *Alloglossie e comunità alloglotte nell'Italia contemporanea. Teorie, applicazioni e descrizioni, prospettive*. Roma: Bulzoni.

Curdt-Christiansen, Xiao Lan & Elizabeth Lanza. 2018. Language management in multilingual families: Efforts, measures and challenges. *Multilingua* 37(2). 123–130.

Čilaš, Ankica, Irena Drpić & Mijo Lončarić. 2007. La lingua dei Croati di Trieste. In J.C. Damir Murković (ed.), *I croati a Trieste*, 471–483. Trieste: Edizioni Comunita Croata di Trieste.

D'Agostino, Mari. 2012. *Sociolinguistica dell'Italia contemporanea*. Bologna: Mulino.

De Houwer, Annick. 2017. Bilingual language acquisition. In Paul Fletcher and Brian MacWhinney (eds.), *The handbook of child language*. 219–250. Hoboken, NJ: Wiley-Blackwell

Ďurovič, Ľubomír. 1983. The case systems in the language of diaspora children. *Slavica Lundensia* 9. 21–94.

Garrett, Peter. 2010. *Attitudes to language*. Cambridge: Cambridge University Press.

Grosjean, François. 2013. Bilingual and monolingual language modes. In Carol Chapelle (ed.) *The Encyclopedia of Applied Linguistics*. Malden, MA: Wiley-Blackwell.

Harwood, Jake, Howard Giles & Richard Y. Bourhis. 1994. The genesis of vitality theory: Historical patterns and discoursal dimensions. *International Journal of the Sociology of Language* 108. 167–206.

Hlavac, Jim. 1999. 32 years on and *still* triggering: psycholinguistic processes as motivation for switching amongst Croatian-English bilinguals. *Monash University Linguistic Papers* 2 (1). 11–24.

Hlavac, Jim. 2003. *Second-generation speech. Lexicon, code-switching and morpho-syntax of Croatian-English bilinguals*. Bern: Peter Lang.

ISTAT [Italian National Institute of Statistics]. 2014. *Linguistic diversity among foreign citizens in Italy Years 2011–2012*. https://www.istat.it/en/archive/129304

ISTAT. [Italian National Institute of Statistics]. 2016. *Bilancio demografico nazionale. Testo integrale*. Roma: Istituto nazionale di statistica.

Jutronić-Tihomirović, Dunja. 1988/1989. Jezično prilagođavanje na sintaktičkom nivou. [Linguistic adaptation on the syntactic level] *Radovi razdjela filoloških znanosti* 18. 51–60.

Karan, Marc E. 2011. Understanding and forecasting ethnolinguistic vitality. *Journal of Multilingual and Multicultural Development* 32(2). 137–149.

Klaić, Bratoljub. 1982. *Rječnik stranih riječi* [Dictionary of Foreign Words]. Zagreb: Nakladni zavod Matice hrvatske.

Krpina, Zdravka. 2016. Nastava hrvatskoga jezika u Italiji [Croatian language instruction in Italy]. *Jezik* 63(4–5). 151–166.

Li Wei. 2018. Translanguaging as a practical theory of language. *Applied Linguistics* 39(1). 9–30.

Matica – Mjesečna revija Hrvatske matice iseljenika. [Matica – Monthly magazine of the Croatian Heritage Foundation]. 2018. Svečano započela hrvatska nastava u Milanu [Instruction in Croatian officially launched in Milan], *Siječanj/Veljača [January/February]* 1–2. 20.

Myers-Scotton, Carol. 2006. Natural codeswitching knocks on the laboratory door. *Bilingualism: Language and Cognition* 9(2). 203–212.

Pereltsvaig, Asya. 2008. Aspect in Russian as grammatical rather than lexical notion: Evidence from Heritage Russian. *Russian Linguistics* 32(1). 27–42.

Polinsky, Maria. 2006. Incomplete acquisition: American Russian. *Journal of Slavic Linguistics* 14. 161–219.
Polinsky, Maria. 2008. Without aspect. In Greville Corbett & Michael Noonan (eds.), *Case and Grammatical Relations, Studies in honor of Bernard Comrie*, 263–82. Amsterdam: John Benjamins.
State Office for Croats Abroad. 2016b. Hrvatsko iseljeništvo u Talijanskoj Republici [Croatian emigrants in Italy]. http://www.hrvatiizvanrh.hr/hr/hmiu/hrvatsko-iseljenistvo-u-republici-italiji/26
Tuttitalia.it. 2019a. Croati in Italia [Croats in Italy]. https://www.tuttitalia.it/statistiche/cittadini-stranieri/croazia/ (accessed 22 September 2018)
Tuttitalia.it. 2019b. Bosniaci in Italia [Bosnians in Italy]. http://www.tuttitalia.it/statistiche/cittadini-stranieri/bosnia-erzegovina/ (accessed 22 September 2018)
Udier, Sanda Lucija. 2006. Položaj glagolskih enklitika u nastavi hrvatskoga kao stranoga jezika za početnike [The position of verbal clitics in the teaching of Croatian as a foreign language to elementary level students]. *Lahor: časopis za hrvatski kao materinski, drugi i strani jezik* [Lahor: Journal for Croatian as a native, second and foreign language] 1(1). 61–68.
Županović Filipin, Nada & Karmen Bevanda. 2015. La commutazione di codice nel bilinguismo croato-italiano: analisi di un tipo testuale. *Italica Belgradensia* 1. 27–48.
Županović Filipin, Nada & Karmen Bevanda Tolić. 2015. Tra due sponde linguistiche: Commutazione di codice in due generazioni di una famiglia bilingue. *Studia Romanica et Anglica Zagrabiensia* 60. 55–83.

Vesna Piasevoli
The Croatian speech of first- and second-generation Croats in Trieste

1 Introduction

Croatians and Italians have historically had a great deal of contact with one another. As countries with long coastlines on opposite sides of the Adriatic Sea, contact has always been close, but at times strained. This led one Croatian historian to pessimistically remark that close proximity "has also at times brought about a darker side to relations characterised by mutual distrust, open enmity and even conflict" (Čoralić 1997: 9). To an extent, this ambivalent sentiment is still felt today in Trieste, an Italian outpost that reaches eastwards towards Croatia's Istrian peninsula. The etymology of the city's name, derived from Indo-European *terg* 'market' (cf. Cro. *trg* 'town square') with the suffix *-este* meaning 'city' perhaps foretold its future development as a magnet for those living in surrounding regions (Benussi 2001). Along with other groups, Croats, as well as Slovenes, have had regular intense contact with Trieste and have resided there for centuries. Glagolitic inscriptions inside churches in Trieste are but one of the numerous symbols of a long-standing Croatian presence in the city (Parovel 2013). At least since the early fifteenth century there were reports of Croats travelling to or transiting through Trieste, *Fin dal 1413 abbiamo notizia del trasporto di genti croate sul Carso triestino* 'Since 1413 we have received notice of the transport of Croatian people to the Karst Plateau of Trieste' (Bonifacio and Cimador 2013: 122). These initial movements of people coincided with the Ottoman incursions towards Venetian and Hapsburg frontier areas in the north of Istria and in Friuli (Čoralić 2001: 59).

Historically, the period in which the presence of Croats in Trieste was perhaps the most 'prominent' was that of the Austro-Hungarian Empire. At that time, Trieste was the Empire's main port and an important trading and commercial centre in its own right (Strčić 2007). Trieste flourished at a time when neighbouring Istria and Dalmatia remained poor and underdeveloped. Sailors from the east coast of the Adriatic Sea and its many islands, from Istria in the north to the Bay of

---

Note: I would like to express my gratitude to Karmen Petrić for assisting me with the composition of this chapter in English and to thank Paula Jakus for her assistance in the formatting and presentation of the chapter.

Vesna Piasevoli, University of Trieste

https://doi.org/10.1515/9781501503917-009

Cattaro in the south, were employed by Trieste-based shipping companies sailing under the Austro-Hungarian flag. It was during this time of the Empire, in the nineteenth century that Croatian, often known under the designation of "Illyrian" (Jurišić 2003: 38), began to be taught in Trieste. There are sources that record not only the presence of Croatian students at Trieste's Nautical Academy, but that instruction in Croatian took place there also (D'Alessio and Diklić 2007: 425–467).

Trieste is the largest urban centre proximate to Istria, located on its northwestern fringe. Many Istrian Croats live, work and study there. There is a substantial number of people who commute to or from Trieste on a daily basis: those from Croatian Istria usually work in hospitality, aged care or have semi-skilled jobs; amongst those heading in the opposite direction, there are Italian-language teachers based in Trieste who commute daily to teach at schools in Buje (It. *Buie*) or Rijeka (It. *Fiume*) in Croatia.

The period after WWI, which witnessed the arrival of fascism, was a very difficult time for Croats, Slovenes and other Slavs living in Trieste. The Slovene *Narodni dom* 'National Hall', a centre not only of the large Slovene community in Trieste, but also of the Croatian and other Slavic minorities, was burnt down in 1920 (Pahor 2007). This ushered in a period in which the official recognition of their presence was reduced to a minimum. Many were required or strongly encouraged to change their surnames, e.g. from *Crnković* to *Neri* or from *Ivanac* to *Giovannini*. In other instances, the final 'ć' was omitted or vowels were added, e.g. *Grgurić* became *Gregori*, *Lovrenčić* became *Laurini*, *Božić* or *Božič* became *Bossi* (Bonifacio and Cimador 2013: 12). Interestingly, it was only wealthy and powerful families, such as the *Kozulich* or *Cosulich* families who were able to retain their original surname ending in '-*ch*'. Common allegiance to the Catholic Church and attendance at Italian-language services also enabled assimilation, something that distinguished Croats from Trieste's Serbian Orthodox residents. But overall, Croats (and Slovenes) in Trieste suffered the effects of a paradoxical policy that sought to render them 'invisible' via assimilation and changing of surnames, and that was also overtly or covertly discriminatory towards its Slavic-origin residents via pejorative terms by which Croats and Slovenes were referred to, regardless of whether they lived within or beyond the city's boundaries. Amongst Trieste's residents, identity negotiation traverses notions of 'long-standing' vs. 'recently-arrived', Friulian Italian vs. Istrian Italian vs. Istrian Croatian/Slovene, Italophone vs. Slavophone, '(economic) migrant' vs. 'refugee', with variation in self-perception, self-presentation and the performance of ethnolinguistic identity.

Immediately after WWII, Trieste's status remained unresolved until the problem of border demarcation was finally settled between Italy and Yugoslavia in 1954. During this time of uncertainty, many residents of Trieste emigrated to overseas countries, and amongst them was a large number of Croats (Strčić 2007).

Notwithstanding an on-going presence in the city, but perhaps because Trieste was usually seen as a 'transit destination', many of the city's Croatian-language institutions are of recent vintage. For example, Croatian-language church services were introduced in 1985, only on a monthly basis, and largely due to the efforts of one family. The outbreak of war in Croatia was a factor that galvanised Trieste's Croats leading to the establishment of organisations that aided refugees from Croatia and Bosnia-Hercegovina. This later led to the organisation of assistance for more recent (economic) migrants to Trieste. In 1992, the *Comitato pro Croazia* 'Committee for Croatia', was established and in 1996, the association formed a branch of the pre-eminent Croatian cultural organisation *Matica hrvatska* 'Matrix Croatica'. In 1994, not long after Croatia's declaration of independence, a Croatian consulate was opened, and in 1999 the *Comunità croata* 'the Croatian Association' was established as a formal organisation. In the same year a Croatian language school was opened in Trieste (Vascotto 2001; Krpina 2016). In 2002, those based in Trieste were instrumental in establishing the *Federazione delle comunità croate in Italia* 'Federation of Croatian associations in Italy' as an umbrella organisation of Croatian communities in Trieste, Rome, Milan, Udine and Molise (Piasevoli 2007).

2 Profile of informants

All informants are well known to the author in her capacity as a teacher of Croatian at school and university level and as an active member of Trieste's Croatian community. Descriptions given here reflect the author's long-term and on-going contact with them. The perspective of the author towards (fellow-) Croatian-speakers is one of in-group member and co-protagonist in shared interactions, as well as one of researcher who has systematically and non-systematically collected linguistic and other data from and about Croatian-speakers in Trieste. The positionality of the author is akin to that of an ethnographic researcher who is a co-member of the sociolinguistic minority, while the author's on-going relationship with the informants has been punctuated here by the formal process of data collection. The data sample collected is the basis of the corpus of examples presented here, and the discussion provided is based on an analysis of this linguistic corpus only.

The data sample contains recorded interviews with five first-generation informants born in Croatia or Bosnia-Herzegovina who migrated in young adulthood (hereafter: 'Gen.1A'), two first-generation informants born in Croatia who migrated as children (hereafter: 'Gen.1B') and three informants born in Italy (hereafter: 'Gen.2'). Interviews lasted from 15 to 36 minutes, and the number of words in Croatian and/or Italian utterances ranged from 641 to 1,680 per informant. Interviews were conducted individually by the author with one informant at a time. The format of the interview was semi-formal, with the author inviting the informants initially to share information about their childhood and formative years. From there, an informal dialogue usually developed and the informants traversed a number of topics, sometimes also switching the perspective from which they spoke, i.e. that of an individual versus that of a member of one or multiple groups. Details on the informants that make up the data sample are given in Table 1 below.

Table 1: Informants' demographic data and linguistic data on their speech samples.

Informant	Generation	Year and place of birth	Approx. length of recorded speech sample (mins.)	No. of tokens	No. of turns	No. of Croatian monolingual turns	No. of Cro.-Ital. bilingual turns	No. of Italian-origin forms
AA	Gen.1A	1934, Gračišće	16	1029	64	49	15	17
NA	Gen.1A	1942, Sali	21	851	56	42	14	14
ZL	Gen.1A	1943, Zagreb	20	817	40	30	10	10
LjJ	Gen.1A	1945, Bihać	23	1067	46	34	12	12
MR	Gen.1A	1960, Lič	18	1059	45	36	9	11
MB	Gen.1B	1943, Nerezine	23	887	92	70	22	27
EO	Gen.1B	1953, Pula	34	1153	136	118	18	19
MŠ	Gen.2	1947, Trieste	36	1680	26	21	5	14
JV	Gen.2	1947, Modena	16	758	40	24	16	18
RP	Gen.2	1989, Trieste	15	641	60	43	17	17
Total			222	9942	605	467	138	159
Ave. per informant			22.2	994	61	47	14	16

In the recorded interviews with informants, the author mostly spoke monolingual Croatian, but the informants were free to draw on either language in the interview. The three right-hand columns in Table 1 show informants' turns and the codes employed in them. Of note is that despite the differing sociolinguistic profiles of the informants across the three generational groups, there are few substantial differences in the proportional contribution of each language or both languages in their turns. About three-quarters of these consist of monolingual Croatian utterances, and about one quarter of bilingual utterances containing Croatian and Italian forms. The informants were told they would be invited to participate in a collection of biographical or personal accounts about Croats living in Trieste.

2.1 Sociolinguistic biographies of the informants

Information on informants' background is provided here, focusing on the acquisition and use of both languages.

Informant AA (Gen.1A, F, 83) was born in 1934 in Istria, in Gračišće near Pazin. She came to Italy with her husband and young son in 1966, and initially lived in a refugee camp. At the age of 83, AA is still a businesswoman in charge of a large workforce. A large number of her employees are Croats, Serbs and Bosnians as well as others from the former SFRY, with whom she uses Croatian. Her son, daughter, as well as her grandchildren understand Croatian, but do not speak it. She says of language in her family before marriage:

> *Moji doma su govorili m'ješano, talijanski i hrvatski; hrvatski jezik kao što je po selima, dijalekt.*
>
> 'My family at home spoke a mixture of Italian and Croatian; the type of Croatian that was spoken across the villages, dialect.'

Informant NA (Gen.1A, F, 75) was born in Sali, on the island of Dugi Otok in 1942. Upon completion of high school, she moved to Trieste and was married there in 1966. She describes her husband's family position towards her in the following way:

> *Rodbina od moga muža uvijek me je gledala kao 'šćava' . . .*
>
> 'My husband's family always considered me a 'šćava' . . . '

The term *s'ciavo* M / *s'ciava* F (presented here in Italian orthographical form) is specific to the Triestine dialect, from old Venetian, and is a form based on one or both possible etymologies: 1) *schiavo* 'slave'; 2) *slavo* 'Slav' (Doria 1984: 59). Another informant, MR, provides the following comment:

> *Šćavi su za Treštine Zlavi, gente dell'est, ljudi s istoka.*
>
> 'For people from Trieste, 'šćavi' are 'Zlavi' [Slavs] 'gente dell'est, people from the east.'

Until her retirement, NA worked as a sales assistant. She is a widow with two adult sons who speak Croatian, although only with relatives. They never attended formal instruction in Croatian. NA attends Croatian events and mass. She reports the following about herself:

> *Malo sam znala talijanski; moj svekar je govorio da sam kao jedna izgubljena ptica. Hrvatski mi je služio za posao. Zapravo, kad su moja djeca bila malena, onda nije bilo hrvatske škole, čak nije bilo poželjno ni čuti ni govoriti hrvatski na ulici ili u autobusu.*

> 'I spoke very little Italian; my father in-law used to say that I was like a lost bird. I used Croatian for work. When my children were little, there was no Croatian school, and it wasn't desirable for one to speak Croatian on the streets or on public transport.'

Informant ZL (Gen.1A, F, 74) was born in 1943 in Zagreb, where she completed high school. She moved to Rome in 1962 for work, and she started speaking exclusively Italian.

> *Moja teta u Njemačkoj veli: „A jesi se ti zaljubila?" „Jesam, u Rim, u grad". Nije onda bilo kao što je sad. To je bilo prije više od 40 godina . . .*

> 'My aunt in Germany said: "Have you fallen in love?" "I have, with Rome, with the city." It was not the same then as it is now. That was more than 40 years ago . . . '

Her mother was Slovenian. Until she started school, she spoke Slovenian at home, but later supressed and forgot it. After retiring, she moved to Trieste, where she became acquainted with members of the Croatian community, with whom she speaks Croatian. She often visits her hometown Zagreb, where she has childhood friends. She is not married and has no children.

Informant LjJ (Gen.1A, F, 72) was born in 1945 in Bihać, Bosnia-Herzegovina. Her mother was Croatian whilst her father was Slovenian. She completed high school in Bihać and then studied in Ljubljana. She moved to Trieste in 1981, when she got married. She is active in Trieste's Croatian community. Her husband is a Slovene from Trieste. Both by birth and marriage she comes from a mixed family, which could be said is a typical family from Trieste. Nowadays, she speaks Slovenian, Italian and Triestine dialect with her husband, while at the beginning of their marriage they used to speak only Slovenian. They have one daughter with whom she speaks in Croatian. With her family, LjJ frequently visits Zagreb where her siblings live. She also visits her old friends who still live in Bihać. She describes her origins in the following way:

> *Ja sam kćerka Slovenca i Hrvatice rodom iz Crikvenice. Moj dido, mamin tata, je bio građevinski inženjer i konstruir'o je ceste i mostove po Austro-Ugarskoj, po Hrvatskoj i po Bosni. Tako je moja mama stigla u Bosnu . . .*

> 'I am a daughter of a Slovene and a Croat from Crikvenica. My maternal granddad was a civil engineer and he built roads and bridges throughout the Austro-Hungarian Empire, in Croatia and Bosnia. That is how my mum came to Bosnia.'

Informant MR (Gen.1A, F, 57) was born in 1960 in Lič, Croatia. She completed high school in Rijeka. After marrying in 1980, she moved to Trieste. She has twin girls who also speak Croatian. Before her children started school, she spoke only Croatian with them, while nowadays she alternates between Croatian and Italian. She travels to Lič every weekend with her husband, sometimes with her daughters as well. She reports the following on her speaking habits at home:

> Ja govorim kako smo mi govorili doma, ne govorim pravilno, književno, ma čak ni moje kćeri ne govoriju zato što sam ja uvijek govorila 'po moju'...
>
> 'I speak as we spoke at home, I don't speak correct standard Croatian, even my daughters don't speak it either because I always spoke Croatian in "my own way"...'

Informant MB (Gen.1B, F, 74) is a Gen.1B-speaker who was born in Nerezine on the island of Lošinj in 1943. Her father was Italian whilst her mother was Croatian but spoke only Italian with her. With her maternal grandparents she spoke only Croatian:

> Nono i nona nisu znali ništa talijanski, samo hrvatski... dijalekt.
>
> 'Granddad and grandma didn't know any Italian, just Croatian... a dialect.'

She finished first grade in Nerezine and then moved to Trieste at the age of 10. She attended school and then worked as a bookkeeper until her retirement in Trieste. Nowadays, she alternates between living in Trieste and Nerezine. In order to improve her language skills, she attended an advanced Croatian course in Trieste organised by the Croatian Community. She has no children and speaks Croatian only with her Croat neighbour from Slavonia.

Informant EO (Gen.1B, F, 64) was born in 1953 in Pula. Her father was Croatian and her mother an Italian from Istria. She learnt Croatian from the children in the refugee camp that she was evacuated to after WWII. She never attended Croatian classes. She arrived in Italy in 1962 and worked as a shop assistant in Trieste using Croatian with some of her customers. Nowadays, she uses Croatian only when holidaying in Istria.

Informant MŠ (Gen.2, M, 70) was born in 1947 in Trieste. His father's family comes from Šibenik, and his mother is from the nearby island of Žirje. His father's family left Šibenik during WWII for political and economic reasons, and later had all their property confiscated. MŠ studied and graduated from the University of Trieste. He speaks Croatian with the members of Trieste's Croatian community and with his relatives in Croatia.

> *Imali smo poznanstva radi trgovine jer dida moj, i pradida, je trgovao sa Trstom, za vrijeme Austrije još, i onda je bila prilika nešto kupiti i slučajno je ostao ...*
>
> 'We knew people thanks to our trading business, my grandfather and great grandfather were trading with Trieste during the Austrian ruling and they happened to stay ... '

Informant JV (Gen.2, F, 70) was born in 1947 in Modena. Her father was a Croat born in Split and her mother was an Italian who taught in the Italian school on the island of Mljet during WWII. Her parents first emigrated to Venezuela and later moved back to Europe, this time to Trieste. JV learnt Croatian from her relatives in Split and the nearby island of Brač. She studied Croatian for one year at Trieste University. She is a musician with two adult children who live in Modena. They do not speak Croatian, nor do they have contact with Croatia. Her younger brother and sister, who live in Trieste, speak Croatian but are not involved with the Croatian community. Her brother's children attend Slovenian classes. During the interview, she endeavoured to speak standard Croatian language. She reported the following:

> *Kući, moja majka i moj tata oni su razgovarali italijanski, ali tamo u Venezueli ja sam imala rodice, moja baka Jerka i tetu. Pa onda ja san samo slušala da oni su razgovarali hrvatski.*
>
> 'At home, my mum and dad were speaking Italian, but in Venezuela I had my cousins, my grandma Jerka and my aunt. I would listen to them speak Croatian.'

The last informant RP (Gen.2, F, 28) was born in 1989 in Trieste. She has a twin sister, their father is half-Italian and half-Croatian from Rijeka, and their mother is the first-generation informant MR. RP was one of the first people to go through formal Croatian schooling and studied Croatian at the University of Trieste. She speaks Croatian mostly on visits to her mother's birthplace, Lič.

3 Abridged narratives of attitudes towards Croats and Croatian-speakers in Trieste

Trieste is home to around 200,000 people – the same number of people that lived in the city 100 years ago when it was still a part of the Austro-Hungarian Empire. It is an ageing city that has experienced a high level of emigration and a low level of immigration in comparison to other cities in northern Italy. Over the centuries, Trieste's Italian heritage has been strongly influenced by the long period of Habsburg administration and centuries-long contact with Slovenes and Croats.

Trieste's character as a 'borderline-city' was only further heightened by the Cold War and its role as a city that was a western outpost almost encircled by the "iron curtain". For Croats in the former SFRY, it was a gateway to the rest of the world. In the 1970s and 1980s, Trieste, especially the area around the square Piazza Ponte Rosso, was the major Western European shopping destination for residents of the former SFRY. Amongst the residents of Trieste, regardless of their linguistic or national background, the city's peripheral or borderline status is a cultural meme that is manifested in everyday language in the following way:

> *Pogotovo preko, oltre Monfalcone è Italia. Znaju reći: Vado in Italia. A ovo? Ovo je Trst, posebna zona.*
>
> 'Especially over there, beyond Monfalcone that's where Italy is. They say: "Vado in Italia" [I'm going to Italy] "And what is this?" "This is Trieste, a special zone".' (NA, Gen.1A, F, 75)

The dialect of Italian spoken in Trieste is a mix of Venetian, spoken along the entire Adriatic coast from the time of the Venetian Empire up to and beyond the time of Austro-Hungarian rule, with influences of German, Greek, Slovenian and Croatian. Loanwords from the latter (with their representation according to standard Croatian orthography given in square brackets) include *baba* [baba] 'old or chatty woman' (Ital. *donna anziana, chiacchierona*), *patoc* [potok] 'brook' (Ital. *ruscello*), *spavar* [spavati] 'to sleep' (Ital. *dormire*), *zima* [zima] 'cold weather' (Ital. *freddo intenso*) with one bearing a semantic meaning different from HMLD. Cro, *cisto* 'broke' (Ital. *squattrinato*) c.f [čisto] = 'clean', (Doria 1984: 44, 155, 442, 660, 810). Ljubičić (2009) features a description of Croatian-origin words in her orthographical representation in Venetian dialects.

Both first- and second-generation informants in this sample report that they freely use Croatian at home and in public situations. However, personal and anecdotal information from an older Gen.1A informant suggests that it was not always like this:

> *Istrijani i Treštini dosta su „skučeni", izvan Rijeke ne postoji više Hrvatska ... Otkuda ste Vi, pita me. Ja kažem, iz okolice Zadra. A ona, mi son' di Fiume ... I gotovo. Dalje ne znaju. Za njih je sve Jugo ...*
>
> 'People from Istria and Trieste are very "limited", there is no Croatia beyond Rijeka ... "Where are you from?" she asks me. I say: "from near Zadar." She says: *mi son' di Fiume* [Trieste dialect for "I am from Rijeka"] and that's it. They don't know any other places. To them everything is Yugo.' (NA, Gen.1A, F, 75)

The use of Croatian in Trieste is recalled by MŠ, one of the oldest Gen.2 informants, in the following way. His comment is provided below via the English gloss only:

> My mother tongue? Even my parents don't know which language I started speaking first, Croatian or Italian . . . I have always been bilingual . . . With my parents I spoke Croatian, but with my peers at school I spoke exclusively Italian. I never mentioned my Croatian background . . . I was almost embarrassed and didn't want to be teased . . . There were many derogatory terms used for Slavs in general, such as *šćavo / s'ciavo*.
>
> . . . in Trieste the situation was not easy . . . there was a lot of hatred towards Slavs . . .
>
> Dad used to say that he was a Dalmatian, not a Croat . . . There was a ban on all Yugoslav assets in Trieste; this only applied to Trieste as they were scared that Tito would annex the city to Yugoslavia if there were too many buildings owned by Yugoslavs.
>
> Therefore, in the post-WWII years the situation was very tense and difficult. There were about 100,000 refugees from Istria, the *esuli* who saw no prospect in staying in Trieste, and who then emigrated to Argentina, America and Australia. My family stayed as we had property, which we had bought before the War . . . however, we also wanted to leave. My father hadn't visited Yugoslavia for 20 years. There were many problems . . . my grandfather was convicted for being wealthy and other things . . . but my mum went every year. When my mum, my brother and I would cross the border in the 1950s, we were often the only ones on the train as no one used to cross the border, the Iron Curtain . . . It was very strict, an hour at the border, although there was no one but us. There were hardly any tourists.

The position that their country of origin had towards them is described in the following way:

> Croats were not well regarded, so even if they had attempted to organise themselves in societies or clubs, they would have had both Italy and Yugoslavia against them. It was not in the interest of Socialist Yugoslavia to have Croats united in a community in which they identified themselves as such, as Croats. Perhaps if they had identified as Yugoslavs, it would have been different.

In relation to his own personal identity, he has the following to report:

> I did a bit of research on the history of both Trieste and Croatia . . . and I found myself having an identity crisis. I didn't know who I was when I was younger. My father was an *apolide*, a stateless person, and I had a green passport, not a red one like those who lived in Yugoslavia, because I lived abroad. We were not recognised in Yugoslavia since for them diaspora people were always the enemy as they were usually against communism . . . I don't know . . . I was not accepted by anyone. All of my schooling has been in Italian, but I visited Croatia every summer, first Zagreb and then Dalmatia. I therefore never lost contact with the language.

It appears that feelings of fear and shame experienced by Croats living in Trieste since the end of WWII had gradually subsided by the 1990s. From then on they reported that they could freely express themselves and openly recount their experiences.

4 Presentation and analysis of spoken data

All Gen.1A and Gen.1B informants endeavoured to speak standard Croatian, particularly at the start of the interview. The effect of monitoring and the observer's paradox is well known (Labov 1972: 209). However, as the interview progressed and when discussing certain topics, informants would often switch between standard Croatian or a dialect or non-standard variety. In view of the occupational background of the interviewer, some felt the need to apologise for switching between dialect and standard Croatian. When talking about anything closely connected to Trieste or Italy, informants use Italian words and switch languages seamlessly. Gen.1A and Gen.1B speakers were educated during the time of former Yugoslavia and their use of Croatian is characteristic of those who acquired it in this period and bears few examples of some of the lexical changes that have occurred since Croatian independence, eg. use of *hiljada* ('thousand' instead of *tisuća*), referring to months by their international names, giving ordinal numbers in Italian etc. Gen.2 speakers' discourse was less spontaneous and in some cases quite self-monitored, at least initially. Gen.2 informants most frequently answered questions with short responses only.

Despite the long-standing presence of Croats in Trieste, a 'stabilised Triestino Croatian koine' has never developed (Čilaš, Drpić and Lončarić 2007: 481) and there is variation in the forms of Croatian used by informants across but also within generational groups. This is reflective of the different geographical areas that they come from and the regiolects spoken there. The abbreviation 'TRS.Cro' is therefore employed not as a designation to refer to a specific variety spoken by Croatian-origin residents of Trieste, but as a hypernym that encompasses the forms found in the data sample presented in this chapter. Examples of informants' speech are presented in this section in such a way that the orthographical representation of items reflects their phonological form: phonologically integrated Italian-origin items are represented according to Croatian orthography; unintegrated forms are presented according to their Italian spelling.

The following phenomena are identified in this chapter: lexical transference, including a break-up of forms according to different parts of speech (4.1); loan translations (4.2); changes in structure (4.3) including the sub-sections: emergence of *jedan* as an indefinite article (4.3.1); personal pronouns (4.3.2); numbers and case marking (4.3.3), case marking in NPs (4.3.4), possessive constructions with *od* 'from' and GEN. (4.3.5), word order changes, including position of clitics, clause-final adverbs, noun and adjective NPs (4.3.6), dependent clause conjunctions (4.3.7.), syntactic calques (4.3.8), syntactic change and verbal aspect (4.3.9); and code-switching (4.4). Examples are presented below that are reflective of phenomena that vary from those found in HMLD.Cro varieties. Information is provided on the total number of examples that vary from HMLD.Cro. At the same time, a quantification of all forms and the number that represent variations from the norm is not included.

4.1 Lexical transference

Terms and realia specific to Trieste or the Italian context are common sources for lexical transfers Examples (1) and (2) contain designations of occupations.

(1) *radila   sam   kao   **ragioniere***
  work-PST.F.SG AUX-1SG like accountant-NOM.M.SG
  'I worked as an **accountant**...' (MB,Gen.1B,F,74)

  Ital.:   Ho lavorato come **ragioniere**...
  HMLD.Cro: Radila sam kao **računovođa**...

(2) ***prete***   *dođe*   *i*   *reče*
  priest-NOM.M.SG come-3SG and say-3SG
  'The **priest** came and said...' (LjJ,Gen.1A,F,72)

  Ital.:   Il **prete** venne e disse...
  HMLD.Cro: **Svećenik** dođe i reče...

Two-word items also occur as intra-clausal insertions:

(3) *kad   je   K.   počela   u   školu   ići*
  when AUX-3SG K. start-PST.F.SG to+ACC school-ACC.F.SG go-INF.
  *sam   našla   **tipo amike**   pravilo*
  AUX-1SG find-PST.F.SG like girlfriend-ACC.F.PL make-PST.N.SG
  se   rođendane
  REFL birthday-ACC.M.PL
  'When K. started school I found **like [female] girlfriends.** There were birthday parties...' (LjJ,Gen.1A,F,72)

  Ital.:   Quando K. ha iniziato la scuola, ho trovato **tipo amiche**, si facevano le feste di compleanno...
  HMLD.Cro: Kad je K. počela ići u školu, našla sam **recimo prijateljice**, pravilo se rođendane...

Most insertions are nouns. Some occur as adjectives where suffix markers of phi-features (here –*a* for FEM.SG) are common to both languages as in (4):

(4) sestra   je   bila   **brava**   u školi
    sister-NOM.F.SG AUX-3SG be-PST.F.SG good-NOM.F.SG school-LOC.F.SG
    'My sister was **good** at school...' (EO,Gen.1B,F,64)

   Ital.:   Mia sorella era **brava** a scuola...
   HMLD.Cro: Sestra mi je bila **dobra** u školi...

Historical language contact and the influence of Venetian Italian on Croatian Čakavian dialects are apparent in the vernaculars of Gen.1A informants who regularly use them. Informants' contact with the (Venetian-based) Triestine dialect has a conserving effect:

(5) muči   se   i   radi   živi   po   **šufitama**
    toil-3.SG REFL and work-3SG live-3SG in+LOC attics-LOC.F.PL
    'People have it hard, working and living in the **attics**' (AA,Gen.1A,F,83)

   Ital.:   Si fatica e lavora, si vive nelle **soffitte**...
   HMLD.Cro: Muči se i radi, živi po **tavanima**...

Here the Triestine dialect form *sufita* 'attic' (Doria 1984: 705) occurs that is congruent to a form in the informant's Istrian dialect, *šufita* with the same meaning. In the following example, a past participle form *corretto* 'correct-PST.PTCP' is inserted which contains phi-features of the donor language, Italian. The *-o* suffix is also congruent to the required morpheme of the recipient language, Croatian that has the multi-feature morpheme *–o* to also mark the features: PTCP.M.SG.

(6) imala   sam   ljubav   s   D.
    have-PST.F.SG AUX-1SG   love-ACC.F.SG with D.
    on   je   **corretto**   greške
    he   AUX-3SG correct-PST.PTCP mistake-ACC.F.PL
    'I was in a relationship with D... He used to **correct** my mistakes.'
    (JV,Gen.2,F,70)

   Ital.:   Ero fidanzata con D... Lui **correggeva** i miei errori
               (**correggere**-INF, **corretto**- PST.PTCP).
   HMLD.Cro: Hodala sam s D... On mi je **ispravljao** greške.

In (6), the Italian-origin insertion is a past participle that follows the Croatian AUX in forming a past tense construction. The features of the Croatian subject *on* ('he') for number (here SG) and gender (here MASC) are congruently marked on the PTCP via the invariable *–o* suffix, which is also the target suffix of an equivalent Croatian past participle: *ispravlja-o* ('correct' PTCP.M.SG).

The total number of lexical transfers uttered by the informants is 31; 24 single-word items and 7 two-word items. Frequency of single-word forms was highest amongst Gen.1B informants (12), with 8 provided by Gen.1A informants, and 4 from Gen.2. Roughly equal numbers of two-word or compound items were produced by speakers of all generations.

4.2 Loan translations

This section adopts Backus and Dorleijn's definition of loan translation (2009: 77) as "usage of morphemes in Language A that is the result of literal translation of one or more elements in a semantically equivalent expression in Language B". In (7) a repetition of the adverb *pomalo* 'slowly' occurs, based on the Italian sequencing of *piano piano* 'slowly slowly' (= 'gradually').

(7) bolja situacija je postala
better-NOM.F.SG situation-NOM.F.SG AUX-3SG become-PST.F.SG
pomalo pomalo kad je pao komunizam
slowly slowly when AUX-3SG fall-PST.M.SG communism-NOM.M.SG
'The situation **little by little** improved with the fall of communism.'
(MŠ,Gen.2,M,70)

Ital.: La situazione è migliorata **piano piano** con il crollo del comunismo
HMLD.Cro.: **Malo pomalo** situacija je postajala bolja kad je pao komunizam.

In (8) the influence of Italian *fare + qualcosa* 'to do + OBJ' is evident in the construction *napraviti + (polovicu) školu* 'to do + (half) school', an otherwise unknown collocation in Croatian:

(8) **škole** sam **napravila polovicu**
school-GEN.F.SG AUX-1SG make-PST.F.SG half-ACC.F.SG
hrvatske polovicu talijanske
Croatian-GEN.F.SG half-ACC.F.SG Italian-GEN.F.SG
'Half of **my schooling was** in Croatian and the other half in Italian.'
(AA,Gen.1A,F,83)

Ital.: **Ho fatto** metà **delle scuole** in croato, metà in italiano.
HMLD.Cro.: **Pola školovanja bilo je** na talijanskom, a pola na hrvatskom.

A similar high-frequency Italian collocation *mettere + qualcosa* 'to put + OBJ' is translated morpheme by morpheme into Croatian in:

(9) kad   sam   **stavila**   **firmu**   tu
    when   AUX-1SG   put-PST.F.SG   firm-ACC.F.SG   here
    'When I **established my firm** here...' (AA,Gen.1A,F,83)

    Ital.:   Quando ho **messo su la mia ditta** qui...
    HMLD. Cro: Kad sam **osnovala firmu/tvrtku** tu...

In (10), the notion of a state of affairs is referred to, ie. existential 'there is', which in Croatian is expressed via the construction *imati* 'to have' + SUBJ-GEN. In Italian, *essere* 'to be' + SUBJ-NOM is the equivalent construction that is given in its Croatian translated form:

(10) **mržnja**   **je**   uvik
     hatred-NOM.F.SG   be-PRS.3SG   always
     'There is always hatred.' (AA,Gen.1A,F,83)

    Ital.:   L'odio **c'è sempre**.
    HMLD.Cro: Uvijek **ima mržnje**-GEN.F.SG

In (11), a Croatian construction based on the Italian model *avere aiuto* 'to have (=receive) help' is employed, which is a converse one compared to its equivalent Croatian construction:

(11) nismo   **imali**   **pomoći**   od   nikoga   nikad
     NEG.AUX-1PL   have-PST.M.PL   help-GEN.F.SG   from+GEN   nobody-GEN   never
     'No-one ever helped us.' (AA,Gen.1A,F,83)

    Ital.:   Non **abbiamo avuto aiuto** da nessuno mai.
    HMLD.Cro: Nikad nam nitko **nije pomogao**.

An Italian construction is translated below which is also converse to its equivalent Croatian one:

(12) **vidim**   **te**   dobro
     see-1SG   you-ACC   well
     'You look good.' (MR,Gen.1A,F,57)

    Ital.:   **Ti vedo** bene.
    HMLD.Cro: Dobro **izgledaš**.

In the sample there are 19 loan translations and 10 of them are in the speech of Gen.1A speakers. This marks loan translations as a comparatively frequent occurrence. The relationship between loan translations and code-switching – the latter relating to an adoption not only of the structure of elements from the other language but their form as well – is looked at in 4.3.8 below. Instances of loan translations in other diaspora varieties of Croatian can be found in AUT.Cro (Ščukanec, this volume), CAN.Cro (Petrović, this volume); AUS.Cro (Hlavac and Stolac, this volume), NZ.Cro (Stoffel and Hlavac, this volume) and ARG.Cro (Skelin Horvat, Musulin and Blažević, this volume).

4.3 Structural innovations

A comparison of the features that Italian and Croatian mark through morphology reveals similarities e.g. gender and number as features of nouns, and long and short forms of object pronouns. But there are differences, such as Italian's larger number of compound verb tenses and subjunctive mood vs. Croatian's distinction of verbal aspect for all verbs (Sočanac 2004). Further, although both languages are pro-drop and SVO at a basic level, there are differences such as Croatian's rich inflectional morphology for NPs while Italian has the category *article* with two forms, definite and indefinite, as in English. This last feature is explored in 4.3.1 below.

4.3.1 *Jedan* and its use as an indefinite article

Nine instances occur where *jedan* 'one' appears to take on the function of an indefinite article. It seems that its primary use is not to express singularity but to qualify the succeeding noun as unspecific in the same way that the Italian INDF. ART *uno* (including all forms *un, un', una*) does:

(13) su   našli   **je'**nu   zadrugu
     AUX-3PL find-PST.M.PL IND.ART-ACC.F.SG co-operative-ACC.F.SG
     'They found **a** co-operative.' (AA,Gen.1A,F,83)

   Ital.:   Hanno trovato **una** cooperativa.
   HMLD.Cro: Našli su Ø zadrugu.

(14) **već**   smrt   Tita   je   bila
     already   death-NOM.F.SG   Tito-GEN.M.SG   AUX-3SG   be-PST.F.SG
     za   Tršćane   **jedan**   veliki
     for+ACC   resident of Trieste-ACC.M.PL   one-NOM.M.SG   big-NOM.M.SG
     događaj
     event-NOM.M.SG
     'The very death of Tito was a big event for the people of Trieste...'
     (MŠ,Gen.2,M,70)

   Ital.:   Già la morte di Tito è stata **un** grande evento per i triestini...
   HMLD.Cro: Već je Titova smrt bila za Tršćane Ø veliki događaj...

These examples are from a Gen.1A and a Gen.2 informant. The use of *jedan* not as a marker of number, but as a form which expresses the singularity of the succeeding noun, appears to be based on influence from Italian. In HMLD.Cro, morphology alone via a *noun*-SG suffix indicates SG number. Distribution of the 9 instances of *jedan* as a translated indefinite article is 5 amongst Gen.1A informants, 1 from a Gen.1B informant, and 3 from Gen.2 informants. The use of *jedan* in article-like constructions is also recorded in other diaspora varieties of Croatian, e.g. CAN.Cro (Petrović, this volume), AUS.Cro (Hlavac and Stolac, this volume) and ARG.Cro (Skelin Horvat, Musulin and Blažević, this volume).

4.3.2 Personal pronouns

As stated, Croatian is a pro-drop language. Verbal morphology indicates the subject, which is usually dropped. A SUBJ PRON typically marks emphasis. In the examples below, the implicature of the informant's utterances does not contain emphasis; the presence of the SUBJ PRON appears overt and marked.

(15) **oni**   su   svi   išli   u
     they-NOM.M.PL   AUX-3PL   all-NOM.M.PL   go-PST.M.PL   to+ACC
     školu   za   vrijeme   Austrije
     school-ACC.F.SG   during+ACC   time-ACC.N.SG   Austria-GEN.F.SG
     sve   su   **one**   bile   intelektualke
     all-NOM.F.PL   AUX-3PL   they-NOM.F.PL   be-PST.F.PL   intellectual-NOM.F.PL
     '**They** all went to school during the time of Austrian rule... **They** were all learned women.' (NA, Gen.1A,F,75)

Ital.: Tutti **loro** hanno frequentato la scuola sotto l'Austria. Tutte **loro** erano intellettuali.
HMLD.Cro.: Svi su išli u školu za vrijeme Austrije. Sve su bile intelektualke.

(16) ***ja*** sam se rodila ***ja*** sam išla u
I AUX-1SG REFL bear-PST.F.SG I AUX-1SG go-PST.F.SG to+ACC
školu ***ja*** volim Trst
school-ACC.F.SG I love-PRS.1SG Trieste-ACC.M.SG
'I was born...I went to school...I love Trieste.' (JV,Gen.2,F,70)

Ital.: Sono nata... Ho frequentato la scuola... Amo Trieste.
HMLD.Cro: Rodila sam se... Išla sam u školu... Volim Trst.

The examples above show a tendency of the speaker to use the SUBJ PRON although its usage appears redundant. Italian is pro-drop like Croatian and the influence of Italian is unlikely here. However, there is some evidence that when a diaspora pro-drop language is in contact with a host-language that is also pro-drop, the pro-drop setting may still undergo some change. For example, diaspora speakers of Veneto Italian in Mexico are recorded to have a slightly elevated incidence of overt subjects when speaking Spanish (Barnes 2010). It is possible that when speaking Veneto Italian, the same phenomenon may occur on the basis of "overmarking", a commonly observed feature in heritage languages (Polinsky 2018: 173). Overt subjects are found in other diaspora varieties of Croatian, particularly where the societally dominant language is English, which does not have pro-drop, e.g. USA. Cro (Jutronić, this volume), CAN.Cro (Petrović, this volume) and NZ.Cro (Stoffel and Hlavac, this volume).

The examples above show that overt subjects are to be found in the speech of speakers from both generations. This begs the question: if the SUBJ PRON is not marking emphasis or contrast, and it is not clear to what extent overmarking may be occurring, particularly in the speech of Gen.1A speakers, then what is its function? There may be 'performance-based' reasons for this: for Gen.2 speakers they may be discourse fillers that allow the speaker to 'buy time' in retrieving or organising the forms that s/he wishes to employ; the SUBJ PRON overtly marks grammatical relations between elements where the speaker may be unsure in speech output how to map out and express these relations via inflectional morphology only. This remains a hypothesis as subject-verb agreement morphology remains otherwise mostly intact.

Analogous to the SUBJ PRON that is usually dropped in Croatian, the unmarked form for an OBJ PRON in non-initial position is the OBJ PRON short form. Long form OBJ PRONS are used for emphasis only. Again, the cause of this phenomenon is not the influence of Italian. In Italian, the short forms of the OBJ PRON are also unmarked for emphasis. In the following example, the speaker employs *both* short and long form. This appears to be motivated by the speaker's desire to use emphasis to distinguish the object, *ga* 'him'-ACC.M.SG from the subject *njegova braća* 'his brothers'. The double production of the OBJ PRON may be a 'misfiring' or an instance of indecision about the use of the short vs. the long form. It also bears a similarity to the repetition of SUBJ forms that can have a high frequency amongst some heritage speakers (Polinsky 2007). An example of 'double-marking' with the clitic and long form of a non-subject pronoun is also reported in the CAN.Cro corpus (see Petrović, this volume).

(17) onda su   **ga**   **njega**   njegova
     then AUX-3PL   he-ACC (SHORT)   he-ACC (LONG)   his-NOM.F.SG
     braća   koja   su   živjela
     brothers-NOM.FSG   who-REL.PRON.F.SG   AUX-3PL   live-PST.N.PL
     u+LOC   Sloveniji   potegnula   u   Ljubljanu
     in   Slovenia-LOC.F.SG   drag-PST.F.SG   to+ACC   Ljubljana-ACC.F.SG
     'Then his brothers who were living in Slovenia brought **him** to Ljubljana.'
     (LjJ,Gen.1A,F,72)

    Ital.:   Poi i suoi fratelli che vivevano in Slovenia l'hanno trascinato a Lubiana.
    HMLD.Cro: Onda su **ga** njegova braća koja su živjela u Sloveniji, povukla u Ljubljanu.

There are eight instances where overt SUBJ and OBJ PRON forms appear. Five were produced by Gen.1A informants and one by a Gen.2 speaker.

4.3.3 Numbers and case marking

In Croatian, numbers require specific case marking on succeeding nominals. After the numbers 2, 3 and 4 (or larger numbers ending in these) GEN.SG case marking is required on succeeding nominals; after the numbers 0, 5, 6, 7, 8, 9 and 10, 20 and so on (or larger numbers ending in these) GEN.PL marking is required. This morphology is different from the morphology of plural forms not preceded by a number which have NOM.PL morphological marking. Seven examples of non-target case marking are recorded, of which five (18) to (22) are presented below:

(18) išli   smo   **svaku**   **godinu**   i   po
    go-PST.M.PL AUX-1PL   every-ACC.F.SG   year-ACC.F.SG   and   for
    čet'ri   **tjedana**   preko   **ljeto**
    four+GEN.SG   week-GEN.M.PL   during+GEN   summer-NOM.N.SG
    'We used to go **every year** for up to **four weeks**, during **summer**...'
    (RP,Gen.2,F,28)

    Ital.:   Andavamo anche **quattro settimane ogni anno**, d'**estate**...
    HMLD.Cro: Išli smo **svake godine**-GEN i po **četiri tjedna**-GEN.SG, preko **ljeta**-GEN...

Plural nouns such as *ljudi* 'people' (M.PL) and irregular plural nouns such as *djeca* 'children' (F.SG) are preceded by a collective (neuter) numeral, such as *dvoje*+GEN.PL 'two', rather than the cardinal number *dva*+GEN.SG or *dvije*+GEN.SG 'two'. In the example below, a regular cardinal number is used with the irregular plural *ljudi*:

(19) to   su   **dvi**   **ljudi**   da   se
    those   be-PRS.3PL two+GEN.SG   people-GEN.M.PL   COMP   REFL
    ideju
    go-PRS.3PL
    '...those are **two people who** are to go...' (RP,Gen.2,F,28)

    Ital.:   Sono **due persone che** vanno...
    HMLD.Cro: To je **dvoje**-NOM.N.SG **ljudi**-GEN.M.PL **koji** idu...

As stated above, a collective (neuter) numeral, such as *dvoje* 'two', rather than the cardinal number *dva*-M or *dvije*-F 'two' is commonly used with nouns denoting humans, eg. *ljudi* 'people', *djeca* 'children'. Succeeding nouns are in GEN. The following example contains a construction based on an Italian model. The equivalent Italian construction has a subject personal pronoun in nominative and a cardinal number:

(20) **mi**   **dva**   smo   govorili   i   dalje
    we-NOM   **two**+GEN.SG AUX-1PL   speak-PST.M.PL   and   still
    slovenski
    Slovenian-ACC.M.SG
    '**us two** continued speaking Slovenian.' (LjJ,Gen.1A,F,72)

    Ital.:   **Noi due** abbiamo continuato a parlare in sloveno.
    HMLD.Cro: **Nas**-'we-GEN' **dvoje**-NOM smo govorili i dalje slovenski.

In Croatian, specific years are expressed by ordinal forms of the number that have GEN.SG marking. In Italian, the cardinal form is used. Use of the cardinal form in Italian appears to account for its use in (21) below:

(21) i   ostala   u   Rimu   do
      and   stay-PST.F.SG in+LOC   Rome-LOC.M.SG   until+GEN
      dve hiljade i sedam
      two thousand and seven
      '...and stayed in Rome until **two thousand and seven**.' (ZL,Gen.1A,F,74)

   Ital.:   ...e rimasi a Roma fino al **duemilasette**-CARDINAL.NO.
   HMLD.Cro.: ...i ostala u Rimu do **dvije tisuće (hiljade) i sedme**-ORDINAL.
              NO.GEN.F.SG.

In (22), the influence of Italian is even clearer, with *ottobre* 'October' preceding a particular year. This is given as a cardinal, rather than as an ordinal number:

(22) od   tamo   smo   došli   tu   u   Trstu
      from there AUX-1PL come-PST.M.PL   here   to+ACC   Trieste-LOC.M.SG
      ottobre   **šezdeset i dva**   brat
      October-NOM.M.SG   sixty-two-CARDINAL.NO.   brother-NOM.M.SG
      u   setembru
      in+LOC   september-LOC.M.SG
      'From there we came here, to Trieste in October **sixty-two**, my brother came in September.' (EO,Gen.1B,F,64)

   Ital.:   Da lì siamo venuti qui, a Trieste, nell'ottobre del **sessantadue**,
              e mio fratello a settembre.
   HMLD.Cro: Otamo smo došli tu, u Trst, u listopadu (oktobru)-LOC **šezdeset druge**-ORDINAL.NO.GEN.F.SG, a brat u rujnu (septembru).

Seven instances of non-target case marking following numerals are provided by two different Gen.1A informants, three are produced by Gen.1B informants, and two are produced by the same Gen.2 informant. Changes in the choice of ordinal vs. cardinal forms of numbers are also recorded in the USA.Cro sample (see Jutronić, this volume).

4.3.4 Case-marking in NPs

Croatian has a rich inflection system for nouns, with morphological marking for case, number and gender. This section focuses on case-marking only. There are innumerable instances in which the case-marking of forms in NPs, i.e. nouns, pronouns, adjectives and determiners conforms to that found in HMLD.Cro. Such instances are termed here 'target'; my focus here is on those instances of 'non-target' case-marking. I apply Ďurovič's (1984: 23) implicativity system of change in case-marking, i.e. an ordering in which morphological markers from the right of the following list may be replaced by those to their left NOM<ACC<GEN<LOC<INS<DAT<VOC. The number of instances of non-target case-marking is summarised below in Table 2:

Table 2: Non-target case realisations and their frequency and distribution across generations.

Target case	Provided case	No. of instances	No. of instances across Gen. groups
ACC	NOM	2	2 x Gen.1B
LOC	ACC	8	3 x Gen.1B; 5 x Gen.2
ACC	LOC	6	1 x Gen.1A; 1 x Gen.1B; 4 x Gen.2
INS	GEN	1	1 x Gen.2

Applying Ďurovič's (1984) implicativity system to the TRS.Cro data and the 17 instances of non-target case-marking found here, it is possible to see that 11 of the 17 examples conform to the predictions of the implicativity scale. While 11 of the instances of non-target case-marking can be accounted for by Ďurovič's (1984) predictions, a larger number – 14 – are those that appear to be based on the movement (ACC) vs. location (LOC) distinction. Sixteen of the 17 examples of non-target case-marking are from Gen.1B or Gen.2 speakers. Below is a selection of these examples:

ACC > NOM

(23) sam   imala   **ona**   dok   smo   bili
     AUX-1SG   have-PST.F.SG   she-NOM.F.SG   while   AUX-1PL be-PST.M.PL
     tamo
     there
     'I had **her** whilst we were there.' (EO,Gen.1B,F,64)

   Ital.:   Ho avuto **lei** mentre eravamo lì.
   HMLD.Cro: Imala sam **nju**-ACC dok smo bili tamo.

This example is noteworthy, as it is usually nouns, adjectives and determiners that are affected when changes in case-marking occur in NPs, but rarely pronouns. In their data from Russian-English bilinguals, Isurin and Ivanova-Sullivan (2008: 77–78) located only three examples from heritage language speakers of case reduction of pronouns. In their Russian-English data, they report that when pronoun forms change, they change from one OBL case to another, not to NOM as in the above example. Non-distinction of the Italian FEM.PERSONAL.PRON *lei* as a subject or object could exert an influence.

The single largest group of non-target forms is the replacement of LOC morphology with ACC forms.

LOC > ACC

(24) *ostavili   kuću   sve*
     leave-PST.M.PL   house-ACC.F.SG   everything-ACC.N.SG
     *sve   tanjure   na   **stol***
     everything-ACC.N.SG plate-ACC.M.PL on+LOC **table**-ACC.M.SG
     'We left the house, everything we had, plates were still on the **table**.'
     (MB,Gen.1B,F,74)

   Ital.:   Abbiamo lasciato la casa, tutto quanto, i piatti sul **tavolo**...
   HMLD.Cro.: Ostavili kuću, sve sve, tanjure na **stolu**- LOC...

(25) *i   na   **Bled**   sam   bio   kad   sam*
     and   to+LOC   Bled-ACC.M.SG   AUX-1SG   be-PST.M.SG   when   AUX-1SG
     bio   mali   ali   stranih   turista
     be-PST.M.SG   little-NOM.M.SG   but   foreign-GEN.M.PL   tourist-GEN.M.PL
     nije   bilo   skoro
     NEG.AUX-3SG   be-PST.N.SG   almost
     '...and I visited **Bled** when I was little, but there were hardly any foreign tourists.' (MŠ,Gen.2,M, 70)

   Ital.:   ...e ho visitato **Bled** quando ero piccolo, ma i turisti stranieri quasi non c'erano.
   HMLD.Cro.: ...i na **Bledu**-LOC sam bio kad sam bio mali, ali stranih turista skoro nije bilo.

In (24) and (25), it is possible to see that there is target case marking of nominals occurring elsewhere in the utterance. The two examples above show target case-marking for other cases, such as GEN and ACC. The substitution of LOC forms with ACC ones in these examples relates, as mentioned, to the 'movement vs. position' distinction that is the semantic basis for the peculiar syntactic forms, and the circumstance that the same prepositions *u* 'in/into' and *na* 'on/onto' govern both cases. In the following example, the same speaker in the same utterance employs an ACC form for a target LOC one, and a LOC one for a target ACC one:

LOC > ACC, ACC > LOC

(26)   *mi*   *smo*   *išli*   *tamo*   *na*   *posjet*   *išli*
        we   AUX-1PL   go-PST.M.PL   there   on+ACC   visit-ACC.M.SG   go-PST.M.PL
        smo   *u*   **Splitu**   *bila*   *sam*   *tamo*
        AUX-1PL   to+ACC   Split-LOC.M.SG   be-PST.F.SG   AUX-1SG   there
        na   **ljetovanje**
        on+LOC   holiday-ACC.N.SG
        '. . .we went there for a visit. We went to Split. I was there on holiday.'
        (JV,Gen.2,F,70)

        Ital.:   . . .siamo andati lì in visita. Siamo andati a Spalato. Ci sono stata in vacanza.
        HMLD.Cro: . . .mi smo išli tamo u posjet-ACC. Išli smo u **Split**-ACC. Bila sam tamo na **ljetovanju**-LOC.

As stated above, the same prepositions *u* and *na* can govern either ACC or LOC. Another instance, this time from a Gen.1A speaker, features *u* twice, the second time with a non-target LOC. This may be a 'performance error', i.e. the –*u* suffix of the previous nominal, *Italiju*, may have influenced production of non-target *kampu*:

ACC > LOC

(27)   *šezdeset i treće*   *sam*   *došla*   *u*   *Italiju*
        sixty-three-GEN.F.SG   AUX-1SG   come-PST.F.SG   to+ACC   Italy-ACC.F.SG
        u   **kampu**
        to+ACC   camp-LOC.M.SG
        'In sixty-three I arrived in Italy to the **refugee camp**. . .' (AA,Gen.1A,F,83)

        Ital.:   Nel sessantatré sono arrivata in Italia nel **campo profughi**.
        HMLD.Cro: Šezdeset i treće sam došla u Italiju u **izbjeglički kamp**-ACC.

INS > GEN

Similar to the prepositions *u* 'to'/'into' and *na* 'on'/'onto', the preposition *s* has multiple meanings that govern different cases: 'with'+INS or *s* 'from'+GEN. In the following example although the use of *s* was related to the meaning 'with'+INS, the case marking of the following nominal was GEN. instead of INS.

(28) *oni   su   tražili   s   fakulteta*
     they-NOM.M.PL AUX-3PL look for-PST.M.PL with+INS faculty-GEN.M.SG
     'They were looking for someone with a **university degree**...' (RP,Gen.2,F,28)

   Ital.:   Cercavano qualcuno con una **laurea**...
   HMLD.Cro: Oni su tražili nekoga s **fakultetom**-INS...

The implicativity model of case change or replacement developed by Ďurovič (1983, 1984) is employed in other studies of diaspora Croatian, such as CAN.Cro (Petrović, this volume) and AUS.Cro (Hlavac and Stolac, this volume).

4.3.5 Possessive constructions with *od* 'from'/'of' + GEN

Some possessive constructions bear 'double' marking of possession via the preposition *od* 'from'/'of' *and* use of GEN. The preposition *od* requires GEN. marking of succeeding nominals. However, HMLD.Cro requires GEN. marking only of the succeeding NP item to show relations of possession. Employment of *od* is indicative of an isomorphic construction based on the Ital. model: object of possession + *di* ('of') + possessor.

(29) *tamo   su   dolazili   direktori   od*
     there   AUX-3PL   come-PST.M.PL.   director-NOM.M.PL.   of+GEN
     banke   tvornice
     bank-GEN.F.SG   factory-GEN.F.SG
     '**directors of banks and factories** used to come there.' (NA,Gen.1A,F,75)

   Ital.:   una volta i direttori delle **banche** e **fabbriche** venivano lì.
   HMLD.Cro: tamo su dolazili direktori **banaka, tvornica**-GEN.F.PL.

(30) *on   je   bio   čovjek   najveći*
     he-NOM AUX-3SG   be-PST.M.SG   person-NOM.M.SG   big-SUPL.NOM.SG
     od   otoka
     of+GEN   island-GEN.M.SG
     'He was the biggest person **of the island**.' (JV,Gen.2,F,70)

   Ital.:   Lui era l'uomo più grande dell'**isola**.
   HMLD.Cro: On je bio najveći čovjek na **otoku**-LOC ('on the island').

There are five instances from each of the three generational groups that make up the 15 instances of 'double-marked' possessive constructions. The 'double-marking' of possession via *od* + GEN is attested in other Italian-Croatian corpora, such as dramas and plays written by Dubrovnik writers including the famous playwright Marin Držić, eg. *jedan čovjek od njegove kvalitati* (Ital.: un uomo della sua qualità, HMLD.Cro jedan čovjek njegove kvalitete) (Deanović 1972: 306). Sočanac (2004) locates many further examples of this use of *od* in GEN. of other examples of literary texts from southern Dalmatia. It is also recorded in another study of diaspora Croatian in contact with Italian (see Županović Filipin, Hlavac and Piasevoli, this volume) as well as in other varieties of diaspora Croatian, e.g. AUT.Cro (see Ščukanec, this volume), USA.Cro (see Jutronić, this volume) and AUS.Cro (see Hlavac and Stolac, this volume).

4.3.6 Word order

As stated, Croatian and Italian are both SVO. Leftward movement of copulas and auxiliaries is possible in both languages so that these can precede the subject. Croatian has clitics whose position is determined by hierarchical relations (Browne 1974) and by sentence prosody; Standard Croatian does not permit clitics in clause-initial position. However, some non-standard varieties, particular Istrian regiolects, feature this. It appears that non-standard, regiolectal models, together with the influence of Italian, account for examples of pre-posed clitics:

(31) *i   sam   ih   pitala   da   li   možem*
    and   AUX-1SG   they-ACC   ask-PST.F.SG   COMP   if   can-PRS.1SG
    da   radim
    COMP   work-PRS.1SG
    'And I **asked them** if I could work.' (AA,Gen.1A,F,83)

    Ital.:   E **ho chiesto loro** se potevo lavorare.
    HMLD.Cro: I **pitala sam ih** mogu li raditi.

(32) *l'jep   je   film   su   mladi*
    nice-NOM.M.SG   AUX   film-NOM.M.SG   be-PRS.1PL   young-NOM.M.PL
    glumci
    actors-NOM.M.PL
    'It's a nice film...the actors are young.' (RP,Gen.2,F,28)

    Ital.:   È un bel film... **sono giovani gli attori.**
    HMLD.Cro: Lijep je film... **glumci su mladi.**

Example (32) above contains a clitic in initial position in the second clause. Leftward movement of clitics here looks to be attributable to the equivalent Italian model.

Another area of contrast between Italian and Croatian is the word order of NPs containing an attributive adjective. In Italian, most attributive adjectives follow the noun. In Croatian, attributive adjectives precede the noun and their placement after it is restricted to poetic or literary language or as rhetorical device marking emphasis. Word order conventions from Italian account for the following example of a post-positioned adjective in (33) below:

(33)   *tamo su   dolazili   **ljudi**   **bogati***
there AUX-3PL come-PST.M.PL people-NOM.M.PL rich-NOM.M.PL
iz   Hrvatske
from+GEN Croatia-GEN.F.SG
'Rich people from Croatia used to go there.' (NA,Gen.1A,F,75)

    Ital.:   Una volta ci andava la **gente ricca** della Croazia.
    HMLD.Cro: Tamo su dolazili **bogati ljudi** iz Hrvatske.

From the same speaker, a further example of a post-posed adjective occurs that also contains *jedan* used in a non-numerical sense (see section 4.3.1 above):

(34)   *to   je   bila   jedna   **familja**   **bogata***
that AUX-3SG be-PST.F.SG one-NOM.F.SG family-NOM.F.SG rich-NOM.F.SG
'That was a rich family.' (NA,Gen.1A,F,75)

    Ital.:   Era una **famiglia ricca**.
    HMLD.Cro: To je bila **bogata obitelj**.

These examples from a Gen.1A informant are the only ones pertaining to constructions in which adjectives precede nouns like in Italian.

In both Italian and Croatian, the position of adverbs is free. In Croatian, the unmarked position of adverbs is post-verbal or, in the case of compound verbs, following AUX and preceding the main verb. A position different from this is marked. In (35) below, the adverb is in clause-final position.

(35) mrko   su   nas   gledali   u   jednom
     strangely AUX-3PL we-ACC   look-PST.M.PL in+LOC some-LOC.M.SG
     restoranu   jer   smo   govorili
     restaurant-LOC.M.SG because AUX-1PL   speak-PST.M.PL
     protiv   komunizma   **glasno**
     against+GEN   communism-GEN.M.SG   loudly
     'They gave us dark looks in a restaurant because we spoke out against communism **loudly**.' (MŠ,Gen.2,M,70)

> Ital.: Ci guardavano di traverso in un ristorante perché parlavamo contro il comunismo **ad alta voce**.
>
> HMLD.Cro: Mrko su nas gledali u jednom restoranu jer smo **glasno** govorili protiv komunizma.

In (35), the position of the adverb *glasno* 'loudly' appears to be influenced by the position of its Italian equivalent. Overall, there are nine examples of word order changes. Six of those are related to the use of clitics at the beginning of clauses – three provided by Gen.1A informants, two by Gen.1B informants, and one by a Gen.2 informant. There are two examples of adverbs at the end of clauses, uttered both by the same Gen. 2 informant.

4.3.7 Dependent clause conjunctions

The influence of Italian conjunctions *che* 'that' and *se* 'if' is apparent in two examples below that introduce a dependent clause:

(36) ja   radim   u   firmi   **da**   prevozi
     I   work-PRS.1SG in+LOC   firm-LOC.F.SG   COMP   transport-PRS.3SG
     kontejnere
     dumpster-ACC.M.PL
     'I work for a company **that** transports dumpsters.' (RP,Gen.2,F,28)

> Ital.: Lavoro in una ditta **che** trasporta i cassonetti.
>
> HMLD.Cro: Radim u tvrtki **koja** se bavi prijevozom kontejnera.

While Ital. *che* 'that' can function as both a conjunction and a relative pronoun, its Croatian equivalent *da* 'that' is a conjunction (or complementizer) only and cannot function as a relative pronoun. Instead, in HMLD.Cro either of the REL. PRON. forms *koji* or *što* would be employed. In the following example *ako* 'if' / 'whether' functions as a conjunction.

(37) ne   znam   **ako** nono   od   moj
     NEG   know-PRS.1SG   if   grandpa-NOM.M.SG   of+GEN   my-NOM.M.SG
     papà   ili ne'ko   je   došao   iz
     dad-NOM.M.SG   or someone-NOM   AUX-3SG   come-PST.M.SG from+GEN.
     Dalmacije
     Dalmatia-GEN.F.SG
     'I don't know **if** my fraternal grandpa or someone else came from Dalmatia...'
     (EO,Gen.1B,F,64)

- Ital.: Non so **se** il nonno di mio papà o qualcun altro sia venuto dalla Dalmazia...
- HMLD. Cro: Ne znam **je li** djed mojega oca ili netko drugi došao iz Dalmacije...

In English, as in Italian, a main clause such as *I don't know* may be followed by a subordinating conjunction such as *if* or *whether* (Italian: *se*) and the finite verb in the subordinate clause typically follows the subject. In the equivalent Croatian construction, the finite verb in the subordinate clause is pre-posed to initial position and followed by the particle *li*. This results in the following structure: *ne znam* ('I don't know') + finite verb + *li*. The structural constituents and word order conventions of Croatian subordinate clauses are often different from those in Italian and this appears to explain why Croatian equivalents of the required Italian constituents are being employed in some of them. There are 3 examples of dependent clause conjunctions with non-target forms, one uttered by a Gen.1B informant and two by a Gen.2 informant.

4.3.8 Syntactic calques

Syntactic calques relate to the transfer of syntactical function or construction in the source language that is imitated in the target language. There are two instances in which syntactic calques appear. One is linked to the use of NEG in a sentence from a Gen. 2 informant. The other is related to the back-shifting of tenses from a Gen. 1A informant. Both instances are presented below.

(38) **uvijek nisam   pustila**   klavir   samo   kad
     always   NEG.AUX-1SG   let go-PST.F.SG   piano-ACC.M.SG   only   when
     sam   bila   na   fakultetu
     AUX-1SG be-PST.F.SG   at+LOC   university-LOC.M.SG
     '**I never stopped playing** piano, only when I was at university.' (JV,Gen.2,F,70)

Ital.: **Non ho mai abbandonato** il pianoforte, solo quando frequentavo l'università.
HMLD.Cro: **Nisam nikad ostavila** klavir, samo kad sam bila na fakultetu.

In all varieties of Croatian, a NEG verb calls also for NEG marking on adverbs. For example, in a negative sentence, a time adverb such as *uvijek* 'always' cannot usually occur and instead, its NEG equivalent *nikada* 'never' is used. In contrast, the Italian adverb *mai* 'always' *can* occur in NEG sentences. This is the only example of a non-target form related to NEG-marking that occurs due to Italian influence. Italian, like English, features a 'back-shifting' of tenses in narratives where a subject is given in a past tense in the first clause and the same subject is referred to in the second clause:

(39) *našla sam dvije prijateljice*
find-PST.F.SG AUX-1SG two+GEN.SG girlfriend-GEN.F.SG
koje **su bile** *iz Hrvatske*
REL.PRON-NOM.F.PL AUX-3PL be-PST.F.PL from+GEN Croatia-GEN.F.SG
'**I found** two friends who **were** from Croatia.' (MR, Gen.1A, F, 57)

Ital.: **Ho trovato** due amiche che **sono venute** dalla Croazia.
HMLD.Cro: **Našla sam** dvije prijateljice koje **su**-PRS iz Hrvatske.

Croatian has neither a sequence of tense convention nor use of a subjunctive in reported narratives such as above. Actions may be reported in the PAST, but reference about subjects of these actions is in the PRES. In Croatian, past tense is used only if it is known that the subjects are no longer alive. For further examples of syntactic calques or transference in other varieties of diaspora Croatian, see Županović Filipin, Hlavac and Piasevoli; and Jutronić; Hlavac and Stolac (all this volume).

4.3.9 Syntactic change and verbal aspect

Verbal aspect is a feature of all Croatian verbs. Morphologically, the 'base' form of a verb can be perfective, e.g. *kupiti* 'to buy', *sresti* 'to meet' with modification of the stem or the ending yielding imperfective forms, *kupovati* and *sretati*. The 'base' form of a verb may also be IPFV, eg. *čitati* 'to read', *gledati* 'to look', to which prefixes are added to yield PFV forms, *pročitati* and *pogledati*. There are ten instances of non-target forms used according to the semantic meaning of the clause. In all ten instances, an expected IPFV aspect form is replaced by a PFV aspect form:

(40) tko   je   imao   puno   djece
     who   AUX-3SG   have-PST.M.SG   lots+GEN   children-GEN.F.SG
     dobio   je   lakše   šećer   brašno
     get-PST.PFV.M.SG   AUX-3SG   easily-COMP   sugar-ACC.M.SG   flour-ACC.N.SG
     'Whoever had a lot of children, **received** sugar and flour more easily.'
     (LjJ,Gen.1A, F,72)

   Ital.:   Chi aveva tanti figli, **riceveva** più facilmente farina, zucchero.
   HMLD.Cro: Tko je imao puno djece, **dobivao**-IPFV je lakše šećer, brašno.

(41) r'jetko   je   tko   **shvatio**   kakva
     rarely   AUX-3SG   who   **understand**-PST.PFV.M.SG what-ACC.F.SG
     će   biti   budućnost
     FUT.AUX-3SG   be-INF   future-NOM.F.SG
     '. . .hardly anyone **understood** what the future would be like. . .'
     (MŠ,Gen.2,M,70)

   Ital.:   Pochi **capivano** come sarebbero andate le cose in futuro.
   HMLD.Cro: Rijetko je tko **shvaćao**-IPFV kakva će biti budućnost.

(42) ja   sam   sa   djecom   uvijek   **došla**
     I   AUX-1SG   with+INS   children-INS.F.SG always   **come**-PST.PFV.F.SG
     ovdje
     here
     'I **would** always **bring** my children here.' (JV, Gen.2, F, 70)

   Ital.:   **Portavo** sempre i miei figli qui.
   HMLD. Cro: Ja sam s djecom uvijek **dolazila**-IPFV ovamo.

For seven instances in which non-target PFV forms are given instead of IPVF ones, the PFV form is the 'base' form for that verb, eg. *došli* 'come'-PST.PFV instead of *dolazili* 'come'-PST.IPFV, *dobio* 'recive' -PST.PFV instead of *dobivao* 'recive' -PST.IPFV, *dali* 'give'-PST.PFV instead of *davali* 'give'-PST.IPFV, *okrenula* 'turn'-PST.IPFV instead of *okretala* 'turn'-PST.IPFV, *shvatio* 'grasp'-PST.IPFV instead of *shvaćao* 'grasp'-PST.IPFV, *uklopili* 'fit in'-PST.IPFV instead of *uklapali* 'fit in'-PST.IPFV and *razmisliti* 'think about'-INF.PFV instead of *razmišljati* 'think about'-INF.IPFV. In two examples the aspect 'partners' are not phonologically similar, *rekla* 'say'-PST.PFV instead of *govorila* 'say'-PST.IPFV and *čula* 'hear'-PST.PFV instead of *slušala* 'hear'-PST.IPFV. (The last example is an example of suppletion, i.e. the use of a verb as an aspectual partner that has a completely different root.) In only one example is the PFV form not the 'base' form *naučiti* 'to learn' (which is PFV by way of prefixation of *na-* on IPFV *učiti* 'to learn').

(43) malo   sam   počela   **naučiti**   hrvatski
     little AUX-1SG   start-PST.PFV.F.SG learn-INF.PFV   Croatian-ACC.M.SG
     imala   sam   neku   gramatiku   od
     have-PST.F.SG AUX-1SG   some-ACC.F.SG   grammar-ACC.F.SG   from+GEN
     moje   majke
     my-GEN.F.SG   mother-GEN.F.SG
     'I started to learn Croatian a little bit, I had a grammar book from my mum.' (JV, Gen.2, F, 70)

    Ital.: Ho iniziato un po' a **imparare** il croato, avevo una grammatica di mia madre.
    HMLD.Cro: Malo sam počela-PFV **učiti-IPFV** hrvatski, imala sam neku gramatiku svoje majke.

A change in the choice of verb forms to convey the semantic content of an utterance, as shown in examples (40) to (43) above, has occurred. This change has occurred on the basis of speakers' conceptualisation of the duration or type of temporal activity being referred to. Duration or type of temporal activity are marked differently in Italian in which, similar to other Romance languages, concepts of aspect and tense are merged, and aspect is consistently marked in some past tenses only. For example, Ital. *passato prossimo* ('recent past') is more likely to be rendered in Cro. via PFV aspect, eg. *ho dato* > *dao*-PFV *sam* ('I gave'), *ho aperto* > *otvorio*-PFV *sam* ('I opened'), *sono ritornato* > *vratio*-PFV *sam se* ('I returned'), but for other examples of *passato prossimo* Cro. IPFV aspect may be more usual, eg. *ho dormito* > *spavao*-IPFV *sam* ('I slept') or *ho camminato* > *hodao*-IPFV *sam* ('I walked'). Some Ital. tenses match up closely with a particular Cro. aspect such as *imperfetto* ('imperfect') with IPFV aspect in the past tense, eg. *mangiavo* > *jeo-*IPFV *sam* ('I was eating'/'I usually ate'), or the *passato remoto* ('remote past') with PFV aspect in the aorist, eg. *io mangiai* > *pojedoh*-PFV.AOR ('I ate'). Other tenses such as *trapassato remoto* ('remote pluperfect'), *futuro anteriore* ('future perfect'), *presente* ('present') and *futuro semplice* ('simple future') do not readily match with a particular aspectual form in Croatian, and corresponding verb forms may yield equivalent IPFV or PFV verbs forms in Croatian.

While *temporal* (i.e. PRES/PAST/FUT) marking remains intact through no reported instances of non-target verb forms in tense marking, the marking of an action as *completed* or *unfolding* (or *iterative*) is not uniform in the speech of all informants. Evidence of non-target marking in some speakers' utterances suggests that aspectual marking of verbs amongst these speakers is open to change. Where a verb marked with the features of one aspect form begins to take on the functions of a verb with the other aspect form, we can speak of a merging of functional distinctions. Where this occurs consistently by the same speaker or across a group, we can speak of this instance of syncretism appearing as a loss of aspect distinction. It is significant that all of the instances feature PFV verbs taking on IPFV functions. It is also significant that nine of the ten PFV verb examples feature verbs for which the PFV is the 'base form' of the verb.

This suggests that where syncretism occurs, it is the morphologically 'more simplex' form of the verb that performs the function of encompassing both aspects. This hypothesis will be looked at in other language contact corpora. This contrasts with Polinsky's (2007) Russian-English data where non-distinction of aspect amongst heritage speakers is conspicuous, but where no obvious tendency towards PFV was ascertainable. Polinsky (2007: 182) argues that the lexicalisation of one aspectual form "depends primarily on telicity". Of the eleven instances of PFV rather than IPFV-marked verbs, 5 were from Gen.1A informants, 1 by a Gen.1B informant, and 6 by Gen.2 informants. The occurrence of 'non-target' choices of aspect amongst Gen.1A speakers is of note, as change in aspect is seldom reported in the speech of adults who 'fully acquired' their L1 in an L1 environment (Polinsky 2007).

The use of PFV verbs in constructions where IPFV verbs would otherwise be expected is recorded in other varieties of diaspora Croatian, e.g. ITAL.Cro (see Županović Filipin, Hlavac and Piasevoli, this volume) and AUS.Cro (see Hlavac and Stolac, this volume).

4.4 Code-switching

Examples of code-switching are those that have longer sequences of words – typically three or more – transferred from Italian. The incidence of Italian-Croatian code-switching in literary texts ranging from the sixteenth to the eighteenth centuries in Dubrovnik (Ital. Ragusa) has been comprehensively studied by Sočanac (2004). The texts are dramas and plays, and tellingly, their linguistic form would have reflected the (bilingual) vernaculars spoken by the city's inhabitants at the time. Sočanac (2004) locates inter-, intra- and extra-clausal code-switching where Italian forms are usually inserted into or alternate with Croatian text, and provides grammatical and theme-based as well as sociolinguistic and pragmatically-based classifications of different categories of code-switching. Regarding thematic features, those related to officialdom and education yielded more code-switches to Italian, while discourse-internal features such as amplification, contrast or use of phraseology account for many other instances (Sočanac 2004: 240–253). Example (44) below contains an intra-clausal code-switch consisting of four constituents.

(44) on   je   bil   **ferito**   **della**
     he   AUX-3SG   be-PST.PTCT.M.SG   wounded(man)-PST.PTCP.M.SG   of
     Prima guerra bio   je   star
     first   war   be-PST.PTCP.M.SG   AUX-3SG   old-NOM.M.SG
     'He was **wounded in the First World War** . . . He was old.' (MB,Gen.1B,F,74)

   Ital.:   Lui era stato **ferito nella Prima Guerra Mondiale**. Era vecchio.
   HMLD.Cro: On je bio **ranjen u Prvom svjetskom ratu**. Bio je star.

In example (44) above, *ferito* 'wounded' occurs as a PST.PTCP, perhaps functioning as an adjective to describe the circumstances of an older family member. The following examples contain inter-clausal code-switches at clause boundaries:

(45) kad   sam   ja   počela   raditi,   **e**   **lei** **lavora**
     when   AUX-1SG I   start-PST.F.SG work-INF   and   she   work-PRS.3SG
     bila   sam   izvan   **šagome**
     be-PST.F.SG   AUX-1SG   outside+GEN   norm-GEN.F.SG
     'When I started working, **and she works**. I defied the **rule**.'
     (NA,Gen.1A,F,75)

   Ital.:   Quando io iniziai a lavorare, **e lei lavora**. Sfidai le **norme**.
   HMLD.Cro: Kad sam ja počela raditi, **a, ona radi**. Bila sam izvan **pravila**.

Here, Ital. *sagoma* (used here in an adapted form *šagome*), an equivalent to *oblik* 'model' is inserted in a construction that is Croatian-based, *izvan pravila* (lit. 'out of the rules'). In the following example, a bilingual homophone *idee/ideje* 'idea'-ACC.F.PL occurs in the third clause of the turn. The fifth clause is an inter-clausal code-switch into Italian.

(46) oni   su   marljivi   sve   znaju   imaju
     they   be-3PL   diligent-NOM.M.PL   everything   know-3PL   have-3PL
     idee   lukavi   su   si   **aiutano**
     idea-ACC.F.PL   shrewd-NOM.M.PL   be-3PL   REFL   help-PRS.3PL
     'They are diligent, they know everything, they have **ideas**. They
     are shrewd. **They help each other**.' (MB,Gen.1B,F,74)

Ital.:	Loro sono diligenti, sanno tutto, hanno le loro **idee**. Sono furbi. **Si aiutano**.
HMLD.Cro.:	Oni su marljivi, sve znaju, imaju **ideje**. Lukavi su. **Pomažu se**.

There are 14 code-switches (sequences of three or more allophone items) in the sample, six uttered by Gen.1A informants, six by Gen.1B informants, and two by Gen. 2 informants. The higher incidence amongst older-generation speakers is accounted for by the larger volume of linguistic data provided by them. But the low incidence amongst Gen.2 speakers is conspicuous; in a larger sample of 76 Gen.1 and 27 Gen.2 speakers of Macedonian in Australia, Hlavac found (2016: 44) the frequency of code-switching is 2.5 times higher amongst younger-generation speakers compared to older ones. This may point to overt monitoring amongst the Gen.2 informants to consciously *avoid* code-switching as a 'conspicuous' marker of 'less fluent proficiency'. It is not clear whether the frequency of code-switches is related to the frequency of loan translations, i.e. a lower incidence of one co-occurs with a higher incidence of the other. This was postulated by Clyne (1991: 175–191) who attributed some instances of code-switching to speakers' apparent unease with apparent replications of structures from the other language. The small size of this sample disallows a systematic matching of the two, but the relatively low frequency of code-switching in this sample is notable.

5 Conclusion

This section re-visits the results from section 4 and provides a cross-generational comparison of the frequency of phenomena across the generational groups. As stated at the start of section 4, the data sample presented is a quantification of forms that diverge from HMLD.Cro. These are quantified in raw numbers and not matched against all instances of possible divergences. To give an example of this, the total number of loan translations is provided *without* reference to the total number of collocations or phrasemes in the sample that would demonstrate how frequently Croatian and how frequently Italian supplies input in the production of collocations or phrasemes.

Numerically, lexical transference is the single most frequent manifestation of the contact situation with 34 examples. This is unsurprising given the frequency and prominence that lexical transfers usually occupy in most studies of language contact phenomena (Haugen 1950; van Hout and Muysken, 1994; Field 2002). Amongst the transfers, the most common categories are nouns and terms associated with the host-society context. Congruent to lexical transfers but reflecting a different category of form-meaning sets, the next most frequent language contact category is loan translations with 19 examples. Within this sample of just under 10,000 tokens, this figure may appear high. To account for this I recount Backus and Dorleijn's (2009: 91) observation that loan translations "may be under-identified since their deviation from the convention norm in the non-contact variety is so minimal that they cannot be identified". Most are two- to three-word loan translations consisting of content morphemes only. In terms of structure, most are also VERB + OBJECT constructions, which supports Dorleijn and van der Heijden's (2000) hypothesis that such a kind of structural collocation appears to be "translation-prone".

There are nine instances of *jedan* 'one' taking on the function of an INDEF. ART. 'Article-like' forms have been recorded in other Slavic languages that, like Croatian, lack articles. For example, in the variety or Russian spoken by some Russian-speaking migrants in America, Laleko (2010: 70) notes the use of the DEM. ADJ *etot* 'this' (cf. Cro. *ovaj*) and Polinsky (2006: 247) records examples of another DEM. ADJ, *tot* 'that' (cf. Cro. *taj*) as well as *etot* as DEF. ART. forms that can occur in American Russian. Polinsky (2006) interprets this use of DEM ADJ as a compensatory strategy to express the function of DEF ART that is otherwise not available in diaspora Russian. The same could be said for this TRS.Cro corpus and the nascent development of an INDEF ART via *jedan*. There appears to be no congruent use of Cro DEM ADJ forms to function as a DEF ART.

As a pro-drop language, subject pronouns are overt in Croatian. Their presence marks emphasis or amplification. However, there are eight instances in which they are used without obvious emphasis or amplification. Italian influence is unlikely here as Italian is also pro-drop. Most instances come from Gen.1A informants, and this may be a feature of some informants' idiolects, particularly of their narrative styles when recounting events.

Numbers require morpho-syntactic marking specific to the final-digit number. The number *jedan* 'one' functions as an adjective, while other numbers function as nouns requiring GEN.SG or GEN.PL markers on quantified nominals. Non-target marking of nouns shows evidence that some speakers replace GEN.SG with GEN. PL, or GEN.PL with GEN.SG, a 'performance error' that can occur among HMLD.Cro speakers, but which is usually promptly corrected. Only Gen.2 informants provide such forms. More conspicuous are non-target numerals with animate subjects together with NOM. pronominal forms, which are GEN in HMLD.Cro. The influence of Italian is clear in accounting for these forms. Similarly, cardinal rather than ordinal forms used in designations of years are also based on equivalent Italian models. Non-target forms are found across all generational groups.

Non-target case-marking occurs in 17 NPs containing nominals. In all instances, OBL forms are the target ones, while in 11 of the 17 instances, case forms are given that follow the predictions of Ďurovič's (1984: 23) implicativity scale of representation of case. The exceptions are ACC > LOC forms that otherwise also represent a special category, more related to a larger process of ACC and LOC syncretism present in some HMLD.Cro varieties, more specifically the 'movement vs. location' distinction. All but one of the case-marking instances are from Gen.1B and Gen.2 speakers. Italian is not a direct influence contributing to these forms. However, Italian is an influence in the construction, *od* 'from' + possessor-GEN, that is 'double-marked'. What this means is that in comparison, HMLD.Cro has GEN. marking on the post-posed possessor only.

Word order changes occur in the form of clitic movement leftwards to initial position and post-posed adjectives. These are influenced by Italian models, and there is influence from Italian in the poly-functionality of Italian conjunctions that are transferred onto Croatian, eg. *da*-COMP 'that' used as a REL.PRON. Syntactic calques from Italian such as *uvijek* 'always' instead of *nikada* 'never' in a NEG sentence, and sequence of tense PAST forms in narratives are also found. The most prominent syntactic change is the replacement of target IPFV verbs with non-target PFV ones that occurs eleven times in the corpus. In nine cases the non-target PFV form is the 'base' form of the verb. This is a possible 'linguistic' cause for these instances, ie. where a lack of distinction in regard to telicity is made, base-form – in most instances here the PFV – becomes the default. Polinsky (2006, 2008) found instances of non-target use of aspectual forms for both target PFV and IPFV verbs, but with many instances of PFV forms occurring in the presence of imperfectivising sentential triggers, such as habitual adverbs – eg. *r'jetko* 'rarely' in (41) and *uvijek* 'always' in (42) above – when predicates are lexically telic. As a result, amongst younger generation speakers, there are initial signs that imperfective verbal aspect becomes replaced with the perfective one, the 'base form' of the verb. This suggests that the morphologically 'more simplex' form of the verb can end up being the form that encompasses both aspects.

Code-switching examples, both intra- and inter-clausal ones, come from speakers of all generation groups. Although the data sample is relatively small, it is of note that a greater frequency of code-switching was *not* observed amongst Gen.1B and Gen.2 informants. The roughly equivalent incidence of loan translations and code-switches suggests that the former is a strategy that is employed either to avoid the latter, or that the transfer and replication of Italian structure onto Croatian forms obviates, to some extent, the functions that code-switching may perform.

In conclusion, there are very few examples of discourse-pragmatic forms that are transferred from Italian, and few prominent phonological features characteristic of Italian. In regard to the latter, it should be said that the phonological inventories of the contributing codes – Croatian Istrian non-standard Štokavian varieties as well as Standard Croatian, and Triestine dialect as well as (regionally-influenced) Standard Italian – bear many similarities and relatively few differences.

References

Backus, Ad. & Dorlejin, Margreet. 2009. Loan translations versus code-switching. In Barbara Bullock & Almeida Jacqueline Toribio (eds.), *The Cambridge Handbook of Linguistic Code-switching*, 75–94. Cambridge: Cambridge University Press.

Barnes, Hilary. 2010. Subject pronoun expression in bilinguals of two null subject languages. In Karlos Arregi (ed.) *Romance Linguistics 2008. Interactions in Romance. Selected Papers from the 38th Linguistic Symposium on Romance Languages (LSRL), Urbana-Champaign, April 2008*, 9–22. Amsterdam: John Benjamins.

Benussi, Cristina. 2001. Dentro Trieste: un po' di storia. In Cristina Benussi, *Dentro Trieste. Voci e volti di ebrei, greci, sloveni, serbi, croati*, 5–24. Trieste: Hammerle Editori in Trieste.

Bonifacio, Marino & Gianni Cimador. 2013. *I Cognomi Triestini e Goriziani. Origini, storia, etimologia dall'Istria al Basso Friuli*. Trieste: Il Piccolo, Lint.

Browne, Wayles. 1974. Serbo-Croatian enclitics for English-speaking learners, *Journal of Slavic Linguistics* 12(1). 249–283.

Clyne, Michael. 1991. *Community languages. The Australian experience*. Cambridge: Cambridge University Press.

Čilaš, Ankica, Irena Drpić & Mijo Lončarić. 2007. La lingua dei croati di Trieste. In J. C. Damir Murković (ed.), *I croati a Trieste*, 471–484. Trieste: Comunità croata di Trieste.

Čoralić, Lovorka. 1997. Povijest [History]. In Natka Badurina, *Hrvatska/Italija, stoljetne veze: povijest, književnost* [Croatia/Italy, centuries-long connections: history, literature], 23–40. Zagreb: Društvo hrvatskih književnika.

Čoralić, Lovorka. 2001. *U gradu svetoga Marka. Povijest hrvatske zajednice u Mlecima* [In the city of St. Mark. A history of the Croatian community in Venice]. Zagreb: Golden marketing.

D'Alessio, Vanni & Olga Diklić. 2007. Studenti croati, il caso della Scuola Nautica. In J. C. Damir Murković (ed.), *I croati a Trieste*, 425–470. Trieste: Comunità croata di Trieste.

Deanović, Mirko. 1972. *Dubrovačke preradbe Molièreovih komedij*. [Dubrovnik adaptations of Molière's comedies] Zagreb: JAZU.

Doria, Mario. 1984. *Grande Dizionario del Dialetto Triestino*. Trieste: Edizioni Italo Svevo.

Dorleijn, Margreet & van der Heijden, Hanneke. 2000. Verbs and their objects in Turkish spoken in the Netherlands. Paper presented at the 10th International Conference on Turkish Linguistics, 16–18 August, Bogazici Üniversitesi, Istanbul.

Ďurovič, Ľubomír. 1983. The case systems in the language of diaspora children. *Slavica Lundensia* 9. 21–94.

Ďurovič, Ľubomír. 1984. The diaspora children's Serbo-Croatian. In Benjamin Stolz, I. R. Titunik & Lubomir Doležel (eds.), *Language and literature theory*, 19–28. Ann Arbor: University of Michigan.

Field, Fredric. 2002. *Linguistic borrowing in bilingual contexts*. Amsterdam/Philadelphia: John Benjamins.

Haugen, Einar. 1950. The analysis of linguistic borrowing. *Language* 26. 210–231.

Hlavac, Jim. 2016. Code-switching, lexico-grammatical features and loan translation: data from a large Macedonian-English corpus. *Philologica Estonica* 1. 38–60.

Isurin, Ludmila & Ivanova-Sullivan, Tanya. 2008. Lost in between: the case of Russian heritage speakers. *Heritage Language Journal* 6(1). 72–104.

Jurišić, Šimun. 2003. *Trst-Trieste-Trešt (i prinosi Južnih Slavena talijanskom gradu)* [Trst-Trieste-Trešt and contributions of South Slavs to an Italian city]. Split: Tehničar-kopirni centar.

Krpina, Zdravka. 2016. Nastava hrvatskoga jezika u Italiji [Croatian language instruction in Italy] *Jezik* 63(4–5). 151–166.
Labov, William. 1972. *Sociolinguistic patterns*. Philadelphia: University of Pennsylvania Press.
Laleko, Oksana. 2010. *The syntax-pragmatics interface in language loss: Covert restructuring of aspect in heritage Russian*. PhD Thesis, University of Minnesota.
Ljubičić, Maslina. 2009. Sui metaplasmi delle parole croate nel dialetto veneto. *Studia Romanica et Anglica Zagrabiensia* 54. 83–110
Pahor, Milan. 2007. Gli sloveni e i croati. In J. C. Damir Murković (ed.), *I croati a Trieste*. 45–72. Trieste: Comunità croata di Trieste.
Parovel, Paolo G. 2013. Alfabeti medievali e moderni della lingua croata. In *La Voce di Trieste*, Trieste: Edigraf.
Piasevoli, Vesna. 2007. La comunità Croata di Trieste ed altre associazioni. In J. C. Damir Murković (ed.), *I croati a Trieste*. Trieste: Comunità croata di Trieste, 495–512.
Polinsky, Maria. 2006. Incomplete acquisition: American Russian. *Journal of Slavic Linguistics* 14(2). 191–262.
Polinsky, Maria. 2007. Reaching the end point and stopping mid way: different scenarios in the acquisition of Russian. *Russian Linguistics* 31. 157–199.
Polinsky, Maria. 2018. *Heritage Languages and Their Speakers*. Cambridge, UK: Cambridge University Press.
Sočanac, Lelija. 2004. *Hrvatsko-talijanski jezični dodiri* [Croatian-Italian language contacts]. Zagreb: Nakladni zavod Globus.
Strčić, Petar. 2007. La storia dei croati. In J. C. Damir Murković (ed.), *I croati a Trieste*, 19–44. Trieste: Comunità croata di Trieste.
Van Hout, Roeland & Muysken, Pieter. 1994. Modeling lexical borrowability. *Language Variation and Change* 6(1). 39–62.
Vascotto, Patrizia. 2001. I croati. In Cristina Benussi (ed.), *Dentro Trieste. Voci e volti di ebrei, greci, sloveni, serbi, croati*, 63–71.Trieste: Hammerle Editori in Trieste.

Croatian in North America

USA

Dunja Jutronić
The Croatian language in the USA: Changes in Croatian syntax as a result of contact with English

1 Introduction

The language of Croatian immigrants in the United States of America (hereafter: USA) and their descendants has been described by a number of language contact researchers, e.g., Jutronić (1974, 1976), Albin (1976), Jutronić-Tihomirović (1980, 1983, 1985), Ward (1980), Filipović (1982, 1984, 1992), Bauer (1983), Gasiński (1986) and also by Lenček and Magner (1976) who edited a volume devoted to this topic, *The dilemma of the melting pot: The case of the South Slavic Languages*. More recently, Zubčić's (2009/2010) detailed bibliography contextualises research on Croatian in the USA with that undertaken on other Croatian-speaking communities in Western Europe and elsewhere.

This chapter deals specifically with changes in Croatian syntax as a result of contact with English in the USA. Earlier studies on Croatian as an immigrant language focused generally on lexical transference, which is perhaps a more readily reportable or conspicuous phenomenon than the transference of syntactic structures. Consequently, it is not surprising that in the investigations of the Croatian language in the USA (hereafter: USA.Cro) little attention has been paid to the description of influences of English on the syntactic level and descriptions of syntactic change are relatively brief. For example, Albin (1976) devotes only a couple of lines to syntactic transference where he states that "syntactic constructions due to E [English] influence rarely occur in our material . . . the most noted is the verb 'go' plus an adverbial particle . . . *Kad je otišao u Jugoslaviju natrag* ('When he went back to Yugoslavia')" (1976: 86–87). Here, *natrag* 'back' is perceived as redundant as the verb *otišao* 'went off' encompasses the notion of 'return', and employment of *natrag* is accounted for due to the form of the English equivalent

---

Note: I would like to thank Prof. Diana Stolac and Dr Jim Hlavac first for their invitation to participate and write this chapter on Croatian in the United States. Second, as my work on the chapter progressed I was greatly helped by their encouragment and helpful assistance. Last but not the least, I am very much impressed by the extraordinary enthusiasm that they put into the realization of this edited volume.

Dunja Jutronić, University of Maribor, University of Split

https://doi.org/10.1515/9781501503917-010

'back'. In a normatively based study, Bauer (1983) lists syntactic "deviations" in an American Croatian newspaper *Zajedničar* 'The Fraternalist' locating instances of non-standard inflections. In Gasiński's (1986: 44) description of émigré speakers' speech there is a short paragraph on the lack of concord between adjectives and nouns but little else on syntax. In another paper written at the time, Jutronić-Tihomirović (1983) touches on the topic of syntactic transference, but with a discussion of general trends only without a comprehensive investigation. The present contribution therefore seeks to advance current descriptions of USA. Cro by re-examining and extending the findings from existing data samples.

This chapter is structured in the following way. The remaining parts of this section present general demographic and sociolinguistic information on Croatian-origin residents in the USA and on Croatian-speakers in that country. Section 2 presents information on the speech community that the informants of this chapter come from. Section 3 contains a presentation and linguistic description of the speech of second-generation speakers and Section 4 contains the conclusion with findings summarized.

1.1 History of contact, vintages of emigration, status

Legend has it that the first Croatian immigrants to America were Dalmatian sailors on Christopher Columbus' ships (Øverland 2000: 66). As a seafaring people, it is likely that many Croats sailed to (and back from) America in the centuries following Columbus' arrival. Still, by the year 1880, it is estimated that there were only approx. 20,000 Croats living in the United States of America. In the following years and beyond the turn of the century, there was large-scale emigration that coincided with waves of emigration from other Eastern European countries (Prpić 1997; Čizmić 1998).

In the immediate post-WWII period, it was mainly political emigrants who arrived, followed in the 1960s by both political and economic migrants. Immigration continued with numbers of war refugees in the 1990s, and mostly well-educated economic migrants from the 1990s to today. The Croatian language has no *de jure* status in the US. The 'melting pot' nature of America's immigration policies means that government-sponsored language-learning resources are allocated to the acquisition and use of English, with little more than token support for the maintenance of heritage languages. The eminent US linguist, Joshua Fishman, reports on how badly these languages fare:

... the newest linguistic resources (actual and potential) of this country have always been so monstrously squandered and destroyed (at worst) or neglected and ignored (at best) that – except for the very most recent immigrants, some of their atypical children, and some rare and very "exotic" other exceptions – the USA has become an overwhelmingly monolingual English-speaking country. (Fishman 2004: 408. Original brackets and punctuation.)

1.2 Number of Croatian-heritage residents, number of Croatian-speakers

US census collections elicit data on "ancestry or ethnic origin" and "does this person speak a language other than English at home". From the 2010 census, the US Census Bureau (2012) reports that there were 414,714 residents with Croatian ancestry. This contrasts with homeland Croatian estimates that claim that 1,200,000 Americans are of Croatian origin (State Office for Croats Abroad 2016a). There are now fifth and sixth-generation Croatian-Americans, most of whom have little or no knowledge of Croatian. US Census collections still group speakers of Croatian together with speakers of Bosnian and Serbian, and the sum total of speakers who speak one of these three languages at home is 269,624 (Ryan 2013). The number of Croatian-speakers of this group is up to one half, i.e. approx. 135,000. To this figure I add those Gen.1 and Gen.2 speakers who have switched to English as their home language, and so I estimate that there are up to 175,000 Croatian-speakers in America.

1.3 Geographic distribution, socio-economic profile

Concentrations of Croats in the US reflect those cities or regions that have experienced economic and industrial expansion that typically attract economic migrants. There are high concentrations of Croats in the following areas: Chicago, New York, Pittsburgh, Cleveland, San Pedro, Los Angeles, Detroit and St Louis (Šipka 2017). Chain migration from Dalmatia and later from northern Croatia and Hercegovina was a feature of early to mid-twentieth-century emigration. Pre-existing networks into which recent immigrants could integrate had consequences on speakers' sociolinguistic and occupational profiles: most immigrants arrived with little or no proficiency in English and lived and often worked in communities in which they continued to regularly use their homeland regiolect; employment was often gained in manufacturing, construction, mining, and in California, in the fish and shipping industries. Post-1980 emigrants tended to have a higher level of education and proficiency in English. Upward mobility amongst second- and third-generation descendants of older vintage migrants, as well as the higher skill profile of more recent, post-1980 migrants to the US account for Croatian-Americans' high household income: in 2005 this was US$ 32,434 compared to the national average of US$ 25,039 (Čuka 2009).

1.4 Infrastructure

As the country that has, over many decades, accepted the single largest single number of Croatian immigrants, there are a vast number of organizations that reflect these emigrants' interests and affiliations: cultural associations – the oldest is the *Croatian American Cultural Center* of San Francisco founded in 1857, the biggest is the *Croatian Fraternal Union* (CFU) founded in 1897; churches – there are over 30 Croatian Catholic parishes across the US (St Jerome Croatian Catholic Church, 2012); political lobby groups, e.g. *Croatian American Association*; sporting associations – mainly in the form of soccer clubs, the first of which was founded in 1922, (Croatian National Soccer Federation of Canada and USA 2016); musical associations, e.g. tamburica through organisations such as the *Milwaukee Croatian Tamburitzans*; or regionally-focused ones – e.g. the *Association of Susak Emigrants in Hoboken, NJ*.

Where offered, Croatian-language instruction is usually provided by Croatian Catholic parishes, that are supported by the *CSAC – Croatian Schools of America and Canada* (HIŠAK Hrvatske iseljeničke škole Amerike i Kanade) that co-ordinates curriculum and resource development (Uldrijan 2011). These schools are supplementary only and are not aligned with mainstream school systems. At university level, there are lectorates at the University of Indiana and University of Iowa that are supported by Croatia's Ministry of Education. Other universities at which Croatian can be studied are University of Kansas, University of Detroit Mercy, and the University of Washington. Some American colleges and universities teach Croatian as part of programs under the designation of Bosnian-Croatian-Serbian, e.g. University of California (Berkeley), University of California (Los Angeles), Yale University and Northwestern University or as part of programs with the name 'Serbo-Croatian', e.g. Stanford University, University of Pennsylvania. Print media in Croatian is small-scale and within most Croatian organisations, English more so than Croatian is becoming the language of media communication. The CFU's newspaper *Zajedničar* 'The Fraternalist' was first published in 1905 in Pittsburgh and today has a circulation of 70,000 copies, but now with only a small number of pages in Croatian. This is reflective of the overall proficiency level in Croatian of most CFU members: at the autumn session of that organization, "English was declared the official language of the CFU (few readers were able to read in Croatian)" (Djuric 2003: 116–117) marking a language shift to English across this organization.

1.5 Domain use, language maintenance and shift

Use of Croatian is restricted to home/family, social networks and religion domains. Throughout the twentieth century, chain migration has been a feature of Croatian immigration to America, and Croatian was a commonly-used language for many newly-arrived migrants: they often gained employment with or through relatives or contacts who organised their passage to America. In the twenty-first century, Gen.1 migrants still report a high use of using Croatian at home – up to 94%. Amongst Gen.2 and Gen.3 members, there is a decrease in use and even reported proficiency, although both Jutronić (1976) and Filipović (2001) were able to gain linguistic data from Gen.2 and some Gen.3 speakers. Šipka (2017) also reports mixed levels of proficiency amongst heritage speakers, and limited opportunities for formal instruction amongst those wishing to acquire the (standard variety of the) language.

1.6 Contacts with Croatia. Host country attitudes towards Croats

In the past, geographical distance between America and Croatia meant that most Croatian-Americans' contacts with Croatia were infrequent. Nowadays, cheaper airplane fares for trans-Atlantic travel allow Croatian-Americans to more readily visit Croatia than throughout most of the twentieth century. Before the outbreak of the Covid-19 pandemic, direct flights between the USA (Philadelphia – Dubrovnik, with American Airlines) had been resumed only as late as June 2019, but inter-continental travel between the US and Croatia had become easier and cheaper over the last 30 years, greatly enabling travel between the two countries.

In the post-WWII era, as migrants from a homeland that was then a communist country, Croatians were afforded attention as well as recognition for their efforts to retain their cultural and religious practices. The 'Ethnic Revival' that occurred in America from the late 1960s onwards led to many second-, third- and fourth-generation descendants of migrants gaining a sense of pride in or positive identification with their ethnic heritage. For Croatians, this movement was punctuated by negative publicity due to an aeroplane hijacking and death of a policeman as a result of the activities of the self-proclaimed Fighters for Free Croatia in September 1976. This meant that many Croatian-Americans invested their energies in damage control of their own self-image and had fewer resources to focus on other community needs, including language maintenance resources. It possibly led to ambivalence amongst some young Croatian-Americans towards their ethnic heritage, with possible commensurate effects on language acquisition and use. Negative perceptions and sentiment did not really abate until the outbreak of the war in Croatia in 1991. Since then, Croatia has become a political and military (NATO) partner of the US, and it is now a popular holiday destination for Americans of Croatian and non-Croatian heritage alike.

2 The speech community

As stated, this chapter is a discussion of syntactic aspects in the speech of second-generation Croatian-Americans, focusing on this generational group due to the claim, as expressed by Hlavac (2003: 329) that, second-generation speakers are "the real 'movers and shakers' in (immigrant) language contact phenomena, especially in regard to switching and language change". This chapter is written with two aims in mind: The first is descriptive, i.e., selected syntactic characteristics are described with up to three examples provided in relation to each. The second aim is a classification of the kinds of changes that occur. In doing so I define here key terms that will be employed in this chapter: *transference*, the process whereby any "form, feature or construction [is] taken over by the speaker from another language, whatever the motives or explanation for this" (Clyne 2003: 76); *convergence*, i.e., "partial similarities increasing at the expense of differences" (Weinreich 1953: 41–42) with the understanding that in this context, convergence affects one language only and is not bi-directional. In other words, this application of the term *convergence* means that Croatian converges towards English and English remains unchanged. Further, there are features of acquisition that point to divergent pathways and instances of incomplete learning or even attrition i.e. changes in Croatian in the USA that indicate a reduction or loss of features (Schmid 2011). This chapter is organized in such a way that the discussion of the changes follows the description of each syntactic characteristic. Analysis is qualitative, not quantitative. Consequently, detailed data on the dispersion and recurrence of forms across the sample of speakers is not provided. The last section on findings and conclusion contains comment on language change in this language contact situation.

This section provides details on a sample of informants from whom recorded spoken language data were gained. Fieldwork research was conducted in Steelton, Pennsylvania, a small community (2010 pop. 5,990) situated 4 miles from Harrisburg. It was founded in 1866, a year after the Pennsylvania Steel Company had erected its first plant nearby. The steel plant prospered and the nearby town grew rapidly in population. Today the plant extends along each bank of the Susquehanna River and still constitutes the core of Steelton since the majority of its inhabitants work in it. Steelton's population includes a variety of ethnic groups – Italians, Hungarians, Germans, Irish and Welsh – and also Croats, along with Serbs, Slovenes and some Macedonians, with the four latter groups making up the largest immigrant cohort in the town. The story of Croatian immigration to Steelton is, in all respects, a typical immigrant story. The first Croatian immigrants arrived between 1880 and 1885, with a larger group following between 1885 and 1890. Most of the settlers came from Vivodina, an area in northern Croatia between Karlovac and the Slovenian border. Others came from the islands of Krk and Dugi Otok. The first immigrants were mostly young men from poor, rural areas and most of them intended to make some money and to return home. Some of them travelled back and forth, while others went back to marry and brought their wives back with them to America. Sometimes it would be years before they were able to save enough money for the *šifkarta* 'ship ticket' for their wives or families to come over. By 1895 there were sixty Croatian families in Steelton. The outbreak of WWI brought an end to all travel and mass immigration. Very few could leave their newly-adopted country and not many newcomers joined them from across the Atlantic. A great majority of Steelton's Croats worked in the steel mill. They did not know English and, as most of them were illiterate and unskilled, they were assigned the physically most demanding tasks at their place of work.

The participants in this sample are 11 older speakers from the second generation and can be considered 'heritage language speakers' amongst whom there can be wide variation in the level of (self-perceived) proficiency (Polinsky 1995). Most of them came from Steelton or from surrounding smaller towns in Pennsylvania; only one is from New York. The informants had, at most, 12 years of schooling and their occupational profiles range from office manager to steelworker, from postmaster to housewife. The informants were interviewed in Croatian by the author and all interviews were recorded. In the initial stages of the interviews I elicited some information on their family background, informants were then asked questions about familiar topics such as their own family, work, what they know about Croatia, community activities, in a semi-structured format. The primary aim was to encourage them to talk spontaneously as they do when they either speak with their parents or with their Croatian friends in order to avoid the artificiality of a formal interview. In addition, a smaller part of the data sample is made up of speech recorded from Croatian-speakers in Steelton, at public and semi-public gatherings. The interviews and informal observations were transcribed and then analyzed. The sociolinguistic questionnaire was given to the informants in order to obtain data on their use of Croatian, within their families and in their community (Jutronić-Tihomirović 1985). What is of importance here is that these informants are not speakers of standard Croatian, since the language they learned from their parents was either Kajkavian (coming from the villages in the area of Karlovac) or a Čakavian dialect (the island of Krk and Dugi Otok). As the interviewer, I accommodated my speech to that of my interlocutors on a number of occasions, especially in relation to Čakavian, in which I have proficiency. The variety of Croatian that the informants speak is a non-standard dialect, acquired in the home/family domain. Most informants received no formal instruction in Croatian and so their familiarity and level of contact with standard Croatian is restricted or even non-existent.

3 Description and analysis of the speech of second-generation speakers

The Croatian vernacular of second-generation Croatian-Americans has a number of grammatical features which both differentiate it from HMLD.Cro, and which show its adoption of features from the socially dominant language in the US, English. As stated in the introduction, these concern the phenomena of transference, to a lesser extent convergence and also language attrition. The focus of this chapter is on the following syntactic features: overt possessive adjectives (Section 3.1); overt (subject) personal pronouns (Section 3.2); word order and use of clitics (Section 3.3); overt (non-subject) personal pronouns (Section 3.4); use of AUX verbs *biti* 'to be' and *htjeti* 'to want', and use of *biti* 'to be' as COP (Section 3.5); possessive constructions (Section 3.6); passive (Section 3.7); numerals and dates (Section 3.8).

3.1 Overt possessive adjectives

Possessive adjectives are found to be used much more often in USA.Cro than in HMLD.Cro. In HMLD.Cro, possession is commonly expressed by dative constructions, e.g., *ona mi je sestra* 'she to me-DAT is sister'. In USA.Cro however, speakers tend to favour a construction such as *ona je moja sestra* 'she is my sister'. This construction is one that is closer to English, where constituents that relate back to the logical subject attract a possessive adjective.

(1) nego   sam   celi   **moj**   život
     but   AUX-1SG   whole-ACC.M.SG   my-ACC.M.SG   life-ACC.M.SG
     'but **my** whole life I...'

HMLD.Cro
nego   sam   c[ij]eli   Ø   život
but   AUX-1SG   whole-ACC.M.SG   Ø   life-ACC.M.SG

(2) je   **moj**   stric   **mi**   je   reka
    yeah   my-NOM.M.SG   uncle-NOM.M.SG   me-DAT   AUX-3SG   say-PST.M.SG
    'yeah, **my** uncle told me'

   HMLD.Cro
   da   stric   **mi**   je   reka(o)
   yes   uncle-NOM.M.SG   me-DAT   AUX-3SG   say-PST.M.SG

In the following example, not only the personal pronoun is overt, the subject pronoun that commences the utterance is also overt and does not occur in an equivalent HMLD.Cro construction:

(3) **ja**   sam   išla   k   **moji**
    I   AUX-1SG   go-PST.F.SG   to+DAT   my-DAT.F.SG [NON-TARGET]
    sestri
    sister-DAT.F.SG
    'I went to **my** sister'

   HMLD.Cro
   išla   sam   k   sestri
   go-PST.F.SG   AUX-1SG   to+DAT   sister-DAT.F.SG

Employment of possessive adjectives in examples (1) to (3) above is not an instance of change or transference as this construction exists in HMLD.Cro. However, its increased frequency in USA.Cro can be considered an example of convergence, as what appears to be happening is that a construction that has no congruent equivalent in English is falling into disuse – the unmarked DAT. construction – while the more marked personal possessive construction that matches closely the equivalent English construction is becoming the unmarked choice. This reduction in differences is in Weinreich's (1953) terms an example of convergence.

There are many further instances in addition to that shown in (3), where subject pronouns are employed overtly in a way that is considered redundant in HMLD.Cro. Croatian is a *pro*-drop language, i.e., non-emphatic subject pronouns are omitted. This sample of spoken data shows a higher incidence of non-required overt subject pronouns, although in studies of written texts of USA.Cro, the same observation is not made (Bauer 1983). Examples of subject pronouns are contained in the following section.

3.2 Overt (subject) personal pronouns

A number of examples are recorded in which personal pronouns in subject position are employed overtly:

(4) **ja** tamo   nemam   ništa   zašto   bi   **ja**
    I   there have-NEG.PRS1SG   nothing why   AUX-COND.1SG   I
    išo   tamo
    go-PST.M.SG   there
    '**I** do not have anything there, why should **I** go there?'

HMLD.Cro
tamo   nemam   ništa   zašto   bih   išao   tamo
there   have-NEG.1SG   nothing why   COND.1SG   go-PST.M.SG   there

(5) **mi** znademo   međ sobom   ali   **mi**   se   toliko   ne   vidimo
   we   know-1PL   among ourselves but   we   REFL   so much   NEG   see-1PL
   mi bili   bliže   more   bit   bilo   više
   we   be-PST.M.PL   closer   can-3SG be INF   be PST.N.SG   more
   ali   **mi**   nismo   blizu
   but   we   be-NEG.1PL   close
   '**We** know each other, but **we** don't see each other that often; if **we** lived nearer, it could be more, but **we** don't live close by.'

HMLD.Cro
međusobno   se   znamo   ali   se   ne   viđamo
among ourselves   REFL   know-1PL   but   REFL   NEG   see-PRS.1PL.ITERATIVE
toliko da   smo   bliže   može   bit   bi   bilo   više
much   if   be-3PL   closer   can-3SG   be-INF   COND   be-PST.N.SG   more
ali   nismo   blizu
but   be-NEG.1PL   close

As in the case of possessive adjectives, employment of subject pronouns is not an instance of overt transference, as the same category exists in HMLD.Cro, but apparently one of convergence where the *unmarked* use of subject pronouns in USA.Cro appears to resemble the near universal use of subject pronouns in English. Use of personal and possessive adjectives in USA.Cro appears to be a case of *transference* from English and other studies of South Slavic languages in predominantly Anglophone diaspora settings come to similar conclusions. For example, in varieties of

Serbian spoken in the USA, Savić reports that "in the variety of Serbian studied here, the pro-drop parameter is being reset in accordance with English syntactic rules" (1995: 387). Where the pro-drop parameter is attrited completely, i.e., where the absence of a subject pronoun is perceived by speakers of USA.Cro as unusual or marked, then we can speak of convergence and structural change. The corpus does not show that this has occurred yet, with employment of overt subject pronouns still being variable. These same findings are found widely in pro-drop diaspora languages in contact with English as a societally-dominant language, e.g. Montrul (2016), Serratrice (2007). Polinsky (2018: 254) views overt subjects as an example of "over-marking" and as a means for "heritage speakers to be clearer in production". It is possible that the 'narrative' and, at times, 'biographical' character of informants' elicited speech results naturally in a higher incidence of personal pronouns, as it would in HMLD.Cro. Overt subjects are recorded also in ITAL.Cro (Županović Filipin, Hlavac and Piasevoli, this volume), TRS.Cro (Piasevoli, this volume), CAN. Cro (Petrović, this volume) and AUS.Cro (Hlavac & Stolac, this volume).

3.3 Word order and use of clitics

Word order, although more flexible in Croatian than in English, plays an important role when several clitics are used in a sentence. In standard HMLD.Cro, clitic forms cannot occur in initial position but their place within a clause is typically second position (c.f. Wackernagel's law – Wackernagel 1892). In other words, they are attached to the first stressed constituent of a clause, with some exceptions such as some conjunctions and other words that send the clitic to third position. Where multiple clitics co-occur, the position of each clitic is determined hierarchically according to the following order:

particle	AUX	DAT	ACC/GEN	REFL	3SG.AUX
1	2	3	4	5	6

As can be seen from the above hierarchy, the 'outlier' is 3SG.AUX, which occupies the last position amongst clitics that are otherwise pre-posed, i.e. in second, third or fourth position. Other clitic forms of auxiliary verbs are in second position of this order (Browne 1974; Udier 2006). In non-standard varieties of Croatian, particularly the Čakavian and Kajkavian dialects that are the heritage varieties of this sample's informants, there can be variation in the placement of clitics that differs from the standard language. The two examples below contain instances in which the 'outlier' *je* (3SG.AUX) is positioned leftwards of its usual position as a finally placed clitic. Very often, instead of using clitics, informants use the full or emphatic form of the pronouns. They do this perhaps to obviate the need to consider the word order constraints of clitics, which apply in not only standard but also non-standard varieties of HMLD.Cro (cf. 3.4).

A number of examples of clitic placement are given below with different clitics used. Clitics are indicated in bold. Comments are given after each example or group of examples.

(6) ja kuham kako **je** **me** mama naučila
I cook-1SG how AUX-3SG me-ACC.SG mother-NOM.F.SG teach-PST.F.SG
'I cook as my mom taught me'

HMLD.Cro
kuham kako **me** **je** mama naučila
cook-1SG how me-ACC AUX-3SG mother-NOM.F.SG teach-PST.F.SG

As touched on above, the 'leftward' movement of the 3SG.AUX clitic in example (6) can be accounted for on the basis of the informants' heritage dialect. In Čakavian dialects Lisac (2003, 2009) reports variation in the position of the reflexive pronoun *se* and also *je*-3SG.AUX. Muljačić (2003) and Jutronić, Tomelić-Ćurlin and Runjić-Stoilova (2016) also locate leftward movement of *je* having an effect on the position of other clitics.

In the following example, (7), 3SG.AUX *je* occurs in initial position, which can occur in both Čakavian and Kajkavian dialects, but only in interrogatives such as *su našli?* (be-AUX.3PL [clitic] 'find' PTCP.3PL) 'did they find it?', instead of *jesu [li] našli* (be-AUX.3PL [full form] 'find' PTCP.3PL) (Vranić 2001; Galović 2017). Example (7) is, however, a declarative sentence, where the initial position of the clitic is highly marked. Conspicuous is also the subject pronoun which is not dropped as it would be in an equivalent HMLD.Cro utterance:

(7) **je** **on** govorio u talijanskom
AUX-3SG he speak-PST.M.SG in+LOC Italian-LOC.M.SG
jeziku
language-LOC.M.SG
'He spoke in Italian.'

HMLD.Cro
govorio **je** na talijanskom jeziku
speak-PST.M.SG AUX-3SG in+LOC Italian-LOC.M.SG language-LOC.M.SG

In relation to Kajkavian, Lončarić (1996: 116) does not report specifically on the position of the 3SG.AUX clitic, but concludes in general terms that "the place of clitics in Kajkavian is relatively freer than in our other dialects, but their position is not completely free". English does not possess the category *clitic pronouns* and there is no transference of morphosyntactic features from English in the informants' speech. In the following example, 3SG.AUX is moved leftward, but to a position not otherwise expected according to the informant's Kajkavian background:

(8) onda **je**   **ju**   primilo   ovdje
    then AUX-3SG her-ACC accept-PST.N.SG here
    '...then she got accepted here.'

   HMLD.Cro
   onda **ju**   **je**   primilo   ovdje
   then her-ACC AUX-3SG accept-PST.N.SG here

In various HMLD.Cro varieties, instances of clitic combinations are often resolved by the elision of *je* where the reflexive *se* occurs. The 3SG.AUX *je* can also be dropped after the pronominal clitic *me* me-ACC. and *te* you-ACC, e.g., *on te vidio* 'he you-ACC. see-PST.PART.' instead of *on te je vidio* 'he you-ACC. be-3SG.AUX see-PST.PART.3SG ('he saw you'). In the Kajkavian dialect of the informant, *je* 3SG. AUX is not dropped, but what is unusual is its placement left of the direct object clitic, *ju* her-ACC.

The above examples related to verbal clitics and the position of their order in the clause relates back to features of Croatian that they learned from their parents. The two examples presented below show clitics in a marked position, emphasized in italics, that cannot be easily accounted for on the basis of the heritage variety of the speaker:

(9) a   ona **je**   učila   **ih**   po hrvatski
    and she AUX.3SG teach-PST.F.SG them-ACC in Croatian-ACC.M.SG
    '...and she taught them Croatian.'

   HMLD.Cro
   a   ona **ih**   **je**   učila   hrvatski
   and she them-ACC AUX-3SG teach-PST.F.SG Croatian-ACC.M.SG

(10) jer   on   **nije**   javio   **se**   njega
    because he-NOM   NEG.AUX-3SG   volunteer-PST.M.SG REFL   him-ACC
    su   uzeli
    AUX-3PL take-PST.M.PL
    'but he did not report himself [volunteer], they took him.'

HMLD.Cro
jer   **nije**   **se**   on   javio   njega
because NEG.AUX.3SG   REFL   he-NOM   volunteer-PST.M.SG him-ACC
su   uzeli
AUX.3PL take-PST.M.PL

As stated, the position of clitics, both verbal and pronouns ones, cannot be accounted for by the informants' heritage variety. In (9), an object pronoun clitic is placed *after* the verb following English word order conventions, but not Croatian ones. In (10), the rightward movement of the reflexive particle *se* after the main verb *javio* appears also to be determined by the linear order of its English equivalent *because he didn't report himself*. In (11), the copula *su* also occurs in a position rightward to its unmarked position, which in HMLD. Cro conditional clauses is preposed to follow immediately after the conditional conjunction *ako* 'if':

(11) *ali   ako **im**   djeca   **su**   oženjena*
    but   if   them-DAT.PL   children-F.SG   be-3PL   marry-PASS.PTCP.F.SG
    onda   je   okay
    then   be-3SG   okay
    '. . .but if their children were married then it is okay.'

HMLD.Cro
ali   ako **su**   **im**   djeca   oženjena
but   if   be-3PL   them-DAT.PL   children-F.SG marry-PASS.PTCP.F.SG
onda   je   okej
then   be-3SG   okay

As in (9) and (10), the influence of an English model, with the copula following the subject *children are married* appears to be present. It is interesting to note that (11) contains an example of the DAT possessive construction. This suggests that a convergence to English has occurred, via an increased frequency of possessive constructions with possessive adjectives analogous to the form of this construction in English. But a complete *loss* or *attrition* of the DAT possessive construction has not occurred, as (11) shows.

It is not clear how the contact situation may influence the order of clitics, as many of the instances of marked or non-standard word order could be attributed to features of the informants' heritage dialect. This explanation is not water-tight as I lack descriptions of the particular local vernaculars of the informants, relating to the period when their parents lived in Croatia at the start of the twentieth century. Another conspicuous feature is that there are no instances of more than two clitics occurring in the same clause. A clustering of three or more clitics is perhaps not a frequent occurrence in spoken varieties of HMLD.Cro corpora, but such an absence of clusters of clitics is unusual. This suggests that informants may use clitics less frequently as part of a strategy to avoid them due to insecurity about their position or syntactic function vis-à-vis other forms. A lower frequency of clitics could also be reflective of a general tendency to employ longer forms instead. The lack of the feature clitic vs. full form pronouns and auxiliaries in English may play a role, but this is less clear, as explored further below.

What is clear is that *je* 'be' 3SG. occurs in positions leftwards from its position in standard HMLD.Cro. A pattern of leftward movement of *je* AUX so that it precedes objects, i.e., *je me, je mi, je ju, je učila ih, nije javio se* in examples (6) to (9) above shows that it is now occupying the position that other *biti*-AUX ('be-AUX') forms occupy. The exception is (9) and (10) where the forms of *biti*-AUX, *sam, su* (be-1SG, be-3PL) are moved rightward but these examples are calqued from English.

It is important to note that many of the instances of clitic ordering in the examples presented are unusual, and an initial observation is that there does not appear to be free variation, but at least a 'freer variation' in comparison to HMLD. Cro conventions. It is possible to say that firstly, there is an influence of home dialects. Third person *je* leftward movement is testified in other varieties of diaspora (namely Burgenland) Croatian, based on historically older varieties of HMLD.Cro dialects (Browne 2010). Secondly, there appears to be the influence of English word order that does not feature a dislocation of verbal auxiliaries rightwards. Avoidance as a feature that could pertain to clitic pronouns is further explored in the following section. Petrović (this volume) also records instances of leftward movement of 3SG.AUX *je* in CAN.Cro.

3.4 Overt (non-subject) personal pronouns

In this section, the form of non-subject personal pronouns is examined. As stated above, pronouns employed in non-initial position usually occur in their clitic form. Full form personal pronouns can occur in any position including initial position while their employment in medial or final position typically conveys emphasis or contrast. In the following examples, neither emphasis nor contrast was apparent from the speaker in regard to intonation or the thematic content of the utterance.

(12)   oni   su   **meni**   mogu   da   naprave
       they-M.PL AUX-3PL me-DAT.LONG-FORM can-PRS3 PL COMP make-3PL
       uzmu   **meni**   pola   jarde
       take-3PL me- DAT.LONG-FORM half+GEN yard-GEN.F.SG
       'they could do this **to me**, they could take **to me** half of yard [= half of **my** yard].'

HMLD.Cro
mogli   su   **mi**   napravit uzeti   **mi**
can-PST.M.PL AUX.3PL me-DAT.CLITIC make-INF take-INF me-DAT.CLITIC
pola   jarda
half+GEN yard-GEN.M.SG

In the following two examples, the overtness of full form OBJ pronouns is accompanied by overt subject pronouns (cf. 3.2). Pronouns are used overtly or rather, the stressed, i.e., longer pronominal forms are used instead of the unstressed, clitic forms. To make this clearer those subject pronouns that are overt and full-form object pronouns are marked in bold in example (13) below in place of narrow glosses.

(13)   ne   da   **ja**   **tebi**   govorim ne   da
       NEG   COMP I [OVERT] you-LONG FORM tell-1SG NEG COMP
       je   **meni**   neko   drugi govorio   to
       AUX-3SG me-LONG FORM somebody else tell-PST.M.SG that-NOM.N.SG
       je   **meni**   **moja**   mat
       AUX-3SG me-LONG FORM my [OVERT] mother-NOM.F.SG
       to   je   **meni**   reko
       that-NOM.N.SG AUX-3SG me-LONG FORM say-PST.3SG
       moj   brat
       my [OVERT] -NOM.M.SG brother-NOM.M.SG
       i   to   su   **meni**
       and   that-NOM.N.SG AUX-3PL me-DAT.FULL FORM
       moji   rekli
       my-NOM.M.PL [family members] say-PST.M.PL
       'It is not that **I** am telling **you** [LONG.FORM], it's not that somebody else told **me** [LONG.FORM]; it's **my** mother who told **me** [LONG.FORM], it's **my** brother who told **me** [LONG.FORM], **my** family told **me** [LONG.FORM].'

HMLD.Cro

ne	da	**ti**		govorim	ne	da	**mi**
NEG	COMP	you-DAT.CLITIC	tell-1.SG	NEG	COMP	me-DAT.CLITIC
je	netko	drugi	govorio	to		**mi**
AUX.3SG	somebody	else	tell-PST.M.SG	that-NOM.N.SG		me-CLIT
je	majka		to	**mi**		je
AUX.3SG	mother-NOM.F.SG		that-NOM.N.SG	me-DAT.CLIT		AUX.3SG
rekao	brat		i	to		su
say-PST.3SG	brother-NOM.M.SG	and	that-NOM.N.SG	AUX.3PL
mi	rekli	moji				
me-DAT.CLIT	say-PST.M.PL	my-NOM.M.SG [family members]

As stated above in relation to subject pronouns and a changing of the pro-drop function in some informants' repertoires, the use of pronouns shows convergence towards English models. It is important to mention that the speakers do not use stressed forms of pronouns primarily because they do not know the clitic forms. Examples (6), (8), (9) and (11) contain evidence that clitics are used in the informant's vernaculars. Further, amongst those informants with a Kajkavian home dialect, there can be dialectal influences that do not mark full forms of personal pronouns as overt to the same extent that these are marked in standard HMLD.Cro.

However, I would like to argue that it is variation or uncertainty in the placement of clitics in USA.Cro that accounts for this. The use of the long pronoun is a marked feature in HMLD.Cro in contrast to the short use of pronouns which is unmarked. There seems to be an emerging pattern, amongst some but not all speakers, for only the full form of the pronoun to be used. This can be accounted for by a lack of distinction of the feature (+/−emphasis) in the pronominal system in English. This means that the full forms of the pronouns are used, by some, without being marked for emphasis as they are in HMLD.Cro. What this means is that in USA.Cro, the feature (+/−emphasis) which in relation to object pronouns can be expressed via full or clitic form is less often expressed via this choice of morphological forms. To make up for this loss of structural choices to provide emphasis distinction, intonational or prosodic forms are employed to compensate for this loss, at least situationally. In other words, the form of a pronoun is now not checked for the feature emphasis, and instead, other linguistic means (e.g. intonation) are pressed into service to express a feature that has been lost formally. I observe here convergence to English as a result of the transference of English models onto the marking of personal pronouns. An attrition of clitic forms has not taken place, however, and this change in the form of personal pronouns is a nascent one only.

This finding is in line with general trends on language change in diaspora settings. In relation to choices within paradigms Polinsky (2018: 165–166) observes that the "phonetically heavier forms" tend to predominate, i.e. that a "form that is perceptually more prominent tends to win, and lighter forms may be lost". This is what appears to be happening with some speakers of USA.Cro in relation to the long vs. short form object pronoun choice. To be sure, and as Section 3.3 shows, clitics (including object pronoun ones) are not completely lost as a grammatical category in heritage speakers' vernaculars, and when speakers use clitics, there are no examples of an erroneous form of the clitic being used. But as Section 3.3 does show, their placement is prone to change. In some cases, change in placement is 'freer'; in other cases, change in placement relates to the non-observation of the anomalous rightward dislocation of the 3SG.AUX *je* which amounts to a regularisation of the word order paradigm of clitics. In CAN.Cro (Petrović, this volume) and NZ.Cro (Stoffel and Hlavac, this volume) instances of overt non-subject pronouns are also recorded.

3.5 Use of AUX verbs *biti* 'to be' and *htjeti* 'to want', and use of *biti* 'to be' as COP

In Croatian, actions that occurred in the past are usually represented via PRF tense, a compound tense that consists of an inflected form of the AUX *biti* 'to be' and the PST.PTCP which agrees with the subject in gender and number. The following instances of omission of AUX *biti* are found:

(14) za   njom   Ø **došla**   Marđi
     after+INS   her-INS.F.SG   come-PST.F.SG   Margie-NOM.F.
     '... after her came Margie'

HMLD.Cro
za   njom   **je**   **došla**   Marđi
after+INS   her-INS.F.SG   AUX-3SG   come-PST.F.SG   Margie-NOM.F

(15) bole (bolje) **Ø mi   se**   **slagali**   nego   oni
     better   we REFL   get along-PST.M.PL   than   they-NOM.M.PL
     'we got along better than they did'

HMLD.Cro
bolje **smo se slagali** nego oni
better AUX-1PL REFL get along-PST.M.PL than they-NOM.M.PL

(16) ja mislim od hrvatsku školu Ø
 I think-PRS.1SG from Croatian-ACC.F.SG school-ACC.F.SG
 finili
 finish-PST.M.PL
 'I think they finished Croatian school.'

HMLD.Cro
mislim da **su finili / završili** hrvatsku školu
think-1SG COMP AUX-3PL finish-PST.M.PL Croatian-ADJ.ACC school-ACC.F.SG

The following example appears in FUT, also a compound tense in Croatian, consisting of the AUX *htjeti* 'want'/ 'will' which is conjugated and the INF. In (17) below, the AUX is omitted.

(17) *pap* ja ne Ø *rabotati* tu
 dad-VOC.M.SG I NEG work-INF here
 'Dad, I will not work here.'

HMLD.Cro
tata Ø **neću rabotati/raditi** tu
dad-VOC.M.SG I NEG.FUT.AUX-1SG work-INF here

Different forms of AUX *biti* ('to be') are omitted: 3SG *je*; 1PL *smo*; 3PL *su* and 1SG of *htjeti*, *ću* ('I will'). The instances of omission of the AUX in the perfect tense cannot be considered examples of the *krnji perfekt* ('truncated perfect') which is a use of the perfect tense without auxiliary occurring in headlines and repetitive narrations. In their samples of diaspora Serbian, Savić (1995) and Dimitrijević-Savić (2008) also locate deletion of the AUX in perfect tense, but only where the AUX is 3SG *je*.

In regard to the speech of second-generation Serbian-Australians, Dimitrijević-Savić (2008) discounts the possibility of English influence on AUX omission in the perfect (or in other English tenses in which the AUX is *be*) as AUX omission does not happen in English for these tenses. Instead, Dimitrijević-Savić (2008: 78) relates AUX *je* omission to the multiple roles that it performs, as a clitic (placed last when co-occuring with other clitics in standard Croatian) and as a non-clitic AUX. As a non-clitic AUX, *je* is omitted when it co-occurs with REFL *se* in both standard and non-standard varieties of Croatian. But forms of the AUX other than 3SG are not omitted, so it is hard to attribute the various forms of AUX that are omitted in this sample to this convention in standard and non-standard varieties of Croatian. While this data sample shows a trend of variable placement of clitic *je* shown in examples (6) to (9) above, an explanation of omission of different forms of the AUX perhaps needs to go beyond looking at the 3SG.AUX *je* form only. One possible account is that the default past tense in English, simple past, consists of one form only. According to this view, omission of the AUX is influenced by English's single-form past simple, while the remaining Croatian verbal form, the past participle, shows agreement with the subject through morphological marking for gender and number. Example (17) is slightly different since the negative form of the auxiliary indicating future tense (*neću* 'I will not') is reduced to just the NEG (*ne* 'not') and there is no finite verb in the clause. It is possible that a 'single-form' past construction in English (i.e. Eng. past simple) and its high frequency in English is a feature being transferred onto Croatian verb constructions consisting of only single forms only. Example (17) may be an 'outlying' instance of AUX omission that cannot be adequately accounted for here.

The following examples record omission of *biti* ('to be') in present tense (existential) utterances where it functions as a copula. Here, omission of *biti* occurs, perhaps conspicuously, in the 3SG. form *je* ('is') only and this is marked below via 'Ø'.

(18) **to   Ø   vražja   Kata**
     that-NOM.N.SG   devilish-NOM.F.SG   Kata-NOM.F.SG
     'that's devilish Kata' [Croatian equivalent for the female first name 'Kate']

     HMLD.Cro
     to   je   vražja   Kata
     that-NOM.N.SG   be-3SG   devilish-NOM.F.SG   Kata-NOM.F.SG

(19) **ona   Ø**   *četrdeset i šest*   *godina*   *stara*
     she-NOM   forty-six+GEN.PL   year-GEN.F.PL   old-ADJ.NOM.F.SG
     'she is 46 years old'

     HMLD.Cro
     ona je   četrdeset i šest   godina   stara
     she   be-3SG   forty-six+GEN.PL   year-GEN.F.PL   old-ADJ.NOM.F.SG

These examples of omission of the copula appear to be an extension by analogy of *je* omission for the perfect tense. As stated, Dimitrijević-Savić (2008) also records instances of 3SG copula omission in her Australian-Serbian sample. Example (19) above contains a dialect-based construction *biti* ('be') + number + *godina* ('year') + *star* ('old'), which is identical to the equivalent English construction. In standard HMLD.Cro, a different construction is required: *imati* ('have') + number + *godina* ('year').

3.6 Possessive constructions

Recalling the first three examples given in this chapter, I have shown that possessive adjectives are used overtly in constructions in which they occur attributively before the noun that they describe. In HMLD.Cro a pre-posed DAT of a personal pronoun is the more frequently employed construction. In the following examples, further possessive constructions are presented. In Croatian, relations of possession can be expressed through a pre-posed attributive such as a personal adjective, e.g. *naše* 'our' *ime* 'name' ('our name'), or a possessive form of a noun, e.g. *majčino* 'mother's' *ime* 'name' ('mother's name'). These are examples of pre-posed, determiner-like possessives. Possession can also be expressed via post-posed GEN constructions, eg., *ime* 'name' *majke* 'mother+GEN' ('mother's name), where GEN morphological markers show the possessive. Comparing the two possessive constructions, the pre-posed one is considered stylistically preferable, at least in standard HMLD.Cro and also in most non-standard varieties. However, there is a restriction to this construction: normally only a simplex (i.e. single-form) possessor can occur in the pre-posed position. If the possessor contains two or more elements, then a post-posed construction is typically employed, eg. *ime* 'name' *naše* 'our+GEN' *majke* 'mother+GEN' ('name of our mother').

In non-standard varieties of Croatian, a further construction is possible that features the preposition *od* 'from' and a pre-posed GEN, with the modifying possessor before the possessed: *od* 'from+GEN' *majke* 'mother+GEN' *ime* 'name' (lit. 'from mother name'). Example (20) below is an example of this dialect-based possessive. The rearrangement of the head noun and its modifiers seems to have much to do with similar structures expressed in English where nouns become (pre-posed) possessives through addition of the apostrophe and -*s* (i.e. via the 'Saxon genitive').

(20) **o[-d]   naše   majke   ime   je**
     of+GEN   our-GEN.F.SG   mother-GEN.F.SG   name-NOM.N.SG   AUX-3SG
     bilo   Grubišić
     be-PST.N.SG   Grubišić
     '**our mother's name** was Grubišić'

HMLD.Cro
ime **naše** **majke** je bilo
name-NOM.N.SG our-GEN.F.SG mother-GEN.F.SG AUX-3SG be-PST.N.SG
Grubišić

The pre-modifying GEN construction with *od* 'from' allows multiple elements to pre-pose and to modify the possessor and example (20) above contains two elements, *naše* 'our' and *majke* 'mother' that occur before *ime* 'name'. As stated, this is in contrast to standard Croatian that allows only one pre-posing element. This construction can also feature the possessed element not only as a subject, but as an object, as shown in (21) below:

(21) zoven **od** *mojega* *muža* **mamu**
 call-1SG of+GEN my-GEN.M.SG husband-GEN.M.SG mom-ACC.F.SG
 'I call **my husband's mother**'

 HMLD.Cro
 zoven **mamu** *mojega* *muža*
 call-1SG mom-ACC.F.SG my-GEN.M.SG husband-GEN.M.SG

This construction is found also where possession is not semantically present, but where the pre-posed modifier is not a possessor but attributively describes the composition of the following noun:

(22) **od** **rezance** **žuhu (juhu)**
 of+GEN noodle-ACC.M.PL soup-ACC.F.SG.
 '...noodle soup.'

 HMLD.Cro
 juhu **s** **rezancima**
 soup-ACC.F.SG with+INS noodle-INS.M.PL.

In (23) below, the preposition *od* 'from' is omitted. But the sequence of elements and case marking indicate that pre-posed *naše majke* our mother+GEN is the possessor of *kuća* 'house':

(23) i **naše** **majke** **kuća** je imala
    and our-GEN.F.SG mother-GEN.F.SG house-NOM.F.SG AUX-3SG have-PST.F.SG
    'and **our mother's house** had. . .'

HMLD.Cro
i **kuća** **naše** **majke** je imala
and house-NOM.F.SG our-GEN.F.SG mother-GEN.F.SG AUX-3SG have-PST.F.SG

Omission of the preposition *od* in (23) is not a feature of the HMLD.Cro dialect of this speaker. The preposition serves the function of showing the relations between the pre-posed two elements (and their case marking) on the one hand, and the possessed element that is in NOM on the other. Omission of the preposition has the effect that it may appear less clear to outsiders that the pre-posed elements modify the possessed element, but to counter this, GEN case marking is still present. To the speaker of this utterance, it is clear that the GEN markers obviate uncertainty about the role of the pre-posed elements. The sequencing of the elements mirrors that of an equivalent English 'Saxon-genitive' constructions that have pre-posed modifiers. I argue that the structure of the equivalent English construction bears an influence on the occurrence of utterances such as those in (21) to (23). What is also apparent, as observed above in relation to example (2) in section 3.1 is that the adnominal possessive DAT construction: *majka* 'mother-NOM' *nam* 'us-DAT' *se* 'REFL' *zove* 'call-3SG' is not the construction that the informant employs. This would be the most unmarked construction in standard HMLD.Cro. (Some non-standard HMLD.Cro varieties still feature the pre-posed *od* construction). The adnominal possessive DAT construction is likely to be familiar to the informant, but I posit that it is not employed here as it is not the most unmarked construction for this speaker and also because the speaker may also avoid constructions with multiple clitics, *nam* 'to us' and *se* REFL. In (24), a three-element modifier, *mojga očeva brata* 'my father's brother's' functions attributively to the object of possession, *či* (*kćer*) 'daughter':

(24) ona Mara mojga očeva **brata** **či (kći)**
    that-NOM.F.SG Mara-NOM.F.SG my-GEN.M.SG father-GEN.M.SG-POSS brother-GEN.M.SG daughter-NOM.F.SG
    'that Mara, the **daughter of my father's brothe**r'

HMLD.Cro
ona   Mara   **kći**   **brata**
that-NOM.F.SG Mara-NOM.F.SG daughter-NOM.F.SG brother-GEN.M.SG
mojega   **oca**
my-GEN.M.SG father-GEN.M.SG.

In (25) a dual-element pre-posed modifier is employed that bears NOM not GEN marking:

(25) *sveta*   *Marija*   *crkva*
     saint-ADJ.F.NOM.SG Mary-F.NOM.SG church-F.NOM.SG
     '**St. Mary's** church'

     HMLD.Cro
     crkva   **svete**   **Marije**
     church-F.NOM.SG saint-ADJ.F.GEN.SG   Mary-F.GEN.SG

Example (25) has neither *od* 'from' nor GEN marking, but contains two pre-posed possessors. It appears as a calque of the equivalent English. Example (25) is not a possessive construction in the semantic sense, as *St. Mary* does not *possess* the church. Rather *St. Mary* is a designation given to the church. Notwithstanding this, GEN marking would otherwise be expected to form this construction. An English-based construction is being employed here in a way that lacks case marking or overt morphology.

The following examples are semantically possessive ones where both *od* 'from' and GEN case marking are omitted, and it is the order of the elements that indicates the hierarchical relations between them:

(26) *pa* *njegova*   *žena*   *sestra*
     then his-NOM.M.SG   wife-NOM.F.SG   sister-NOM.F.SG
     '... then **his wife's sister**'

     HMLD.Cro
     pa   **sestra**   **njegove**   **žene**
     then sister-NOM.F.SG   his-GEN.M.SG   wife-GEN.F.SG

Example (26) was not readily understandable to the author when she heard this: it was my knowledge of the broader context *and* my familiarity with the dialect-diaspora possessive constructions employed by the informants that enabled me to understand the relations. These line up, as the gloss shows, in a way that follows English possessive construction word order.

In example (27), it appears that the phrase *mat i otac* 'mother and father' or *mat ili otac* 'mother or father' has become a fixed expression in the informant's repertoire that remains in NOM even when it is the possessor of the following noun:

(27) kad   dojedu   na   **mat**   ili   **otac**
      when   come-3PL   on+ACC   mother-NOM.F.SG   or   father-NOM.M.SG
      kuću
      house-ACC.F.SG
      'when they come to my **mother's or father's house**'

HMLD.Cro
kad   dođu   u   **kuću**   matere   ili
when   come-3PL   in+ACC   house-ACC.F.SG   mother-GEN.F.SG   or
oca
father-GEN.M.SG

The interesting feature in examples (26) and (27) is not only the pre-positing under the influence of home dialects and English but the use of NOM in the possessive constructions. This is interesting because even if there may be changes to the case system or changes in speaker's case repertoires, I expect that nouns adjacent to each other with a particular relationship between them (possessive-GEN, directional-DAT) will still bear case marking to show these relationships between respective constituents. Genitive case-marking and *od* 'from' are present in examples (20) and (21), while in (22) *od* is followed by non-target ACC case marking. In (23) and (24), *od* is omitted but GEN case marking is retained. In (25) to (27), a progression of change in possessive constructions is most apparent with both *od* and GEN case marking absent. Primary causation for this appears to be the *od* construction in the informants' homeland dialects, that can undergo both loss of case marking and loss of *od* with a word order sequencing resembling that of English possessive NPs. A further possessive in example (28) shown here, contains a two-element modifier *moj oče[-v]* 'my father's' in NOM preceding the object of possession:

(28) najprije   je   bio   **moj**   **oče[-v]**
     first of all-ADV AUX-3SG   be-PST.M.SG   my-NOM.M.SG   father-NOM.M.SG
     brat
     brother-NOM.M.SG
     'first it was **my father's brother**'

HMLD.Cro
najprije   je   bio   **brat**   **mojega**
first of all-ADV AUX-3SG   be-PST.M.SG.   brother-NOM.M.SG   my-GEN.M.SG
oca
father-GEN.M.SG

In the final example (29) presented here, a pre-posed modifier results in a change of meaning. In English, a *steel factory* manufactures steel. Here, the pre-posed modifier is logically the product that the factory produces. In all varieties of Croatian, the product must be post-posed, i.e. *fabrika željeza* 'factory of steel'. A pre-position of *željezo* 'steel', even in its adjectival form, yields the meaning *factory made of steel*.

(29) u   **železni**   **fabriki**
     in   steel-ADJ.LOC(?).F.SG   factory-LOC.F.SG
     'in the steel factory'

HMLD.Cro
u   **fabrici**   **žel[-j]eza**
in   factory-LOC.F.SG   steel-NOUN.GEN.N.SG

Instances of *od* 'of'/'from' as a periphrastic marker of possession, with or without GEN marking of the succeeding possessor, are recorded in MOL.Cro (Ščukanec, Breu and Vuk, this volume), AUT.Cro (Ščukanec, this volume) and NZ.Cro (Stoffel and Hlavac, this volume).

3.7 Use of passive

Croatian has passive constructions that, like English, feature 'be' (*biti*) as AUX, with the passive participle. Passive voice is much less frequent in Croatian than in English, and is usually marked as high register, formal or impersonal. The following passive constructions are found in the sample:

(30) moj   je   brat   ubijen
     my-NOM.M.SG AUX-3SG   brother-NOM.M.SG   kill-PASS.PTCP.M.SG
     'my **brother was killed**'

Example (30) above is not conspicuously high register or marked in HMLD.Cro. The same utterance is given below in active voice to show how this construction would otherwise be expressed:

    Active voice equivalent:
    ubili   su   **mi**   **brata**
    kill-PST.M.PL   AUX-3PL   me-DAT   brother-ACC.M.SG

The following two examples (31) and (32) are conspicuously higher in register and are marked as such in HMLD.Cro with equivalent forms.

(31) ručak   je   bio   donesen
     lunch-NOM.M.SG   AUX-3SG   be-PST.M.SG   bring-PASS.PTCP.M.SG
     '... the dinner **was brought**.'

    HMLD.Cro
    donijeli   su   ručak
    bring-PST3PL   AUX-3PL   lunch-ACC.M.SG

(32) trešnje   su   bile   ubrane
     cherry-NOM.F.PL AUX-3PL   be-PST.F.PL   pick-PASS.PTCP.F.PL
     '... cherries **were picked**.'

    HMLD.Cro
    ubrali   su   trešnje
    pick-PST.3PL   AUX.3PL   cherry-ACC.F.PL

Examples (30) to (32) above are all grammatically well-formed, but sound conspicuously high-register, particularly considering the level of register generally used by the informants. Croatian passive particles bear suffixes that pattern according to verb group and these are not, in contrast to English, co-morphemic with past participle suffixes. As a result, they represent a separate and discrete grammatical category that is characteristically acquired later than other morphological forms. External influence is a likely influence in the occurrence of these passives, as the unmarked English equivalent for this clause is a passive construction. The influence of equivalent English constructions is perhaps not the only factor that accounts for the passive constructions found in the examples above. The incidence of the passive in (30), for example is I contend, due to a preference for possessive pronoun forms, as well as an avoidance of the adnominal possessive construction, *ubili su mi* (me-DAT CLITIC) *brata* 'they killed my brother'.

In these examples, a Croatian verb in active voice with 3PL marking would be the unmarked equivalent, as shown above. Another equivalent construction employed in Croatian is reflexive. In the following instances (33) and (34), passives are employed for constructions which would otherwise be REFL in HMLD. Cro. The use of passive changes the meaning of the utterance as in the following example:

(33) tako **smo** u Rimu **slikani**
 so AUX-1PL in+LOC Rome-LOC.M.SG photograph-PASS.PTCP.M.PL
 'So **we were photographed** in Rome' [= 'So we took photos (of ourselves) in Rome']

 HMLD.Cro
 tako **smo** **se** slikali u Rimu
 so AUX.1PL REFL take photos-PST.M.PL in+LOC Rome-LOC.M.SG

(34) on **je** **bio** **prevaren** u
 he-NOM AUX-3SG PST.M.SG deceive-PASS.PTCP.M.SG in+LOC
 njegovoj odluci
 his-LOC.F.SG decision-LOC.F.SG
 '**He was deceived** in his decision.' (= 'He made a mistake in the decision he made')

 HMLD.Cro
 on **se** **prevario** u svojoj
 he-NOM REFL deceive-PST.M.SG in+LOC own-REFL.POSS.PRON.LOC.F.SG
 odluci
 decision-LOC.F.SG

The meaning of both utterances in (33) and (34) is reflexive and in HMLD.Cro, a reflexive construction would be used requiring REFL *se*. Instead, (33) and (34) contain passive clauses in which the grammatical subject appears alone without referential information that the subject is also the recipient of the verb. This alters the meaning of the utterances. In (34) *on je bio prevaren* 'he was deceived' the informant (evident from the context) meant that he deceived himself, i.e. *on se prevario* 'he deceived himself' which has the reflexive pronoun *se*. By turning it into a passive sentence the speaker changed the meaning from 'he deceived himself' to 'he was deceived'. The use of passive resulted in an unintended change in the meaning. Further, in (34), the possessive pronoun *njegovoj* 'his' is employed but where the subject is the same as the possessor of the object, then the possessive pronoun *svoj* 'own' must be used. If the possessive pronoun *njegov* 'his' is used, this indicates that the possessor of the object is *not* the same as the grammatical subject. But the grammatical subject is the same as the possessor of the object, and this USA.Cro utterance contains an unintended meaning.

3.8 Numerals

The influence of English on Croatian numerals is generally not looked at in studies on diaspora communities, although Gasiński (1986: 40) provides six examples from emigrants' speech in which times of day, days of the week, months and years are supplied by English, one of which is (35):

(35) ja   sam   partio   iz   Dubrovnika   **in**
     I   AUX-1SG depart-PST.M.SG   from+GEN   Dubrovnik-GEN.M.SG in
     najtinówtri   mej first
     nineteen o three   May first
     'I departed from Dubrovnik **in 1903 May first**.'

In the sample, there are other such phonologically integrated transfers such as *ejtin najdinajn* 'eighteen ninety-nine' (HMLD.Cro *tisuću osamsto devedeset devete* 'thousand eight hundred ninety ninth') in the speech of first-generation speakers. In Croatian, ordinal numbers are used not only for dates, as in English, but also for years. A feature of the sample that some dates given in Croatian are sequenced according to USA English, that has the month first. In answer to the question: *kad si rođen(-a)* or *kad ste rođeni?* 'When were you born?', these are some responses:

(36) kolovoz   **jedanajstog**
     August-NOM.M.SG   eleventh-GEN.M.SG.ORDINAL
     'August **eleventh**'

   HMLD.Cro
   jedanajstog   kolovoza
   eleventh-GEN.M.SG.ORDINAL   August-GEN.M.SG

(37) *jula*   **osam**
   july-GEN.M.SG   eight-CARDINAL
   'July **eight**'

   HMLD.Cro
   osmog   *jula / srpnja*
   eighth-GEN.M.SG.ORDINAL   july-GEN.M.SG

(38) *februar*   ***dvajstosam***
   February-NOM.M.SG   twenty eight-CARDINAL
   'February **twenty eight**'

   HMLD.Cro
   dvadesetosmog   *februara / veljače*
   twenty eighth-GEN.M.SG.ORDINAL   February-GEN.M.SG

In example (36) the date is given as an ordinal number *jedanaestog* 'eleventh' in USA.Cro, as it is in HMLD.Cro, but following the month, which remains in NOM case while in HMLD.Cro, the month is given in GEN. (In Croatian, the name of the month and the ordinal are in NOM only when the date is used in a general sense, eg., *dan rada je prvi*-NOM. *svibanj*-NOM lit. 'Day of Labour [= Labour Day] is first May'.) For specific dates, as in above, GEN is used. In (37), the month is given in GEN, but the cardinal form of the date is given, not the ordinal form. The cardinal form is reflective of most varieties of contemporary USA English in which this form is now widely used. Example (38) has the pre-posed month in NOM and a cardinal for the date. The lexico-grammatical features of USA English dates and numerals are transferred into USA.Cro here, *without* the form of the lexemes. To be sure, there are many instances of times, dates and years code-switched into English in the sample. In any case, the constituent order conventions of USA English dates have been adopted, with variation in use between ordinal and cardinal numbers for dates themselves.

The way years are expressed is also different between both languages. For example, the year *1971* in Croatian is always expressed in the following syntactic form: *tisuću* 'thousand-ACC.F.SG. *devetsto sedamdeset* 'nine hundred seventy' (all numerals CARDINAL)' *i* 'and' *prva* 'first-NOM.F.SG.ORDINAL'. The final number is an ordinal form that is an adjective that agrees in case and gender with *godina* 'year' NOM.F.SG. Specific years, as with dates, require GEN marking of the final ordinal. Years in English are more frequently expressed as two numerical units: 'nineteen – seventy-one' (19–71). This pattern is taken on by Croatian bilinguals. The answers given below were the answers to the question: *Kad su se rodili roditelji?* 'When were your parents born?'

In example (39) the year is first given with HMLD.Cro sequencing – including GEN.F.SG marking and the ordinal form for the final number – followed by the same number with English sequencing via Croatian lexemes.

(39) mat   se   rodila
      mother-NOM.F.SG   REFL   born-PST.F.SG
      devetsto i pete,   **devetnast i pete**
      nine hundred and fifth- GEN.F.SG.ORDINAL nineteen and fifth-GEN.F.SG.ORDINAL
      'Mother was born in **nine hundred and five, nineteen and five** (=1905).'

      HMLD.Cro
      mat   se   rodila
      mother- NOM.F.SG   REFL   born-PST.F.SG
      (tisuću) devetsto i pete
      (thousand) nine hundred and fifth-GEN.F.SG ORDINAL

In (40) the year is first given with HMLD.Cro sequencing – but with a cardinal form of the final number – followed by English numerical sequencing containing a composite number consisting of Croatian *devetnajest* 'nineteen' and English *o tu* 'o two'. This example contains a juxtaposition of two syntactic realizations with the first in Croatian and the second one in English:

(40) otac   se   rodil   **devesto dvije**
      father-NOM.M.SG   REFL   born-PST.M.SG   nine hundred and two-F.ORDINAL
      devetnajest   **o tu**
      nineteen-CARDINAL   o two
      'My father was born in **nine hundred two, nineteen o two.**'

      HMLD.Cro
      otac   se   rodil   **(tisuću) devetsto druge**
      father-NOM.M.SG   REFL   born-PST.M.SG   (thousand) nine hundred-CARDINAL
                                                  two-GEN.F ORDINAL

Addresses also contain numbers – house or apartment numbers. In answer to the question, *koja ti je adresa?* 'what's your address?' or *gdje živiš?* 'where do you live?' the following responses were collected:

(41) **četiri šesnajst**   *Park Side Road*
    four sixteen-CARDINAL   Park side Road
    'four sixteen (=416) Park Side Road'

    HMLD.Cro
    ulica Park Side   **četiri sto šestnaest**
    road-NOM.F.SG Park Side four hundred sixteen-CARDINAL

(42) **tri osamdeset**   *Summer Street*
    three eighty-CARDINAL   Summer Street
    'three eighty (=380) Summer Street'

    HMLD.Cro
    Summer Street   **tristo osamdeset**
    Summer Street   three hundred eighty-CARDINAL

Sequencing of the numbers used in addresses is modelled on USA English that reduces numbers in the hundreds column to single figure digits, resulting in omission of the word 'hundred'. This occurs in examples (41) and (42) above. In his discussion of the reasons why an English-based sequencing pattern is present in speakers' production of numbers and dates, Gasiński (1986: 41) suggests that speakers intentionally employ such forms as an overt marker signalling their own and their interlocutors' bilingualism. I disagree and suggest that US.Cro speakers habitually provide their personal details in English and this becomes an entrenched way that they utter them, regardless of whether they're speaking Croatian or English. Giving the house number in Croatian may be an 'on-the-spot' strategy that sometimes bears a clearly English model, e.g. *tri osamdeset* 'three eighty'= '380'.

Years, dates, numbers etc. are referentially simplex items, i.e. they refer to one single designation, either a particular year, a certain date or specific address. But they are lexically and morphologically complex as they are rendered via compound constructions that, in Croatian, bear morphological marking that distinguishes case and gender, as well as cardinal from ordinal forms. The examples show a retention of GEN case marking and ordinal forms amongst some speakers, while amongst others, cardinal numbers are used rather than ordinals. This change appears to be more frequent than a change of case marking from GEN to NOM. A further example (43), illustrates this overall trend well:

(43) *prosinca* *sedamnajstog* dev... eh...
December-GEN.M.SG seventeenth-GEN.M.SG.ORDINAL nine... ah...
devetnajst ***osam***
nineteen-CARDINAL eight CARDINAL
'December seventeenth...ni....ah.....**nineteen eight**' [=1908].

Example (43) bears GEN marking for both the (traditional) designation of the month and the ordinal form of the date. But the 'month-then-date' sequencing in USA English is adopted. Following this, the speaker attempts to produce Croatian sequencing of the year, but is unable to, and produces an English-based calque with a cardinal rather than ordinal form. Thus, the most conspicuous incidence of transference is that of number or date or number *sequencing*, followed by a change from ordinal to cardinal numbers. Both of these are directly attributable to the contact situation where GEN case marking changes to NOM only in relation to initial-position months. Further, cardinal numbers do not usually bear case marking so the shift from ordinal to cardinal numbers obviates the presence of any overt case morphology.

4 Findings and conclusions

I summarize here the most important findings related to the phenomena of transference, convergence and language attrition in USA Croatian. In the category of overt possessive adjectives there is convergence to English without transference since the structure is known or already used in Croatian. There is a preference for more marked constructions similar to English (*moj stric* 'my uncle' instead of just *stric* 'uncle'). This construction is considered redundant in HMLD.Cro but is increasingly becoming the unmarked choice in USA.Cro. The use of more marked constructions seems to be related to the avoidance of adnominal DAT construction, i.e. *ona je moja sestra* 'she is my sister' instead of *ona mi je sestra* 'she me DAT is sister'.

The use of overt subject personal pronouns in USA.Cro, e.g. *ja radim* 'I work-1SG' instead of *radim* 'work-1SG' shows convergence towards the English use of personal pronouns. In other words, there is transference of the English syntactic feature of near-universal presence of the subject personal pronoun which is redundant in HMLD.Cro since the doer of the action is indicated in the verb. With such usage it is possible to perhaps posit this as a first sign of the attrition of the pro-drop feature in the speech of immigrant Croatians. The presence of subject pronouns can be seen as a contact influence similar to the use of possessive pronouns that are common in English but less common in HMLD.Cro.

In the case of overt (non-subject) personal pronouns there is transference from English that does not distinguish long from short forms with long forms being preferred, eg. *ja sam **njoj** dala dolar* 'I [OVERT] AUX **her** [FULL FORM] gave dollar'. It is interesting to note that long forms occur in clauses that themselves tend to bear an SVO word order. What is perhaps even more significant, the favouring of long forms also obviates the need for particular word order conventions to be followed that that are not SVO. This is closely connected to a re-alignment or a change of clitics placement, and a general tendency towards avoiding clitic forms, e.g. *dala sam dolar **njoj*** 'I gave a dollar to **her** [FULL FORM]' instead of *dala sam **joj** dolar* 'I gave **her** [CLITIC] a dollar. There is a gradual loss of the long vs. short (non-subject) pronoun distinction in favour of the long form as the default. Findings from other languages in diaspora settings suggest that the employment of the full form is congruent to a strategy of overt marking or favouring phonetically heavier forms. For heritage speakers, these have greater form-meaning transparency (Polinsky 2018).

There is a rather complex situation in relation to the general use of clitics in USA.Cro. First of all, in the placement of clitics there is no obvious sign of transference as English does not have this feature. Secondly, there is obvious influence from home dialects which have different rules for clitic placement that are freer than those of standard HMLD.Cro. Thirdly, there are cases where the English word order is reflected in the positioning of clitics. Fourthly, there is one interesting change or innovation in the 'regularization' of clitic ordering paradigm so that the 'outlier' *je* 'be-AUX.3SG' is no longer post-posed to the right. Instead, there is a leftward movement of *je*. This change is therefore affecting an 'outlying' AUX or clitic so that it is more similar to other clitics in regard to its position. This process is well documented in other studies of heritage languages. Over-regularizations of syntactic (including word-order) paradigms occur with decreased frequency or even elimination of irregular forms, e.g. Montrul (2004) for American Spanish, Polinsky (2006) for American Russian. Further, there is a change in position of the REFL clitic *se* in relation to other clitics as well which is not readily identifiable as an over-regularization strategy.

In compound tenses it is possible to find cases of deletion of AUX forms of *biti* 'be', e.g. 3SG *je*; 1PL *smo*; 3PL *su* in examples such as *za njom Ø došla Marđi* 'after her came Margie'. It is possible that transference of the model from English which is a 'single-form' simple past tense is an influence here. This change is not related to changes in *je* position (see the comment on clitics) because it is not only *je* that is deleted but various forms of AUX are omitted, e.g. *hrvatsku školu* [Ø of AUX *su* 'be-3PL'] *finili* 'they finished Croatian school'. The influence of the non-standard home variety and the informal conversational style of the data collection setting may play a role in this.

There are a number of things to be said about possessive constructions. First, there are pre-posed constructions with an *od* + GEN sequencing that is congruent to English, but also determined by home dialectal constructions, e.g. *od naše majke ime* 'our mother's name'. Second, there is some avoidance of the adnominal DAT construction, such as *majka mi se zove* 'mother-NOM me-DAT REFL call-3SG' 'mother me-DAT is called' and instead forms such as *moja majka se zove* 'my mother-NOM REFL call-3SG' occur. Third, a loss of case marking in some instances and a linear word order that resembles English possessive construction word order are ascertainable that exemplify convergence to English, e.g. *zoven od mojega muža mamu* 'I call from my-GEN husband-GEN mother-ACC', i.e. 'I call my husband's mother'. However, the catalyst here may well be the home dialect construction that resembles the English Saxon genitive construction. Fourth, innovation can be observed in the change of GEN to NOM forms, and word order patterning that resembles English possessive patterns. This even extends to semantically non-possessive constructions, e.g. *sveta Marija crkva* ('St. Mary's church'). Fifth, phrases such as the following are encountered, e.g. *Pero*-M.NOM *Graša*-GEN.M *brata*-GEN.M.SG. *Lovra*-GEN.M.) with a likely meaning of *Lovro, brata Pere Graša* ('Lovro, Pero Grašo's brother'), which is a clear example of structural change in USA.Cro. In such cases, what points to the attrition of syntactic relations is the combination of non-target use of morphological inflections together with a word order pattern that is marked in any variety of HMLD.Cro.

There are further instances of variation and signs of nascent changes in some speakers' repertoires in relation to the way that hierarchical relations are expressed via case marking, or amongst some, via analytic constructions and stricter, English-modelled word order. Sentences like *ovo moj rođak očev bukva* ('this my-NOM cousin-NOM father's-POSS.SG.M book-SG.F') meaning 'this is my cousin's father's book' are not readily comprehensible without a knowledge of the speaker's immediate context. It is interesting that Savić in her investigation of the Serbian syntax of émigré speakers reports that: "The analysis of the Serbian/English utterances indicates that Serbian word order is still well preserved in all the speakers . . . " (1995: 489–490). Complete retention of all syntactic categories appears to be less so the case in this corpus.

In the instance of the use of passive there are no structural differences between two languages. Passive sentences in HMLD.Cro are less frequently used than in English since they are associated with a higher, more elevated register. But in the use of passive in USA.Cro it is possible to talk of transference from English and thus convergence to English patterns as passive sentences are less marked and not felt to be as related to a high register in USA.Cro. Furthermore, a related change to do with production of passive at the expense of other constructions is the avoidance or lower frequency of reflexives, which is congruent to change in the use of the reflexive particle *se* in the ordering of clitics.

Dates and numbers show strong transference from English models, leading to convergence to English. There is sequencing according to English models, e.g. *jula osam* 'July 8'. There is also some attrition of GEN marking, e.g. *februar dvajstosam* 'February twenty-eight'. This example also shows the change or innovation in the use of cardinal numbers, e.g. *dvajsosam* 'twenty-eight' rather than ordinal, e.g. *dvadeset osmi* 'twenty eighth' for dates and years. The phrase *tri osamdeset* ('three eighty' = 380) is calqued on the English model, a longer form characteristic of HMLD.Cro instead of *tristo osamdeset* ('three hundred and eighty'). These constructions would not be readily understood by HMLD.Cro speakers as such and are, indeed, contact-based innovations.

In discussions of changes in the non-dominant language, a common opinion is that under the influence of the dominant language, the non-dominant language undergoes simplification: "language contact, especially when extensive L2 learning is involved, is a main source of complexity reduction (grammar simplification)" (Miestamo, Sinnemaki and Karlsson 2008: viii). The changes in Croatian syntax here do not always confirm this position. On the contrary, in some instances, there are changes that amount to complexification, even in cases of apparent attrition. What has to be distinguished when discussing possible language complexification is from which standpoint we are talking. Miestamo, Sinnemaki and Karlsson (2008: x) say that "two basic approaches to complexity are distinguished: the absolute one where complexity is seen as an objective property of the system, and the relative one: complexity as cost/difficulty to language users". The type of complexification I am talking about here is structural complexity. Discussing the resetting of the pro-drop parameter in Australian Serbian, Dimitrijević-Savić notices that there is no simplification: ". . . the resetting of the pro-drop parameters in AS [Australian Serbian] results from contact-induced changes that makes AS, more similar to English but does not result in the simplification of AS" (2008: 66). The same is true for USA.Cro in being reset according to English syntactic rules and, in some instances, it features more complex categories than HMLD.Cro or it features apparently redundant forms. The resetting of the pro-drop parameters in USA.Cro, the use of possessive pronouns, the use of emphatic (long form) of pronouns used redundantly, and long forms of clitics are examples of structural change and possibly complexification as they co-exist in most speakers' vernaculars alongside equivalent structures that are in line with those found in HMLD.Cro.

Simplification is also usually connected with attrition. This is the case with Croatian morphology where first signs of the loss of, for example, morphological endings, are considered to be simplification of the structural system. But in many of the clause- and phrase-long examples that have been presented such as the possessive constructions, simplification is not really apparent, and the phenomena recorded cannot be attributed to one source only. Another case in point is the transference of numerals calqued on the English pattern which cannot be considered an example of simplification. Simplification which is usually associated with attrition, i.e. the wholesale loss of expressing numerals, dates, addresses etc. is not yet clearly apparent as the structural components of two codes are contributing to expression of referential content. It is not the case that the structural features of speakers' vernaculars have been replaced by English-based models only. Instead these co-occur, with some variation, with the structural features of their home (non-standard/dialectal) Croatian varieties acquired from their first-generation parents.

References

Albin, Alexander. 1976. A Yugoslav community in San Pedro, California. *General Linguistics* 16(2–3). 78–94.

Bauer, Ivan. 1983. Syntactic deviations in an American-Croatian newspaper: An approach to the phenomena of linguistic borrowing. *Folia Slavica* 6(2). 253–263.

Browne, Wayles. 1974. Serbo-Croatian enclitics for English-speaking learners. *Journal of Slavic Linguistics* 12(1). 249–283.

Browne, Wayles 2010. Syntactic studies in Burgenland Croatian: The order of clitics. *Balkanistica* 23. 21–41.

Clyne, Michael. 2003. *Dynamics of language contact*. Cambridge: Cambridge University Press.

Croatian National Soccer Federation of Canada and USA. 2016. *Member clubs*. http://hnnsavez.com/sample-page/about/ (accessed 1 Sept. 2019)

Čizmić, Ivan. 1998. Iseljavanje iz Hrvatske u Ameriku kao dio europskih migracijskih tijekova [Emigration from Croatia to America as an aspect of European migration waves]. *Društvena istraživanja: časopis za opća društvena pitanja* 7(1–2). 127–146.

Čuka, Anica. 2009. Hrvati u SAD-u prema novijim američkim popisima stanovnika, Migrantske zajednice, udruženja i društvene aktivnosti u Sjevernoj i Južnoj Americi: komparativni prikaz Hrvatska-Slovenija, [Croats in the US according to recent census collections, migrant communities, associations and social activities in North and South America: a comparative description of Croatia and Slovenia.] *Zbornik radova sa znanstvenog skupa održanog u Zagrebu 3. travnja 2009*. 45–58. Zagreb: Institut za migracije i narodnosti.

Dimitrijević-Savić, Jovana. 2008. Convergence and attrition: Serbian in contact with English in Australia. *Journal of Slavic Linguistics* 16(1). 57–90.

Djuric, Ivana. 2003. The Croatian Diaspora in North America: Identity, Ethnic Solidarity and Formation of a "Transnational National Community". *International Journal of Politics, Culture and Society* 17(1): 113–130.

Filipović, Rudolf. 1982. Serbo-Croatian in the United States: Croatian dialects in contact with American English. In Roland Sussex (ed.), *The Slavic languages in Emigre Communities*, 23–31. Edmonton: Linguistic Research Inc.

Filipović, Rudolf. 1984. Croatian dialects in the United States: Sociolinguistic aspects. *Folia Slavica* 6(2). 278–292.

Filipović, Rudolf. 1992. Croatian dialects as markers of Croatian ethnicity in the United States. *Dubrovnik* 5. 185–193.

Filipović, Rudolf. 2001. Croatian dialects in the United States: sociolinguistic conditions for the maintenance of a dialect. *International Journal of the Sociology of Language* 147. 51–63.

Fishman, Joshua. 2004. Language maintenance, language shift, and reversing language shift. In Tej Bhatia & William Ritchie (eds.), *Handbook of bilingualism,* 406–436. MA: Blackwell.

Galović, Filip. 2017. Zapisi s terenskih istraživanja kajkavskih govora [Notes from field work of Kajkavian dialects]. Unpublished manuscript.

Gasiński, Thaddeus. 1986. English elements in the speech of the Croatian immigrant community of Santa Clara Valley, California. *Zbornik Matice srpske za filologiju i lingvistiku* 29(2). 31–45.

Hlavac, Jim. 2003. *Second-generation speech. Lexicon, code-switching and morpho-syntax of Croatian-English bilinguals.* Bern: Peter Lang.

Jutronić, Dunja. 1974. The Serbo-Croatian language in Steelton, PA. *General Linguistics* 14. 15–34.

Jutronić, Dunja. 1976. Language maintenance and language shift of the Serbo-Croatian language in Steelton, Pennsylvania. *General Linguistics* 16(2-3). 166–168.

Jutronić, Dunja, Marijana Tomelić-Ćurlin & Anita Runjić-Stoilova. 2016. *Libar o jeziku Marka Uvodića Splićanina* [A book about the language of Marko Uvodić Splićanin]. Split: Filozofski fakultet u Splitu.

Jutronić-Tihomirović, Dunja. 1980. The effect of dialectal variations on the adaptation of loanwords. In Roland Sussex (ed.), *The Slavic Languages in Emigré Communities*, 61–75. Carbondale: Linguistic Research.

Jutronić-Tihomirović, Dunja. 1983. A contribution to the study of syntactic interference in language contact. *Folia Slavica* 6(2). 310–320.

Jutronić-Tihomirović, Dunja. 1985. *Hrvatski jezik u SAD* [The Croatian Language in the United States]. Split: Logos.

Lisac, Josip. 2003. *Hrvatska dijalektologija 1. Hrvatski dijalekti i govori štokavskog narječja i hrvatski govori torlačkog narječja* [Croatian Dialectology 1. Croatian dialects, vernaculars of the Štokavski dialect and Croatian vernaculars of the Torlački dialect]. Zagreb: Golden marketing –Tehnička knjiga.

Lisac, Josip. 2009. *Hrvatska dijalektologija 2. Čakavsko narječje* [Croatian Dialectology 2. The Čakavian Dialect]. Zagreb: Golden marketing – Tehnička knjiga.

Lenček, Rado & Thomas Magner (eds.). 1976. *The dilemma of the melting pot. The case of the South Slavic languages.* University Park: Pennsylvania State University Press.

Lončarić, Mijo. 1996. *Kajkavsko narječje.* [The Kajkavian Dialect] Zagreb: Školska knjiga.

Miestamo, Matti, Kaius Sinnemaki & Fred Karlsson (eds.). 2008. *Language complexity, typology, contact, change.* Amsterdam/Philadelphia: John Benjamins.

Montrul, Silvina. 2004. *The Acquisition of Spanish. Morphosyntactic Development in Monolingual and Bilingual L1 Acquisition and in Adult L2 Acquisition*. Amsterdam: John Benjamins.
Montrul, Silvina. 2016. *The Acquisition of Heritage Languages*. Cambridge, UK: Cambridge University Press.
Muljačić, Željko. 2003. Jedno novo vrelo u proučavanju sintakse i paremiologije [A new source in the research of syntax and paremiology]. In M. Moguš (ed.), *Hrvatski dijalektološki zbornik* [Croatian Dialectology Journal] (12). 125–149. Zagreb: HAZU.
Øverland, Orm. 2000. *Immigrant minds, American identities*. Urbana and Chicago: University of Illinois Press.
Polinsky, Maria. 1995. American Russian: Language loss meets language acquisition. In Wayles Browne (ed.), *Formal Approaches to Slavic Linguistics. Cornell Meeting*, 370–406. Ann Arbor: Michigan Slavic Publications.
Polinsky, Maria. 2006. Incomplete Acquisition: American Russian. *Journal of Slavic Linguistics* 14. 161–219.
Polinsky, Maria. 2018. *Heritage Languages and Their Speakers*. Cambridge, UK: Cambridge University Press.
Prpić, Jure. 1997. *Hrvati u Americi* [Croats in America]. Zagreb: Hrvatska matica iseljenika.
Ryan, Camille. 2013. *Language use in the United States: 2011*. https://www.census.gov/prod/2013pubs/acs-22.pdf. (accessed 1 Sept. 2019)
Savić, Jelena. 1995. Structural convergence and language change: Evidence from Serbian/English code-switching. *Language in Society* 24(4). 475–492.
Schmid, Monika. 2011. *Language attrition. Key topics in sociolinguistics*. Cambridge: Cambridge University Press.
Serratrice, Ludovica. 2007. Cross-linguistic influence in the interpretation of anaphoric and cataphoric pronouns in English-Italian bilingual children. *Bilingualism: Language and Cognition* 10, 225–238.
State Office for Croats Abroad. 2016a. Hrvatsko iseljeništvo u SAD-u [Croatian emigrants in the USA]. http://www.hrvatiizvanrh.hr/hr/hmiu/hrvatsko-iseljenistvo-u-sad-u/35 (accessed 4 Sept. 2019)
St Jerome Croatian Catholic Church. 2012. Hrvatske župe u Americi i Kanadi [Croatian parishes in America and Canada]. http://www.stjeromecroatian.org/hrv/usacanada.html (accessed 4 Sept. 2019)
Šipka, Danko. 2017. Bosnian/Croatian/Serbian heritage speakers in four major U.S. metropolitan areas: resources for the attainment of full professional linguistic proficiency. *East/West Journal of Ukrainian Studies* 4(1). 33–61.
Udier, Sanda Lucija. 2006. Položaj glagolskih enklitika u nastavi hrvatskoga kao stranoga jezika za početnike [Position of verbal clitics in the teaching of Croatian as a foreign language for beginners]. *Lahor* (1). 61–68.
Uldrijan, Ivan. 2011. Katoličke misije i župe – prave čuvarice hrvatskoga jezika. [Catholic missions and parishes – genuine protectors of the Croatian language] Interview: dr. Vinko Grubišić, professor emeritus University of Waterloo, Canada http://www.glas-koncila.hr/index.php?option=com_php&Itemid=41&news_ID=19283 (accessed 1 Sept. 2019)
US Census Bureau. 2012. *Total ancestry reported*. https://factfinder.census.gov/faces/tableservices/jsf/pages/productview.xhtml?pid=ACS_12_1YR_B04003&prodType=table (accessed 4 Sept. 2019)

Vranić, Silvana. 2001. Iz paških čakavskih govora [About the Čakavian Dialects from Pag], *Hrvatski dijalektološki zbornik* [*Croatian Dialectology Journal*] 12. 151–167.
Wackernagel, Jakob. 1892. Über ein Gesetz der indogermanischen Wortstellung, *Indogermanische Forschungen* 1. 333–436
Ward, Charles. 1980. Intrafamiliar patterns and Croatian language maintenance in America. *Studies in Ethnicity – The East European Experience in America*. 3–14.
Weinreich Uriel. 1953. *Languages in Contact*. The Hague: Mouton.
Zubčić, Sanja. 2009/10. Speech of Croatian emigrants in the overseas countries and countries of Western Europe: The level of research attained. *Croatian Studies Review* 6. 141–162.

Canada

Ivana Petrović
Features in the speech of Croatian-speakers in the greater Toronto area

1 Introduction

This chapter is concerned with the contact between English and Croatian in the Croatian immigrant community in Toronto, Canada. A sociolinguistic description of language use in the community foregrounds a presentation of features of Croatian as spoken by first- and second-generation Croatian-Canadians, particularly focusing on those features that diverge from the Croatian spoken in the homeland.

Winford's (2003: 33) notion of "unequal" or asymmetrical bilingualism could be applied in the context of Croatian-English contact in Canada. English exists as the socially dominant language in the immigrant situation, but English is not the linguistically dominant variety for all speakers in this bilingual community. Generally, first-generation speakers, those who as adolescents or adults left Croatia (Gen.1A in Haugen's terms), remain linguistically dominant in Croatian; this remains their language of choice for communication with other members of the community. Second-generation speakers, those born in Canada and those who arrived as young children (Gen.2 and Gen.1B in Haugen's terms), are linguistically dominant in English. Despite the fact that for most of them Croatian was the language they were mainly exposed to in childhood and very often the first language they learned chronologically, formal schooling in English and its role as the language of their social environment strongly influenced their linguistic development, and therefore they later became dominant in that language.

In the context of North America, a body of research literature from both a homeland and a diasporic perspective exists on Croatian-English contact in the USA, e.g. Albin and Alexander (1972), Filipović (1979, 1984, 1991, 2001), Jutronić (1974, 1976), Jutronić-Tihomirović (1982, 1985), and Magner (1976) with one study on French-English-Croatian trilingualism by Ćosić (1992/1994). Canada is a multilingual, multi-ethnic, and multicultural society, and the study of bilingualism, language contact, language policy as well as bilingual education has a long and rich tradition (e.g. Edwards 1998). However, there has been relatively little research into the speech and language practices of the Croatian ethnic minority living in that country. To date, the most detailed published work that examines the speech

Ivana Petrović, University of Split

of Croatian immigrants in Canada remains Surdučki's (1978) comprehensive monograph *Srpskohrvatski i engleski u kontaktu* 'Serbo-Croatian and English in Contact'. The book examines two different contact situations: indirect contact between English and Serbo-Croatian in Yugoslavia (the term *Serbo-Croatian* was the designation for the official language in the then Socialist Republic of Serbia where Surdučki was based), and direct contact between the languages in Canada. The volume includes a list of English loanwords recorded in the speech of Serbian and Croatian immigrants living in Canada. Surdučki (1978) also discusses adaptation of these loanwords, primarily focusing on morphological adaptation and briefly examines phonological and graphemic adaptation. In addition to this book, Surdučki also deals with émigré language varieties in Canada in some of his other works: in Surdučki (1966, 1967) English loanwords in immigrant press are analysed, and in Surdučki (1983, 1984) he again compares the contact between English and Serbo-Croatian in Yugoslavia and in Canada. In terms of other research of Croatian spoken in Canada, a brief examination of forms of address between homeland and immigrant Croatian is provided by Juričić and Kess (1978), while a detailed description of intra-family language practices is provided by Starčević's (2014) ethnographic study of two Gen.1A parents and their two Gen.1B children. Further, and most recently, language maintenance of Croatian amongst Gen.1 and Gen.2 speakers has been an area of close interest for the author of this chapter (Petrović 2017, 2018).

This chapter addresses the following question: What types of change or innovation are observable in the speech of Croatian-speakers in Canada? Change or innovation are examined in relation to lexical, morpho-syntactic and semantic features. The influence of English is examined in accounting for change or innovation. Reference is also made to other studies on Croatian as a diaspora language to see if and how findings in other countries, especially those other Anglophone countries of the New World, are congruent to findings made here. Background information is provided on a larger group of Croatian-speakers in Toronto in a summary of language use features across domains to contextualise the situation of bilingual Croatian-Canadians.

This chapter is structured in the following way. The remaining parts of this section present general demographic and sociolinguistic information on Croatian-origin residents in Canada and on Croatian-speakers in that country. Section 2 presents information on the informants and the collection of sociolinguistic data and spoken language data from them. Section 3 contains information on the data sample, while section 4 gives a brief description of sociolinguistic features of the informants and information on self-reported proficiency in Croatian use of the language in intra-family settings. Section 5 presents examples of bilingual speech, focusing on lexical, structural features as well as loan translation. Section 6 contains the conclusion with findings summarized.

1.1 History of contact, vintages of emigration, status

There is evidence of the presence of Croatians in Canada as early as the mid-sixteenth century as crew members or sailors on colonizing expeditions (Rasporich 1982: 11). Large-scale migration of Croatians to North America began at the end of the nineteenth century. (See Jutronić this volume.) The US was the most popular destination for young, mostly uneducated men in search of a better life in the New World, but a number of them came to Canada, usually by way of the US, and worked mostly in the mining, fishing, and logging industries. They typically came with no intention to stay permanently. Notwithstanding most migrants' planned desire to return, there were clusters or settlements of Croats in the late nineteenth century on the west coast, in British Columbia. Sizeable numbers of Croatian immigrants did not begin to arrive in Canada until after WWI, with large numbers settling mainly in or around urban centers in Ontario. By far the largest number of Croatians came to Canada in the post-WWII period, especially in the 1960s and 1970s, with further economic migrants and refugees arriving in the 1990s, during and after the wars in Croatia and Bosnia-Herzegovina. Croatian has no official status in Canada.

1.2 Number of Croatian-heritage residents, number of Croatian-speakers

The number of Croatian-heritage Canadian residents has grown steadily over the last 20 years as the following figures from successive census collections reveal: 1996–84,495 (Statistics Canada 2016a); 2001–97,050 (Statistics Canada 2016b); 2006–110,880 (Statistics Canada 2014a); 2011–114,880 (Statistics Canada 2019a); 2016–133,970 (Statistics Canada 2019b). Canada allows multiple declarations of ethnic origin and the increase in those claiming Croatian heritage is partly attributed to an increase of residents who claimed it alongside another heritage. In 1996 the number of those who nominated 'Croatian' alongside another category of heritage was 29,220 or, as a percentage of the total number of Croatian-heritage Canadians, 34.5% (Statistics Canada 2016a). In the following years the number of those who claim dual heritage has increased. The numbers and percentages of those claiming Croatian heritage alongside another for the following years are (with percentages in brackets): 2001–38,880 (40%) (Statistics Canada 2016b); 2006–54,475 (49.1%) (Statistics Canada 2014a); 2011–63,055 (54.9%) (Statistics Canada 2019a); 2016–78,370 (58.5%) (Statistics Canada 2019b).

While the number of those who claim Croatian ancestry has been increasing, census data show that the percentage of Croatians who speak the language and use it at home has been decreasing. The Canadian census asks two questions in relation to language use/proficiency: "What language(s), other than English or French, can this person speak well enough to conduct a conversation?" and "What language does this person speak most often at home?" In the 2006 census, the number of residents who answered 'Croatian' to these questions was 72,685 (65.5% of all Croatian-heritage residents) (Statistics Canada 2014b) and 22,165 respectively (Statistics Canada 2014c). As a percentage, this showed the linguistic profiles of all Croatian-heritage residents were the following: 65.5% 'could conduct a conversation in Croatian', while 19.9% 'spoke mostly Croatian at home'. For 2011, the number of residents who answered 'Croatian' to these questions were 63,445 (55.2% of all Croatian-heritage residents) and 18,730 (16.3% of all Croatian-heritage residents) respectively (Statistics Canada 2015). From the 2016 census collection data, the data are 69,840 (52.1%) and 16,775 (12.5%) (Statistics Canada 2019c). This shows a progressively decreasing number of Croatian-Canadians who report being able to functionally communicate in Croatian and in using Croatian as their main home language. It is possible that by answering 'Croatian' to the first question, some residents may answer 'English' to the home-language question, where this language is used alongside Croatian. I estimate that the number of Croatian-speakers in Canada, including unreported residents who have passive (aural) skills only, to be between 90,000 and 100,000.

1.3 Geographical distribution, socio-economic profile

Data from the 2016 census show that the majority of Croatian-origin Canadians live in Ontario (82,220), with 37,460 living in Toronto (Statistics Canada 2019b). Large numbers are found elsewhere in Canada or other parts of Ontario: Vancouver (15,670), Hamilton (13,655), Kitchener (4,920), Calgary (6,265), and Montreal (5,230) (Statistics Canada 2019a). Toronto's community is well organized with numerous social, cultural, and religious institutions as well as many ethnic businesses. Those who arrived in the 1960s and 1970s tended to live in specific immigrant neighborhoods of Toronto (Grubišić 1984). In the last few decades, residential patterns have changed. Toronto's Croatian-Canadian community is now dispersed across a broader geographical area across the greater metropolitan area of Toronto. Although there is a long-standing (albeit small) Croatian community in largely Francophone Montreal, our discussion here focuses on Croats in the largely Anglophone provinces of Canada, and on contact with English.

The socio-economic profile of Gen.1 migrants was or remains lower than that of other Canadians. Their children (and grandchildren) as well as more recent migrants have had much greater access to education and they typically work in fields and settings that are more highly-skilled and better paid. As such, they are 'well established' in Canadian society, meaning that are represented in a large variety of segments of Canadian society. The socio-economic profile of Croatian-Canadians today is likely to be close to the average socio-economic profile of Canadians in general.

1.4 Infrastructure

As stated, the Croatian community in the Toronto area features numerous social, cultural, and religious institutions as well as many ethnic businesses. The Catholic Church plays a major role as the hub of the community life, providing not only religious services but also co-ordinating educational and cultural activities. There are nineteen Croatian Catholic parishes in Canada, most of them now offering services in both Croatian and English, with some of them also printing news bulletins for their congregations. Croatian TV and radio channels are available on demand, or via subscription. Locally-produced radio programming in Croatian is broadcast weekly in some major Canadian cities, usually for one or two hours, The first Croatian language school was established in Toronto in 1961 by Croatian Catholic priests (Sopta 2012). Enrolments for supplementary instruction in Croatian (after school on weekdays or on Saturdays) increased greatly and another school was opened in nearby Mississauga in 1977, with enrolment numbers staying high throughout the 1980s (Bubrin 1994; Granic 2009). Today, elementary and secondary-level Croatian language classes are funded by the Ontario government as part of the International Languages Program. Courses in Croatian language and culture are offered at the University of Toronto and Waterloo University. In general, community-based activities of Croatians living across southern Ontario usually take place in Toronto and its surrounding urban areas. Elsewhere, the Croatian Catholic parishes and Croatian community centres in Vancouver, Edmonton, Montreal and other urban centres are the focus of activities for smaller communities in other parts of the country.

1.5 Domain use, language maintenance and shift

In the past, high residential concentrations of Croats in some urban areas not only facilitated the settlement of newcomers but also the establishment of a transposed diaspora community. These close-knit networks represented transnational communities in which use of the heritage language amongst Gen.1 speakers and Gen.2 speakers was greatly enabled, as well as the observation of religious and cultural traditions. Use of Croatian is generally restricted to the home/family, friendship, leisure and religious domains. It is rare now for it to be used at workplaces, either with workmates or customers/others. It remains the dominant and favoured language of most

Gen.1 speakers. For Gen.2 speakers it is used in intra-family interactions with older interlocutors (parents, grandparents), but with same-age ones such as siblings and peers, English is more predominant, with or without code-switching into Croatian.

Proficiency in and use of Croatian is highly favourable but not axiomatic in contemporary constructions of 'Canadian Croatianness'. Even if younger Croatian-Canadians do not speak the language well or often, they usually still maintain a sense of Croatian ethnic identity and often still have close social ties with other Croatians. At a macro-social level, language maintenance efforts amongst Croatians (as well as other ethnic groups) are supported by Canada's policies of multilingualism and multiculturalism. As a result, alongside acquisition of English, immigrants to Canada do not experience undue pressure to shift to English and heritage language maintenance is encouraged.

1.6 Contacts with Croatia. Host society attitudes towards Croats

The great geographical distance between the two countries makes frequent travel to Croatia a challenge, resulting in fewer opportunities for contact with friends and relatives in the homeland. Before the outbreak of the Covid-19 pandemic that halted or severely curtailed travel between Canada and Europe, In June 2018 direct flights between Toronto and Zagreb had been resumed after an absence of any direct flights between the two countries that had lasted 27 years. This had made air travel more accessible and affordable. The majority of Croatians in Canada have travelled to Croatia at least once in their lifetime with many older Croatian-Canadians visiting the country on a yearly basis, usually during summer. Younger generation members visit less regularly, often combining a trip to Croatia with visits to other European destinations as well. In the main, Canadian 'mainstream' or 'host' society has a generally positive attitude towards Croats. They represent a group that started to come to Canada in sizeable numbers not until the post-WWII era with the stereotypical image for first-generation speakers being that of hard-working migrants working in laborious and often less desirable occupations.

2 Data collection and informants

The data that this chapter is based on was collected in the Croatian immigrant speech community in Toronto, Ontario. Aside from the fact that it is the biggest area of Croatian settlement in Canada, the Toronto community was chosen because the researcher had lived there throughout the period of data collection and had contact with a number of community members, which facilitated and accelerated the search for informants. The majority of informants were recruited through contacts with relatives and friends (some of whom were also part of the study) and a smaller number through snowball sampling. The data collection process consisted of two phases. The first phase involved the collection of speech data in 2007 and the second phase the collection of questionnaire data in 2013.

In the first phase of the study, 22 informants (11 first-generation and 11 second-generation Croatian-Canadians) were interviewed; the interviews were recorded and later transcribed verbatim for analysis. The purpose of the interview was to obtain samples of natural speech of informants. A semi-structured interview was chosen as an appropriate method. Topics of the interview were broad and questions were open-ended; informants talked about their life in Croatia and Canada (their childhood, education, work, and family life), migration and the process of adaptation to new circumstances, various Croatian community organizations, participation in the social life of the community, cultural differences between the two countries, etc. Before the interview, basic demographic information such as age, place of birth, educational level attained, and length of time living in Canada was gathered. As previously mentioned, there were 22 informants (9 females and 13 males); all actively involved in the community. One informant arrived in Canada in the mid-1950s, five arrived in the late 1960s/early 1970s, and five in the late 1990s/early 2000s. Out of the 11 Gen.2 informants, 10 were Canadian-born, while one was born in Germany and arrived in Canada at the age of 3 with her parents. Her age at emigration allows her to be grouped as a Gen.2 informant.

In the second phase of the study, 220 participants (110 first-generation and 110 second-generation Croatian-Canadians) completed a sociolinguistic questionnaire. The questionnaire, constructed on the basis of relevant literature and previous studies of immigrant speech (e.g. Hlavac 2003, Šabec 1992), consisted of two versions (one for first-generation participants and one for second-generation participants) that differed only slightly. It contained 41 questions, both open- and close-ended, covering demographic and linguistic information (self-reported proficiency in Croatian and English, language use in the family domain, and language attitudes). The questionnaire was written in both Croatian and English and participants were instructed to use whichever language they preferred. As a rule, first-generation participants responded in Croatian and second-generation participants responded in English. Demographic characteristics of participants who were involved in the second phase of the study are presented in Table 1. The survey and interview samples were similar in terms of demographic characteristics.

Table 1: Demographic characteristics and information on the education level of informants from the sociolinguistic questionnaire.

	Gen. 1	Gen. 2
No. of informants	110	110
Female / Male	58.2% / 41.8%	54.5% / 45.5%
Ave. age / Age range	58.6 / 28–84	33.1 / 14–54
Ave no. of years residing in Canada / Range of years	33.6 / 2–57	32.6 / 13–54
Highest education level attained		
Primary (Elementary school)	29.1%	0.0%
Secondary (High school, College)	67.3%	44.5%
Tertiary (Undergraduate, Graduate)	3.6%	55.5%

3 Sample

Some recordings with informants involved in the first phase of the study were completed individually and some in groups of two or three informants of the same generation. Approximately 10 hours of data was recorded and later transcribed. Considering that shorter interview segments were selected for analysis (approximately 15–20 minutes for individual interviews and 20–40 minutes for group interviews), 4 hours and 40 minutes of recorded data (approximately 27 000 words in total) constitutes the corpus on which the analysis is based. Transcription was performed manually. Utterance boundaries were determined according to pauses longer than 3 seconds and syntactic and semantic coherence.

The interviews were conducted in Croatian. Since the researcher is a native speaker of Croatian, using Croatian as the main language of communication seemed to be the most natural choice. However, informants were reminded to use whichever language they preferred, Croatian or English. As informants knew that the interviewer herself was bilingual, it was predicted that they would feel comfortable using either Croatian, English, or that they would code-switch between the two. However, the fact that the interviewer spoke Croatian probably led them to use more Croatian than they normally would in communication with other members of the community. In most cases, first-generation informants spoke Croatian with only occasional English-origin insertions, or even less commonly with phrase- or clause-length alternations into English. Second-generation informants very often commenced their responses in Croatian, but often code-switched to English, and moved between both languages. Table 2 below presents the sample in terms of number of words in Croatian and English as well as number of monolingual and bilingual utterances of informants.

Table 2: Number of words and utterances for both generations from recorded spoken language sample.

	Gen. 1	Gen. 2	Total
No. of informants	11	11	22
Utterances			
Croatian (monolingual)	601	315	916
English (monolingual)	2	109	111
Bilingual	192	409	601
Total	795	833	1 628
Lexical items			
Croatian words	13 588	10 341	23 929
English words	391	2 497	2 888
Total	13 979	12 838	26 817
Ave. no. of Cro. words per informant	1 235	940	1 087
Ave. no. of Eng. words per informant	35	227	131
Percentage of Eng. proper nouns in the total no. of Eng. words	22.5%	3.8%	0.7%

Table 2 shows that Croatian was the language predominantly used in the sample. The total number of Croatian words is significantly higher than the total number of English words for both generations. Proportionally, the speech of first-generation informants was overwhelmingly Croatian-dominant, with 97% of their speech consisting of Croatian lexemes or forms. Amongst the second generation informants, the equivalent percentage was 80%. The majority of utterances produced by first-generation informants were monolingual Croatian utterances (75.6%), followed by bilingual utterances (24.1%) and an insignificant number of monolingual English utterances (0.3%). Second-generation speakers' utterances were predominantly bilingual (49.1%), followed by monolingual Croatian utterances (37.8%) and monolingual English utterances (13.1%). A substantial number of the English-origin forms (mainly single-item insertions) in the speech of first-generation speakers are proper nouns (22.5%). Amongst the second-generation speakers, proper nouns make up a much smaller proportion (3.8%) of the much larger number of English-origin insertions and alternations. In this study, all English-origin items that were used in an otherwise Croatian conversation are considered code-switches. This is in line with Thomason's (2001: 132) definition of code-switching as "the use of material from two (or more) languages by a single speaker in the same conversation". In Thomason's opinion, code-switching is a mechanism that can bring about contact-induced change. Myers-Scotton (2002: 104) sees code-switching as both a mechanism and an outcome of change. When viewed as a structural mechanism, it is considered the main catalyst of convergence (Myers-Scotton 2002: 247). This chapter adopts a division of code-switching into: intra-clausal switching, inter-clausal switching, and extra-clausal switching.

Intra-clausal switching refers to switching within a clause, as in examples (1) and (2) below. English-origin elements are marked in bold. Data on the informant who produced the example utterance are provided in brackets at the end of each example. Gen. 1 or Gen. 2 refers to informant's generation status, 'M' or 'F' indicates gender of the informant, and the number indicates informant's age. The orthographical representation of items reflects their phonological form: phonologically integrated English-origin items are represented according to Croatian orthography, while unintegrated forms are presented according to their English spelling.

(1) ...i treći puta su nas primili, dobili smo sve dokumente, **legal** dokumente, prošli smo kroz cijeli **procedure** da bi se došlo ovdje kao **landed immigrants** i tu smo došli...
'...and third time we were accepted, we got all the documents, **legal** documents, we went through the whole **procedure** to come here as **landed immigrants** and we came...' (Gen.1,F,58)

(2) ...jer oni nisu nikad bili tamo, oni ne ide na misu, ne idu u hrvatski **picnic**...
'...because they were never there, they don't go to mass, they don't go to Croatian **picnic**...' (Gen.2,M,31)

Inter-clausal switching refers to code-switching that occurs at clause boundaries, as in examples (3) and (4) below:

(3) ...**I'm from Greece, I'm from Italy whatever, oh I'm Croatian** i nekako se osjećaš već bliže, **Canadians they don't... they don't understand the family, the big family, the eating, drinking, family comes first...**
'...**I'm from Greece, I'm from Italy whatever, oh I'm Croatian** and somehow you already feel closer, **Canadians they don't... they don't understand the family, the big family, the eating, drinking, family comes first...**' (Gen.2,F,27)

(4) . . .*ako, ako se neko radovao,* **they had some mental problems,** *to je svak mrzio,* **I'm telling you**. . .
'. . .and if, if somebody was looking forward to it, **they had some mental problems**, everybody hated that, **I'm telling you**. . .' (Gen.2,M,22)

Example (4) above has four clauses, each with a different subject. The switch between perspectives that occurs between the clauses is accompanied by a code-switch. The change in subject and perspective from one clause to another is a feature reported for alternational, inter-clausal code-switching (Muysken 2000: 96).

Extra-clausal switching refers to switching of "discourse-specific elements" (Hlavac 2003: 47), such as discourse markers or tags, before, after or between clauses as in examples (5) and (6):

(5) . . .*znaš kakav je on,* **so** *ja sam došla i ostala*. . .
'. . .you know what he is like, **so** I came and I stayed. . .' (Gen.1,F,43)

(6) . . .**yeah,** *obukao sam kopačke prvi put, i ovdje su, još uvik ih imam.. moje prve kopačke*. . .
'. . .**yeah**, I put my football boots on for the first time, and they're here, I still have them, my first pair of football boots . . .' (Gen.2,M,35)

Hlavac (2006) notes that among second-generation speakers of Croatian in Australia of all categories of code-switches, extra-clausal code-switches are the most numerous. He further observes that English-origin discourse forms co-occur with Croatian discourse forms, and that high incidence of certain English discourse markers such as *so* and *yeah* could be attributed to their polyfunctionality. In Hlavac's (2016) research on the speech of two generations of Macedonian-Australians the most common form of code-switches were extra-clausal code-switches.

Table 3 below shows a statistical break-down of code-switching according to its occurrence within, at or external to clause boundaries for both generations of informants.

The majority of code-switches in the sample were intra-clausal, insertional switches (55.6%), followed by extra-clausal (30.5%) switches, and inter-clausal, alternational code-switches (13.9%). There are differences between the two generations of informants in terms of the number and type of switches. As mentioned, the data show that first-generation informants did not engage in code-switching as often as second-generation informants and rarely switched between clauses. The occurrence of code-switching depends on various factors: the formality of

Table 3: Frequency of code-switching type according to clause-boundary.

	Gen. 1	Gen. 2	Total
Intra-clausal switching	152	361	513
Inter-clausal switching	5	123	128
Extra-clausal switching	96	185	281
Total	253	669	922

situation, the relationship between interlocutors, or the topic of conversation. Hlavac (2012: 50) pointed out that code-switching is so frequent in the speech of his informants that "its occurrence is relatively unmarked". The data here show that code-switching is a communication strategy employed habitually and unremarkably by the members of the Toronto speech community. It appears to be an unmarked choice for second-generation speakers when interacting with other bilinguals in the community. First-generation speakers, however, exhibit greater variability in terms of the frequency of switching. For some first-generation speakers, code-switching is also a relatively unmarked form of speech, but for others it may be more marked.

4 Language use in the community

In this section, the responses on self-declared language proficiency in English and Croatian and reported language use according to domain from the sociolinguistic questionnaire are presented and discussed.

4.1 Language proficiency

A great majority of first-generation informants (95.5%) named Croatian as the language they know best and all second-generation informants named English as the language they know best. These results are not surprising and conform to the classic three-generation language shift pattern recorded amongst immigrant communities in North America: the first-generation maintains the heritage language, the second-generation is bilingual, but dominant in the majority language, and a complete shift to the majority language may occur in the third generation (Fishman 1966; Veltman 1983). However, this is just a general pattern and does not account for considerable intra-group differences. For example,

4.5% of first-generation informants named English as the language they know best. Details of this group are interesting as they depict a somewhat less common first-generation immigrant experience. In general terms, they are highly educated and affluent professionals, in exogamous marriages, who have been living in Canada for a long time, and who rarely use Croatian. They report now being linguistically dominant in English, although they all reported not knowing any English before coming to Canada.

In total, only a relatively small percentage (13.6%) of all first-generation informants knew some English before migration to Canada. This is indicative of the profile of Croatian immigrants who arrived in the 1960s and 1970s. Examination of the biographical data of those who did have proficiency in English revealed that nearly all of them belonged to a more recently arrived wave of Croatian immigrants. Within this particular group, many were able to acquire proficiency in English before emigration which was something not found amongst previous generations of Croatian immigrants. Those who mostly arrived in the 1960s and 1970s, generally had little or no education and did not speak English. As a result they had to settle for lower-wage jobs. Amongst those first-generation informants with no knowledge of English, less than half (46.4%) attended formal instruction in English after arrival in Canada. The average age at which they started to learn English, either formally or in non-formal environments (e.g. workplace) was 23.3.

Regarding the language proficiency of second-generation informants, all nominated English as the language they know best. They are linguistically dominant in English and use Croatian for in-group communication with first-generation community members. Further, 92.7% of them stated that they had regularly attended Croatian language classes, usually taught on Saturday mornings, mostly because their parents insisted that they do so. Hlavac (2003: 343) reports a similarly high percentage of second-generation informants in Australia who reported receiving formal instruction in Croatian – 85%.

4.2 Domains of language use

In exploring patterns of language use amongst the larger, sociolinguistic sample, a domain-based framework (Fishman 1965), was adopted. In terms of the domains or "contextualized spheres of communication" as Clyne (2003: 20) defines them, the responses indicate that the two languages cover distinct functional domains. Generally, English is the language of workplace and education; Croatian, on the other hand, is the language of family and religion. The family or home domain has been considered by many as having the central role in language maintenance efforts by various ethnic minorities (e.g. Fishman 1991; Pauwels 2016).

Therefore, the main goal in analysing the domains of language use in the community is to investigate and describe the inter- and intra-generational communication patterns within the family domain. In Table 4 the results of questionnaire analysis with regard to language use in the family domain are presented.

Table 4: Choice of language in interactions with family members of succeeding and preceding generations, and of the same generation.

Generation	Question	Eng.	Eng. with some Cro.	Cro. with some Eng.	Cro.	Total
Gen. 1	Which language do you speak with your children?	6.7%	11.5%	39.5%	42.3%	100%
	Which language do you speak with your grandchildren?	17%	13.8%	27.7%	41.5%	100%
Gen. 2	Which language do you speak with your mother?	9.1%	20.9%	29.1%	40.9%	100%
	Which language do you speak with your father?	4.6%	19.3%	32.1%	44%	100%
	Which language do you speak with your siblings?	59%	35.2%	2.9%	2.9%	100%

Table 4 shows that Croatian is the language primarily used for communication between parents and children. Most first-generation informants report that they use Croatian (42.3%) or Croatian with some English (39.5%) when speaking with their children. There is only a small decrease in the reported use of Croatian, or Croatian with some English with grandchildren. This is a comparatively high percentage, considering that for some informants, their grandchildren would come from ethnically exogamous families in which Croatian is not used as much as in ethnically endogamous families.

Second-generation informants report that they mostly use Croatian (40.9%) or Croatian with some English (29.1%) in communication with their mother. Similar results are reported about communication with their father; however, a slight rise in the use of both Croatian (44%) and Croatian with some English (32.1%) is registered. Surprisingly, the finding is consistent with the results obtained by Hlavac (2003) who found that the language his second-generation Croatian-Australians use with their fathers is "more Croatian-dominant" (Hlavac 2003: 21) than the language they use with their mothers even though previous research in the Australian context emphasized the role the mother plays in maintaining a minority language (Pauwels 1995). One possible explanation for these findings could be the differences in perception of paternal and maternal behaviours and expectations in traditional Croatian families, as recounted by a second-generation informant:

(7) ...kad pričam s materom, **I'm completely comfortable speaking, it doesn't matter** ako ću pričat.. pričat engleski ili hrvatski.. znam da, da.. otac očekiva hrvatski.
'...when I'm talking with my mom, **I'm completely comfortable speaking, it doesn't matter** if I will speak.. speak English or Croatian.. I know that, that my father expects Croatian.' (Gen.2,M,35)

In terms of language choice in communication between second-generation participants and their siblings, Table 4 shows that they mostly use English (59%) and English with some Croatian (35.2%), which is again in line with Hlavac's (2003) findings.

5 Features of Croatian as spoken in Canada

In regard to categories distinguished in this chapter, I employ the terms *transfer* and *transference* as defined by Clyne (2003). I employ these terms viewing them as synonymous to Thomason and Kaufman's (1988: 37) notion of *borrowing* which they define as "the incorporation of foreign features into a group's native language by speakers of that language: the native language is maintained but is changed by the addition of the incorporated features." Transference refers to both lexical and structural elements, i.e. phonological, morphological, and syntactic features can be transferred. The transference of lexemes is the most frequent and usually the most conspicuous outcome of language contact. Structural transference tends to occur only in situations of widespread bilingualism amongst or within groups whose languages are in extended and intense language contact, as is the case with the Croatian-English bilinguals of this sample.

5.1 Lexical change

Typically, lexical items often appear as the most initial examples of language contact (Thomason 2001). The reasons for transference are varied: 'lexical need' relating to referents that do not have an equivalent in the recipient language and these transfers fill a 'lexical gap' and are known as *cultural loans* (e.g. Matras 2009) or *cultural borrowings* (e.g. Myers-Scotton 2002). Further, where code-switching is an unmarked variety, items that constitute lexical input from English may themselves be unmarked. They may signify items or concepts specific to Canada or Toronto. At the same time, they need not be culturally-specific items, and they can still co-occur with Croatian-origin equivalent items.

Listed here are some categories of lexical transfers found in the corpus: cultural loans – *đinđerela* – 'ginger ale', *imigrejšn* – 'immigration', *bankrupsi* – 'bankruptcy'; nouns (that co-occur with their Croatian equivalents) – *demiđ* – 'damage', *nejber* – 'neighbour', *šapa* – 'shop', *kena* – 'can'; verbs: *agrijati se* (REFL) – 'to agree', *tičati* – 'to teach', *fonati* – 'to phone'; adjectives: *bizi* – 'busy', *fultajm* – 'full time', *laki* – 'lucky', *najs* – 'nice', *pjur* – 'pure'; adverbs: *komplitno* – 'completely'; discourse markers: *dacit* – 'that's it', *jes* – 'yes', *ju nou* – 'you know', *kaman* – 'come on', *eskjuzmi* – 'excuse me', *sori* – 'sorry', *okej* – 'okay', *ja* – 'yeah'. The last item is not a direct transfer from English, but a form that some of those with a knowledge of German have come to use. These speakers appear to be transferring the poly-functionality of Eng. *yeah* onto a German-origin discourse marker that is rarely used and even then only in some northern Croatian dialects. In these speakers' Croatian repertoires *ja* has become a conventionalised discourse marker with a large number of functions similar to *yeah*. Influence from the discourse norms of German- or Scandinavian-origin interlocutors who may transfer this feature into their English may be a cause for this too. Lexical transfers and foreign origin discourse markers are found in other varieties of diaspora Croatian, e.g. AUT. Cro (Ščukanec, this volume), ITAL.Cro (Županović Filipin, Hlavac and Piasevoli, this volume), TRS.Cro (Piasevoli, this volume), AUS.Cro (Hlavac and Stolac, this volume), NZ.Cro (Stoffel and Hlavac, this volume), ARG.Cro (Skelin Horvat, Musulin and Blažević, this volume).

Below in examples (8) and (9), English-origin verbs, phonologically and morphologically integrated into Croatian, in an otherwise Croatian utterance are presented. In (10) and (11) phonologically integrated English-origin discourse markers are shown.

(8) ...*ako imaš povišen* **blad prešr**, *moraš bit skroz* **okej** *da bi* **se** *ja* **agrijala** *da te pošaljem*...
 '...if you have elevated **blood pressure**, you have to be completely **ok** for me to **agree** to send you...' (Gen.1,F,64)

(9) ...*učila je engleski, djecu* **tičala**, *otišla je za* **ikspirijens**.
 '...she was teaching English, teaching kids, she went for the **experience**.' (Gen.1,M,68)

(10) . . .*mi smo svi došli manje-više slično,* **ju nou,** *došli smo prazni kufera, prazni ruku. . .*
'. . .we all came here more or less in a similar way, **you know,** with empty suitcases, empty hands. . .' (Gen.1,M,55)

(11) . . .*moraš otić u poštu da platiš,* **okej** *okreneš se, ideš u poštu, oh a uplatnica, pa zar nema uplatnice,* **o no,** *to je u knjižari. . .*
'. . .you have to go to the post office to pay, **ok** you turn around, you go to the post office, oh what about money order form, aren't there any money order forms, **oh no,** that is in the bookstore. . .' (Gen.1,F,43)

All the transfers presented here so far are, to various degrees, phonologically integrated into Croatian. English-origin words are generally phonologically integrated in the speech of first-generation informants, from whom examples (8) to (11) are drawn, and less so in the speech of second-generation informants. Some speakers use both phonologically integrated and unintegrated English-origin words, sometimes even in the same sentence:

(12) . . .*ja neću nikad izgubit moj* **akcent,** *ja još uvijek imam* **accent**. . .
'. . .I will never lose my **accent,** I still have my **accent**. . .' (Gen.1,F,58)

While some transfers found in the corpus show complete phonological integration, some are only partially integrated. These forms, in which phonemes from both languages are combined, are called *compromise forms* (Clyne 1991: 174; Hlavac 2003: 36). For example, [pʊpjularno] in (13) below contains phonological elements from both Croatian *popularno* [pòpulārno] and Canadian English *popular* [pʊpjʊlər]. Another example, reported also by Hlavac (2003: 88), is *tat* [tat] (14), a combination of Croatian *tata* [tàta] and English *dad* [dæ:d].

(13) . . .*dobro je, samo nije* **pʊpjularno** . . .
'. . .it's good, it's just not popular [pʊpjʊlər]. . .' (Gen.2,M,23)

HMLD.Cro . . .dobro je, samo nije **popularno** [popularno]. . .

(14) . . .*ali kad vidim moj prijatelj Syd, njegov* **tat** *je Kinez*. . .
'. . .but when I see my friend Syd, his dad is Chinese. . .' (Gen.2,M,31)

HMLD.Cro . . .ali kad vidim svog prijatelja Syda, njegov **tata** je Kinez. . .

As in example (13) some transfers are also morphologically adapted to the recipient language, as shown in (15) and (16) below. It has been observed that the phonological, morphological and syntactic integration of English-origin items decreases from the first generation to the second. To demonstrate how English-origin items are morphologically integrated, glosses showing the morphological features are given in the following examples:

(15) ja   bi   volila   popit
     I   COND.AUX   like VPST.PTCP.F.SG drink-INF.
     čašu   vina   sa   malo   **đinđerelom**
     glass-ACC.F.SG   wine-GEN.N.SG   with+INS some   ginger ale-INS.F.SG
     '...I would like to have a glass of wine with some ginger ale...' (Gen.1, F, 72)

(16) i   on je   reko   da   sam
     and   he AUX.3SG   say-PST.PTCP.M.SG   COMP   AUX-1SG
     radila   u   tako nekom   **ofisu**
     work-PST.PTCP.F.SG   in+LOC like   some-LOC.M.SG   office-LOC.M.SG
     '...and he said that I worked in some office...' (Gen.1,F,43)

In examples (15) and (16) above, morphological integration occurs with target morphological marking, i.e. morphological marking that is congruent to a HMLD. Cro standard or non-standard variety that is the first or heritage language of the informants.

5.2 Structural change

As can be seen on the basis of the types of lexemes that are transferred from English into Croatian, the language contact situation here appears to be at the level of second lowest intensity, i.e. *slightly more intense contact* on Thomason's (2001: 70) four-grading scale of contact intensity, ranging from *casual contact* to *intense contact*. Examples of structural transfer are looked at in this section to enable a description of the degree of intensity that is displayed in the morphosyntactic features of informants' spoken Croatian. The following features are examined: morphological inflections of case, subject pronouns, forms of non-subject personal pronouns, use of reflexive pronouns, use of possessive pronouns, word order of clitics, prepositions and semantic transference, loan translations, and *jedan* 'one' as a nascent indefinite article.

5.2.1 Case system

Croatian has a rich case-marking system with seven cases (nominative, genitive, dative, accusative, vocative, locative, and instrumental) and three major declension patterns. A number of studies of heritage Croatian in countries where English is the dominant language have shown variation in case marking as compared to HMLD.Cro e.g. Jutronić (1974) and Hlavac (2003). In her study of the speech of members of Croatian community in Steelton, Pennsylvania, Jutronić (1974) observed the increased use of the nominative case in place of other cases. She interpreted it as not necessarily a direct influence of American English, but a possible result of "the forgetting process" (Jutronić 1974: 22), i.e. due to attrition amongst first-generation speakers or incomplete acquisition amongst second-generation speakers. Hlavac (2003: 310), who studied the speech of second-generation Croatians in Australia, found that in his corpus 91% of all Croatian NPs receive target case marking. However, as he points out, this percentage includes nominals with 'zero' endings i.e. NOM.M.SG and ACC.M.SG.INANIM nouns. When these forms are not counted, the percentage of target realizations for GEN, LOC, INS, and DAT is 75% (Hlavac 2003: 310). In examining case marking of nominals in his data, Hlavac (2003) applied Đurovič's (1983) model of implicativity. In Đurovič's (1983) explanation of the reduction of the case system among immigrant children in Sweden, the seven cases are ordered as follows: NOM. ACC. GEN. LOC. INS. DAT. VOC., with cases to the left lost last and cases to the right lost first. Hlavac (2003: 314) found that the majority of non-target case realizations in his sample are congruent to Đurovič's (1983) model of implicativity. Furthermore, Hlavac (2003: 320) concludes that the change in case marking of Croatian NPs could be attributed to both external and internal influences. The external influence that Hlavac identifies is the significant percentage (32%) of NPs with phonologically and morphologically integrated English-origin nouns that bear non-target case morphology, where a 'carry over' effect of the English-origin items is that case markers are reduced at a greater rate than for Croatian-origin lexemes in NPs. Đurovič's (1983) implicativity scale is employed as model in the description of case-marking in NPs from other data samples, such as those from ITAL.Cro (Županović Filipin, Hlavac and Piasevoli, this volume), AUS.Cro (Hlavac and Stolac, this volume) and NZ.Cro (Stoffel and Hlavac, this volume).

In the corpus studied here there is variation between the generations, between speakers of the same generation, and even within the speech of the same speaker in regard to marking of phi-features of nouns, noun modifiers and pronouns. Whereas the speech of first-generation informants is characterized by a use of cases identical to that of HMLD.Cro speakers, the speech of second-generation informants contains various examples of non-target case realizations. As previously reported by Jutronić (1974) and Hlavac (2003), the data reveal examples in which the NOM case replaced ACC, GEN and INS, as well as examples in which the ACC replaced LOC. A quantification of all NPs from the sample and their morphological features is not provided here.

Examples presented below are grouped according to the expected target-case form, followed by an arrow → with the actual case form employed by the informant:

Accusative → Nominative

(17) i   za   **cijela**   **ta**   **sjeverna**
     and   for+ACC   whole-NOM.F.SG   that-NOM.F.SG   north-NOM.F.SG
     američka   **mreža**
     American-NOM.F.SG   network-NOM.F.SG
     '...and for the entire North American network...' (Gen.2,M,35)

HMLD.Cro
i   za   **cijelu**   **tu**   **sjevernoameričku**
and   for+ACC   whole-ACC.F.SG   that-ACC.F.SG.   north-American-ACC.F.SG
mrežu
network-ACC.F.SG

(18) to   je   bilo   vrlo   važan
     that-NOM.N.SG. AUX-3SG   be-PST.PTCP.N.SG   very   important-NOM.M.SG
     jedan   dan   za   **svi**   **Hrvati**
     one-NOM.M.SG   day-NOM.M.SG   for+ACC   all-NOM.M.PL   Croatian-NOM.M.PL
     '...that was a very important day for all Croatians...' (Gen.2,M,35)

HMLD.Cro
to   je   bio   Ø (jedan)   vrlo
that-NOM.N.SG.   AUX-3SG   be-PST.PTCP.M.SG   Ø (one)   very
važan   dan   za   **sve**
important-NOM.M.SG   day-NOM.M.SG.   for+ACC   all-ACC.M.PL
Hrvate
Croatian-ACC.M.PL

In examples (17) and (18) above, ACC forms for two NPs are represented via NOM forms. Significantly, both NPs are part of larger prepositional phrases (PPs), and the prepositions govern the case for succeeding NP forms. Semantically, the hierarchical and relational meaning of all forms in the examples is clear, as the preposition *za* 'for' makes clear what the relationship is between *važan dan* 'important day' and *svi Hrvati* 'all Croats', where the NP *svi Hrvati* bears non-target case-marking (i.e. NOM instead of ACC). In Hlavac's (2003: 310) sample, only 171 (5%) of the 3,128 direct object NPs have non-target ACC case marking. But of these 171 non-target ACC NPs, 112 or 65% of them are preceded by a preposition (Hlavac 2003: 323). The presence of prepositions alone does not induce non-target case marking in NPs, but amongst those NPs with non-target case marking alone, there is a greater likelihood that a preposition will precede these, which is what is shown in examples (17) and (18).

Genitive → Nominative

(19) every   Saturday   jesam   od   **prvi**   do
      every   Saturday   be-1SG   from+GEN   first-NOM.M.SG.   to+GEN
      osmi   razred   svake   subote
      eighth-NOM.M.SG.   grade-NOM.M.SG   every-GEN.F.SG   Saturday-GEN.F.SG
      osim   ljetna   doba
      except+GEN   summer-NOM.F.SG   time-NOM.F.SG
      '...every Saturday, I did, from first to eighth grade except in summertime...'
      (Gen.2, M, 35)

      HMLD.Cro
      every   Saturday   jesam   od   **prvog**   do
      every   Saturday   be-1SG   from+GEN   first-GEN.M.SG.   to+GEN
      osmog   razreda   svake   subote
      eighth-GEN.M.SG   grade-GEN.M.SG   every-GEN.F.SG   Saturday-GEN.F.SG
      osim   u   ljetno   doba
      except+GEN   in+ACC   summer-ACC.N.SG   time-ACC.N.SG

(20) imam   puno   **Hrvati**   **prijatelji**   ali
      have-1SG   many+GEN   Croatian-NOM.M.PL   friend-NOM.M.PL   but
      imam   dosta   **Kanađani**   ili **Kinezovi**
      have-1SG   many+GEN   Canadian-NOM.M.PL   or Chinese-NOM.M.PL
      'I have lots of Croatian friends, but I also have many Canadian or Chinese friends'. (Gen.2,M,19)

      HMLD.Cro
      imam   puno   **prijatelja**   **Hrvata**   ali
      have-1SG   many+GEN   friend-GEN.M.PL   Croatian-GEN.M.PL   but
      imam   dosta   **Kanađana**   ili **Kineza**
      have-1SG   many+GEN   Canadians-GEN.M.PL   or Chinese-GEN.M.PL

Analogous to examples (17) and (18), example (19) above contains two prepositions that govern the GEN while the succeeding adjectives and noun bear NOM morphology. In (20), there are two adverbs of quantity *puno* and *dosta* that require GEN marking on following nominals. As shown above in regard to ACC non-target inflections, the relational meaning of all elements to each other remains clear as the prepositions and adverbs of quantity express these. What is also apparent in (19) is that an adverbial phrase with *no* preposition is rendered with a target GEN structure, *svake subote* 'every+GEN Saturday+GEN'. This shows that in this informant's repertoire, GEN is not 'lost' as a morpho-syntactic category of which he has a command. Instead, it is vulnerable to reduction only in PPs or APs containing prepositions that otherwise express hierarchical and relational meaning.

Instrumental → Nominative

(21) *ne   volim   party anymore too much   you know   samo   bit*
NEG   like-1SG   party anymore too much   you know   only   be-INF
*sa   **ljud**i   koje   znam*
with+INS   people-NOM.M.PL   REL.PRON-ACC.M.PL   know-1SG
familija   takve   stvari
family-NOM.F.SG   such-NOM.F.PL   thing-NOM.F.PL
'. . .I don't like to party anymore too much, you know, only to be with people that I know, family, that kind of thing. . .' (Gen.2 M,21)

HMLD.Cro
ne   volim   više ići na tulume previše   znaš   samo   biti
NEG   like-1SG   party anymore too much   you know   only   be-INF
*s   **ljudima**   koje   znam   familija*
with+INS   people-INS.M.PL   REL.PRON-ACC.M.PL   know-1SG   family-NOM.F.SG
takve   stvari
such-NOM.F.PL   thing-NOM.F.PL

(22) *jer   ja   sam   se   družio   i   sa*
because   I   AUX-1SG   REFL.   hangout-SG.M.PST.PTCP   and   with+INS
njeni   prijatelji
her-NOM.F.PL   friend-NOM.F.PL
'. . .because I was hanging out with her friends as well. . . .' (Gen.2,M,22)

HMLD.Cro
jer   družio   sam   se   i   s
because   hang out-PST.PTCP.M.SG   AUX-1SG   REFL   and   with+INS
njenim   **prijateljima**
her-INS.M.PL   friend-INS.M.PL

Examples (21) and (22) reveal non-target nominal inflections following a preposition *s* 'with' that governs INS that pattern in a similar way to the PPs and APs presented in examples (17) to (20).

Other instances of non-target case-marking by second-generation informants include ACC forms that replace LOC as in (23) and (24).

Locative → Accusative

(23) *da   je   ova   stvarno jedna   dobra*
      that   be-3SG this-NOM.F.SG   truly   one-NOM.F.SG   good-NOM.F.SG
      *država   jer   živimo   u   **mir***
      country-NOM.F.SG   because   live-1PL in+LOC peace-ACC/NOM.M.SG.
      '...that this is truly a good country because we live in peace...' (Gen.2,M,35)

HMLD.Cro
da   je   ovo   stvarno dobra   država
that   be-3SG this-NOM.N.SG   truly   good-NOM.F.SG   country-NOM.F.SG
*jer   živimo   u   **miru***
because   live-1PL   in+LOC   peace-LOC.M.SG

(24) *u   srcu   ja   sam   Hrvat   jer   kad*
      in+LOC   heart-LOC.N.SG   I   be-1SG   Croat-NOM.M.SG because   when
      *sam   ja   u   **Hrvatsku**   imam   osjećaj   da*
      be-1SG   I   in+LOC   Croatia-ACC.F.SG have-1SG feeling-ACC.M.SG COMP
      sam   kući
      be-1SG   home-DAT.F.SG
      '...in my heart I'm Croatian because when I'm in Croatia I feel that I'm home.' (Gen.2,M,31)

HMLD.Cro

ja	sam	u	srcu	Hrvat	jer	kad
I	be-1SG	in+LOC	heart-LOC.N.SG	Croat-NOM.M.SG	because	when

sam	u	**Hrvatskoj**	imam	osjećaj	da
be-1SG	in+LOC	Croatia-LOC.F.SG	have-1SG	feeling-ACC.M.SG	COMP

sam	kući
be-1SG	home-DAT.F.SG

In (23) above, a preposition governing LOC case, *u* 'in', does not yield LOC marking on the following nominal, *mir* 'peace' ACC.M.SG. In (24), after the same preposition, a FEM nominal is given in its ACC form *Hrvatsku* 'Croatia' ACC.F.SG. To be sure, the ACC marking here for target LOC forms is non-standard. I consider them to be non-target forms, notwithstanding a non-distinction in morphology marking between ACC and LOC in some regiolects of Dalmatia and southern Herzegovina (Brozović and Ivić 1988; Jutronić-Tihomirović 1989). In (24), there is also a target LOC form, *u srcu* 'in heart-LOC.N.SG' and there is also *kući*, a form which is an adverb, but etymologically derived from a DAT construction, i.e. *kući* 'house-DAT.F.SG' In Croatian, syncretism has occurred between LOC and DAT and occurrence of these forms indicates that a loss of the LOC has not occurred in this informant's repertoire, but that it is subject to reduction in PPs.

All of the examples presented above (17) – (24), are congruent to Ďurovič's (1983) model of implicativity, where in the instances of non-target case-marking, those cases to the left replace cases to the right. It appears that in the corpus studied here there is general tendency that non-target-realizations of cases conform to Ďurovič's (1983) implicativity principle.

5.2.2 Increased use of overt subject pronouns

Croatian, in contrast to English, is a pro-drop (null-subject) language and as such it allows for subject pronouns to be omitted. In Croatian, the presence of a subject pronoun is usually overt and typically indicates emphasis or contrast. Increased use of personal pronouns in subject position was observed in the speech of both generations of informants. Example (25) shows the use of the subject pronoun *ja* 'I' (as do examples (22) and (24) above) while in example (26) the pronoun *oni* 'they' occurs when there was no conversationally referential feature such as emphasis or contrast.

(25) ...*ja ne radim sada, ja sam u školu, ali ja mislim da to pomaže u poslu...*
'... I don't work now, I go to school, but I think that it helps with your work...' (Gen.2,M,21)

HMLD.Cro ... ne radim sada, idem u školu, ali mislim da to pomaže u poslu ...

(26) ...*oni kad su bili mali, su samo hrvatski govorili, **oni** kad su došli u kindergarten.. **oni** su bili newcomers...*
'...when they were little, they only spoke Croatian, when they started kindergarten, they were newcomers...' (Gen.1,F,58)

HMLD.Cro ...kad su bili mali, samo su hrvatski govorili, kad su došli u vrtić.. bili su došljaci...

A quantification of overt subject pronouns is not provided here. However this is a feature that is present in the speech of Gen.2 *and* Gen.1 informants, as (26) above shows. Example (26) above is in line with Otheguy, Zentella and Livert's (2007) observation that Gen.1 speakers of a pro-drop language can begin to use overt subjects in the diaspora setting. Jutronić (1974: 24–25, this volume), who reports the same tendency in the speech of her Croatian-American informants, attributes overt personal pronouns in subject position to the influence of English which is not pro-drop. Many studies in countries where English is the societally dominant language record an elevated use of overt subjects in heritage languages that have pro-drop, such as Spanish (e.g. Silva-Corvalán 1994; Montrul 2016) or Italian (e.g. Sorace and Filiaci 2006; Serratrice 2007). Polinsky (2018: 254) sees attrition of null pronouns as an example of a more broad-scale trend: overt subject pronouns allow "heritage speakers to be clearer in production" and are a form of overmarking that can occur in other areas of performance as well. Overt subjects are recorded also in ITAL.Cro (Županović Filipin, Hlavac and Piasevoli, this volume), TRS.Cro (Piasevoli, this volume) and AUS.Cro (Hlavac & Stolac, this volume).

5.2.3 Increased use of full form pronouns

In Croatian there are two forms of object personal and reflexive pronouns, the short (unaccented or clitic) form and the full (accented) form. Short forms are generally the unmarked choice while full forms are obligatory only when in clause-initial position, after prepositions and to show emphasis or contrast. In the corpus of speech of both first- and second-generation Croatian-Canadians, many examples of full form object pronouns were located where clitic forms would otherwise be expected. Jutronić (1974: 25) argues that there is a preference for the full form among many speakers of USA.Cro due to the complexity of syntactic patterns required when unaccented forms are used. (For further examples of overt full form object pronouns in NZ.Cro see Stoffel and Hlavac, this volume.) The argument made by Jutronić (1974; see also Jutronić this volume) is in line with general observations on the language of heritage speakers that a choice of two forms within the same paradigm often leads to one form predominating (Polinsky 2008). In (27), (28), (29), and (30) full forms of Croatian pronouns were used although there was no apparent reason for emphasis or contrast.

(27) . . .to što ja ne znam jezik, to **mene** nikad nije zbunilo. . .
'. . .the fact that I don't know the language, that has never intimidated me. . .' (Gen.1,F,43)

HMLD.Cro   . . .to što ja ne znam jezik, to **me** nikad nije zbunjivalo. . .

(28) . . .to **meni** nije bilo jasno. . .
'. . .I didn't understand that. . .' (Gen.2,F,41)

HMLD.Cro   . . .to **mi** nije bilo jasno. . .

(29) . . .oni su **njemu** rekli da mi to nismo znali. . .
'. . .they told him that we didn't know that. . .' (Gen.1,F,54)

HMLD.Cro   . . .rekli su **mu** da to nismo znali. . . / . . . oni su **mu** rekli da to nismo znali . . .

In Croatian, the word order position of a clitic pronoun is less flexible than that of a full form pronoun. Full form pronouns can occur in any position, including clause-initial and -final position. But clitic pronouns are subject to, at least in standard HMLD.Cro, a stricter word order position, and clitics *cannot* occur in initial position. Their position, immediately or anywhere after initial position, is determined hierarchically according to the following order;

particle	AUX	DAT	ACC/GEN	REFL	3SG.AUX
1	2	3	4	5	6

In examples (27) to (29) above, the position of the full form pronoun is identical to that of the equivalent clitic, i.e. in initial position after a determiner or in second position after an AUX. In example (30) below, both the form and the position of the full form are non-target.

(30) . . . i ona kaže ajme kako bi to bilo da ne vidim roditelji devetnest godina.. baš je taka sudbina **njoj** bila. . .
'. . .and she says oh my, what would it be like not to see my parents for nineteen years.. that was exactly her destiny. . .' (Gen.1,F,72)

HMLD.Cro . . .i ona kaže ajme kako bi to bilo da ne vidim roditelje devetnaest godina.. baš **joj** je takva bila sudbina. . .

The relationship between *sudbina* and the subject is one of possession. The most unmarked representation of this is an adnominal DAT construction, usually with a clitic form. In accounting for the use of the full form forms there do not appear to be changes in word order that may offer a clue as to why this is happening: examples (27), (28) and (30) show word patterns that are no different from those of HMLD.Cro. Example (29) bears overt subject as well as object pronouns in general, but a clitic could occur in exactly the same position that the full form pronoun was given. In USA.Cro, there is some evidence that word order changes occur as an accompanying feature that favour the use of full form pronouns, i.e. that full form pronouns still occur, even discounting those word order changes such as fronting that require a full form (see Jutronić, this volume). As stated, in the language of diaspora speakers, choices within paradigms tend to be reduced, but this does not explain why full form object pronouns are sometimes replacing clitic ones, rather than clitic pronouns full form ones. Polinsky (2018: 165–166) argues that the "phonetically heavier forms" tend to predominate because their form make the function of the constituent more transparent. Less prominent forms are perceptually less transparent and therefore less amenable to diaspora speakers as bearers of syntactic relations.

5.2.4 Word order: Clitics

As outlined in Section 5.2.3, position of clitics is subject to strict word order rules in Croatian. In example (31) the problem is with the placement of clitics – unaccented forms of some pronouns (personal and reflexive), verbs, and the conditional particle *bi*. In Croatian, clitics cannot stand by themselves. They are connected to the preceding accented word, and together they form a single accentual unit (Browne 1975; Browne and Alt 2004). Rules governing the placement of clitics in a sentence forecast that in (31) the conditional particle *bi* and *me* ('me-

ACC') would be grouped together. However, this does not happen and the subject *tata* 'dad' precedes the object pronoun, which (here in its non-target DAT form) is given in both its clitic *mi* 'to me' and its full form *meni* 'to me' immediately following the COMP *da* 'that'.

(31) ...to meni.. je malo žao 'cause ja mislim **da bi** tata mogao **mi meni** više naučit kako bi trebala pričat [hrvatski]...
'...for me it's a bit sad, because I think that my dad could teach me more about how I should speak [Croatian]...' (Gen.2,F,41)

HMLD.Cro ...to mi.. je malo žao jer mislim **da bi me** tata mogao više naučiti kako pričati [hrvatski]...

In example (32) the same clitic *mi* ('me-DAT') would be expected to precede AUX *je* 'be-3SG'. According to the rules for placement of clitics in a sentence, AUX clitics are in second position, except for the AUX *je* which is an exception, an 'outlier' that is placed at the end (Browne 1975).

(32) ...nije da mi je neugodno, ali.. volila bi je .. volila bi .. **da je mi** .. lakše .. da se ne moram toliko trudit...
'...it's not that I'm uncomfortable, but I'd like I'd like **that** [it] **is to me** [= 'for it'] it to be easier [for me], for me to not have to go to so much effort... have to try so hard' (Gen.2,F,41)

HMLD.Cro ...nije da mi je neugodno, ali voljela bih **da mi je** lakše, da se ne moram toliko truditi...

In (32), leftward movement of AUX *je* 'be-3SG' occurs which cannot be attributable to any non-standard varieties of HMLD.Cro. It is possible that *je* as an outlier to the usual, second position for AUX is susceptible to movement leftwards. Jutronić (this volume) also records instances of this same phenomenon. In example (33) the subject pronoun *ja* comes first amongst the clitics, preceding AUX *sam* where it should otherwise follow it. This could be interpreted as a patterning of the English model that requires that the subject precedes the verb in all declarative sentences.

(33) ...kad **ja sam** išao doma nekoliko ljudi su išli unutra...
'...when I was going home, several people came in...' (Gen.2, M, 31)

HMLD.Cro ...kad **sam ja** išao doma... nekoliko ljudi je išlo unutra...

Changes in placement of clitics were also reported by Jutronić (1974) amongst Croatian-speakers in the US, and by Hansen, Romić and Kolaković (2013) amongst Croatian-speakers in Germany.

5.2.5 Omission of reflexive pronouns

Reflexive verbs are much more common as a category of verb forms in Croatian compared to English, and reflexive constructions are more common than in English with many reflexive verb constructions also expressing passive voice. In Croatian the verb *igrati* 'to play' can be used reflexively, *igrati se* 'to play + REFL' to denote playing in a general sense, or as a transitive verb with a direct object, e.g. *igrati igru* 'to play a game'. The omission of the reflexive pronoun *se* in example (34) indicates that the verb was used transitively, when in fact it was supposed to be used reflexively.

(34)   S. *i oni bi samo* **igrali**...
       '...S. and they just want to play...' (Gen.2,F,27)

       HMLD.Cro   S. i oni bi **se** samo igrali...

A similar case is example (35) with the verb *snaći se* 'to manage', where the reflexive pronoun *se* was omitted:

(35)   ...*ako idem danas .. u Hrvatsku .. ja možem* **snać** *malo*...
       '...if I were to go to Croatia today, I can partially manage...' (Gen.2,M,28)

       HMLD.Cro   ...da idem danas.. u Hrvatsku.. ja bih **se** mogao malo snaći...

The absence of the REFL particle is likely to be attributable to influence from English equivalents in which REFL is not present. A quantification of all reflexive verbs in the sample was not undertaken, and I make no claim here that this is a widespread occurrence. Omission of the reflexive particle is perhaps conspicuous due to its relative infrequency, i.e. it tends not to be an 'expected' feature of heritage speakers' vernaculars. But where changes occur, it appears that the particle is omitted, rather than added for non-reflexive verbs, and reflexive clitic dropping is a finding in line with observations on another Slavic language spoken in a diaspora setting, American Russian (Polinsky 2006). Other studies of Croatian in a diaspora setting indicate that this may be a less categorical trend, e.g. Hlavac and Stolac (this volume) also report 14 instances of reflexive particle omission, but they also locate 8 instances where it occurs in non-reflexive constructions.

5.2.6 Non-target use of possessive pronouns

In addition to forms specific to number (SG or PL) and person (1st 2nd or 3rd) Croatian has a further possessive pronoun that can be used for any number or person, *svoj*, which is the unmarked choice in most constructions in which possessive pronouns occur. Analogous to subject pronouns, possessive pronouns that are specific to the number and person of the subject, e.g. *moj* 'my', *tvoj* 'your' etc. are overt, and usually used only to emphasise or contrast the subject. In the third person, for both singular and plural use of *svoj* is obligatory; use of third person possessive pronouns such as *njegov* 'his', *njezin* 'her' or *njihov* 'their' indicate that the possessor of the object is *not* the same as the grammatical subject. In (36) the 3PL possessive pronoun *njihov* 'their' is employed, instead of *svoj*. But in (36) the grammatical subject is the same as the possessor of the object, and the utterance contains an unintended meaning:

(36) imaju   taj   cilj   da   čuvaju
     have-3PL   that-ACC.M.SG   goal-ACC.M.SG   COMP   maintain-3PL
     njihov   jezik
     their-ACC.M.SG   language-ACC.M.SG
     '...they have the goal of maintaining their language...' (Gen.2,M,35)

   HMLD.Cro
   imaju   za   cilj   da   očuvaju
   have-3PL   for+ACC   goal-ACC.M.SG   COMP   maintain-3PL
   svoj   jezik
   own-REFL.POSS.ACC.M.SG   language-ACC.M.SG

A similar situation is with examples (37) and (38) where *moje* 'my' was used instead the reflexive possessive *svoje*.

(37) zašto   ja   ne   bi   zadržao   **moje**   ime
     why   I   NEG   COND.AUX   keep-PST.M.SG   my-ACC.N.SG   name-ACC.N.SG
     i   prezime
     and   last name- ACC.N.SG
     '...why wouldn't I keep my first and last name...' (Gen.1,M,64)

   HMLD.Cro
   zašto   ja   ne   bih   zadržao   **svoje**
   why   I   NEG   COND.AUX   keep-PST.M.SG   own-REFL.POSS.ACC.N.SG
   ime   i   prezime
   name-ACC.N.SG   and   last name-ACC.N.SG

(38) meni   je   svejedno ja izmolim **moje**
     me-DAT be-1SG same   I   pray-1SG my-ACC.N.SG
     '...it's all the same to me, I do my prayers...' (Gen.1,F,43)

HMLD.Cro
meni   je   svejedno ja izmolim **svoje**
me-DAT be-1SG same   I   pray-1SG own REFL.POSS.ACC.N.SG

Both (37) and (38) are from Gen.1 informants. While all examples of non-target morphology marking for case are from Gen.2 informants, it is of interest that examples of overt subject pronouns and a re-alignment of the use of possessive pronouns according to English models are present in the speech of older, Croatian L1 informants. Amongst Gen.2 speakers of USA.Cro, Jutronić (this volume) locates a conspicuous over-use of possessive pronouns – but not *svoj* in particular – that she attributes to the reduced use of DAT constructions in expressing relations of possession. She attributes this to the transference of syntactic models from English. Transference is also located as the reason for the over-use of *svoj* in ITAL.Cro (Županović Filipin, Hlavac and Piasevoli, this volume) where the lexico-semantic features of Italian *suo* 'his/her/its' appear to be transferred onto those of Croatian *svoj*.

5.2.7 Prepositions and semantic transference

The role of prepositions is to express relations (of place, time, etc.) between other elements of the sentence. Croatian prepositions govern cases i.e. they determine the case of the noun. In example (39) the preposition *iz* 'from' was used. Its use appears to be due to the equivalent English construction in which the preposition *from* is used. In Croatian, the notion of 'translation from' one language into another is rendered via the preposition *s* 'off/from' + GEN. (This preposition is not to be confused with the homophonous preposition *s* 'with' + INS) The semantic field of the English preposition *from* is applied to the Croatian preposition *iz* 'from' so that *iz* functions as the preposition expressing 'transfer from language to another', a function that is otherwise performed by *s*.

(39) ...pretežno moram privest **iz** engleski na hrvatski kada ću pričat hrvatski...
     '...I usually have to translate *from* English into Croatian when I speak Croatian...' (Gen.2,F,41)

HMLD.Cro ...pretežno moram prevesti **s** engleskog na hrvatski kad govorim hrvatski...

In (39) above, NOM. rather than GEN. case marking is present after the preposition *iz* that governs GEN. case (cf. section 5.2.1). A similar instance of semantic transference of the referential field of an equivalent English preposition is shown in (40) below, where *u* 'in' (+ LOC) is employed by the informant, based on the English construction 'in+ name of language':

(40) ...*ja ne znam kako se to kaže **u** hrvatski, ja ne znam*...
'... I don't know how to say that in Croatian, I don't know...' (Gen.2,M,28)

    HMLD.Cro ...*ne znam kako se to kaže **na** hrvatskom, ne znam*...
'...I don't know how to say that *in* Croatian, I don't know...' (Gen.2,M,28)

In HMLD.Cro the preposition *na* 'on' (+LOC) is used to perform this function. As in (39), there is NOM. rather than LOC. case marking on the succeeding nominals.

5.2.8 Loan translations

Influences of English on Croatian spoken in Canada can be seen in calquing of certain constructions where whole phrases, collocations, and idiomatic expressions are modelled according to English patterns. Examples (41), (42), (43), (44), (45), and (46) are structurally based on English phraseological or collocational structures that have been transferred 'element for element' into Croatian. The examples contain only Croatian lexemes and morpho-syntactic features, but the word-for-word sequencing of certain phrases or clusters of words is unknown in HMLD.Cro. This understanding of semantic loan translations is in line with Backus and Dorleijn's (2009: 77) definition of loan translations as "any usage of morphemes in Language A that is the result of the literal translation of one or more elements in a semantically equivalent expression in Language B."

(41) ...*a ovde naši ljudi **rade duge sate** i mizeran poso.. i ponosan je samo da zaradi*...
'...our people here **work long hours** at tedious jobs and is proud simply to be earning...' (Gen.1,F,55)

    HMLD.Cro ...*ovdje naši ljudi **dugo ostaju na poslu** i rade teške poslove i ponosan je samo da zaradi*...
'...here our people **stay at work for a long time** and work hard manual jobs and he is proud simply to be earning...'

Example (41) above contains a translated version of the metaphor *work long hours*, while (42) below features a high-register item, *formulirati* 'to formulate' with the meaning of 'to form (friendships)':

(42) ...i.. imao sam priliku imat i.. **formulirat prijateljstvo** sa Hrvatima...
'...and I had a chance to have and.. **form friendships** with Croatians...'
(Gen.2,M,35)

    HMLD.Cro ...imao sam priliku **sklopiti prijateljstvo** s Hrvatima...
    '...I had a chance to **construct friendships** with Croatians...'

(43) ...*radila san u jednoj plastičnoj tvornici*.. *di se kosmetika pakuje*...
'...**I worked in a plastics factory**.. where cosmetics are packaged...'
(Gen.1,F,64)

    HMLD.Cro ...radila sam u **tvornici plastike**, gdje se pakira kozmetika...
    '...I worked in a **factory of plastic**, where cosmetics are packaged...'

Example (43) above contains a pre-posed modifier that results in a change of meaning. In English, a *plastics factory* manufactures plastic. Here, the-preposed modifier is logically the product that the factory produces. In all varieties of Croatian, the product must be post-posed, i.e. *tvornica plastike* 'factory of plastic'. A pre-position of *plastika* 'plastic(s)', even in its adjectival form, yields the meaning *factory made of plastic*.

(44) ...*je li voliš ovi majica, ovi je dvadeset dolara, je li voliš*.. *o* **ne volim kako to stoji na nju**...
'...do you like this shirt, this one is $20, do you like it.. oh I **don't like how it looks on her**...' (Gen.2,F,22)

    HMLD.Cro ...sviđa li ti se ova majica, košta 20 dolara, sviđa li ti se.. o **ne sviđa mi se kako joj to stoji**...
    '...do you like this shirt, it costs $20, do you like it.. oh I **don't like how it stands on her**...'

Example (44) contains a loan translation of part of an English phrase 'SUBJ [clothing] *look on* OBJ [person]'. The PREP *na* is the Croatian equivalent of *on*, and it is employed followed by the PRON *nju* 'her-ACC', referring to the person. The equivalent HMLD.Cro structure is 'SUBJ [clothing] *stajati* 'stand' IND.OBJ+DAT [person]'.

Use of clitics pronouns alters the word order so that the DAT object is preposed: *joj* 'her+DAT' *to* 'that' *stoji* 'stand-3.SG'.

(45) ...*ja probam,* **neki puta ja pričam hrvatski nazad**...
 '...I try, **sometimes I speak Croatian back**...' (Gen.2,M,28)

   HMLD.Cro ...*pokušavam, ponekad ja* **odgovaram** *na hrvatskom*...
   '...I try, sometimes I **answer** in Croatian...'

(46) ...*on da dođe ovdje i da vidi da* **može napravit pare***, on bi osto*...
 '...if he were to come here and see that he **could make money**, he would stay...' (Gen.1,F,51)

   HMLD.Cro ...*da on dođe ovamo i da vidi da* **može zaraditi novaca**, *on bi ostao*...
   '...if he were to come here and see that he **could earn money**, he would stay...'

Examples (45) and (46) contain translations of English phrases *speak* OBJ [language] *back* and *make money*. The collocations *pričati nazad* 'speak back' and *napraviti pare* 'make money' do not exist in HMLD.Cro. Loan translations are found widely in other varieties of diaspora Croatian (see Ščukanec; Piasevoli; Hlavac and Stolac; Stoffel and Hlavac; Skelin Horvat, Musulin and Blažević, all this volume).

5.2.9 Use of *jedan* 'one' as an indefinite article

In three examples (18), (23) and (43) above, the ADJ *jedan* 'one' preposes Croatian nominals. They are repeated here with narrow glosses:

(18) *to*   *je*   *bilo*   *vrlo*   *važan*
   that-NOM.N.SG   AUX-3SG   be-PST.PTCP.N.SG   very   important-NOM.M.SG
   jedan   *dan*   *za*   *svi*
   one-NOM.M.SG   day-NOM.M.SG for+ACC   all-NOM.M.PL
   Hrvati
   Croatian-NOM.M.PL
   '...that was **a** very important day for all Croatians...' (Gen.2,M,35)

(23) da   je   ova   stvarno **jedna**   dobra
     that be-3SG this-NOM.F.SG truly   one-NOM.F.SG good-NOM.F.SG
     država
     country-NOM.F.SG
     '...that this is truly **a** good country...' (Gen.2,M,35)

(43) radila   san   u   **jednoj**   plastičnoj
     work-PTCP.SG.F AUX-1SG   in+LOC   one-LOG.F.SG   plastic-NOM.SG.F
     tvornici...
     factory-NOM.SG.F
     '...I worked in **a** plastics factory...' (Gen.1,F,64)

The HMLD.Cro equivalents do not feature *jedan* whose use would slightly alter the meaning of the utterance. In (18), (23) and (43), *jedan* does not perform the function of expressing numerical quantity of the following nominal, which from the morphological (i.e. SG) suffix of the nominal is clear. Instead, *jedan* expresses specificity about the following nominal which is mentioned for the first time, and therefore appears to be taking on the function of an indefinite article. To be sure, *jedan* can take on functions in HMLD.Cro that go beyond marking numerical quantity. For example, *jedan* can function as a determiner that emphasises the distinctiveness of the following nominal, in the same way that *one* can do this in English e.g. *ona je jedna uspješna sportašica* 'she is one successful sportswoman'. This use, however, is stylistically marked as it emphasises the following nominal's particularity. In examples (18), (23) and (43) *jedan* does not mark the succeeding nominals as particular or peculiar. Use of *jedan* in these instances represents an example of the nascent development of *jedan* as an indefinite article. Similar instances of *jedan* with an article-like function are reported in other varieties of Croatian spoken in diaspora settings (see Piasevoli; Hlavac and Stolac; Skelin Horvat, Musulin and Blažević, all this volume).

6 Conclusion

The aim of this chapter was to explore the influence of English (majority language) on Croatian spoken in Canada (minority language). The focus was on the features of Croatian as spoken in Canada that differ from the features of homeland Croatian. From a corpus of approx. 27,000 words based on interviews conducted with 22 Croatian-English first- and second-generation bilinguals, instances of lexical, morpho-syntactic and semantic features are identified that diverge from those of HMLD.Cro. Lexical items are a conspicuous feature of all informants' speech, with around 10% of the total corpus consisting of English-origin forms. Almost all grammatical categories are represented: nouns, verbs, adjectives, adverbs and discourse markers. The presence of English-origin lexical transfers can be in the form of single-word or short insertions, or phrase- or clause-long alternations from English. English-origin items tend to occur as single-item insertions only in the speech of first-generation informants, and are almost always phonologically and morphologically integrated. Amongst second-generation speakers, the incidence of English-origin items is higher, especially that of alternations, and there are variable degrees of phonological and morphological integration of these.

Second-generation speakers are also those informants amongst whom morpho-syntactic changes are apparent. Instances of non-target case marking such as ACC > NOM, GEN > NOM, INS > NOM, LOC > ACC are reported, which are congruent to a case implicativity hierarchy that describes the forms drawn on when case morphology is reduced (Ďurovič 1983). The presence of prepositions in instances of reduced case morphology is registered, with prepositions potentially increasing the likelihood of non-target case marking in succeeding NP constructions, which is compatible to Hlavac's (2003) findings.

In the speech of both second- and first-generation speakers, increased use of overt subject pronouns was observed when no emphasis or contrast was intended, thereby showing the direct influence of English upon Croatian spoken in the community. This is a finding common to many studies that look at pro-drop heritage languages in contact with English. What is also of interest is that the speech of both generations of speakers abounds with full forms of non-subject pronouns where short forms would be expected. This is again apparently traceable to English – as English does not distinguish between full form or clitic pronouns. But perhaps the overt use of both subject and object pronouns can be seen as a wider trend of "overmarking", i.e. more overt or direct form-mapping that can occurs with pronouns, as it can with other categories (Polinsky 2018: 184, 254).

In regard to word order, amongst second-generation informants, changes in the word order of clitics are observed, with instances of leftward movement of subject pronoun to precede AUX. This is presumably modelled according to the fronted placement of subjects in English declaratives.

In some instances, verbs requiring the reflexive particle *se* lack it. This again can be attributed to English influence as reflexive constructions are much less common in English. Data from American Russian show similar instances of reflexive particle omission (Polinsky 2006). Omission may be evidence that an unstressed particle such as *se* which does not have a full-form equivalent lacks "perceptual salience" (Polinsky 2018: 165) and is therefore susceptible to attrition.

Similarly the reflexive possessive pronoun *svoj* that is used to indicate that the possessor of the object is the same as the grammatical subject can be replaced with 3rd person possessive pronouns. When this occurs, this results in a meaning change and indicates that the object of possession belongs to someone else.

Likewise, Gen.2 informants are seen to transfer the semantic field of English prepositions to Croatian prepositions. This shows a direct influence of English on Croatian spoken by the informants. Loan translations are also an example of impact of English; whole phrases, collocations, and idiomatic expressions containing Croatian lexemes and morpho-syntactic features are modelled according to English patterns. These loan translations are present in the speech of both generations of informants. Another innovation, also observed in both groups of informants, is the use of ADJ *jedan* 'one' before nominals, thus functioning as an indefinite article, which is non-existent in Croatian.

This chapter shows that speakers' repertoire in Croatian is undergoing changes due to contact with English. The English influence is most obvious at the lexical level. However, the analysis also showed a number of morpho-syntactic features of bilingual Croatian that diverge from the monolingual Croatian spoken in the homeland. Findings here suggest that some of those features could be a product of structural convergence toward English (e.g. use of the nominative in place of other cases, increased use of overt subject pronouns, non-target use of possessives, omission of reflexive pronouns, changes in the word order of clitics, formation of loan translations, etc.). However, some changes could also be internally motivated, or, as Thomason (2001: 62) points out, "multiple causation" may be a possible explanation as a change could have more than one cause. In conclusion, it could be speculated that systematic changes in Croatian as spoken in Canada are, for the most part, a result of specific language contact conditions. While contact with English may not be the only factor influencing the change in Croatian spoken in Canada, it is certainly the primary motivator of change.

References

Albin, Alexander & Ronelle Alexander. 1972. *The speech of Yugoslav immigrants in San Pedro, California*. The Hague: Martinus Nijhoff.
Backus, Ad & Margreet Dorleijn. 2009. Loan translations versus code-switching. In Barbara Bullock & Almeida Jacqueline Toribio (eds.), *The Cambridge handbook of linguistic code-switching*, 75–93. Cambridge: Cambridge University Press.
Browne, Wayles. 1975. Serbo-Croatian enclitics for English-speaking learners. In Rudolf Filipović (ed.), *Contrastive analysis of English and Serbo-Croatian*, Vol. 1, 105–134. Zagreb: Institute of Linguistics, University of Zagreb.

Browne, Wayles & Theresa Alt. 2004. *A handbook of Bosnian, Serbian, and Croatian.* Durham, NC: Duke University, SEELRC.
Brozović, Dalibor & Pavle Ivić. 1988. *Jezik, srpskohrvatski/hrvatskosrpski, hrvatski ili srpski* [Language, Serbo-Croatian/Croato-Serbian, Croatian or Serbian]. Zagreb: Jugoslavenski leksikografski zavod Miroslav Krleža.
Bubrin, Vladimir. 1994. Thirty-five years of Croatian heritage language in Toronto. In Marin Sopta & Gabriele Pietro Scardellato (eds.), *Unknown journey: A history of Croatians in Canada, vol.14,* 101–106. Toronto: Multicultural History Society of Ontario.
Clyne, Michael. 1991. *Community languages: The Australian experience.* Cambridge: Cambridge University Press.
Clyne, Michael. 2003. *Dynamics of language contact.* Cambridge: Cambridge University Press.
Ćosić, Vjekoslav. 1992–1994. Sociolingvistički status hrvatskih iseljenika u Quebecu [The sociolinguistic status of Croatian emigrants in Quebec]. *Radovi Razdjela filoloških znanosti* 22(23). 27–45.
Ďurovič, Ľubomír. 1983. The case systems in the language of diaspora children. *Slavica Lundensia* 9. 21–94.
Edwards, John (ed.). 1998. *Language in Canada.* Cambridge: Cambridge University Press.
Filipović, Rudolf. 1979. Proučavanje hrvatskih dijalekata u SAD [The study of Croatian dialects in the United States]. *Bilten Zavoda za lingvistiku* 3. 4–19.
Filipović, Rudolf. 1984. Croatian dialects in the United States: Sociolinguistic Aspects. *Folia Slavica* 6. 278–292.
Filipović, Rudolf. 1991. Neposredni jezični dodiri u hrvatskim dijalektima u SAD [Indirect language contact in the Croatian dialects in the United States]. *Senjski zbornik* 18. 31–40.
Filipović, Rudolf. 2001. Croatian Dialects in the United States: Sociolinguistic Conditions for the Maintenance of a Dialect. *International Journal of the Sociology of Language* 147. 51–63.
Fishman, Joshua A. 1965. Who speaks what language to whom and when? *La linguistique* 1(2). 67–88.
Fishman, Joshua. 1966. *Language loyalty in the United States.* The Hague: Mouton.
Fishman, Joshua A. 1991. *Reversing language shift.* Clevedon: Multilingual Matters.
Granic, Stan. 2009. First steps: Božidar Vidov and the early Croatian language schools in Canada. *Canadian Ethnic Studies* 41(1). 29–46.
Grubišić, Vinko. 1984. Croatians in Toronto. *Polyphony* 6(1). 88–91.
Hansen, Björn, Daniel Romić & Zrinka Kolaković. 2013. Okviri za istraživanje sintaktičkih struktura govornika druge generacije bosanskoga, hrvatskoga i srpskoga jezika u Njemačkoj [A framework for research on syntactic structures of heritage Croatian, Bosnian and Serbian as spoken by the second generation in Germany]. *Lahor* 15. 9–45.
Hlavac, Jim. 2003. *Second-generation speech: Lexicon, code-switching and morpho-syntax of Croatian-English bilinguals.* Bern: Peter Lang.
Hlavac, Jim. 2006. Bilingual discourse markers: Evidence from Croatian-English code-switching. *Journal of Pragmatics* 38. 1870–1900.
Hlavac, Jim. 2012. Psycholinguistic, metalinguistic and socio-psychological accounts of code-switching: a comparative analysis of their incidence in a large Croatian-English sample. *Suvremena lingvistika* 73. 47–71.
Hlavac, Jim. 2016. Code-switching, lexico-grammatical features and loan translation: data from a large Macedonian-English corpus. *Philologia Estonica Tallinnensis* 1. 38–60.
Juričić, Želimir B. & Joseph F. Kess. 1978. Sociolinguistic dimensions of respectful address: A comparative study of native and immigrant Croatian. In Zbignier Folejewski, Edmund

Heier, George Luckyj & Gunter Schaarschmidt (eds.), *Canadian contributions to the VIII International Congress of Slavists (Zagreb-Ljubljana 1978)*. 103–116. Ottawa: Canadian Association of Slavists.
Jutronić, Dunja. 1974. The Serbo-Croatian language in Steelton, PA. *General Linguistics* 14. 15–34.
Jutronić, Dunja. 1976. Language maintenance and language shift of the Serbo-Croatian language in Steelton, Pennsylvania. *General Linguistics* 16. 166–186.
Jutronić-Tihomirović, Dunja. 1982. The effect of dialectal variations on the adaptation of loanwords. *International Journal of Slavic Linguistics* 5. 63–73.
Jutronić-Tihomirović, Dunja. 1985. *Hrvatski jezik u SAD [Croatian language in the United States]*. Split: Logos.
Jutronić-Tihomirović, Dunja. 1989. Jezično prilagođavanje na sintaktičkom nivou [Linguistic accommodation at the syntactic level]. *Radovi razdjela filoloških znanosti*. 18. 51–60.
Magner, Thomas F. 1976. The melting pot and language maintenance in South Slavic immigrant groups. *General Linguistics* 16. 59–67.
Matras, Yaron. 2009. *Language contact*. Cambridge: Cambridge University Press.
Montrul, Silvina. 2016. *The Acquisition of Heritage Languages*. Cambridge, UK: Cambridge University Press.
Muysken, Pieter. 2000. *Bilingual speech. A typology of code-mixing*. Cambridge, UK: Cambridge University of Press.
Myers-Scotton, Carol. 2002. *Contact linguistics: Bilingual encounters and grammatical outcomes*. Oxford: Oxford University Press.
Otheguy, Ricardo, Ana Celia Zentella & David Livert. (2007). Language and dialect contact in Spanish in New York: Toward the formation of a speech community." *Language*, 770–802.
Pauwels, Anne. 1995. Linguistic practices and language maintenance among bilingual men and women in Australia. *Nordlyd* 11. 21–50.
Pauwels, Anne. 2016. *Language maintenance and shift*. Cambridge: Cambridge University Press.
Petrović, Ivana. 2017. Očuvanje hrvatskog jezika u Kanadi [Croatian Language Maintenance in Canada]. *Migracijske i etničke teme* 33(1). 7–36.
Petrović, Ivana. 2018. Croatian as a heritage language in Canada. *Zbornik radova Filozofskog fakulteta Sveučilišta u Splitu* 11. 59–72.
Polinsky, Maria. 2006. Incomplete acquisition: American Russian. *Journal of Slavic Linguistics* 14. 161–219.
Polinsky, Maria. 2018. *Heritage Languages and Their Speakers*. Cambridge, UK: Cambridge University Press.
Rasporich, Anthony, W. 1982. *For a better life: za bolji život: a history of the Croatians in Canada*. Toronto: McClelland and Stewart.
Serratrice, Ludovica. 2007. Cross-linguistic influence in the interpretation of anaphoric and cataphoric pronouns in English-Italian bilingual children. *Bilingualism: Language and Cognition* 10, 225–238.
Silva-Corvalán, Carmen. 1994. *Language Contact and Change: Spanish in Los Angeles*. Oxford: Oxford University Press.
Sopta, Marin. 2012. *Hrvati u Kanadi [Croats in Canada]*. Zagreb: Institut društvenih znanosti Ivo Pilar.
Sorace, Antonella & Francesca Filiaci. 2006. Anaphora resolution in near-native speakers of Italian. *Second Language Research*. 22, 339–368.

Starčević, Anđel. 2014. *Hrvatski i engleski jezik u dodiru: hrvatska iseljenička obitelj u Kanadi* [Croatian and English in contact: a Croatian immigrant family in Canada], PhD Dissertation. University of Zagreb.

Statistics Canada. 2014a. *2006 Census of Canada, Ethnic Origin, Single and Multiple Ethnic Origin Responses and Sex for the Population of Canada, Provinces, Territories, Census Metropolitan Areas and Census Agglomerations*. https://www12.statcan.gc.ca/census-recensement/2006/dp-pd/tbt/Rp-eng.cfm?LANG=E&APATH=3&DETAIL=0&DIM= 0&FL=A&FREE=0&GC=0&GID=0&GK=0&GRP=1&PID=92333&PRID=0&PTYPE= 88971,97154&S=0&SHOWALL=0&SUB=0&Temporal=2006&THEME=80&VID=0& VNAMEE=&VNAMEF= (accessed 15 September 2020).

Statistics Canada. 2014b. *2006 Census of Canada, Various Languages Spoken, Age Groups and Sex for the Population of Canada, Provinces, Territories, Census Metropolitan Areas and Census Agglomerationsi*. https://www12.statcan.gc.ca/census-recensement/2006/dp-pd/ tbt/Rp-eng.cfm?LANG=E&APATH=3&DETAIL=0&DIM=0&FL=A&FREE=0&GC=0&GID=0& GK=0&GRP=1&PID=89189&PRID=0&PTYPE=88971,97154&S=0&SHOWALL= 0&SUB=0&Temporal=2006&THEME=70&VID=0&VNAMEE=&VNAMEF= (accessed 25 September 2020).

Statistics Canada. 2014c. *2006 Census of Canada, Detailed Language Spoken Most Often at Home, Other Language Spoken Regularly at Home, Mother Tongue, Age Groups and Sex for the Population of Canada, Provinces, Territories, Census Metropolitan Areas and Census Agglomerations*. https://www12.statcan.gc.ca/census-recensement/ 2006/dp-pd/tbt/Rp-eng.cfm?LANG=E&APATH=3&DETAIL=0&DIM=0&FL=A&FREE=0& GC=0&GID=0&GK=0&GRP=1&PID=94817&PRID=0&PTYPE=88971,97154&S=0& SHOWALL=0&SUB=0&Temporal=2006&THEME=70&VID=0&VNAMEE=&VNAMEF= (accessed 25 September 2020).

Statistics Canada. 2015. *NHS Profile, Canada, 2011, Non-official languages spoken*. https://www12.statcan.gc.ca/nhs-enm/2011/dp-pd/prof/details/page. cfm?Lang=E&Geo1=PR&Code1=01&Data=Count&SearchText=Canada&SearchType= Begins&SearchPR=01&A1=Non-official%20language&B1=All&Custom=&TABID=1 (accessed 15 September).

Statistics Canada. 2016a. *1996 Census, Profile of Census Divisions and Subdivisions, Total population by ethnic origin*. https://www12.statcan.gc.ca/datasets/Rp-eng. cfm?TABID=2&LANG=E&APATH=3&DETAIL=0&DIM=0&FL=A&FREE=0&GC=0&GID= 199773&GK=0&GRP=1&PID=35782&PRID=0&PTYPE=3&S=0&SHOWALL=0&SUB=0& Temporal=1996&THEME=34&VID=0&VNAMEE=&VNAMEF=&D1=0&D2=0&D3=0&D4=0& D5=0&D6=0 (accessed 15 September 2020).

Statistics Canada. 2016b. *2001 Census, Ethnic Origin, Sex and Single and Multiple Responses for Population, for Canada, Provinces, Territories, Census Metropolitan Areas and Census Agglomerations*. https://www12.statcan.gc.ca/datasets/Rp-eng.cfm?LANG=E&APATH=3& DETAIL=0&DIM=0&FL=A&FREE=0&GC=0&GID=0&GK=0&GRP=1&PID=62911&PRID=0& PTYPE=55440&S=0&SHOWALL=0&SUB=0&Temporal=2001&THEME=44&VID=0& VNAMEE=&VNAMEF= (accessed 15 September 2020).

Statistics Canada. 2019a. *2011 National Household Survey, Ethnic Origin, Single and Multiple Ethnic Origin Responses, Generation Status, Age Groups and Sex for the Population in Private Households of Canada, Provinces, Territories, Census Metropolitan Areas and Census Agglomerations*. https://www12.statcan.gc.ca/nhs-enm/2011/dp-pd/dt-td/ Rp-eng.cfm?LANG=E&APATH=3&DETAIL=0&DIM=0&FL=A&FREE=0&GC=0&GID=0&

GK=0&GRP=1&PID=105396&PRID=0&PTYPE=105277&S=0&SHOWALL=0&SUB=0& Temporal=2013&THEME=95&VID=0&VNAMEE=&VNAMEF= (accessed 15 September 2020).

Statistics Canada. 2019b. *2016 Census of Canada, Ethnic Origin, Single and Multiple Ethnic Origin Responses, Generation Status, Age and Sex for the Population in Private Households of Canada, Provinces and Territories, Census Metropolitan Areas and Census Agglomerations.* https://www12.statcan.gc.ca/census-recensement/2016/dp-pd/ dt-td/Rp-eng.cfm?APATH=3&DETAIL=0&DIM=0&FL=A&FREE=0&GC=0&GID= 0&GK= 0&GRP=1&LANG=E&PID=110528&PRID=10&PTYPE=109445&S=0&SHOWALL= 0&SUB=0&THEME=120&Temporal=2016&VID=0&VNAMEE=&VNAMEF= (accessed 15 September 2020).

Statistics Canada. 2019c. *2016 Census. Census Profile.* https://www12.statcan.gc.ca/ census-recensement/2016/dp-pd/prof/details/page.cfm?Lang=E&Geo1=PR&Code1= 01&Geo2=PR&Code2=01&SearchText=Canada&SearchType=Begins&SearchPR=01&B1= Language&TABID=1&type=0 (accessed 25 September 2020).

Surdučki, Milan. 1966. English loanwords in the Serbo-Croatian immigrant press. *Canadian Journal of Linguistics* 12(1). 52–63.

Surdučki, Milan. 1967. English loanwords in the Serbo-Croatian immigrant press. *Canadian Journal of Linguistics* 12(2). 123–135.

Surdučki, Milan. 1978. *Srpskohrvatski i engleski u kontaktu* [Serbo-Croatian and English in contact]. Novi Sad: Matica srpska.

Surdučki, Milan. 1983. Standardni srpskohrvatski i iseljenički srpskohrvatski u kontaktu sengleskim: sličnosti i razlike [Standard Serbo-Croatian and immigrant Serbo-Croatian in contact with English: similarities and differences]. *Zbornik Matice srpske za filologiju i lingvistiku* 26(2). 101–108.

Surdučki, Milan. 1984. English-Serbo-Croatian Contacts in Canada and Yugoslavia. *Melbourne Slavonic Studies* 18. 15–26.

Šabec, Nada. 1992. *Linguistic and sociolinguistic constraints on English-Slovene code switching.* University of Zagreb: Faculty of Humanities and Social Sciences. PhD dissertation.

Thomason, Sarah. 2001. *Language Contact. An Introduction.* Edinburgh: Edinburgh University Press.

Thomason, Sarah & Terrence Kaufman. 1988. *Language contact, creolization, and genetic linguistics.* Berkeley: University of California Press.

Veltman, Calvin. 1983. *Language shift in the United States.* Berlin. Mouton de Gruyter.

Winford, Donald. 2003. *An introduction to contact linguistics.* Oxford: Blackwell.

Croatian in the southern hemisphere

Australia

Jim Hlavac and Diana Stolac
Features in the Croatian speech of three generations of Croatian-Australians

1 Introduction

This chapter examines Croatian-speakers in Australia and looks at aspects of the Croatian speech of three generations of speakers. Two datasets form the basis of this chapter, containing samples of speech from nearly 200 speakers. The samples of speech were collected over a 21-year time period, from 1996 to 2017, and are based on a variety of data collection methods.

This chapter is structured in the following way. The remaining parts of this section present general demographic and sociolinguistic information on Croatian-origin residents in Australia and on Croatian-speakers in that country. Section 2 presents information on data collection with details of the different groups of information and different collection periods that make up both datasets. Section 3 presents data on informants' sociolinguistic profiles. Section 4 presents and discusses select examples from both datasets according to the following: lexical and pragmatic transference; semantic transference and loan translations; code-switching; morphology and syntax. Section 5 contains the conclusion with findings summarized.

1.1 History of contact, vintages of emigration, status

Aborigines have inhabited Australia for approximately 60,000 years, and the presence of White Europeans is, in comparative terms, a very recent phenomenon. After the arrival of British colonisers in Australia in 1788, it was not until the gold rush years after 1850 that small numbers of Croatian migrants – perhaps 'pioneers' or 'adventurers' would be a more accurate term – began to arrive in that country. Šutalo, a Croatian-Australian historian, records that by 1890 there were approximately 850 Croats in Australia (2004: 16). Sizeable migration did not commence until the post-WWII period. We can distinguish the following waves: former soldiers and office-bearers (and their families) of the former NDH in the late 1940s and early 1950s; political refugees from the FNRJ/SFRJ in the early 1960s; mostly

Jim Hlavac, Monash University
Diana Stolac, University of Rijeka

https://doi.org/10.1515/9781501503917-012

economic migrants in the late 1960s to the early 1980s. During this last period, over 95,000 people left the SFRJ and settled in Australia, with Croats forming the single largest ethnic group of this wave of immigrants (Tkalčević 1992). Chain migration was a feature of this wave, as well as previous ones (cf. Mesarić-Žabčić 2014). A fourth wave were refugees from the wars in Croatia and Bosnia-Herzegovina arriving in the 1990s. A fifth wave consists of skilled or tertiary-educated economic migrants who have been arriving since 2000.

Croatian has no official status in Australia, but its de facto status is that of a 'community' (or 'ethnic') language (Clyne 2005; Community Languages Australia 2018). This means that Croatian is one of the nearly 200 languages for which there are government-sponsored translation and interpreting services, one of the languages in which publicly-funded radio and media provides programs, and it is one of the languages taught as a mainstream school subject within the education systems of some of Australia's six states and two territories. The official recognition of the designation 'Croatian language' occurred in Australia before it did in the SFRJ: translation and interpreting services and radio programs were provided in Croatian in 1975, with recognition of it as a school subject occurring in 1980 (Hlavac 2003: 14). In 2016, a disproportionately high number of Croatian-speakers have Australian citizenship – 95.9% – compared to 82.4% of all Australian residents.

1.2 Number of Croatian-heritage residents, number of Croatian-speakers

Data from the 2016 census collection shows that 133,268 Australian residents claimed Croatian ancestry (ABS 2016). This is an increase from 126,264 in the 2011 census and from 105,747 recorded in the 2001 census (ABS 2011). Even then, demographers reported that these figures appeared low, with Price (2001) estimating that there were about 146,000 Australians with Croatian heritage. Census collections also record responses to the question "what language do you speak at home". This question captures those Croatian-speakers who use the language at home, but not those who do not (e.g. those in exogamous relationships, many Gen.2 and Gen.3 speakers). Over the last 20 years there has been a steady decrease in those speaking Croatian at home according to the last four census collections with the highest number recorded in 2001: 69,152 (1996); 69,850 (2001); 63,612 (2006); 61,547 (2011); 56,889 (2016), (ABS 2016). Adding those who have proficiency in Croatia but whose home language has shifted from Croatian to English, we estimate that the number of Croatian-speakers in Australia is currently approximately 90,000.

1.3 Geographic distribution, socio-economic profile

Data presented here are based on responses to the 2011 census collection for the group 'home language users of Croatian'. These data contain an over-representation of older and more Croatian-dominant residents as many younger speakers and those whose home language is no longer Croatian are not included. There are 22,879 Croatian-speakers in New South Wales, mainly in Sydney, with smaller numbers in Wollongong. A further 22,168 reside in Victoria, mainly in Melbourne with a significant further group in Geelong. Settlement reflects the profiles of Gen.1 speakers who lived in areas accessible to industrial, manufacturing and other service industries. There are older communities in Western Australia and South Australia that worked in the fishing industry (Fremantle, Port Lincoln) and in mining (Kalgoorlie, Cooper Pedy). Further Croats live and work in rural areas with grape-growing, fruit-growing, tobacco-growing and sugar cane industries across Victoria, South Australia, New South Wales and Queensland.

Overall, those speaking Croatian at home have slightly lower rates of educational level, higher rates of trade certificate completion, and significantly lower income levels than the general Australian population (SBS 2014). These statistics do not include many Gen.2 and Gen.3 speakers, and the overall rates of average income amongst Croatian-Australians are likely to be only slightly lower than the national average.

1.4 Infrastructure

Earlier this century, Šutalo (2004: 217) wrote that "there are over 250 Croatian clubs and societies in Australia devoted to a huge spectrum of activities and interests – social, language, sporting (soccer, golf and bocce), folkloric, drama, literary, musical, arts, religious, women's, students' and senior citizens' clubs". This is still the situation in 2021. The most prominent institutions are the 15 Croatian Catholic centres across the country with four in Melbourne and three in Sydney, and approximately 50 Croatian soccer clubs across the country. The annual Croatian-Australian soccer tournament that has been held for over 50 years brings together dozens of clubs that otherwise compete in various state and regional leagues. Soccer clubs, Sydney Croatia and Melbourne Croatia were both once champions of the then National Soccer League. Reflecting the demography of the community, there are Croatian aged care facilities in Sydney, Canberra, Perth and Geelong.

Croatian-language media is published in print form via two weekly newspapers, Hrvatski Vjesnik ('The Croatian Herald', Melbourne) and Domovina ('Homeland', Sydney). State-funded radio, namely SBS (Special Broadcasting Service) transmits four one-hour programs in Croatian weekly with Croatian films and the main 30-minute daily news bulletin from Croatia (središnji Dnevnik HRT-a) transmitted on SBS television. A dozen other radio stations across the country transmit regular programs in Croatian.

Since the 1980s, Croatian has been recognised as a mainstream school subject within the Australian education system. This means that it is taught and assessed in the same way as other subjects, and students may study Croatian from year 1 to year 12, and study the language for their Higher School Certificate. For example, in Victoria, Croatian is taught onsite at four centres of the Victorian School of Languages on Saturdays to approximately 500 students at all levels. It is also taught via distance learning to students in more remote areas. Similar arrangements exist in New South Wales, with other states and territories able to share and access curriculum and resources. One school, Holy Family Catholic Primary School in Geelong, Victoria, has Croatian as a mainstream school subject which is learnt by Croatian and non-Croatian children alike. Croatian language and culture has been taught at the Croatian Studies Centre, Macquarie University (Sydney) since 1984.

1.5 Domain use, language maintenance and shift

Language maintenance amongst Gen.1 speakers is high with over 80% of those born in Croatia (regardless of their age at migration) speaking Croatian as their home language. For these speakers, Croatian remains their dominant language for a variety of domains: personal (e.g. 'inner speech', dreaming, counting quickly), home/family (e.g. spouse, same-age family members, children, grandchildren), social life/leisure (e.g. sport, church). It is often widely used in further domains alongside English: media (e.g. radio, print media); workplace/shopping/neighbourhood (Hlavac 2009). Amongst Gen.2 speakers, Croatian is the dominant language used in the home/family domain. In some domains, Gen.2 speakers most often report using *both* languages: language selection can be determined by the generational membership of other interlocutors; with peers, code-switching may be the default vernacular used. These bilingual domains are: personal domain (e.g. swearing, talking to animals), social life/leisure domain (e.g. picnics, soccer matches, discos or *zabave*); family domain with one's own spouse/partner and children (Hlavac 2009).

From the 2011 census, more detailed data show that just under two-thirds of these are residents born outside Australia (50.2% in Croatia, 7.3% in Bosnia-Herzegovina) while 35.3% were born in Australia. This points to a sizeable number of over 20,000 Gen.2 speakers who claim Croatian as their home language, while there are over 2,831 Gen.3 speakers of Croatian (grandparents born in Croatia). The figure for Gen.3 speakers from the 2016 census has even grown slightly to 2,975. Croatian is therefore a mid-level to highly maintained language in Australia, not maintained by Australian-born generations as well as languages such as Macedonian or Greek (Hlavac 2015), but maintained more so than languages such as German (Winter and Pauwels 2006).

1.6 Contacts with Croatia. Host society attitudes towards Croats

The 'tyranny of distance' is a meme of Australian literature referring to the country's isolation from other areas of the world as an inescapable obstacle. Those who left Croatia to come to Australia, particularly those who came by ship – a journey that often lasted two months – knew very well that returning home would be a difficult and expensive undertaking. Therefore, amongst Croatian immigrants there developed a deep sense that Australia would be their new home, usually forever. This accounts for the extensive number of clubs or organisations and the physical presence of churches, schools, soccer grounds, social clubs etc. that were a testimony to their intentions to establish 'their own version of Croatia' on the other side of the world.

Three developments have occurred that have facilitated closer contacts with Croatia: affordable inter-continental airfares; electronic media and tools such as Skype; and the ageing of the large wave of 1960s and 1970s migrants, who are now retired and more regularly visit their homeland. In fact, return migration is now a prominent feature of this group, and also of some younger groups. Croatian-Australian sociologist Colic-Peisker (2010: 54) reports that "since 2003, for the first time in the history of Australian Croatians, return migration numbers started to exceed permanent arrivals from Croatia to Australia". To younger Croatian-Australians, Croatia has multiple attractions: a place to visit relatives, a holiday destination and a launching pad to visit other European countries. For some with the means and time, Croatia is the country in which they spend the Northern summer, returning to Australia in October for the Southern summer. Reflecting the numerical strength of Australia's Croatian community, Australia was the first non-European country to recognise Croatia's independence, early in 1992. A key feature of mainstream Australians' perceptions of Croatians is their contribution to sport. There have been Croatian-Australians who have excelled at sports such as cricket, rugby, tennis and Australian Rules Football, playing at the highest level. The most conspicuous contribution has been to Australian soccer: over

40 Croatian-origin players have represented Australia in the national soccer team over the last 30 years.

1.7 Language-focused studies of Croatian-Australians

As stated in 1.2 and 1.4 above, descriptions of Croatian settlement in Australia, such as those by Tkalčević (1992) and Šutalo (2004), document the demographic and socio-economic profiles of Croats in Australia and the establishment of churches, clubs, sporting associations, schools, businesses and other organisations. Language is not a focal point of these historical accounts, perhaps because the sociolinguistic features of the Croatian-speaking community were thought to be known by all and therefore not needing overt mention: first-generation migrants (before the 1980s) typically had little or no proficiency in English at the time of their arrival and their children acquired Croatian at home. The home/family domain was and remains the setting in which Croatian is most often used, followed by the domains friendship/social interactions and religion. For some, Croatian is or was used at some workplaces, e.g. with workmates or customers. These were the findings from the first author's (Hlavac 2003) study of 100 second-generation speakers' profiles that included the collection of sociolinguistic responses on speakers' language use.

Further to a collection of sociolinguistic data, the same source (Hlavac 2003) features an analysis of lexical and morpho-syntactic features in the Croatian speech of second-generation speakers, with a particular focus on the incidence and form of English-Croatian code-switching and its structural properties. Other studies from this dataset focus on 'trigger words' that can precipitate 'unconscious' or unintended code-switching (Hlavac 1999a), phonological properties of integrated English-origin lexemes in Croatian (Hlavac 1999b), and interjections and discourse markers (Hlavac 2003, 2006). There are a number of other studies on Croatian spoken in Australia: Doucet (1990) provides a brief account of English lexical and phraseological insertions into the Croatian speech of first-generation speakers; Škvorc (2006) does the same in relation to the speech of second-generation speakers; Clissa (1995) completed a study on language shift and diglossia amongst speakers of the micro-language Molise-Croatian (see Chapter 3), who had migrated from central Italy to Western Australia.

Other studies looking at Croatian-speakers have looked at the role of Croatian Studies at Macquarie University as a tertiary-level centre that not only teaches Croatian but also researches Croatian settlement in Australia, e.g. Budak (2008). A community-based perspective on the profiles and activities of Croatian-

Australians is provided by Šutalo (2010) who, on the topic of Croatian language instruction, locates a gradual but steady decline in interest in and attendance at Croatian schools. Šutalo bemoans the fewer opportunities for formal instruction compared to past decades, but also identifies language proficiency as an attribute needed by those born in Australia who, at that time, were required to demonstrate proficiency in Croatian to apply for Croatian (and therewieh EU) citizenship (see Hlavac, this volume). From a sociological perspective, Lalich (2010) describes the transnational spaces that Croatian-Australians occupy and how these shape their linguistic repertoires. Focussing on the Croatian Catholic Centres in New South Wales, Mesarić Žabčić (2010) identifies these as key hubs of not only Croatian-language church-related activities, but as centres that teach and promote the Croatian language inside and outside their premises. Stolac (2017a) examines the language of returnees to Croatia, including many from Australia, while in studies from Stolac and Vlastelić (2018) and Stolac (2019) data on agreement and other syntactic categories are presented in the Croatian speech of second- and third-generation speakers living in Australia, as well as in other Anglophone countries.

2 Details of informants

As stated, this chapter presents examples drawn from two datasets that contain recordings of the Croatian speech of Croatian-Australians. The first dataset is from 1996, and consists of 88 Gen.2 informants and 12 Gen.1B informants who arrived in Australia before commencing school (< 5 years of age). Both groups, thus, have similar acquisitional and sociolinguistic profiles, and the informants from this group all resided in Melbourne. Dataset 1 was collected by the first author who is based in Melbourne. Dataset 2 consists of recorded collections of the speech of Gen.1A, Gen.1B, Gen.2 and Gen.3 speakers from six cities: Melbourne, Geelong, Sydney (including Gosford), Canberra, Brisbane and Hobart. Dataset 2 is from the second-named author, based in Rijeka, who collected these on fieldwork trips to Australia in 2010, 2014, 2015 and 2017. We refer to all samples of data that we have collected as the combined Australian Croatian (AUS.Cro) datasets. Table 1 below gives a statistical outline of the AUS.Cro datasets with details on the number of informants from each generational group and the place of data collection.

Table 1: Number of informants from both AUS.Cro datasets by generational affiliation and locality of data collection.

Period/s of data collection	Locality of data collection	Gen. 1A	Gen. 1B	Gen. 2	Gen. 3	Total
Dataset 1 1996	Melbourne	0	12	88	0	100
Dataset 2 2010–2017	Melbourne	13	2	6	2	23
	Geelong	5	4	7	1	17
	Sydney	10	4	13	7	34
	Canberra	5	2	1	0	8
	Brisbane	3	1	1	0	5
	Hobart	4	1	1	0	6
Total		40	26	117	10	193

The 100 informants from dataset 1 were contacted via the first-named author's family, work and social contacts (14 informants), then by the 'snowball effect' via informants already contacted and interviewed (51 informants), and through ethnically-affiliated organisations: educationally-based across five settings (32 informants); political organisations (3 informants). Most (77) informants were interviewed individually, while the remaining 23 were interviewed with or in the presence of siblings, friends, grandparents, spouses or workmates. Some of the informants were related to each other and many knew each other; thus, there are likely to be multiplex social networks shared amongst many informants. There was an equal ratio of male to female informants and their ages ranged from 16 to 32.

Sociolinguistic data on the informants that make up dataset 1 were gained via an 80-question survey personally administered to the informants after the first-named author had engaged in a spoken interaction with them. Data relating to informants' spoken language come from a corpus of 10–12 minute segments from these spoken interactions (lasting between 14 and 47 minutes), which were audio-recorded and then transcribed.

In dataset 2 there is greater heterogeneity of informants, not only across four generational groups, but across their vintages of immigration. Thus, dataset 2 includes Gen.1A informants from the large wave of post-WWII migrants, together with their children (Gen.2) and grandchildren (Gen.3). Dataset 2 also includes informants from the 1990s – both refugees of war and economic migrants (Gen.1A, Gen.1B), and in some cases their adult children (Gen.2). Gen.1A (and Gen.1B) informants of older vintages of migration tend to have a higher degree of involvement in intra-community activities. The informants from this latter group tend to have a higher level of education and had a higher level of proficiency in English upon arrival in Australia.

Contact with informants was established initially via the relatives of the second author's husband, and through the 'snowball' effect. Further informants were contacted via ethnically-affiliated organisations. Information relating to the sociolinguistic features of dataset 2 was gained via semi-structured interviews conducted with them at their homes, at their workplaces or at Croatian community gatherings. Data relating to the informants' spoken language come from audio-recordings and transcribed notes. There was an almost equal ratio of male (46) to female informants (47), and an age range from 17 (Gen.3) to 76 (Gen.1A). Details of informants are represented after examples in the following way: dataset 1 or 2 (D1 or D2); generation (Gen.1A, 1B, 2 or 3); gender (F or M) and age (e.g. 25).

3 Sociolinguistic description of informants' language use

The Gen.2 informants from dataset 1 bear the following sociolinguistic features: communication from and to the preceding generation/s (parents, aunts, uncles, grandparents) is predominantly Croatian, with some reporting a higher use of 'only Croatian' in the speech of older interlocutors to them, compared to the Gen.2 informants with their older family members. With siblings, both older and younger, the most common choice of language is English. However, up to 40% of informants report that code-switching or bilingual speech is the most common variety used with brothers and sisters. Over a third reported having 'mostly Croatian' friends, while nearly half reported that the proportion of Croatian and non-Croatian friends was roughly equal. With (similarly-aged) Croatian friends, 63% reported that 'both Croatian and English' were the variety most commonly used. The majority attend Croatian-specific social events such as picnics and *zabave* ('semi-formal social gatherings with speeches, food, drink and dancing') at which 76% claim they use both Croatian and English. In regard to ethnic-specific youth organisation, sporting and folklore events in Melbourne, the majority of informants reported that they attend these and most of this group report using 'both languages' with not only older but also same-age interlocutors.

Three quarters of the informants in dataset 1 report attending religious services where language choice reflects the generation of the interlocutor: previous-generation parishioners (Croatian), same-age parishioners (English/both languages), younger parishioners (English). Forty percent report praying in Croatian, compared to 25% in

English. Media consumption is variable, with English dominating as the language for paper-based and electronic sources, but a certain level reported also listening to, viewing and reading Croatian-language media, based either in Australia or Croatia. Interestingly, 37% reported using Croatian at their (part- or full-time) workplace, with Croatian-speaking interlocutors such as clients and customers, followed by workmates. Only 28% use Croatian in a transactional sense to buy goods or consume services, while 41% have neighbours with whom Croatian is used.

The profiles of the informants that make up dataset 2 are quite mixed and this can be accounted for on the basis of their differing generational affiliations and vintage of migration. The linguistic repertoires of Gen.1A migrants determine language choice in various domains, and the likely interlocutors and constellations of these domains. Amongst older-vintage informants, Croatian is used overwhelmingly, and amongst some older females, restricted acquisition of English meant that Croatian was the *only* code that could be used. Notwithstanding this, phonologically and morphologically adapted transfers from English are frequently heard in the Croatian speech of these speakers; these have usually been acquired from the bilingual speech of their children. While older vintage Gen.1A (and Gen.1B) speakers' social and leisure networks are based on ethnically-affiliated organisations, amongst younger vintage Gen.1A (and Gen.1B) speakers this is much less frequently the case. Amongst the Gen.2 speakers of both groups, those from an older vintage of migration have usually attended (supplementary) formal instruction in Croatian, while younger-generation Gen.2 speakers are likely to have acquired (standard) Croatian via more frequent visits back to Croatia, as well as through formal instruction in Australia.

On the basis of observations from the second author, those Gen.2 and Gen.3 students who attended formal instruction in Croatian in Saturday morning schools and/or *vjeronauk* 'religious instruction given in Croatian' appear to have more highly advanced linguistic skills, not only aural/oral macro-skills, but also reading and writing ones. At the same time, it is hard to isolate the effect of formal instruction without systematically observing the linguistic profiles of attendees and non-attendees of formal instruction, especially where school attendance usually brings with it a range of additional Croatian-language settings that provide further input for acquisition, e.g. social networking, shared homework projects, assessment tasks requiring contact with older speakers.

The Gen.1A, Gen.1B and Gen.2 informants of more recent immigration vintages avail themselves of electronic means to enable direct communication with family and friends in Croatia via WhatsApp, Viber or Skype and electronic media to a greater degree than older vintage migrants. At the same time, the level of tech-savviness of their children and grandchildren (Gen.2 and Gen.3 members) means that these younger speakers can now and sometimes do readily avail themselves of the same tools to contact family members and friends, as well as media based in Croatia. The significance of this is that these are Croatian-language settings that the younger speakers *themselves* have come to and created, independent of the home- or school-based measures to encourage minority language use.

The effects of linguistic models and inter-generational communication cannot be understated. This was particularly evident amongst many of the Gen.1B speakers from dataset 2. Where grandparents also migrated with these younger (child/teenage) Gen.1B migrants it was observed that Croatian language use at home and Croatian proficiency level in general appeared much stronger.

Mirroring the sociolinguistic profiles of the Gen.2 informants from dataset 1, the Gen.1B, Gen.2 and Gen.3 speakers of dataset 2 report that their passive aural skills are stronger than their active oral ones, while reading and especially writing skills, in comparison to aural/oral skills, are much less developed. The functional restrictedness in which Gen.2 and Gen.3 speakers have acquired Croatian has commensurate effects on their Croatian proficiency level (De Houwer 2007; Lanza & Svendsen 2007). This functional restrictedness is directly related to specific settings where there has been input in Croatian. Thus, the home/family settings, social/friendship networks, and faith-based activities (for those who attend formal services) are domains in which younger speakers can functionally communicate in Croatian. In some others, such as the workplace, education or transactional domains, language use is much more variable. What is evident in these latter domains is that even where speakers have Croatian proficiency, this is restricted to a particular register, and there is limited command of other registers that feature specific lexical forms and phraseological or collocational constructions. This is a challenge well known to heritage language teachers: to work with and encourage younger speakers to use the existing forms and registers of which they have a developing command; and to provide input and models of further genres of spoken and written expression that have other registers featuring lexical forms and constructions *without* creating the impression amongst younger speakers that their existing proficiency level is inferior or deficient (Kagan 2005; Cvikić, Jelaska & Kanajet Šimić 2010).

4 Presentation and analysis of spoken Croatian data

This section presents a variety of features present in the AUS.Cro samples. These are divided into the following four sections: lexicon and pragmatics (4.1); calques, loan translations and semantic transfers (4.2); code-switching (4.3); and morphology and syntax (4.4). To provide a picture of how frequent English-origin elements are in the speech of the single-largest generation group, we present below data on these, according to their syntactic position and number or elements. As Table 2 shows, the number of extra-clausal transfers, within which we include discourse markers, affirmatives and negatives, interjections and expletives, is far greater than the number of inter-clausal and intra-clausal ones.

Table 2: Number of extra-clausal, inter-clausal and intra-clausal transfers from dataset 1.

	Single items	Multiple items	Total
Extra-clausal transfers	2,516	172	2,688
Inter-clausal transfers	137	140	277
Intra-clausal transfers	962	296	1,258
Total	3,615	608	4,223

4.1 Lexicon and pragmatics

English-origin lexical forms are found in the speech of all informants across all generations. There are differences in the overall frequency of English-origin items between the Croatian-speakers across both AUS.Cro datasets according to generation. In general terms, frequency is lowest amongst Gen.1A informants, with successive increases in frequency in the speech of speakers of the subsequent generations: Gen.1B, Gen.2, Gen.3.

In regard to dataset 1 that consists of 100 10–12-minute segments of speech, the relative frequency of monolingual and bilingual turns in the speech of the Gen.2 speakers can be seen in Table 3:

Table 3: Number of turns and examples of transfers across dataset 1.

	Number (& Percentage)
Turns	5,677
Monolingual Croatian turns	3,043 (53%)
Monolingual English turns	311 (6%)
Non-lexicalised turns (e.g. turns consisting of *uh-huh* or *mm* only etc.)	47 (1%)
Turns containing transfer/s (or code-switch/es)	2,276 (40%)
English-origin items	4,223

In the repertoires of Gen.1A speakers, English-origin items are phonologically integrated into Croatian. For many of these Gen.1A speakers, their phonological repertoires do not allow any other option as phonological transference from Croatian is clearly apparent in their English speech. Morphological integration of English transfers also occurs in the speech of Gen.1A speakers where the syntactic role of these requires morphological inflections. In regard to speakers of subsequent generations, the presence of phonological and morphological integration of lexical items steadily decreases according to generation. For most Gen.1B speakers and for all Gen.2 and Gen.3 speakers, phonological integration is an *optional* occurrence as these speakers can pronounce items according to either Croatian or English phonology. Morphological integration is also variable amongst speakers of later generations; there is a tendency for speakers of each subsequent generation to employ these less and less, particularly in relation to nouns, while transferred verbs usually attract morphological markers (see below Table 4).

Table 4: Number of integrated and unintegrated transfers according to part of speech.

Grammatical categories	Integrated transfers No. of tokens (and %)	Unintegrated transfers No. of tokens (and %)
Nouns (common nouns)		
a) single/simplex items	165 (81%)	624 (65%)
b) compound items	0	62 (6%)
Total common nouns	165 (81%)	686 (71%)
Adjective + noun	0	117 (2%)
Adjectives	12 (6%)	92 (10%)
Adverbs	3 (1%)	36 (4%)
Verbs	24 (12%)	10 (1%)
Number + noun	0	6 (1%)
Adverb + adjective	0	5 (1%)
Conjunctions	0	3 (0%)
Noun + preposition	0	2 (0%)
Adjective + adjective + noun	0	2 (0%)
Noun + conjunction + noun	0	1 (0%)
Preposition + adjective	0	1 (0%)
Determiner + adjective + noun	0	1 (0%)
Total	**204 (17%)**	**962 (83%)**
(Plus proper nouns)	143	1,168

In dataset 1 there are approx. 148,000 lexical tokens, of which there are 204 English-origin transfers that are phonologically and/or morphologically integrated (excluding 143 proper nouns) and 962 unintegrated transfers (excluding 1,168 proper nouns). Table 4 below provides an overview of the grammatical categories of both categories of transfers.

Across both samples, there are a number of English-origin forms that are frequent and widespread, e.g. *area, traffic, rubbish, rent* (noun and verb), *picnic, hospital, boss, movie, holiday* or *high school*. These lexical items tend to occur in their phonologically (and to a lesser extent morphologically) integrated form in the speech of younger-generation (as well as Gen.1A) speakers. For some younger speakers, forms such as *erija/arija* 'area', *trafika* 'traffic', *renta* 'rent' and *rabiš* 'rubbish' appear to be perceived as Croatian-origin forms. For example, two Gen.2 informants reported using them in Croatia and learning, to their surprise, that they were English-origin and not Croatian-origin items. Instances of integrated transfers that are commonly used are the following two examples: *bila je jaka trafika* 'be-PAST.F.SG AUX-be-3SG strong-NOM.F.SG traffic-NOM.F.SG', 'the traffic was heavy'; *stanuje u toj eriji* 'reside-3SG in+LOC that-LOC.F.SG area-LOC.F.SG' 's/he lives in that area'.

In dataset 1, just on half of the integrated transfers occurred more than once across the sample. In contrast, 71% of a much larger number of unintegrated transfers occurred as nonce transfers. This is evidence of a slight tendency for transfers of higher recurrence to be integrated rather than unintegrated. Instances of unintegrated transfers are the following:

(1) .. *ima baš onaj **sauce** na njega što je najbolje..*
.. it has that **sauce** on it which is the best.. (D1,Gen.2,F,25)

The following utterance has two transfers, both part of a larger NP:

(2) .. *prije nego što ja dođem normalno.. ali, yeah.. osim, um.. **minutes** za **meetings** kad imamo sastanak, nema koga za tu dužnost, za taj posao...*
.. before I arrive, of course.. but, yeah.. apart from, um.. **minutes** for **meetings** when we have a meeting, there's no one for that duty, for that job...(D1,Gen.2,F,28)

Transfers may or may not co-occur alongside their Croatian equivalents. Of the 204 integrated transfers in dataset 1, 62% of them co-occurred with their Croatian equivalent/s. This does not mean that they co-occur within the speech of the same speaker; rather, it refers to their recurrence across the dataset as whole. This is a macro- rather than micro-linguistic application of the notion of recurrence. In example (3) below, *manuals* occurs as a hyponym to the preceding item *knjiga* 'book'.

(3) .. *ako oni kažu da moraš nešto tri puta okrenuti.. moraš to napravit.. ako kaže da stane za pol sata, moraš stat pol sata.. sve po knjigi, po* **manuals**.. *kako se zove..*
.. if they say that you have to turn it around three turns.. that's what you have to do.. if it's said that it should rest for half an hour, you have to stop half an hour.. everything by the book, by the manuals.. how it's called. (D1,Gen.2,M,32)

While most integrated and unintegrated transfers are nouns, a number of them belong to other parts of speech. In the NP shown in example (4) the adjective *easy-going* appears as the first adjective in an NP consisting of three components: ADJ+ADJ+N.

(4) *Dobro, kakav je ambijent, kakva je atmosfera?*
Okay, what's the ambience, what's the atmosphere like? (J.H.)

Kao **easy-going** *obiteljsko atmosfera. Ljudi su tamo došli sjedit za dan i sunčat se ili samo kao.. kao komotno..*
Like **easy-going** family atmosphere. People have come to sit and sun themselves for the day or just like.. like [to be] comfortable. (D1,Gen.2,F,19)

While example (4) presents a single-occurring English-origin adjective in a longer NP, transfers from English can include all components of multi-item NPs, such as ADJ+N, N+N, DET+ADJ+N. Table 4 does not include discourse markers. Discourse markers are a functional rather than grammatical category and are discussed below in 4.1.3. What is evident from Table 4 and the examples shown above is that amongst the lexical items transferred from English, nouns are the most prominent category. This is a common observation made in a large number of language contact situations e.g. Heath (1989), Thomason (2001).

4.1.1 Gender assignment

English is a language that lacks grammatical gender and assignment of Croatian gender to English-origin common and proper nouns is determined almost exclusively by the phonotactic characteristics of the transfer, in particular its word-final phonological features: those ending with a consonant are M., while those ending in *-a* or *-ə* are usually F. Those Croatian nouns that end in *-o* or *-e* are usually N, but, in relation to many English-origin transfers now used in HMLD.Cro, e.g. *bendžo* 'banjo' M, and *vaterpolo* 'waterpolo', M a recent tendency towards allocating *–o* transfers to masculine gender has become apparent. Of the 851 common nouns that are English-origin transfers in dataset 1 (proper nouns are excluded here), the Croatian gender assigned to them is recognisable either through morphological markers on the transfer, e.g. *svakakvi za.. **karpenteriju**, za što ja radim* 'all sorts for+ACC.. carpentry-ACC.F.SG for which I work', ('all sorts for.. the carpentry F that I work for'), *i vidiš bishopa* 'and see-2SG bishop-ACC.M.SG' ('and you see the bishop M') or through attributive adjectives that bear phi-features indicating gender, *to je stara arija* 'that be-3SG old-NOM.F.SG area-NOM.F.SG' ('that's an old F area').

In most instances, however, morphological markers on the transfer or preceding, or other attributives are absent. In such instances, gender assignment is not overt, e.g. *težak je bio zrak i **polušen** od te fabrike* 'heavy was the air and **pollution** (M?) from that factory', *nema **concrete**, ništa* 'there's no concrete (M?), nothing'. The word final consonant of *polušen* (phonologically integrated) and *concrete* (phonologically unintegrated) suggest that they would be likely to be assigned masculine gender. In both samples, there appear to be no apparent instances of *-a* suffixation on consonant-final words and subsequent feminine assignment, as Filipović (1986: 129) reported for a small group of English transfers in HMLD.Cro (eg. *farma* F 'farm'). In a small number of instances, assignment to M or F is not clear where a portmanteau suffix (here ACC.PL) does not show a distinction between M and F: *drugi stric je imao **orandže**, on je gore živio u..* 'other uncle had **oranges**-ACC. PL.M or F, *he lived up in. . .*'. ('My other uncle had oranges. He lived up in. . .')

Where the gender of a phonologically or morphologically integrated noun can be clearly identified, in most cases (79%) it is masculine, with the remaining 21% feminine. There are no neuter nouns identified. The high occurrence of mor it is phologically integrated transfers assigned to the masculine gender is not surprising. Surdučki (1978: 288), Jutronić-Tihomirović (1985: 33) and Filipović (1986: 130) all report a tendency to integrate transfers as masculine nouns. In other varieties of diaspora Croatian, such as AUT.Cro (see Sčukanec, this volume) and ITAL.Cro (see Županović Filipin, Hlavac and Piasevoli, this volume), a tendency to assign masculine gender to transferred nouns is also observed. Phonological and graphemic form plays the most important role in gender assignment. Surdučki (1978: 288–230.) reports that nearly 90% of the 2402 recorded transfers in the speech of Croatian immigrants in Canada are adapted as masculine nouns. Amongst the phonologically unintegrated transfers occurring in dataset 1, a similarly high percentage of those transfers that can be constituents of NPs, e.g. nouns, adjectives and determiners show a tendency to be masculine through any of the following: morphological marking of preceding or succeeding attributive adjectives; through determiners; or through succeeding predicative adjectives.

4.1.2 Verbs

Verbs make up only a relatively small percentage of the English-origin transfers: 12% of the integrated transfers and only 1% of the unintegrated transfers. The much higher percentage of integrated compared to unintegrated verbs sets this part of speech apart from all others as the category that is most likely to be integrated. Verbs play a central role in the morpho-syntactic grid of utterances and it is this role that appears to account for why they usually attract morphological markers. Morphological markers overtly show the role of the transfer as a verb. In example (5), a suffix is attached to the multi-syllable English verb *overhaul*:

(5) i   dok   ne   overhaulamo..   to   su   veliki   *landing gears*
    and   until   NEG   overhaul-1PL   that   be-3PL   big-NOM.M.PL   landing gears
    jesi   li   ikad   vidio   *landing gears*
    AUX-2SG   PARTICLE   ever   see-PST.M.SG   landing gears
    'And until we overhaul.. those are big landing gears. Have you ever seen landing gears..?' (D1, Gen.2,M,32)

Example (5) above features the verbal suffix *–amo*, the PRES-1PL form of an *–ati* (INF.) verb. The suffix *–ati*, along with the suffix *–ovati* are the most commonly employed suffixes that English-origin forms attract in Croatian. Croatian has six verb groups, each with different INF suffixes, and most English-origin verbs in both datasets are assigned to these two groups. The suffixes *–ati* and *–ovati* are the most commonly used ones for English-origin transfers in HMLD.Cro as well (Filipović 1961, 1980). Example (6) contains another *–ati* verb in 1PL, *paintamo* 'we paint', and a verb with the suffix *–ovati* that retains this form in its 1PL form, *silovamo* 'we seal', instead of the infix *–ova–* undergoing the change to *–uje–*, i.e. form, *silujemo*. (The latter form *silujemo* means 'we rape'):

(6) sada   radin   na   pripravljan   krove   stare
    now   work-1SG   on   prepare-1SG   roof-ACC.M.SG   old-ACC.M.SG
    ponovljujen   krove   peren   i   promjenin   ploče
    repeat-1SG   roof-ACC.M.SG   wash-1SG   and   change-1SG   tile-ACC.F.PL
    i   ciment   **radimo**   **silovamo**   **paintamo**   takve
    and   cement-ACC.M.SG   work-1PL   seal-1PL   paint-1PL   such-ACC.F.PL
    stvari
    thing-ACC.F.PL
    Now I work on.. I prepare old roofs.. I repeat [=renew] roofs, I clean and change tiles and cement, **we work, we seal, we paint**.. things like that. (D1,Gen.1B,M,32).

Other instances of integrated verbs include the following verb *debajtovati* 'to debate': *to je sve kao, moraš **debajtovati** zato.. issues, you know...to je dobro* 'that's all like, you have to **debate** because.. issues, you know...that's good', and the verb *smelovati* 'to smell': *onda ne smiješ potrošit, uvijek piše: "Nemoj potrošit voda".. i **smelova** kao, nekako kao od, um, chlorine..* 'then you're not allowed to use, everywhere it is written: "Don't waste water".. and it **smells** like, somehow like of, um, chlorine'. In NZ Cro, the most common Croatian verb suffixes for English-origin verbs are *–iti* and *–ati* (see Stoffel and Hlavac, this volume), while in ARG.Cro, it is *–irati* (See Skelin Horvat, Musulin and Blažević, this volume). The INF form and all PRES tense forms of English verbs (except for PRES-3SG) lack overt morphology marking them as verbs, and this enables affixation of a Croatian verbal suffix to clearly show the phi-features of the integrated verb. However, the form of most English PAST tense verbs clearly identifies them as verbs and distinguishes them from other parts of speech. This raises the question of whether the INF form functions as the base form to which Croatian PAST tense markers are affixed. In example (7) below, a past tense form of the verb *scream* occurs, to which a suffix is added:

(7) i   taj   na   pijesku   je
     .. and   that-NOM.M.SG   on+LOC   sand-LOC.M.SG.   AUX-3SG
     kažeo   je   rekao   [am]   you know   je
     tell-PST-3SG AUX-3SG say-PAST.M.SG   um   you know   AUX-3SG
     skr.. skrim<u>dio</u>
     scr.. scream+**ed**+PAST.M.SG
     '.. and the one on the sand told, said, um.. you know.. scr.. screamed..'
     (D1, 5,Gen.2,F,17)

The form *skrimdio* contains past tense markers from both languages, *–ed* and *–io* PAST.M.SG, i.e. 'double morphology' Myers-Scotton (1993: 109–112). The English past tense marker is mostly likely an unanalysed form, retained perhaps for phonotactic reasons, while the Croatian PAST tense marker marks the clause's syntactic relations, showing agreement with the male subject antecedent. There are six other PAST tense verbs in both datasets (all of them English regular verbs) and all have Croatian PAST tense markers only:

drajvala je.. 'drive-PAST.SG.F AUX-3SG' 'she **drove**..';

*i tako je **fulfilovao**..* 'and such AUX-3SG fulfil-PAST.SG.M' 'and as such he **fulfilled**..';

*čovjek koji je **fiksao** televizije..* 'man REL.PRON AUX-3SG fix-PAST.M.SG television-ACC.PL.F' 'the man who **fixed** televisions..';

jer oni su ga, um.. kao **tajpovali** 'because they AUX-3PL him-ACC, um.. like tape-PAST-PL.M' 'because they, um.. like **taped** him'.

Amongst the unintegrated verbs from English are verbs that are given in their past participle form, such as *taken* in example (8):

(8) ne   možu   kazat   gdje   je   ova
    NEG   able-1SG say-INF   where   AUX-3SG   this-NOM.F.SG
    slika   er   **taken**
    picture-NOM.F.SG   er   taken
    'I can't say where this picture was.. er.. **taken**.' (D1,Gen.2,M,20)

Croatian has passive past participles analogous to English past participles, but with phi-features marked. In (8), the suffix *-en* marks *taken* as a past participle, which appears to be sufficient for its syntactic role to be clear. Agreement with its antecedent subject in terms of gender, otherwise a feature of Croatian passive past participles, is not marked, i.e. *taken* does not attract the suffix NOM.F.SG *-a* for it to agree with *slika-*'picture-NOM.F.SG'. At the same time, the speaker hesitated twice in this example and this may indicate that he was unsure or conscious of his delivery and the level of syntactic congruency within a VP consisting of a Croatian AUX and an English past participle. Another example is: *I kada je bio osamljen.. bio je..* **fixated** *na televiziju i to..* 'And when he was lonely.. he was.. **fixated** on television and that..' Here, hesitation is also apparent in two places, where an English-origin past participle functions as a predicative adjective.

In the following instance, an English-origin verb *bat* occurs as an INF following a Croatian modal. Its position after the inflected Croatian modal clearly marks it as an INF: *..obidva teams trebaju* **bat** *i onda to je to, i završi.* '.. both teams have to **bat** and then that's that, and it finishes'. In the following instance, an unintegrated verb occurs in a syntactic role that, in English, would be fulfilled by an INF form. This syntactic role is performed in Croatian via the construction *da* 'that' + PRES. But the verb *escape* here does not bear PRES markers:

(9) jedna   žena   koja   je   vozila
    one-NOM.F.SG   woman-NOM.F.SG   REL.PRON.F.SG   AUX-3SG   drive-PST.F.SG
    autobus   ona je   pomagala   djecu   da
    bus-ACC.M.SG   she AUX-3SG   help-PAST.F.SG children-ACC.F.SG COMP
    escape
    escape
    '..one woman who was driving the bus.. she, um.. helped the children.. to..
    escape' (D1,Gen.2,F,17)

Hesitation phenomena are present here too. In the following example, it is not morphology but marked word order that makes the syntactic function of the English-origin verb clear:

(10) ne   ne   on   radi   taj   posao   i   ja   njega
     no   no   he   work-3SG   that-ACC.M.SG   job-ACC.M.SG   and   I   him-ACC
     supervise
     supervise
     'No, no, he does that job and I **supervise** him.' (D1,Gen.2,M,27)

In example (10), the order of the pronouns in the second clause is marked with the overt, full form of the ACC pronoun *njega* 'him' (clitic form: *ga*) preceding the English-origin verb *supervise*. Croatian is SVO like English, but Croatian can be SOV, particularly when the object is a pronoun and where this occurs clause-final position of the verb is not marked. This, together with the overt ACC pronoun *njega* mark *supervise* as the verb, even though the verb lacks Croatian verbal morphology. Further examples of transferred verbs and morphosyntactic changes that co-occur with these are given below in 4.4.2.

4.1.3 Affirmatives, negatives and discourse markers

This section focuses on affirmatives, negatives and discourse markers as the most frequent category of English-origin items found in the speech of informants across all generations and both datasets. Sometimes these groups of items are termed 'extra-clausal' forms, i.e. forms that have a function that is discourse-specific and subject to minimal syntactic restrictions. This means that regardless of whether they occur within a clause or at a clause boundary, they are syntactically 'outside' the morpho-syntactic grid of the clause and are not bound by this (Maschler 2000; Matras 2000; Blankenhorn 2003). Some researchers report that affirmatives, negatives and discourse markers are a category that can be adopted *en masse* and that displace most or all forms that were previously employed e.g. Salmons (1990) and Goss & Salmons (2000). Example (11) below contains multiple examples of *yeah*:

(11) *uvijek imaš kontakt... s klijentima..?*
     you always have contact with... your clients..? (J.H.)

   Yeah, *ja sam to već naučila. Sada ima već četiri godine da ja to radim, i jest..* **yeah**, *i to sam počela od.. ne znam, ima duže vremena što to radim, i svaki dan*

*ima drugčije, pričaš sa drugi narod, um.. drugčiji je posao, posao se mijenja.. i, **yeah** baš.. ne znam što bi drugo radila.. (smije se).. naučila sam već..*
'**Yeah**, I have already got used to it. It's now four years that I've been doing it and it is.. **yeah**, and I started off.. I don't know, it's been some time that I've been doing it, and every day there's different, you talk to different people, um.. the work's different, work changes.. and **yeah**. Really.. I don't know what else I'd do.. (laughter).. I've already got used to it.' (D1,Gen.2,F,26)

The first instance of *yeah* at the start of the turn is a straightforward affirmative. The second instance has the function of a pause filler and linking device. The third and last instance in (11) above appears also as a pause filler, and almost as a precursor to the finishing utterance of the informant's turn. While the dictionary meaning of *yeah* is that of an affirmative, in example (11) above, the second and third instances of *yeah* are examples of its use as a pause-filler and linking device, and as a precursor to turn-termination (Hlavac 2006). Here, it is not only the polyfunctionality of *yeah* that has been adopted in this speaker's repertoire, it is the *form* of *yeah* as well as its many functions that have become a part of her Croatian-English speech. This breadth of functions is not performed by its Croatian equivalent *da*, and this accounts for why amongst the affirmative and affirmative-like forms found in dataset 1, *yeah* is the form that is used in nearly 80% of instances as shown in Table 5.

Table 5: Frequency of English and Croatian affirmatives and affirmative-like forms.

Form	No. of tokens and % of total	No. of speakers	Ave. no. of tokens per speaker
English			
yeah	2,252 (79%)	99	23
yep	7 (0%)	6	1
yes	3 (0%)	1	3
English + Croatian			
yeah + da	23 (1%)	17	1
yeah + finite form of *biti* 'to be' (e.g. *jesam* 'I am')	4 (0%)	4	1
da + yeah	22 (1%)	15	1
Croatian			
da	400 (14%)	50	8
repetition of Cro. VP (e.g. *imam* 'I have')	9 (0%)	8	1
Finite form of *biti*	8 (0%)	6	1

Table 5 (continued)

Form	No. of tokens and % of total	No. of speakers	Ave. no. of tokens per speaker
Non-lexical			
uh-huh	66 (3%)	36	2
mm	46 (2%)	26	2
Total	2,840		

The form *yeah* has a high frequency due to its polyfunctionality. The same does not apply to the English negative *no*. In dataset 1, where negative forms are employed, most often it is a Croatian form, i.e. *ne* 'no' that is used, which occurs 144 times and makes up 55% of all negatives. When English negatives are used, non-standard *nah* (65 times = 25%) is more frequent than *no* (53 times = 20%).

We look now at other discourse markers that have a high frequency in English: *you know, so* and *like* (Sankoff et al. 1997: 203; Schiffrin 1987: 316). Miller (2009: 318) reports, on the basis of a spoken data sample of Australian English, that these three forms, along with *well* are the four most commonly used discourse markers in Australia. Table 6 below shows the number of instances that these English-origin discourse markers are used across the sample, together with their Croatian equivalents, and the number of speakers (given in brackets) amongst whom these forms are recorded.

Table 6: Frequency of English and Croatian discourse markers.

Discourse marker	English		Croatian		Total
	No. of tokens	No. of speakers	No. of tokens	No. of speakers	
you know – znaš/znate	153	36	112	24	265
so (conj.) – te	90	28	4	3	
– pa			11	7	125
– tako da			20	18	
so (end of turn) – i tako	13	6	8	8	21
like – kao	41	14	191	71	232

The comparison of frequency of English-origin discourse markers and their Croatian equivalents shows that *so* and to a lesser extent *you know* are more common than comparable Croatian discourse markers. The much higher frequency of *so* is partly accounted for by the larger number of forms available in Croatian that function as conjunctions usually between a cause and its effect. Overall, *you know* and *znaš* (2SG informal) / *znate* (2SG formal/2PL generic) are the most common discourse markers, which indicates that informants frequently refer to or appeal to knowledge believed to be shared between them and other interlocutors. As stated *so* is poly-functional as a conjunction, end of turn marker, and frequently also as a pause-filler or 'floor-holder' and these multiple functions account for its high incidence. The functions that *like* can perform are perhaps less apparent. Romaine and Lange (1991) state that "..discourses introduced by *like* preserve the pragmatic force of reduced responsibility conveyed by the indirect mode, but allow the speaker to sidestep the syntactic and semantic problems of incorporation" (1991: 272). Employment of *like* in bilingual speech as a punctor, hedge and/or adverbial approximant indicates that pragmatic transference of the variety of functions that *like* can perform in English is a likely cause for the high incidence of *kao* in Croatian speech. Transferred discourse markers are reported on in other diaspora varieties of Croatian such as ITAL.Cro (see Županović Filipin, Hlavac and Piasevoli, this volume), NZ.Cro (see Stoffel and Hlavac, this volume) and ARG.Cro (see Skelin Horvat, Musulin and Blažević, this volume).

4.2 Semantic transfers, loan translations and de-semanticised verbs

This section presents examples of semantic transference, loan translation and instances of desemanticised verbs. Instances in which the semantic features of an English equivalent have been transferred onto a Croatian-origin lexeme include the following:

(12) .. *da samo **prakticiram** nešto u glazbi..*
'just to **practise** something in music..' (D1,Gen.2,M,19).

HMLD.Cro: da samo **vježbam** nešto u glazbi. [*prakticirati* = to practise medicine/law]

(13) .. *ne volim ništa što je **predebelo***
'I don't like anything that is **too fatty**' (D1,Gen.2,F,19)

HMLD.Cro: ne volim ništa što je **premasno**. [*predebelo* = too obese].

(14) .. *meksikansko.. to je nice,* **vrućo**.. *to je isto..*
'Mexican.. that's nice, **hot**.. that's also..' (D1,Gen.2,F,21)

HMLD.Cro: meksikansko.. to je ukusno, **ljuto**.. to je isto. [*vruće* = hot (in temperature, not spiciness)]

(15) .. *da bude prave* **kondicije**.
'for there to be the right **conditions**' (D2,Gen.3,M,adult – age unknown)

HMLD.Cro: da budu pravi **(pred-)uvjeti**. [*kondicija* = state of physical fitness]

(16) *Nekada na trening* **guram sebe prejako**.
Sometimes at training I **push myself too hard**. (D2,Gen.3,F,adult – age unknown)

HMLD.Cro: Na treningu **se** nekada **naprežem previše**.

(17) *Imali smo* **slabe tomatuse**.
We had **poor tomatoes** [a poor tomato season]. (D2,Gen.3,M,adult – age unknown)

HMLD.Cro: Imali smo **slab urod rajčica**.

We next look at loan translations and adopt Backus and Dorleijn's definition (2009: 77) of this category referring to the "usage of morphemes in Language A that is the result of literal translation of one or more elements in a semantically equivalent expression in Language B". This definition is analogous to the notion of calques, a term more frequently used by Croatia-based researchers, that refer to "a more or less faithful reproduction of a foreign-language item [or items] via an item [or items] in the lexicon of the recipient language" (Turk 2013: 45. Our translation. Square brackets added).

In both datasets we find examples of loan translations in which strings of morphemes or components are transferred into the other language: e.g. *uzeti fotografiju/sliku* 'take a photograph/picture', cf. HMLD.Cro *fotografirati/slikati* 'to photograph'/'to picture'; *držiti se lijevo* 'to keep to the left', cf. HMLD.Cro *voziti po lijevoj traci/strani* 'drive on the left lane/side'; *daj mi ruku!* ('give me a hand!'), cf. HMLD.Cro *pomozi mi!* 'help me!'. Examples of loan translations in other diaspora varieties are also recorded, such as AUT.Cro (see Ščukanec, this volume), TRS. Cro (see Piasevoli, this volume), CAN.Cro (see Petrović, this volume) and ARG.Cro (See Skelin Horvat, Musulin and Blažević, this volume).

(18) *onda mama nije htjela **doći mene dobit***
'then mum didn't want **to come and get me**' (D1,Gen.2,M,22).

HMLD.Cro: onda mama nije **me htjela pokupiti**
'then mum didn't want to pick me up'.

(19) *Glumica Demi Moore **je bila unutra***
'the actress Demi Moore **was in it**'. (D1,Gen.2,M,18).

HMLD.Cro: **u filmu je glumila** Demi Moore 'in the film acted Demi Moore'

(20) *on se riješio da se ubije **kroz piću***
'he decided to kill himself **through drink**'. (D1,Gen.2,M,24)

HMLD.Cro: riješio se da se ubije **pićem**
'he decided to kill himself by means of drink'.

(21) *.. bio je na party jedan i **zadnji čovjek** što sam mislio **da ću ga ikad vidjet** ovdje u Australiji*
'.. he was at a party and the **last person** that I thought **I ever will see here** in Australia' (D1,Gen.2,M,24).

HMLD.Cro: Bio je **posljednji čovjek kojega sam očekivao vidjeti** na zabavi ovdje u Australiji
'he was the last person that I expected to see at an event here in Australia'

(22) *Morala sam, onaj.. **napravit malo prijatelji**, ali..*
'I had to, um.. **make a few friends**, but..' (D1,Gen.2,F,20).

HMLD.Cro: morala sam, onaj.. **sklopiti prijateljstva**, ali..
'I had to, um.. form friendships..'

Example (22) contains the verb *napravit* 'to make' where in HMLD.Cro employ a more semantically specific verb *sklopiti* 'to form' would be employed. In HMLD.Cro the verb *napravit* 'to make', and other verbs such as *imati* 'to have' and *dati* 'to give' (cf. *daj mi ruku* – 'give me a hand') are identified by Peti-Stantić, Japirko and Kežić (2016: 209) as the Croatian verbs that are thought to most likely function as light verbs (*lagani glagoli*) for Croatian phrasemes or constructions in which the verb bears little semantic-referential content ('de-semanticised verbs'). In NZ.Cro, verbs such as *učiniti* 'to do' and *znati* 'to know' are used in DO-verb constructions (see Stoffel and Hlavac, this volume). In the AUS.Cro datasets, we observe the transference of more de-semanticised functions of *have* and *work* onto their Croatian equivalents *imati* and *raditi* in the following DO-verb examples:

(23) **imam** *čaj popodne*
'I **have** tea in the afternoon'. (D2,Gen.2,F,65)

HMLD.Cro: **pijem** čaj popodne (lit.) 'I drink čaj in the afternoon'

(24) *vidim da svi* **imaju lijepi dan** *tu..*
'I see that all people are **having a nice day** here' (D1,Gen.2,M,20).

HMLD.Cro: vidim da svi ljudi tu **lijepo se provode** (lit.) 'I see that all people are **spending their time nicely**'

(25) *ja* **radim** *sada tri predmeta, ovaj.. semestar*
'I am **doing** now three subjects, this.. semester' (D1,Gen.2,F,20).

HMLD.Cro: ja sada **učim** tri predmeta, ovaj.. semestar. (lit.) 'I am now **studying**...'

(26) *.. sada sam u juniversitetu i kurs što sada* **radim** *je...*
'now I am at university and the course that I am now **doing** is...' (D1,Gen.2, M,20).

HMLD.Cro: sada sam na faksu i ono što sada **studiram** je...(lit.) 'now I'm at uni and that which I am now **studying** is..'

(27) *i on tu* **radi building** *i to kao, on radi na, um.. kako se prave kuće..*
'and he **does building** here and that like, he works on, um.. how houses are made' (D1,Gen.2, M,18).

HMLD.Cro: on **je** tu **građevinski radnik**.. (lit.) 'he **is** here **a construction worker**.'

(28) *oh,* **radim** *utege nekada, i* **igram šport**.. *nogomet igram za..*
'oh, I **do** weights sometimes, and I **play sport**.. I play soccer for..' (D1,Gen.2,M,17).

HMLD.Cro: oh, **dižem** utege nekada, i **bavim se sportom**.. nogomet igram za. (lit.) 'oh, I **lift** weights sometimes, and **engage in sport**, I play soccer for'.

Apart from *biti* (copula, AUX verb) and *imati* 'to have', the verb *raditi* 'to work/do' is the most commonly used verb. There are 627 instances of *raditi* in its various tense and conjugational forms. Many instances (269) of *raditi* relate to its use in its full semantic sense, eg. **radim** *u mali butik u gradu* 'I **work** in a small boutique in the city', or to its use in other phraseological constructions, eg. **radilo** *se od jednoga čovjeka* 'it was **about** one man'. However, 58 instances of *raditi* show that it is used as a largely de-semanticised verb where the semantic-referential content of the utterance is contained largely by NPs, as examples (25) to (28) have shown.

In some instances, the calques contain transferred forms from the English constructions. The English-origin transfers are underlined in the instances below:

(29) *tri, četiri kilometra.. i isto tribam* **hodat pas za walk**, *so.. to je isto važno..*
'three, four kilometres.. and also I need **to walk the dog for a walk**, so.. that's also important'. (D1,Gen.2,F,17).

HMLD.Cro: tri, četiri kilometra.. i isto tribam **izvoditi psa u šetnju** tako da.. to je isto važno.

(30) *on igra.. možda za Portland ili neko tako, um..* **ja ne znam za sure**, *ali igrao je..*
'he plays.. maybe for Portland or some such, um.. **I don't know for sure**, but he played (D1,Gen.2,M,21).

HMLD.Cro: on igra.. možda za Portland ili nešto tako, um.. **ne znam pouzdano**, ali. . .

(31) *Kad popravljaš auto, što brže, što brže napraviš* **da bude ready za customer** *i tako sve..*
'When you are repairing a car, [it's to be done] as fast as possible, as fast as possible you do it for it **to be ready for the customer** and everything like that (D1,Gen.2,M,27).

HMLD.Cro: . . . da bude **spremno za klijenta**.

Time expressions frequently occur in English as code-switches, but there are instances in which elements of English time constructions are replicated in Croatian. Croatian time expressions often feature the use of particular case forms: GEN to express specific dates and time periods; INS to express 'at the start of' or 'at the end of'. The calqued time expressions below contain a different use of cases. (For equivalent examples in USA.Cro, see Jutronić, this volume.)

(32) **na kraj** *listopada* on+ACC end-ACC.M.SG October-GEN.M.SG
'**at the end** of October' (D2,Gen.2,M,32)

HMLD.Cro: **krajem** listopada. end-INS.M.SG October-GEN.M.SG

Another time expression features target INS case, but with a preposition *s* 'with' that is overt and a time marker *zaključak* 'conclusion' that is atypical:

(33) **sa zaključkom** *siječnja*, with+INS conclusion-INS.M.SG. January-GEN.M.SG
'by the end of January'. (D2,Gen.2,F,18)

HMLD.Cro: **krajem** *siječnja* end-INS.M.SG January-GEN.M.SG

(34) **na treći** *dan* on+ACC third-ACC.M.SG day-ACC.M.SG
'**on the third** day' (D2,Gen.2,F,46)

HMLD.Cro: **trećega dana** third-GEN.M.SG. day-GEN.M.SG

The last example that we present in this section contains both a time expression, but also an example of the transfer of English pragmatic norms in expressing a request to an unknown person, i.e. via use of the conditional and expressed as an interrogative:

(35) **Biste li bili tako ljubazni odgovoriti** *po trideset prvi svibanja?*
'**Would you be so kind** as to reply by the thirty-first of May?' (D2,Gen.2,M,20)

HMLD.Cro: **Lijepo vas molim da odgovorite** *do trideset i prvog svibnja.*
'Kindly you-ACC request-1SG that respond-2PL by thirty-first of May.'

The HMLD.Cro equivalent for this is a two-clause declarative statement. An interrogative containing a conditional construction is possible, but marked as extremely or even overly polite: **Biste li bili toliko ljubazni da odgovorite** *do trideset i prvog svibnja?*

4.3 Code-switching

As Table 2 showed, most English-origin items in the corpora occur as singly-occurring items or in lexically simplex units (e.g. compound nouns or NPs). Longer stretches that consist of multiple items are less frequent, but still occur in both samples. Nearly half occur as intra-clausal code-switches:

(36) .. *samo je kao.. kako on.. um..* **comes to terms with**.. *um.. ta žena koja je umrla..*
'.. it's only like.. how he.. um.. **comes to terms with**.. um.. that woman who died..' (D1,Gen.2,F,17).

HMLD.Cro: .. *kako on.. um..* **se miri s time**.. *um.. da je ta žena umrla. . .*

(37) *kino volim jako jer.. kino mogu **get away** (smije se).. **from everything**.*
'cinema I like a lot because.. cinema I can **get away**.. (laughter).. **from everything**.' (D1,Gen.2,F,26).

HMLD.Cro:...jer.. u kinu mogu **pobjeći**...**od svega**.

As examples (36) and (37) above show, code-switches often contain or are commenced by phrasemes supplied by English. The phrasemes are common and perhaps likely to be 'high-frequency' ones in the English repertoires of the speakers. The phrases occurring in (36) and (37) are comparable (English-language) ones to those in loan translation examples (18) to (22) that entirely consisted of Croatian constituents, or to those that consisted of constituents from both languages, as in examples (29) to (31). Further examples of phrases that form clauses of their own, i.e. inter-clausal code-switches, are the following:

(38) *četiri godina.. dosta, **need a change, so**.. vidjet ću, ne znam.*
'four years.. enough, **need a change, so**.. I'll see, I don't know.'
(D1,Gen.1B,F,27).

HMLD.Cro: četiri godine.. su dosta, **treba mi promjena**, tako da..vidjet ću, ne znam.

(39) *onda to nema, **it's out of control**, to je sad, **like**..*
'then it isn't there, **it's out of control**, that is now, **like**...' (D1,Gen.2,M,17).

HMLD.Cro: onda toga nema, to **je izmaklo kontroli**, to je sad, **kao**..

(40) *kroz te probleme.. znaš, **deal with the problems**, kako bih rekao.*
'through these problems.. you know, **deal with the problems**, how I would say it.' (D1,Gen.2,M,24).

HMLD.Cro: kroz te probleme.. znaš, **nositi se s problemima**, kako bih rekao.

As can be seen from many of the examples, most instances of code-switching are not flagged. This reflects the linguistic practices of most informants for whom bilingual speech is an unmarked variety in many contexts. But some code-switches are flagged such as (36) and (40) above. In dataset 1, bilingual speech is usually not accompanied by hesitation phenomena, but where these do occur, they are more likely to occur in the proximity of English-origin items (whether single-or multiple-word items), and appear to be surface-level evidence of lexical retrieval difficulties or of monitoring of language selection. It has been suggested by Hlavac (2011) these perform the function of facilitating the incorporation and comprehension of 'other language' text, at least partly as a hearer-centred strategy. In some cases, the phrase-or clause-length code-switches occur as variations or repetitions of immediately preceding Croatian text:

(41) *ako mi idemo za previše..* ***for too long***, *onda.. dojadit će nam*, **you know.. it's going to be boring.. so..** *rekli smo da ćemo tamo bit..*
'if we go for too long…**for too long**, then.. we'll get fed up with it, **you know.. it's going to be boring.. so..** we said that we'll be there..' (D1,Gen.2,M,17)

In example (41) the first code-switch, *for too long*, appears as repetition and therefore as emphasis for the immediately preceding Croatian phrase *za previse* 'for too long'. The second code-switch commences with a discourse marker, *you know*, marking shared knowledge or beliefs, and the following clause *it's going to be boring* is a stylistic variation to the referential content of what was just previously expressed in Croatian, *dojadit će nam* (Hlavac 2012).

4.4 Morphology and syntax

This section presents examples of largely monolingual Croatian speech lacking lexical or semantic input from English. We focus here on noun phrases and features thereof, including use of *jedan* 'one' as a determiner, verbs and their valency word order, syntactic transference and other features of syntax.

4.4.1 Noun phrases

Noun phrases (NPs) containing nouns are presented in this section, while those containing pronominals are not examined here and are touched on in section 4.4.3. Croatian nouns are marked for the features case (see below 4.4.1.1), gender (see below 4.4.1.2) and number (see below 4.4.1.3).

4.4.1.1 Case
There is not an isomorphic relationship between feature-marking for CASE and nominal suffix. Rather, nominal suffixes are portmanteau forms that mark all three features, CASE, GENDER and NUMBER. At the same time some suffixes are not perceived as overt as they are realised with a -Ø ending, ie. NOM.M.SG. or ACC.M.SG.INAMINATE (Barić et al. 1990: 69–92). In addition, all NOM case nominals, whether singular or plural, are considered to be 'base' or 'unmarked' forms.

We are reminded of Jakobson's (1936) description of the Russian case system and other studies that look at case in within universal markedness theory, e.g. Wurzel (1984), Herbert (1986) and Dressler (1987).

In examining NPs contained in both datasets, we frame our analysis according to Ďurovič's (1983, 1984, 1987, 1988) large-scale study of Serbocroatian/Croatian-speaking children aged 4–18 in Sweden. A quantitative analysis of case-marking of nominals and pronominals in his sample revealed two prominent phenomena: reduction of the case system and variation in the use of cases. Ďurovič posited that a reduction in the number of cases used by speakers could be systematic, i.e. that certain patterns in speakers' NP case-marking could be discerned, and that there was likely to be a hierarchical basis to selection of case.

For example, Ďurovič hypothesised that the presence of GEN in an informant's grammatical system implies that the cases, NOM and ACC, are also part of the same system. His system of 'case implicativity' suggests that a 'complete' case system is most likely to have the following ordering of cases: NOM, ACC, GEN, LOC, INS, DAT, VOC. The term 'ordering' refers to the implicative character of the cases. What this means is that the presence of any case in a system implies the presence of all other cases 'to the left', but says nothing about the cases 'to the right', i.e. if a speaker was able to produce locative NPs, this meant that they had full command of NOM, ACC, GEN, but did not mean that they necessarily had full command of the following cases to the right. i.e. INS, DAT and VOC. Ďurovič's (1983) implicativity scale is employed as a model in the description of case-marking in NPs from other data samples, such as those from ITAL.Cro (see Županović Filipin, Hlavac and Piasevoli, this volume), CAN.Cro (see Petrović, this volume) and NZ.Cro (Stoffel and Hlavac, this volume).

In syntactic environments requiring oblique cases, such as LOC, INS or DAT Ďurovič (1983) reports that the ACC is used as the default case: ".. the accusative must be considered a "praepositionalis generalis"." (1983: 26. Double-inverted commas his.). Employment of LOC, INS or DAT with a default case is congruent, as Ďurovič (1983) writes, with Jakobson's (1936) categories of *Randkasus* ('peripheral case') for LOC, INS and DAT, while NOM, ACC and GEN occupy the status of *Vollkasus* ('base case').

Examination of case marking of nominals in this study is not micro-linguistic. It is not possible here to provide a detailed profile of case systems of individual informants. Instead, sum totals of NPs recorded in the sample of the 100 informants from dataset 1 are provided. Overall numbers of NPs with 'target' case marking are firstly compared with numbers of NPs with 'non-target' case marking. In Table 7, the total number of 'target' and 'non-target' nominals is provided according to each case.

Table 7: Target and non-target case realisations of nominals in dataset 1.

Case	No. of target realisations (and %)	No. of non-target realisations (and %)	Total (and %)
NOM	2463 (100%)	0	2463 (26%)
ACC	3128 (95%)	171 (5%)	3299 (35%)
GEN	1403 (86%)	279 (14%)	1682 (18%)
LOC	936 (74%)	330 (26%)	1266 (14%)
INS	410 (86%)	67 (14%)	477 (5%)
DAT	104 (79%)	27 (21%)	131 (2%)
(VOC)[1]	0	0	
Total	8444 (91%)	874 (9%)	9318

Table 7 above that 91% of speakers' Croatian NPs have target case marking. This indicates in the first place, that across the sample, speakers' case systems have not 'broken down' and that nominals have a very high likelihood of bearing correct morphological markers. Predictably, there are no instances of nominatives realised with 'non-target' forms. The nominative is, as stated above, perceived to be the 'base' or 'least marked' form and is unlikely to be replaced with more 'peripheral' or 'more marked' forms. However, when the number of nominatives is excluded, the percentage of non-target realisations rises from 9% to 15%, and when both nominatives and accusatives are excluded the percentage of non-target realisations for the remaining four cases rises to 25%.

In general, there is a tendency for the cases listed further down the table to have a lower overall frequency and a higher percentage of non-target forms. This in itself is not confirmation of Ďurovič's (1983) hierarchy of implicativity as the data in Table 7 do not indicate whether non-target realisations are always realised with other case forms above or below in the table (or to the left or to the right to use Ďurovič's analogy). For instance, it is not automatically evident from Table 7 whether non-target genitives are replaced with case forms from above ('to the left' in Ďurovič's hierarchy) or below ('to the right' in Ďurovič's hierarchy). The higher number of non-target forms for the cases LOC, INS and DAT for instance suggests though that these cases are most likely to be reduced first and be replaced by other ones by default. This is indirect support for Ďurovič's (1983) model.

---

[1] Vocative case forms are found in the sample, but only as non-target realisations of other cases. There are no instances where the VOC is a target case form.

The LOC case remains noteworthy because it occupies a mid-point on the hierarchy in terms of incidence with 936 tokens (which amounts to more than twice the number of instrumentals, 410, but only two-thirds of the number of genitives, 1403) while being the case that is most often realised with non-target forms (26% of locatives are 'non-target, while the overall average is only 9%). Locatives occur much more frequently than instrumentals and datives, which justifies their position preceding these two cases within Ďurovič's (1983) hierarchy, but at the same time they are realised far more than the other two 'succeeding' cases with non-target forms. When considering the frequency of NPs and case marking, it is instructive to note Kostić's (1986) results of an examination of the frequency of NP case forms in a corpus of 2 million words, based on a collection of Croatian and Serbian non-fiction and literary texts. Kostić (1986: 78) excludes the few instances of VOC tokens and records the following distribution of case marking across approx. 650,000 NPs, including pronouns: NOM (32.9%), GEN (28.3%), ACC (19.8%), LOC (10.7%), INS (6.3%) and DAT (2.1%). The frequency of respective case forms recorded in Kostić's (1986) corpus is similar to the frequency of respective case forms shown in Table 7 above, with the exception of ACC preceding GEN in frequency rather than following it.

In Table 8 below, the non-target case realisations in our informants' NPs are presented and matched with Ďurovič's (1983) hierarchy of implicativity of cases. In Table 8 below, the case form that would have been expected ('target case form') is presented first, followed with an arrow pointing to the non-target case form that was realised by the speaker. As stated, Ďurovič's (1983) model is based primarily on the premise that 'choice' of default forms is necessarily specified by the 'implicational nature' of the case system, and where 'case restrictedness' occurs, certain outcomes (in terms of morphological forms) can be predicted. Those realisations that are congruent to Ďurovič's (1983) model of implicativity (ie. default forms chosen 'to the left') are provided in standard (non-italic) script. Those realisations that are *not* congruent to his model (i.e. forms chosen 'to the right') are provided in italic script. Thus, examples of GEN replaced by NOM or ACC, as hypothesised by Ďurovič (1983), are in standard, non-italic script, while examples of GEN replaced by LOC, INS or DAT are in italic script as they are counter to the expectations of Ďurovič's (1983) model.

The findings for non-target case realisations in Table 8 show that the overwhelming majority of such instances are congruent to the predictions of Ďurovič's (1983) model of implicativity. Of the 874 instances of non-target realisations 801 (92%) are replaced by cases 'to the left' on the implicativity hierarchy. Morphosyntactic features of nominals in this sample are shown to be very similar to those found in Ďurovič's (1983) sample. On the basis of data here this is strong evidence to support his model of implicativity of cases where case systems

Table 8: Target cases and their non-target case realisations presented according to Ďurovič's (1983) model of case implicativity: NOM, ACC, GEN, LOC, INS, DAT, VOC.

Target case		Non-target realisation	Singular	Plural	Total
NOM			\multicolumn{3}{c}{No non-target realisations recorded}		
ACC	→	NOM	88	24	112
ACC	→	GEN	8	2	10
ACC	→	LOC	41		
ACC	→	INS	1	$= 3^2$	$= 49^3$
ACC	→	DAT	4		
GEN	→	NOM	152	47	199
GEN	→	ACC	47	24	71
GEN	→	LOC	0		
GEN	→	INS	0	$= 5^2$	$= 9^3$
GEN	→	DAT	4		
LOC	→	NOM	18	6	24
LOC	→	ACC	276	11	287
LOC	→	GEN	14	2	16
LOC	→	INS	2	0	2
LOC	→	VOC	1	0	1
INS	→	NOM	32	9	41
INS	→	ACC	11	6	17
INS	→	GEN	5	2	7
INS	→	DAT	1	0	1
INS	→	VOC	1	0	1
DAT	→	NOM	7	11	18
DAT	→	ACC	5	2	7
DAT	→	GEN	2	0	2
Total congruent to Ďurovič's model (Standard script)			657	144	801
Total non-congruent to Ďurovič's model (Italic script)			63	10	73
Total			**720**	**154**	**874**

of speakers of diaspora Croatian undergo change. As Table 8 also shows, there is little difference between the singular and plural forms of nouns in regard to the incidence of target-case realisations. Similarly, there is little difference in the level of target case realisations between masculine (87%), feminine (93%) and neuter (91%) nouns (Hlavac 2000: 486).

---

2 The plural forms for LOC, INS and DAT are collapsed into one form, *-ima* for M, N and F.II nouns, and *-ama* for F.I nouns. Instances cannot therefore be allocated to any one of these three cases and are listed as a combined total.

3 Due to formal non-distinction of the cases LOC, INS and DAT in the plural only a combined total for all three cases can be provided.

4.4.1.2 Gender

While case-marking of NPs is a feature that is prominent in many descriptions of the speech of diaspora speakers, there are other features of NPs such as marking of gender that are of note. In dataset 1, there are 4,266 FEM NPs (excluding pronouns), of which 356 are FEM II nouns, i.e. nouns that have a word-final consonant and a different system of declension compared to FEM nouns ending in –*a*. The large number of F.II nouns in the sample is partly accounted for by the frequency of the F noun *stvar* 'thing', that occurs in the commonly-used phrase *i takve stvari* 'and things like that'. There are 11 eleven examples of F.II nouns being declined as M nouns. Their consonant-final structure accounts for why speakers may re-classify them in their repertoires in this way. (See Ščukanec, Breu & Vuk, this volume.) Amongst the examples of assignment to masculine are three instances of *stvar* 'thing' and three of feminine *noć* 'night'.

(42) *većina* **isti** **stvar** *kroz*
majority-NOM.F.SG **same**-NOM.M.SG **thing**-NOM.M.SG through+ACC
cijeli *film*
whole-ACC.M.SG film-ACC.M.SG
'...mainly the same thing through the whole film.' (D1,Gen.2,F,21).
HMLD.Cro: *većinom* **ista** *stvar*...

(43) *dnevnik* *gledam* *skoro* **svaki**
main news bulletin-ACC.M.SG view-1SG nearly **every**-ACC.M.SG
noć
night-ACC.M.SG
'I watch the main news bulletin nearly **every** night'. (D1,Gen.2,F,19).
HMLD.Cro:...*skoro* **svaku** *noć*.

Morphological marking for the feature GENDER in NPs does not otherwise diverge from that found in the speech of HMLD.Cro speakers.

4.4.1.3 Number

In both datasets 1 and 2, there are eight instances of non-congruent marking of number between an attributive and its head noun, e.g. *izgleda* 'appear-3SG' *na* 'on+LOC' *ovoj* 'this-LOC.F.SG' *slikama* 'picture-LOC.F.PL' 'it looks like on this pictures' (D2,Gen.1B,F,27). A more frequent occurrence than non-congruence of NUMBER marking between internal consituents of an NP in dataset 1 is the occurrence of a singular subject NP with plural marking on the verb. The examples given below relate to morphological features beyond the NP, i.e. subject-verb agreement. It appears that the lexico-semantic features of some English nouns have influenced those of their Croatian equivalents, and this has had consequences on number marking of some NPs. The subject NPs that these relate to are all instances of nouns whose equivalents in English, even where these occur as singular forms, attract plural marking of the verb, such as *police, fire brigade, audience* or *government*. In HMLD. Cro, these grammatically SG nouns co-occur with SG verbal morphology only. In the AUS.Cro sample there are Croatian SG nouns that co-occur with PL verb morphology.

(44) i   tamo **su**   znaš   **mafija**   **dali**
 and there AUX-3PL know-2SG **mafia-SG** **give**-PST.3PL
 novac   da   kupe
 money-ACC.M.SG COMP buy-3PL
 '.. and there, you know, the mafia-SG gave-3PL money so that they could buy..' (D1,Gen.2,M, 22)

(45) i   **ima**   **svit**   što   **jedu**   kao **imaju**
 and have-3SG **people**-NOM.M.SG REL.PRON **eat**-3PL like **have**-3PL
 piknik
 picnic-ACC.M.SG
 '.. and there are people-SG who <u>are</u> eating like having a picnic.' (D1,Gen.2,F,19)

(46) imam   želju   i   također **moja**
 have-1SG wish-ACC.F.SG and Also   **my**-NOM.F.SG
 obitelj   **žele**   da   se   vratimo..
 family-NOM.F.SG **wish**-3PL COMP REFL return-1PL
 'I have the desire and.. as well.. my family-SG wish-PL that we return.' (D1,Gen.2,F,20)

(47) većina   **imaju**   tako osam   deset
 majority-NOM.F.SG   **have**-3PL such eight ten
 'The majority have like eight, ten..' (D1,Gen.2,F,21)

A peculiarity of Australian English is that designations of football (or soccer, rugby or any sporting) teams that are SG also attract PL verb marking:

(48) isto kad   **Melbourne Kroacija**   **igraju**
 same when **Melbourne Croatia**-NOM.F.SG   **play**-3PL
 utakmice   tamo
 match-ACC.F.PL   there
 '.. also when Melbourne Croatia-SG play-PL matches there..' (D1,Gen.2,M,22)

In examples (44) to (48) above, the English equivalents of the Croatian subjects, *mafia, people, family, majority* and *Melbourne Croatia* are all SG nouns which co-occur with PL marking on verbs. Transference of the lexico-semantic features of this small number of English nouns results in these AUS.Cro NPs attracting plural morphology for verbs. Singular subjects with PL marked verbs occur also in the AUT.Cro and HUN.Cro corpora, albeit for reasons that appear to be pragmatic rather than lexico-semantic (see Ščukanec this volume, and Ščukanec, Breu & Vuk this volume).

4.4.1.4 Employment of *jedan* 'one' as a nascent indefinite article

As shown above in section 4.1, there are 9,318 NPs in dataset 1. In a small number of these – 209 – forms of the Croatian number *jedan* M 'one' (*jedna* F, *jedno* N) occur. Although a number, *jedan* is declined as a DEM ADJ, i.e. it bears phi-features of its noun head. In most cases, *jedan* is used in a numerical sense to refer to 'one' of something, e.g. *imam dvije sestre i **jednog** brata* 'I have two sisters and **one** brother'. In other instances its use in NPs relates to a quantification in a more general sense, e.g. *samo za **jedno** vrijeme, samo šest mjeseci smo bili tamo* 'just for **a certain amount of** time, we were there just six months', while in others it is found in idiomatic set phrases, e.g. *to je u **jednu** ruku.. teško pitanje, tu sve ovisi o . . .* 'in **one** sense that's.. a hard question, here everything depends on . . .'. These uses of *jedan* are no different from the way speakers of HMLD.Cro employ *jedan* attributively in NPs. But, further to this, *jedan*, although a number, can denote specification of the succeeding noun. In many instances where this occurs, it is accompanied by intonational features, here that of emphasis (shown via upper case in the example below only):

(49) *To je radilo o **JEDNOM** ubojstvu, ako se ne varam, od **JEDNE** žene koja je planirala sve protiv svog muža.*
'it was about **A** murder, if I'm not mistaken, by **A PARTICULAR** woman who was planning everything against her husband' (D1,Gen.2,F,17)

The intonational features of example (49) mark both instances of *jedan* as a DET ADJ that denotes a specification of the following noun. In the 209 NPs that contain *jedan* functioning attributively, there are 23 instances where its use is *not* accompanied by pragmatic or prosodic features and where specification is *not* readily ascertainable:

(50) *sam jednu godinu učila.. ah.. film-making sa <u>jedan</u> direktor iz Hrvatske.. to je.. XXX.. ne znam kako se preziva..*
I studied one year.. ah.. film-making with <u>a</u> [film] director from Croatia.. that was.. XXX.. I don't know his surname.. (D1,Gen.2,F,26)

In example (50) the second incidence of *jedan* appears redundant. The succeeding noun is singular, countable and unspecified – features that typically require use of the indefinite article in English, and this appears to be the reason why it occurs. Of note is that the following noun is *direktor*, a Croatian noun but used here in a sense in which semantic transference from English is evident. The word *direktor* in Croatian means 'company director' or 'school principal', but not 'film director' (which is *redatelj*). In example (51), another English-origin transfer co-occurs with a seemingly redundant use of *jedan*.

(51) *...ali je **fun**, bilo je <u>jedan</u> dobri **ekspirijens** isto smo išli znaš onaj **boogie boarding**, kao **surfing**, kao **surfing**.. imaš **veliki board**..*
*...but it's **fun**, it was <u>a</u> good **experience** also we did, you know, that **boogie boarding**, like **surfing**, like **surfing**.. you have [a] **big board**..* (D1,Gen.2,M,30)

Example (51) has a number of English-origin transfers, and *ekspirijens* 'experience' is one of them. Here, preceding *jedan* functions as an indefinite article as it describes a noun that is singular, countable and previously unmentioned. Interestingly, there is no use of *jedan* in front of *veliki board* at the end of the utterance, which is also singular, countable and previously unmentioned. What examples (50) and (51) indicate is that in some NPs containing English-origin nouns (or Croatian nouns that bear semantic features of English equivalents), the grammatical features of these nouns can sometimes be 'carried over' into the Croatian structure of the NPs in which they occur, resulting in occurrence of *jedan* as a form functioning as an indefinite article. There are fewer examples of *jedan* functioning in this way in 'Croatian-only' NPs, but some are still found:

(52) *... ima <u>jedan</u> glavni glumac, on.. proba da kao živi normalno život i. ...*
.. there's <u>a</u> lead actor, he.. tries to, like, live normally life and...(D1,Gen.2,F,20)

(53) *.. igraju kolo, <u>jedna</u> ulica, možda bi bila <u>jedna</u> glavna ulica u <u>jednu</u> selu, um.. rekao bi..*
.. they're doing [a] ring-dance, <u>a</u> street, maybe it could be <u>a</u> main street in <u>a</u> village, um.. I'd say.. (D1,Gen.1B,M,31).

Examples (52) and (53) contain only Croatian lexemes and morphemes and occurrence of *jedan* here appears to be evidence of the emergence of its use as an article-like form in *some* speakers' repertoires in only *some* instances. But as stated, statistically, *jedan* is found to perform an article-like function in only 23 of the 209 NPs containing *jedan*. The vast majority of the 9,318 NPs do not contain *jedan* used as a determiner with an article-like function. Examples of use of *jedan* as an indefinite article are found in TRS.Cro (see Piasevoli, this volume), CAN. Cro (see Petrović, this volume) and ARG.Cro (see Skelin Horvat, Musulin and Blažević, this volume).

4.4.2 Verbs and valency

The AUS.Cro datasets contain a very large number of verbs or VPs: over 15,000. As noted above in 4.1.2, verbs pattern differently from nouns and other parts of speech as they are less commonly transferred from English, and when transferred, they are much more likely to be morphologically (and phonologically) integrated. While there are a sizeable number of NPs that feature English transfers (usually nouns, less commonly adjectives) and a smaller number that show innovations in case, number and gender marking, there are proportionately fewer VPs that bear evidence of comparable innovations. This section presents a number of examples relating to the following: verb morphology, in particular conjugational suffixes; verbs used reflexively without a reflexive particle and verbs used transitively with a reflexive particle; verb valency; and aspect marking.

Leaving aside the instances of SG subjects that co-occur with PL verbs (see above 4.4.1.3), instances of subject-verb non-agreement are rare. A conspicuous example is one in which an impersonal construction is normally used. In example (54), the logical experiencer of the action is the subject of the verb *smetati* 'to disturb', which is not conjugated and remains in its INF form. In HMLD.Cro the experiencer of the action is in DAT and a 3SG form of *smetati* is employed.

(54) **ja** ne **smetati** hladno
 I NEG **disturb**-INF cold-ADJ.NOM.N.SG
 'I do not mind the cold.' (D2,Gen.2,F,25)

 HMLD.Cro:
 ne **smeta** mi hladno [vrijeme]
 NEG **disturb**-3SG me-DAT cold-ADJ.NOM.N.SG [weather-NOM.N.SG]

More frequent are instances in which verbs are used with a reflexive meaning, but which lack the reflexive particle *se* 'self':

(55) *spremaju   oni   za   dugačak   put*
     prepare-3PL they   for+ACC long-ACC.M.SG trip-ACC.M.SG
     'they're preparing for a long trip' (D2,Gen.2,F,42)

   HMLD.Cro: *spremaju **se** za dugačak put.*

In the AUS.Cro datasets, there are 14 examples of non-occurrence of the reflexive particle where it is otherwise required. None of the examples that lack the reflexive particle are rendered incomprehensible due to its absence. Conspicuous amongst the 14 examples is that eight of them are impersonal constructions. Five of the examples of non-occurrence feature the verb *sviđati se* 'to please', which is a verb where the experiencer is encoded as a DAT participant, and the verb phrase contains a third-person subject referent and the REFL *se*. Semantically, the construction in English that is closest to this is 'to like'.

(56) *druge   serije   to   ne   **sviđa***
     other-NOM.F.PL   series-NOM.F.PL   that-NOM.N.SG   NEG   please-3SG
     ***me**   nego   je   to*
     me-ACC   rather   be-3SG   that-NOM.N.SG
     '.. other series.. that doesn't please me [= I don't like that].. instead that's..
     (D1,Gen.2,M,22).

   HMLD.Cro: *druge serije.. to mi 'me-DAT' se ne sviđa.. nego je to..*

In example (56), not only does *sviđati se* lack the reflexive particle, the valency of the verb has changed so that the logical experiencer of the verb is a direct object, rather than an indirect object with DAT case marking. Conversely, there are eight instances of reflexive particles occurring where these are *not* required syntactically.

(57) ***mene**   **se**   to   više   ne   interesira*
     me-ACC   REFL   that-NOM.N.SG   more   NEG   interest-3SG
     'That no longer interests me' (D1,Gen.2,M,23).
     HMLD.Cro: *mene to više ne interesira.*

In sum, there are more instances of reflexive verbs occurring without the REFL participle *se*, than employment of *se* with otherwise non-reflexive verbs. Reflexive verbs are much less frequent in English compared to Croatian. A lower incidence of reflexive verbs in English can have the effect that these non-reflexive verbs bear influence on their Croatian equivalents that are reflexive. This phenomenon can occur in relation to both "naturally reflexive" verbs (Alexiadou and Schäfer 2014) as in (55), as well as inherently reflexive ones such as *sviđati se* 'to please + REFL' in (56). Data from a CAN.Cro sample shows further examples of reflexive verbs lacking the reflexive particle *se* (see Petrović, this volume). Instances of innovations in the valency of some verbs are also found. These number 13 in all, and often relate to the marking of indirect objects. Example (58) contains such an instance.

(58) ali volio bih pružit **djecu**
but like-PAST.SG.M COND-1SG provide-INF **children-ACC.F.SG**
malo bolju priliku
little-ADV better-ACC.F.SG opportunity-ACC.F.SG
'but I'd like to provide my children with a slightly better opportunity..'
(D1,Gen.2,M,31).

HMLD.Cro: ali volio bih pružiti djeci-DAT malo bolju priliku.

The last feature of verbs presented here is aspect. All Croatian verbs are marked for aspect, which shows whether the activity is bounded, commenced or completed (PFV), or an enduring or repetitive action, or one that was interrupted and resumed (IPFV). There are ten instances in the AUS.Cro samples in which aspectual marking of the verb is not congruent to the temporal features expressed in speakers' utterances. In all instances, it is a PFV form of the verb that is employed where HMLD.Cro would require an IPFV form:

(59) uvijek se nešto njemu **dogodio** i on
always REFL something him-DAT happen-PST.PFV.M.SG and he
'Something always happened to him and he.. ' (D1,Gen.2,F,20)

HMLD.Cro: Uvijek se nešto njemu događalo-PST.IPFV.N.3SG i on..

(60) svaki mjesec možda dva
every-NOM.M.SG month-NOM.M.SG perhaps two+SG.GEN
puta to mi je ja to
time-GEN.M.SG that-NOM.N.SG me-DAT be-3SG I that-NOM.N.SG
shvatim kao da je to često
understand-1SG.PFV like COMP be-3SG that-NOM.N.SG often-ADV
'every month maybe two times that was.. to me.. I understand that like that that's often..' (D1,Gen.2,M,18).

HMLD.Cro: .. to mi je, ja to shvaćam-1SG.IPFV kao da je to često..

There are over 15,000 verbs in dataset 1 and only ten instances of a verb form occurring whose aspectual marking is not congruent to the referential content or temporal-marking. It is of note, though, that where non-target aspect marking occurs, all examples show that a PFV replaces an IPFV form.

4.4.3 Word order

This section focuses on pronouns, clitics and adverbs. Croatian is pro-drop and subject pronouns are usually overt, typically marking emphasis or contrast. Discourse-internal features usually account for their use (or more commonly their non-use). In the AUS.Cro datasets, there are a large number – approx. 470 – of subject pronouns whose production is not overt and not accompanied by intonation features to mark emphasis or contrast. To be sure, the number of dropped subject pronouns is far larger than this number, and the pro-drop function is found in the speech of *all* speakers. Production of subject pronouns is not accompanied by changes in verb morphology such that agreement specification is lost. Example (54) above appears as a fairly rare exception to this tendency and a 'reduction' of conjugational morphology to a 'base' form such as INF or PRES.3SG does not usually occur. Instead, subject pronouns co-occur with verbs that agree with them in person and number. Example (61) contains such an example.

(61) .. ali kad sam završila **ja** školu, ono.. drugu godinu otkad sam **ja** završila, oni su..

...but when **I** finished school, um.. the second year since **I** finished school, they.. (D1,Gen.2,F,21).

Croatian is SVO and the first instance of *ja* 'I' in example (61) occurs *after* both verb forms and is syntactically conspicuous through its post-verbal position. A conspicuous characteristic of both datasets is that the subject pronoun that was overt was 1SG *ja* 'I'. Both datasets contain a large number of personally related narratives and speakers were often recounting events and at the same time marking their own positionality in these. There appeared to be rhetorical features in their Croatian speech that resembled the way they would be likely to recount these events in English. (We cannot test this claim as we do not have recordings of their English speech). We suggest that subject pronouns in English function not only as a grammatical category; they are forms that convey positional and relational information and are always there as *potential* carriers of rhetorical emphasis. In Croatian, they need not be there, and where rhetorical emphasis occurs, it can be conveyed by *either* an overt subject pronoun, or intonational emphasis on the finite verb. So, English has subject pronouns that are always there as (potential) carriers of rhetorical or discourse-specific features (along with their mandatory function as subject marker). We argue that this feature that is available to them in English and that is likely to be employed by them in their English speech is transferred into their Croatian speech. Overt subject pronouns are therefore not only an example of the transference of grammatical features, but an example of transference of Australian English pragmatic norms involving the function of 'I' (and other pronouns, but less often) as carriers of discourse-specific positional and relational content that is transferred onto the use of *ja* (and other Croatian pronouns, but less often). Thus, we see *ja* 'I' as an example of the transference of pragmatic norms of narrative structure that have 'I' as not only a grammatical feature, but a speaker-positional one as well.

In Croatian, direct object (ACC) and indirect object (DAT) pronouns have two forms: a full (or long) form and a clitic (or short) form. Full forms pattern the same way as subject pronouns and are considered overt while the clitic form is the unmarked or default form. Clitics cannot occur in clause-initial position. But full form pronouns can occupy any position within a clause, including initial and final position. The order in which clitics occur in standard HMLD.Cro is shown below in Table 9:

Table 9: Order of clitics and short forms in standard HMLD.Cro.

particle	AUX [exc. 3SG.]	DAT	ACC/GEN	REFL	3SG.AUX
1	2	3	4	5	6

In example (62), a full form pronoun, *nju* 'her-ACC' is used (together with an overt subject pronoun *mi* 'we'). The position of the full form *nju* between the AUX *smo* 'be-1PL' and the main verb *vidjeli* 'see-PST-PL.M', is where a clitic form of the pronoun *je* 'her-ACC' would be expected:

(62) skoro   godinu   dana   otkad   mi   smo
     almost year-ACC.F.SG   day-GEN.M.PL   since   we   AUX-1PL
     nju   vidjeli
     her-ACC.F.SG   see-PAST-M.PL
     '.. almost a year since we saw **her**' (D1,Gen1B,F,27)

As can be seen from Table 9 and example (62), the position of object or reflexive pronoun clitics in subordinate clauses is *after* the AUX verb, but *before* the main verb. Thus, the word order of Croatian subordinate clauses is often (S)OV. In English, subordinate clauses retain SVO word order. More frequent and conspicuous in the AUS.Cro samples are examples of full form pronouns that occur in post-(main)verb position:

(63) obadva su   se   ovdje rodili   mama je
     both   AUX-3PL REFL here   give birth-PST.M.PL   mum   AUX-3SG
     imala   **njih**   kad   je   bila   devetnaest
     have-PST.F.SG   **them**-ACC.M.PL   when AUX-3SG   be-PST.F.SG nineteen
     'Both were born here.. mum had **them** when she was nineteen.'
     (D1,Gen.2,M,17)

   HMLD.Cro:. . .mama **ih**-ACC.CLITIC je rodila kada je imala devetnaest.

(64) ja bi   rađe   da   pošaljem   **njih**   u
     I   COND dear-COMPARATIVE   COMP send-1SG   **them**-ACC to+ACC
     privatnu   školu
     private-ACC.F.SG school-ACC.F.SG
     'I would rather send **them** to a private school' (D1,Gen2,M,23)

   HMLD.Cro: ja bih radije da **ih**-ACC.CLITIC šaljem u privatnu školu.

In the AUS.Cro samples, there are 33 examples of full-form object pronouns, most of them occurring *after* the main verb. It is not clear whether it is the production of full form pronouns that leads to their post-positioning after main verbs. Alternately, there may be a tendency amongst some speakers for SVO patterns in subordinate clauses to lead to the selection of full form pronouns as typically only these can occur in a post-main-verb position. Or, it could be that both patterns are emerging contemporaneously in the repertoires of some speakers. In sum, the end result in these examples is that constructions emerge that are closer to English equivalents and unknown in any variety of HMLD.Cro. (See Jutronić, this volume.)

There are over 50 examples of clitic ordering in the AUS.Cro samples that are not congruent to the word order conventions of standard HMLD.Cro as shown in Table 9 above. These are not presented here as conventions of clitic order in a number of non-standard and regional varieties of HMLD.Cro are known to differ from *standard* Croatian, and therefore cannot be clearly identified as possible examples of language contact.

4.4.4 Syntactic transference

In this section, we present examples of noun phrases that contain multiple attributives. We view the examples that we present in this section as innovations that relate not only to noun phrases but also to word order changes and thus indicative of a more widespread change in some speakers' repertoires. In Croatian, there are no limits on the number of pre-posed attributives that precede a noun as long as each attributive relates only to the head noun. Attributives in Croatian are ordered in a way similar to that of English NPs: demonstrative, possessive, temporal, size, colour, narrow specification + noun. Where an attributive describes another and not the head noun, this usually needs to be post-posed after the head[4] (Katičić 1991: 382) – note the position of *s kratkim rukavima* 'with short sleeves' in an example NP below:

> onaj   tvoj   prvi   veliki   plavi   prugasti   prsluk   s kratkim rukavima
> that   your   first   big   blue   striped   waistcoat   with short sleeves
> 'That first, big, blue, striped, short-sleeved waistcoat of yours.'

In English, attributives that describe another attributive (*short sleeved*) can still be pre-posed before the head noun as shown above. (In English, a demonstrative *and* a possessive determiner cannot co-occur as pre-posed attributives and *your* is post-posed here).

In the AUS.Cro samples, there are examples of NPs with attributives that internally relate to each other and not to the head noun only:

(65) za   Uskrs   ja   sam   išo   u
      for+ACC   Easter-ACC.M.SG   I   AUX-1SG   go-PST.SG.M   to+ACC
      crkvu   **u**   **devet**   **sati**   misa
      church-ACC.F.SG   **at**   **nine**   **hour**-GEN.M.PL   mass-NOM.F.SG
      'At Easter I went to church, to nine o'clock mass'. (D2,Gen.2,M,19)

   HMLD.Cro: Za Uskrs sam išao u crkvu na misu **u devet sati.**

---

4 In Croatian, there are some instances in which an attributive that describes another attributive can pre-pose the head noun. This can occur in high register or literary texts and the attributive itself is usually in instrumental case, as shown underlined in this example NP: *nekoliko uskih, strmih kamenom popločenih ulica* 'several narrow, steep, stone paved streets'.

(66) idemo   u   **Harry Potter Studio**   izlet
     go-1PL   to+ACC   Harry Potter Studio-NOM/ACC.M.SG   excursion-ACC.M.SG
     'We're going on a Harry Potter Studio excursion'. (D2,Gen.2,F,25)

   HMLD.Cro: Idemo na izlet u **studio Harryja Pottera**.

(67) onda   smo   na   internet   gledali
     then   AUX-1PL   on+LOC   internet-ACC.M.SG view-PAST.PL.M
     hrvatski   *Uskrs*   *pjesme*
     Croatian-ACC.M.SG   Easter-ACC.M.SG   song-ACC.F.PL
     'Then on the internet we watched Croatian Easter songs'. (D2,Gen.2 M,19)

   HMLD.Cro: Onda smo na internetu gledali **hrvatske**-ACC.F.PL **uskrsne**-
   ACC.F.PL pjesme

(68) morala   sam   uzeti   *moj*   *prvu*
     must-PST.F.SG   AUX-1SG   take-INF   my-NOM.M.SG   first-ACC.F.SG
     pomoć   *certifikat*   jer   je
     aid-ACC.F.SG   certificate-ACC.M.SG   because be-3SG
     istečen
     expire-PASSIVE.PTCP.M.SG
     'I had to take **my first aid certificate** because it is [= had] expired.'
     (D2,Gen.3,F,adult – age unknown)

   HMLD.Cro: morala sam položiti tečaj da dobijem **svjedodžbu** o osposo-
   bljenosti za pružanje **prve pomoći** jer je [prijašnja] svjedodžba istekla.

Examples (65) to (68) contain pre-posed attributives that internally contain components that determine their 'internal' head: in (65) *devet* 'nine' is a numeral that functions as an attributive to the following noun *sati* 'hours',[5] *u* 'at' preceding *devet sati* renders it an 'internal adverbial phrase of time'; in (66), the multi-item attributive *Harry Potter Studio* itself consists of a proper noun that is an attributive to *Studio*. In example (67), the attributive *hrvatski* 'Croatian' describes not *pjesme*

---

5 Some (e.g. Rutkowski 2002) argue that numerals in Slavic languages such as Polish should be considered grammaticalised nouns. From this perspective, *devet sati* 'nine o'clock' could be considered a compound noun consisting of two parts. We acknowledge the validity of this view, but as the grammatical role of numerals is not our focus here, we employ the conventional description of numerals as pre-modifiers of nominals.

'songs' but *Uskrs* 'Easter', and *hrvatski Uskrs* appears as an internal NP preceding the head noun *pjesme*. To be sure, both 'Croatian' (e.g. *hrvatske*-ACC.F.PL) and 'Easter' (e.g. *uskrsne*-ACC.F.PL) can be attributives to *pjesme*-ACC.F.PL 'songs', i.e. *hrvatske uskrsne pjesme* as shown in the HMLD.Cro equivalent. In (68) both the personal adjective *moj* 'my' and an NP *prvu pomoć* 'first aid' are attributives to another noun *certifikat* 'certificate'.

Examples (65) to (68) show that within NPs, 'internal' DET+NOUN islands can exist, where marking of phi-features relates to an internal head only, and not the head noun of the larger NP. This innovation is a change in the word order pattern of NPs. It is also a change in the position of 'bundles of referential content' that show a small and only emerging trend towards positions that equivalent English utterances occupy.

The following examples are uncommon ones and feature negation. Negation in Croatian (Stolac 2017b), as in all Slavic languages, is different from English and Germanic languages through the feature of 'negative concord' that requires that clauses with indefinite pronouns or adverbs also become negative pronouns or adverbs where the verb predicate contains a negative (Fitzgibbons 2008). The context of the following example was an informal chat between the second author and the informant about her future plans:

(69) *Hoćeš li dugo ostati u Hrvatskoj?* (D.S)
 Nikad znaš
 'You never know' (D2,Gen.2,F,33)

 HMLD.Cro: nikada **ne** znaš

In (69), the negative form of the adverb *ikada* 'ever', namely *nikada* 'never' occurs, as required in Croatian, but the NEG in the verb predicate is absent. This is unusual as negation of the adverb occurs only where there is a NEG verb. In English, negation can but need not be marked by *not* preceding the verb; negation can be marked via negative forms of adverbs such as *never, nowhere, not. . .any* or *no*, which, where they occur, are the sole markers of negation in a negative clause. Another similar example is recorded; this time from a Gen.3 speaker:

(70) *Nikad kažeš*.
 'You never say that' (D2,Gen.3,M,35)

 HMLD.Cro: Nikad **ne** govoriš o tome. ['Never NEG speak-2SG about that']

Negative adverbs *without* a NEG verb are uncommon in diaspora Croatian, although Mønnesland (1989: 97) reports a similar example from Norway-born children: *niko je mogao dati pare* 'no one could give any money' and identifies the Norwegian equivalent *Ingen kunne gi penger* as the likely source of influence, cf. HMLD.Cro: *niko **ni**je mogao dati pare*. Starčević (2014: 238) also locates similar examples from a Gen.2 speaker in Canada, e.g. *barem bi znala abecedu il brojit, al ja ne mislim da sam ja ništa znala* 'at least I would have known the alphabet or how to count, but I don't think that I knew nothing'. Cf. HMLD.Cro: *barem bi znala abecedu il brojit, al ja ne mislim da ja **ni**sam ništa znala*. Instances of negative marking on adverbs and not on verbs are also recorded in HUN.Cro (see Ščukanec, Breu and Vuk, this volume).

We conclude this section with an example of agreement marking within an NP containing a numeral following the rules of English syntax rather than those of Croatian. In English, all nouns succeeding a numeral with a numerical quantity of two (2) or more are marked with plural, i.e. *–s*. In Croatian, numerals that end in *jedan* 'one' (–1), such as those between 21 and 91 inclusive, that is *dvadeset i jedan* (lit. 'twenty and one' – '21'), *trideset i jedan* (lit. 'thirty and one' – '31', *četrdeset i jedan* (lit. 'forty and one' – '41') etc., require the succeeding noun to be in the singular. The syntactic feature of *jedan* 'one' being singular overrides the fact that a number such as '21' or '31' logically refers to a plural number of referents. In (71), a second-generation speaker relates the number of apartments that her cousin manages on the island of Korčula:

(71) moja   rodica   na   Korčuli   radi
     my-NOM.F.SG cousin-NOM.F.SG   on+LOC   Korčula-LOC.F.SG work-3SG
     u   turizam   i   ima   dvadeset i **jedan**
     in+LOC   tourism-ACC.M.SG   and   have-3SG   twenty and **one**
     apartmani
     apartment-NOM.M.<u>PL</u>
     'My cousin in Korčula works in tourism and has twenty-one apartment<u>s</u>.'
     (D2,Gen.2,F,25)

In HMLD.Cro, the last NP would be: *dvadeset i jedan apartman*-ACC.M.SG. For a fuller analysis of this, see Stolac (2019: 294–295) and Stolac and Vlastelić (2018). This example of non-agreement in number between the numeral and the succeeding NP is analogous to examples (45) to (49) above that contain grammatically singular subjects, e.g. *mafija* 'mafia', *svit* 'people'/'folk', *moja obitelj* 'my family' that are conceived of as designating a referent that is logically plural that requires plural-marking on verbs.

4.4.5 Lexical and syntactic transference

This last section presents examples containing lexical transfers or code-switching that themselves appear to be catalysts of morphosyntactic innovations, although we are hesitant to locate causality in this direction only; it could be that morphosyntactic innovations facilitate the insertion of lexical transfers or the activity of code-switching. In example (67) below, there is only one (phonologically integrated) lexical transfer employed, *remember*:

(72) to   je   možda   najbolje   što
      that-NOM.N.SG be-3SG   perhaps   best-NOM.N.SG   INDF.PRON.ACC
      sam   ja   **što**   ja   **rememba**   yeah
      AUX-1SG   I   INDF.PRON.ACC   I   **remember**   yeah
      '. . .that's maybe the best [thing] that I have, that I remember.. yeah.'
      (D1,Gen.2,M,20)

   HMLD.Cro. to je možda najbolje što sam, čega-INDF.PRON.GEN se-REFL ja sjećam-1SG

The verb *rememba* is not *morphologically* integrated, i.e. its verbal morphology does not show Croatian phi-features and this necessitates production of the subject pronoun *ja* 'I' for this to be made clear. The verb *rememba* is used here transitively, with the experiencer *ja* 'I' marked in subject position, and the experienced *što* 'what-INDF.PRON.ACC' as a direct object. This is a construction that is different from the equivalent Croatian one that has a reflexive verb *sjetiti se* PFV / *sjećati se* IPFV and the experienced object in GEN. The verb *rememba* is not only a lexical import into Croatian, it co-occurs with a SBJ + DIR.OBJ construction that is otherwise not known in HMLD.Cro. To see if this new construction is specific to this example containing the transfer *remember*, or if the SBJ + DIR.OBJ construction may be an emerging construction that is otherwise found in AUS.Cro, we look at all examples where *sjetit se / sjećati se* 'to remember' occur in the sample. There are 19 examples and 17 of these contain an accompanying REFL particle. In the first place, this statistic tells us that in the vast majority of instances the notion of 'remember' is expressed via Croatian, rather than English lexemes, and that the target lexico-grammatical features of the Croatian verb are also employed. However, there are two examples in which there is no REFL and the experienced action is in ACC case, ie. a DIR.OBJ.

(73) kao **neke**   stvari   ne   **sjećam**   baš
     like **some**-ACC.F.PL **thing**-ACC.F.PL NEG **remember**-1SG really
     dobro   kao   gdje   su   mjesta
     good-ADV like where be-3PL place-NOM.N.PL
     . . .like some things I don't remember really well, like.. where the places. . .(D1,Gen.2,M,22)

Example (73) is one of the two examples in which *sjetiti se / sjećati se* is employed without a REFL with the experienced object in ACC. As there are instances with Croatian lexemes only in which the REFL is not employed and the object occurs as an ACC, we cannot clearly locate causality: it could be that production of *rememba* brings about accompanying morpho-syntactic changes; it could be that grammatical transference shown by the replication of an English-based construction SBJ + DIR.OBJ enables the insertion of the lexical transfer *rememba*; it could be that both phenomena are occurring contemporaneously and causality is coming from both directions and combining to result in a form such as *rememba*.

5 Conclusion

A large number of phenomena are presented in this chapter and this conclusion summarises the findings of both datasets. Lexical transference from English is widespread with a general correlation of quantity of input from English and likelihood of phonological and/or morphological integration of transfers according to generational membership of the speaker – from Gen.1A, through to Gen.1B, Gen.2 and Gen.3. English-origin lexical transfers can function as 'additions' to speakers' repertoires, but need not as is shown by 62% of the integrated transfers that co-occur with Croatian equivalents (at least across the sample, if not within the same speaker's speech). There is some evidence that integrated transfers are more recurrent and more widespread than unintegrated transfers: 50% of the integrated transfers occur two or more times across dataset 1, while 71% of the unintegrated transfers are nonce occurrences.

Unsurprisingly, nouns predominate as the most widespread part of speech, with adjectives (usually co-occurring with English-origin nouns) the second most highly represented category. Verbs are rarely transferred, but where this occurs, these are likely to be morphologically integrated. English-origin items are most likely to occur as single-word transfers, rather than within multiple-word code-switched segments. The single largest number of English origin transfers occur 'outside' clause boundaries as discourse-motivated 'extra-clausal' transfers that are not part of the morphosyntactic grid of clauses.

Poly-functional *yeah* is used as an affirmative, pause-filler, turn-terminator as well as other functions. The frequency of English-origin discourse markers represents not only an instance of pragmatic transference – the adoption of the features of Australian English when speaking Croatian – but also, to an extent, the adoption of the pragmatic *forms* themselves. Examples of these are *you know, so* and *like*.

Phraseological calques are recorded as well as loan translations of equivalent English discourse segments. We note their incidence, and hypothesise that for some speakers, their occurrence may be motivated by a desire to avoid multiple-item code-switching into English. At the same time, we hypothesise that other speakers may employ multiple-item transfers to avoid the semantic or structural 'mixing' of their languages that calquing may represent. Amongst some calques, we locate employment of *raditi* 'to work' as a desemanticised *do*-verb, where referential content is carried by the NPs. An apparent reliance on NPs as the main carriers of referential content in some utterances is ascertainable in the speech of some speakers.

In regard to structural characteristics, a number of observations can be made. Amongst Gen.1A, Gen.1B and Gen.2 informants, there is little evidence to support the oft-mentioned hypothesis that oblique case marking is a category that undergoes attrition. There are comparatively few examples to show that this is happening: 91% of NPs have 'target' case marking. Even where NPs in NOM case are excluded, the percentage of instances of non-target case rises to only 15%. Where non-target case marking occurs, our data support the expectations of Ďurovič's (1983) model of case implicativity in relation to the employment of other cases to express syntactic relations of indirect object (DAT), instrumental (INS) or locative (LOC). This finding is congruent to Polinsky's (2018: 2014) observation that "case restructuring is subject to pressures from one-to-one mapping and overgeneralization".

A number of instances of changes in gender marking are reported on the basis of phonotactic or consonant-final features of some FEM.II nouns that attract MASC marking. The number of these is far greater than the number of non-target forms recorded in relation to number, while almost no non-target forms are found in relation to person. The small number of non-target number forms relate to grammatically SG nouns that are the subjects of PL verbs on the basis of influence of the lexico-semantic marking of equivalent English nouns such as *family* or *majority*, which usually co-occur with PL verbal marking in English. These findings are congruent to diaspora varieties of other languages with morphological marking of person, number and case, e.g. American Hungarian (Fenyvesi 2000) or marking of person, number, gender and case, e.g. American Russian (Polinsky

2000). A distribution of non-target forms shows that those relating to gender are more numerous than those relating to number. In turn, non-target forms relating to number are more numerous than those relating to person. These findings from Sections 4.4.1.2 and 4.4.1.3 are congruent to Harley and Ritter's (2002) hierarchical conceptualisation of phi-features. Gender is, they argue, more prone to change than number or person.

There are a small number of examples of *jedan* 'one' being employed as an indefinite article, and this appears to be emergent in only a small number of speakers' repertoires. Use of *jedan* as an article-like form occurs preceding English-origin nouns as well as preceding Croatian nouns. This development is one that appears to go beyond use of *jedan* as a "presentative marker" and one that has the functions of a "specific indefinite marker" (Belaj and Matovac 2015: 4), a term that refers to referents "known to the speaker but presumed to be unknown to the hearer, with the difference that the participant [referent] is not expected to be a major [focus of] discourse". This is a nascent development occurring in HMLD.Cro as well (Belaj and Matovac 2015).

There are few examples of verb valency change, and comparatively few examples of change found in Croatian reflexive verbs that are statistically much more frequent than they are in English. Few examples of non-target use of verbal aspect occur. Where these occur, PFV forms replace IPFV ones.

Subject pronoun overtness is a comparatively commonplace feature of AUS. Cro. We locate pragmatic features, i.e. the dialogic and narrative features that pertained in the data collection situations as a primary cause of this, ahead of structurally-based changes that may be precipitating the loss of pro-drop. At the same time, we do not discount that changes in pragmatic function can and do lead to structural realignments. To an extent, an analogous change is also found in some speakers' repertoires in which object pronouns are employed in the overt or full form, rather than via clitics. Word order changes on the basis of avoidance of use of clitics are not recorded. The position of adverbs is changing in some instances, which can be partly accounted for on the basis of the lesser reliance of verbs as carriers of referential content. Within some NPs, there are instances of multiple pre-posed attributives that do not bear agreement markers with the phi-features of the head noun. Changes in feature marking within NPs (Section 4.4.4.) are mirrored by fewer examples of changes occurring in VPs (Section 4.4.5). This finding is congruent to a general trend observed across many heritage languages that nominal morphology is more susceptible to change than verbal morphology (Polinsky 2018).

This chapter presented examples from two datasets that encompass speakers of different generations and of different vintages of emigration. In regard to the latter feature, there is little evidence that the linguistic forms used by more recently arrived Gen.1 speakers are different to those used by Gen.1 speakers of older vintages of migration. Admittedly, this remains a very general observation as this feature was not applied as a variable in categorising different groups of speakers. Similarly, the speech patterns of Gen.2 speakers whose parents are from older vintages of migration do not, at least superficially, stand out as different from those of Gen.2 speakers of more recently arrived parents. Further, the small number of examples from Gen.3 speakers allows us to make only the most general of statements that features of their speech appear similar to those of most Gen.2 speakers.

References

ABS (Australian Bureau of Statistics). 2011. Quick Stats for 2011 Census Collection. http://www.censusdata.abs.gov.au/census_services/getproduct/census/2011/quickstat/0 (accessed 12 April 2019).

ABS (Australian Bureau of Statistics). 2016. Data analysis of 2016 Census. http://www.abs.gov.au/websitedbs/censushome.nsf/home/Data (accessed 12 April 2019).

Alexiadou, Artemis & Florian Schäfer. 2014. Towards a non-uniform analysis of naturally reflexive verbs. In Robert Santana-LaBarge (ed.), *Proceedings of the 31st West Coast Conference on Formal Linguistics*, 1–10. Somerville, MA: Cascadilla Proceedings Project.

Backus, Ad & Margreet Dorleijn. 2009. Loan translations versus code-switching. In Barbara Bullock & Almeida Jacqueline Toribio (eds.), *The Cambridge Handbook of Linguistic Code-switching*, 75–94. Cambridge: Cambridge University Press.

Barić, Eugenija, Mijo Lončarić, Dragica Malić, Slavko Pavešić, Mirko Peti, Vesna Zečević & Marija Znika. 1990. *Gramatika hrvatskoga književnog jezika, 2. izdanje* [Grammar of the Croatian literary language, 2nd ed.]. Zagreb: Školska knjiga.

Belaj & Branimir Darko Matovac. 2015. On the article-like use of the indefinite determiners *jedan* and *neki* in Croatian and other Slavic languages. *Suvremena lingvistika* 79. 1–20.

Blankenhorn, Renate. 2003. *Pragmatische Spezifika der Kommunikation von Russlanddeutschen in Sibirien. Entlehnung von Diskursmarkern und Modifikatoren sowie Code-switching*. Peter Lang, Frankfurt am Main.

Budak, Luka. 2008. Najstariji izvandomovinski studij, uz 25. obljetnicu hrvatskih studija na Sveučilištu Macquarie u Sydneyu [The oldest university-level program outside Croatia: On the occasion of the 25th anniversary of Croatian Studies at Macquarie University]. *Croatian Studies Review* 5(1). 177–184.

Clissa, John. 1995. *Language shift and diglossia among the Italo-Croatian migrants from the Molise in Western Australia. A preliminary study*. Perth: University of Western Australia. MA thesis.

Clyne, Michael. 2005. *Australia's language potential*. Sydney: University of New South Wales Press.

Colic-Peisker, Val. 2010. The Croatian community in Australia in the early 21st century: a demographic and socio-cultural transition. *Croatian Studies Review* 6. 53–68.

Community Languages Australia. 2018. Language policy. http://www.communitylanguagesaustralia.org.au/language-policy/ (accessed 12 April 2019).

Cvikić, Lidija, Zrinka Jelaska & Lana Kanajet Šimić. 2010. Nasljedni govornici i njihova motivacija za učenje hrvatskoga jezika [Heritage speakers and their motivation for learning Croatian]. *Croatian Studies Review* 6(1). 113–117.

De Houwer, Annick. 2007. Parental Language Input Patterns and Children's Bilingual Use. *Applied Psycholinguistics* 28(3). 411–424.

Doucet, Jacques. 1990. First generation Serbo-Croatian speakers in Queensland: language maintenance and language shift. In: Suzanne Romaine (ed.). *Language in Australia*, 270–284. Cambridge, UK: Cambridge University Press.

Dressler, Wolfgang. (ed.) 1987. *Leitmotifs in natural morphology*. Amsterdam: John Benjamins.

Ďurovič, Ľubomír. 1983. The case systems in the language of diaspora children. *Slavica Lundensia* 9. 21–94.

Ďurovič, Ľubomír. 1984. The diaspora children's Serbo-Croatian. In Benjamin Stolz, I. R. Titunik & Lubomir Doležel (eds.), *Language and literature theory*, 19–28. Ann Arbor: University of Michigan.

Ďurovič, Ľubomír. 1987. The development of grammar systems in diaspora children's language. *Slavica Lundensia* 11. 51–85.

Ďurovič, Ľubomír. 1988. The concept of diaspora language. *Slavica Lundensia* 12. 7–9.

Fenyvesi, Anna. 2000. The affectedness of the verbal complex in American Hungarian. In Anna Fenyvesi & Klara Sándor (eds.) *Language contact and the verbal complex of Dutch and Hungarian: Working papers from the 1st Bilingual Language Use Theme Meeint of the Study of Language Contact, 11–13 November, 1999, Szeged, Hungary*. 94–107. Szeged: JGyTF Press.

Filipović, Rudolf. 1961. The morphological adaptation of English loan-words in Serbo-Croat. *Studia Romanica et Anglica Zagrabiensia* 11. 91–104.

Filipović, Rudolf. 1980. Transmorphemization: Substitution on the morphological level reinterpreted. *Studia Romanica et Anglica Zagrabiensia* 25. 1–8.

Filipović, Rudolf. 1986. *Teorija jezika u kontaktu*. [A theory of languages in contact] Zagreb: Školska knjiga.

Fitzgibbons, Natalia. 2008. Freestanding Negative Concord Items in Russian. *Nanzan Linguistics: Special Issue* 3(2). 51–63.

Goss, Emily & Joseph Salmons. 2000. The evolution of a bilingual discourse marking system: Modal particles and English markers in German-American dialects. *International Journal of Bilingualism* 4(4). 469–484.

Harley, Heidi & Elizabeth Ritter. 2002. Person and number in pronouns: a feature geometric analysis. *Language* 78. 482–526.

Heath, Jeffrey. 1989. *From code-switching to borrowing: A case study of Moroccan Arabic*. London: Kegan Paul International.

Herbert, Robert. 1986. *Language universals, markedness theory, and natural phonetic processes*. Berlin: Mouton de Gruyter.

Hlavac, Jim. 1999a. 32 years on and still triggering: Psycholinguistic processes as motivation for switching amongst Croatian-English bilinguals. *Monash University Linguistics Papers* 2(1). 11–24.

Hlavac, Jim. 1999b. Phonological integration of English transfers in Croatian: Evidence from the Croatian speech of second-generation Croatian-Australians. *Filologija* 32. 39–74.

Hlavac, Jim. 2000. *Croatian in Melbourne: lexicon, switching and morphosyntactic features in the speech of second-generation bilinguals*. Melbourne: Monash University. PhD thesis.

Hlavac, Jim. 2003. *Second-generation speech. Lexicon, code-switching and morpho-syntax of Croatian-English bilinguals*. Bern: Peter Lang.

Hlavac, Jim. 2006. Bilingual discourse markers: Evidence from Croatian-English code-switching. *Journal of Pragmatics* 38(11). 1870–1900.

Hlavac, Jim. 2009. Hrvatski jezik među Australcima hrvatskog jezika [Croatian language maintenance amongst Croatian-Australians]. In Jagoda Granić (ed.), *Jezična politika i jezična stvarnost* [Language Policy and Language Reality], 84–94. Zagreb: Croatian Applied Linguistics Society.

Hlavac, Jim. 2011. Hesitation and monitoring phenomena in bilingual speech. A consequence of code-switching or a strategy to facilitates its incorporation? *Journal of Pragmatics* 43. 3793–3806.

Hlavac, Jim. 2012. Psycholinguistic, metalinguistic and socio-psychological accounts of code-switching: a comparative analysis of their incidence in a large Croatian-English sample. *Suvremena lingvisika / Contemporary Linguistics* 73. 47–71.

Hlavac, Jim. 2015. Language maintenance and sociolinguistic continuity among two groups of first-generation speakers: Macedonians from Aegean Macedonia and the Republic of Macedonia. In John Hajek & Yvette Slaughter (eds.), *Challenging the monolingual mindset*, 131–148. Bristol: Multilingual Matters.

Jakobson, Roman. 1936. Beitrag zur allgemeinen Kasuslehre. *Travaux du Cercle Linguistique de Prague* 6. 240–288.

Jutronić-Tihomirović, Dunja. 1985. *Hrvatski jezik u SAD.* [The Croatian language in the US] Split: Logos.

Kagan, Olga. 2005. In support of a proficiency-based definition of heritage language learners: The case of Russian. *International Journal of Bilingual Education and Bilingualism* 8(2–3). 213–221.

Katičić, Radoslav. 1991. *Sintaksa hrvatskoga književnog jezika* [A syntax of the Croatian literary language]. Zagreb: Hrvatska akademija znanosti i umjetnosti / Globus Nakladni zavod.

Kostić, Đorđe. 1986. *Operativna gramatika srpskohrvatskog jezika* [An operational grammar of Serbo-Croatian]. Beograd: Prosveta.

Lalich, Walter. 2010. The Croatian language in the expanding transnational space. *Croatian Studies Review* 6(1). 31–52.

Lanza, Elizabeth & Bente Svendsen. 2007. Tell me who your friends are and I might be able to tell you what language(s) you speak: social network analysis, multilingualism and identity. *International Journal of Bilingualism* 11(3). 275–300.

Maschler, Yael. 2000. What can bilingual conversation tell us about discourse markers? *International Journal of Bilingualism* 4(4). 437–445.

Matras, Yaron, 2000. Fusion and the cognitive basis for bilingual discourse markers *International Journal of Bilingualism* 4(4). 505–528

Mesarić Žabčić, Rebeka. 2010. Katolička crkva kao nositelj očuvanja hrvatskog identiteta u državi New South Wales u Australiji [The role of the Catholic Church in the preservation of Croatian identify in New South Wales, Australia]. *Croatian Studies Review* 6(1). 129–140.

Mesarić-Žabčić, Rebeka. 2014. The phenomenon of overseas chain migration to Australia. *Croatian Studies Review* 10. 133–150.

Miller, Jim. 2009. *Like* and other discourse markers. In Pam Peters, Peter Collins & Adam Smith (eds.), *Comparative studies in Australian and New Zealand English*, 317–337. Amsterdam: John Benjamins.

Mønnesland, Svein. 1987. Norwegian interference in the language of Yugoslav children in Norway. *Slavica Lundensia*. 11, 87–99.

Myers-Scotton. Carol. 1993. *Duelling Languages: Grammatical Structure in Codeswitching*. Oxford: Clarendon Press.

Myers-Scotton, Carol. 2002. *Contact Linguistics. Bilingual Encounters and Grammatical Outcomes*. Oxford: Oxford University Press.

Peti-Stantić, Anita, Hrvoje Japirko & Marin Kežić. 2016. Koliko su lagani tzv. lagani glagoli u hrvatskom? [How light are so-called 'light' verbs in Croatian?] *Filološke studije* 14. 202–225.

Polinsky, Maria. 2000. The composite linguistic profile of speakers of Russian in the US. In Olga Kagan and Benjamin Rifkin (eds.) *The Learning and Teaching of Slavic Languages and Cultures*, 437–465. Bloomington, IN: Slavica.

Polinsky, Maria. 2018. *Heritage Languages and Their Speakers*. Cambridge, UK: Cambridge University Press.

Price, Charles. 2001. The ethnic character of the Australian population. In James Jupp (ed.), *The Australian people: an encyclopaedia of the nation, its people and their origins*, 78–85. Cambridge, UK: Cambridge University Press.

Romaine, Suzanne & Deborah Lange. 1991. The use of like as a marker of reported speech and thought: A case of grammaticalization in progress. *American Speech* 66(3). 227–276.

Rutkowski, Paweł. 2002. Numerals as grammaticalised nouns: A generative approach. *Interlingüística* 13(3). 317–328.

Salmons, Joe. 1990. Bilingual discourse marking: code switching, borrowing and convergence in some German-American dialects. *Linguistics* 28. 453–480.

Sankoff, Gillian, Pierrette Thibault, Naomi Nagy, Hélène Blondeau, Marie-Odile Fonollosa & Lucie Gagnon. 1997. Variation in the use of discourse markers in a language contact situation. *Language Variation and Change* 9. 191–217.

Schiffrin, Deborah. 1987. *Discourse Markers*. Cambridge University Press, Cambridge UK.

Starčević, Anđel. 2014. *Hrvatski i engleski jezik u dodiru: hrvatska iseljenička obitelj u Kanadi*. [Croatian and English in contact: an immigrant Croatian family in Canada]. PhD dissertation. Faculty of Humanities and Social Sciences, University of Zagreb.

Stolac, Diana. 2017a. Odnos nasljednoga jezika i standardnoga hrvatskog jezika u govoru povratnika. [The relationship of heritage language and Standard Croatian in the speech of returnees]. In Marin Sopta, Vlatka Lemić, Mijo Korade, Ivan Rogić & Marina Perić Kaselj (eds.), *Hrvatska izvan domovine (II.)* [Croatia outside the homeland II.], 675–683. Zagreb: Centar za istraživanje hrvatskog iseljeništva & Centar za kulturu i informacije Maksimir.

Stolac, Diana. 2017b. Genitive of negation in the Croatian language. *Jezikoslovlje* 18(1). 101–123.

Stolac, Diana. 2019. Sročnost u jeziku Hrvata u Australiji [Syntactic agreement in the language of Australian Croats]. In Ivana Vidović-Bolt (ed.), *Zbornik s međunarodnoga znanstvenog skupa Komparativnoslavističke lingvokulturalne teme (KOMPAS)* [Edited volume of KOMPAS, an international conference on comparative Slavic and linguistic-cultural themes], 289–297. Zagreb: Srednja Europa.

Stolac, Diana & Anastazija Vlastelić. 2018. Agreement in the language of Croats living in English-speaking countries. *Paper presented at the 2nd International Conference on Multilingual Education in Linguistically Diverse Contexts (MELDC18)*, University of Malta, Valetta, 30–31 August.

Surdučki, Milan. 1978. *Srpskohrvatski i engleski u kontaktu*. [Serbo-Croatian and English in Contact] Novi Sad: Matica srpska.

Škvorc, Boris. 2006. Hrvatski uokviren engleskim: jezik australskih Hrvata kao prvi i drugi jezik [Croatian framed by English: the language of Australian Croatians as their first and second language.]. *Lahor. Časopis za hrvatski kao materinski, drugi i strani jezik* [Lahor. Journal of Croatian as a native, second and foreign language] 1(1). 15–26.
Šutalo, Ilija. 2004. *Croatians in Australia. Pioneers, Settlers and their Descendants*. Kent Town, SA: Wakefield Press.
Šutalo, Ilija. 2010. The future of the Croatian community and identity in Australia. *Croatian Studies Review* 6(1). 7–30.
Thomason, Sarah. G. 2001. *Language contact. An introduction*. Edinburgh: Edinburgh University Press.
Tkalčević, Mato. 1992. *Hrvati u Australiji* [Croats in Australia]. Zagreb: Nakladni zavod Matice hrvatske.
Turk, Marija. 2013. *Jezično kalkiranje u teoriji i praksi. Prilog lingvistici jezičnih dodira* [Linguistic calquing in theory and practice. A contribution to language contact linguistics]. Zagreb: Hrvatska sveučilišna naklada & Filozofski fakultet Sveučilišta u Rijeci.
Winter, Jo & Anne Pauwels. 2006. Language maintenance in friendships: second-generation German, Greek and Vietnamese migrants. *International Journal of the Sociology of Language* 180. 123–139.
Wurzel, Wolfgang. 1984. *Flexionsmorphologie und Natürlichkeit*. Berlin: Akademie-Verlag.

New Zealand

Hans-Peter Stoffel and Jim Hlavac
Croatian dialect speakers from Dalmatia and their linguistic contact with English and Māori in New Zealand

1 Introduction

Croatian immigrants and their descendants in New Zealand (Aotearoa in the Māori language) have been characterised by their Dalmatian-Adriatic origin ever since the arrival of the first settlers in the second half of the 19th century. They came from the coastal areas between Omiš and the Peninsula of Pelješac, its hinterland between Imotski and the estuary of the Neretva River, and from the islands of Brač, Hvar, Vis and Korčula. Their speech, here subsumed under the designation of New Zealand Croatian (hereafter NZ.Cro) was and remains dialect-based. Many NZ Croatians have relatives who migrated from the same areas of Dalmatia to North and South America, and to Australia. Several of the varieties of Croatian spoken in those countries are likely to be similar to NZ.Cro and comparisons are occasionally made with other diaspora varieties of Croatian in the English-speaking 'New World' (Albin 1976, Albijanić 1982; Filipović 1985; Jutronić-Tihomirović 1985).

On the other hand, there are also several features which are unique to NZ.Cro and this chapter presents speech and sociolinguistic data on a diaspora community going back to its pre-WWI pioneers. The earliest first-generation migrants all worked as *gumdiggers* excavating the fossilised resin of the fallen kauri trees in the north of NZ. They formed linguistic enclaves resulting in the creation of a vocabulary of widely used professionalisms encompassing lexical transfers and adaptation patterns that became recurrent across the speech community.

The history of the Croatian community in NZ has been extensively researched. The community's main chroniclers are Trlin (1979), Jelicich and Trlin (1997), Jelicich (2008) and Dragicevich (2017). Monographs from Croatia-based authors include those by Čizmić (1981), Klarić (2000) and Božić-Vrbančić (2008), while a brief historical overview is also given by Stoffel (2009). The theme of Croatians and Croatian settlement in New Zealand has been written about by the NZ-born Croatian-origin writer Amelia Batistich (1915–2004) who is known throughout NZ through her stories and novels, all written in English.

Hans-Peter Stoffel, University of Auckland
Jim Hlavac, Monash University

https://doi.org/10.1515/9781501503917-013

In regard to the language of NZ Croatians, the first author of this chapter has investigated the speech of Croatian immigrants from Dalmatia in contact with English and Māori, with an emphasis on the 'language of the gumdiggers', on sociolinguistic aspects and the history of their linguistic integration into the host society.[1] His findings have been published in some 20 articles that have appeared between 1970 and 2013 and are mentioned in this chapter where relevant. Only Besides him, Jakich (1975) provided a description of the transference of features from NZ English onto NZ.Cro amongst speakers in the Wellington area and later published a short survey on NZ.Cro (1987) while in her study Janković-Kramarić (2001) concentrates on the ethnic identity of Auckland Croatians. A comparison with studies on Croatian in North America (Albin 1976; Jutronić 1976, Jutronić-Tihomirović 1985; and Surdučki 1978) is given in this chapter, while a previous study (Stoffel 1991) provided a comparative overview of morphological adaptation of loanwords across different diaspora settings. A distinguishing feature of the description of Croatian in New Zealand is that there are linguistic maps on NZ.Cro and on the northern area of NZ where data for Sample A (see below Table 1) was taken in an international linguistic atlas (Stoffel 1996).

This chapter is structured in the following way: The remaining parts of this section present general demographic and sociolinguistic information on Croatian-origin residents in New Zealand and on Croatian-speakers in that country. Section 2 presents information on data collection with details of the different groups of information and different collection periods that make up both datasets. Section 3 presents data on informants' sociolinguistic profiles with mention of a small number of trilingual Croatian-Māori-English families and trends in language maintenance and shift. Section 4 presents and discusses examples of linguistic data across the following fields: lexicon; pragmatics, i.e. discourse markers; semantics and loan translations; code-switching; morphosyntax. Section 5 contains the conclusion with findings summarised.

1.1 History of contact, vintages of emigration, status

New Zealand has, since the arrival of the British in the late eighteenth century, become a destination country for modest numbers of immigrants. In contrast to Australia, New Zealand does not have a national policy of multiculturalism, but an official policy of biculturalism, identifying Māori and Pākehā/European-descent New Zealanders as

---

[1] The first author, Hans-Peter Stoffel, wishes to express his gratitude to the University of Auckland Grants Committee for supporting data collection and field work across various time periods.

the two major ethnic groups, with Māori (te reo Māori) and English as its two main languages. In practice, there is some publicly-funded translation and educational support for other languages, such as Croatian that have no de jure status in New Zealand. By the end of the nineteenth century Croatians were one of the three major Continental European immigrant groups in NZ, along with Germans and 'Scandinavians'. Nowadays, Croatian is numerically a small language outnumbered by other, mainly Asian and Pacific languages spoken by more recent migrants. There have been five waves of Croatian immigration to New Zealand: the 1890s until World War I (approximately 5,000 arrivals); the 1920s (around 1,600 arrivals); the 1930s (about 600 arrivals); "a fluctuating flow from the late 1940s until the early 1970s (approximately 3,200 arrivals) and the latest during the 1990s" (Jelicich and Trlin 1997: 280). There are up to five generations of Croatian-New Zealanders, with some 23% of them having mixed Māori-Croatian parentage (Statistics NZ 2013; cf. also Božić-Vrbančić 2008). The median age of the group in 2013 was around 40; just over 50% of those declaring themselves Croatians had arrived in NZ more than 20 years ago.

1.2 Number of Croatian-heritage residents, number of Croatian-speakers

In the 2013 census collection, there are 2,673 New Zealand residents whose ethnicity is listed as 'Croatian' (Statistics NZ 2013). This number appears very low, considering long-standing and sizeable migration from Dalmatia over the last 125 years. In-group members estimate the number is much higher, e.g. 40,000 (Janković-Kramarić 2001) with a media source stating that "over 100,000 New Zealanders have Croatian heritage" (Fuseworks Media 2008). The total number of Croatian-speakers is similarly unclear. Census collections in NZ group Croatian with Serbian (under the term 'Serbo-Croatian'), of which there were 5,349 residents who reported speaking these languages at home. The actual figure of Croatian-speakers, with varying levels of proficiency, is higher. By subtracting the number of Serbian-speakers included within the designation 'Serbo-Croatian', and adding those who are likely to have proficiency as Gen.2 and Gen.3 second speakers but who did not declare this, there are likely to be up to 10,000 Croatian-speakers in NZ.

1.3 Geographical distribution, socio-economic profile

About 77% of all Croatians live in Auckland, especially its western suburbs, or in rural areas further north, centred around the towns of Dargaville, Whāngārei and Kaitāia (8.8%). The small settlement of Waiharara with its Sts. Cyrill and

Methodius Church north of Kaitāia is surrounded by a number of farms run by Croatians. Smaller groups live in Wellington (8.2%) and elsewhere in the North Island. Only about 5% live in the South Island (Statistics NZ 2013).

Within roughly 100 years Croatians have moved from the gumfields in the North (where they excavated the resin of fallen Kauri trees) to virtually all occupations in the highest ranks both in the private and the state sector. They belong to average and above average income groups. While the median income is NZ$29,500 and 38.7% are below this, there is also a considerable group with a high income of over NZ$70,000, and there have often been Croatian names on New Zealand's Rich List. Croatians also report a higher rate of university education, 27%, compared to the national average of 20%. Croatians' upward mobility can be attributed to their initial hard work as 'gumdiggers' or as fishermen, later establishing themselves as winemakers, farmers or owners of fishing businesses, or working self-employed or salaried in urban professions.

1.4 Infrastructure

There are two major clubs in Auckland: the Croatian Cultural Society and the Dalmatian Cultural Society with substantial club premises, with other smaller clubs in other towns as well. Only one specifically Croatian Catholic church exists. Language instruction is offered in clubs but usually just once a week and often just for short periods and for lower levels only. At Auckland University it is now sometimes taught only as a continuing (adult) education course. At higher levels funding is a problem. Modern colloquial Croatian is now more available due to access to electronic media in Homeland Croatian and to the influence of recent immigrants. There are Croatian football (soccer) and bocce (buće or boće) clubs in Auckland, and reflective of their integration into New Zealand society, also a Croatian rugby and cricket club.

1.5 Domain use, language maintenance and shift

Croatian dialects transposed to New Zealand in the late nineteenth century were passed on to New Zealand-born descendants. Croatian as spoken in New Zealand is still mostly dialect-based and the Dalmatian dialects are often mixed with elements from New Zealand English. It is spoken by older first-generation and second-generation speakers and it occupies a lower status in terms of prestige as expressed by speakers themselves, e.g. 'that mixed language' or *onaj pidžin* 'that pidgin' which still wields value as a marker of familiarity and locality.

As outlined above, exogamy is a feature of about half of Croatian family units (Jelicich and Trlin 1997) having the effect that only limited opportunity or effort is made to transmit the language on to the following generation. Even in endogamous households, transmission of the language is variable, and even where this happens, active use of it often ends when children leave the parental home. Inter-generational transmission of the dialect, and interest in the standard language is more widespread among families with a deeper interest in all things Croatian in general.

Language shift to English appears to be rapid beyond the first generation: 86% of those identifying as 'ethnic Croatians' born overseas claim proficiency in 'Serbo-Croatian' while the figure for those born in New Zealand is only 18% (Statistics NZ, 2013). At the same time, over 95% of all 'ethnically declaring Croatians' report proficiency in English, regardless of birthplace. Professed attitudes towards maintenance are high, but active involvement in language maintenance efforts is less enthusiastic, as evidenced by low attendances at classes offering instruction in Croatian.

1.6 Contacts with Croatia

Because of the 'tyranny of distance' felt by many living in the Antipodes, contact with Croatia was minimal until the 1950s but increased steadily from then until becoming frequent and even regular from the late 1980s. Electronic communication, cheaper airfares (in relation to income) and in- and out-migration have promoted contact, including linguistic interchange. Further immigration, as well as return migration have increased levels of contact as well.

1.7 Host society attitudes towards Croatians

The host society's attitude is clearly borne out by the title of Andrew Trlin's book published in 1979, *Now Respected, Once Despised*. Nowadays Croatians are highly regarded members of the Pākehā and the Māori host communities (Božić-Vrbančić 2008). The general standing of Croatians has also been enhanced by their contribution to cultural activities and public life in general. People such as New Zealand-born writer Amelia Batistich (1915–2004) and the painter Milan Mrkusich (1925–2018), as well as the considerable number of Croatians occupying public office as mayors and MPs have contributed to this. Along with them are the considerable number of Croatian-origin sportspeople, many of whom have represented New Zealand at the highest level.

2 Details of informants and data collection

Data that make up the sample for the sociolinguistic description (section 3) and for the presentation of linguistic data (section 4) come from various corpora and field work collections conducted over a number of years by the first author. There are three samples that form the largest part of the data corpus on which this chapter is based. The first sample (Sample A) is a collection of speech recordings together with sociolinguistic surveys that were undertaken in the 1970s and 1980s. Amongst the first-generation (hereafter 'Gen.1') informants of that sample were 8 pre-WWI informants, 'the pioneers' who had been in NZ for over 60 years. They had had very little if any formal schooling in Croatian prior to emigration. Second-generation (hereafter 'Gen.2') informants were middle-aged (40–50), while third-generation (hereafter 'Gen.3') informants were of school age or young adults. Sample A is the main sample from which examples of spoken NZ.Cro are presented here. The other two samples are collections of sociolinguistic data undertaken subsequent to Sample A. These collections took the form of questionnaires with follow-up interviewing of some informants as well.

Sample B was gained from Croatian-heritage Gen.2 and Gen.3 speakers who were attending formal instruction in Croatian at the University of Auckland. Sample C was gained from a random survey of residents with Croatian surnames in the telephone directory of Greater Auckland in 1990, which yielded 61 informants over three generations (Montgomery 1993; Stoffel 1994, 1996). A methodological detail in relation to data collection is that many potential informants could not participate as they had or claimed to have little or no proficiency in Croatian. Thus, this chapter presents data that is indicative of those New Zealanders who have proficiency in Croatian, but which may not be indicative of all Croatian-origin New Zealanders.

Table 1 presents an outline of the periods of data collection and the number of informants according to generation.

Table 1: Data samples and details on informants.

	Sample A			Sample B		Sample C	
Period of data collection	1970s–1980s			1981		1990	
Type of data	Recorded speech, socioling. questionnaires			Sociolinguistic questionnaires		Sociolinguistic questionnaires	
Gen. membership	Gen.1	Gen.2	Gen.3	Gen.2	Gen.3	Gen.1	Gen.2
No. of informants	19	21	3	8	8	22	31
Age ranges	70–90	40–50	12–25	18–20	18–20	70–90	45–75

All Gen.1 informants were born overseas with their L1 being the Štokavian-Ikavian or Šćakavian dialects of the coastal or hinterland areas of Dalmatia, or the Čakavian-Ikavian dialects spoken on islands along the Adriatic coast. The subsequent generations – Gen.2 and Gen.3 informants are NZ-born and English-dominant. Historically, the Gen.1 informants settled in rural areas in the northern-most 350 km of NZ with its provincial towns of Kaitāia and Dargaville. Many also settled in NZ's largest city Auckland, especially in its central and western suburbs, which still had a country atmosphere in the first half of the twentieth century.

Across all generations, social networks were close and supportive both in the country towns and in Auckland. Contacts with the outside world were less intensive for women on isolated farms. Contact with Croatia was mostly by letter after permanent settlement and arrival of more women from Dalmatia had started, but from the 1960s onwards travel to their former homeland, Yugoslavia, became a more frequent occurrence. The majority of the informants in country areas were blue-collar workers and farmers, those in Auckland white-collar workers.

Sample A informants were recorded in one-to-one interviews, but whenever possible larger groups (couples, families, social gatherings) were interviewed and recorded which enabled intra-group interaction and minimised the presence of the field-work researcher. Contact with many informants was substantial and recurrent: at least a quarter of the Sample A informants were visited several times over a period of one to five years for further interviews and later for casual visits. The oldest of them had passed away by the mid-1990s but contact was maintained with many of the Gen.2 and Gen.3 speakers until the mid-2000s. Unless stated otherwise, examples presented in this chapter are from Sample A.

The fieldworker and data-collector for the linguistic examples presented in this chapter is the first author, who, although not being an in-group member, collected a number of corpora from the speech community through systematic elicitation and data-gathering tools. But as a New Zealand co-resident, dialect speaker and fellow immigrant, and as a linguist not from the home-country sent to 'test their knowledge of Croatian' he became a peer or familiar contact person for many speakers of NZ.Cro. The length of recorded data with individual informants varies between 15 minutes to an hour or more per session. The original aim of recording informants' speech was to investigate vocabulary related to the men's employment – excavation of kauri resin – which then opened up to other topics of conversation. In addition to these formal samples, the contact of the first author with NZ.Cro speakers was substantial and on-going over the 43 years that he spent in the country. The perspective of the first author is therefore an ethnographic one, as observer or participant, as researcher or pedagogue, as acquaintance or friend to many if not most of the informants. Along with recorded interviews and sociolinguistic questionnaires, the first author's collected fieldwork includes taped radio broadcasts, collections of club notices, a large corpus of student language work, and hundreds of hours of systematic and non-systematic personal observation. In addition to examples from Sample A, there are some examples provided in this chapter that come from the first author's personal observations – these are marked as such (i.e. Stoffel – notes from research corpora). The first author counts himself particularly fortunate to have collected data not only from the pre-WWI pioneers, but also from the small group of Gen.2 Croatian-Māori-English trilinguals.

Examples of informants' speech are presented in section 4 in a way so that the orthographical representation of items reflects their phonological form: phonologically integrated English-origin items are represented according to Croatian orthography; unintegrated forms are presented according to their English spelling.

3 Sociolinguistic description

As stated above in section 2, the L1 for Gen.1 informants was a central-Dalmatian dialect. The Gen.1 early pioneers were exclusively monolingual Croatian dialect speakers when they arrived and formed linguistic enclaves. Remarkably, many came into contact with Māori before English: their fellow gumdiggers were usually Māori from whom they learnt some Māori; English was acquired to sell the gum resin at markets. For most of the Gen.2 and many of the Gen.3 speakers, NZ.Cro was the L1 in the home until they started school where, well into the 1960s, pressure to assimilate was strong and an 'English-only' sentiment pervaded. For some younger speakers, NZ.Cro was not only chronologically, but still 'emotionally' their L1. But in reality English became their dominant language in a way comparable to speakers in other, established Croatian communities such as those in Pennsylvania (Jutronić 1976) or the Dalmatian emigrants in California (Albin 1976).

During the assimilationist era, which in NZ lasted until the 1960s, sections of the host society were not positively inclined towards Croatians. This did not bother Gen.1 informants, or so they said, but "it was bad for the children". This led to assimilation and inter-marriage with other European communities, e.g. the Irish, who were also Catholic, and Māori (Stoffel 1982). This then hastened language shift to English, or at least to the use of both English and NZ.Cro at home, or in the case of the Dalmatian/Māori families, to English, Māori and NZ.Cro: *Māori su se šlagali š namin puno više nego ingleški narod*. 'The Māori got along with us much better than the English people' (Gen.1, Sample A). Croatians closer to Auckland fared better, and since the 1960s the concept of integration rather than assimilation has prevailed.

In regard to informants' self-reported oral and aural skills in Croatian, Gen.1 and Gen.2 informants are able to engage in conversation with others via NZ.Cro.

(The NZ census uses a similar formulation to gauge residents' linguistic skills.) While Gen.1 speakers report high levels of fluency, Gen.2 informants provided more varied responses on self-rated linguistic proficiency: good 40%; fair 30%; poor 30%. Gen.3 informants could often not sustain a conversation in NZ.Cro and reported usually code-switching or reverting to English. The Sample A informants, perhaps unsurprisingly, listed "understanding and listening to music", including weekly broadcasts in Croatian, as key language-based activities. But these were passive skills and promoted language maintenance amongst younger generation speakers only marginally.

At the time of the interviews in the 1970s and 1980s the first author had to consider only three domains in which Croatian was still used: 'family', 'neighbourhood', and 'community' with religion included in the latter. Gumdigging had long ceased as an occupation. This had a commensurate effect on the 'language of the workplace' that (mainly male) informants in the north of the country used. For those who established viticulture and horticultural businesses or farms, Croatian remained to an extent a workplace code. For those who became shop owners or white-collar workers, often moving south to the outer suburbs of western Auckland, the domain 'occupation' was largely Anglophone.

In the family domain, Gen.1 parents of a more recent vintage used both languages with children. In families with Gen.2 parents, either *both* languages or, much more often, English only, were used inter-generationally. Many Gen.2 and Gen.3 informants from Samples B and C commented that their parents' use of Croatian with them was: "the odd word", "rarely", "parents still use Croatian between themselves and with visitors but wouldn't speak it with us". Language shift to English had occurred for many by the third generation. For those in Auckland's western suburbs with its market gardens and vineyards, both Croatian and English were used in the neighbourhood domain. Maintenance of Croatian was higher for those in the isolated North in the neighbourhood domain, with more Croatian than English used, even amongst some Gen.2 speakers.

At community functions, such as club gatherings and festivities, including church and religious events, both languages were used. Language choice was oriented towards the generation and perceived proficiency in English or Croatian of the interlocutor. In studies of intra-group communication in Auckland in 1990 it was found that the influence of location and degree of formality in the relationship of the speakers on the language used in a particular situation was minor, and that age and whether a person was born and brought up in NZ or Croatia was more important than other criteria (cf. Montgomery 1993:10; Stoffel 1994). This feature guiding language choice could be applied to all samples. In some smaller settlements in the North, 'Croatian-only' or 'both languages' were used at public gatherings, often due to the presence of those still with little

English. Official business at club gatherings was discussed mainly in English. English was used, or followed by Croatian, for general announcements to all present, regardless of generation – a practice also observed in other ethnic clubs in NZ.

3.1 A brief description of Croatian-Māori-English trilingual families

An important sub-group from Sample A are families in which the (pioneer) husband from Dalmatia married a Māori woman who he had met on the gum fields. Data presented in this sub-section relate to Gen.1 and Gen.2 informants from Sample A. In the case of one Gen.1 informant who was the only member of the household who spoke Croatian, the home languages were English and Māori – the latter having been acquired by him. Croatian was not passed on to his wife or children who spoke Māori and English only (Stoffel 1988a: 367). A more unusual case is that of another Gen.1 Croatian husband who was illiterate when he arrived in NZ. He acquired some literacy with the assistance of his Māori wife (Stoffel 1988a: 368) who could hold a conversation in NZ.Cro 'at intermediate level'. His Māori wife acquired enough NZ.Cro and 'textbook Croatian' to compose letters to relatives back home in a form of standard Croatian. Some of their children also knew NZ.Cro but gradually lost it once they had left the family home. This type of mixed Dalmatian/Māori family generally considered itself Māori.

The fieldwork also included contact with the children (all Gen.2 men) of these mixed marriages. These informants rated their Croatian as 'fair', but their competence compared favourably with that of many Gen.2 informants of endogamous unions. While Croatian was spoken little in the home domain, it was spoken in the neighbourhood and at gatherings but there it had to compete with Māori. These families also regarded themselves as Māori (Stoffel 1988a: 367–68). Neither the wives nor children knew any Croatian but they took part in community events such as dancing *kolo* (a circle dance that features dancers linking arms) or playing *tamburica* (a traditional stringed instrument).

3.2 Integration into NZ society, language maintenance and language shift

At the beginning of their immigration to NZ some 80% of all Croatians went to the gumfields in the rural areas of the North. By the 1990s the great majority had moved to the provincial towns and to Auckland. Demographic and social factors such as concentration, continuity of settlement and endogamy were still strong features relating to those residing in Auckland's rural western suburbs and were factors supporting language maintenance. However, the profiles of Gen.3 informants in Auckland from sample A, and both Gen.2 and Gen.3 informants in Auckland from Samples B and C showed that education, social and economic mobility, together with increased exogamy, were now all clear-cut factors promoting language shift (Conklin and Lourie 1983: 53). Although immigration was continuing, it was minimal, and rather ominously Montgomery (1993:12) relates that "[n]ew immigrants will find that their NZ relatives' first language is English . . .". The cessation of new arrivals is reflected in the figure of only 3,500 "Yugoslav-born" [mostly Croatians] reported in census collections in the 1970s (Jelicich and Trlin 1997). This was yet another language shift factor and the community was concerned about its future and language maintenance. Unexpectedly, there would be a new influx of Croatian immigrants in the 1990s with a higher level of education and prior knowledge of English.

Questions regarding identity and maintaining and learning Croatian always received strong affirmative responses from informants of all samples. But more than 50% of respondents added qualifications, such as "is it realistic?" or "not at the expense of New Zealand or English". When asked where language should be learned the answer was mostly: "in the home, before school begins" which is often not congruent with what was found to be the case, at least from younger generation informants who reported on their home language(s). The informants from Sample C were less categoric about language maintenance, but gave a larger variety of responses about how this could be achieved: "teaching it after entry to school like a foreign language", "teaching it for travel", "for visiting relatives" or as "one of the BA options at university". The results of the Sample C survey led those analysing the results (Montgomery 1993; Stoffel 1994, 1996) to conclude that "the ardour for maintaining Croatian in Auckland was not matched by practical commitment, particularly in Gen.2 and Gen.3 [in 1990] . . ." (Montgomery 1993: 11). For most of the informants of these samples NZ.Cro in its dialect form offered little prestige and had formidable competition from English. But it has continued to hold an emotional value for many.

In all samples A, B and C, language maintenance is found to be best achieved in endogamous families who strive to maintain it, who have links with Croatia, and who are conscious of the need for its transmission to the following generation, or in the case of Gen.1 people only, those living alone. One Gen.2 informant argued that "with a special effort" it is also possible to maintain NZ.Cro in mixed households but there are few of these in the present samples, and the Māori/Croatian/English examples of trilingualism are now a thing of the past.

The NZ-born informants regarded themselves as New Zealanders of Croatian heritage. While they were still bilingual, many of their Croatian-origin friends were bicultural but no longer actively bilingual. In New Zealand a knowledge of the language was not regarded as a necessary part of Croatian heritage. This raises the question of the non-standard variety of NZ.Cro as a disincentive or handicap for its transmission (Clyne 2003: 53). In regard to instances in which formal instruction was offered, a problem that arose was that what was learnt or at least heard at home was not what they would learn in the clubs or at university where a standard variety of HMLD.Cro was taught. For example, dialectal forms such as *trpeza* (NZ. Cro 'table': HMLD.Cro 'dinner-table') became *stol* (HMLD.Cro 'table') and *katriga* or *katrida* 'chair' became *stolica* (HMLD.Cro 'chair'). Classes with formal instruction in Croatian have been available in Auckland from the major clubs, but these were taught by volunteers and only once a week and did not automatically continue to higher stages. The main problem was to attract and to hold on to younger students. Proficiency in Croatian amongst younger speakers was very variable and English soon became their dominant language. Standard HMLD.Cro was generally regarded highly, but at the same time criticised, especially by older Gen.1 speakers, when it was seen to contain too many "foreignisms" "contaminating the once beautiful Croatian language", or when they felt visitors from the homeland emphasized their knowledge of the standard too insensitively. These arguments are perhaps often 'pressed into service' by diaspora speakers who otherwise have few means to express their uneasiness towards standard, formal varieties to which they have (had) little access.

Support from the linguistic homeland, Croatia, has become a factor promoting LM amongst some, with travel to/from the homeland (visiting relatives, language courses, group travel of sporting clubs) frequent already prior to 1990. Since then, electronic and digital media have opened the way to practically unlimited direct and daily connections with Croatia. With more arrivals since 1990, the number of Croatian-speakers in NZ has increased. However, with language shift occurring with the older vintages of migration, the variety of Croatian spoken in NZ in the years to come may well be that of a transposed standard. Apart from language shift, integration into the host society also manifests itself in the preference for NZ food, NZ body language, adoption of NZ lifestyle and customs beginning already amongst Sample A informants and later most NZ Croatians. The changes of surnames remain, however, mostly confined to minor adaptations "to please [the] local population" (Gen.1, Sample A, pioneer, in English) and not carried out by all families with the same name: <Jeličić> to <Jelicich>, pronounced [ˈdʒɛlɪsɪtʃ], or <Brljević> to <Brylevich>.

4 Linguistic analysis of NZ Croatians' speech

An important consideration in language contact research is the form of the heritage language that is undergoing contact. In this case, it is not a standard variety of Croatian, but a group of central Dalmatian Štokavian-Ikavian or Šćakavian dialects and Čakavian-Ikavian dialects spoken mainly on the islands which were the L1 of all Gen.1 informants in this chapter. An important point of reference is the *Čakavisch-Deutsches Lexikon* 'Čakavian-German Dictionary' (Hraste, Šimunović, and Olesch 1979; hereafter 'ČDL') that describes the Čakavian dialects that were the homeland and heritage varieties of many of the Sample A informants. A further valuable source for all Dalmatian dialects is the *Dictionary of the Split dialect* by Magner and Jutronić (2006). Short descriptions of the Split dialect (Magner 1978; Stoffel 1994) and of the local dialects made at the time of the first author's recordings in the 1970s-80s (Šimundić 1971; Kaštropil 1970; Šimunović 1979) have been used for comparison and contrast. Albin's (1976) data from San Pedro also contains accentuated texts that are from emigrants with a similar dialect background. These comparisons allow a more informed analysis of features that may seem, at first glance, to be contact-induced when, in fact, they already existed in the homeland and were simply reinforced by the contact situation, as in the following:

(1) na   učilištu   **pasala**   dobro
at+LOC school-LOC.N.SG **pass**- PST.3SG.F well
'At school... she **passed** [her exams] well' (Gen.1, personal observation)

This example, containing what looks to be a morphologically integrated form of *pass* is most probably *not* a direct calque of Eng. 'to pass an exam'. A similar expression is given as an illustrative example in the ČDL (1979: 781):

(2) sin   mi   je   **paso**   sve
son-NOM.M.SG PRON.DAT 1SG AUX-3SG **pass**-PST.M.SG all-ACC.M.PL
ežame
exams-ACC.M.PL
'My son passed all exams'.

Example (2) shows that *pasat* 'to pass' (cf. Venetian Ital. *spassare* 'to pass') is or was a lexical form available in the informant's home language with the referential meaning 'to pass'. Use of *pasat* is likely to be reinforced by the homophonous form of its English equivalent, but the form itself is not a lexical transfer, even though it appears to be one. This underlines the need to have access to the form of speakers' home or heritage variety, which in this contact situation is rarely a standard one.

This section contains the following sub-sections, organised according to commonly reported contact linguistic phenomena and the incidence of these in the sample: 4.1 lexical transference, with further sub-sections presenting nouns, verbs, and derivation, suffixation; recurrence and co-occurrence with equivalent forms; 4.2 discourse markers; 4.3 semantic transference and loan translations; 4.4 code-switching; 4.5 morphosyntactic change, with further sub-sections on prepositions and periphrastic constructions, pronouns and agreement and non-agreement.

4.1 Lexical transference

In this section, lexical items that are of English or Māori origin are presented and examined. These are labelled here 'lexical transfers', a term that refers to the transfer of lexemes that occur in NZ.Cro speech. This term has no definitive criteria beyond 'transfer into' NZ.Cro and lexical transfers may or may not display any of the following: phonological, morphological and/or grammatical integration; high or low frequency in a speaker's repertoire; recurrence across speech community; apparent 'lexical need' for their occurrence; status as part of indigenous lexicon; metalinguistic awareness; result of diachronic process (Schatz 1989; Muysken 2000; Hlavac 2003). Lexical transfers presented here are mostly single-item or 'collocationally simplex' forms. These are typically, but not always, 'embedded' or 'inserted' in longer stretches of NZ.Cro speech. A strict distinction between lexical transfers and code-switching is not made here. Many of the same criteria listed above can apply to code-switches. Code-switches are distinguished here as multiple-item units or longer stretches of 'talk' from the other language (cf. 4.4).

As in other émigré settings, conspicuous examples of lexical transfer are realia which were new to the immigrants (see also Ščukanec; Piasevoli; Županović, Hlavac and Piasevoli; Jutronić; Petrović; Hlavac and Stolac; Skelin Horvat, Musulin and Blažević, all this volume). In the NZ.Cro sample, this includes forms such as *bordinauz* 'boarding-house' (Gen.1), *titra* 'ti-tree' (Gen.1), but also high-frequency words and phrases such as *plenti* 'plenty' (Gen.1–3), *juzit* 'to use' (Gen.1–3) and *trajat* 'to try' (Gen.1–3). English is not the only donor language for transfer. Transfers from Māori enter NZ.Cro either directly from the Māori language or via New Zealand English (hereafter: 'NZ.Eng'). The two most common in Sample A (Gen. 1–3) are: *tangi* 'funeral', and *kai* 'food'. Most transfers from Māori relate to Māori culture and society or denote NZ flora and fauna.

Phonological adaptation, at least for Gen.1 speakers, included frequent modification of consonants, e.g. *andervet* 'hundredweight', *šćudent* 'student', *nort* 'the North'. Vowels do not have a glide, and unstressed, reduced vowels of NZ.Eng are realised in a multitude of ways. NZ.Eng [ɜː] is rendered as [e], e.g.

edigedi 'hurdy-gurdy' (gumwashing device like an old washing machine), *bas* or *bos* 'bus' NZ.Eng [bɒs], *padek* 'paddock'. The phoneme /h/ does not exist in many speakers' dialects, resulting in *potol* for 'pothole', or *Teapua* for the place name 'Te Hāpua'. But amongst some speakers, standard Croatian /x/ is employed as an equivalent for /h/, e.g. *po* [*poć*] *na holidej* 'go on a holiday'. Surdučki (1978: 347) and Hlavac (2003: 61) also report variable employment of /x/ amongst speakers who do not have it in their home language variety.

In regard to morphological adaptation, there are two types of adaptation: paradigmatic and suffixal substitution. Adaptation occurs on the basis of word-final structure which follows Croatian word-final morphophonology. Almost all transfers of nouns are subject only to paradigmatic substitution; verbs are adapted by way of suffixal substitution; adjectives sometimes undergo no morphological adaptation, e.g. *bizi* 'busy', but they can have comparative desinences: e.g. *hardije* [hard-COMPARATIVE-ADJ-NOM.N.SG] 'harder' – *to je malo hardije* . . . 'this one [pointing to a piece of gum] is a bit harder' . . . (Stoffel – notes from research corpora).

Comparative adjectives can also be expressed by English-modelled periphrastic constructions, resulting in a 'double comparative' structure, characteristic also of non-standard varieties of English, including NZ English:

(3) **nomber ten** je više **streta**
 number ten be-3SG more **straighter**
 '[Road] **Number ten** is more **straighter**.' (Gen.1, Sample A)

The largest lexical field are occupation-specific terms relating to gumdigging, created by the Gen.1 pioneers. They consist of well over 200 different words and expressions and were used widely by all Gen.1 informants. These transfers were almost all completely adapted to the phonological system of NZ.Cro. This conforms to Jutronić's observations (1974:16) but contrasts with Albin (1976: 83) who found "unassimilated" transfers "rather common" in the speech of some of his Gen.1 informants. In NZ.Cro just a few transfers were only partially adapted morphologically, e.g. *gali* 'gully', but their fully-adapted doublets were used much more frequently: *gala* 'gully'. Phonological and morphophonological modification in the integration process of lexemes in NZ.Cro in many ways is found to follow the patterns of adaptation of transfers from Italian in the informants' home dialects in Croatia.

4.1.1 Nouns

The great majority of transferred lexemes are nouns, most of them ending in –Ø. Most are therefore assigned masculine gender in Croatian. Instances of epenthesis occur, e.g. *švanap* 'swamp', cf. *u švampiman* [in+LOC swamp-LOC.M.PL] 'in the swamps'. This occurs due to the phonotactic rules of some speakers' varieties that lead to *s* in initial position in consonant clusters becoming post-alveolar ʃ. Similarly, phonotactic conventions of some speakers do not allow nasal-initial consonant clusters leading to a change of nasal consonant from bilabial *m* to alveolar *n* in medial position between two vowels, cf. *kanap* in example (4) below. Other examples of changes according to phonotactic features of speakers' Croatian varieties are *špir* 'spear', *dos* or *dost* 'dust' (cf. Filipović 1961).

Instances of nouns with final vowels can lead to re-classification, here as an ADJ due to the suffix *–i*, e.g. *Sidni* 'Sydney' – *u Sidnom smo stali* . . . [in+LOC Sydney-ADJ.LOC.M.SG stay-PST.M.PL] 'In Sydney we stayed . . .' (Gen.1, Sample A). A change in the word class of an item from the donor language (noun) to the recipient language (adjective) is unusual, but possible where the item's features are congruent to a recipient paradigm (Field 2002: 17). (Cf. In Croatian, there are other place names for countries that are adjectives, e.g. *Hrvatska* 'Croatia', *Njemačka* 'Germany'). The city, *Grozny*, capital of Chechnya is also an adjective and declined in oblique cases, e.g. *u Groznom* in+LOC Grozny-ADJ.LOC.M.SG 'in Grozny'). Final plurals in <s>, phonetically [s] or [z], were reinterpreted as singular forms: *bojz* 'boy-SG' and *bojzi* 'boy-PL'. This is in line with Field's (2002:15) observation that items are perceived as monomorphemic in the recipient language, regardless of whether they may be multi-morphemic in the donor language:

(4) **pablik vorks**   *je*   **suplaja**   **kanap**
    public works   AUX-3SG   **supply**-PST.M.SG **camp**-ACC.M.SG
    'Public works supplied the camp'. (Gen.1, Sample A).

Transferred nouns ending in *-a* are less frequent. Adding *-a* can occur for monosyllabic words with a long vowel or in words with nasals or liquids but no clear-cut pattern can be established: e.g. *resa* 'race', *goma* 'gum', *marketa* 'market', *gambelja* 'gamble', *tanga* 'water tank', *šanda* 'shanty', e.g. *u nas je bilo . . . timber za učinit mu šandu* 'we had timber for him to build a shanty'. Apart from source words in *-a* there are some words ending in */i/* with specific consonant clusters that replace */i/* with -a or add the desinence -a. Some have lesser-used doublets keeping the */i/*, e.g. *titri*, or with *–a*, e.g. *titra* 'ti-tree', e.g. *sve u titran* 'everything was covered in ti-trees'. Word-final */ou/* can also be replaced by *–a*, e.g. *šal(ad)* 'shallow', e.g. *kopat na šal(ad)i* 'to dig on shallow land'. A number of word-final adaptations in */i/* to *-ija* can be explained by rhyme analogy with similar words in *-ija* denoting shops or places of work, eg *bučerija* 'butchery', cf. HMLD.Cro *pašticerija* 'pastry shop' (Magner and Jutronić 2006: 122). Just as the English-origin forms found in the speech of Gen.1 speakers reflect (or reflected) the contexts of their daily life, so too do those found in the speech of younger-generation speakers:

(5) *On rabota u* **Inland Revenue**.
'He works at the **Inland Revenue** [Department]'. (Gen.2. Sample A)

(6) *Moran pisat* **paper** *radi* **honours degree**.
'I have to write a **paper** for my **honours degree**.' (Gen.3. Sample A)

Transfers from English into NZ.Cro are comparable, though not completely identical, with those in other English-speaking countries. Thus, the phonological form of NZ English <box> resulted in *boksa* 'box' and *boksica* 'little box' (cf. *baksa* and *baksica* based on the North American forwarded pronunciation of the lower vowel – Albin and Alexander 1972: 71; Surdučki 1978: 44). (For further examples of the morphological and/or phonological integration of lexical transfers in other diaspora Croatian corpora, see: Ščukanec; Piasevoli; Županović Filipin, Hlavac and Piasevoli; Petrović; Hlavac and Stolac; Skelin Horvat, Musulin and Blažević, all this volume.) Lexical transfers occur in phrases that are based on a Croatian equivalent of an English collocation, e.g. *ić šopin* 'to go shopping' (Gen.1–3). Most single-item transfers are nouns or adjectives + nouns, and verbs. The examples given above are phonologically integrated, shown through the use of Croatian orthography here, and in the case of verbs, also morphologically integrated. Morphological integration is variable, usually depending on the generation of the speaker, e.g. *u* [in+LOC] *šediman* [šed-LOC.M.PL] *na* [on+LOC] *vorfu* [vorf-LOC.M.SG] 'in the sheds on the wharf' (Gen.1, Sample A). Gen.1 speakers morphologically integrate transfers except for proper nouns of Māori origin. Example (7) below contains an unintegrated Māori-origin place name from a Gen.2 speaker:

(7) otišli   su   u   **Wajharara**
    go-PST.M.PL AUX-3PL   to+ACC   **Waiharara**-NOM.F.SG
    'They went to **Waiharara**' (Gen.2, Sample B)

A narrower representation of the above form from this Gen.2 speaker would be [wɔj'haɹaɹə] which is its pronunciation in NZ.Eng; Gen.1 speakers are likely to pronounce it as [vaj'hararə]. The following example illustrates phonological integration going in an unexpected direction. Here, English-origin transfers remain phonologically and morphologically unintegrated into the Croatian grid of the utterance, but the *Croatian* items that form the morphosyntactic grid are subject to strong phonological transference from English:

(8) ona [ˈɔnə]   je[jə]   **artist**   piše[ˈpʰiʃə]   **books**
    she   be-3SG   **artist**   write-3SG   **books**
    'She's an **artist**; she writes **books**'. (Gen.2, Stoffel – notes from research corpora)

Integration of transfers can be prosodic too. Stress could fall on the preceding word (in the following in **bold**), where the transfer is preceded by a conjunction or preposition, e.g. on ima **i** fon. 'he's got the phone, **too**', **na** farmu '**on to** the farm'. Proclisis or accent shift to a preceding preposition or conjuction that is then prosodified with the succeeding word is a feature of many speakers' homeland varieties.

4.1.2 Verbs

All Gen.1 and most Gen.2 speakers adapt verbs by way of suffixal substitution into the *-i* or *-a* conjugations, e.g. *špira(va)t* 'to spear' (more specifically, 'to locate the gum using a long, thin spear') with PRS.1SG *špira(je)-n* 'I spear' and PST.1SG: *špira(-la) san* 'I speared', cf. *špira san gomu sa špiron* 'I searched for the gum with a spear'; *špeli(va)t* 'to spell', *špelivaš* PRS.2SG 'you spell'. In one transfer, *oškrepat* 'to scrape' PFV the addition of the prefix *–o* is modelled on the HMLD. Cro equivalent *ostrugati* 'to scrape'. Otherwise, the form of HMLD.Cro equivalents does not have a decisive factor in the morphological adaptation of lexical transfers. One poly-semantic English verb is recorded with two different meanings in NZ.Cro as well: *bakat* 'to back', e.g. *bakat karu* 'to back out a car' (= 'to drive a car in reverse') and the following meaning 'to back a horse' as in (9):

(9) konja   trče   ja   san   u   kući   ja   mogu
    horse-PL   run-3PL   I   be-1SG   in+LOC   house-LOC.F.SG   I   can-1SG
    bakat   ili   dat   komu   da   me   **baka...**
    back-INF or   give-INF   someone-DAT   COMP   me-ACC   **back-3SG**
    'The horses are running... I am at home, I can back them [bet on them] or give [money] to someone to back me [to bet on a horse on my behalf]....'. (Gen.1, Sample A)

As stated, English-origin verbs are almost always morphologically integrated. Further examples are, e.g. *implojit* 'to employ', *šprejit* 'to spray', *trajat* 'to try', *vokat* 'to walk', *ringat* 'to ring'/'to telephone'. The suffix *–ati* is found to be the most common verb suffix for transfers in AUS.Cro, along with *–ovati* (see Hlavac and Stolac, this volume), while in ARG.Cro, the most productive suffix is *–irati* (see Skelin Horvat, Musulin and Blažević, this volume). The form *ringat* 'to ring'/'to telephone' is a conventionalised transfer, found in many Croatian diaspora settings (Surdučki 1978; Hlavac 2003). Here, in example (10), the object of *ringat* 'to ring' is in DAT, as shown in this line from a humorous skit written by and for NZ Croatians:

(10) *Pipica   ja   ću   ti   **ringat**   lejta   kad   nisi*
     Pipitsa   I   FUT.AUX-1SG you-DAT **ring-INF** later when be-2SG.NEG
     bizi   *adio*
     busy   addio
     'Pipitsa, I'll **ring**-DAT you **later** when you aren't **busy**. Bye for now.'
     (Stoffel 2011: 391)

Most examples of *ringat* 'to ring' have an ACC object, cf. examples (25) and (32) below. To those recently arrived from the homeland, the transfer *ringat* was a source of delight as they associated it with 'ring a bell'. Gen.2 and Gen.3 speakers did not generally realise the fun of it all. An example of a morphologically (and phonologically) unintegrated verb from a Gen.2 speaker is given below:

(11) *u   Živogošće   ja   ću   **meet**   moje*
     in+LOC Živogošće-NOM.N.SG I FUT.AUX-1SG **meet**-INF my-ACC.M.PL
     rođake   tute
     relative-ACC.M.PL there
     'In Živogošće I will **meet** my relatives there' (Gen.2, Sample A)

Most English-origin verbs that appear in the infinitive are integrated. But it is perhaps not insignificant that the few verbs that remain unintegrated are infinitive forms as in (11) above, where morphological agreement with the subject is not required.

4.1.3 Derivation, suffixation, recurrence and co-occurrence with equivalent forms

Derivation and suffixation of transfers is evident in the gumdiggers' vocabulary that contains a wealth of fully integrated forms that attract suffixes, yielding semantic extensions, e.g. *maor-ski* (Māori-ADJ) 'Māori', *maor-ka* (Māori-FEM) 'female Māori', *inglez-ica* (English-FEM) 'Englishwoman'[='female New Zealander'], *drenčić* (drain-DIMIN) 'little drain', *padek* 'paddock' > *padekat-prepadekat* 'to dig up the gum systematically over a whole paddock'. These suffixes such as -*čić* and

-ina are productive in the homeland dialects of the speakers, and occur with Italianisms borrowed into varieties of HMLD.Cro (Gačić 1979:40; Stoffel 1983). A number of key-words in the gumdigging vocabulary have equivalents in the form of calques (see below section 4.3). They were used either in initial interviews, or when writing to the first author, or in written questionnaires. In (12) below, one speaker employs a commonly heard transfer, *gomdiger* 'gumdigger' uttered in casual speech.

(12) bilo je **plenti gomdigera**
 be-PST.3SG.N AUX-3SG plenty+GEN gumdigger-GEN.M.PL
 'There were **plenty of gumdiggers**' (Gen.1, Sample A)

In example (12), not only does *gumdigger* occur as a morphologically and phonologically integrated transfer, phonologically integrated *plenty* bears the grammatical features of Croatian equivalents *puno* 'lots of' or *mnogo* 'many', both of which govern GEN. This results in *gumdigger* appearing in its GEN.M.PL form. (Existential constructions such as in (12) containing *bilo je* 'there was/were' or *ima* 'there is/are' have the logical subject as a GEN, regardless of adverbs.) The following excerpt taken from the same speaker contains the Croatian equivalent form. Monitoring of his speech is apparent and it seems that he was aware of the more formal situation in which the interview was conducted. He wanted to say *gomdigera* but immediately replaced it by the more formal *smolokopača*, whose features show that it is GEN.M.PL following the construction *bilo je* 'there were':

(13) *Bilo je g. . . smolokopača, koji nisu znali ni čitat ni pisat.*
 'There were g. . . resin-diggers, who could neither read nor write'. (Gen.1, Sample A)

In the following example the integrated lexical items *separat* 'to separate' and *krima* 'cream' have a collocational relationship that results in the construction *za krimu učinit* 'to make cream'. This construction, *za* 'for' +INF ('in order to' +INF) exists in the speaker's home variety: dual causation is likely here:

(14) a na ruku tribalo **separat**
 and on+ACC hand-ACC.F.SG must-PST.3SG.N **separate**-INF
 mliko za **krimu** učinit
 milk-ACC.N.SG for+ACC **cream**-ACC.F.SG make-INF
 '. . .and by hand one had to **separate** the milk in order to make **cream**' (Gen.2, Sample A)

The main verb *separat* 'to separate' is phonologically integrated and most likely also morphologically integrated. The ending is not NZ.Eng -*eıt*, but -*at* which is a Croatian (dialect and/or truncated) infinitive suffix. A similar example of the use of the preposition *za* 'for' meaning 'in order **for** me to' is to be found in example (15):

(15) dok   san   ćapa   mjesto   na   brodići
     until   AUX-1SG   grab-PST.1SG.M   place-ACC.N.SG   on+LOC   boat-LOC.F.SG
     za   doć   ovamu   nort
     for   come-INF   here   north
     'until I grabbed a place on a small boat in order to come up north...'
     (Gen.1, Sample A)

Here, however, the expression 'in order [for me] to' rendered via *za* 'for' + INF is one found also in HMLD.Cro non-standard varieties; influence from both Dalmatian dialects and English are apparent.

4.2 Discourse markers

Discourse markers are unevenly spread over the samples but do occur in all of them and in the speech of speakers of all three generations. The most frequent discourse markers in the samples were unadapted *y'(ou) know* (Gen.2 and Gen.3 speakers), *ju no* 'you know' (Gen.1 and Gen.2 speakers) and *znate* 'you know-2PL' (Gen.1 and Gen.2 speakers). Their frequency is high and congruent to their frequency in AUS.Cro (Hlavac 2003: 145; Hlavac and Stolac, this volume). Other frequently-used discourse markers are *well*, *anyway* (in the sense of *bilo kao bilo*, lit.: 'was as was'), *I mean* and its equivalent, *ja minin* 'I mean-1SG' (in the sense of *hoću reći*, lit.: 'I want to say'). Other less frequent ones are *you see*, *that's right*, *actually*, *that's it* and *really*. These are usually phonologically adapted in the speech of Gen.1 speakers and unadapted in the speech of Gen.2 and Gen.3 speakers. Largely unadapted discourse markers are recorded in other diaspora Croatian samples, e.g. ITAL.Cro (Županović Filipin, Hlavac and Piasevoli, this volume) and ARG.Cro (Skelin Horvat, Musulin and Blažević, this volume).

An ever more frequent discourse marker is *eh* which is used widely in NZ English. Hay, Maclagan and Gordon (2008: 81, 108) point out that the particle *eh* is used in many parts of the country – "the farther north you are in the country the more common it tends to be" – and also commonly found in Māori English speech. All examples recorded in Sample A are from the North. The following is from a Gen.2 trilingual Māori speaker:

(16) *dica, oni idu. . .uči, što zovu kola,* **eh,** *dansi. . .*
'the children, they go. . .they learn what they call kolos, **eh,** dances. . .'.
(Gen.2, Sample A)

4.3 Semantic transference and loan translations

This section presents examples in which Croatian lexical items are employed that bear transference of semantic features of an English homophone or equivalent. For example there are a variety of terms that refer to and mean 'money': *lira*-SG. and *lire*-PL. 'money' based on Italian *lira*. Further, the form *lira st(e) rlina* as a compound of the Italian-origin form *lira* and an English-origin item *pound sterling* existed in speakers' homeland dialects, as well as the term *funta* 'pound'. In NZ.Cro *lira* and *funta* and less frequently *pena* (penny) were used up until (and beyond) the introduction of decimal currency in 1967, with *dolar* and *sent* (both usually unintegrated) being added afterwards. Forms such as *bušak* attested as a homeland dialect form (ČDL 1979: 93 – Wald = 'forest') acquired the additional meaning of 'specific NZ bush', even though on first glance this form appears as an adapted lexical transfer directly from NZ.Eng *bush*.

This section also presents examples of calques or loan translations, defined by Backus and Dorleijn (2009: 77) as "usage of morphemes in Language A that is the result of literal translation of one or more elements in a semantically equivalent expression in Language B". There are two wide-spread calques used across all three generations: *ić u slike* 'go to pictures' [= 'go to the cinema', HMLD.Cro 'ići u kino'] and *donit pijat* 'bring plate' [= as a guest, bring a plate of food to an event]. The latter is commonly used as a verbal and written request before gatherings, *molim, donesite pijat* ('please bring-2PL.IMP plate'). (The form *pijat* is not a transfer from English, but a Dalmatian regionalism.) The calque *donit pijat* is not only an example of semantic transference, but pragmatic transference and the adoption of New Zealand social mores. In the homeland, it is inconceivable that anyone invited to an event could be asked to bring to it a plate of food to share.

In the speech of almost all informants English-based verb+noun or verb+adjective constructions are found calqued in NZ.Cro with de-semanticised dummy verbs such as *učinit* 'to do', *bit* 'to be', *hodit* 'to go/walk', *ić* 'to go' and *znat* 'to know' that are 'pressed into service' as DO-verbs, followed by nouns drawn from Croatian or English:

učinit 'to do, to make'
*učinit **šandu*** 'to construct a shanty', *učinit **good living*** 'to have a good life'

bit 'to be'
*bit **surprised*** 'to be surprised', *bit **stabilised*** 'to be stabilised', *bit **engaged*** 'to be engaged'

(h)odit za + INS 'to go out for'
*gredin za **groceries*** 'I go out (shopping) for groceries'

ić + GERUND 'to go+gerund'
*ić **contracting**,* 'to go contracting', *ić **shopping*** 'to go shopping'

znat + GERUND 'to know how to + gerund'
*ja znan **driving** pa mogu po vanka...* 'I know driving [know how to drive] and so can go out...'

These examples show a trend towards analytism and are a sign of convergence towards the lexico-semantic structures of English. This includes a shift in the items that bear referential content, from verbs to nouns or adjectives, cf. *učinit good living* 'to have a good life'. vs HMLD.Cro *uživati (u životu)* 'to enjoy oneself (in life)'. In a similar way, in AUS.Cro, the verb *raditi* 'to do'/'to make' is employed as a light verb in DO-constructions (see Hlavac and Stolac, this volume). In our NZ.Cro corpus, we locate translations of English phrasal verb constructions, as in example (17):

(17) *ja **gledan** za nj u **garden***
 I **look**-1SG **for**+ACC him-ACC.M in+LOC **garden**
 'I am **looking for** him in the **garden**' (Gen.1, Sample A)

The above example features an extension of the semantic field of *gledat* 'to look' to encompass 'to search', and an adoption of the phrasal verb collocation *to look for* with the Croatian equivalent *za* for the preposition *for*. This differs from standard and dialect varieties of HMLD.Cro that have the forms *tražiti* and *iskat* 'to look for' respectively (Magner and Jutronić 2006). Both these forms are formally and semantically unrelated to *gledat* 'to look'. Example (18) below contains an instance of word order based on an equivalent English construction in which the preposition is dislocated from the interrogative pronoun and appears in clause-final position:

(18) **šta** se smiješ **od**
     what REFL laugh-2SG **from**
     'What are you laughing about?' (Gen.2, Stoffel – notes from research corpora)

HMLD.Cro requires dative marking on the object, i.e. *čemu* 'what-DAT' *se*-REFL *smiješ* laugh-2SG?

4.4 Code-switching

In a conversation, code-switching can be inter-clausal, intra-clausal and extra-clausal (which we apply to discourse markers). Code-switching depends on structural *and* sociolinguistic criteria and varies substantially according to situation and individual informants. When code-switching "the speaker is crossing over into the other language rather than transferring *something*, a lexical item or unit, from one language to another" (Clyne 2003: 75). Code-switching relates to lexical items, either single-item (or compound-item) insertions or multiple-item alternations. The place within a clause where a speaker may code-switch may be internal to it, i.e. *intra-clausal* code-switching, or at a clause boundary, i.e. *inter-clausal* code-switching. The former may more likely be an example of *embedding* or *insertion*, while the latter may be more typical of *alternation*. Instances of dates, numbers and amounts (see Jutronić, this volume) may be a catalyst for intra-clausal code-switching:

(19) *Doša san u* **New Zealand.. nineteen fifteen**
     'I came to **New Zealand.. nineteen fifteen**'. (Gen.1, Sample A)

(20) *Sada guveran neće zajimat ovin mladin farmarin preko..* **eighty thousand dollars**
     'Now the government will not lend these young farmers over.. **eighty thousand dollars**'. (Gen.1, Sample A)

Some code-switches are immediately followed by their NZ.Cro equivalents, which can represent self-corrections or instances of emphasis:

(21) *...narod nije zna..* **what to do..** *što će činit.*
     people did not know.. **what to do..** what they will do. (Gen.1, Sample A)

The following are instances of inter-clausal code-switching. As with the previous example, repetition can occur as emphasis and in (22) it seems to amplify the repair or clarification made by the speaker:

(22) *Kopali smo smolu dvi noge.. dvi stope do tri stope...* **I mean two foot, three foot...**
'We were digging the resin *dvi noge* [= two human feet].. *dvi stope* [= measurement of two feet] to three *stope*... **I mean two feet, three feet...**'. (Gen.1, Sample A)

A subordinating conjunction is here the point where a code-switch occurs:

(23) *Ja nisan nikad reka Inglezu da san Hrvat* **'cause he don't know what that is.**
'I never told an Englishman [= English-speaking NZer] that I am a Croatian **'cause he don't know what that is.**' (Gen 1, Sample A)

An interlocutor-specific code use can account for some examples of inter-clausal code-switching where the speaker code-switches when addressing different interlocutors:

(24) **Oh, you've bought a section** ['sekʃn]... *Oni su kupili sekšon* ['sekʃon].
'**Oh, you've bought a section** (plot of land)... They have bought a section' (Gen.2, Stoffel – notes from research corpora)

In example (24), the first utterance is addressed to English-speaking acquaintances, after which the Gen.2 speaker turned to his Gen.1 parents to report the same information to them using a loanword phonologically integrated in a way characteristic of the speech of Gen.1 speakers. He does this because this is one of a firm number of words in the repertoire of Gen.1 speakers that is an established transfer fully integrated into NZ.Cro and is perceived as such. Had he transferred this word directly from NZ.Eng, as a Gen.2 speaker his pronunciation of the form would have been unintegrated and indistinguishable from NZ.Eng ['sekʃn].

In the excerpt below, the speaker commences in NZ.Cro and code-switches to repeat the reported speech of another and herself, in the language this was given in:

(25) *Mate me ringa, govori,* **"tell you, hard luck". I say: "no, no".**
'Mate rings me and says, **"I tell you, hard luck". I say: "no, no..."**.' (Gen.1, Sample A)

The immediacy of phrases commonly used in English appears to precipitate an inter-clausal code-switch as shown in (26):

(26)   ... *i oni su nas primili u njihovu kuću i* **treated us like one of the family**
'...and they took us into their house and **treated us like one of the family.**'
(Gen.2, Sample A)

In (26), the 3PL subject is the same as the possessor of the object. In constructions like this, a specific possessive pronoun *svoj* 'own' is used, rather than the possessive pronoun *njihov* 'their'. The Gen.2 speaker's use of the 3PL possessive pronoun *njihov* 'their' indicates that the possessor of the object is *not* the same as the grammatical subject. But here the grammatical subject is the same as the possessor of the object, and the utterance contains an unintended meaning. Instances of change in grammatical markers are explored further in the following section. What is also conspicuous in (26) is that *oni* 'they' is the subject to both the Croatian predicate *su nas primili* 'took us in' and an English predicate *treated us* (...). Here, we have two co-ordinating clauses, the first in Croatian and the second in English and the past-tense predicates in both languages are controlled by the same subject.

4.5 Morphosyntactic features – change and convergence

Morphosyntactic change occurs in the speech of all generations but is most present in the basic structures of the speech of Gen.2 and Gen.3 speakers. It is not always clear whether a given morphosyntactic change or apparent instance of convergence to English models is caused by direct contact with English, or whether it is a case of indirect change or both. It is important to recall that the linguistic variety which was the younger speakers' first or heritage language was already undergoing change at the time they acquired it – that is, the homeland Dalmatian dialects of their parents and grandparents as Gen.1 speakers often featured lexical structural and semantic innovation and that was then the variety which younger speakers heard and acquired. For Gen.2 and Gen.3 speakers, the model provided to them was no longer a monolingual, homeland-based one, but a Dalmatian dialect that had been in contact with English, sometimes for up to decades. Further, many of the homeland dialects had particular characteristics such as analytic constructions similar to those found in English. For example, the ČDL (1979: XLV-XLVI) lists a number of features of Dalmatian Čakavian dialects relevant to the study of indirect change here: convergence of the desinences in the declension of nouns; reduction of the number of verb tense forms found to only three, i.e. PRS., PRF. and FUT. 1; an extension of the semantic radius of a number of prepositions. These characteristics – in particular their frequency and recurrence – may have undergone change after contact with English commenced. But we are careful to attribute these solely to the influence of English – it is perhaps more likely that contact with English is a catalyst for their prominence or higher incidence, and in the expansion of analytic constructions to other forms. Stoffel (1988b: 383) describes the coalescence of these two influences in regard to certain constructions as "reinforced categories".

4.5.1 Nouns

In regard to nouns, there is convergence of the inflectional plural suffixes for DAT, LOC and INS via *–in* (M, N) and *–an* (F) as alternatives to *-ima(n)* and *-ama(n)*, e.g. *farmarin* ('farmer'-DAT/LOC/INS.M.PL) and *titran* ('ti-tree'-DAT/LOC/INS.F.PL). Convergence of LOC and ACC in spatial use, e.g. location-specified utterances normally requiring LOC: *živin u kuću* ('live-1SG in+ACC [instead of LOC] house-ACC.F.SG') 'I live in the house', has the result that ACC case markings are employed for these, as they are in utterances containing movement, e.g. *iden u kuću* ('go into+ACC house-ACC.F.SG') 'I go into the house'.

We locate changes in case-marking, and with these also changes in word order. A variable but general reduction to a two-case system of NOM and OBL is observable amongst some Gen.2 and Gen.3 speakers. In the singular, MASC nouns in DIR.OBJ position are not distinguished according to the feature animacy, while minimal FEM.SG desinences are NOM *-a* plus a *casus generalis* ending in *-u*. A reduction of morphological markers to express grammatical relations is compensated by a more strict word order, whereby SVO(indirect)O(direct) becomes more frequent than SVO(direct)O(indirect). The latter is the unmarked word order in most varieties of HMLD.Cro. This results in utterances such as:

(27) ja pišen **ambassador** pismo
I write-1.SG **ambassador**-NOM.M.SG letter-ACC.N.SG
'I am writing the ambassador a letter' (Gen.3, Sample Λ).

HMLD.Cro.: pišem 'write'-1SG pismo 'letter'-ACC.N.SG ambasadoru 'ambassador'-DAT.M.

(28) on je da libar **žensku**
he AUX-3SG give-PST.M.SG book-ACC.M.SG **woman**-ACC.F.SG
'He gave a book to the woman' (Gen.2, Sample A).

HMLD.Cro.: dao 'give'-PST.M.SG je AUX-3SG libar 'book'-ACC.M.SG ženi 'woman'-DAT.F.SG.

The reduction of desinences in the declension of nouns shows a further shift towards a pattern of plural desinences in *-i* (MASC.) and *-e* (FEM.) for all cases. However, the frequency of this emerging pattern depends on individual speakers and their idiolect. There has already been convergence of LOC, DAT, and INS on the one hand, and VOC and NOM on the other which is a feature of HMLD.Cro varieties. What we observe is that Ďurovič's (1984: 23) implicativity system of change in case marking, i.e. an ordering in which morphological markers from the right of the following list may be replaced by those to their left NOM<ACC<GEN<LOC<INS<DAT<VOC also applies to the NZ.Cro data. The same implicativity scale in regard to case marking is employed in studies on other diaspora varieties of Croatian, e.g. ITAL.Cro (see Županović Filipin, Hlavac and Piasevoli, this volume), CAN.Cro (see Petrović, this volume) and AUS.Cro (see Hlavac and Stolac, this volume). At the same time, there is no one speaker with a NOM and OBL system only. Lexicalised forms which informants may have heard from parents or grandparents, such as *čaša čaja* 'glass'-NOM.F.SG 'tea'-GEN.M.SG – 'cup of tea' (Gen.2, Sample A) or *sa bason* 'with'+ INS 'bus'-INS.M.SG – 'by bus' (Gen.2, Sample A) occur in the speech of younger-generation speakers. They may be 'unanalysed constructions' that bear marking for cases that are otherwise not always marked in the same way elsewhere in their speech; they may be instances that occur in variable systems in which case marking is likely to be more present in some constructions, while in others, strategies such as periphrastic prepositional phrases, word order, or overt pronouns obviate the perceived need for OBL case marking. Example (29) is likely to be an example of an 'unanalysed construction' present in the repertoire of the informant who otherwise irregularly marks possessive constructions with GEN marking:

(29) od   majke   ćer
      from+GEN   mother-GEN.F.SG   daughter-NOM.F.SG
      'mother's daughter' (Gen.2, Sample A).

This pre-posed possessive construction is found in HMLD.Cro dialects, as well as in other varieties of diaspora Croatian and other Slavic émigré languages (Sussex 1993) (cf. standard HMLD.Cro *majčina kći* 'mother'-POSS.NOM.F.SG 'daughter'-NOM.F.SG). The example below bears evidence of a variable system in which the presence of other elements appears to account for the variation in case markers showing grammatical relations:

(30) u   mojoj   materin   kuća
      in+LOC   my-LOC.F.SG   mother-POSS.NOM.M.SG   house-NOM.F.SG
      '... in my mother's house' (Gen.3, Sample A).

In the above example, the preposition *u* 'in' marks the spatial relations, while linear sequencing marks *mojoj* and *materin* as pre-posed attributive forms to the object of possession *kuća*. The sequence of forms, following an English word order, marks relations, not morphology which is inconsistent across all three forms for case and gender (cf. 4.5.3 below and Jutronić, this volume). A HMLD. Cro equivalent would have different sequencing: *u kući moje matere* 'in house-LOC.F.SG my-GEN.F.SG mother-GEN.F.SG'.

While standard HMLD.Cro has three different endings for PRS.3PL verb conjugation -*u*, -*e* and –*aju*, in NZ.Cro all PRS.3PL verbs end in –*u* (encompassing also the endings –*idu* or -*edu*), e.g. *implojit* 'employ-INF', *imploju* 'employ-3PL'. An –*iti* verb in HMLD.Cro would be expected to have a PRS.3PL ending –*e*, i.e. *imploje*. This is in line with some non-standard varieties of HMLD.Cro that also feature a –*u* ending for all 3PL forms. Thus, the 3PL suffix on transfers such as *imploju* or *implojidu* is not an example of morphological simplification that is unique to the diaspora setting. Further, there is a tendency to integrate transferred verbs as biaspectual verbs, in particular via the affix -*at*, less frequently -*it*, both of a biaspectual quality in NZ.Cro, with a possible iterative extension in -*(va)*- such as *ring-a-va-t* 'ring-INF' (Stoffel 1988c) (cf. also 4.5.3).

In regard to prepositions, there is periphrastic use of *s(a)* 'with' in INS constructions expressing 'by means of', e.g. *došli smo s kočon* 'we came by coach-INS.M.SG', *sa karon* 'by car-INS.M.SG' (Gen.2, Sample A) and *ja rabotan sa jedan ruka* 'I work with+INS one-NOM.M.SG hand-NOM.F.SG' (Gen.3, Sample A). Periphrastic use of *s(a)* is also a feature of many HMLD.Cro non-standard varieties. Possessive constructions contain overt use of *od* 'of' in constructions that do not require the preposition as GEN marking achieves this, e.g. *riba od mora* 'fish from sea-GEN.N.SG' 'sea fish'. English equivalents such as *seafood* or *salt-water fish* appear to have no influence here, as they have a pre-posed attribute that modifies the agent of possession. A pre-posed construction is also what is contained in the more common HMLD.Cro form, *morska riba* 'sea-ATTRIB fish'. In Čakavian dialects of Croatian, *od* 'of' has eight meanings/functions including to denote quality, but the functions of *od* are further extended based on those of its English equivalents, *of* and *about*, e.g. *Bilo je grades od gome* 'There were grades of gum-GEN.F.SG' (Gen.2, Sample A), *Što mislin od ova* ... ? 'What do I think about this.. ?' (Gen.3, A), *Wellington je capital od Nove Zelande* 'Wellington is the capital of New Zealand-GEN.F.SG' (Gen.2, Sample A), and *na dvadeset i prve od devetoga* 'on the twenty-first-GEN.F.SG of the ninth-GEN.M.SG [month]' (Gen.2, Sample A). The *od* constructions here feature either the transference of the functions of *of* or *from*, or as in the case of the last two instances, periphrastic use of *od*. Of note is that non-target case-marking (i.e. reduction of INS and GEN to NOM or ACC) on the succeeding nominals is recorded in only two of the eight examples given here. Transference of the function of *for* onto *za* 'for' denoting a time duration is clear in the following: *ima san šermilkera za dvadeset i dvi godina*, 'I had a sharemilker[2] for twenty-two years' (Gen.1, Sample A). In equivalent HMLD.Cro varieties, including non-standard ones, duration is expressed via the time period only without a preposition.

4.5.2 Pronouns

Croatian is pro-drop and subject personal pronouns are usually overt, marking emphasis or contrast. A number of examples in this chapter contain instances of overt subject pronouns. In regard to object personal pronouns, there is a short form and a long form, with the short form being the unmarked choice in most instances, and the long form indicating emphasis or contrast. As in example (28), in example (31) below, the subject pronoun is overt, and only the long form of the object pronoun occurs:

(31) **ja**   dajen   libar   **nju**
     I   give-1SG   book-ACC.M.SG   her-ACC.F
     'I give the book to her' (Gen.2, Sample A).

   Cf. the HMLD.Cro equivalent in a congruent dialect:
   dajen 'give'-1SG   *joj* 'her'-DAT.F   *libar* 'book'-ACC.M.SG

Both the subject pronoun, by its occurrence, and the object pronoun, through the long form are overt. The development of a two-case system results in a change of case marking for OBL morphology from DAT to ACC only. The word order also follows an English rather than HMLD.Cro model. (For equivalent examples of object pronoun forms and word order in USA.Cro, see Jutronić, this volume.) A similar example is (32) below, with target morphology but overt pronouns:

(32) **ja**   ću   ringat   **nju**
     I   FUT.AUX-1SG   ring-INF   **her**-ACC.F.
     'I am going to phone her' (Gen.2, Sample A).

---

2 A sharemilker is a person who shares work on a dairy farm for a share of the profit, and sometimes has his or her own herd (Reed Dictionary of New Zealand English 2001: 1053).

In an unmarked utterance where the OBJ 'she' is not emphasised, this would be rendered via a clitic pronoun *je* 'she-ACC.F' that would not occur in sentence-final position but preceding the second verb, i.e. *ja ću je ringat*.

4.5.3 Verbs

Example (32) above contains the verb, *ringat* 'to ring', mentioned above in section 4.1.2. NZ.Cro speakers' verbal system integrates verbs with the affixes *-a-va/-i-va* as biaspectual and we regard *ringat* 'to ring' and *ringavat* 'to ring' as alternative means for the integration of the same English-origin verb, whereby the forms in *-a-va-t*, which are much rarer, can have an iterative character. This diaspora situation seems to reflect that in [HMLD] Čakavian where verbs in *-at* are generally of Romance origin and are bi-aspectual, and additional imperfective forms in *-o-vat-* have also evolved (ČDL 1979:XL). Magner and Jutronić (2006) generally treat such verbs as instances of a perfective and imperfective verb pair. Of the 78 transferred verbs in NZ.Cro only seven show formal aspectual marking, all exclusively by way of prefixation. All others are biaspectual (Stoffel 1988c). English does have a limited aspectual system, but does not formally distinguish aspect in a paradigmatic way as Croatian or other Slavic languages do. However, on the basis of the data, it is not possible to establish if the whole NZ.Cro verbal system, not just transferred verbs, is moving towards a one-form-biaspectual system. Within the samples there are examples such as *odgovorit* 'to answer-PFV' or *kupit* 'to buy-PFV' used biaspectually, i.e. with both perfective *and* imperfective (i.e. duration, repetition) functions. It is noted here that the PFV verb is employed as the default for both aspects. (For data on the extended use of PFV verbs in other diaspora varieties, see: Županović Filipin, Hlavac and Piasevoli; Piasevoli; Hlavac and Stolac, all this volume.). However, in the NZ.Cro corpora, there were also Gen.2 (Sample A) informants who clearly distinguished the forms of each aspectual pair, e.g. *kupovat*-IPFV and *kupit*-PFV 'to buy' and their use of the respective form was grammatically, not lexically (i.e. stylistically) based.

We can observe levelling and thus further examples of convergence of forms, mostly in the speech of Gen.2 and Gen.3 speakers. These are instances of internal modification and reduction of forms rather than contact-induced change. There are not many of these forms but the tendency is, as with aspect, towards one base form: *peren* 1SG 'I wash', *pereš* 2SG, *pere* 3SG ... *pereju* 3PL yielding, by analogy, the INF *peret* 'to wash' rather than *prat*. A similar occurrence is recorded for PST.PTCP forms: *zoven* PRS.1SG 'I call', *zoveš* PRS.2SG etc. This then yields *zovili* 'call'-PST.M.PL rather than *zvali*. The possessive suffix *–ov* is added to a noun *otac* 'father' resulting in *otacov* 'father's' while in all HMLD.Cro varieties, the equivalent form is *očev*. (The first two consonants undergo assimilation and reduction to an affricate.) Contact appears to be responsible for the occurrence of many passive constructions that are conspicuous through appearing as English-based calques:

(33) *Dargaville je   setlina   na   drugi*
       Dargaville AUX-3SG   settle-PASS.PTCP.NOM.F.SG   in+ACC   different-ACC.M.SG
       način
       way-ACC.M.SG
       'Dargaville was settled in a different way' (Gen.1, Sample A).

4.5.4 Agreement and non-agreement

One of the most significant single contact-induced changes is lack of agreement, especially in instances involving natural gender such as *moj mama* 'my-MASC' 'mother-FEM' or:

(34) **on**   *je*   **starija**   *nego*   **njegov**
       he-NOM.M.SG   be-3SG   older-NOM.F.SG   than   his-NOM.M.SG
       sestra
       sister-NOM.F.SG
       'He is older than his sister' (Gen.2, Sample A).

Here there is a mismatch in the marking of gender between the M subject and a F predicate, and within the NP that features a M attribute describing a F noun. It seems that the younger-generation speakers are not aware of this phenomenon even when they are otherwise reasonably fluent. An example of lack of agreement in verbal forms is:

(35) *ako još   **želite**   tikete   **telefoniraj***
       if   still **wish**-2PL ticket-ACC.M.PL   **telephone**-2SG.IMP
       'if you still want-2PL tickets, ring-2SG...' (Gen.2. Written circular)

In example (35) the first verb in the written circular is 2PL *želite* 'you wish', while the imperative in the same sentence that is directed at the same addressees is 2SG *telefoniraj* 'telephone'. In general, a lack of agreement of the features gender, number and case amongst constituents within the same NP or VP is uncommon. Where instances of this occur, they are usually to be found in the speech of Gen.2 and Gen.3 speakers, such as in the example *ja rabotan sa jedan ruka* 'I work with one-NOM.M.SG hand-NOM.F.SG' above in section 4.5.1. A lack of agreement of morphological forms is not a characteristic of Gen.1 speakers, and seems to be clearly a consequence of language contact which features the convergence of NZ.Cro closer to English.

5 Conclusion

A detail mentioned in section 2 which is re-stated here is the number of New Zealanders of Croatian origin who declined to participate in linguistic fieldwork elicitations or from whom no data could be gained due to little or no proficiency in Croatian. Language shift to English was rapid in the assimilationist first half of the 20th century. Later on, many children to whom language was insufficiently transmitted (especially in mixed marriages) soon 'abandoned' their heritage language and shifted completely to English once they reached adulthood. We must also remember that the taped samples include only those who were still able to speak the language. Younger speakers willing to participate in recorded interactions numbered about a third of all those who were approached as potential informants to be part of Sample A in the 1970s. Similarly only about a third of those who were approached to complete the questionnaire-only survey in 1990 actually did so (Sample C). Therefore, the speakers recorded here, are, in many ways those whose speech has been captured before or at the cusp of a 'turnover' of their dominant, matrix language (Myers-Scotton 1998). This is usually followed by abandonment and language shift. A portrayal of NZ Croatians would be incomplete if it did not note that English has become the dominant or even sole language for Gen.2 and Gen.3 members, and even many Gen.1 members use Croatian only infrequently.

To outsiders from the homeland, the most noticeable feature of NZ Croatians' speech is 'foreign' words and atypical constructions while members of the New Zealand's host society Anglophone majority may recognise a 'foreign' accent as a sign of language contact. Less noticeable but more far-reaching are, as we have seen, the effects of prolonged language contact such as a levelling of paradigms, calquing of grammatical and semantic structures, and a tendency towards analytic constructions which require a stricter word order, especially when coupled with a gradually increasing paucity of the lexicon. The first author's observations of NZ.Cro over more than 40 years indicate that these phenomena are common and widespread (cf. "recurrent synchrony", Stoffel 1993: 87) with some variation depending on individuals and amongst individual families as well.

A distinguishing feature of this speech community is its longevity – notwithstanding language shift to English – there are third- and now even fourth-generation descendants of the original settlers who arrived at the end of the nineteenth century. The sociolinguistic features that prevailed then, both in the homeland and in New Zealand, determined the linguistic features that characterise NZ.Cro still today: the heritage language is based on Dalmatian Štokavian- and Čakavian-Ikavian dialects and the contact languages were NZ.Eng and an indigenous language, Māori. For some early settlers, acquisition of a knowledge of English occurred at the same time as an acquisition of a knowledge of Māori. Although there are few active trilingual speakers today, it is likely that many of those in Croatian-Māori marriages or those who were the products of them had at least some proficiency in all three languages – the social conditions of the time and subsequent anthropological research (Božić-Vrbančić 2008) strongly suggest this. Alongside English, Māori was a donor language for terms and realia that were little known to the early settlers. In some cases, forms from Māori entered NZ.Cro 'directly'; perhaps more commonly, English was the intermediary language for their entry. In either case, NZ.Cro stands as a rare example in which a transposed, immigrant language bears a significant number of forms and features not only from the socially dominant language English, but also from an indigenous language.

The homeland varieties of most New Zealand Croatians, the central Dalmatian dialects, bear evidence of language contact with superstrate Venetian Italian. This means that some forms which appear as transfers from English such as *pasat* 'to pass' are established forms in the heritage language; English *pass* may have no effect or it may have a reinforcing effect on the use of these items in speakers' repertoires. Amongst Gen.1 speakers, lexical transfers are usually phonologically and morphologically integrated into NZ.Cro; integration can also be prosodic through transfers being embedded into prepositional phrases in which word stress moves leftwards from the transfer onto the preposition. While nouns predominate as the forms transferred – particularly in the area of gumdigging, the livelihood of the earlier settlers – there are adjectives that bear examples of integration via comparative suffixes –*ije* or pre-posed periphrastic adverbs (*više* 'more') that co-occur with English-origin (comparative) adjectives such as *streta* ('straighter'). Suffixation also applies to nouns such that diminutive, feminine or adjectival suffixes are affixed to English-origin transfers.

There are cross-generational differences in the incidence and type of integration that occurs. In the repertoires of Gen.2 and Gen.3 speakers, English-origin items typically remain phonologically and morphologically unintegrated except in instances where an item appears to be an established loan in the vernaculars of Gen.1 speakers so that younger speakers acquire such lexical items in the same way they acquire other Croatian lexical items; the English origin of some of these forms may not even be obvious to some speakers. In some cases, though, the phonological adaptation can go in other directions, where all lexemes and morphemes are supplied from Croatian, but unmistakably English-origin features of phonology such as aspiration of plosives or centralisation of unstressed vowels lead to the impression that younger speakers are 'speaking Croatian with an English accent'.

Verbs, like other forms, are integrated into NZ.Cro with the specific dialectal features of the heritage variety, i.e. with *-u* or *-iju* forms in 3PL. Of note is that the features such as aspect in transferred verbs such as *-at* and *-it* can be biaspectual and their iteration occasionally overtly represented via infixes such as *-a(va)-* or *-i(va)-*. Amongst some younger speakers, PFV verbs are used with both PFV and IPFV functions, but this is not (yet) a widespread phenomenon.

Discourse markers such as *y'(ou) know*, *well* and *anyway*, reported from other Croatian diaspora settings in Anglophone countries also occur commonly in NZ.Cro. Specific though to NZ.Cro is the discourse marker *eh*, which is transferred from the speech of English speakers, particularly by NZ.Cro speakers of Māori origin.

Semantic transfers and loan translations abound – this is, we contend, characteristic of long-standing bilingualism with forms such as *ić u slike* 'go to the pictures' and *donesite pijat* 'bring a plate' representing calques produced spontaneously by Gen.1 speakers which have become conventionalised constructions acquired as heritage language items no different from non-calqued constructions by Gen.2 and Gen.3 speakers. These calques, although semantic, bring with them a linear ordering of forms based on English syntax and their popularisation leads to analytically-based word order patterns such as verb+DIR.OBJ, *učinit good living* 'to have a good life', verb+gerund *znan driving* 'I know how to drive'. The effect of this tendency towards more analytic constructions is on the one hand a reduction of reflexive or other constructions that require OBJ marking of nominal constituents. This is the general tendency, but the tendency or drift towards analytic constructions can lead to structures that are syntactically *more complex* than HMLD.Cro equivalents as the example *ja gledan za nj u garden* 'I look for him in the garden' shows, where HMLD.Cro requires a DIR.OBJ only after the verb. (See Jutronić, this volume.) An even more pronounced example is right-clefted *od* 'from [=about]', in the utterance *šta se smiješ od?* 'What are you laughing about?'

Code-switching occurs both as embedded items and alternated passages. Realia, numbers, dates and amounts transferred from English are typical examples of the former. Phraseological constructions, reported speech, and code-switched repetitions as a form of emphasis or amplification are among the many apparent reasons for alternations into English. Along with lexical transfers, structural changes are the most conspicuous features of NZ.Cro particularly in the speech of Gen.2 and Gen.3 speakers. Replication of constructions via calques, as mentioned above, leads to linear patterns of English-based word order. This is, in view of the syntactic features of NZ.Cro, part of a broader tendency in which syntactic relations between items within a clause are marked increasingly via word order and less so via morphology. This is a process still occurring and it may be that language shift to English will occur amongst these Gen.3 speakers before their NZ.Cro vernaculars are reduced to a two-case (NOM and OBJ only) system. To be sure, this has not yet happened. In some instances, case convergence had already occurred in non-standard HMLD.Cro dialectal varieties that is the heritage language of most speakers. This relates to the convergence of the space vs. motion distinction with the effect that ACC morphology marks nominal phrases in LOC (Jutronić-Tihomirović 1985). Amongst some speakers, the use of the ACC as a general OBL case is observable, at least for FEM nouns. Along the same lines, examples of 'target' case-marking may be more accurately described as fossilised forms that regularly occur in some speakers' repertoires, e.g. *od majke ćer* with 'intact' GEN morphology while their vernaculars may not otherwise feature possession-marking via Croatian GEN constructions.

Overall, we see Ďurovič's (1984) implicativity scale confirmed that describes the replacement of marking for OBL cases according to the following hierarchy: NOM<ACC<GEN<LOC<INS<DAT<VOC. Perhaps even more conspicuous are examples of NPs within which there is non-congruence in feature-marking for case and/or gender, resulting in NPs such as *u mojoj materin kuća* with a combination of target LOC markers and non-target NOM ones, and target FEM suffixes with non-target MASC ones. Although comparative data of all NPs with and without prepositions are not available it appears that non-agreement in feature-marking and reduction in case-marking is more widespread in NPs *with* prepositions than in those without. The apparent 'over-use' of prepositions in some NPs, e.g. *bilo je grades od gome* 'there were grades of gum', is attributable to the influence of the original central Dalmatian dialects that feature this, with English playing a role of re-enforcing these constructions that match their English equivalents word for word. This last point reiterates the need for the features of the homeland or heritage vernacular to be kept in view as the 'point of comparison' for descriptions of innovation and change, rather than a version of the standard language, which in almost no cases here is the home variety of the recorded speakers.

In a geographical sense, NZ.Cro represents the 'most distant' variety of Croatian used outside the homeland. It is, as stated, a 'long-standing' variety that has been maintained, partly due to the relative geographical and social isolation of its speakers, at least in the first half of the twentieth century. It is now seriously threatened by language shift to English. If and when NZ.Cro does disappear in the repertoire of individuals it is because they are simply abandoning it, but not because it has reached an end-point on a continuum of possible change or attrition: "the ultimate reason for the demise is not structural decay but rather speech behaviour and attitudes caused by the external setting" (Stoffel 2000: 815).

References

Albijanić, Alexander. 1982. San Pedro revisited: Language maintenance in the San Pedro Yugoslav Community. In Roland Sussex (ed.), *The Slavic Languages in Emigre Communities*, 11–22. Edmonton: Linguistic Research Inc.
Albin, Alexander & Ronelle Alexander. 1972. *The Speech of Yugoslav Immigrants in San Pedro, California*. The Hague: Martinus Nijhoff.
Albin, Alexander. 1976. A Yugoslav Community in San Pedro, California. *General Linguistics* 16 (2–3). 78–94.
Backus, Ad & Margreet Dorleijn. 2009. Loan translations versus code-switching. In Bullock, Barbara & Almeida J. Toribio (eds.), *The Cambridge Handbook of Linguistic Code-switching*, 75–93. Cambridge: Cambridge University Press.
Božić-Vrbančić, Senka. 2008. *Tarara: Croats and Maori in New Zealand. Memory, Belonging, Identity*. Dunedin: University of Otago Press.
Clyne, Michael. 2003. *Dynamics of Language Contact*. Cambridge: Cambridge University Press.
Conklin, Nancy Faires & Margaret A. Lourie. 1983. *A host of tongues: Language communities in the United States*. New York: Free Press.
Čizmić, Ivan. 1981. *Iz Dalmacije u Novi Zeland*. [From Dalmatia to New Zealand] Zagreb: Globus.
Dragicevich, Kaye. 2017. *Pioneer Dalmatian Settlers of the Far North*. Awanui: Willow Creek Press.
Ďurovič, Ľubomír. 1984. The Diaspora Children's Serbo-Croatian. In B. Stolz, I. Titunik & L. Doležel (eds.), *Language and Literature Theory*, 19–28. Ann Arbor: University of Michigan.
Field, Fredric. 2002. *Linguistic borrowing in bilingual contexts*. Amsterdam: John Benjamins.
Filipović, Rudolf. 1961. The morphological adaptation of English loan-words in Serbo-Croat. *Studia Romanica et Anglica Zagrabiensia* 11. 91–104.
Filipović, Rudolf. 1985. Croatian dialects in the United States: Sociolinguistic aspects. *Folia Slavica* 6(3). 278–292.
Fuseworks Media. 2008. NZ celebrates 150 years of Kiwi-Croatian culture. http://www.voxy.co.nz/politics/carter-nz-celebrates-150-years-kiwi-croatian-culture/5/1618
Gačić, Jasna. 1979. Romanski elementi u splitskom čakavskom govoru. [The Romance elements in the Čakavian vernacular of Split] *Čakavska rič* 1. 3–55.
Hay, Jennifer, Margaret Maclagan & Elizabeth Gordon. 2008. *New Zealand English*. Edinburgh: Edinburgh University Press Ltd.
Hlavac, Jim. 2003. *Second-generation speech. Lexicon, code-switching and morpho-syntax of Croatian-English bilinguals*. Bern: Peter Lang.
Hraste, Mate, Petar Šimunović & Reinhold Olesch. 1979. *Čakavisch-Deutsches Lexikon*. Teil 1. Wien: Böhlau.
Jakich, Miranda. 1975. *A Personal Description of the Interference Occurring in the Serbo-Croatian/English Language Contact Situation in New Zealand*. Extended Essay for M.A. Wellington: Victoria University.

Jakich, Miranda. 1987. The Yugoslav Language in New Zealand. In Walter Hirsch (ed.), *Living Languages: Bilingualism & Community Languages in NZ*: 117–124. Auckland: Heinemann.

Janković-Kramarić, Judita Florentina. 2001. *Ethnic Identity Among the Croatian Community in Auckland*. Auckland: University of Auckland. MSc. thesis in Psychology.

Jelicich, Stephen. 2008. *From Distant Villages. The Lives and Times of Croatian Settlers in New Zealand, 1858–1958*. Auckland: Pharos Publications Ltd.

Jelicich, Stephen & Andrew Trlin. 1997. Croatian. In Penny Griffith, Ross Harvey & Keith Maslan (eds.), *Book & Print in New Zealand. A Guide to Print Culture in Aotearoa*, 276–281. Wellington: Victoria University Press.

Jutronić, Dunja. 1974. The Serbo-Croatian Language in Steelton, Pennsylvania. *General Linguistics* 14 (1). 15–34.

Jutronić, Dunja. 1976. Language Maintenance and Language Shift of the Serbo-Croatian Language in Steelton, Pennsylvania. *General Linguistics* 16 (2–3). 166–186.

Jutronić-Tihomirović, Dunja. 1985. *Hrvatski jezik u SAD*. [The Croatian language in the USA] Split: Logos.

Kaštropil, Ivo. 1970. Neke značajke govora Blata i Vele Luke. [Some characteristics of the vernacular of Blato and Vela Luka] In Marinko Gjivoje (ed.), *Zbornik otoka Korčule* 1. 86–90. Zagreb: KPD Bratska sloga.

Klarić, don Ante. 2000. *Povijest hrvatske katoličke misije Sv. Leopolda B. Mandića u Aucklandu (Novi Zeland) (1904.-1999.)*. [A history of the Croatian Catholic Mission of St. Leopold B. Mandić in Auckland]. Split: Dalmacija papir.

Magner, Thomas. 1978. Diglossia in Split. *Folia Slavica* 1(3). 400–436.

Magner, Thomas F. & Dunja Jutronić. 2006. *Rječnik splitskog govora. Dictionary of Split Dialect.* Durieux: Dubrovnik University Press.

Montgomery, Keith. 1993. *Language Maintenance and Language Shift – Patterns of Croatian in Auckland*. Auckland: University of Auckland. [Unpublished] MA Extended Essay.

Muysken, Pieter. 2000. *Bilingual Speech*. Cambridge: Cambridge University Press.

Myers-Scotton, Carol. 1998. One way to dusty death: the Matrix Language Turnover Hypothesis. In Lenore Grenoble & Lindsay Whaley (eds.), *Endangered Languages*, 289–306. Cambridge: Cambridge University Press.

Reed Dictionary of New Zealand English. 2001. (Third Edition). Auckland: Reed Publishing.

Schatz, Henriette. 1989. Code-Switching or Borrowing. *International Journal of Applied Linguistics* 83(1). 125–162.

Statistics NZ. 2013. Ethnic group profiles: Croatian http://www.stats.govt.nz/Census/2013-census/profile-and-summary-reports/ethnic-profiles (accessed 24 November 2016).

Stoffel, Hans-Peter. 1982. Language Maintenance and Language Shift of the Serbo-Croatian Language in a New Zealand Dalmatian Community. In Roland Sussex (ed.), *The Slavic Languages in Emigre Communities*, 121–139. Carbondale, Edmonton: Linguistic Research Inc.

Stoffel, Hans-Peter. 1983. Secondary Derivation from English Loanwords in New Zealand Serbo-Croatian Dialects. *Wiener Slawistischer Almanach* 12. 293–299.

Stoffel, Hans-Peter. 1988a. Slavisches in Polynesien. Zum serbokroatisch-Māori-englischen Sprachkontakt in Neuseeland. In Boris Christa, Wolfgang Gesemann, Marko Pavlyshyn, Helmut W. Schaller, Hans-Peter Stoffel & Roland Sussex (eds.), *Slavic Themes. Papers from Two Hemispheres*, 349–370. Neuried: Hieronymus.

Stoffel, Hans-Peter. 1988b. Veränderungen morphosyntaktischer Strukturen in slavischen Auswanderersprachen. In Peter Brang (ed.) *Schweizerische Beiträge zum 10. Internationalen Slavistenkongress in Sofia, September 1988* (Slavica Helvetica 30). 339–359. Bern: Peter Lang.
Stoffel, Hans-Peter. 1988c. Bi-Aspectual Loan-Verbs in Migrant Serbo-Croatian. *New Zealand Slavonic Journal 1988*, Part I: Serbo-Croatian Colloquium Papers, 1–7.
Stoffel, Hans-Peter. 1991. Common Trends in the Morphological Adaptation of Loanwords in Serbo-Croatian Migrant Dialects. In Vladimir Ivir & Damir Kalogjera (eds.), *Languages in Contact and Contrast*, 417–429. Mouton: Berlin, New York.
Stoffel, Hans-Peter. 1993. Slavic Languages in the 'New World': Cases of Migranto-before-Death? *Australian Slavonic and East European Studies* 7(1). 75–89.
Stoffel, Hans-Peter. 1994. Dialect and Standard Language in a Migrant Situation: The Case of New Zealand Croatian. *New Zealand Slavonic Journal 1994*. 153–170.
Stoffel, Hans-Peter. 1996. The Dalmatians and Their Language. In Stephen Wurm, Peter Mühlhäusler & Darrell T. Tryon (eds.), *Atlas of Languages of Intercultural Communication in the Pacific, Asia, and the Americas*, Vol.II.1. Texts. 191–194. Berlin & New York: Mouton de Gruyter. [+ vol. I: *Maps*, Map 22, with Chris Corne, and Map 24, with James Northcote-Bade].
Stoffel, Hans-Peter. 2000. Slav Migrant Languages in the New World. In Lew Zybatow (ed.). *Sprachwandel in der Slavia. Die slavischen Sprachen an der Schwelle zum 21. Jahrhundert. Ein Internationales Handbuch.* Vol. 2 (Linguistik International 4), 805–829. Bern: Lang Verlag.
Stoffel, Hans-Peter. 2009. From the Adriatic Sea to the Pacific Ocean. The Croats in New Zealand. *Asian and African Studies* 18(2). 232–264.
Stoffel, Hans-Peter. 2011. The Joy of "Migranto". Dalmatian Skits as a Source for the Study of Croatian-English Language Contact in New Zealand. In Wolfgang Pöckl, Ingeborg Ohnheiser & Peter Sandrini (eds.), *Translation – Sprachvariation – Mehrsprachigkeit. Festschrift für Lew Zybatow zum 60. Geburtstag*, 407–422. Frankfurt a.M.: Peter Lang.
Surdučki, Milan. 1978. *Srpskohrvatski i engleski u kontaktu. Rečnik i morfološka analiza engleskih pozajmljenica u standardnom jeziku i jeziku Srba i Hrvata iseljenika u Kanadi.* [Serbo-Croatian and English in contact. A dictionary and morphological analysis of English borrowings in the standard language and in the language of Serb and Croat emigrants in Canada] Novi Sad: Matica srpska.
Sussex, Roland. 1993. Slavonic languages in emigration. In: Bernard Comrie & Greville Corbett (eds.) *The Slavonic Languages*, 999–1036. London: Routledge.
Šimundić, Mate. 1971. *Govor Imotske krajine i Bekije* [The speech of the Imotski County and Bekija]. Sarajevo: Akademija nauka i umjetnosti BiH.
Šimunović, Petar. 1979. Einführung. In Mate Hraste, Petar Šimunović & Reinhold Olesch (eds.). *Čakavisch-Deutsches Lexikon*. Teil 1. XII–XLVII. Wien: Böhlau.
Trlin, Andrew. 1979. *Now Respected, Once Despised. Yugoslavs in New Zealand*. Palmerston North: Dunmore Press Ltd.

Argentina

Anita Skelin Horvat, Maša Musulin and Ana Gabrijela Blažević
Croatian in Argentina: Lexical transfers in the speech of bilingual Croatian-Spanish speakers

1 Introduction

In this chapter, aspects of the language of Croatian migrants and their children and grandchildren in Argentina are presented. The Croatian community in Argentina is sizeable; depending on the source, estimates suggest there are between 250,000 and 500,000 Argentinian residents of Croatian background (Sinovčić 1991; Antić 2002). Emigration to Argentina started as early as the middle of the eighteenth century with large numbers settling in Argentina throughout the nineteenth century and the first part of the twentieth century (Sinovčić 1991; Šprljan 2014a, 2014b). Croats and their descendants live across all parts of the country. In many towns and cities there are various cultural organizations, and in several places, formal language instruction is organised as well. Argentina is known as a country of migrants and in many cities there are concentrations of Croatian settlers that organise festivals and other activities that mark their presence in Argentina. Croatian is therefore one of a number of transposed, 'immigrant' languages that are spoken in Argentina, alongside the dominant language, Spanish.

This chapter is structured in the following way. The remaining parts of this section present general demographic and sociolinguistic information on Croatian-origin residents in Argentina and on Croatian-speakers in that country. Section 3 gives details on the methodological tools employed to gain data from informants, together with some discussion on their acquisition of Croatian according to their generational membership. Section 3 presents sociolinguistic data on the language use of informants, whose speech forms the data sample for this chapter. Section 4 presents and discusses select examples from both datasets

---

Note: All three authors would like to express their gratitude to the University of Zagreb for two financial grants awarded in 2015 and 2016 that supported the field work and collection of data on which this chapter is based. Further, the authors would like to express their sincere thanks to the Central State Office for Croats Abroad for financial support of the following project *Jezični identiteti hrvatske iseljeničke zajednice u Argentini* 'Linguistic identities of the Croatian emigrant community in Argentina' that was awarded in 2016.

Anita Skelin Horvat, Maša Musulin and Ana Gabrijela Blažević, University of Zagreb

https://doi.org/10.1515/9781501503917-014

according to the following: lexical and pragmatic transference, loan translations and morphosyntactic change. Section 5 contains the conclusion with findings summarised.

1.1 History of contact, vintages of emigration, status

Argentina is largely a country of immigrants and is well known for its history of accepting immigrants. In the nineteenth century President Sarmiento launched a program that targeted European immigrants in a measure to both populate and modernize the country. Croats have been and remain a group that has benefitted from the legacy of targeted European immigration, and in general, host country attitudes towards them are positive. This is why Argentina is home to the largest Croatian émigré community in Latin America and Buenos Aires was usually the first place that emigrants to South America arrived in.

There have been several waves of immigration to Argentina over the last 150 years: late nineteenth century; early twentieth century (economic migration from Dalmatia and southern parts of Croatia); the inter-war period (economic migration from all parts of Croatia); immediate post-WWII period (largely political migration) (Sinovčić 1991; Šprljan 2004). Prior to WWI, small colonies of Croatian immigrants existed in other Latin American countries, such as Chile, Peru, Bolivia, Uruguay and Brazil, and there was also emigration to Venezuela in the inter-war years. However, Argentina remained the country with the largest number of Croatian settlers, with sizeable numbers not only in Buenos Aires, but also in other towns (Antić 2002). Antić (2002) records that there was also considerable mobility of Croatian settlers within Latin America, with many migrants 're-migrating' to other areas or countries due to employment or climatic reasons.

The earliest available documents (personal letters from the 1920s) indicate that immigration to Argentina reaches back to the 1860s, with larger numbers starting to arrive after 1881 when Argentina's economy began to expand rapidly (Antić 2002). There are accounts from young Dalmatian men about La Boca (the harbour area of Buenos Aires) as well as those who later settled in the province of Santa Fe, often in Rosario, its largest city. Antić (2002) estimates that at the beginning of the twentieth century, there were some 25,000 Croats in Argentina, with 4,000 to 5,000 in Buenos Aires, and this number rose to 130,000 before WWII. This was due, in large part, to the restrictive immigration policies of the US that led to immigrants settling in other parts of the Americas.

In Argentinian national or immigration records, it is hard to identify and quantify the total number of Croatian migrants, due to the fact that these documents typically record immigrants' 'country of origin'. Šprljan (2004: 46–47) gives the example of his grandfather and changing 'countries of origin': he was born in 1911 and lived in the same place until emigration to Argentina in the 1940s – the Austro-Hungarian Empire, Kingdom of Serbs, Croatians and Slovenians, Kingdom of Yugoslavia, Federal People's Republic of Yugoslavia. Most Croats in these early years worked in the maritime industry or agriculture. During this period some early migrants gained fame and repute, e.g. Nikola (Nicolás) Plantić, who arrived in 1748 and became a professor at the University in Córdoba, or Ivan Vučetić (Juan Vucetich), who emigrated from the island of Hvar in 1882 and who was the worldwide pioneer of dactyloscopy (i.e. science of finger-printing) (Šprljan 2004). Croatian has no official status in Argentina.

1.2 Number of Croatian-heritage residents, number of Croatian-speakers

The Croatian community in Argentina is sizeable. As stated, estimates range from 250,000 (Central State Office for Croats Abroad 2019) to a figure somewhere between this and 500,000 (Sinovčić 1991; Antić 2002). A respected member of the Croatian community, Joza Vrljičak, estimates the number to be 422,000 (personal communication). He bases this on the identification of 116,000 persons with a Croatian surname from the Argentinian electoral register, with factors such as demographic growth, and the fact that women in Argentina do not pass on their surname to their children, taken into account. There are no Argentinian official statistics about size or number of migrant groups. Due to a long history of immigration there are now Croatian-Argentinians of the third and fourth generations. It is difficult to estimate how many still actively use Croatian due to the lack of statistical data.

1.3 Distribution, socio-economic profile

Croats are dispersed all over Argentina, but the biggest communities live in Buenos Aires, Rosario and Córdoba. The lack of official statistics means that we can only make very general remarks about the educational profile of our sample, based on questionnaire responses, where educational level is often indicative of socio-economic profile. A high percentage (37%) have a university degree, 17% have had some sort of higher education and 32% finished secondary school. These figures are higher than the national average, and in general, it is possible that the socio-economic profile of Croats is slightly higher than that of the general population.

1.4 Infrastructure

There are many cultural associations, mainly folkloric groups, but also language schools for children, as well as print and electronic media. These are located in Buenos Aires as well as in 23 other localities across Argentina. The Croatian Ministry of Science and Education supports the teaching of Croatian at two cultural centres, the *Centro Juvenil Argentino-Croata* and at the *Circulo Croata*, both in Buenos Aires. There is also language instruction provided at the two Croatian Catholic parishes in Buenos Aires, and instruction is also provided in Rosario and Córdoba. Rosario is where the *Hola* project was established in 1998 for the teaching of Croatian, under the auspices of the Croatian Heritage Foundation and in collaboration with Spanish language students from the University of Zagreb. Gadže (2017) records that over the years, there have been 52 books published in Croatian or about Croatia, with the most famous one being the periodical *Studia Croatica* founded in 1960. *Studia Croatica* is a Spanish-language journal that publishes Croatian-themed academic and scientific papers. There are three radio programs *Croacias totales* 'Total Croatia' in Buenos Aires, *Croacia en mi corazón* 'Croatia in my heart' in San Justo, and *Bar croata* 'Croatian bar' in Rosario that transmit programs in both Croatian and Spanish.

1.5 Domain use, language maintenance and shift

Intra-family and cross-generational settings are the domains in which Croatian is used most, and the main linguistic models for younger speakers are their grandparents or older family members. From interviews it is difficult to predict the future of Croatian in Argentina: there are some third and fourth generation members that are able to speak Croatian, and there are some second-generation ones who lack any proficiency. Factors influencing this are endogamy, proximity of grandparents, community involvement, level of contact with Croatian, opportunity to receive formal instruction, notions of identity and connectedness with Croatia.

1.6 Contacts with Croatia, host country attitudes towards Croats

Related to the last point in the previous section, levels of contact between Argentina and Croatia are much higher today than they were in the past. The affordability of inter-continental air travel and the availability of electronic media and communication tools are responsible for this. Our data sample of 337 informants shows that over 80% have visited Croatia, with some having visited the country up to five times.

2 Methodology and details of informants

The data presented in this chapter were collected during three weeks of field research in the three largest cities, Buenos Aires, Córdoba and Rosario. The field work involved the collection of recorded spoken language, sociolinguistic and ethnolinguistic vitality data via questionnaires, as well as the collection of data relating to language contact between Croatian and Spanish and its consequences. The aim of the field work was to document the position of Croatian within the community, the use of language within different generations and the changes that the language is going through, including the influence of Spanish on it. The research data presented in this chapter consists of two samples. The first is a sample of 337 sociolinguistic questionnaires completed by first-generation informants (N=1; 0.3%), second-generation informants (N=177; 53%) and third or fourth generation informants (N=156; 46%). The age of informants ranged from 17 to 90. Nearly two-thirds (65%) of the participants (N=219) were women and 34% men (N=114). The second sample presented here is based on an analysis of transcribed recorded interactions with 12 Croatian-speakers who are part of a larger group of 44 speakers who were interviewed by the authors. The 12 informants of the second sample consist of: 5 Gen.1 speakers with an age range of 71 to 92; 5 Gen.2 speakers with an age range of 43 to 69; 1 Gen.3 speaker aged 21; and 1 Gen.4 speaker aged 32. Most informants of the second sample participated in providing data for the first sample, except the interviewed Gen.1 participants.

The authors relied mainly on ethnically affiliated institutions and existing contacts within these institutions to contact and interview potential informants. The authors make no claim about this smaller sample being representative of the wider Croatian-Argentinian community, and it is hard for us to assess whether features of the speech of less ethnically affiliated Croats are similar to those presented here. All interviews lasted about 1 hour or longer. The total length of the interviews recorded with informants in the second sample is 13 hours and 26 minutes.

Most of the Gen.1 informants included in this analysis attended primary school in Croatia and one of them went to high school there. They usually came to Argentina with other family members relatives, but also often left other members of their immediate family behind in Croatia. The range of contact with the remaining family members varies from no contact to very frequent. Regarding contact with other Croats in Argentina, the situation varies between cities. Of the five first-generation informants, two of the three informants living in Buenos Aires lived almost completely surrounded by Croats and only one of them had a more varied circle of friends along with Croatian ones. The informant from Córdoba mentioned she had close contact and still meets with other Croats, while the informant from Rosario identified a difference in the vintage of migration and different political convictions as reasons why she had little contact with other Croats in her area.

The four second-generation informants are all children of endogamous marriages and their parents spoke only Croatian at home. The three informants from Buenos Aires grew up closely connected with the Croatian community and attended Croatian language classes. Although the single informant from Córdoba did not attend language classes, all four second-generation informants are today very active members of their local Croatian community.

The third-generation informant grew up with frequent contact with Croatian as all grandparents were Croatians and very active in the community. This informant spent two semesters studying Croatian in Croatia. The fourth-generation informant has Croatian origins only on his father's side and did not have much contact with the language until his adult years. He spent a couple of months in Croatia visiting family but did not undertake formal instruction in the language.

3 Sociolinguistic description of informants' language use

In most diaspora communities language occupies a special status. Croatian minority groups in Argentina see their ancestral language as a component of a cultural and historical heritage that they are trying to maintain. Not every Argentinian with Croatian roots speaks the language, but almost all Croatian-Argentinians (or at least those who were interviewed) are aware of the danger of losing the language. For this reason, Croatian language courses have become a prominent part of the community's activities, notwithstanding their modest financial resources. In Buenos Aires, the *Mala škola* ('Little school') has been instructing children in language, folk-dancing and traditional singing since 1954. In Rosario, home to a large Croatian community, Croatian is taught by teachers sent from Croatia, who have proficiency in Spanish, within the auspices of the *Hola* program.[1] Classes

---

[1] The *Hola* program was initiated by locally-born community members in their capacity as community leaders and as honorary members of the Croatian diplomatic corps – Pablo Soto Bog-

are also organized in surrounding localities as well. In Córdoba, the *Kolito*, as it is called (compound of Cro. *kolo* 'circle dance' + Span. *–ito* diminutive, meaning 'little kolo') is organized every Saturday at the *Hrvatski dom / Hogar croata* 'Croatian House' where traditional songs and dancing are taught, with some language instruction as well. Scholarships to study Croatian in Croatia have been awarded to younger-generation Croatian-Argentinians by the Central State Office for Croats Abroad, and the same body financially supports many cultural activities organised by Argentina-based Croatian associations (Central State Office for Croats Abroad 2019). The Croatian embassy in Buenos Aires and the honorary consulates in Córdoba and San Miguel de Tucumán also provide support for locally-focussed cultural initiatives. Surmising the factors that may be conducive to language maintenance, we observe that institutional support (coming here from the country of origin, rather than the country of emigration), along with status and demography may be factors that can contribute to the ethnolinguistic vitality of a group (Giles, Bourhis and Taylor 1977).

In interviews it was often mentioned that those from the same town or area who had already emigrated before quite often determined the choice of destination for subsequent immigrants. In the larger cities with a higher concentration of Croats, there were (and are still) some neighbourhoods with a large number of Croatian-origin residents, who themselves describe it as a support network, even as 'a kind of family'. Amongst many informants from these areas, we can observe features that conform to Fishman's (2001: 451–171) nexus of the "home-family-neighbourhood community".

In regard to descriptions of the languages that informants have proficiency in, two questions were posed. The first, *What is your mother tongue?* was intentionally ambiguous knowing that for some informants mother tongue is the first language they have learned and for some the language of the family or their heritage language. And for that reason the second question clearly relates to linguistic dominance, *What is the language you know best?* Although almost all (N=316, 94%) of the first group informants (questionnaire answers) report a higher level proficiency in Spanish than Croatian, when asked which of the two they consider their mother tongue, 33.3 % (N=112) chose Croatian. An additional 3.3% (N=11) selected both Spanish and Croatian, as can be seen in the following Figure 1.[2]

---

danić (Chile) and Lucija Zizich (Rosario, Argentina). Since its inception, 58 students from Zagreb University with Spanish proficiency have taught in this program in 11 localities across South America (Hrvatska matica iseljenika 2019).

2 Only one Gen.1 speaker completed the sociolinguistic questionnaire. However, 5 Gen.1 speakers participated in the recorded interviews. The reason why four Gen.1 speakers did not complete

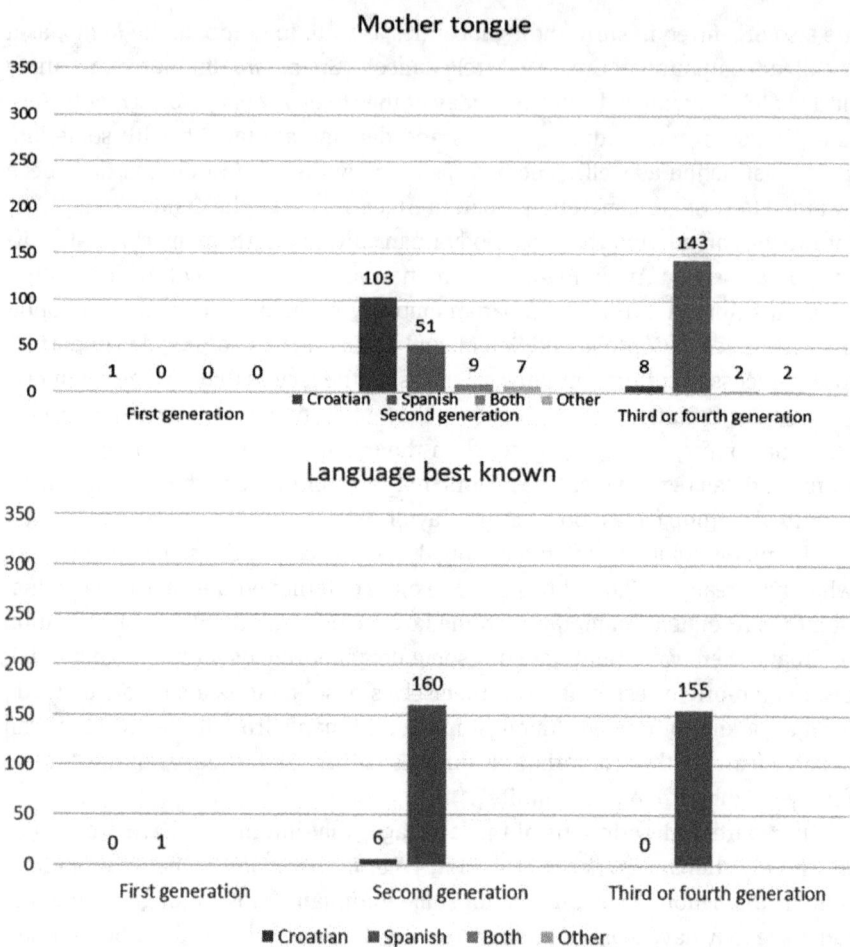

Figure 1: Self-reported descriptions of informants' 'mother tongue' and their dominant language.

Although oral proficiency in Croatian may be variable for some informants, many consider it an important symbol of identity and thus, their 'mother tongue', regardless of their ability to actively use it. A very large percentage of informants (82.8 %) stated that they considered the language important, as they wanted to maintain relations with the homeland of their ancestors. An even higher percentage (85.5%) believed that Croatian culture could only be understood through the

---

the sociolinguistic questionnaire was due to their advanced age (71 to 92 years) and our reluctance to subject them to a rather long and demanding questionnaire.

language. Almost half mentioned the importance and instrumental function of language proficiency as a means to obtain Croatian citizenship (47.2%).[3]

In terms of other organisations that support or facilitate Croatian-language institutions, it has most often been Catholic clergymen or members of religious orders who have been teachers and providers of formal instruction in Croatian. In particular, members of religious orders, both brothers (most often Franciscans) and nuns were responsible for Croatian-language teaching provided for school-age children. Church services were and are still held in Croatian in Buenos Aires, and members of the Croatian Catholic clergy co-ordinate religious and non-religious Croatian-language activities that enable interaction between Croatian-speakers, e.g. folk-dancing groups, learning and playing of traditional instruments, celebrating Croatian festivities and so on.

There are also various other mostly informal organisations, often in private premises because other cities in Argentina don't have a Croatian church. They usually exist under the name *Hrvatski dom* (or *Hogar croata* 'Croatian house') or *Hrvatski kulturni centar* (or *Centro cultural croata* 'Croatian cultural centre'). Gatherings are usually on Sundays or festive days. For example, traditional dances are organised every week for younger children and adults at the *Hrvatski dom* in Córdoba and *Hrvatski kulturni centar* in Buenos Aires.

4 Presentation and analysis of spoken Croatian data

In this section, only some instances of cross-linguistic influence between Croatian and Spanish in the language of bilingual Croatian-Spanish speakers in Argentina are presented. The elements presented here – these are also the most frequently occurring ones in the data sample based on the transcribed interviews with the 12 informants,[4] – are lexical transfers (or according to some authors code switches),

---

3 Prior to 2020, during some periods, persons of Croatian-origin born outside Croatia were required to have a "knowledge of the Croatian language and the Roman-script alphabet" (orig.: "poznavanje hrvatskog jezika i latiničnog pisma") if they wished to apply for Croatian citizenship through descent (Središnji državni portal 2020). At the time of data collection this requirement was still in place and so acquisition of Croatian, at least for some, may have been partly motivated by the desire to gain Croatian citizenship.
4 We provide information about the generation to which the informants belong and their age. Gen.1 members are those who moved to Argentina aged 14 or older, while Gen.2 members are those born in Argentina to Gen.1 parents, or who migrated at a very early age. Gen.3 members are the children of Gen.2 ones, and Gen.4 members are the children of Gen.3 ones.

semantic transfers primarily due to calquing and code switching. Below, we briefly discuss features of the most frequent elements, lexical transfers and code-switches, providing a definition here based on different theoretical approaches.

Even though it could be seen that lexical transference and code switching are rather different phenomena it is still not easy to differentiate them. According to Matras (2009: 106), lexical borrowing usually refers to the use of vocabulary from one language in another while code-switching is "spontaneous language mixing in the conversation of bilinguals". During the process of lexical transference a lexical item can be changed on different levels and with different outcomes. There are different sociolinguistic circumstances that shape the contact language situation in general, and transference processes in particular. Lexical transference is usually the first one occurring in a language contact situation, while the transference of other language elements, and especially structural change, happens usually only within situations of more intense contact between languages. Code-switching is understood here as "the use of two language varieties in the same conversation" (Myers-Scotton 2006: 239) and usually includes longer sequences of lexical items from the other language (cf. Myers-Scotton 2006). Excerpts from the linguistic sample are given in each of the following sections. Information is given on the informant from whom an excerpt is taken, which includes the informant number, their generational membership and their age. Thus, the following information in brackets (12, Gen. 2, 69) identifies the speaker as being informant number 12 and as a second-generation speaker who was aged 69 at the time of data collection.

4.1 Lexical transfers and loan translations

Interviews were conducted predominantly in Croatian. We therefore consider Spanish lexemes to be transfers where both meaning and the phonemic shape of the word are imported. Because the speakers are Spanish-Croatian bilinguals, these imported elements typically remain unintegrated at the phonological level, i.e. bilingual speakers do not (always) substitute phonemes particular to Spanish with the equivalent ones from Croatian. In previous studies on Croatian in contact situations, Filipović (1986) distinguished three levels of integration depending on the type: complete, partial and free phonological integration (or 'transphonemisation') and null, partial and complete morphological integration (or 'transmorphemisation'). In our corpus, various degrees of integration for both types are found.

Within the corpus of lexical transfers identified, we firstly present nouns (4.1.1) as the most common part of speech transferred, followed by adjectives

(4.1.2), verbs (4.1.3), adverbs (4.1.4), discourse markers (4.1.5) and loan translations (4.1.6). Integrated as well as unintegrated groups of nouns relate to what Myers-Scotton (2002: 239) describes as two types of transfers: cultural borrowings, which include names for objects, institutions and culture of the Argentinian society and core borrowed forms that "duplicate already existing words in the L1." Myers-Scotton (2002: 239) considers that cultural borrowings usually appear abruptly while core ones "usually begin life in a recipient language when bilinguals introduce them as singly occurring codeswitching forms". We agree that it is difficult to make a distinction between lexical transference and code-switching in the language of the bilinguals. Some of our examples could be analysed as either lexical transfers or single-word code-switches.

4.1.1 Nouns

We commence our examination of lexical transfers by looking first at nouns. Amongst these, examples of cultural borrowings are conspicuous and we begin our discussion with this sub-group. These are mostly nouns including the names of some cultural symbols that are multi-word items both with and without phonological and morphological integration (see Piasevoli; Jutronić; Petrović; Hlavac and Stolac; Stoffel and Hlavac, all this volume). Integration into Croatian usually occurs and is usually ascertainable due to the morphological differences between Croatian and Spanish, i.e. Croatian nouns and other nominal classes of words have declinations, while in Spanish that is not the case. Morphological integration of Spanish nouns includes mostly applying nominal inflection onto lexical transfers (Matras 2009), e.g. assigning Croatian phi-features to Spanish-origin items. In the examples provided in this and in the following sections Croatian is identifiable as the matrix language while Spanish is the embedded language (Myers-Scotton 2002). In some instances, we find what appear to be the opposite: Croatian-origin items with Spanish suffixes, eg. *kolito* 'little kolo' derived from Croatian *kolo* 'circle dance' with the Spanish diminutive ending *-ito*. The form *kolo* and more particularly *kolito* are used in the *Spanish* speech of Croatian-Argentinians, and as a diminutive form, then 're-borrowed' back into Croatian spoken in Argentina, as a Croatian-origin item that is a cultural borrowing specific to the Spanish-language, and subsequently, Croatian-language speech of Croatian-Argentinians. It is has also become the name for a children's folk-dancing group based in Córdoba. Below is a lexical transfer that represents a cultural borrowing specific to the setting of the speaker's workplace.

(1) jer   ja   kako radim   na   Pravnom   fakultetu,
    because I   as   work-1SG at+LOC Law-LOC.M.SG Faculty-LOC.M.SG
    ovo   mi   je...   **barcito**...
    this me-DAT be-3SG... barcito ['little coffee bar']
    'As I work at the Law Faculty, this is my **barcito** (= little coffee bar=)...'
    (12,Gen.2,69)

Cultural borrowings are mostly names for different institutions, streets, holidays, food, specific products, etc. and primarily serve to fill a perceived lexical gap (Myers-Scotton 2002; Matras 2009; Dewaele and Li 2014).

(2) jer   kak' slavimo   tu   **veinticinco de mayo** Željko
    because   as   celebrate-1PL here the 25th of May   Željko
    pravi   ovaj uvijek   **asado**   i   napravimo
    prepare-3SG this always   roast meat-ACC.M/N.SG   and make-1PL
    empanade   i   onda   reko'   **bueno** a   kod
    empanada-ACC.F.PL   and then   say-1SG.PAST   fine   and at+GEN
    mog   **consuegra**   jedemo   **locro**
    my-GEN.M.SG consuegro-GEN.M.SG   eat-1PL   Argentinian stew-ACC.M/N.SG
    taj   dan
    that-ACC.M.SG day-ACC.M.SG
    'Because, as we celebrate here **veinticinco de mayo** (the '25th of May') Željko prepares, um, always **asado** ('roast meat') and we make **empanadas** and then I said, **bueno** ('fine'), and at my **consuegro**'s (= father-in-law's) house we eat **locro** (= Argentinian stew) that day. (3,Gen.1,61)

In (2), we see that alongside four cultural transfers, two other Spanish-origin forms occur, *bueno* 'fine' and *consuegro* 'father-in-law of one's own son or daughter'. The form *consuegro* can perhaps also be considered a cultural transfer: the term may denote a Spanish-speaking person; or the term may denote a Croatian-origin person referred to in a way characteristic of Argentinian social relations. (Croatian, like English, does not have a discrete lexeme for this designation and employs a semantically periphrastic construction similar to that in English.) The occurrence of *bueno* 'fine' can be seen as the transference of verbatim direct speech, i.e. the speaker used this form as a way to signal his readiness to take leave from celebrations at Željko's house.

(3) jako zgodno i   kad   smo   imali...   priredbu
    very nice   and when AUX-1PL have-PAST.M.PL   event-ACC.F.SG
    de fin de años   svaki   se   obuko   u...
    end-of-school celebration everyone REFL   put- PAST.M.SG on...
    'really nice and when we had.. an event **de fin de años** (= end-of-school celebration), everybody put on...' (3,Gen.1,74)

Some instances of lexical transference are flagged through phrases preceding or succeeding them. An instance is given in (4) that also contains the Croatian translated equivalent of the second lexical transfer, *derecho internacional*:

(4) ona je   učila   kako se   kaže   **abogacía** tu
    she AUX-3SG study-PST.F.SG   how   REFL say.3SG   advocacy   here
    predaje... **derecho internacional** međunarodno   pravo.
    teach-3SG   international law   international- ACC.N.SG. law-ACC.N.SG
    'She taught, what's it called?... **abogacía (=advocacy)** ... here she teaches **derecho internacional (=international law)**, international law.' (2,Gen.1,72)

The instances given above are all examples of Spanish-origin items that are not phonologically or (overtly) morphologically integrated into Croatian. Examples (5) and (6) below contain insertions *cuadra* 'block' and *empresa* 'firm' that are both phonologically and morphologically integrated.

(5) ali sa   Malinom smo   bili   ovdje jer   ovdje
    but with+INS   Malina   AUX-1PL be-PAST.PL.M   here   because   here
    na   tri   **cuadre**   ovako u   ulici
    on   three+GEN   block-GEN.F.SG   like   in+LOC   street-LOC.F.SG
    Peru mi smo   živili   u   jednoj
    Peru we AUX-1PL live-PAST.M.PL   in+LOC   one-LOC.F.SG
    cuadri   a   ona je   živjela   u
    block-LOC.F.SG   and she AUX-3SG live-PAST.F.SG   in+LOC
    drugoj   ovako
    another-LOC.F.SG   like this
    'But with Malina we were here because across three **cuadra (=block)**', like in Peru street, ehm.. we lived in one **cuadra (= block)** and she lived in another, like this... (7,Gen.1,74)

(6) ovaj   od   osam   do   šest se   radi   ili   do   četiri
    well   from   eight   until   six   REFL   work-3SG or   until four
    već   ovisi   u   kojoj   si   **empresi**
    rather depend-3SG   in+LOC   which-LOC.F.SG   be-2SG   firm-LOC.F.SG
    'Well, from eight to six are the working hours, or until four, it depends on which **empresa (=firm)** you work in.' (3,Gen.1,74)

(7) i   onda   ima   **primose**   ona   ima
    and   then   have-3SG   cousin-ACC.M.PL   she   have-3SG
    dvoje   djece
    two+GEN   children-GEN.F.SG
    'And then she has **primose (=cousins)**, she has two children.' (3,Gen.1,74)

4.1.2 Adjectives

Spanish-origin adjectives are also located in our corpus, along with verbs and adverbs. But adjectives as well as the other parts of speech remain less frequent than nouns that are the most readily transferred category. Adjectives are generally less transferable than nouns and only a relatively small number of adjectives were recorded in the corpus. Matras (2009: 188) makes the observation that adjectives tend to occur as attributives and to be syntactically integrated (and recognizable) as such through the adoption of morphology from the recipient language. Most of the adjectives in our sample are used predicatively (as a part of nominal predicative) and they do not attract the morphology of the recipient language, Croatian. Instead, they retain the morphological features of the donor language, Spanish, as shown in examples (8) to (12) below:

(8) na   primjer   približava   se   neki   ono
    for+ACC   example-ACC.M.SG   approach-3SG   REFL   some-NOM.M.SG   like
    šta   ja   znam   čovjek   koji   izgleda   ono
    what   I   know-1SG   man-NOM.M.SG   who-NOM.M.SG   appear-3SG   like
    aj ajmo   reć   tako   to   **peligroso**   ono
    le let's   say-INF   such   that   dangerous   like
    'For example, some, like, what do I know, man approaches who looks, like, le.. let's say, pretty, um, **peligroso (=dangerous)**, um. . . (8,Gen.3,21)

In example (8), *peligroso*–M.SG 'dangerous' bears Spanish morphological marking. It does not attract overt Croatian marking for the feature M.SG that requires a consonant-final suffix, e.g. *peligros* (?) or *peligrosan* (?). Thus, *peligroso* is a 'bare' form. We observe also that it is an adjective used predicatively and that it is dislocated from the noun it refers back to across a clause boundary and other hesitation features.

In example (8) the M.SG form of the Spanish adjective is congruent to the morphological features of the Croatian subject, *čovjek* 'man' NOM.M.SG. In example (9), the demonstrative pronoun *to* NOM.N.SG 'that' is the subject while the Spanish adjective *tremendo* NOM.M.SG 'tremendous' bears an *–o* suffix. In Croatian, the *–o* suffix coincides with the morphological marking of neuter rather than masculine. The morphological marking of *tremendo* is congruent morphologically with neuter marking of the Croatian neuter subject.

(9) sí, sí   to   ko   god   ti   veli
     yes, yes   that-NOM.N.SG   who   ever you-DAT.SG   say-3SG
     to   je   **tremendo**
     that-NOM.N.SG   be-3SG   tremendous-M.SG
     'Yes, yes, that whoever tells you, that is **tremendo (=tremendous)**.'
     (3,Gen.1,74)

A similar coincidence occurs in the following example, where the Spanish adjective *paciente* 'patient' M/F.SG has an *–e* suffix. In Croatian, an *-e* suffix marks an adjective as FEM.PL, which conforms to the feature marking of the Croatian subject, *gospođe* 'ladies' NOM.F.PL.

(10) erm   gospođe   su   tolko   pažljivi
     er   lady-NOM.F.PL   be-3PL   so   attentive-NOM.M.PL
     i   **paciente**   kako   se   kaže
     and   patient-M/F.SG as   REFL   say-3SG
     'Erm, ladies are so attentive and... **paciente** (=patient) as they say'
     (5,Gen.2,69)

The morphological suffix of *paciente* is *–e*, a form that in Croatian marks an attributive or noun as FEM.PL and, on first glance, appears to be morphologically integrated into the Croatian morphosyntactic grid of the clause. But in Spanish, the morphological marking of *paciente* is M/F.SG. In Spanish, the plural form to agree with *gospođe*–F.PL would be *pacientes*–F.PL, e.g. *las damas son pacientes* – 'the ladies are patient'. It appears the speaker has employed the 'base' form of the adjective of 'patient', *paciente* rather than one that reflects Spanish F.PL morphological marking. Further, the Croatian adjective closer to the subject *gospođe*, namely *pažljivi* 'attentive' is marked morphologically as MASC.PL. There is apparent discordance in the marking of attributives and of their head nouns. Where concordance does occur, such as that between *gospode*-F.PL and *paciente*-F, it is probably co-incidental.

In example (11) the subject in the second clause is 2PL, and the predicative adjective is required to agree with the gender and number of the subject -*i* for M.PL, -*e* for F.PL. The morphological suffix of the Spanish adjective is neither –*i* nor –*e*. But its form is clearly plural, *ridículos*-M.PL.

(11) kad   govore   o   manjinama   reko'
     when   talk-3PL about+LOC minority-LOC.F.PL   say-PST.M.PL
     nemojte bit   **ridículos**
     don't-2PL be-INF   ridiculous-M.PL
     'When they talk about minorities, I said, don't be **ridículos (=ridiculous)**.'
     (3,Gen.1,74)

In example (11) *ridículos* 'ridiculous' bears Spanish M.PL marking. The form of this predicate adjective does not change when referring back to a Croatian subject that has M.PL marking. In Croatian, the morphological suffix -*i* marks adjectives as masculine plural. A form such as *ridículosi* (?) 'ridiculous-M.PL' is not attested.

We observe that predicatively employed Spanish adjectives bear default or unmarked masculine morphology, and usually SG and only sometimes PL-marked morphemes. Spanish adjectives bear these forms regardless of whether the Croatian subject also bears these features, or whether the form of the adjective's suffix coincides with the features of a target suffix in Croatian. Looking beyond root forms of adjectives, Matras (2009: 190) reports that comparative and superlative forms of the adjective can be transferred, more usually in situations of long-term, prolonged contact. In our corpus one example of a non-positive form is recorded:

(12) ovi   su   vam   **mejores**   koji   imaju
     these   be-3PL   you-DAT.PL   better-M.PL   who-NOM.M.PL   have-3PL
     dulce de leche to   je   **dulce**   to
     dulce de leche   that-NOM.N.SG   be-3SG   sweet- M.SG   that-NOM.N.SG
     je   slatko   od   mlijeka   znate
     be-3SG sweet-NOM.N.SG   from+GEN   milk-GEN.N.SG   know-2PL
     'These are **mejores** (=better), that have **dulce de leche** (=sweetened caramel milk), that is **dulce** (=sweet), that is sweet from milk, you know.'
     (1,Gen.2,43)

Here, the Spanish comparative adjective[5] is not given in its default M.SG form, but in a form that is M.PL to agree with the Croatian subject *ovi* 'these'-NOM.M.PL. In this way, example (12) patterns in a way similar to (11).

4.1.3 Verbs

In our corpus, transferred verbs occur as both phonologically and morphologically integrated forms. Integrated verbs in our corpus usually have Croatian conjugational endings added on the Spanish root. Spanish has three main verb classes according to infinitive endings *-ar*, *-er* and *–ir*. Croatian has six verb classes according to infinitive endings and present tense forms. In relation to the integration of Spanish verbs into Croatian a pattern becomes recognisable that Spanish verbs ending in *-ir* attract the Croatian verbal suffix *–irati*, a suffix commonly used for transferred verbs (Jernej 1959; Skok 1955); e.g. *traducir* > *tradusirati* 'translate', *transmitir* > *trasmicirati* 'transmit'. Examples (13) and (14) contain such integrated verbal forms:

(13) *ja   sam   u   Italiji   **tradusirala**   ja   sam*
     I   AUX-1SG   in+LOC   Italy-LOC.F.SG   translate-PST.F.SG   I   AUX-1SG
     *svršila   ovaj   za   **traduktoru***
     finish-PST.F.SG   this   for+ACC translator-ACC.F.SG
     'In Italy I **tradusirala** (=translated), I finished this [course].. to become a **traduktora** (=translator).' (3,Gen.1,74)

(14) *mi..mislim   ja   se   **trasmicira**   prema   od*
     th.. think-1SG   I   REFL   transmit-3SG   towards   from+GEN
     didove   od   didovi   do
     grandfather-ACC.M.PL   from+GEN   grandfather-NOM.M.PL   to+GEN
     unuke   i   poslije   do, do   trećeg
     grandchildren-ACC.M.PL   and   after   to, to+GEN   third-GEN.M.SG
     I thi.. think it is **trasmicira** (= passed on) towards, from grandfathers, from grandfathers to grandchildren and later, to, to.. the third. . . (9,Gen.4,32)

A further example of a Spanish-origin verb with the *–irati* suffix is given in example (15). This example contains an instance of phonological integration

---

[5] In some grammars the form *mejores* is considered not only a comparative form but also a superlative form. In this example *mejores* could be understood as a superlative form.

where a change in consonant occurs from Span. *grabar* 'to record' to *gravar*. Both /b/ and /v/ have the same pronunciation in Spanish as a bi labial voiced stop or fricative. It is not clear why /b/ is replaced by /v/ to yield *gravar*. Example (15) also shows that a Spanish –*ar* verb can also attract the –*irati* suffix in Croatian:

(15) i   on   je   reko   da   sada   su   dobili
     and   he   AUX-3SG   say-PST.M.SG   that   now   AUX-3PL   receive-PST.M.PL
     jednu   pomoć   iz   Hrvatske   i
     one-ACC.F.SG   assistance-ACC.F.SG from+GEN   Croatia-GEN.F.SG   and
     onda   **graviraju**   jedan   CD
     then   record-3PL   one-ACC.M.SG   CD-ACC.M.SG
     'And he said that they now received a help from Croatia and then they **graviraju** (=record – Span. **grabar**) one CD.' (7,Gen.1,74)

Other Spanish verbs ending in -*ar* take on the conjugational pattern of the fifth verb class in Croatian where present tense is formed with -*a*-; e.g. *poblar* > *pueblati* 'to populate'.

(16) ako   se   manjine   ne, ne   pueblaju   sa
     if   REFL   minorities-NOM.F.PL NEG   **pueblaju** (=populate) with+INS
     Argentincima   uvijek   će   biti
     Argentinian-INS.M.PL   always   FUT.AUX-3SG   be-INF
     'If minorities don't, don't **pueblaju** ('= populate' > 're-produce') with Argentinians, it will always be...' (3,Gen.1,74)

Because of the small number of transferred verbs we cannot make any general conclusions about the adaptation of verbs. However, it is interesting to note that the Croatian verbal suffix employed in three of the four examples shown here is –*irati*. This suffix is the most widely used one in Croatian for transferred verbs, particularly those from Romance languages such as Italian or French, congruent to Spanish here. In contrast, in English-Croatian contact situations, the following verb suffixes are found to be more productive: –*ati* and –*ovati* in AUS.Cro (see Hlavac and Stolac, this volume); or –*iti* and –*ati* in NZ.Cro (see Stoffel and Hlavac, this volume). There are some Spanish verbs that appear to occur in an unintegrated form, or at least in a form that is ambiguous. For example, in (17), the verb form, *toca* occurs. It can be analysed as the Spanish PRS.3SG form of *tocar* 'to touch', which as an intransitive verb in this case refers to an obligation that someone has. Alternatively, it can be analysed as a transferred verb integrated into Croatian – *tok-a* PRS.3SG of *tokati* 'it's my turn'.

(17) ja   sam   njih   pozvala   doma   kod   tate
     I   AUX-1SG them-ACC   invite-PST.F.SG home   at+GEN   dad-GEN.F.SG
     u   kuću   jer   sam   rekla   tati
     in+ACC   house-ACC.F.SG   because   AUX-1SG say-PST.F.SG   dad-DAT.F.SG
     reko   sad   **me**   **toca**
     say-PST.M.SG   now   me-ACC   touch-3SG
     I invited them to my dad's house, cause I said to dad, he said, now **me toca** (=it's my turn') (3,Gen.1,74)

In (17), the object pronoun *me* ('me'-ACC) that precedes *toca/toka* does not provide us with further information on the linguistic affiliations of this phrase, as the form *me* is common to both Spanish and Croatian and in both languages it can pre-pose the finite verb. We therefore provide two accounts for what is happening in (17). The first is that it is an entirely Spanish phrase, albeit a truncation of the full phrase *me toca a mí* 'it's my turn'. The second one is a verb integrated into Croatian that has attracted 3.SG marking as an –*ati* verb, i.e. *tokati* 'to touch' that is preceded by its object *me* ('me' ACC.SG.CLITIC). The only problem with the second account is that *me toka* 'it's my turn' appears as a non-transparent and rather strange-sounding phrase; it is unknown in HMLD.Cro, but this is not to say that a construction OBJ + *tokati* is not inconceivable in the repertoires of Croatian-Argentinians. There would need to be further instances such as *ga toka* 'his turn' (?) or *nas toka* 'our turn' (?) for this to be verified as an integrated verb that has functions beyond set idioms such as *me toca / me toka*.

Another type of Spanish verbal construction that is found in the corpus is the construction of the type 'reflexive + impersonal 3SG', e.g. *se acabó* 'that's it, it's over'. Example (18) contains the following instance of it:

(18) već   kad   mi   se   rodila   prva
     already   when   me-DAT   REFL   bear-PST.F.SG   first-NOM.F.SG
     kćer   kao   da   sam   ja   rekla   se
     daughter-NOM.F.SG like   COMP   AUX-1SG I   say-PST.F.SG   se-REFL
     acabó   tu   živim   to   moram   prihvatiti
     finished   here   live-1SG   that-ACC.N.SG   must-1SG   accept-INF
     When my first daughter was born, it was like I said, **se acabó** (= that's it, it's over), I live here, I have to accept that. (3,Gen.1,74)

In example (18), the transferred form together with a reflexive particle constitutes an entire clause. Syntactically, the code-switch is independent of the morphosyntactic features of the surrounding clause as it occurs as an inter-clausal insertion.

4.1.4 Adverbs

Adverbs also make up a smaller number of transfers compared to nouns. In our corpus seven adverbs and adverbial phrases are documented, *directamente* 'directly', *totalmente* 'totally', *aparte* 'apart', *también* 'also', *acá* 'here', *así*, 'like that', *por ahí* 'there', as well as NPs with adverbial function such as *lo mismo* 'the same'. In Spanish there are two groups of adverbs regarding form. One group is made of adverbs based on the FEM. form of the adjective and the suffix + *-mente*. The other group is made up of adverbs with diverse forms. In our corpus both forms of adverbs are used. In Croatian, adverbs derived from adjectives bear the following morphological marking: NOM.N.SG. Croatian adverbs bear this morphological marking regardless of the features of the verbs or adjectives that they qualify.

(19) sam   ga   našo   i   da   ja
     AUX-1SG   him-ACC   find-PST.M.SG   and that I
     i   ništa   ok   **directamente** ništa
     and   nothing okay   directly   nothing
     I found him and that I... and nothing, okay, **directamente** (=directly/absolutely) nothing. (5,Gen.2,69)

(20) **claro**   oni   govore   nemaju   problema
     clearly   they-M.PL   speak-3PL   have-NEG.3PL   problem-GEN.M.SG
     miješani   brak   ne   možeš   ti   ja   ne
     mixed-NOM.M.SG   marriage-NOM.M.SG   NEG   can-2SG you   I   NEG
     pozovem   moje   kćeri   **aparte**   moje
     invite-1SG   my-ACC.F.PL   daughter-ACC.F.PL   apart-ADV   my-ACC.M.PL
     zetove   **aparte**   smo   svi   zajedno
     son-in-law-ACC.M.PL   apart- ADV   be-1PL   all-NOM.M.PL   together
     Claro (=clearly), they speak, they don't have any problems... mixed marriage. You can't... I don't invite my daughters over **aparte** (=separately), my sons-in-law **aparte** (=separately), we are all together. (3,Gen.1,74)

(21) svi   mi   slavimo   Uskrs   sa
     all-NOM.M.PL   we   celebrate-1PL   Easter-ACC.M.SG   with+INS
     pisanicama   **acá** nosimo   jelo   blagosloviti
     decorated eggs-INS.F.PL here   carry-1PL   food-ACC.N.SG   bless-INF
     All, we celebrate, um... Easter with decorated eggs, **acá** (= here), we take food to be blessed. (3, Gen.1, 74)

Example (21) shows the use of adverbs with a low level of morphosyntactic dependence on other constituents in the clause, which appears to facilitate their insertion as Spanish-origin items in clauses that otherwise have Croatian as the matrix language.

4.1.5 Discourse markers

Some adverbs appear to be performing a function more akin to a discourse marker than a conventional adverb, and in some instances the boundaries of use as an adverb or as a discourse marker are hard to delineate. As Matras (2009) remarked, discourse markers and connectors are highly transferable classes of words and Spanish discourse markers are transferred into the Croatian speech of the informants of this sample. Very often they serve as fillers, tags, markers of hesitation or as interjections and so forth. Transferred discourse markers are recorded in other diaspora Croatian samples, e.g. AUS.Cro (Hlavac and Stolac, this volume) and NZ.Cro (Stoffel and Hlavac, this volume). They occur in different positions within the sentence, between clauses, within clauses, or as items that appear, at least in a syntactic sense, extraneous to the surrounding talk and function as forms that relate to the overall organisation of discourse, i.e. as 'extra-clausal' transfers and/or codeswitches (Hlavac 2006). An instance of one is *claro* meaning 'indeed', 'clearly' or 'of course' contained in example (20). *Claro* has a number of functions in Spanish: agreement marker; back-channelling marker; marker of certainty in the exposition of talk etc. Its polyfunctionality makes it an amenable candidate to be transferred.

The discourse markers recorded in our corpus are: *bueno* 'okay'/'right'/'well', which occurred 38 times: *claro* 'clearly'/'indeed'/'of course', which occurred 10 times; and *sí* 'yes', which occurred 22 times but which was used by only two of our informants. *Bueno* and *claro* mostly have the functions of an utterance-opener or a hesitation marker used between clauses, while *sí* is also used as an intensifier (sometimes used twice or even three times – see above example (9)) and usually it was placed at the beginning or the end of a clause.

(22) tako   da   imate   **bueno** još   ima   dosta   za   istraživati
      so   that   have-2PL   well   still have-3SG   enough   for research-INF
      'So, you have, **bueno** (=well), there is still a lot of things to research.'
      (5,Gen.2,69)

(23) i   **bueno**   to   je   bio   rat
      and   well   that-NOM.N.SG   AUX-3SG   be-PST.M.SG   war-NOM.M.SG
      And, **bueno** (=well), that was the war. . . (2,Gen.1,72)

(24) ja   svake   godine   njima   šaljem
     I   every-GEN.F.SG year-GEN.F.SG them-DAT   send-1SG
     pismo   sí
     letter-ACC.N.SG   yes
     'Every year I send them a letter, **sí** (= yes)'. (2,Gen.1,72)

Matras (2009: 194) states that connectors are "high on the borrowing hierarchy", giving as one of the examples the documented frequent use of Spanish connector *pero* 'but' along with *bueno* 'well' in Central American and Pacific languages due to the contact with Spanish. In our corpus the use of the Spanish conjunction *pero* and interjection *ay* (expressing pain or dismay) are recorded as well.

(25) nije   da   su   oni   čisto   izolirani   **pero**
     be-NEG.3SG   that be-3PL   they   cleanly isolated-NOM.M.PL   but
     govoriti   ne   govore
     speak-INF   NEG   speak-3PL
     'It's not that they're completely isolated, **pero** (=but)... to speak, they don't speak... (3,Gen.1,74)

The use of some expressions could be seen as modifiers, e.g. *más o menos* 'more or less' and *no importa* 'does not matter', which is also used as an exclamation. In our examples these two expressions occur as discourse-motivated, extra-clausal code-switches that express the position of the speaker.

(26) znam   francuski   znam   talijanski   onda
     know-1SG   French-ACC.M.SG   know-1SG   Italian-ACC.M.SG   then
     se   ja   sa   ovim   **más o menos**
     REFL   I   with+INS   these-INS.M.PL   more or less
     I know French, I know Italian... then I with this **más o menos** (=more or less)... (6,Gen.2,67)

(27) čokljava   ćorava   šepava   **no importa**   ja   idem
     lame-NOM.F.SG   blind-NOM.F.SG   limping-NOM.F.SG   not important   I   go-1SG
     'Lame, blind, limping **no importa** (= it doesn't matter), I go...' (3,Gen.1,74)

4.1.6 Loan translations

In our corpus, examples of words and phrases that are literally reproduced from Spanish into Croatian as loan translations are also documented. The notion of loan translation can be conceived of in different ways (Haugen 1950; Muhvić-Dimanovski 1992). We adopt Backus and Dorleijn's (2009: 79) conceptualisation of the term to refer to the replication of semantic expressions from a donor language with equivalent morphemes in the recipient language. Loan translations are found in other diaspora Croatian corpora, e.g. AUT.Cro (Ščukanec, this volume), TRS.Cro (Piasevoli, this volume), CAN.Cro (Petrović, this volume), AUS.Cro (Hlavac and Stolac, this volume) and NZ.Cro (Stoffel and Hlavac, this volume). We find a number of examples of loan translations that occur only once within the sample, but also some that occur multiple times. Two examples (28) and (29) of loan translations[6] that occur more than once from two or more speakers are presented below:

(28) znali   bi   **uzest**   koji   tramvaj
     know-PST.M.PL COND   take-INF   which-ACC.M.SG   tram--ACC.M.SG
     ili   koji   autobus
     or   which-ACC.M.SG   bus-ACC.M.SG
     'They were known to **take** whichever tram or whichever bus.' (12,Gen.2,69).

In this example the Spanish collocation verb *tomar* 'to take' + mode of transport is transferred in Croatian where the usual construction that is used is 'verb of motion + mode of transport-INS'.

(29) i   jezik   je   **nema**   **ništa**   **vidjeti**
     and   language-NOM.M.SG be-3SG   have-NEG.3SG   nothing   see-INF
     sa   španjolskim
     with+INS Spanish-INS.M.SG
     'And the language **is nothing to see with** (=has nothing to do with/no connection with) Spanish (12,Gen.2,69)

Here the collocation *nada que ver con* (lit.) 'nothing to see with', meaning 'to have nothing to do with/to have no connection with' is translated word for-word into Croatian. To speakers of HMLD.Cro, this loan translation is incomprehensible, and comprehension of it requires a knowledge of the structure of the Spanish source phrase.

---

6 For more examples with more detailed analysis, see Skelin Horvat and Musulin (2018).

4.2 Morphosyntactic change

In this section, we focus on one structural feature apparent in the speech of some speakers: the conspicuous use of *jedan* 'one' in contexts in which the numerical value of the succeeding noun is neither important nor obvious. Spanish possesses the grammatical feature of article, with indefinite and definite forms. The indefinite form of the article in Spanish is *un/una*, which is the same form used to express the number 'one'. (Indefinite articles in many languages are often derived from the number *one* as is the case in German and French.) Croatian does not possess articles as a grammatical category.

The following examples contain *jedan* 'one' where its use appears to resemble that of an indefinite article. Silić (1992–1993: 405) states that in Croatian, such a structure is more frequent and more "spontaneous" than the structure Ø + *noun*. A more widely used form is attributive *neki* 'a certain', which is pre-posed and which can also assume article-like functions (Silić 1992–1993). In relation to *jedan* 'one' in Croatian, Belaj and Matovac (2015: 4) describe its incidence preceding a noun as something that can occur when a speaker wishes "to introduce a discourse participant [i.e. a nominal lexical form] known to the speaker but presumed to be unknown to the hearer, with the difference that the participant is not expected to be a major discourse participant", i.e. as a lexical referent that is not likely to recur in the communicative interaction. On a five-point scale ranging from use of *jedan* as a numeral to that of a generalized article, Belaj and Matovac (2015: 4) term these instances "non-specific indefinite markers", i.e. at just one stage before developing into a generalized article. Other uses of *jedan* include employment of it as an approximate quantifier, here co-occurring with a logically plural noun, e.g. *Bit će* **jedno** *sto knjiga hrvatskih u kući, nema više od toga, to je sve što imam.* 'There will be **about** one hundred Croatian books in the house, no more than that, that's all I have.'

In our corpus there are 187 instances of *jedan* being used in a way that is approaching that of an article. (For further descriptions of *jedan* used in this way, see: Piasevoli; Petrović; Hlavac and Stolac, all this volume.) Occurrence of *jedan* in this ARG.Cro corpus includes instances where it precedes not only Croatian nouns but Spanish ones as well. In a number of the examples, the determiner *neki* instead of *jedan* could have been used. In most of these examples there was otherwise no apparent reason for a determiner to occur at all. In relation to the examples where the determiner *jedan* precedes a Spanish noun, this could be explained as the Spanish transfer also 'pulling with it' the lexico-grammatical feature of article-marking with it, so that *jedan* takes the place of the Spanish article that would otherwise precede such a transfer in an equivalent Spanish construction. Examples (30) and (31) demonstrate this:

(30) ja   pošto   sam   imala   ovako **jednu**
     I   because AUX-1SG have-PST.F.SG   like   one-ACC.F.SG
     bolsitu   **nada más**   uzmem   **bolsitu**   i
     little bag-ACC.F.SG   nothing more   take-1SG little bag-ACC.F.SG   and
     krenem.
     take off-1PL.
     'I, because I had like **a little bag, nothing more**, I take **little bag** and take off...' (11,Gen.1,88)

(31) bio   je   tako inteligentan   onda je
     be-PAST.3SG.M   AUX-3SG   so   intelligent-NOM.M.SG   then AUX-3SG
     išao   u   dobio   **jednu**   **becu**
     go-PST.3SG.M   to   get-PST.3SG.M   one-ACC.F.SG   scholarship-ACC.F.SG
     'He was so intelligent, then he went to... he got **a scholarship**. (2,Gen.1,72)

In other examples, which are more numerous, *jedan* precedes not a Spanish-origin transfer but a Croatian noun. As stated above, *jedan* does occur as an attributive preceding nouns in HMLD.Cro, but it is usually stylistically marked or it indexes discourse-specific features such that it appears as a 'presentative' marker (Belaj and Matovac 2015: 4) or as a 'reference' marker (Heine and Kuteva 2006: 104). Example (32) is an instance of this:

(32) za   mene   je   to   bila   **jedna**
     for+ACC   me-ACC   AUX.3SG   that   be-PST.F.SG   one-NOM.F.SG
     ogromna   emocija   emocija   jer
     huge-NOM.F.SG   emotion-NOM.F.SG   emotion-NOM.F.SG   because
     'For me that was **a** huge emotion.. emotion.. because...' (7,Gen.1,74)

The item *emocija* 'emotion' is given twice and preceded by an adjective that amplifies the illocutionary effect of *emocija* itself. Here, *jedan* has a 'presenting' function, as it does in HMLD.Cro. But in most instances where *jedan* occurs ahead of a Croatian noun, there is no obvious discourse-specific feature present. It is likely that Spanish is the cause for an increased incidence of *jedan* in utterances that do not contain emphasis or stylistic marking that would otherwise account for its occurrence. Example (33) contains two such instances:

(33) **jedan** čovjek piso **jednu**
one-NOM.M.SG man-NOM.M.SG write-PAST.3SG one-ACC.F.SG
knjigu o mala škola u
book-ACC.F.SG about+LOC little-NOM.F.SG school-NOM.F.SG in
Campo Fermo mala škola
Campo Fermo little-NOM.F.SG school-NOM.F.SG
'**A** man wrote **a** book about the small school in Campo Fermo, the small school.' (5,Gen.2,69)

From example (15) above, we present again that part that contains *jedan* preposing a Croatian noun that itself is uncountable, *pomoć* 'help/assistance'. We repeat this here as example (34):

(34) sada su dobili **jednu** pomoć
now AUX-3PL receive-PST.M.PL one-ACC.F.SG assistance-ACC.F.SG
iz Hrvatske
from+GEN Croatia-GEN.F.SG
'Now they received **a** help from Croatia...' (7, Gen.1, 74)

Example (34) shows that amongst some speakers in some constructions, *jedan* is being used as a non-specific indefinite marker *independent* of the lexicogrammatical features of the succeeding Croatian noun, which in this instance are 'non-countedness'. It is probable that the NP structure of (34) can be attributed to the structure of an equivalent Spanish NP, where the NP *una ayuda/asistencia* is a well-formed NP.

5 Conclusion

From our analysis, in terms of frequency it is found that nouns, followed by adverbs, verbs, discourse markers, then adjectives are the most commonly occurring Spanish-origin items in this ARG.Cro sample to Croatian. The frequency of items according to parts of speech differs little from the frequency of particular groups of lexical transfers reported in other language contact situations, e.g. Matras (2009), Field (2002). Many Spanish-origin nouns occur as subjects or inanimate direct objects and do not attract Croatian morphological markers. (Non-marking of inanimate direct objects applies to consonant-final transfers assigned masculine gender.) Those Spanish-origin nouns that occur in NPs as objects or parts of larger PPs that attract oblique marking usually also receive it. In relation to Spanish-origin adjectives, most function as predicates. We observe that in some instances, Spanish adjectival suffixes (such as word-final -*o*) sometimes coincide with the morphological form that would be required from the recipient language, Croatian, as in the case of NOM.N.SG adjectives. In other instances though, their morphological marking is clearly provided from the donor-language only. Predicative adjectives are, in a linear sense, often somewhat dislocated from their controlling subjects. It would be speculative for us to suggest that predicative adjectives not adjacent to their subject heads are prone to non-agreement as there is no evidence for this happening in monolingual Croatian utterances, i.e. 'long-distance' dependencies between nouns, adjectives and other classifiers still attract target Croatian morphological marking. Instead, we offer a different explanation. It is possible that the absence of Croatian morphological marking is due to the *phonotactic* form of the Spanish-origin adjectives: speakers may perceive this to be an obstacle for speakers to morphologically integrate Spanish-origin transfers into Croatian in a way that they consider felicitous.

In contrast to nouns and adjectives, Spanish-origin verbs are almost always morphologically integrated. This confirms an observation made by almost all other researchers looking at Croatian in contact situations as a recipient language of transferred verbs (e.g. Filipović 1980; Gasiński 1986; Hlavac 2003). Conventions for the phonological and morphological integration of foreign-origin verbs in HMLD.Cro outlined by Filipović (1986: 137) are replicated in this corpus. Thus, we report that Spanish *–ir* verbs attract the Croatian *–irati* suffix: *traducir > tradusirati* 'translate', *transmitir > trasmicirati* 'transmit'. An *–ar* verb, *grabar* 'to record' also attracts the *–irati* suffix, yielding *graviraju* 'they record'. Another verb *pueblaju* 'they populate' functions as a Croatian *–ati* verb, derived from the equivalent Spanish verb *poblar* 'to populate'. Two Spanish-origin verbs occur that do not appear to be morphologically integrated. Surrounding items provide evidence for why they remain unintegrated. The first occurs with its reflexive particle in Spanish *se acabó* 'it's finished' and functions as an extra-clausal code-switch, i.e. the verb is part of a 'stand-alone' alternation not integrated into morphosyntactic grid of the clause. The second instance is not so clear cut, but it is more likely that *me toca* is a truncated form of *me toca a mí* 'it's my turn', and thus, like *se acabó*, an extra-clausal code-switch.

Adverbs and discourse markers occur as unintegrated forms, both phonologically and morphologically. It is possible that the polyfunctionality of some of them, such as *bueno* 'okay' or 'well' and *claro* 'indeed', 'clearly', 'of course' and from this their higher incidence in Spanish is an enabling factor to account for their occurrence in otherwise Croatian speech. Discourse-internal evaluative markers such as *no importa* 'not important' occur as extra-clausal switches, while there is at least one occurrence of *sí* 'yes' in clause-final position as a terminator

(Hlavac 2006). Some loan translations also occur, with one notable one requiring a knowledge of Spanish and back-translation from it to be understandable: *nema ništa vidjeti sa* 'have-NEG nothing see with' = 'have no connection with'.

This chapter has also recorded many instances of a conspicuous use of *jedan* 'one' with a function that is not associated with a numerical value. Instead, *jedan* is being used by some speakers and in some constructions as a "non-specific indefinite marker" (Belaj and Matovac 2015). Its employment preceding lexical transfers is perhaps understandable where the lexico-grammatical features of the Spanish-origin are 'carried over' resulting in election of *jedan* as an equivalent of the Spanish indefinite article, where this would be used in an equivalent, monolingual Spanish NP. But *jedan* is also recorded preceding Croatian nouns as a non-specific indefinite marker in the same way as it precedes Spanish-origin items. We see here a nascent development of an indefinite article form that is attributable to contact with Spanish.

The corpus presented is modest in the number of tokens and informants recorded. This prevents us from making conclusive assertions about general tendencies in ARG.Cro. We look forward to examining data in our larger corpus that contains a further 32 informants who were also recorded to see if these linguistic patterns recur or not.

References

Antić, Ljubomir. 2002. *Hrvati i Amerika* [Croats and America]. Zagreb: Hrvatska sveučilišna naklada – Hrvatska matica iseljenika.

Backus, Ad. & Margreet Dorleijn. 2009. Loan translations versus code-switching. In Barbara E. Bullock & Almeida Jacqueline Toribio (eds.), *The Cambridge handbook of linguistic code-switching*, 75–94. Cambridge: Cambridge University Press.

Belaj, Branimir & Darko Matovac. 2015. On the article-like use of the indefinite determiners *jedan* and *neki* in Croatian and other Slavic languages. *Suvremena lingvistika 79*. 1–20.

Central State Office for Croats Abroad. 2019. *Croatian diaspora in Argentina* http://www.hrvatiizvanrh.hr/en/hmiu/croatian-diaspora-in-argentina/16 (accessed 31 January 2019).

Dewaele, Jean-Marc & Wei Li. 2014. Attitudes towards code-switching among adult mono- and multilingual language users. *Journal of Multilingual and Multicultural Development* 35(3). 235–251.

Field, Frederic. 2002. *Linguistic borrowing in bilingual contexts*. Amsterdam: John Benjamins.

Filipović, Rudolf. 1980. Transmorphemization: Substitution on the Morphological Level Reinterpreted. *Studia Romanica et Anglica Zagrabiensia*. 25.

Filipović, Rudolf. 1986. *Teorija jezika u kontaktu*. [Theory of languages in contact]. Zagreb: Jugoslavenska akademija znanosti i umjetnosti / Školska knjiga.

Fishman, Joshua. 2001. *Can threatened languages be saved? Reversing language shift revisited*. Clevedon: Multilingual Matters.

Gadže, Paula. 2017. Uloga medija u očuvanju identiteta Hrvata u Buenos Airesu i Rosariju [The role of media in the maintenance of identity amongst Croats in Buenos Aires and Rosario]. In Vesna Kukavica (ed.) *Hrvatski iseljenički zbornik*. [Croatian Émigré Almanac] 226–240. Zagreb: Hrvatska matica iseljenika.

Gasiński, Thaddeus. 1986. English elements in the speech of the Croatian immigrant community of Santa Clara Valley, California. *Zbornik Matice srpske za filologiju i lingvistiku* 29(2). 31–45.

Giles, Howard, Richard Bourhis, & Donald Taylor. 1977. Towards a theory of language in ethnic group relations. In Howard Giles (ed.), *Language, ethnicity and intergroup relations*, 307–348. London: Academic Press.

Haugen, Einar. 1950. The analysis of linguistic borrowing. *Language* 26(2). 210–231.

Heine, Bernd & Tania Kuteva. 2006. *The changing languages of Europe*. Oxford: Oxford University Press.

Hlavac, Jim. 2003. *Second-generation speech. Lexicon, code-switching and morpho-syntax of Croatian-English bilinguals*. Bern: Peter Lang.

Hlavac, Jim. 2006. Bilingual discourse markers: Evidence from Croatian-English code-switching. *Journal of Pragmatics* 38. 1870–1900.

Hrvatska matica iseljenika [Croatian Heritage Foundation] 2019. *Hola-predavanja hrvatskoga jezika i kulture u Argentini* [Hola instruction in the teaching of Croatian language and culture in Argentina]. https://matis.hr/programi/hola-predavanja-hrvatskoga-jezika-i-kulture-u-argentini-2/ (accessed 31 January 2019).

Jernej, Josip. 1959. Glagoli na –irati u XVII. i XVIII. stoljeću [Verbs ending in *-irati* in the 17th and 18th centuries]. *Filologija* 2. 31–40.

Matras, Yaron. 2009. *Language contact*. Cambridge: Cambridge University Press.

Muhvić-Dimanovski, Vesna. 1992. *Prevedenice – jedan oblik neologizama* [Loan translations – one category of neologisms]. Zagreb: HAZU.

Myers-Scotton, Carol. 2002. *Contact linguistics. Bilingual encounters and grammatical outcomes*. Oxford: Oxford University Press.

Myers-Scotton, Carol. 2006. *Multiple voices. An introduction to bilingualism*. Malden, MA: Blackwell.

Silić, Josip. 1992–1993. Aktualizator *jedan* u hrvatskom jeziku (uvodna razmišljanja). [The lexeme *jedan* as a marker of immediacy in Croatian (Initial considerations)]. *Filologija* 20(21). 403–413.

Sinovčić, Marko. 1991. *Hrvati u Argentini i njihov doprinos hrvatskoj kulturi. Pregled hrvatskog tiska objavljenog u Argentini od 1946. do 1990.* [Croats in Argentina and their contribution to Croatian culture. An overview of print media published in Croatian in Argentina from 1946 to 1990]. Buenos Aires: Entre Rios.

Skelin Horvat, Anita & Maša Musulin. 2018. Nema ništa vidjeti sa španjolskim – Un esbozo de los calcos hispanocroatas. [There's nothing to see with Spanish = There's no connection with Spanish – An outline of calques used by Croats in Latin America] In Nina Lanović, Maslina Ljubičić, Maša Musulin, Petar Radosavljević & Sanja Šoštarić (eds.), *Poglavlja iz romanske filologije: u čast akademiku Augustu Kovačecu o njegovu 80. rođendanu*, [Chapters in Romance philology: in honour of Prof. August Kovačec, member of the Croatian Academy of Sciences and Arts, on the occasion of his 80th birthday.] 91–105. Zagreb: FF Press.

Skok, Petar. 1955. O sufiksima -isati, -irati i -ovati [About the suffixes -isati, -irati, and -ovati]. *Jezik* 4(2). 36–43.

Središnji državni portal [Central Government Portal] (2020). *Stjecanje hrvatskog državljanstva* [Applying for Croatian citizenship]. https://gov.hr/moja-uprava/drzavljanstvo-i-isprave/hrvatsko-drzavljanstvo/stjecanje-hrvatskog-drzavljanstva/1719

Šprljan, Cristian. 2004. Historia de la inmigración croata en Córdoba [A history of Croatian immigration to Córdoba]. *Studia Croatica* 45(146). 1–217.

Šprljan, Cristian. (2014a). *Croacia y los croatas desde la Argentina: Discursos, notas, artículos y recuerdos (2003–2013)*. [Croatia and Croats from Argentina: Discourses, notes, articles and memories] Córdoba: Brujas.

Šprljan, Cristian. (2014b). *Los inmigrantes croatas: quiénes son y cómo vinieron*. [Croatian immigrants – who they are and where they came from] Córdoba: Brujas.

Conclusion

Jim Hlavac and Carol Myers-Scotton
Intra-clausal code-switching and possessive constructions in heritage varieties of Croatian: An MLF-based examination

1 Introduction

This chapter is the last in this edited volume and our intention was for this chapter to provide an overview of and to revisit the main findings in relation to lexical, semantic and structural innovations reported in chapters 5 to 14. However, even a cursory review of the great number of innovations recorded across these ten chapters would go beyond the bounds of a concluding chapter. This last chapter is not a conclusive one in relation to all types of data presented in the previous chapters. Instead, we restrict our review and revisiting of chapters 5 to 14 to two main areas as we see that these two areas are well represented in the examples across a number of chapters. These two areas are intra-clausal code-switching and possessive constructions; hence, the title of this chapter. We are interested to see if or how examples from these two areas can be described and accounted for in terms of the Matrix Language Frame (MLF) model (Myers-Scotton 2002), a model that has widely applied to data from contact linguistic corpora featuring heritage speakers, e.g. Bolonyai (1998), Fuller and Lehnert (2000), Schmitt (2000), Hlavac (2003), Smith (2006), He (2013) and Fairchild and Van Hell (2017). The profile of many but not all heritage language speakers is one of high-level bilingualism. In in-group interactions, the heritage language is typically *a* language that can be commonly used, but it is perhaps rarely the sole language used. It may be that the use of both languages – i.e. bilingual speech – is the unmarked variety in many situations, and a monolingual variety of the heritage language or the socially-dominant language would be marked. These situations are ones in which 'classic code-switching' typically occurs (Myers-Scotton 2002: 8).

The goal of this chapter is to show how the possibility of combining lexical and structural elements in bilingual NPs, VPs and possessive constructions can be explained in terms of the content-based elements (nouns) from one language that call or control grammatical morphemes in the other language. This

Jim Hlavac, Monash University
Carol Myers-Scotton, Michigan State University

argument follows from the MLF model of bilingual clauses. This model assumes certain asymmetries between the roles of the participating languages. The structurally more dominant language is called the Matrix Language (ML) and the other language is called the Embedded Language (EL).

The MLF was introduced in Chapter 2, and in this chapter we briefly re-visit the main aspects of it and also introduce the general principles of the 4-M model, a classification of morphemes according to the role they play at the level of speech production. We foreground here how the MLF and the 4-M model apply to heritage languages in general, and to the data sets of Croatian spoken as a heritage language. In this chapter, we look at instances of speech containing lexical items from two languages and at instances of structural change. We are also interested in seemingly unusual instances that possibly pose a challenge to the general trends and patterns that we know of in contact linguistics, and possibly also to the expectations of the 4-M model. We see these examples as insights into what outcomes can occur amongst speakers in different bi- or multi-lingual settings, with many of them being speakers of Croatian as their non-dominant language.

This chapter locates examples amongst those presented in chapters 5 through to 14 to see how the ML contributes particular types of morphemes to integrate lexical and structural material from the EL. In Section 2 we identify and examine examples of intra-clausal code-switching involving EL single items, usually nouns but also some verbs. Section 2 also presents EL islands that are multiple-item chunks such as NPs, PPs or multiple items of a VP. In Section 3 we look at structural properties of possessive constructions and at the types of morphemes that are supplied by each (or both) language(s). Section 4 summarises our observations and analysis and relates these back to our understanding of heritage languages.

To reiterate the components of the model, the MLF is based on the premise that in bilingual clauses (or CPs – projections of complementizer) one language is superordinate to the other through it determining the structural frame of the clause. This language is the Matrix Language (ML). The MLF model identifies the ML as the language that satisfies two principles, the Morpheme Order Principle and more importantly, the System Morpheme Principle:

> The Morpheme Order Principle predicts that where a singly occurring lexeme from the Embedded Language occurs together with any number of Matrix Language ones, the surface morpheme order will be that of the Matrix Language;
>
> The System Morpheme Principle predicts that all grammatical relations external to their head constituent (i.e. which participate in the sentence's thematic role grid) will come from the Matrix Language. (Myers-Scotton 2002: 59)

The understanding that different morphemes perform different roles in structure premises these principles. This brings us to the 4-M model. This is a model that analyses and identifies the structural roles of different types of morphemes that distinguishes four categories. The argument is that they differ in terms of their semantic and syntactic properties, but also in terms of how they are accessed at abstract levels in language production. The four categories of morphemes are *content morphemes, early system morphemes, bridge late system morphemes* and *outside late system morphemes.*

The implication of the 4-M model on analyses of bilingual speech is that it gives not only a description of different types of morphemes; it makes predictions about which language – the ML or the EL – contributes which type of morpheme. A detailed explanation of the 4-M model and a comprehensive description of the four types of morphemes is given in Myers-Scotton (2002) and Myers-Scotton and Jake (2017).

In simple terms, *content morphemes* are conveyors of semantic meaning and also often pragmatic meaning and nouns and verbs are the most typical examples. In the process of speech production, concepts, realia or entities are *lemmas* (in psycholinguistic terms) elect content morphemes. Content morphemes, particularly nouns, can readily traverse language boundaries and content morpheme nouns are usually the most frequent type of transfers in bilingual corpora. Further to this,

> some aspects of speaker intentions may not be realized through . . . content morphemes. [S]ome semantic and pragmatic concepts such as definiteness and plurality or completeness or progressive are required to further realize intentions.
> (Myers-Scotton and Jake 2017: 344)

While content morphemes typically relate to denotative values, other features such as plurality or possession are shown not by content morphemes but by system ones. For example, expressing plurality in English, typically a plural *–s* suffix will achieve this, and as a morpheme, plural *s* is an early system morpheme. It does not denote an entity as such but a feature of an entity, and it can occur only with its content morpheme head.

We focus in particular on the last two types of morphemes, and re-state their defining characteristics. In the 4-M model, the two further groups of morphemes distinguished are what are called *late system* morphemes. They have this label as they are structural units only, and not activated until a later stage of speech production (in hierarchical terms and not in terms of linear, online production). They are units that build larger constituents. The late system morphemes that are labelled *bridge* system morphemes are determined according to their function of joining phrases or even clauses together. For example, in English, a relationship between a possessor and a possessee can be marked by *of*, and in a complex phrase such as *the cover of the book*, the preposition *of* is a bridge system morpheme as it marks the relationship between the two phrases. Conjunctions or complementizers such as English *that* are also bridge system morphemes.

The last type of morphemes are *outsider late system* morphemes. These "depend for their form on information *outside* their immediate maximal projection" (Myers-Scotton 2002: 75). Outsiders are grammatical morphemes that contribute to well-formed syntactic constructions. Outsider late system morphemes bear features of the grammatical relations external to their head constituent and across the whole clause or CP. Examples of these are subject-verb agreement markers, clitics and most instances of case affixes. Outsiders themselves do not add meaning; instead they make more transparent the structure of the clause in which they appear.

We now turn our attention to examples of intra-clausal code-switching that include insertions or items from the EL into the ML. We note that although Croatian is likely to be the ML due to the psycholinguistic and sociolinguistic features of the communicative settings from which the data samples are taken, we do not take this as assumed and we rely on morphosyntactic criteria to identify the ML, and in particular on system morphemes as evidence for the linguistic code that is supplying these as the ML. In some instances, as foregrounded in Chapter 2, the morphosyntactic grid of a clause itself may bear evidence of structural change. Instances of these are looked at closely to see if there appears to be structural input from not one but two linguistic codes. In such cases, the ML itself, in an abstract sense, may be an amalgam of two varieties, which is labelled a Composite Matrix Language.

2 Code-switching and the presence of embedded language forms or islands

This section re-presents examples from select chapters and examines how forms from the EL occur in speakers' Croatian speech. We are particularly interested in which morphemes are supplied by the EL and which by the ML. The ML, as stated, is identifiable as the language that provides the frame of a clause's morphosyntactic grid. System morphemes that occur in a clause are typically from the ML, and one group of morpheme, the outsider late system can be provided only by the ML. This is a prediction from the System Morpheme Principle outlined in section 1. In this section we commence by looking at some examples of singly occurring content morphemes from the EL. As stated, nouns are the most frequent example of content morphemes. From chapter 6 that focused on Croatian-speakers in Austria we re-present example (9), shown here as (1). A Gen-1A speaker is recalling the reception that many migrants received after their arrival in Austria. In the narrative, a German content morpheme *Ausländer* 'foreigner' appears as a phonologically integrated transfer that also receives Croatian morphological marking:

(1) taj   nekakav   stav   prema
    this-NOM.M.SG kind of-NOM.M.SG attitude-NOM.M.SG towards+LOC
    auslenderima
    foreigner-LOC.M.PL
    'This kind of attitude toward **foreigners**...' (Gen.1A,40,F)

    HMLD.Cro: Takav stav prema **strancima**...

Example (1) is not a full clause but an NP *taj nekakav stav* 'this kind of attitude' followed by a PP, *prema auslenderima* 'towards foreigners' and the EL item is the noun within the PP. Within the PP the preposition head *prema* 'towards' governs LOC case, and the following noun attracts LOC case marking. The LOC case marking is shown in the inflection *auslender**ima*** 'foreigner-LOC.M.PL'. The morphological inflection –*ima* is a multi-feature morpheme that indexes not only case but also the other phi-features of number and gender. It is the fact that -*ima* marks case that allows us to classify -*ima* as an outsider system morpheme. The 'pull-down' principle means that if a multi-feature morpheme contains information on case or relations outside its maximal projection, it is its role as an outsider system morpheme that takes precedence, leading to the 'whole' (multi-feature) morpheme being considered an outsider (Myers-Scotton 2002: 82).

The following example is taken from the ITAL.Cro corpus from chapter 8. A Gen.1A speaker is asking another member of her family to have a look at things cooking in the kitchen. Example (8) in that chapter is given below, re-numbered as (2). It contains another transfer, this time from Italian, namely *casseruola* F 'saucepan':

(2) **amore** ti   prego   daj   pogledaj   jel   ima
    love   you-ACC   beg-1SG   give-2SG.IMP look-2SG.IMP AUX-3SG   have-3SG
    vode   u   tom   **casseruolu**
    water-GEN.F.SG   in+LOC   that-LOC.M.SG saucepan-LOC.M.SG
    '**darling, please** take a look to see if there is water in that **saucepan**'
    (Gen.1,[22],F,52)

We focus on the last item in example (2) above, the Italian-origin form *casseruola*-F 'saucepan' which is integrated not as a feminine noun but as a masculine one, i.e. *casseruolo*-M 'saucepan'. This has occurred probably due to the influence of the gender of its Croatian equivalent, *lonac*-M. In this PP, the preposition *u* 'in' here governs LOC and the subsequent noun and its determiner attract LOC marking, along with the phi-features of masculine and singular contained in the multi-feature morpheme –*u*. Here, the system morpheme is supplied by the ML, Croatian. Examples (1) and (2) show how outsider system morphemes supplied by the ML integrate EL items into the morphosyntactic grid of the ML.

We now look at an instance in which two EL items occur together as a subject NP. This example is from the NZ.Cro data of chapter 13 and example (12) from it, here re-numbered (3). A male Gen.1A speaker is recalling the type of employment that many young men engaged in in the first decades of the twentieth century. As stated in chapter 13, the clause commences with a Croatian verb *bilo je* 'there was/were'. This is an existential construction and the logical subject, if it is countable and plural, receives GEN.PL marking.

(3) *bilo*   *je*   **plenti**   *gomdigera*
     be-PTCP.3N.SG   AUX-3SG   plenty(+GEN?)   gumdigger-GEN.M.PL
     'There were **plenty of gumdiggers**' (Gen.1,Sample A)

There are two English-origin transfers in example (3). We look firstly at the second item, *gomdigera* 'gumdigger-GEN.M.PL'. At the level of the clause or CP, the construction *bilo je* 'be-PTCP.3N.SG + AUX-3SG' requires the subject to have GEN.PL marking and *gomdigera* 'gumdigger-GEN.M.PL' bears such marking. Looking now at the preceding transfer, *plenti*, this is an adverb of quantity in the sense of *plenty of*. Croatian equivalents for it are *mnogo* 'many' and *puno* 'lots of' and both these forms require the following nominal to be GEN. If *plenti* attracts the same case marking features as its Croatian equivalents – and this is shown in example (3) with a question mark – then within the maximal projection *plenti gomdigera* 'plenty of gumdigger-GEN.M.PL' we can posit that GEN.PL marking is generated at this hierarchal level too. Overall though, in our analysis if the relationship between constituents across the CP determines GEN marking for the logical subject of the CP, then the GEN.M.PL -*a* marking of *gomdigera* is an outsider system morpheme. As in (1) and (2), the outsider system morpheme is supplied by the ML.

The following example is taken from the AUT.Cro corpus from chapter 6 where it is example (7). We re-number it here as (4). It features a Gen.1A speaker talking about assistance offered to children in their acquisition of German:

(4) *doduše   imaju   i   takozvane*
    admittedly   have-3.PL.PRES   and   so-called ACC.M.PL
    Sprachtrainere
    language coach-ACC.M.PL
    'It is true that they also have so-called **language coaches**.' (Gen.1A,61,M)

In (4), the German-origin lexeme *Sprachtrainer* 'language coach/es' is the DIR.OBJ of the verb *imaju* 'have-3PL'. Here, inflectional marking reflects relations outside the maximal projection of the head. An outsider system morpheme from Croatian integrates the EL item into the frame of the clause via the multi-feature morpheme –*e* that indexes case (ACC) alongside gender (M) and number (PL).

We find instances of further DIR.OBJ forms and other constituents from the EL that are integrated into the clause via ML outsider system morphemes where relations across the clause require such marking. The following example is taken from the ARG.Cro corpus from chapter 14 where it is example (2) re-numbered here as (5). A Gen.1A speaker is describing how a public holiday is celebrated in her family. There are six lexical transfers, including a date, and a code-switch quote, *bueno* 'fine'. We focus on the Spanish-origin transfers, *asado* 'roast meat', *empanade* 'empanadas', *consuegra* 'father-in-law' and *locro* 'Argentinian stew'.

(5) *jer   kak'   slavimo   tu*   **veinticinco de mayo**   *Željko*
    because   as   celebrate-1PL here   the 25th of May   Željko
    pravi   ovaj   uvijek   **asado**   *i   napravimo*
    prepare-3SG this   always   roast meat-ACC.M/N.SG   and   make-1PL
    empanade   *i   onda   reko'*   **bueno** *a   kod*
    empanada-ACC.F.PL   and   then   say-1SG.PAST   fine   and   at+GEN
    mog   **consuegra**   *jedemo*
    my-GEN.M.SG   consuegro-GEN.M.SG   eat-1PL
    locro   *taj*   *dan*
    Argentinian stew-ACC.M/N.SG   that-ACC.M.SG   day-ACC.M.SG
    'Because, as we celebrate here **veinticinco de mayo** ('25th of May') Željko prepares, um, always **asado** ('roast meat') and we make **empanadas** and then I said, "**bueno**" ("fine"), and at my **consuegro**'s ('father-in-law's') house we eat **locro** ('Argentinian stew') that day.' (3, Gen.1, 61)

In example (5) we find some EL items receive Croatian morphemes while others do not. Looking at the two that do not, *asado* 'roast meat' and *locro* 'Argentinian stew', we note their phonotactic structure with word final –*o*. Nouns in Spanish ending in –*o* are almost always masculine. In Croatian, nouns with word final –*o* are usually neuter, although many recently established transfers such as *logo*

'logo', *kino* 'cinema' and *vaterpolo* 'waterpolo' are assigned masculine gender. In any case, both transfers are direct objects. Regardless of which Croatian gender they are assigned, the target morphological marker is –Ø, as neuter singular and masculine singular non-animate nouns have the same zero marking for both the nominate and accusative. Although *asado* 'roast meat' and *locro* 'stew' appear to be bare forms, in fact, the Croatian frame of the CP does not require them to have overt morphological marking.

The EL transfers *empanade* 'emapanadas' and *consuegra* 'father-in-law' do contain morphological marking. We will start with *consuegra* which occurs in a PP with the head *kod*+GEN 'at', a preposition similar to German *bei* or French *chez*. The head, the preposition *kod* 'at' determines the morphological form of the transfer, *consuegro* 'brother-in-law', yielding *consuegra* 'brother-in-law GEN.M.SG'. Croatian is the supplier of the outsider system morpheme to integrate the EL item into the ML PP. The other EL item is *empanade* 'empanadas-ACC.F.PL' which bears Croatian morphological marking it a direct object. Its SG form is *empanada* which determines its allocation in Croatian as a feminine noun. Within the CP or clause, its role as DIR.OBJ yields the multi-feature inflection -*e*, an outsider late system morpheme which encodes the features case (ACC), gender (F) and number (PL).

EL forms that are predicate adjectives also occur. Example (6) below, is from the ITAL.Cro corpus of chapter 8 where it is listed as (5). A Gen.3 speaker is making a comparison about the quality of food in another country to that in Italy. Here, an EL adjective *sana* 'healthy-F.SG' occurs in an ML predicate:

(6) hrana   nije   tako **sana**   zdrava
    food-NOM.F.SG be-NEG.3SG so   healthy-NOM.F.SG healthy-NOM.F.SG
    k'o u   Italiji
    as in+LOC   Italy-LOC.F.SG
    'The food is not as **sana** ['healthy']... healthy as in Italy.' (Gen.3,[9],M,9)

In Croatian, as in Italian, predicate adjectives bear the phi-features of their antecedent subject. The subject here is *hrana* 'food-NOM.F.SG'. Morphology of Croatian predicate adjectives is determined by relations across the CP. The morphological marker that *sana* 'healthy-NOM.F.SG' receives is the morpheme -*a*, an outsider system morpheme. The form *sana* 'healthy-NOM.F.SG' is clearly based on the Croatian antecedent subject *hrana* 'food-NOM.F.SG', and not on an Italian equivalent. (All Italian equivalents are masculine and would require congruent marking on the predicate adjective, resulting in *sano* 'healthy-NOM.M.SG', e.g. **il** *cibo* / **il** *mangiare non è sano* 'healthy-NOM.M.SG'.) The presence of the Croatian equivalent of *sana* 'healthy-F', namely *zdrava* 'healthy-F' that immediately follows the EL item is not significant. The production of an ML equivalent item immediately following the EL one need not be indicative of an infelicity or perceived incongruence of EL *sana* within the Croatian CP. It is not uncommon for EL items to be closely followed by their ML equivalents (Hlavac 2011: 3082).

We now move to those examples from the chapters where morphological integration is absent but otherwise required in the morphosyntactic grid of the ML, Croatian. We are keen to look for reasons why ML system morpheme marking is not present in these instances. Our first instance of this is taken from the AUT. Cro corpus of chapter 6, marked there as example (12) and shown here as (7). A Gen.2 speaker is recalling events surrounding her exams in her final year at secondary school. A German-origin adjective+noun NP *mündliche*-F.SG *Matura*-F.SG 'oral school leaving exam' is inserted into a larger Croatian PP.

(7) ja   sam   išla   na   svoj   **mündliche**
    I   AUX-1SG   go-PST.F.SG   to+ACC   my [own]-ACC.M.SG oral-F.SG
    Matura   otišla   sa   ***Fieber***
    school leaving exam-F.SG   leave-PST.F.SG with+INS   temperature-ø
    'I went for my **oral school leaving exam**, left home with a **fever**. . .'
    (Gen.2,22,F)

The head of the PP is the preposition *na* 'to'+ACC. Following the preposition is the possessive pronoun *svoj* 'my [own]'. We have marked *svoj* 'own-ADJ' as ACC.M.SG as it follows the preposition *na*+ACC, but in fact *svoj* 'own-ADJ' has no overt morphology: the form for ACC.M.SG is the same as the base form, i.e. -Ø. Following *svoj* 'own-ADJ' is the EL island, *mündliche*-F.SG *Matura*-F.SG 'school leaving oral exam'. The morphology marking the adjective *mündliche* 'oral-F.SG' is feminine, i.e. *-e* 'F.SG' is supplied by the EL, German, and the noun *Matura* 'school leaving exam' is itself feminine.[1] So, *mündliche Matura* 'oral school leaving exam' is an EL island as it contains two lexemes with at least three morphemes that show internal structural-dependency relations. As an EL island *mündliche Matura* does not have any affixed Croatian morphological markers and it is not optimally integrated into the ML. Although it is not optimally integrated, this example does not contravene the System Morpheme Principle, as the morphological marking on *mündliche*-F.SG *Matura*-F.SG shows it to be an adjective-noun pair that is in

---

[1] Historically, the form *Matura* 'A-levels' or 'school leaving certificate' is one that entered Croatian from Austrian German some time ago, and the Croatian form *matura* still has the same meaning as Austrian German *Matura*. But *Matura* here is clearly an EL form. If it were a Croatian form, it would bear an ACC inflection, i.e. *maturu*-ACC.F.SG, as it follows the preposition *na* 'to-ACC' requiring ACC case marking.

its German 'base', i.e. NOM form, and neither item bears markers external to the head constituent.

It is likely that the forms *mündliche* 'oral-F.SG' and *Matura* 'final school leaving exam' frequently collocate together and *mündliche Matura* can be considered a lexically complex but conceptually simplex item in speakers' repertoires. It is a template form that is transferred from German as a (structurally) complex unit and is congruent to other formulaic expressions that commonly form EL islands (Backus 1996; Myers-Scotton 2002: 140–146).

ML system morpheme markers are absent also from other constituents in example (7): *Fieber* 'fever' is a singly-occurring EL item at the end of the clause. It is within a PP that has the preposition *sa* 'with+INS' as its head. The transfer *Fieber* consists of a content morpheme and is a bare form that lacks system morphemes from either language. As such, it does not contravene the System Morpheme Principle. The same Gen.2 speaker who produced (7) also produced the following example (8), which is presented as example (13) in chapter 6. The topic of her speech is still on her secondary school years. Here, the entire PP is an EL island.

(8) i **mit ausgezeichnetem Erfolg** sam
    and with+DAT excellent-DAT.M.SG success-M.SG AUX-1SG
    maturirala
    graduate-PTCP.F.SG
    'And **with excellent grades** I graduated from high school.' (Gen.2,22,F)

The EL island that is formally a PP is *mit ausgezeichnetem Erfolg* (lit.) 'with excellent success' and this functions as a manner expression. This is a category that is identified by Myers-Scotton (1993: 144) as being a common one in the Implicational Hierarchy of EL Islands: "other time and manner expressions (NP/PP adjuncts used adverbially)". Formally, the PP contains EL content and system morphemes, e.g. the second constituent, the ADJ *ausgezeichnetem* 'excellent-DAT.M.SG' has an EL outsider system morpheme suffix that is required by the preceding EL constituent, its head *mit*+DAT. The items within the EL island are assembled according to the requirements of the elements of the EL items themselves co-occuring with each other, rather than the EL 'imposing itself' as the provider of structure.

We present a third example from this same Gen.2 speaker that contains the same transfer found in example (1) above, namely *Ausländer* 'foreigners'. In the re-presented example, numbered here as (9), *Ausländer* 'foreigners' is not only morphologically but also phonologically unintegrated.

(9) tamo   nije   bilo   ovih   **Ausländer**
    there   NEG.AUX-3SG   be-PST.N.SG   these-GEN.M.PL   **foreigner-**(PL)-ø
    što   kažu
    what-ACC say-3PL
    'There were not any **foreigners** there, as they call them.' (Gen.2,22,F)

As mentioned for example (3), existential constructions with *bilo je* 'there was/ were' have the logical subject in GEN. This same rule applies also to NEG existential sentences such as (9) with the construction *ne* NEG + *biti* 'be' + subject-GEN. In (9) above, the preceding determiner *ovih* 'these-GEN.M.PL' has GEN marking. But *Ausländer* 'foreigner' does not receive overt ML marking. It occurs in its 'base' German form. As it happens, the PL form of *Ausländer* 'foreigners' is the same as its SG form. So, we can consider it to be marked at least for number (+PL). But marking for GEN is absent, and *Ausländer* 'foreigners' here is a bare form. There are no outsider system morphemes provided by German, and the System Morpheme Principle is not contravened.

This brings us to ask why ML system morphemes occur with some EL forms and not with others in instances when the feature marking of relations within a maximal projection of head would otherwise require these. In the first place, EL islands that consist of multiple (i.e. two or more) constituents as in (7) and (8) do not contain ML morphological markers, and contain EL morphemes. We see this as the structure of EL items calling bridge and outsider system morphemes that result in EL islands (Myers-Scotton and Jake 2017: 346). When single-occurring EL forms occur, they receive ML markers where their syntactic role requires these according to Croatian morphosyntax, and where outsider system morphemes occur, they are supplied by Croatian. Examples (1) to (6) show how this occurs.

Looking back at the instances of single-occurring EL forms in (7) and (9) we observe that the Gen.2 speaker who produced them has a pattern of not marking German-origin forms with Croatian morphemes to integrate them into the Croatian morphosyntactic grid of her CPs. The same speaker otherwise has target marking for phi-features on Croatian constituents, and system morphemes, including outsider ones, are supplied from Croatian elsewhere in her utterances.

It may be that it is not just coincidental that there is an absence of outsider system morphemes on EL items, and that the speaker is a Gen.2 one. Differences in the speech of Gen.2 speakers compared to Gen.1 speakers occur and are reported on (e.g. Jake and Myers-Scotton 2002). As outlined in chapter 2 in relation to other studies on Croatian as a diaspora language, data from Gen.2 speakers showed that EL forms receive ML morphological markers in only 11%

to 50% of situations in which these would otherwise be required, depending on the speaker (Albijanić 1982: 18). The equivalent percentage for Gen.1 speakers is found to be much higher – 99%. Non-election of system morphemes on EL forms may be a first step that can lead to changes in the marking of system morphemes on *ML* forms, although this need not be the case, and certainly not an automatic consequence. We still keep this in mind as we move to further examples taken from chapters 5 to 14 of this volume.

We now look at instances of intra-clausal code-switching between the constituents of compound verbs, i.e. where the AUX verb is supplied by the ML but the main verb comes from the EL. The compound tense constructions that we will be looking at are mostly past tense ones, or constructions consisting of ML *biti* 'be' + EL participles. The default tense used to describe past actions in Croatian is the perfect tense which consists of the AUX *biti* 'be' and a past participle that bears feature marking of its subject for gender and number (but not person). We now look at an instance where a code-switch occurs between ML *biti* 'be' and an EL main verb in a passive-origin stative construction. From chapter 11 and the AUS.Cro corpus, we have the following example, numbered here as (10). A Gen.2 speaker is looking at a picture and trying to associate where it could be from.

(10) *ne   možu   kazat   gdje   je   ova*
     NEG   can-1SG say-INF where   AUX-3SG   this-NOM.F.SG
     slika   er   **taken**
     picture-NOM.F.SG   er   taken
     'I can't say where this picture was.. er.. **taken**.' (8,Gen.2,M,20)

The predicate in (10) is derived from a passive construction. In the ML, passive constructions have the AUX verb *biti* 'be' followed by a passive participle. The AUX verb *biti* 'be' is the same AUX used in *active* past tense constructions as well. In contrast to English, in Croatian, it is the PTCP that marks a past tense construction as passive or active. The morphological suffixes of PST.PTCP forms used in an active past tense (perfect) construction are -*o* M.SG; -*la* F.SG; -*lo* N.SG. These are different from the PTCP forms usually employed in a passive construction of any tense: -*n* M.SG; -*na* F.SG; -*no* N.SG. In contrast, in English, it is the AUX that distinguishes active from passive voice: *have* for active present perfect and *be* for passives of any tense. The form of the English PST.PTCP is the same, whether employed in active present perfect tense constructions or in passive constructions.

Example (10) has the EL item *taken* that appears as a bare form. It does not receive overt ML morphology to show agreement in gender and number with its antecedent subject, i.e. it does not receive a morphological suffix such as NOM.F.SG -*a* for it to agree with *slika* 'picture-NOM.F.SG', yielding something like *taken-a* (?). In the absence of ML morphological markers, we look at how we can classify *taken*. The form *taken* is an irregular past participle form, and like other irregular past tense forms in English, it is likely that these "are present in the mental lexicon as units and not assembled on line" (Myers-Scotton 2005: 343). Further, past participles derived from passive constructions commonly function as predicative adjectives with little sense that they are structurally derived from an active to passive transformation. This is also what Bolonyai (2005) finds for the small number of English bare-form past participles in speech where Hungarian is the ML. When they function as adjectives, they can be classified as content morphemes that lack any system morphemes.

Chapter 13 contained another passive past participle which we give here as example (11). A Gen.2 speaker is describing a male person known to her and how he behaved during periods of loneliness.

(11) *i   kada   je   bio   osamljen   bio*
and when be-3SG be-PST.M.SG left alone-PASS.PTCP.M.SG   be-PST.M.SG
*je   **fixated** na   televiziju   i   to*
be-3SG   fixated   at+ACC   television-ACC.F.SG   and   that-ACC.N.SG
'And when he was lonely.. he was.. **fixated** on television and that..'
(Gen.2,F,26)

Example (11) also has a passive-based construction as in (10). While (10) is a present tense construction *je* 'be-PRS.3SG' + *taken*, (11) has a past tense construction *bio* 'be-PST.PTCP.M.SG' *je* 'be-PRS.3SG' + *fixated*. As in (10), there is hesitation that precedes the participle *fixated*. While *fixated* may formally be classified as a past participle based on an active to passive voice transformation, use of the verb in its active form, *to fixate*, is unusual, e.g. 'it fixated me'(?). Its use is strongly restricted to the passive where its function is that of a stative or adjectival passive. We therefore classify *fixated* as a content morpheme, similar to other English adjectives that lack any system morphemes.

Examples (10) and (11) featured code-switches between ML *biti* 'be' and EL participles within the same clause. The following example (12) from the TRS.Cro sample of Chapter 10 also contains a code-switch between ML *biti* 'be' as an AUX followed by an EL past participle form *corretto* 'correct-PST.PTCP' from Italian. The example comes from a Gen.2 speaker who is recounting when she was in a relationship with *D.*, a Gen.1-speaker of Croatian, and the influence that he had on her:

(12) *imala   sam   ljubav   s   D.*
    have-PST.F.SG AUX-1SG   love-ACC.F.SG with   D.
    *on **je**   **corretto**   greške*
    he   AUX-3SG   correct-PST.PTCP   mistake-ACC.F.PL
    'I was in a relationship with D. . . He used to **correct** my mistakes.'
    (JV, Gen.2, F,70)

> Ital.:   Ero fidanzata con D. . . Lui **correggeva**-IPRF i miei errori
>   (**correggere**-INF, **corretto**-PST.PTCP).
> HMLD.Cro: Hodala sam s D. . . On mi je **ispravljao** greške.

We firstly outline a few things about past and compound verb tenses in both Italian and Croatian, before looking at the morphology of *corretto* 'correct-PST.PTCP' and how it fits into the grid of this ML clause. Most Italian verbs – all transitive ones and most others – have the AUX *avere* 'have' for the formation of the recent past tense (*passato prossimo*), and those verbs with *avere* 'have' have an -*o* suffix on the PST.PTCP regardless of the subject's gender, number or person. The only exception to this is when an object pronoun preceding *avere* and this object pronoun is feminine and/or plural. Therefore, for *avere* verbs in the recent past, it is usually only the AUX that checks the subject's features of gender, number and person.[2] An Italian past participle with the AUX *avere* does not check for the gender and number of the antecedent subject of the clause, and the suffix morpheme is usually –*o*. This is also the morphological suffix required for a Croatian PST.PTCP to check the feature marking of the antecedent M.SG subject, namely *on* 'he'. The form of the suffix of the EL PST.PTCP –*o* coincides with the form of the required ML outsider system morpheme.

Further, the sense of the past tense action being described in (12) is a repetitive, habitual activity that in Italian would be expressed via imperfect tense (i.e. *correggeva* 'correct-IPRF.3SG') rather than recent past. Employment of an EL verb form in the recent past represents an adaptation of the verb tense used to the features of the Croatian verb tense system.

We look now at a code-switch taken from the NZ.Cro corpus of chapter 13 (example 25) that is classified there as an inter-clausal code-switch. A Gen.2

---

[2] In Italian, there is also a smaller group of intransitive verbs and verbs of motion that for recent past have the AUX *essere* 'be' followed by the PST.PTCP. For these verbs requiring *essere* in the recent past, *both* AUX and PST.PTCP bear morphology that is checked with the subject for gender and number. This is an important distinction: an Italian past participle with the *essere* AUX bears an Italian multi-feature outsider system morpheme that checks features outside their maximal projection of head, i.e. gender and number of the antecedent subject of the clause.

speaker is recalling how their family was accepted by others, evidenced by being invited to others' houses. An ML pronoun, *oni* 'they' is the subject of an ML clause, and then of an EL clause that occurs after a co-ordinating conjunction *i* 'and':

(13) *i*   *oni*   *su*   *nas*   *primili*   *u*
      and   they-NOM.M   AUX-3PL   us-ACC   accept-PST.M.PL   to+ACC
      njihovu   *kuću*   *i*   **treated us like one of the family**
      their-ACC.F.SG   house-ACC.F.SG   and   treated us like one of the family
      '. . .and they took us into their house and **treated us like one of the family**.' (Gen.2, Sample A)

In (13) *oni* 'they' is the subject to both the Croatian predicate *su nas primili* 'took us in' and an English predicate *treated us like one of the family*. Here, we have two co-ordinating clauses, the first in Croatian and the second in English and the past-tense predicates in both languages are controlled by the same subject. The co-ordinating conjunction at the point of the code-switch is *i* 'and', a bridge system morpheme. Conjunction bridge system morphemes can be supplied by either ML or EL, because "although bridges join two constituents together, they are invariant placeholders satisfying well-formedness conditions for the larger unit" (Myers-Scotton and Jake 2009: 352). The subject of both clauses, Croatian *oni* 'they' 'NOM.M.3PL' is an item consisting of two morphemes: content morpheme *on-* 3.person; (multi-feature) outsider system morpheme *-i* 'NOM.M.PL' that indexes grammatical information outside the maximal projection. So, the ML subject *oni* 'they' controls an EL predicate that is an EL island consisting of a common formulaic phrase: *treat* + OBJ + *like one of the family*.

We look now at an example in which part of the predicate is provided by the ML, and another part by an EL island. Similar to examples (10) to (12), the point of the code-switch is between ML *biti* 'be' and a participle from the EL. The example is numbered as (44) in chapter 9 and we re-number it here as (14). A Gen.1B speaker is recounting what happened to her father in WWI.

(14) *on*   *je*   *bil*   **ferito**   *della*   **Prima**
      he   AUX-3SG   be-PST.PTCP.M.SG   **wounded**-PST.PTCP.M.SG   of   First
      guerra   *bio*   *je*   *star*
      war   be-PST.PTCP.M.SG   AUX-3SG   old-NOM.M.SG
      'He was **wounded in the First World War** . . . He was old.' (MB,-Gen.1B,F,74)

Ital.:   Lui è stato **ferito nella Prima Guerra Mondiale**. Era vecchio.
HMLD.Cro: On je bio **ranjen u Prvom svjetskom ratu**. Bio je star.

Example (14) is different from the previous example of a Croatian-Italian code-switch within a VP in example (12) because here the construction is a passive one. We digress briefly to outline how (past tense) passive constructions are structured in each language. In the ML, Croatian, past passive constructions consist of three constituents: AUX *biti* 'be (NUMBER-PERSON)' + PST.PTCP *biti* 'be (GENDER-NUMBER)' + PASS.PTCP '*main verb* (GENDER-NUMBER)'. Thus, constituents of past passive constructions in the ML, Croatian, contain marking for number and person on the first constituent (*be*-PRES), and marking for gender and number on the second (*be*-PST.PTCP) and third (*main verb*-PASS.PTCP) constituents of the VP. Looking now at the EL, the past passive in Italian is expressed in a similar but not identical way as it is in Croatian: AUX-*essere* 'be (NUMBER-PERSON)' + PST.PTCP-*essere* 'be (GENDER-NUMBER)' + PST.PTCP (GENDER-NUMBER), noting that the form of the third constituent, the PST.PTCP, *does* check with the antecedent subject, so that gender, (-*o* M or -*a* F) and number (-*i* M.PL or -*e* F.PL) are marked on the PST.PTCP. Thus, there is a high degree of equivalence, but not complete equivalence, between Croatian and Italian past passive constructions.

We see in (14) how the first two constituents of the past passive VP are supplied by Croatian, the AUX *je* 'be-3SG' followed by the first PST.PTCP *bil* 'be-PST.PTCP.M.SG' and the code-switch occurs between *bil* 'be-PST.PTCP.M.SG' and *ferito* 'wound-PST.PTCP.M.SG', the second and third constituents of the VP. As stated, in Italian, the PST.PTCP in the past passive construction checks for gender and number, and *ferito* 'wound-PST.PTCP.M.SG' agrees with the subject *on* 'he' for both of these features. As such, *ferito* consists of the content morpheme *feri-* 'wound' and –*to*, an outsider system morpheme. Further, in example (14), the suffix -*to* is not congruent to the morphological marking of a Croatian M.SG PASS.PTCP which has a word-final consonant ending of -*n* or -*t* (cf. the HMLD.Cro equivalent given above is *je bio ranjen* 'wound-PASS.PTCP.M.SG' 'He was wounded'). Thus, example (14) contravenes the System Morpheme Principle. This contravention is the catalyst for the EL island that immediately follows. Feature-marking across the clause is now supplied by Italian which leads to this language now providing the frame in the ensuing EL. The EL form *ferito* 'wound-PST.PTCP.M.SG' has triggered a code-switch, and this trigger is a structural one, not a form-based one such as homophonous, phonotactically similar or ambiguous forms that are "at the intersection of two languages" (Clyne 1991: 193) that can often trigger code-switching. Instead, it has been triggered by the structural infelicity of the EL now taking on the role of feature checking beyond the maximal projection across the CP to supply outsider system morphemes. Most EL islands are not extensive enough to contain outsider system morphemes, but in instances of triggered code-switching they can occur (Myers-Scotton 2002: 142) and the principle that outsider system morphemes resist transfer leads to the occurrence of EL islands as a consequence of this principle (Myers-Scotton 2008).

Examples (12) and (14) show us that Croatian verbs can combine with forms from Italian in compound verb constructions. Chapter 9 also contains an example from the ITAL.Cro corpus, numbered as (49) and re-numbered here as (15) which itself contains a compound verb, this time with the EL main verb in the infinitive. Here, a Gen.2 speaker is addressing a fellow Gen.2 speaker.

(15) Mari' jesi ti išta **decidere** kad i gdje ćeš
Mari' AUX-2SG you anything decide-INF when and where will-2SG
in vacanza dimmi ti **prego** jer ni ja ne znam
on holiday give:me-DAT you please because nor I NEG know-1SG
'Mari', have you **decided** anything [on] when and where to go **on holiday**? **Please tell me** because I don't know either' (Gen.2,F,21)

In examples (10) and (11), we saw how bare form EL participles not contravening the system morpheme principle could co-occur with ML AUX verbs in bilingual VPs. In other instances, we saw how the occurrence of EL outsider system morphemes is attributable to speakers with a changed, composite ML as in example, (12) while in (14) we saw how an EL participle bearing an outsider system morpheme precipitated an EL island. Example (15) is different and we seek to account for why an INF occurs here, and not a PST.PTCP as in the previous examples.

To start with, in (15) the speaker here is addressing a family member and uses 2SG forms. The ML AUX *jesi* 'be-INT.2SG' agrees with the 2SG subject *ti* 'you'. The main verb is an EL form, Italian INF form *decidere* 'decide-INF' and not the EL PST.PTCP *deciso* 'decided'. Italian *decidere* 'to decide' is a verb that takes *avere* 'have' in the recent past and the PST.PTCP form *deciso* usually does not change unless there is a preceding object pronoun, and the gender or number of the antecedent subject does not determine its form. We draw attention to the form of *deciso* 'decide-PST.PTCP' which contains an outsider system morpheme suffix *–so*, and in particular the word-final vowel *–o*. While this suffix satisfies the requirements of Italian structure in the formation of a PST.PTCP, this suffix is not congruent to the form of an equivalent Croatian PST.PTCP. The equivalent Croatian PST.PTCP form would have been *odlučila* 'decide' PST.PTCP.F.SG. The Croatian PST.PTCP has feature marking that checks with the subject's features of number, and importantly, also gender – which here is feminine. A feminine singular subject results in the PST.PTCP bearing an outsider system morpheme suffix *–la*. In Croatian, a PST.PTCP that has a word-final *–o* suffix can only occur with a masculine singular subject. The Italian PST.PTCP suffix *–o* is not congruent to the Croatian feminine singular subject. This appears to be the obstacle for the PST.PTCP form to be employed, and instead the INF is employed.

Example (15) contains no contravention of the System Morpheme Principle, but we see here that the phonotactic form of the EL constituent appears to have an influence on which grammatical form may be elected: if the EL form bears a morphological suffix that marks it, in terms of ML morphology, as not congruent to the gender of the ML subject, then such a suffix is disallowed, and the baseline form is employed, here the INF *decidere*. This explanation is congruent to what we saw in examples (10) and (14). In those examples, the participles had word-final *–o* suffixes and their antecedent subjects were masculine.

We have seen above in examples (10) to (14) that Croatian auxiliaries can combine with English and Italian participles in compound constructions; or we see at least that English and Italian participles functioning as adjectives derived from passive constructions can combine with Croatian *biti* 'be' where *biti* is employed either as an auxiliary or as a copula. We also see in example (15) that there are limits to this where the phonotactic form of an EL PST.PTCP is disallowed if it is overtly not congruent to ML morphological suffixes required, at least for the feature gender.

We come now to equivalent examples involving German and Croatian. Similar to Italian, German has two AUX verbs for the perfect tense, *haben* 'have' which is by far the most commonly used AUX, and *sein* 'be' that is used in combination with some intransitive verbs and some verbs of motion. From chapter 5, we present example (4) which is re-numbered here as (16). As in (7) and (8) above, a Gen.2 speaker is talking about his final year at secondary school:

(16) *ja sam devedeset četvrte* **Abitur machen**
I AUX-1SG ninety-four-GEN.F.SG A levels make-INF
'I did in [19] ninety-four my *Abitur* [A-levels].' (7,Gen.2,M,41)

Example (16) relates to the description of a past action: the speaker mentions when he completed his final school year. Croatian is the ML and the clause commences with a Croatian subject and the AUX *sam* 'be-1SG'. After the ADV phrase of time *devedeset četvrte* 'ninety-four', a common collocation from German is produced, *Abitur machen* 'to do one's A-levels'. The verb *machen* appears in its baseline or INF form, not as a PAST.PTCP *gemacht* that would be used in a German perfect construction. This looks similar to example (15) where the Italian EL verb was an INF rather than a PST.PTCP – in that instance due to formal non-congruence between an Italian PST.PTCP and the Croatian subject. In (16), the verb form contains neither past tense morphology of the EL (*gemacht* 'make-PST. PTCP'), nor that of the ML (*mach-ao*? 'make-PST.PTCP.M.SG'). In either case, there is no outsider system morpheme supplied from either language that would check the form of the verb with other features across the CP such as tense, person and gender. So, the System Morpheme Principle is not contravened. Instead, the EL island consists of two bare forms: the verb *machen* is in its baseline form, as stated; the noun *Abitur* is also in its baseline form without a determiner or other attributives.³ This is a common two-word phrase and the default construction to express 'doing one's A-levels' in Germany. It may be that because *Abitur machen* is a 'tight-knit' collocation, it resists affixation of ML morphemes that would integrate it into the clause.

We look at this further by re-presenting another Croatian-German compound verb construction, reported on in Chapter 5, presented there as (3) and re-numbered here as (17). A Gen.2 speaker is reporting on one of her first jobs which involved working at a trade fair.

(17) svi   koji   su   tamo na
     all-NOM.M.PL   REL.PRON-NOM.M.PL   AUX-3PL   there at+LOC
     sajmu   radili   isto su   bili   kao
     trade-fair-LOC.M.SG work-PST.M.PL   also AUX-3PL   be-PST.3PL   like
     Nijemci   meni   isto su   svoj   posao
     German-NOM.M.PL   me-DAT   also AUX-3PL   own-ACC.M.SG   job-ACC.M.SG
     haben   den   ernst   genommen
     AUX-3PL   it-ACC.M.SG   seriously   take-PST.PTCP
     '.. all who worked there at the trade fair, they were also like Germans to me. Also, their work, they **took it seriously.**' (12, G2, F, 31)

In (17), we have an EL German main verb inflected as a PST.PTCP. We are interested to see how and why this German PST.PTCP appears here. The excerpt shown in (17) starts in Croatian, and this is the ML at the start of the last clause, *isto su svoj posao* 'also AUX-be.3PL own job'. The direct object in this clause *posao* 'job-ACC.M.SG' is further described in a right-clefted construction that contains the EL phraseme (*etwas*) *ernst nehmen* 'to take (something) seriously'. The verb phrase *ernst nehmen* is a collocation like *Abitur machen* contained in (16). In (17) there is an EL PST.PTCP *genommen*, but it does not appear to combine with the ML AUX *su* 'be-3PL'. Instead, the EL AUX *haben* 'have-3PL' precedes it. The code-switch to German is not flagged and there is no conspicuous break in the clause. It appears that when constructing this part of her turn online, the Gen.2 informant sought to employ the German phraseme in a past tense meaning. In order to do so using a German perfect construction featuring *genommen*, the speaker provides also the EL AUX and anaphoric determiner *den* 'it-ACC.M.SG' which has *posao* 'job-

---

3 *Abitur* could be but need not be preceded by determiners such as *das* 'the' *Abitur*, cf. *ich habe vierundneunzig **das** Abitur gemacht*, or *mein* 'my' *Abitur*, cf. *ich habe vierundneunzig **mein** Abitur gemacht*.

ACC.M.SG' as its antecedent. Here, there appears to be structural non-congruence of the German perfect tense compound verb construction with its Croatian equivalent such that the Croatian perfect tense AUX cannot combine with a German PST.PTCP in the same way that it can with an English or Italian one. Because of the apparent lack of congruence, the German perfect tense construction occurs in an EL island.

When we look at other data sets where a Slavic language is the ML, and German the EL, we find a similar tendency. For example, Goldbach (2005) studies the speech of 14 Russian-dominant bilinguals living in Berlin. Amongst the relatively small number of instances of code-switching, two show German verbs that are employed in compound verb constructions where the German AUX also co-occurs with the German PST.PTCP:

(18) *a   теперь   Ира   с   Машей   там*
     and   now   Ira   with+INS   Maša-INS.F.SG there
     *поссорилась   Ира ну как она   сказала   **war***
     argue-PST.REFL.F.SG   Ira well   she   say-PST.F.SG AUX.PST.SG
     eingeschnappt   *потому что   Маша*
     take offence-PST.PTCP   because   Maša
     '... and now, Ira and Maša... had an argument there. Ira, well, she said, **got in a huff**, because Maša...'

(19) *я   щас   нажимала   вот   теперь* **hat**   *er* **gespeichert**
     I   now   press-PST.F.SG like   now   AUX-3SG   he   save-PST.PTCP
     послушно **ganz normal**   *спасибо*
     obediently quite normally   thank you
     'I just pressed it right now. **It saved it**... as it should. **Completely normally**. Thank you.' (Goldbach 2005: 74)

In the two excerpts above from Goldbach (2005), all constituents of the German compound verbs occur in EL islands. These EL islands occur as free-standing, inserted clauses: *war eingeschnappt* 'she got in a huff' and *hat er*[4] *gespeichert* 'it saved it'. Admittedly, this is probably a necessity because in the present and past tense structures of the ML, Russian, there are no AUX forms employed with which a German EL main verb could co-occur. The EL verbs from German occur as EL islands containing both a German AUX and German main verb. But we can

---

[4] The masculine pronoun *er* 'he' likely refers back to Ger. *Rechner* M / *Komputer* M 'computer' or possibly back to Russ. компьютер M 'computer' which is also masculine.

still make the observation that there appears to be less structural equivalence between German EL verbs occurring in CPs where the ML is a Slavic language.

We also identify another distinguishing feature about German EL verbs with the function of a PST.PTCP – that these are marked not only by their suffix *–t* or *–en* but also by their prefix *ge–*. Phonotactically, verbs from other Germanic languages such as English, can readily and easily allow *ge–* prefixation to form past participles, e.g. *geoutsourced* 'outsourced', *gestylt* 'styled' or *gephotoshoppt* 'photoshopped'. But the phonotactic structure of lexical items from other languages is not usually so closely aligned to German, and historically one of the more recently employed suffixes in German to integrate foreign lexemes (usually of Romance origin) is *–ieren*. Significantly, foreign-origin verbs with the *–ieren* suffix do not have *ge–* prefixes. Even when German is the EL, not the ML, German verbs occupying the function of PST PTCP as EL items do not readily integrate into bilingual VPs.

We come now to an example of double-marking of past tense. Example (20) is taken from chapter 13 where it is presented as example (7). The speaker is recounting a scene that she witnessed when at the beach and when a man nearby reacted to seeing a shark in the water. This utterance is characterised by production difficulties. In all, three verb forms are produced. The first *kažeo* 'told' is a non-target form of the M.SG form of the past participle of *kazati* 'to tell', namely *kazao* 'tell-PST.PTCP M.SG.', i.e. the present tense stem *kaže-* is over-generalised as the form to be used in past tense as well. The speaker appears to realise that this is non-target and produces another form synonymous to *kazao* 'told', namely *rekao* 'say- PST.PTCP.M.SG', i.e. 'said'. The form *rekao* 'said' is target. This is then followed by a hesitation marker *um*, a hedge *you know*, and a false start *skr..*, then the double-marked past participle *skrimdio* 'screamed+PST.PTCP.M.SG' is produced to conclude the turn:

(20) i   taj   na   pijesku   je   kažeo
     .. and   that-NOM.SG.M   on+LOC   sand-LOC.SG.M.   AUX-3SG   tell-PST-3SG
     je   rekao   [am] **you know**   je
     AUX.3SG   say-PAST.M.SG   um   **you know**   AUX-3SG
     skr.. skrimdio
     scr.. scream+**ed**+PAST.M.SG
     '.. and the one on the sand told, said, um.. **you know.. scr.. screamed..**'
     (5,Gen.2,F,17)

The form *skrimdio* contains past tense markers from both languages *-ed* and *-io* PST.M.SG and is an instance of 'double morphology' (Myers-Scotton 2002: 91–93). The English regular past tense suffix *-ed* is an outsider system morpheme (Myers-

Scotton 2005: 338) and so is the Croatian past participle marker *–io* (M.SG). This example contravenes the Early System Morpheme Hypothesis that predicts that "only early system morphemes may be doubled in classic codeswitching" (Myers-Scotton 2002: 92). In addition to the conspicuous hesitation and monitoring phenomena evident in (20) above, the Croatian speech of the same informant shows examples of the following: non-agreement in numerals and nouns; non-agreement between NP constituents for the features, number, gender and case; prepositions non-target case marking of succeeding nouns; case marking of nominal direct objects; frequent employment of integrated and unintegrated English-origin verbs; frequent pauses and false-starts.

We list these production phenomena not as an 'escape hatch' from the requirements of the Early System Morpheme Hypothesis; instead we contend that the speaker's anticipational production of a possibly 'incongruous' form is the reason, or at least one of the reasons, why such hesitation phenomena occur. The speaker herself flags this code-switch as conspicuous and there are a number of metalinguistic processes that indicate that the speaker may see the form as a production error that she is conscious of, or possibly as a hypercorrection. What we suggest is that speakers such as the one who produced (20) are likely to be going through the first stages of the Matrix Language Turnover. What this means is the frame for their ML when they 'use Croatian' is no longer a monolingual variety of that language, but a Composite Matrix Language whose structural characteristics are supplied mostly from Croatian, but to an extent also from English.

3 Multi-morphemic possessive constructions

The previous section presented and discussed examples of code-switching in which lexical contributions from the EL are evident. In this section we examine examples of possessive constructions in which not lexical, but structural contribution from the EL appears to be evident. The examples are all taken from Croatian-English contact situations from New Zealand, the USA and Australia.

In Croatian, possession can be expressed via pre-posed attributive + nominal constructions, or via post-posed GEN constructions where the possessee precedes the possessor. The pre-posed attributive construction is more common (in both the standard and most dialects) and is considered stylistically preferable. Pre-posed attributives are usually adjectival forms derived from nouns, e.g. *dijete* 'child-N' > *dječji* 'child's-ADJ', that yield ADJ+N constructions such as *dječja torba* 'children's bag'. Adjectives derived from nouns are clearly identifiable as such via adjectival suffixes such as *–čji, -ski, -ički, -av(a)n, -ast, -njav* that are the most common ones of the 151 adjectival suffixes that exist in standard Croatian (Babić 1991: 351–353). Personal names and nouns denoting family members can also attract adjectival suffixes, with *-ov* being the most common one for masculine nouns and *-in* for feminine ones, e.g. *Stjepan* 'Steven' + *-ov* = *Stjepanov* 'Steven's', *teta* 'aunt' + *-in* = *tetin* 'aunt's'. As attributive forms, they also attract morphological markers to mark the phi-features of case, gender and number. Morphology marking phi-features is affixed after the adjectival suffix. So, the Croatian equivalent of a phrase such as *Steven's sister* would consist of: a content morpheme *Stjepan* 'Steven'; an early system morpheme *-ov* as a possessive adjectival form that marks one feature only (possession); and an outsider late system morpheme that marks multiple features (case, gender, number) *-a* 'NOM.F.SG'; the possessee *sestra*. Together, these yield: *Stjepanova* 'Steven-POSS.NOM.F.SG' *sestra* 'sister-NOM.F.SG'.

Further to this, there is a limit to the number of other attributives that can occur in these constructions. A determiner (e.g. *ta* 'that-NOM.F.SG') can occur in initial position preceding the other two constituents, e.g. *ta Stjepanova sestra*, lit. 'that Steven's sister' (or 'that sister of Steven'), while attributive adjectives (e.g. *mlađa* 'younger-NOM.F.SG') can occur in medial position only, e.g. *Stjepanova mlađa sestra* 'Steven's younger sister'. But two adjectival forms that are both derived from nouns cannot co-occur in these constructions in the way that they can in English, e.g. **Stjepanovo sestrino dijete* 'Steven's sister's child'. Instead, a post-posed GEN construction is required, e.g. *dijete Stjepanove sestre* 'child-NOM.N.SG of Steven's-GEN.F.SG sister-GEN.F.SG', i.e. 'child of Steven's sister'.

We now look at instances in which ML content morphemes denoting personal names or members of a family are employed in possessive constructions. We focus our attention on the two system morphemes affixed to these, the early system morpheme marking possession and the outsider marking phi-features. The following example is taken from chapter 14, example (29) is re-numbered here as (21). A NZ-born Gen.3 speaker is talking here about home life.

(21) *u   mojoj   materin   kuća*
      in+LOC   my-LOC.F.SG   mother-POSS (NOM.M.SG?)   house-NOM.F.SG
      '... in my mother's house' (Gen.3, Sample A).

HMLD.Cro
u   kući   moje   matere
in+LOC   house-LOC.F.SG   my-GEN.F.SG   mother-GEN.F.SG
'... in the house of my mother'

We see in (21) that there is non-congruence in the feature marking of attributive forms and the possessee. We firstly look at the word order characteristics of this example and then look at system morphemes. Stoffel and Hlavac (this volume) point out that the possessee noun *kuća* is preceded not only by two pre-posed forms, but by the preposition *u* 'in'. This kind of construction is permitted in Croatian PPs where all attributive forms must relate to the final-occurring nominal but HMLD.Cro does not allow preceding attributives to relate internally to each other. In (21), we see that this rule of PP structure is contravened: the attributive *mojoj* 'my' relates to another attributive *materin* 'mother's' rather than *kuća* 'house', the possessee. At an abstract level of speech production, there is not only Croatian but also English contribution in this speaker's conceptualisation and production of PPs (Myers-Scotton 2002: 202–203). We are reminded that the example is from a Gen.3 speaker, and English is their dominant language.

We focus now on the system morphemes of example (21). The possessee noun is *kuća* 'house'. The head is the preposition *u* 'in' that requires LOC case marking for all succeeding constituents. The constituent immediately following *u* 'in' has target case marking: *mojoj* 'my-LOC.F.SG'. The following constituent is *materin*. This consists of the content morpheme *mater* 'mother-F.SG' and the early system morpheme marking possession *-in*. There are no further overt morpheme forms in the constituent, and we represent the marking of the phi-features with a question mark as (NOM.M.SG?), i.e. morphological marking that yields an –Ø ending. Target case-marking for this constituent would be *majčinoj*, i.e. mother+POSS+LOC.F.SG'. The last item is the head noun, *kuća* 'house-NOM.F.SG' which occurs in its NOM, 'baseline' form without oblique marking showing LOC. Matrix language outsider morphemes that are otherwise required on the final three constituents are realised in a variable way: *mojoj* 'my-LOC.F.SG' – target; *materin* 'mother-POSS. (NOM.M.SG?)' – absent; *kuća* 'house-NOM.F.SG' – non-target.

The constituent *materin* is of most interest to us and we observe that this form contains an early system morpheme *-in* showing possession, but no system morpheme showing phi-features. Even if case were not to be marked, we would expect gender to be marked because the feminine gender of its head noun, *kuća* 'house', appears to be known to the speaker. This would have yielded *materina* 'mother+POSS+NOM.F.SG'. But, as stated, the outsider system morpheme marking phi-features is absent. We contend that the production of one system morpheme and the absence of another system morpheme is not accidental. Although there are no lexical items supplied by English in the form of EL forms, the input of English structure at an abstract level appears evident. In an equivalent English construction, possessive suffixes are required, but not markers showing phi-features. Feature-marking appears to be co-determined by the structure of both contributing languages: possessive-marking is required by both Croatian and

English and is present; phi-marking is required by Croatian only and is variable in its realisation. Possessive-marking is determined at the 'lemma level' of speech production, while phi-marking is determined at the 'formulator level' of speech production (Myers-Scotton 2002: 24). We see this example, albeit in isolation, as providing an insight into the linguistic outcomes of a matrix language that is composite and not provided by one linguistic code only.

A similar example is reported in chapter 10 from the USA.Cro corpus that is mentioned in the final section of that chapter that is glossed below as example (22). A Gen.2 speaker is talking about family heirlooms shown to the data collector.

(22) ovo   moj   rođak
     this-NOM.N.SG my-NOM.M.SG   relative-NOM.M.SG
     očev   bukva
     father-POSS.NOM.M.SG book-NOM.F.SG
     'this [is] my cousin's father's book'

HMLD.Cro
ovo   je   knjiga   oca   mog
this-NOM.N.SG be-3SG book-NOM.F.SG father-GEN.M.SG my-GEN.M.SG
rođaka
relative-GEN.M.SG
'this is the book of the father of my cousin'

Example (21) was a possessive construction consisting of three items; example (22) has a possessive construction with four items. Looking at this four-item predicate nominative, we see that the head, *bukva* 'book', is NOM.F.SG. The form *bukva* is an English-origin transfer *book* that has been integrated phonologically and morphologically, and assigned feminine gender (cf. HMLD.Cro *knjiga* 'book-F'). We see hierarchical relationships such that there are intermediate projections within the NP between the constituents *rođak* 'cousin' and *očev* 'father's' (i.e. *rođak* + *očev* = 'cousin's father's') that are allowed in English, but not in Croatian. As with example (21) above, we focus on markers of possession.

In example (22), both *rođak* and *očev* function as possessors and are expected to attract morphological marking that shows this. Instead, only *očev* 'father's' bears possessive marking, i.e. *otac* 'father' + *-ev* 'POSS' = *očev* 'father-POSS', while *rođak* 'cousin' lacks a possessive suffix, in this case *–ov*, e.g. *rođakov* 'cousin-POSS'. As is also clear from the gloss, there is non-agreement in gender between the head *bukva*-F and the preceding attributives that all bear -Ø suffixes, or default NOM.M.SG marking. So, phi-markers are apparently absent from the attributives, and the only possessive marker that occurs is the suffix *-ev* in *očev* 'father-POSS', the form which immediately precedes the possessor of the head, *bukva*. To summarise, outsider system morphemes that would otherwise be required on the last four constituents of this phrase are absent.

We posit that it is a composite matrix language that is the basis of the ML of this utterance and we see that Croatian and English structure contribute to possessive marking, at least in relation to that constituent that is closest to the NP head. Phi-marking that is determined by input from Croatian structure only, is variable, as in example (21). Jutronić-Tihomirović (1985: 61) records two further possessive constructions in which no possessive markers are present. These are both from Gen.2 speakers.

(23) *na   mat   ili   otac   kuću*
     on+LOC mother-NOM.F.SG or   father-NOM.F.SG house-ACC.F.SG
     'at mother's or father's house'

   HMLD.Cro
   kod   kuće   matere   ili   oca
   at+GEN house-GEN.F.SG mother-GEN.F.SG or   father-GEN.M.SG
   'at the home of my mother or father'

(24) *kod   njezina   Kata   kuću*
     at+GEN her-NOM.F.SG Kata-NOM.F.SG house-ACC.F.SG
     'at her [cousin's/friend's?] Kata's house'

   HMLD.Cro
   kod   kuće   njezine   Kate
   at+GEN house-GEN.F.SG her-GEN.F.SG Kata-GEN.F.SG
   'at the home of her [cousin/friend?] Kata'

In examples (23) and (24), morphological markers showing phi-features are absent from all attributive constituents preceding the noun head of the PPs. Further, possessive markers –*ov* or *-ev* for masculine nouns (e.g. *otac* + *-ev* = *očev* 'father's') and –*in* for feminine ones (e.g. *majka* + *-in* = *majčin* 'mother's'; *Kata* + *-in* = *Katin* 'Kate's') are absent as well. In contrast to examples (21) and (22) in which possessive marking is apparent partly via structural information supplied by Croatian and partly from English via English word order conventions, in examples (23) and (24), it appears that possessive marking is determined by structural information supplied by English only, where an English-based word order sequence is the only marker to show the relationship between possessors and possessees. As in other language contact situations in which a matrix language turnover is occurring, lexical items are supplied from what used to be the sole matrix language, while the morphosyntactic grid increasingly follows the structural rules of what was the embedded language, here English.

In (23) and (24), there is only one ML outsider system morpheme in each of the examples, and in both examples it is given in a non-target ACC form *kuću* 'house-ACC.F.SG' rather than its GEN form *kuće* 'house-GEN.F.SG'. For comparison, the HMLD.Cro equivalent utterances have outsider system morphemes on all nominals. So, structural relations within the phrases are not clearly shown via outsider morphemes supplied by Croatian. Instead, word order marks relations of possession between constituents. The attributive forms have baseline marking of NOM.M.SG or NOM.F.SG where otherwise GEN, in addition to possessive suffixes, would be expected. (Or at least we posit that these forms would have been used in the Croatian repertoires of these speakers' parents and grand-parents.) Therefore, it seems that case-marking is not an amenable or available strategy to these speakers to express relations of possession. The only instance of OBL case marking is, as mentioned, the noun that is the head in both examples, *kuću* 'house-ACC.F.SG'. The ACC case marking of *kuću* is not congruent to the case required from the preposition heads, *na*+LOC and *kod*+GEN respectively. But the speakers appear to consider this a form that is an object or an object argument of the valence of the PPs overall. The morphological form that they employ to mark this is a non-NOM form, namely ACC, which may be the main or even only non-NOM form in their repertoire of active nominal inflections.

We note, as is pointed out in chapters 8, 9, 10, 11, 12 and 13 that changes in case marking can occur in the speech of some heritage language speakers. A scale of implicativity of case marking (Ďurovič's 1983) is employed in many of these chapters in an attempt to quantify the extent of changes in case marking and to systematise the tendencies where the marking of more 'peripheral' cases is supplied using the markers of less oblique cases. Although there are no reports of speakers' repertoires being reduced to a two-case system only (e.g. NOM with ACC as the default non-NOM) amongst some speakers, the ACC may be commonly employed as a default OBL marker, with instances of other case forms found irregularly or in fossilised constructions. We conclude this section with an example not taken from chapter 12, but from Hlavac (2003: 272) which is an excerpt from the speech of a 20-year old Gen.2 speaker in Melbourne. He was recalling the place of residence of his relatives on his mother's and father's side.

(25) am   imam   moja   **mamin's**   sestra
     um   have-1SG my-NOM.F.SG   mum+in-**POSS**.NOM.M.SG+'s   sister-NOM.F.SG
     je   tu   i   sve   moj   *tata*'s
     be-3SG here   and   all-NOM.N.SG   my-NOM.M.SG   dad-NOM.M.SG+'s
     family je   sve   u   Zagreb
     family   be-3SG   all-NOM.N.SG   in+LOC   Zagreb-NOM.M.SG
     'Um, I have my mum's sister.. is here and.. all my dad's **family** is all in Zagreb' (Gen.2,M,20)

HMLD.Cro
am   imam   ... mamina   sestra   je   tu
um   have-1SG   ... mum-POSS+NOM.F.SG   sister-NOM.F.SG   be-3SG   here
a   čitava   šira   porodica   mog
and   all-NOM.F.SG   wider-NOM.F.SG   family-NOM.F.SG   my-GEN.M.SG
tate   je   u   Zagrebu
dad-GEN.M.SG   be-3SG   in+LOC   Zagreb-LOC.M.SG
'Um, I have... mum's sister is here and the whole wider family of my dad is in Zagreb'.

Example (25) contains two possessive constructions. The possessor *mamin's* in the first construction, *moja mamin's sestra* has possessive morphology from both Croatian and English, *-in* and *-'s*. Possessive markers in both languages are bridge late system morphemes. So, we can see how both languages contribute not only abstract structure in this possessive construction, but also surface morphemes as well. Composite input is evident beyond this: in the same first CP, the possessive construction is the OBJ of the verb *imam* 'have-1SG', but the possessive construction lacks ACC markers that show this syntactic role. English structure does not require feature marking of nominals' syntactic roles across the CP, while Croatian structure does require this.

The second possessive construction in (25) above *sve moj tata's family* has its only possessive marker supplied from English, *-'s*. The head of the NP is an EL form *family*, and this may play a role in the production of English *-'s* and the non-production of Croatian *-in*. (Although *tata* 'dad' is a masculine noun, it ends in *-a* and attracts the feminine possessive marker *-in*.) The contribution of English structure is evident elsewhere as the sequencing of the possessive construction follows English structure rules that allow intermediate projections between attributives, i.e. *moj + tata* within a larger NP which is not allowed in HMLD.Cro.

The equivalent construction in HMLD.Cro has the possessee first followed by the possessor in GEN: *čitava* 'whole-NOM.F.SG' *šira* 'wider-NOM.F.SG' *porodica* 'family-NOM.F.SG' *mog* 'my-GEN.M.SG' *tate* 'dad-GEN.M.SG'. As in the first clause, the second clause does not contain feature marking for case, such as Ľubomír case required after *u* 'in+LOC'. Example (25) shows how contribution from the structures of both languages is evident. Most content morphemes are supplied by Croatian, but their word order shows that English structure is co-determining the morphosyntactic grid in the way that the possessive constructions appear as templates of English ones. What is conspicuous is the contribution of structure not only at an abstract level but of English forms as well, such as early system morpheme -'s. A re-structuring of word order conventions based on EL models is reported in other comparable studies. Ivanova-Sullivan (2014) and Isurin and Ivanova-Sullivan (2008) report patterns showing evidence of a rigid word order among speakers of Russian as a heritage language where homeland Russian allows flexibility.

4 Conclusion

This chapter has selected two types of language contact phenomena that recur amongst some categories of examples across chapters 5 to 14. In general, singly occurring items from the EL are integrated into the ML frame via ML system morphemes, usually outsider system morphemes. In Section 2, examples (1) to (6) show how singly occurring EL forms are integrated into the morphosyntactic grid of the ML via outsider system morphemes, usually inflections that indicate phi-features. Examples (1) to (6) are typical of most of the examples presented throughout this volume.

In this concluding chapter, alongside typical instances in which EL items are integrated into the ML grid of the clause via Croatian outsider system morphemes, we have also deliberately chosen those examples, shown above as examples (7) to (25) that appear conspicuous or peculiar in the way that surface-level forms and/or structure are combined from Croatian as the ML and another language as the EL. We have done this to test the predictions of the 4-M model. Application of the 4-M model to the examples enables a classification of morphemes and their roles. This classification provides us with the framework to explain how various morphemes appear in bilingual clauses, and how they contribute to structure therein.

Examples (7) to (9) contain a mix of EL islands and singly-occurring bare forms. While bare forms are not optimally integrated into the ML morphosyntactic, there is no contravention of the System Morpheme Principle as no outsider system morphemes are supplied by the EL. It is possible that psycholinguistic features, i.e. non-dominance in the ML, are a factor in accounting for bare forms, as these forms are far more frequent in the speech of speakers of the second- and subsequent generations. We are cognisant of the possibility that social factors may play a role in this and that there could be a sociolinguistic basis to non-marking. Bare forms may be a linguistic marker of generational membership that younger-generation speakers employ to distinguish themselves from first-generational speakers whose production of EL forms typically features phonological transference and morphological marking from Croatian. Cross-generational comparison for the feature of morphological integration of EL items show substantial difference between Gen.1 speakers (very high level of morphological integration via outsider system morphemes) and Gen.2 speakers (low to moderate level of morphological integration via outsider system morphemes) (Albijanić 1982). This difference in the linguistic behaviour of speakers (at least in relation to EL forms) according to generation is attested here in the chapters of this volume that match generational membership with linguistic forms (see Sčukanec; Županović Filipin, Hlavac and Piasevoli; Piasevoli; Hlavac and Stolac; Stoffel and Hlavac, all this volume) as well as in studies on heritage languages elsewhere (Polinsky 2008, 2016). Second-generation speakers typically use two (or more) codes on a regular basis, usually in in-group settings and are protagonists of what is often termed 'classic code-switching' (Myers-Scotton 2002: 8). This is a hypernym that encompasses an array of bilingual speech forms from minimal EL input that is fully integrated to considerable EL input that is variably integrated to very extensive EL input such that the code that supplies the nominal ML has itself become bilingual.

The samples also contain past tense forms from the EL that appear to be outsider system morphemes. For example, an English irregular PST.PTCP occurs in example (10) but such irregular past tense forms are elected as content morphemes different from regular past tense forms. Further, the function of some past participles as in (11) is that of an adjective, derived from a passive construction, which points to it being a content rather than a system morpheme.

In example (12), the form of the EL PST PTCP coincides with the target outsider system morpheme suffix of an ML PST.PTCP–*o* ending. There is evidence to show that the frame that determines the speaker's production in Croatian is a Composite Matrix Language in which structural input, including that of outsider system morphemes, can be supplied by both contributing languages. In (13), the occurrence of an EL outsider system morpheme in an English regular past participle triggers an EL island, while an outsider system morpheme on an Italian EL PST.PTCP in a passive construction in (14) also results in the same outcome: a triggered EL island.

Most forms and tenses of German EL verbs have structural (phonotacticly-based) non-congruence with the other, Croatian forms in compound VPs, and this results in EL islands with full German VPs. These full German VPs could almost be classified as inter-clausal alternations rather than as intra-clausal EL islands as shown in examples (16) and (17), as well as in further data from German as an EL in otherwise Russian speech. There is one instance only of double marking of past tense with Eng. *-ed* co-occuring with Cro. *-io*. The example contains conspicuous production features – these could be a consequence as much as a cause of duplication of an outsider system morpheme. Further phenomena point to the evidence that the speaker's matrix language is undergoing change such that English structure is contributed at an abstract level and also at the surface level.

Looking at the examples presented in Section 3 that are all from Croatian-English settings, we see that at the conceptual level of speech production, speakers' intentions are expressed via lemmas provided by Croatian. At the next level, English structure determines the word order of constituents in possessive constructions. Amongst other things, English structure allows intermediate projections internal to the larger PP or NP. At the formulator level, Croatian supplies morphemes that mark possession, at least in (21) and (22), and in one instance in (25). But at the predicate-argument level, Croatian input is less evident as feature marking for phi-features is variable; in fact it sometimes applies within intermediate projections between pairs of attributives, e.g. *moj* + *rođak*-M 'my relative' that are not congruent to the clause's head *bukva*-F 'book' in (22), and *njezina* + *Kata*-NOM.F 'her Kathy' that are not congruent to *kuću*-ACC.F 'house' in (24) while in (21) there is non-congruence across all three constituents. We summarise these phenomena according to the 4-M model in the following way. We see three different results of the input of English structure at the predicate-argument structure level: first, possession expressed via word order sequencing with possessive markers supplied from Croatian in their 'bare' form, i.e. without further marking on relations elsewhere in the CP in examples (21) and (22); second, possession expressed solely via English-based word order sequencing with the absence of possessive morphology from either language in examples (23) and (24); third, possession expressed via English-based word order sequencing with possessive morphology supplied by either language, or even by both as in example (25).

Word order is clearly not a surface morpheme, but we observe that input of English structure in the form of word order conventions is, amongst some speakers, co-determining the realisation of semantic and pragmatic intentions of an utterance. In this way, word order is analogous to an early system morpheme, i.e. features of the lexical head such as the possessive NPs in (21) to (25) determine word order form. We posit that word order, as a feature analogous to an early system morpheme, is more susceptible to replacement or change than bridge late system morphemes such as Croatian possessive markers *-ov* and *-in* and that change in word order is likely to have been a precursor to change in possessive marking. But we lack data that extensively and longitudinally display this and this remains a hypothesis only.

In all examples re-presented in this chapter, Croatian supplies all or nearly all content morphemes. But Croatian supplies fewer late system morphemes than it does in equivalent HMLD.Cro constructions, and in some cases late system morphemes are absent or bear marking that is not congruent to features present elsewhere across the CP. EL outsider system morphemes are very rare, and their occurrence results in a triggered EL island, or they result from an ML that itself has a composite morphosyntactic frame. In general, though, outsider system morphemes are supplied from Croatian, and co-occur with EL forms to integrate these into the ML.

This chapter has collated examples from chapters 5 to 14 in regard to intra-clausal code-switching and possessive constructions only. As stated in Section 1, the 'conclusive' character of this chapter relates to these two phenomena only and we have not revisited and reviewed the other groups of lexical, semantic and structural innovations that together relate to a considerable number of examples.

Indeed, there are very many instances of structural features across the different data-sets that call for further investigation: the use of *jedan* 'one' as a marker signalling indefiniteness; case-marking and the role of prepositions as analytic means to convey syntactic relations; employment of *od* 'of' / 'from' as an analytic marker of possession together with GEN (or even instead of GEN); word order and a drift towards SVO; subject pro-drop; clitic placement; clitic vs. long forms of object pronouns; changes in pragmatic inference co-occurring with long form object pronouns; frequency of Croatian light or DO-verbs with EL nouns or gerunds to replicate common VP structures that exist in the EL. Nor have we addressed the instances of loan translations and the recurrence of transferred lexico-semantic constructions found in many chapters. We welcome further studies that will examine these and other contact linguistic phenomena in the speech of heritage language speakers.

References

Albijanić, Aleksandar. 1982. San Pedro revisited: Language maintenance in the San Pedro Yugoslav Community. In Roland Sussex (ed.) *The Slavic Languages in Emigre Communities*. 11–22. Edmonton: Linguistic Research Inc.

Babić, Stjepan. 1991. *Tvorba riječi u hrvatskom književnom jeziku*. [Word formation in the Croatian Literary Language]. Zagreb: Hrvatska akademija znanosti i umjetnosti / Globus Nakladni zavod.

Backus, Ad. 1996. *Two in one. Bilingual Speech of Turkish Immigrants in The Netherlands*. Tilburg: Tilburg University Press.

Bolonyai, Agnes. 1998. In-Between Languages: Language Shift/Maintenance in Childhood Bilingualism. *International Journal of Bilingualism*, 2(1). 21–43.

Bolonyai, Agnes. 2005. English verbs in Hungarian/Englsh codeswitching. In James Cohen, Kellie McAlister, Kara Rolstad & Jeff MacSwan (eds.) *Proceedings of the 4th International Symposium on Bilingualism*. 317–327. Somerville, MA: Cascadilla Press.

Clyne, Michael. 1991. *Community Languages. The Australian Experience*. Cambridge, UK: Cambridge University Press.

Ďurovič, Ľubomír. 1983. The case systems in the language of diaspora children. *Slavica Lundensia 9*. 21–94.

Fairchild, Sarah & Janet Van Hell. 2017.Determiner-noun code-switching in Spanish heritage speakers. *Bilingualism: Language and Cognition*. 20(1). 150–161.

Fuller, Janet & Lehnert, Heike. 2000. Noun phrase structure in German-English codeswitching: Variation in gender assignment and article use. *International Journal of Bilingualism*, 4(3). 399–420.

Goldbach, Alexandra. 2005. *Deutsch-russischer Sprachkontakt. Deutsche Transferenzen und Code-switching in der Rede Russischsprachiger in Berlin*. Frankfurt/M. Peter Lang.

He, Agnes Weiyun. 2013. The wor(l)d is a collage: multi-performance by Chinese heritage language speakers. *The Modern Language Journal*, 97(2). 304–317.

Hlavac, Jim. 2003. *Second-generation speech. Lexicon, code-switching and morpho-syntax of Croatian-English bilinguals*. Bern: Peter Lang.

Hlavac, Jim. 2011. Hesitation and monitoring phenomena in bilingual speech: a consequence of code-switching or a strategy to facilitate its incorporation? *Journal of Pragmatics* 43(15). 3793–3806.

Isurin, Ludmila & Ivanova-Sullivan, Tanya. 2008. Lost in Between: The Case of Russian Heritage Speakers. *Heritage Language Journal*, 6(1). 72–104.

Ivanova-Sullivan, Tanya. 2014. *Theoretical and Experimental Aspects of Syntax-Discourse Interface in Heritage Grammars*. Leiden: Brill.

Jake, Janice & Carol Myers-Scotton. 2002. Second generation shifts in sociopragmatic codeswitching patterns. In Aleya Rouchdy (ed.) *Language contact and language conflict in Arabic. Variations on a sociolinguistic theme*. 317–330. London: Routledge.

Jutronić-Tihomirović, Dunja. 1985. *Hrvatski jezik u SAD* [The Croatian Language in the United States]. Split: Logos.

Myers-Scotton, Carol. 1993. *Duelling Languages. Grammatical Structure in Codeswitching*. Oxford: Clarendon Press.

Myers-Scotton, Carol. 2002. *Contact Linguistics. Bilingual Encounters and Grammatical Outcomes*. Oxford: Oxford University Press.

Myers-Scotton, Carol. 2005. Supporting a differential access hypothesis: code switching and other contact data. In Judith Kroll & Annette de Groot (eds.) *Handbook of bilingualism. Psycholinguistic approaches*. 326–348. Oxford: Oxford University Press.

Myers-Scotton, Carol. 2008. Language contact: why outsider system morphemes resist transfer. *Journal of Language Contact*, 2. 21–41.

Myers-Scotton, Carol & Janice Jake. 2017. Revisiting the 4-M model: Codeswitching and morpheme election at the abstract level. *International Journal of Bilingualism*, 21(3). 340–366.

Polinsky, Maria. 2008. Gender under incomplete acquisition: heritage speakers' knowledge of noun categorization. *Heritage Language Journal*, 6(1). 40–71.
Polinsky, Maria. 2016. Structure vs. use in heritage language. *Linguistics Vanguard* 2(1). doi:10.1515/lingvan-2015-0036
Schmitt, Elena. 2000. Overt and covert codeswitching in immigrant children from Russia. *International Journal of Bilingualism*, 4(1). 9–28.
Smith, Daniel. 2006. Thresholds leading to shift: Spanish/English codeswitching and convergence in Georgia, U.S.A. *International Journal of Bilingualism*, 10(2). 207–238.

Subject index

4-M model
- 4 different types of morphemes (Myers-Scotton 2002) 23, 628–629, 655
- 4 characteristics of sprachbunds: multilateral, multidirectional, mutual, multilingualism (Friedman, this volume) 187, 205, 210–211

acceptability ratings of model sentences 44 see also proficiency
accusative case see case
acquisition see also divergent attainment, proficiency
- first language acquisition 46
- 'frozen' 40
- restricted acquisition 39, 502
adjectives 36, 58, 126, 127, 138, 142, 148, 152–153, 178, 264–266, 293, 296, 333, 344, 347, 350, 371–372, 382–383, 387, 394, 396–397, 462, 468, 482, 513, 567–569, 574–575, 586, 604, 608–611, 614, 619, 620, 634–635, 639, 644, 650, 656, 666–667
adnominal dative constructions 427, 473 see also case, dative
adstrate influence 191, 205, 207–208 see also convergence, superstrate influence
adverbial phrases 108, 147, 160–162, 167, 173, 468, 644
adverbs 36, 58, 142, 149, 153, 155, 159–162, 169–170, 173, 177, 193, 200, 270, 272, 293, 374, 387, 395, 397, 462, 468, 482, 540, 546–547, 552, 572, 586, 605, 608, 614, 621, 632
adversative clauses see clauses
affirmatives 61, 134, 506, 518–519, 550 see also discourse markers
- yeah 61, 510, 518–520, 548, 550
affixes 35
agglutinative morphology 37 see also morphology
Albania 190
Albanian 5–6, 188, 191, 193–194, 198
- Arbanasi Albanian 6

alternation 50, 53, 55, 131–133, 135, 137, 176, 341, 454–455, 482, 576, 587 see also code-switching
American Croatian (USA.Cro) 405, 412–415, 421–422, 433–434, 437–440
American-Croatians 65, 78, 407–410, 412
American English-Croatian bilinguals 78
analytic constructions 31, 35, 51, 70, 149, 152, 177, 198–199, 201–202
analytic marking 37, 578–579, 587
analytism 36, 74, 575
andative deontic passive see passive voice constructions
animacy (grammatical) 141, 579
antecedent 234, 236, 238–239, 644
aorist see verb tenses/forms
Arabic 8–9, 14
Arabic-English bilinguals 50
archaic forms 105, 117, 140, 144, 176
areal linguistics 70, 197
Argentina 1, 4, 12, 16, 18, 22–23, 595–601, 603, 605, 609 Argentinian Croatian
Argentinian Croatian (ARG.Cro) 618, 620, 622, 633
Argentinian-Croatians 597, 599–601, 605, 613
Aromanian 188, 191, 194
'arrested development' 40 see also divergent attainment
articles 163–166, 179, 618, 621
- definite 72, 74, 163–165, 195, 197
  - postposed definite article of Balkan Slavic 197
- indefinite 74, 163–165, 179, 197, 265, 278, 371, 376–377, 464, 480–481, 483
  - *jedan* as nascent indefinite article 20–21, 72, 198, 208, 265, 271, 278, 350, 371, 376, 377, 386–387, 396, 464, 466, 480–481, 483, 523, 612, 618–619
asymmetrical 52
'attractiveness' 51
attributive forms 68, 138, 147, 151, 164, 165, 166, 169, 178, 267, 277–278, 387, 543

https://doi.org/10.1515/9781501503917-016

Subject index

attrition 41–42, 44, 289, 291, 311, 313–315, 465, 471, 482, 588 *see also* 'forgetters'
awareness of linguistic affiliations of lexemes 56
Australia 9–14, 16, 21, 83, 108, 638
Australian Croatian (AUS.Cro) 570, 573, 575, 580, 638
Australian-Croatians 63, 493, 496, 500–501, 503, 555
Austria 2–4, 6, 9–12, 15–19, 23, 33, 251–261, 269, 278–279, 301, 304–305, 308 *see also* Burgenland
Austrian Croatian (AUT.Cro) 251, 278, 632, 635 *see also* Burgenland Croatian
Austrian-Croatians 261 *see also* Burgenland Croats
Austro-Hungarian Empire 6, 9, 252, 361–362, 368, 370, 597
autochthonous languages 3, 5
auxiliaries 21, 151–153, 188, 190, 200–202, 234, 352, 354, 357, 386, 638, 643–644 *see also* clitics
avoidance strategies 141

back-channeling 615
Balkan languages 189, 205, 207, 209
Balkan Romany *see* Romany
Balkan Slavic 196, 190–208 *see also* Slavic (Common)
- medieval 196
Balkan sprachbund 16–17, 37, 70–71, 187–190, 195, 198, 202, 204–208
Balkans 70, 187–188, 190–192, 194, 199–200, 204–205
bare forms *see* uninflected forms
base language *see* baseline
baseline 43, 52, 78
Belgium 177, 189
bi-aspectual verb transfers *see* verbal aspect
biculturalism 80
bilingual compound verbs 67 *see also* verbs
bilingual discourse 50, 227
bilingual mode *see* mode
bilingual speakers 62, 71–72, 74, 77
bilingual speech 33, 46, 51–52, 79–80, 258, 448, 501–502, 521–522, 557, 627–628, 630, 655, 656 *see also* code-switching

bilingual written texts 79
bilingualism 37, 285, 289, 291, 296, 311, 320, 330
Bolivia 596
borrowings 29, 35, 49, 53, 54, 79, 114–120, 124, 133, 147, 154, 166, 175, 226, 243, 461 *see also* code-switching
- conventionalised borrowings 121, 131, 133
- nonce 264
- taxonomies of borrowability 36, 38
Bosnia-Hercegovina 111, 217, 219–220, 252–253, 256, 259, 286, 295, 321–323, 352, 363, 366, 449
- Hercegovina 108, 112
Bosniaks 6
Bosnian 5–6, 8, 10, 14, 81, 193, 198–199, 220, 221, 251, 255, 261, 265, 324, 407, 408, 443
Bosnian/Croatian/Serbian 254, 261, 324
Bosnian-speakers 82, 365
Bošnjak-Croats (in Hungary) 112, 115, 127, 130, 143
bound morphemes 32, 58, 66
Brazil 596
bridge late system morphemes 629–630, 641, 654, 657
Bulgaria 195–196
Bulgarian 8, 38, 188, 190–193, 199, 202
Burgenland 3, 8, 10, 15, 17, 33, 102–103, 105–108, 112, 113, 118–121, 170, 189
Burgenland Croatian (BGLD.Cro) 33, 101, 103, 105–108, 116–118, 120–121, 124, 126, 128–132, 140, 147–151, 153, 159–160, 162–163, 166–170, 175–176, 251, 253, 255, 419
- codification of supra-regional standard 33
- grammar books 33
- textbooks 33
Burgenland Croats 101, 103, 105–106, 108, 112–113, 119, 252–253, 279

calques 29, 35, 62, 63, 105, 128–130, 139, 155, 167, 175–177, 179, 196, 197, 271, 332, 335, 338, 344, 353–354, 371, 389–390, 397, 505, 523, 526, 550, 572, 574, 584, 587, 604

Subject index — **663**

Canada 1, 4, 9, 11–13, 16, 18, 21, 23–24, 30, 40, 79, 443, 448–454, 460–462, 478, 481, 483, 513, 547, 559, 630–634, 638, 640, 643, 648–650, 653, 658
Canadian Croatian (CAN.Cro) 447–450, 475
Canadian-Croatians 69, 447–448, 451, 453, 471
cardinal numbers 380, 434–437, 440 *see also* numerals
case 196, 264, 267, 269, 289, 292, 303, 550, 568, 579–582, 584, 588
- ablative 197
- accusative 32, 121–123, 127, 134, 138–139, 141–144, 150, 161, 164–165, 168, 174, 177, 193, 195, 234, 238–240, 264–265, 267, 269, 271–272, 274–276, 289, 292–294, 299, 301, 304–306, 321, 346–348, 351–356, 372–380, 382–385, 388–389, 391–392, 394, 412, 416–418, 423, 426, 429, 431, 439, 464, 466, 457, 468, 469–470, 476–477, 480, 482, 508–512, 519–520, 522–528, 532–533, 535–541, 565, 568–573, 575, 579, 582–584, 588, 606–608, 611–614, 616–617, 619–620, 631, 633–635, 637, 639–640, 645–646, 652
- accusative-experiencer construction 68
- accusative as default oblique case marker 69, 525
- acquisition thereof 409
- dative 193, 195, 234, 236, 285–286, 291–295, 297, 299, 301, 303–305, 308, 309, 311–313, 334, 336–339, 345, 352, 354–355, 412–413, 418–421, 425, 427, 429, 431–432, 437, 469–470, 473–474, 477, 479, 523, 524, 525, 526, 531–533, 535, 543, 565, 570–571, 576, 579–580, 582, 606, 609–610, 613, 616, 636, 643, 645 see also dative constructions
- decrease in case distinctions 38, 195, 528, 579, 582, 588, 653
- genitive 69, 121–122, 133, 140, 141, 143–146, 155, 164, 168, 171, 173, 196–197, 234–235, 292, 295, 304, 307, 309, 332, 335–337, 350–351, 353, 356, 374–375, 377, 379–392, 394, 396, 420, 424–426, 427, 428–430, 433–435, 437, 440, 467–468, 478, 519–520, 523–526, 537, 572, 580–581, 588, 606–607, 610–614, 616, 632–634, 637, 644, 648–649, 651–654, 658
- implicativity (in Ďurovič's terms) *see* implicativity
- instrumental 69, 143–144, 148, 155, 269, 289, 305, 338, 348, 356, 382, 384–385, 391, 422, 426, 464–465, 468–469, 477, 519–520, 523–526, 537, 543, 575, 579, 581, 607, 612, 614, 616, 617, 635–636, 646
- comitative instrumental 143, 177
- locative 69, 127, 138, 140–145, 148, 176, 234, 238, 289, 348–349, 356, 373, 379, 381–384, 388–389, 397, 416, 430, 432, 464, 466, 469–470, 478, 481, 506, 510, 515, 525, 526, 528, 529, 530, 543, 544, 547, 550, 565, 568–570, 573, 575, 579–581, 588, 606–608, 610–611, 620, 631–645, 647, 649–650, 652–654
- locative/allative 197
- nominative 234, 236, 238–239, 289, 293, 299, 301, 304–309, 332–338, 340, 344–346, 348, 372–375, 377, 379–383, 385–387, 389, 391, 394, 413, 416, 418, 420, 421–424, 426–431, 465–470, 480–481, 483, 510, 513–515, 517, 523, 525–526, 528–531, 536–537, 539, 543–544, 547–550, 565, 569, 571, 579–580, 584, 588, 608–617, 619–620, 631, 634, 636, 639, 641, 645, 647, 649, 650, 651, 652, 653, 654
- oblique/non-nominative 67–68, 76, 267, 289–290, 347–348, 383, 550, 580, 650, 653
- vocative 69, 140, 144, 195, 289, 423, 524–526
case affixes *see* case-marking
case-marking, 20–21, 38, 68–69, 138, 333, 338–339, 344–348, 356, 371, 379, 381, 383, 385, 396–397, 426–429, 436, 437, 439, 465, 467, 470, 478, 482, 579–582, 588, 630–632, 635, 648, 650, 653, 658
casus generalis 579
Celtic languages 189

Central State Office for Croats Abroad
(*Središnji državni ured za Hrvate izvan Republike Hrvatske*) 12, 25, 251, 321, 359, 407, 443, 595, 597, 601, 603, 622
chain migration 407, 494
Chile 82, 596, 603
Chinese 9, 14
citizenship 220, 229, 260, 322, 331, 494, 503, 603
– Croatian Citizenship Law (2012) 83
– proficiency as a pre-requisite for citizenship 83
– changes to law in 2020 83, 94
clauses 38, 630, 631–634, 639–642, 645–646, 654–655, 657
– adversative 166
– concessive 172
– dependent 371, 388–389
– relative 37, 171
– subordinate 52, 167, 172–174, 238, 240, 389
cleft constructions 81, 353
clitics 152, 166–170, 179, 191, 193, 201, 206, 207, 244, 275, 360–361, 371, 386, 387, 388, 412, 415–424, 427, 432, 438, 440–441, 442–443, 471–475, 482, 540–541, 552, 630, 658
– clitic placement 81, 542
  – Wackernagelian rule 192, 415
– leftward fronting of clitics 170, 474
– pronominal clitics 192, 583
code 55
code-copying 53–54, 64–65 see also code-switching
code-mixing 55 see also code-switching
code-switching 13, 18, 19–23, 29, 34, 50–53, 55, 57, 60, 78, 80, 81, 85, 102–103, 108, 114, 117, 119, 130–135, 137, 176, 177, 179, 222, 225–226, 233, 235–237, 243, 244, 251, 258, 261–264, 270, 278–279, 288, 290, 312, 326, 329–330, 332, 340–341, 343–344, 354–357, 371, 376, 393, 395, 397, 452, 455–458, 462, 483, 484, 493, 498, 501, 505, 521, 548, 550, 554–555, 557, 561, 566, 576, 577, 587, 604–605, 613, 616, 621, 627–628, 630, 633, 638–640, 648, 650, 652, 654, 655, 658, 661, 665

– attitudes towards 257–258, 262 see also language attitudes
– awareness of 278–279
– bi-directional 50
– 'classic code-switching' 60, 233, 263, 627, 648, 656
– definition 56
– extra-clausal 60–61, 81, 126, 128, 131, 456–458, 506, 576, 615, 621
– flagged 278–279 see also flags
– inter-clausal 50, 60, 61, 81, 50, 133, 243, 456–458, 506, 521, 576–577, 613
– intra-clausal 18, 23, 55, 60, 81, 137, 225, 233–237, 243, 357, 372, 394, 576, 627–628, 630, 638, 640, 656
– trigger words 263, 340, 344, 501
codification and standardisation 7–8, 105, 116, 118, 151
Cognitive Grammar 55, 291, 292, 294, 314
collocations 113, 116, 121, 170, 374, 375, 395, 396, 478, 480, 483, 504, 572, 617, 644–645
Common European Framework of Reference for Languages (CEFRL) 83
communicative networks 3, 24 see also domains
commercial/transactional domain see domains
communicative competence 48, 224, 229–230, 260 see also competence
'community languages' (Australia) 39, 494 see also ethnic languages, heritage languages
comparative 149, 153, 154, 177, 178, 567, 610–611 see also superlative
competence (in Chomsky's terms) 40, 42, 62, 75, 195, 289, 329 see also performance
complementiser, projection of (CP) 119, 241, 628, 637, 647
– bilingual CPs 75
complexification 52, 440
Composite Matrix Language 24, 39, 42, 75, 630, 648, 652, 656 see also 4-M model
compound nouns 131, 148, 374 see also nouns
compound numerals see numerals
compound sentences 274, 279

Subject index — 665

compound tenses 272, 278–279, 422–423, 638, 640, 643, 645, 646
concord 151–152
conditional constructions 65, 152–153, 155–156, 172, 276, 473, 520
congruent lexicalisation 53, 61–62
conjugation 611–612
conjunctions 59, 119, 126, 137, 166, 171–172, 203, 244, 273, 276, 279, 333, 371, 388–389, 397, 418, 508, 522, 570, 577, 615–616
connectors *see* conjunctions
constraints (on code-switching) 51
contact induced change 110, 151, 162, 169, 175, 195, 583–584 *see also* language change
contact linguistics 4, 9, 14–17, 24, 206, 291, 293, 334
content morphemes 38, 629, 631, 636, 639, 641–642, 649–650, 655–656, 658
– inflectionless content morphemes 59 see also system morphemes
content words 36
context 48
conventionalised borrowing *see* borrowings
convergence 7, 17–18, 22, 65, 66, 70, 75, 187–188, 207–208, 225, 233, 237–240, 243, 354, 410, 412–415, 418, 421, 437, 439, 440, 443, 575, 578, 579, 580, 583, 585, 588
– bi-lateral phenomena 70
– complex convergent processes 193
– multi-lateral phenomena 70, 189, 206, 208
– pattern replication 65
– uni-lateral phenomena 70
co-ordination 37
co-ordinative sentences 166, 578
copula *see* verbs
couplets (forms given in both languages) 135–137
creoles 29, 34, 74
Croatia 3–11, 15, 17, 19–20, 22, 24, 217–222, 224–226, 231, 252–254, 256–261, 286, 288, 295, 303, 305, 306, 332, 361–363, 366–370, 390, 449, 452–453, 469–470, 475

Croatian 251–279, 285–286, 313, 319, 320, 323–324, 494
Croatian Catholic centres/missions/parishes, 221, 226, 229, 231, 254, 408, 451, 500–501, 556, 598, 603 *see also* religion
Croatian diaspora 1, 3, 4, 9, 10, 12, 24, 569, 573, 581, 587
Croatian emigrants 320, 322–323
– no. of Croatian-origin emigrants in
 – Argentina 597
 – Australia 494–495
 – Canada 449–450
 – Germany 219–220
 – Norway 286
 – USA 407
– geographic distribution across host countries
 – Argentina 597
 – Australia 495
 – Austria 253–254
 – Germany 220–221
 – Italy 322
 – New Zealand 555–556
 – Norway 287
 – USA 407–408
– socio-economic profile in host societies
 – Argentina 597
 – Australia 495
 – Austria 253–254
 – Canada 450–451
 – Germany 220–221
 – Italy 322
 – New Zealand 555–556
 – Norway 287
 – USA 407–408
– infrastructure in host societies (e.g. associations, sporting clubs, schools)
 – Argentina 598
 – Australia 495–496
 – Austria 254–255
 – Canada 451
 – Germany 221
 – Italy 323–324
 – New Zealand 556
 – Norway 287
 – USA 408

- contacts with Croatia of Croatian-speakers in
  - Argentina 598–599
  - Australia 497–498
  - Austria 256–257
  - Canada 452
  - Germany 222–223
  - Italy 324–325
  - New Zealand 557
  - Norway 288
  - USA 409–410
- Croatian Fraternal Union (*Hrvatska bratska zajednica*) 408
- Croatian Heritage Foundation (*Hrvatska matica iseljenika*) 598
- Croatian language 1–13, 15–24, 188–194, 197–201, 203, 206–208
- Croatian language – homeland (HMLD. Cro) 5, 16, 40, 65, 103, 106, 109, 113, 118, 120–121, 123–135, 137, 142–144, 146–157, 159–165, 167–176, 190, 412–440, 463–470, 472–473, 478–480, 482, 564, 568, 570, 572–576, 579–583, 587–588
  - Anglicisms in 79
  - as baseline 40, 78
  - dialects/regiolects 31, 62, 78, 429, 556, 572, 574, 578 see also Čakavian, Kajkavian
    - Dalmatian 31, 175, 560, 556, 565, 573–574, 578, 586, 588
    - Hercegovinian 192
    - Istrian 373, 386, 397
    - north Croatian 462
    - rural 33
    - Slavonian 33
    - Split 31, 565
  - dialect vs. standard use 79, 557, 564–65
  - non-standard 150, 157, 168, 178, 350, 352, 356, 412, 441, 542
  - standard 105, 113, 115, 117–118, 161, 330, 367–369, 371, 386, 397
- Croatian language – immigrant/heritage varieties 82–83, 165, 273, 286, 385–386, 390, 393
  - non-standard 31, 40
- proficiency level 75, 555, 557–558, 561, 564, 585–586 see also proficiency
  - children's proficiency level 80
- standard 31, 40, 81
- typological features 31
- vernacular 40, 48
- Croatian language – as a foreign language 48
- Croatian or Serbian 7–8
- Croatian-Americans *see* American-Croatians
- Croatian-Argentinians *see* Argentinian-Croatians
- Croatian-Australians *see* Australian-Croatians
- Croatian-Canadians *see* Canadian-Croatians
- Croatian-Māori-English trilingualism *see* trilingualism
- Croatian-speakers 1, 3–6, 8–12, 15–19, 21, 24, 40, 217–220, 229, 230, 244, 251, 252, 253, 255, 257, 279, 285–286, 319, 321–322, 363, 368, 595, 597, 599, 603
  - of Homeland Croatian 47, 53, 78, 294–295, 303–304, 306, 308, 310–311
    - in Bosnia-Herzegovina 40
    - in Croatia 40
    - in Montenegro 40
    - in Serbia 40
  - of immigrant/heritage varieties of Croatian
    - no. of speakers in
      - Argentina 597
      - Australia 494–495
      - Austria 253
      - Canada 449–450
      - Germany 219–220
      - Italy 322
      - New Zealand 555
      - Norway 286
      - USA 407
- Croatians 361–363, 365, 368–371
- Croaticum 326–327
- Croato-Serbian 7–8, 198
- cross-linguistic influence 47, 237, 240, 244
- cross-linguistic accessing 80
- cultural transfers 606, 609
- Czech 6, 8, 202, 293, 295

Subject index — **667**

Čakavian 6–7, 104, 108, 111, 167, 190, 192, 200, 352, 360, 373, 411–412, 415–416, 442, 444, 565, 578, 581, 583
Čakavian Ikavian 559, 565, 586

Danish 58
Danish-Croatian contact 58, 81
dates 433–434, 436–437, 440, 576, 587, 633
see also numerals, time expressions
dative case see case
dative constructions 19, 105, 121, 139–141, 143–145, 148, 150, 157, 164, 167–169, 172, 295, 308, 311 see also case, dative
– as radial category 293, 296, 309, 312
– dative as indirect object 290, 293–295, 303–305, 309, 313
– dative-experiencer construction 67
– directional dative 293, 295, 310, 312
– free dative 293–294, 307, 309
– frequency of dative 298
– governed dative 293, 309, 311
– of metonymic extension 293, 305
– possessive dative 294, 301, 307, 309, 311, 413
declarative sentences 274
declension classes/paradigms 119, 123, 139, 140, 142, 143, 144, 145, 194
default past tense see verb tenses
definite article see articles
definiteness 74 see also articles
demonstratives 163, 164
demonstrative adjectives 263
demonstrative pronouns 197, 266, 268, 609
Denmark 81
dependent clauses see clauses
determiners 68, 234, 236, 240, 241, 382–383, 472, 481, 513, 554
diachronic analysis 3, 14–17, 24–31, 34, 37, 102, 151, 154
dialect 55
diaspora communities 18, 39, 95, 102, 107, 118, 120–122, 125, 129–130, 135, 159, 170, 175, 179, 187–191, 193–194, 203–208, 217, 225–226, 228, 233, 235, 240–241, 243–244, 261, 270, 285, 291, 295, 302–303, 317, 321, 326, 336–337, 370, 376–378, 385, 386, 390, 393, 396, 414–415, 419, 422–423, 428, 433, 438, 571, 587, 554, 571, 602, 637
diaspora language varieties 16, 187–188, 203, 205, 207, 553, 580, 583
diaspora language speakers 285, 289, 294, 295, 303, 305, 308, 313, 473, 564 see also heritage language speakers
dictionaries 105, 115 117, 119
– foreign words in Croatian 30, 54
– Molise Croatian-Croatian-Italian 33
diglossia 325
direct objects see objects
directionality (of cross-linguistic influence) 187, 189–191, 205, 207–208 see also convergence
discourse 55, 71
discourse-pragmatic features 52, 233
discourse markers 21–22, 61, 126–131, 134, 155, 176, 203, 334–335, 356, 457, 462, 482, 501, 506, 512, 518, 520–22, 550, 555, 557, 559, 566, 573, 576, 587, 615, 620–621
– eh 573–574, 587
– you know 515, 520–523, 531, 534, 550
– znaš / znate ('you know' 2SG/PL) 520–522, 531, 534, 546
divergent attainment 41–42, 44, 70, 85, 289–290
DO-verbs (lagani glagoli) 67, 524, 557, 574–575
domains 29, 47–48, 81, 218, 222, 228–232, 255, 258–260, 288, 448, 451, 453, 458, 460, 498, 501–502, 504
– commercial/transactional 48, 255, 450–451, 502, 504
– domain-based language use 18, 21, 79, 82
  – in Argentina 598
  – in Australia 496–497
  – in Austria 255
  – in Germany 222
  – in Italy 324
  – in New Zealand 556–557
  – in Norway 288
  – in USA 409
– home/family 288, 324, 328, 409, 412, 451, 498, 504

- media 48, 267, 321, 324, 328, 494, 497–498, 500, 502, 503, 504, 598
  - print media 254
  - radio 224, 242, 451, 498, 559, 598
  - social media 224, 259
  - television 224, 231, 256, 268, 297, 451, 498
- neighbourhood/neighbours 48, 328, 498, 502, 561–562, 601
- social life/friends 48, 255, 255, 258–260, 451, 498, 501–502
- workplace 48, 64, 322, 328, 405, 410–411, 423, 437, 442, 460, 498, 502, 504, 561

dominance (linguistic) 40, 43, 49–50, 81, 258, 275 *see also* proficiency
donor language 61, 69, 608, 617, 621
double marking of features 178, 379, 385–386, 397, 471, 482, 647
double prefixing 162
dummy pronouns *see* pronouns
Dutch 13–14, 50, 57, 75, 76, 77, 82,
- émigré Dutch 13
- nominal subjects and objects 75
Dutch-Croatian bilinguals 68, 75

early system morphemes *see* system morphemes
'economy' (linguistic) 32
education 21, 47, 48, 107, 113, 221–222, 224, 242, 261, 287–288, 297, 496, 498, 501, 504, 556, 563, 597–598
- bilingual primary schools 107
- entry into formal school system in host society 40, 321
- Croatian instruction for children outside Croatia 82–83, 113, 221, 254–255, 287, 323, 327, 331, 363, 408, 451, 460, 498, 501–503, 554, 598, 603
- university programs 93
embedded language 23, 52, 61, 234, 236–237, 243, 576, 587, 605 *see also* matrix language
embedded language (EL) islands 141, 628, 635–636, 637, 641–644, 646, 655
emblematic markers (of identity) 203

emigration, vintages 4, 10, 16, 17, 24, 39, 102, 117, 176, 493, 500, 552, 596
- Argentina 596–597
- Australia 493–494
- Austria 252
- Canada 449
- Germany 218–219
- Italy 320–322
- New Zealand 554–555
- Norway 286
- USA 406–407
endogamy 10, 46, 329, 557, 562–564, 598, 600 *see also* exogamy
English 2–3, 8–9, 13, 20–22, 30, 189–194, 198, 200–201, 203, 210, 433–434, 436–437, 546, 553–557, 559–571, 573–575, 577–579, 581–588, 629–630, 632, 638–639, 644, 646–657
- New York Jewish English 53
English-Croatian contact 30, 58
equivalence 50–51, 510, 520, 525, 531, 539, 549, 570, 572, 576, 587, 588
- 'gap' 71
- 'mismatch' 71
equivalence constraint 51
error analysis 81
Esuli (Ital. 'exiles') of Italian-origin from Croatia 325 *see also* Italians
ethnic businesses *see* domain, transactional
ethnic languages 39 *see also* heritage languages
'Ethnic Revival' (in North America) 409
ethnicity 79
European Charter on Minority or Regional Languages 219
European Economic Area Agreement 286
European Union 10–11, 24, 252
- Croatia's accession to EU in mid-2013 83
evidential categories 198
existential constructions 155, 171, 375, 632, 637
exogamy 46, 119, 189, 288, 329, 460, 494, 557, 562–563, 585 *see also* endogamy
external influence *see* language change
extra-clausal code-switching *see* code-switching

Subject index — **669**

false starts 298, 299, 648 *see also* hesitation phenomena
family language (incl. policy) 49, 80, 218, 222, 224, 231, 320, 329–330, 448, 452, 598 *see also* domains, home/family
- grandchildren 450, 460
- grandparents 324, 328, 496, 598, 600
- siblings 327, 330
feminine declension class 127, 265–267, 269, 278504, 632, 634–635, 640–641, 643, 649, 651
- class II nouns 142
filler words 237, 615 *see also* hesitation phenomena, pauses
Finno-Ugric 5, 17, 49
first-generation *see* Gen.1, Gen.1A, Gen.1B
first language acquisition *see* acquisition
flags 263, 270, 341, 607 *see also* code-switching, flagged
folk dancing 496, 562, 574, 600, 603, 605
footing 344
'foreign influence' 32
'forgetters' 42, 45 *see also* attrition
formal schooling 113, 116, 556, 564 *see also* education
forms of address 448
formulaic expressions 113
fourth-generation speakers *see* Gen.4
FPRY (Federal People's Republic of Yugoslavia) 7, 9, 597 *see also* SFRY, Kingdom of Yugoslavia
free (invariant) morphemes 35, 38
French 6, 8, 198
frequency-based perspective 51, 506
'frozen acquisition' *see* acquisition, divergent attainment
function words 36
functional restrictedness 39, 45, 47, 222
future markers 200
future tense *see* verb tenses/forms

gender 143, 145–146, 264–266, 267–278, 567, 581, 584, 588, 638, 640, 642–644, 648–651
- as a grammatical category 194, 373, 376, 382

gender agreement patterns across NPs 145
gender assignment of nouns 120, 122, 124, 176, 194, 206, 265
- influence of gender of Croatian equivalent 632
- influence of word-final consonant 57, 513, 530, 550
- of formerly neuter nouns 142
- to feminine 58, 120
- to masculine 57, 120–121, 123, 176, 266–269, 278
- to neuter 58
genealogical similarity/relatedness 62
generation 1 (Gen.1) 2, 11, 20–21, 24, 45–46, 50, 58, 78, 80, 82, 220, 222, 224–226, 229–232, 234, 236, 243–244, 258–259, 285, 289, 303, 310, 323, 327, 329–331, 332–333, 341, 343. 356, 407, 409, 443, 452–455, 457, 458, 460, 463, 465, 482, 553, 558–570, 572–573, 575–578, 582, 584–587, 599–600, 603, 606–607, 635–636, 638, 646, 648, 651, 661
generation 1A (Gen.1A) 47–48, 50, 257–263, 265–269, 272–275, 277–278, 280, 282–284, 286, 292–293, 297–298, 300, 307–312, 363–367, 369, 371–382, 384–391, 393–396, 443, 448, 500–503, 506, 508, 510, 549, 550, 631–633
generation 1B (Gen.1B) 46–48, 50, 70, 80–81, 85, 257–258, 261–274, 277, 293, 300–302, 304, 306–307, 309–310, 312, 363–364, 367, 371–374, 377, 381–383, 388, 389, 393- 395, 397, 443, 448, 500, 502–504, 506, 508, 514, 521, 530, 535, 549 550, 533, 535, 641
generation 2 (Gen.2) 10, 18–21, 22, 24, 46, 47, 48, 50, 70, 78, 80, 81, 82, 95, 224–232, 234–236, 238, 240–243, 255–263, 265, 266, 268–269, 271, 274, 276, 285, 288–289, 291, 296, 299–300, 302–308, 310, 326–328, 330–333, 341–342, 354–357, 364, 367–369, 371, 373–374, 377, 378–386, 388–389, 391–393, 395–397, 406–407, 409–410, 412, 423, 443, 448, 451–453, 456–457, 461, 463, 466–469, 471–472, 474–481,

483, 494, 496, 498, 500–504, 506, 508, 510, 512, 514–515, 517–519, 522–526, 530–534, 536–537, 539–540, 542–544, 546–550, 554–556, 558–563, 569–574, 576, 577–587, 598–599, 601, 603–604, 635–637, 641, 644–645, 647, 651, 653, 656
generation 3 (Gen.3) 10, 19, 22, 47, 50, 229–230, 232, 253, 327–328, 332, 342, 355, 409, 494, 496, 500–506, 508, 523, 544, 546, 549, 554, 555, 558–561, 563, 569, 571, 573, 578–581, 583–588, 599–600, 634, 649–650
generation 4 (Gen.4) 47, 599, 600, 611
generational membership 45–47, 125, 594, 656 *see also* Gen.1, Gen.1A, Gen.1B, Gen.2, Gen.3
generative paradigm 290
genitive case *see* case
German 1, 3, 5–6, 9, 13–14, 18, 19, 30, 32–33, 57, 65, 67, 72, 101–103, 105–106, 108, 118–120, 123, 125, 128, 130, 132–133, 135–137, 151–152, 154–155, 162, 163, 167–171, 175–178, 187, 197–198, 251–279, 462, 631–635, 637, 644–646, 647, 656–657
– Austrian German 6, 126, 150, 169, 261, 277
– compound nouns 272, 278
– compound verbs 65
– 'guestworker German' spoken by Croatians 80
– influence 32
– non-standard 239
– syntactic rules 66
– word order 66
German-Croatian contact 30, 102, 105, 217–218, 226, 230, 235, 243
– *Essekerisch/esekerski govor* 'Esseker speech' 33
German-Croatian bicultural identity 221, 224
German-Croatian bilinguals 65–66, 72, 81–82, 225, 237
German-Hungarian-Croatian trilingualism *see* trilingualism
German-speakers 103–104, 117, 252

Germanic language family 5, 14, 17, 189, 203, 546
Germans 555
– ethnic Germans from Slavonia, Syrmia and Baranya (*Volksdeutsche*) 11, 252
Germany 1, 4, 9, 11, 12, 16, 18, 23, 80, 82, 102, 119, 217–222, 224–226, 229, 231–232, 236, 239, 243–244
gerunds *see* verb tenses/forms
grammatical change *see* structural change
grammatical 'deviation' 34, 79
grammatical replication 65, 549
grammaticalisation 71–72, 74, 155
grandchildren *see* family language
grandparents *see* family language
graphemic integration *see* integration
Greece 6, 119
Greek 5–6, 9, 188, 193–195, 198
– Ancient 6
guest workers (*Gastarbeiter*) 102, 217–219, 221, 245, 251–253, 256, 329
Gujarati 194

Habsburg Empire *see* Austro-Hungarian Empire
head constituent 628, 630, 636
Hebrew 9
hedges 278, 647 *see also* hesitation phenomena, pauses
heritage language speakers 39, 68, 275, 379, 383, 393, 471–472, 627, 653, 658
– definition 40, 43
heritage language teachers 504
heritage languages 3, 13–14, 16, 19–20, 24, 39, 85, 102, 238, 289, 292, 303, 312, 458, 565, 578, 585–588
hesitation phenomena 278, 298, 609, 615, 639, 647–648 *see also* pauses
Hindu 303
history of contact between Croatian-speakers and host countries
– Argentina 596–597
– Australia 493–494
– Austria 252
– Canada 449
– Germany 218–219
– Italy 320–322

Subject index — **671**

- New Zealand 554–555
- Norway 286
- USA 406–407

home/family domain *see* domains
host societies 10, 16, 17, 24, 221–222
- host societies' attitudes towards Croats in
  - Argentina 598–599
  - Australia 497–498
  - Austria 256–257
  - Canada 452
  - Germany 222–223
  - Italy 324–325
  - New Zealand 256–257
  - Norway 288
  - USA 409–410

homophone (bilingual) 344, 394, 477
Hungarian 5, 13–14, 17, 30, 33, 44, 101–103, 105, 111, 113–120, 123, 126–127, 129–131, 134–135, 141–143, 151, 160–162, 170, 172–174, 177, 197, 639
- American Hungarian 551
- aspectual particles 159 see also verbal aspect
- influence of 32
- standard 33
- regiolects 33

Hungarian Baranya Croatian (HUN-Bar.Cro) 101, 172, 179
Hungarian Croatian (HUN.Cro) 103, 111, 117, 123, 127–130, 134–135, 141, 148–149, 151–152, 154, 160, 162–163, 170, 174, 176, 177, 179
Hungarian-Croatian contact 113
Hungarian Pomurje Croatian (HUN-Pom.Cro) 101, 148–149, 151, 153, 155–157, 162, 174, 177–178
Hungarian-speakers 103, 117
Hungarians 411
Hungary 3, 10, 13–15, 17, 103, 105–107, 111–117, 148
hybrid nouns 145

idiolects 116, 126
idiomatic expressions 137, 203, 301, 478, 483 *see also* phrasemes/phraseological constructions

Ijekavian 112 *see also* Croatian language, dialects/regiolects
Ikavian 108, 112 *see also* Croatian language, dialects/regiolects
Illyrian (Movement) 6, 362
imperfect tense *see* verb tenses/forms
imperfective verbal aspect *see* verbal aspect
impersonal constructions 59, 67, 142, 149, 537
implicativity 80, 382, 385, 396, 465, 470, 482, 525–526, 528–550, 580, 588 *see also* case
'imposition' 49
incomplete acquisition 41, 465 *see also* divergent attainment
indeclinable forms 123, 147, 155–156
indefinite articles *see* articles
indefiniteness (as a category) 72, 170, 198 *see also* definiteness
Independent State of Croatia 9, 11
indirect objects *see* objects
individual variation *see* variation
Indo-Aryan 194, 210
Indo-European 194, 203, 207
infinitives 198, 235, 573
infixes 77, 140, 149, 152, 178
inflection affixes/categories 35, 37, 44, 57, 71, 264
innovation 192, 195–196, 199, 201–202, 207
input 39, 41 *see also* divergent attainment, proficiency
- different input 41
- reduced input 39, 41, 47
insertions 50, 53, 55, 61, 108, 113, 132–134, 137, 138, 176, 454–455, 482, 576 *see also* code-switching, intra-clausal
instrumental case *see* case
integration 119, 122–126, 131, 176, 251, 264–270, 273, 501, 508–510, 512–515, 536, 548–549, 604–605, 607–609, 611, 632–633, 635–636, 648, 651, 655
- graphemic 30, 54, 78, 79, 448
- morphological 30, 31, 50, 57–60, 78, 79, 108, 113, 116, 120, 123–125, 127, 129, 176, 264, 268, 333, 508, 554–565, 567, 570, 573, 586, 604, 609–610, 621, 635, 656

- non-integration 123, 127, 166, 263, 268–269, 456, 569, 573, 586, 604–605, 612, 636, 648
- phonological 30, 31, 54, 57–59, 60, 78, 113, 118, 120, 122–127, 131, 176, 263, 269, 278, 333–334, 356, 371, 433, 448, 456, 461, 463–464, 482, 508, 560, 566, 569, 572–573, 577, 586, 604–605, 607, 611, 621, 631, 636, 651, 656
- semantic 54
- transphonemisation 125

inter-clausal code-switching *see* code-switching
interference 34, 49, 54 *see also* transference
inter-generational transmission 49, 114, 449, 504, 557
inter-generational variation *see* variation
interjections 61, 203, 237, 501, 506, 615–616
interlingual identification 51
internal influence *see* language change
internationalisms 137
interrogative pronouns *see* pronouns
inter-speaker variation *see* variation
interstrate influence 207 *see also* convergence
intonation unit 298
intra-clausal code-switching *see* code-switching
intra-familial language *see* family language
intra-generational interactions 81
intra-group communication/settings 19, 116–117
intransitive verbs *see* verbs
Ireland 11–12
isomorphism 51, 72, 76, 525
Istro-Romanian 6
Italian 1, 5–6, 8–9, 20, 32–33, 72, 101–102, 109, 111, 120–121, 123, 125–126, 128, 130, 133–134, 137–141, 145–147, 153, 156–160, 163–165, 167, 170, 176–177, 189, 192–208, 631–632, 634, 639, 641–644, 646
- definite article 197
- dialects/regiolects 33, 108, 110, 118, 124, 143, 149
  - *fiumano* (in Rijeka) 33
- Friulian 362
- Istrian 362
- Molise 108, 129, 135, 142, 165, 176
- southern 107–108, 151, 178
- Triestine 367, 368, 378, 407
- Venetian 5, 30, 320, 361, 365, 369, 373, 378, 565, 586
- Veneto 378
- *zaratino* (in Zadar) 33
- imminentive constructions 155
- influence of 32, 196, 201, 374, 378–379, 381, 386, 388, 396, 572
- present progressive 160
- recent past (*passato prossimo*) 640
- standard 110, 124, 135, 147, 153, 192, 200, 397

Italian Croatian (ITAL.Cro) 631, 634, 643 *see also* Triest Croatian (TRS.Cro)
Italian-Croatian bilinguals 72, 320, 326, 356
Italian-Croatian contact 30, 320
Italian-speakers 361, 411
- from Istria, Rijeka & Croatian Littoral 11

Italy 1, 3–4, 10–12, 15–19, 23, 101–102, 109, 111, 363, 365, 367–370, 371, 384
iterative verbs *see* verbs

jedan 'one' as a nascent indefinite article *see* articles
JUBA 'jugoslaviska barn' ('Yugoslav children') project 80 *see also* case implicativity
Judaeo-Spanish (Ladino)/Judezmo 6, 188, 208

Kajkavian 6–7, 17, 101, 104, 112, 115, 117, 127, 137, 144, 147, 150, 157, 167–168, 190, 192, 200, 352, 360, 411, 415–417, 421, 442
Kingdom of Serbs, Croats and Slovenes 7, 9, 596 see also Kingdom of Yugoslavia, Yugoslavia, FNRY, SFRY
Kingdom of Yugoslavia 597 *see also* Kingdom of Serbs, Croats and Slovenes, Yugoslavia, FNRY, SFRY
kinship terms 202–204, 307
Kosovo 6, 190, 195
Kruč (Molise) 108–109, 111, 121–123, 125–126, 140, 145–147, 155–157, 164

Subject index — **673**

L1 43, 47, 264, 268, 295, 289–291, 295, 297
– chronologically first learnt 257
– speakers 36
L2 43, 47
– speakers 36, 83
language attitudes 18, 21, 79, 217–218, 225–230, 232, 257, 288, 298, 324, 328–330, 557, 589
– affective reactions 81
language change
– contact-induced/external influence 31–32, 35, 67, 70, 74, 103, 431
– definition 35
– causation (dual, multiple) 35, 572
– inter-dialectal influence 31
– internal influence 31, 70
language contact 4–5, 8–9, 13–18, 217, 225–226, 233, 243–245, 251
language death 228
language maintenance 17, 34, 49, 79, 80, 82, 107, 117, 222, 228, 232, 246, 254–255, 258–260, 288, 324, 328–331, 324, 448, 451–452, 498, 554, 556–557, 560–561, 563 *see also* language shift
– of heritage Croatian in
  – Argentina 598
  – Australia 496–497
  – Austria 255
  – Canada 451–452
  – Germany 222
  – Italy 324
  – New Zealand 556–557
  – Norway 222
  – USA 409
language of instruction 113 *see also* education
language policy 251, 258, 260
language shift 34, 79, 113, 117, 177, 222, 228–229, 458, 501, 554–556, 561–564, 585, 588 *see also* language maintenance
Latin 5–6, 116, 192, 197, 199, 203, 207
lemmas 629, 657
lexical borrowing 34, 115–116, 120, 604 *see also* borrowing, lexical transference
lexical gap/compensation strategy 56, 241, 462, 606

lexical items 30, 34, 81, 55, 263–264, 274, 278, 455, 461, 464–465, 478, 483, 493, 501, 504, 506, 508–510, 512, 520–521, 523, 548–549, 555, 566–567, 586
lexical transference 14, 20, 22, 53, 77–79, 80, 81, 85, 225, 270,
lexical transfers 19, 22, 57, 78, 118, 120, 123, 125, 263–264, 267, 270, 278, 372, 374, 395, 553, 565–566, 569–570, 574, 586–587, 604–605, 607–608, 620, 633
– nouns 57
lexicon 4–8, 13–14, 16–17, 19–22, 37, 41, 45, 48–49, 53, 81, 102, 115–116, 119, 176–177, 192, 205–207, 290–291, 312–313
lexico-grammatical features 620, 622
lexico-semantic structures 575
Light Walpiri 74
linear congruence 51 *see also* word order
lingua franca 205
lingua receptiva 253, 255, 259
linguistic exclaves 16, 17, 24, 101, 103, 252, 321, 553, 560
linguistic identity 113–114, 117, 598, 602
– bilingual linguistic identity 81
linguistic proficiency *see* proficiency
loan translation 8, 18–22, 50, 53, 62, 63, 64, 78, 79, 116, 129–131, 177, 225–226, 233, 241, 279, 332, 335–337, 339, 356, 371, 374, 395–397, 464, 478, 480, 483, 493, 505, 521–523, 550, 554, 566, 574, 587, 604–605, 616–617
loanblends 78
loanshifts *see* semantic transference
loanwords 31, 34, 53, 54, 115–116, 118–125, 166, 176, 264, 278, 369, 448, 554, 577
locative case *see* case
longitudinal study of speakers 45
long forms of object forms *see* pronouns, objects

Macedonia 188, 190–191, 195–196, 203–204, 209
– Aegean Macedonia 195
Macedonian 38, 188, 190–194, 199, 202, 203, 204, 206–208, 395
– Eastern 192
– Western 192–193, 202, 206, 207

Macedonians 411
macro-skills *see also* proficiency
- listening 46, 47
- reading 230–231, 260, 502, 504
- speaking 46, 47, 217–218, 220–221, 226, 230–232, 237
- writing 81–82, 230, 502, 504
Māori 190–191, 553–555, 557, 560, 562–563, 566, 569, 571, 573, 586–587
Māori-Croatian families 80
Māori-English-Croatian trilingualism *see* trilingualism
marginal passages 62
markedness 31, 51–52, 139, 344, 356, 525, 627
- unmarked forms 114, 132–133, 136, 151, 163–164, 235, 305, 307, 312, 413, 437
masculine declension 122–123, 141, 144
masculine gender 120, 123, 142, 176, 513, 529, 530, 567, 609–610, 620, 633–634, 643–644, 646, 649, 652, 654
Matica hrvatska ('Matrix Croatia') 254
matrix language 38, 50, 52, 53, 75, 235–237, 270–271, 326, 355, 605, 615 *see also* embedded language
Matrix Language Frame 23, 32, 38, 52, 53, 628
Matrix Language Turnover 38, 648
maximal projection 76, 630–632, 637, 641–642
media *see* domains, media
metalinguistic features 115, 343
metonymic extension 293, 295, 305, 309
minority language 39 *see also* heritage language
minority schools *see* education
mixed language 29, 34, 117, 460, 481 *see also* code-switching
mobility 107
modal particles 237
modal verbs *see* verbs
mode, monolingual/bilingual (in Grosjean's terms) 45–46, 341 *see also* bilingual speech
Molise 189, 191–192, 200, 205, 208, 319, 321, 323, 325

Molise Croatian (MOL.Cro) 33, 101–102, 108–111, 121, 125–126, 128, 130, 133, 137–141, 145–147, 151–155, 162–165, 167, 170, 176, 189–208, 321, 501
- grammar of 33
Molise Croats 101–102, 108–109, 118
Molise Italian *see* Italian
monitoring 327, 334, 342 *see also* self-correction
mono-morphemic forms 35
Montenegrin 6, 8, 193, 199
Montenegrins 6
Montenegro 5–8, 324
mood 155, 173
Morpheme Order Principle 628
morphemes 85
- surface 75
morphological calques 18
morphological change 13–14, 22, 44, 71, 78
morphological features 7, 19–20, 22, 54, 81, 347, 379, 382, 462, 464–465, 482, 579, 580
morphological suffixes 32, 439, 609–610
morphological integration *see* integration
morphologically non-integrated forms *see* integration
morphology 34, 37, 102, 128, 144, 146, 148, 150, 154, 179, 194–196, 202, 206, 208, 291, 376–379, 383, 428, 437, 440, 448, 461, 464, 481–482, 493, 505, 515, 531, 533, 536, 540, 548, 552, 642, 646–647, 650, 651 654
morpho-syntactic borrowing 34
morpho-syntactic change 54, 354, 355, 567, 566, 578 *see also* structural change
morpho-syntactic features 80, 126, 128, 154, 160, 237, 263, 448, 468, 478, 481–483, 501, 514, 518, 549, 630, 632, 635, 637, 653, 655, 658
morpho-syntactic grid 75, 514, 518, 550, 569
morphosyntax 45, 53, 269, 289
movement vs. position distinction 31, 142, 177, 382
- in Dalmatian and southern Hercegovinian dialects 470
multilingualism 187, 188, 196, 206

multi-morphemic forms 35
Mundimitar (in Molise)108–109, 121–122, 126, 140, 146–147, 156

negation/negative forms 37, 156, 166, 169, 546
neighbourhood *see* domains
Netherlands 81, 311
neuter gender 121–122, 140–141, 144–145, 148, 164, 266, 513, 529, 609
– in Molise Croatian 142
newspapers (as a data source) 78, 224, 231, 254, 269, 497 *see also* domains, media
New Zealand 2–4, 10–12, 16, 21–22, 553–559, 563–564, 566, 571, 574, 576, 581–582, 585, 586, 648
– Pākehā 554, 557
New Zealand Croatian (NZ.Cro) 190, 553–554, 558–564, 566–567, 569–570, 574–577, 580–581, 583, 585–588, 632, 640
nicknames 333
nominal forms 195, 289
nominal system 206, 208
nominalisation 148
nominative case *see* case
nominal prefixes 32
nominal suffixes 32, 57
non-congruence 178, 644, 646, 650, 656 *see also* subject + verb (non-)agreement
non-countedness 620
non-dominant (language) 49–50 *see also* proficiency
non-standard language 5, 7–8, 16
normativism 105, 117, 132, 146, 162 *see also* purism
North America 78, 108
North Macedonia 195
North Slavic 199, 200
Norway 4, 12, 16, 18–19, 23, 81, 285–287, 290, 296–297,
Norwegian 57, 73, 285, 288–289, 297, 300, 304–305, 307, 547, 557
Norwegian-Croatian bilinguals 72, 74, 81
noun phrases (NPs) 64, 149, 234, 356, 465, 466, 467, 512, 513, 526, 520, 523, 525, 526, 528, 530–531, 533–534, 536, 543, 546, 550, 552, 614, 620, 627–628, 630–632, 636, 648, 650–652, 654, 656–657

nouns 36, 57, 68, 121, 127, 263–266, 268, 270, 278, 335, 339, 344, 346–348, 350, 372, 376, 380, 382–383, 387, 395–396, 455, 462, 465, 477, 482, 508–510, 512, 513, 520, 523, 529–531, 533–534, 536, 544, 547, 549, 550, 552, 559, 566–568, 574–575, 578–580, 586, 588, 605, 608, 614, 618–620, 627–635, 641, 643, 645, 648, 652–654, 658
– gender 335, 356
– proper 455
number (as a grammatical category) 68, 254, 256, 258–259, 262, 266, 276, 278–280, 302, 364, 372, 376, 380–382, 384–387, 403–404, 637–638, 640, 642–643, 648–649
numerals 20–21, 80, 167, 202, 265, 374, 379, 384, 386, 403–404 433–434, 436–437, 440, 544, 547, 554, 576, 587 *see also* dates
– compound numerals 179, 423
– low numerals 37
– ordinal numbers 371, 381, 396, 433–437, 440

objects 346, 352, 353, 378–379, 587
– direct 68, 75, 242, 234, 242, 336, 338, 346, 348, 353–355, 537, 541, 548, 633–645, 648
– indirect 68, 290, 293–295, 304–305, 308–309, 313, 338, 537, 541, 550
– object pronouns see pronouns
oblique case marking *see* case
Oceania 4, 11, 12, 16
od 'from'/'of' + possessor-GEN 397, 430, 581 *see also* possessive constructions
Old Church Slavonic 192, 195, 200
ordinal numbers *see* numerals
Ottoman Empire 190, 196, 19
out-group members 110
overgeneralisation 67, 550
'over-marking' 71, 74 *see also* morphological features

paradigms 70
participles *see* verb tenses/forms

particle 126–128, 152, 156, 159, 161, 166, 168–169, 176, 178, 201
passive voice constructions 21, 139, 153, 155, 162–163, 412, 430–433, 439, 440, 475, 517, 584, 638–639, 642, 644, 656
– andative deontic passive 163
– mediopassive 32
past participles *see* verb tenses/forms
past perfect *see* verb tenses/forms
past tense *see* verb tenses/forms
pattern replication 64, 131, 162
paucal forms 146, 162, 345 *see also* numerals
pauses 298, 300, 519, 648 *see also* hesitation phenomena
perfect tense *see* verb tenses
perfective verbal aspect *see* verbal aspect
performance (in Chomsky's terms) 40, 290 *see also* competence
performance error 384, 396
periphrastic constructions 35, 143, 150, 356, 581
person (as a grammatical category) 68, 271, 299–302
personal pronouns *see* pronouns
phi-features 371, 373, 465, 513, 515, 517, 546, 548, 552, 605, 631–632, 634, 637, 649–650, 652, 657
phonological features 268
phonological interference *see* phonological transference
phonological integration *see* integration
phonological transference 78–79, 85
phonologically non-integrated *see* integration
phonology 13, 15, 20, 35, 41, 48, 49, 102, 291, 560, 569, 571–573, 577, 586
– phonological features 14, 22, 37, 54, 80–81, 102, 123, 126, 128–129, 133, 140, 161
phonotactic features 57, 120, 122, 125, 176, 265–266, 269, 278, 512, 550, 568, 621, 633, 642–644, 647, 656
phrasemes/phraseological constructions 85, 103, 128, 176–177, 203, 338, 521, 524, 566, 569, 577, 580, 586–588, 607, 613–614, 616
phraseological calques 205

picture/story descriptions 44, 80
pidgins 29, 34, 74
pleonastic forms 149, 253
pluperfect *see* verb tenses/forms
plural marking 58, 547, 629
– English plural '-s' 66
pluralia tantum 149 *see also* numerals
Polish 74, 188, 202
polyfunctionality 519–520
polysemy copying 65, 67, 155, 164, 242
– bilingual polysemy 81
Pomurje Croats 101, 111–113, 189 *see also* Hungarian Pomurje Croatian
portmanteau forms 513, 523
Portuguese 151
possession via preposition *do* 'to' 196
possessive adjectives 20, 333, 412–414, 418, 425, 437
possessive constructions 20–21, 23, 197, 200, 259, 273, 276, 312, 290, 291–292, 296, 349, 371, 385, 386, 412, 425–427, 429–430, 441, 580, 581, 629–630, 648–654, 657–658
possessive pronouns 340, 476, 483, 578
post-positioned adjectives 169, 387 *see also* word order
post-World War II period 406, 409, 449 *see also* World War II
pragmatics 1, 8, 14, 22, 35, 41, 45, 48, 237, 493, 505–506, 520, 522, 533, 541, 550, 552
– pragmatic inference 38
– pragmatic markers/particles 126, 130
– pragmatic norms 61
– pragmatic transference 78, 79, 80
predicative forms 68, 146, 148, 151, 178, 234–235, 242, 267, 292, 295, 297, 578, 584, 634, 638, 641, 648, 651, 657
prefixation 154, 159–160
prefixes 63, 124, 149, 159–162, 178, 192, 570
preposed modifiers 427, 543–544, 552, 581
prepositional phrases (PPs) 292, 294, 296, 308, 621, 628, 634, 636, 640, 642, 644, 650, 663
prepositions 38, 119, 121, 128, 138–139, 143, 147–148, 159, 166, 170, 175, 177, 178, 282, 272, 274–275, 333, 338, 344,

345–350, 356, 384, 385, 425–427, 464, 466–468, 471, 477, 482–483, 566, 570, 573, 575, 578, 580–582, 586, 588
- increased use of 38, 206
- preposition calquing 192

present tense *see* verb tenses
preteritum *see* verb tenses
print-media *see* domains
proclisis (accent shift) 570 *see also* clitics
pro-drop 20–21, 275, 279, 376–378, 396, 413, 415, 421, 437, 440, 470–471, 482, 540, 552
proficiency level 45, 60, 21, 40, 70, 119, 187, 225, 243, 285, 299, 311, 319–320, 324, 328–331, 356, 448, 450, 453, 458, 460, 504, 602
- as a component of Croatian identity 84
- first language acquisition 46
- heritage speakers' acquisition of standard Croatian 92, 564
- restricted acquisition 39, 502 *see also* divergent attainment
- self-rated 18, 49, 81
- supplementary mother-tongue education 80

pronominal constructions 289, 294
pronouns 37, 68, 192, 202, 234, 238–239, 266–270, 274–276, 279, 289, 292, 302, 305, 307, 312, 413, 415–416, 418, 421–422, 432–433, 437–438, 518, 528, 530, 540–542, 546, 552, 555, 566, 580, 582
- dummy 240–241
- interrogative 575
- object 420, 472–474, 482, 640, 643
  - long forms 122, 164, 167, 472, 541
  - short forms 122, 164–165, 168
- personal 20–21, 371, 377, 380, 413, 425, 464, 470–471
- non-subject 275, 279
- relative 171, 173, 238–239, 388
- stressed 421
- subject 275–276, 279, 377, 378, 413–414, 420–422, 464, 470–471, 476, 477, 482–483, 540–541, 582 see also pro-drop
- vs nominals 19

pronunciation 332, 355
prosody 22 *see also* stress
psycholinguistic features 46, 52, 232, 289, 629–630, 655
Punjabi 194
purism 116 *see also* normativism

question tags 237, 615

radio *see* domains, media
reading *see* macro-skills
recurrence 54, 56, 73, 410, 510, 566, 571, 578
- 'Frequency Theory' (Maslov 1974) 77
reduced use 39, 222, 228
referentiality 192, 197, 206
reflexive constructions 157, 163, 168, 273, 338, 416–418, 432, 440, 464, 471, 475, 482–483, 536–537, 539, 548, 552, 554, 613, 621
- particle *se* 417, 537
reflexive verbs *see* verbs
refugees, of war 256, 494
register 163, 168, 238, 504, 543
- high 430–431, 439
- narrow repertoire 40, 42
regularisations 70, 74
reinforced categories 565, 579, 588
relative clauses *see* clauses
relative pronouns *see* pronouns
relativiser 119
religion 48, 222, 258–259, 288, 323, 331, 363, 409, 450–451, 500–501, 561
re-migration *see* return migration
repair 298–301, 576 *see also* monitoring
reported speech 50, 555, 577, 587
restricted acquisition *see* proficiency level
restrictedness of input *see* input
retrieval / planning problems 300, 522
   see also hesitation phenomena, pauses
return migration to Croatia 84, 92, 220, 327, 557, 596
- returnee children 82
- returnee children's proficiency level in Croatian 92
rhetorical amplification/emphasis 297

Romance language family 5, 17, 154, 159, 166, 175, 188–189, 191, 194, 197–199, 203, 207–208
Romania 188, 191
Romanian 6, 188, 191, 193, 199
Romany 6, 8, 188, 194, 198, 219
rural lifestyle 103–104, 112
Russian 8–9, 44, 49, 76, 187–188, 646, 655, 657
– American Russian 53, 475, 482, 551
– case system 525
– homeland Russian 76
– heritage Russian 44, 76, 303
Russian-English contact 383, 393, 438
Russian-German contact 177
Ruthenian 6

school *see* education
second-generation *see* Gen.2
self-correction 342–343 *see also* monitoring, repair
semantic change 53
semantic features 34, 41, 45, 48, 81, 102, 119–121, 123, 134, 154–155, 158, 160, 162, 171, 175, 241, 273, 286, 293–294, 306, 311, 332, 448, 477, 481, 505, 522, 574, 604, 617
semantic-pragmatic theta-bundles 64
semantic transference 20, 22, 55, 62, 64, 78–79, 85, 505, 585 *see also* transference
'semi-speakers' 108 *see also* functional restrictedness
separable verbs *see* verbs
Serbia 5, 7–8, 190, 195, 295, 324
Serbian 5, 8, 193, 198–199, 208, 210, 220, 221, 245, 254–255, 261, 265, 292, 324, 362, 407–408, 415, 423, 425, 439–441, 443, 448, 555
– in Australia 440, 425
– Torlak (Prizren-Timok) dialects 195
Serbian-speakers 81–82
Serbo-Croatian 7–8, 113, 188, 198, 448, 483, 555, 557
Serbs 6–7, 9, 365, 411
settings 48

SFRY (Socialist Federal Republic of Yugoslavia) 7, 9, 11 218–219, 256, 261, 365, 369 *see also* Kingdom of Yugoslavia
short forms *see* pronouns, object
simplex forms 131, 134, 137
simplification 222, 228, 440–441
Slavic (Common) 101, 107–109, 119, 152, 154, 157, 159, 160–161, 163, 166, 169, 188, 190–197, 199–203, 206–208 *see also* Balkan Slavic
Slavic languages 5–6, 8, 17, 295, 308, 325, 646
– in diaspora settings 580
– micro-languages 119, 154
Slavs 325
Slovak 6, 8, 116, 202
Slovak-speakers 103
Slovakia 3, 10, 15, 17, 33, 101, 103–107, 194
Slovene 7–8, 190, 199–200, 202, 325, 366, 368–369, 380
Slovenes 361–362, 366, 368, 411
social conditions and linguistic outcomes 33, 188
social life/friends *see* domains
social media *see* domains, media
social mores and proficiency levels 36
social networks 222, 256–257, 288, 324, 328–331, 409, 502 *see also* domains, social life/friends
Socialist Republic of Croatia 7
societally-dominant language 16, 47, 103–104, 289, 292, 443, 471, 586, 627
socio-demographic data 229
socio-economic profiles 10, 17, 322
sociolinguistic features 4–5, 10, 14–15, 17–19, 21, 52, 80, 102–103, 107, 110, 112, 132, 188, 217–218, 225, 228–230, 232, 244, 251, 257–258, 277, 279, 453, 493, 503–504, 553–554, 558, 560, 576, 586, 630, 656
socio-psychological factors 18
Sorbian 199, 202, 219
South America 4, 10–12, 16
south-east Europe 37
South Slavic languages 38, 70, 190, 199–200, 414, 442

Subject index — **679**

Spanish 3, 6, 9, 13–14, 22, 151, 198, 595, 598–601, 603–613, 615–620, 633
- in USA 438

Spanish-Croatian bilingualism 604

speech community 3, 14–15, 42, 553, 559, 566, 585

speech production 75, 77–78, 81, 589, 628–629, 650–651, 657 see also speaking skills

sports 222, 226, 231, 323
- Australian Rules Football 497
- bocce 495, 556
- cricket 497, 556
- golf 495
- rugby 497, 500, 531, 556
- soccer 221, 254, 408, 495–496, 498, 500–501, 525, 531, 556
- tennis 500

sprachbund see Balkan sprachbund, adstrate influences

sprachinseln see linguistic exclaves

status (de jure or de facto) of the Croatian language in
- Argentina 596–506
- Australia 493–494
- Austria 252–253
- Canada 449
- Germany 218–219
- Italy 320–322
- New Zealand 554–555
- Norway 286
- USA 406–407

story re-counting see picture descriptions

stress 275 see also prosody

structural change 34, 37, 44, 55, 62, 70–72, 80–81, 415, 439–440, 604, 628, 630
- 'restructuring' 71

structural features 103, 139, 189

structural interference see structural transference

structural transference 19, 64, 66, 74–75, 119, 461 see also transference

subject pronouns see pronouns

subject-verb (non-)agreement 38, 178, 354, 648, 651, 630

subjects 75

- non-canonical 67
- overt 82, 552, 582
- post-verbal 82

subordinate clauses see clauses

subordination 37

suffixation 125, 154

suffixes 58

suo (Italian 3SG possessive pronoun) 20, 339, 356 see also 'svoj'

superlative 149, 177–178, 610–611 see also comparative

superstrate influence 191, 205, 207–208 see also adstrate influence

supplementary mother-tongue instruction see education

supra-regional code 118 see also codes

surname changes 362, 564

svoj (reflexive possessive adjective) 20, 339, 356, 476, 477, 483, 578, 635, 645 see also reflexive constructions

swearing see taboo expressions

Sweden 80, 289, 465

Swedish 81, 194

Switzerland 11–12, 24, 189

synchronic analysis 10, 13–16, 24, 34, 102, 151, 155 see also diachronic analysis

syncretism 31, 44, 105, 140, 144, 146, 177, 393, 397

syntactic non-congruence 139

syntactic interference – see syntactic transference

syntactic pattern replication 81

syntactic transference 55, 65, 70, 78–80, 85, 102, 116, 147, 543 see also transference

syntactic features 37, 65, 81, 251, 288, 405–406, 410, 412, 415, 419, 434–435, 438–440, 442

syntax 34, 45, 290–291, 338–339, 354, 405, 406, 439–440, 442–443, 493, 505, 523, 547, 555, 557

synthetic constructions 35, 149, 199, 454, 461, 464, 472–473, 477

System Morpheme Principle 628, 630, 635–637, 642, 643–644, 655

system morphemes 38, 66, 648–650, 652, 654- 658 *see also* 4-M model (Myers-Scotton 2002)
– bridge system morphemes 38,
– early system morphemes 38, 629, 647–650, 655, 657
– outside system morphemes 38, 631–634, 636, 637, 640–644, 653, 655–658

Šćakavian 559, 565
Štokavian 6–7, 17, 101, 104, 108, 111–112, 115, 119, 124, 190, 200, 352, 360, 397
– Ikavian 559, 565, 586
švapčarenje 'speaking Swabian [=German]' 33

taboo expressions 202, 231
television *see* domains, media
telicity 77 *see also* verbal aspect
tense *see* verb tenses/forms
tests (diagnostic) 80
thematic role 38
third-generation speakers *see* Gen.3
time expressions 526 *see also* dates
toponyms 332–345, 349, 356
transactional domain *see* domain
transference 44, 54, 67, 85, 228, 231, 241–243, 405–406, 410, 413–414, 417, 421, 437–441, 461, 464, 477–478, 533, 566, 569, 574, 581, 629, 631–634, 636, 642, 651
transfers 50, 54, 79, 85, 117–120, 122, 125, 128, 137, 176, 263–270, 273, 278, 461–462, 464, 477, 483, 553, 566–567, 569–572, 581, 586–587
– definition of 56
transitive verbs *see* verbs
translation (tasks) 44, 375, 377, 494
transmission of heritage language *see* inter-generational transmission
transnational communities 244 *see also* heritage speakers
'transparency of categories' *see* analytism
transphonemisation *see* integration
trigger words *see* code-switching
Triest Croatian (TRS.Cro) 371, 382, 396, 639 *see also* Italian Croatian (ITAL.Cro)

trilingualism
– Burgenland Croatian-Croatian-German 33
– Croatian-Māori-English 22, 554, 560, 562, 586–587
– German-Hungarian-Croatian 103
tuđice see dictionaries of foreign words in Croatian
Turkish 5, 8, 30, 33, 50, 188, 190–191, 195, 198, 202–203, 205, 208, 311
– influence 32
– Ottoman Turkish 5
– West Rumelian 188, 190, 205, 209
Turkish-Dutch bilingualism 50
Turkism 190, 204
turn terminator 519
typological change 32, 37, 70
typological distance 52
typological comparison 34

Ukrainian 6
uninflected forms 200, 332–333, 345–346, 609, 634, 636–639, 643–644, 655–657
unmarked *see* markedness
Upper Sorbian 119
Urdu 303
Uruguay 596
USA 3–4, 9–14, 16, 18, 20–21, 23, 79, 651
usage-based approach 34 *see also* recurrence
utterance-opener 615

valence 21, 67, 139, 273, 336, 338–339, 351, 356–537, 539, 552, 653
variation
– individual 42
– inter-generational 19
– inter-speaker 295, 299, 302–303, 313
Venetian Empire 108
Venetian Italian *see* Italian, dialects/regiolects
Venezuela 596
verb phrases (VPs) 234–235, 240–241, 627, 643, 647, 656
verb tenses/forms 373, 376, 389–390, 392, 397 *see also* verbs

Subject index — 681

- aorist 31–32, 154–155, 178, 199, 202, 208, 392
- future tense 190, 192, 198–201, 207
  - de-obligative 151–152, 158, 178
  - of probability 151
  - volitive 151–152
- gerunds 155
- imperfect 31, 152–155, 178, 192, 199, 202, 640
- participles 64, 108, 146, 153, 155 see also past participles
- past 73, 373, 390, 392, 503, 510, 515–517, 539, 541, 543–544, 638–642, 644–647, 656–657
  - irregular 71, 639, 653, 656
  - as default in Croatian 31, 73
- past participles 160, 179, 357
- past perfect 152, 155, 178
- perfect 31, 73, 124, 152–156, 158–159, 172, 178, 638, 640, 644, 646–647
- pluperfect 72–73, 81, 192, 199–202 see also past perfect
  - in Croatian 72
  - in Norwegian 72
  - obligatory marking of sequence of past actions 74
  - present 153, 155–156, 178, 639, 647
- verbal aspect 20, 159, 176, 351, 357, 397–398, 371, 376, 390, 397, 536, 539–540, 552, 583, 587
  - bi-aspectual verb transfers 79, 124, 581, 583, 587
  - imperfective 32, 76, 124, 152, 154, 158, 178, 390, 397, 539, 548, 552, 583
  - perfective 32, 76, 200, 390, 397, 539, 548, 552, 583
- verbal prefixes or suffixes 32, 77, 334, 575, 612, 617
- verbs 31, 36, 59, 118–119, 124, 132, 141, 143, 153–154, 157, 159, 162–164, 462, 473, 475, 482, 508, 514, 536, 549, 565–567, 569, 570–571, 574–575, 581, 583, 586–587, 611–613, 617, 638, 642–643, 645–646

- bi-transitive 68
- copulas 21, 236, 240, 241, 386, 418, 424–425
- intransitive 293, 308–309, 311, 338, 612
- iterative forms 382, 581, 583
- modal 151–153, 166, 201, 274, 517
  reflexive 69 see also reflexive constructions
- separable 118, 176, 178, 272–273, 278
- transitive 338, 475
  vernacular 110, 115–118, 133–135, 146, 158–159, 373, 393, 412, 419, 421, 422, 440, 441, 442, 475 see also macro-skills, speaking
  vocative see case
  vowel quantity/quality 164

West Slavic 201
workplace see domains
word order 8, 20–21, 37, 81, 135, 139, 143, 166–170, 179, 207–208, 234, 240–241, 244, 273–274, 289, 292, 312, 360–361, 371, 386–389, 397, 422, 412, 415–416, 418–419, 429, 438–439, 464, 472–473, 480, 482, 483, 552, 575, 579–580, 581–582, 585, 587, 588, 652–653, 655, 657–658
- of clitics 416, 419, 438
- linear, English-based 587
- SVO 37, 69, 274, 376, 386, 438, 518, 540, 542, 579, 658
- SOV 37, 167, 518
World War I 107, 449
World War II 107, 362, 367–368, 370, 411
writing see macro-skills

Yiddish, 6, 9, 14
- influence on English 189
Yugoslavia 362, 370–371, 448 see also Kingdom of Yugoslavia, FPRY, SFRY

zero ending 122, 142 see also uninflected forms

Author index

Many of the authors cited in the chapters of this volume have Croatian surnames which contain graphemes that are not used in the English alphabet, e.g. ⟨đ⟩ or ⟨ž⟩. Further, some other authors of Slavic origin have surnames with particular graphemes congruent to those found in the Croatian alphabet. We therefore list authors' surnames according to the order of letters in the Croatian alphabet which is the following:

Aa Bb Cc Čč Ćć Dd Dždž Đđ Ee Ff Gg Hh Ii Jj Kk Ll Ljlj Mm Nn Njnj Oo Pp [Qq] Rr Ss Šš Tt Uu Vv [Ww Xx Yy] Zz Žž

Two further non-Croatian surnames, 'Ďurovič' and 'Øverland', are listed after ⟨Đ⟩ and ⟨O⟩ respectively.

Aalberse, Suzanne 16, 25, 41, 86
Adamou, Evangelia 119, 179
Aikhenvald, Alexandra 70, 86
Albijanić, Aleksandar 58–59, 78, 86, 553, 589, 638, 656, see also Albin, Aleksandar
Albin, Aleksandar 78, 86, 405, 441, 447, 483, 567, 569, 553–554, 560, 565, 567, 569, 589 see also Albijanić, Aleksandar
Alexander, Ronelle 78, 86, 447, 483, 569, 589
Alexiadou, Artemis 533, 545
Aligheri, Dante 321–322, 357
Alt, Theresa 473, 484
Amengual, Mark 90
Andersen, Roger 289–290, 313
Anić, Josip 80, 82, 95
Anić, Vladimir 30, 86, 204, 208
Antić, Ljubomir 595–596, 622
Appel, René 63, 86
Asenova, Petja 190, 205, 208
Auer, Peter 55, 86

Backus, Ad 16, 25, 29, 34, 41, 50, 52, 55, 63, 86, 88, 271, 279, 335, 357, 374, 396, 398, 478, 483, 516, 545, 574, 589, 617, 622, 636, 659
Babić, Stjepan 145, 179, 649, 658
Babić, Zrinka 87, 180 see also Jelaska, Zrinka
Balenović, Katica 79, 86, 88
Barics, Ernő 110, 112, 179 see also Barić, Ernest
Barić, Ernest 111, 112, 113, 179 see also Barics, Ernő
Barić, Eugenija 87, 180, 289, 313, 522, 545, 547

Barnes, Hilary 378, 398
Barron-Hauwaert, Suzanne 46, 86
Başbağı, Ragıp 88
Batarilo, Željko 255, 279
Bauckus, Susan 40, 88
Bauer, Ivan 79, 86, 405–406, 413, 441
Bedore, Lisa M. 330, 357
Beganović, Jasminka 82, 86
Belaj, Branimir 198, 208, 350, 357, 544–545, 618–619, 622
Bencsics, Nikolaus 33, 87, 105, 116, 179–180 see also Benčić, Nikolǧa; Benčić, Nikolaus
Benčić, Nikola 33, 87, 146, 179, 186 see also Bencsics, Nikolaus; Benčić, Nikolaus
Benčić, Nikolaus 33, 87, 104–105, 116, 179 see also Bencsics, Nikolaus; Benčić, Nikola
Benmamoun, Elabbas 43–45, 68, 87, 179–180
Bentahila, Abdelelai 51, 87
Benussi, Cristina 361, 398
Berghaus, Jasmin 124, 154, 181
Berg-Seligson, Susan 51, 87
Bernstein, Basil 55, 87
Berruto, Gaetano 325, 357
Bevanda, Karmen 326, 359 see also Bevanda Tolić, Karmen
Bevanda Tolić, Karmen 326, 359 see also Bevanda, Karmen
Bhatia, Archna 289, 314
Bhatt, Rakesh 289, 314
Bialystok, Ellen 314
Bičanić, Ante 7, 25, 86, 93
Binder, Theo 33, 54, 87

Birdsong, David 87–88, 90
Blankenhorn, Renate 512, 545
Blazsetin, István 110, 112, 179
Blažević, Ana Gabrijela XI, 22, 128, 165, 198, 235–236, 243, 270, 273, 335, 337, 376–377, 462, 480–481, 510, 515–516, 531, 566, 569, 588, 573, 595
Błaszczyk, Izabela 74, 87
Blondeau, Hélène 548
Boerger, Karin M. 357
Bohman, Thomas M. 357
Bolonyai, Agnes 41, 43, 52, 75, 87, 627, 639, 659
Bondi Johannessen, Janne 14, 25
Bonifacio, Marino 361–362, 398
Bourhis, Richard 329, 358, 601, 623
Božić, Saša 251–254, 279
Božić-Vrbančić, Senka 80, 87, 553, 555, 557, 586, 589
Brabec, Ivan 33, 87
Breu, Walter IX, 17, 33, 87–88, 101, 107–110, 119, 121–122, 124, 137, 141–143, 146, 149, 151–155, 162–166, 169, 179–181, 189, 191, 195–197, 199–204, 206, 208, 235, 241, 243, 251, 319, 430, 527, 529, 540
Brčić, Karmen 81, 95, 99
Brinton, Donna 40, 88
Browne, Wayles 168–169, 181, 353, 357, 386, 398, 415, 419, 441, 473–474, 483–484
Brozović, Dalibor 8, 25, 31–32, 88, 470, 484
Bubrin, Vladimir, 451, 484
Budak, Luka 498, 545
Bullock, Barbara 237, 245
Bunis, David 188, 208
Busch, Brigitta 251, 260, 280
Bybee, Joan 34, 88, 546

Chafe, Wallace 290, 294, 298, 313
Chan, Brian Hok-Shing 52, 88
Chomsky, Noam 40, 42, 290, 313
Cimador, Gianni 361–362, 398
Clissa. John 80, 88, 498, 545
Clyne, Michael 14, 25, 40, 46, 54, 62, 66, 85, 88, 133, 138, 177, 181, 335, 340–341, 344, 357, 395, 398, 410, 441, 459, 461, 463, 484, 494, 545, 564, 576, 589, 643, 659
Colic-Peisker, Val 497, 545

Conklin, Nancy Faires 563, 589
Consani, Carlo 325, 358
Corbett, Greville 145, 181
Cormack, Michael 260, 280
Csenar-Schuster, Agnjica 87, 179, 185
Csirmaz, Anikó 178, 181
Crnić Novosel, Mirjana 33, 97
Curdt-Christiansen, Xiao Lan 330, 358
Cvikić, Lidija 48, 83, 88, 503, 546

Čapo, Jasna 223, 245
Čilaš, Ankica 325, 333, 358, 371, 398
Čizmić, Ivan 221, 245, 406, 441, 553, 589
Čoralić, Lovorka 361, 398
Čuka, Anica 408, 441

Ćosić, Vjekoslav 79, 88, 447, 484

D'Agostino, Mari 325, 358
D'Alessio, Vanni 362, 398
Dahl, Östen 35, 88, 178, 181
Daller, Michael H. 43, 88
Davies, Eirlys 51, 87
De Angelis, Gessica 233, 245
De Houwer, Annick 46, 88, 330, 358, 503, 546
De Jong, Nivja H. 88
Deanović, Mirko 386, 398
Delić, Dragana 80, 98
Dell'Aquila, Vittorio 228, 245
Demirçay, Derya 34, 50, 86, 88
Desideri, Paola 358
Dewaele, Jean-Marc 281, 622
Dieser, Elena 185
Diklić, Olga 362, 399
Dimitrijević-Savić, Jovana 423–424, 440–441
Dixon, Robert 70, 86
Djuric, Ivana 408, 441
Dobos, Balázs 114, 181
Doleschal, Ursula 88, 251, 280
Doria, Mario 365, 369, 373, 398
Dorian, Nancy C. 228, 245
Dorleijn, Margreet 63, 86, 271, 279, 335, 357, 374, 396, 398, 478, 483, 516, 545, 574, 589, 617, 622
Doucet, Jacques 80, 88, 498, 546
Dragicevich, Kaye 80, 88, 553, 589

Dressler, Wolfgang 523, 546
Drettas, George 179
Drpić, Irena 325, 333, 358, 371, 398
Dryer, Matthew 70, 88
Dubinina, Irina 44, 88
Dunbar, Robert 260, 281

Đuravonić, Vlasta 99

Ďurovič, Ľubomír 80, 90, 97, 289–290, 303, 313–314, 348–349, 356, 358, 382, 385–386, 398, 465, 470, 482, 484, 523–526, 543, 546, 580, 588, 589, 653, 659

Edwards, John 447, 484
Edwards, Malcolm 67, 89

Faarlund, Jan T. 289, 314
Fairchild, Sarah 627, 659
Fairclough, Marta 14, 25, 990
Fenyvesi, Anna 13–14, 25, 90, 173, 183, 543, 546
Field, Frederic 15, 25, 29, 36, 54, 57, 89, 395, 398, 568, 589, 620, 622
Filiaci, Francesca 490, 485
Filipović, Rudolf 30, 50, 78, 89, 405, 409, 442, 447, 484, 508–509, 546, 553, 568, 589, 604, 621–622
Finka, Božidar 87, 104, 179–180, 182
Finka, Jasna 87, 180
Fishman, Joshua A. 9, 25, 29, 49, 89, 406–407, 442, 458–459, 484, 601, 622
Fitzgibbons, Natalia 539, 546
Flecken, Monique 43, 90
Föglein, Gizella 113, 182
Fonollosa, Marie-Odile 548
Franceschini, Rita 257, 280
Frančić, Anđela 86
Frankovics, György 110, 112, 179
Franks, Steven 146, 168, 182
Friberg, Ann Christin 80, 90
Friedman, Victor A. VII, IX, 17, 70–71, 90, 187–188, 190–195, 198, 202, 205, 208–209
Fuchs, Zuzanna 179, 185
Fuller, Janet 52, 75, 90, 627, 659

Gačić, Jasna 572, 589
Gadže, Paula 598, 623
Gafaranga, Joseph 177, 182
Gagnon, Lucie 548
Gal, Susan 29, 90, 117, 182
Gallis, Arne 295, 308, 314
Galović, Filip 416, 442
Gardner-Chloros, Penelope 54–55, 67, 89–90
Garrett, Peter 330, 358
Garza, Anel 14, 25
Gasiński, Thaddeus 57, 59–60, 63, 79, 90, 405–406, 433, 436, 442, 621, 623
Genevska-Hanke, Dobrinka 43, 92
Gertken, Libby 43, 90
Giles, Howard 329, 358, 601, 623
Gillam, Ronald B. 357
Glovacki-Bernardi, Zrinjka 30, 54, 90, 217, 245
Gołąb, Zbigniew 188, 191, 194, 197, 209
Goldbach, Alexandra 176–177, 182, 646, 659
Goldberg, Adele 160, 182
Goldstein, Ivo 30, 86
Golubović, Biljana 30, 90
Gordon, Elizabeth 573, 589
Gorjanac, Živko 110, 115, 124, 182
Goss, Emily 512, 546
Granic, Stan 451, 484
Grahovac-Pražić, Vesna 79, 86
Grbić, Jadranka 113, 182 see also Grbić Jakopović, Jadranka
Grbić Jakopović, Jadranka 251, 253, 280 see also Grbić, Jadranka
Greene, Kai 357
Greenberg, Robert 8, 25
Gregor, Esma 176, 182
Grković-Major, Jasmina 70, 90, 91
Grosjean, François 45, 90, 341, 358
Gross, Steven 233, 243, 245
Grošelj, Robert 70, 90
Grotzky, Johannes 91, 90
Gruber, Barbara 251, 253, 255, 280
Grubišić, Vinko 450, 484
Guazzelli, Francesca 358
Gumperz, John J. 270, 280
Gürel, Ayşe 285, 289, 314
Gvozdanović, Jadranka 68, 75, 81, 90
Győrvári, Gábor 131, 182
Gyurok, János 114, 182

Hadrovics, László 30, 90, 105, 159–162, 183
Hakuta, Kenji 314
Halmari, Helen 51, 90
Hamp, Eric P. 191, 197, 207, 209
Hansen, Björn 65–67, 69, 81, 90, 217, 242, 245, 475, 484
Harley, Heidi 544, 546
Harwood, Jake 329, 358
Haspelmath, Martin 36, 74, 91, 202, 211
Hasselmo, Nils 62, 91
Haugen, Einar 40, 46, 91, 285, 314, 395, 398, 447, 617, 623
Haukioja, Jussi 290, 314
Hay, Jennifer 573, 589
He, Agnes Weiyun 627, 659
Heath, Jeffrey 507, 546
Heine, Bernd 32, 35, 51, 65, 70–72, 74, 91, 172, 183, 197, 210, 619, 623
Herbert, Robert 523, 546
Hergovich, Katalin 110, 114, 183
Hinrichs, Ljiljana 198, 210
Hinrichs, Uwe 198, 210
Hlavac, Jim III, IX-XI, 1, 19, 21, 23, 29, 46, 51, 53, 58–59, 61–63, 66, 80, 91, 120–122, 125–126, 128, 130, 133, 135, 137, 143, 150–151, 159, 165, 175, 183, 188, 190, 194, 197, 210, 235–237, 240, 243, 245, 255, 264, 266, 270, 273, 275–278, 280, 319, 326, 329, 335, 337, 344, 348–351, 353, 358, 376–378, 385–386, 390, 393, 395, 398, 405, 410, 415, 422, 430, 442, 453, 457–463, 465–467, 471–472, 475, 477, 480–482, 484, 493–494, 496–499, 508, 510, 513, 515, 517, 521–523, 526, 546–547, 553, 566–567, 569–571, 573, 575, 580, 583, 589, 605, 612, 615, 617–618, 621–623, 627, 635, 650, 653, 656, 659
Hornstein Tomić, Caroline 223, 245
Houtzagers, Peter VII, 104, 106, 110, 112, 150, 183
Hraste, Mate 565, 589
Hržica, Gordana 83, 91
Hudeček, Lana 86
Husband, Charles 254, 280
Hymes, Dell 48, 91

Iannaccaro, Gabriele 228, 548
Iannacito, Roberta 189, 192, 200, 210
Ilievski, Petar 187, 193, 210
Isurin, Ludmila 9, 25, 383, 398, 655, 659
Itkonen, Esa 290, 314, 546
Ivanova-Sullivan, Tanya 383, 398, 655, 659
Ivezić, Zoran 80, 95
Ivić, Milka 292, 314
Ivić, Pavle 31–32, 88, 303, 314, 470, 484

Jake, 92 nice 50, 52, 75, 91, 94, 187, 210–211, John, 233, 243, 245, 629, 637, 641, 659
Jakich, Miranda 80, 91, 554, 589–590
Jakobson, Roman 923, 547
Janda, Laura 290–291, 293–295, 303, 305–309, 311–312, 314
Janković-Kramarić, Judita Florentina 554–555, 590
Japirko, Hrvoje 67, 95, 517, 548
Jašar-Nasteva, Olivera 205, 210
Jazidžija, Antonia 33, 98
Jeftić, Nadežda 81, 95
Jelaska, Zrinka 83, 88, 503, 546 see also Babić, Zrinka
Jelicich, Stephen 553, 555, 557, 563, 590
Jensen, John 13, 26
Jernej, Josip 611, 623
Jessner-Schmid, Ulrike 233, 245
Johanson, Lars 49, 51–52, 54–55, 64–65, 67, 92, 292, 314
John, Michael 253, 280
Joseph, Brian D. 187, 190–194, 202, 209–210
Joshi, Aravind 52, 92
Jurčević, Katica 223, 245
Juričić, Želimir B. 448, 484, 546
Jurić, Tado 221, 245
Jurišić, Šimun 362, 398
Jutronić, Dunja X, 20, 58, 78, 92, 126, 147, 170, 175, 194, 197, 275–276, 296, 335, 350, 353, 378, 381, 386, 390, 405, 409, 416, 442, 447, 449, 465–466, 471–475, 477, 485, 519, 536, 554, 560, 565–568, 575–576, 581–583, 587, 590, 605 see also Jutronić-Tihomirović, Dunja

Jutronić-Tihomirović, Dunja 2, 25, 31, 50, 58, 65, 78, 92, 356, 405–406, 411, 442, 447, 470, 485, 508, 547, 548, 553–554, 588, 590, 652, 659 see also Jutronić, Dunja

Kagan, Olga 40, 88, 503, 547
Kahl, Thede 188, 210
Kan, Seda 88
Kanajet Šimić, Lada 83, 88, 503, 546
Kapović, Mate 70, 92, 97
Karall, Kristina 33, 92, 105, 183
Karan, Marc E. 331, 358
Karlsson, Fred 440, 442
Kaštropil, Ivo 565, 590
Katičić, Radoslav 537, 547
Kaufman, Terrence 15, 26, 29, 33–34, 38, 49, 66, 97, 187, 211, 461, 487
Kenesei, Istvan 173, 183
Kerecsényi, Edit 112, 183
Kess, Joseph, F. 298, 314, 448, 484
Kežić, Marin 67, 95, 517, 548
Kinda-Berlaković, Andrea Zorka 107, 184 see also Kinda-Berlaković, Zorka
Kinda-Berlaković, Zorka 87, 179, 186 see also Kinda-Berlaković, Andrea Zorka
Kinder, John 135, 184
King, Tracy 168, 182
Kipp, Sandra 14, 25
Kiss, Katalin É. 169, 173, 184
Kitanics, Máté VII, 111, 184
Klaić, Bratoljub 30, 54, 92, 334, 358
Klarić, don Ante 553, 590
Klatter-Folmer, Jetske 13, 25
Kolaković, Zrinka 69, 81, 90, 475, 484
Köpke, Barbara 43, 92, 285, 289–291, 311, 315
Koschat, Helene 184
Koschat, Jelka 87, 105, 179, 186
Kosnick, Kira 254, 280
Kostić, Đorđe 525, 547
Koufogiorgiou, Andromahi 188, 210
Kresić, Marijana 81, 92, 217, 233, 245 see also Kresić Vukosav, Marijana
Kresić Vukosav, Marijana IX, 1, 18, 118, 121, 129, 133, 217, 223, 245, 320, 335 see also Kresić, Marijana

Krle, Risto 203, 210
Kroon, Sjaak 13, 25
Krpina, Zdravka 323, 358, 363, 399
Kunzmann-Müller, Barbara 275, 280
Kupisch, Tanja 41, 92
Kuteva, Tania 32, 35, 51, 65, 70–72, 74, 91, 172, 183, 197, 210, 619, 633
Kuzmić, Ludvig 87, 185, 193

Laakso, Johanna 228, 246
Labov, William 92, 189–190, 210, 371, 399
Laleko, Oksana 396, 399
Lalich, Walter 499, 547
Lan, Xiao 93, 358
Langacker, Ronald 290–293, 312, 314
Lange, Deborah 515, 548
Langenthal, Péter 110, 184
Langston, Keith 8, 25
Lanza, Elizabeth 330, 358, 503, 547
Lasić, Josip 82, 92
Ledgeway, Adam 192, 210
Lehnert, Heike 627, 659
Lenček, Rado 405, 442
Leung, Constant 48, 92
Levelt, Willem 299, 314
Levine, G. 41, 92
Li, Wei 29, 92, 344, 358, 606, 622
Lichtblau, Albert 253, 280
Lie, Svein 289, 314
Lindstedt, Jouko 35–37, 70, 93, 188, 210
Lisac, Josip 7, 25, 31, 93, 416, 442
Livert, David 43, 94, 471, 485
Lončarić, Mijo 87, 144, 179–180, 184, 186, 313, 325, 333, 358, 371, 398, 417, 442, 545
Lourie, Margaret A. 563, 589
Lucas, Christopher 42, 70–71, 93
Lukenda, Marko 87, 180, 281

Ljubešić, Marta 81–82, 93, 217, 222, 246
Ljubičić, Maslina 30, 93, 369, 399

Maclagan, Margaret 91, 573, 589
MacSwan, Jeff 52, 93
Magner, Thomas 79, 93, 405, 442, 447, 485, 565, 568, 575, 583, 590
Magnusson, Kjell 81, 93

Mahootian, Shahrzad 52, 93
Makarova, Anastasia 163, 181
Malić, Dragica 313, 545
Mamić, Mile 87, 180
Mandić, Živko 115, 184
Manfredi, Stefano 14, 25
Maretić, Tomo 198–199, 201, 210
Maschler, Yael 512, 547
Masica, Colin 190, 194, 210
Maslov, Yurij 76–77, 93
Matovac, Darko 198, 208, 281, 350, 357, 544–545, 618–619, 622
Matras, Yaron II, 64–65, 72, 93, 127, 131, 162, 175, 184, 206, 210, 263, 278, 281, 462, 485, 512, 594, 604–606, 608, 610, 615–616, 620, 623
Menac-Mihalić, Mira 87, 180
Mesarić Žabčić, Rebeka 494, 499, 547
Michaelis, Susanne Maria 36, 74, 91
Miestamo, Matti 440, 442
Mihaljević, Milan 81, 93
Mihaljević, Milica 86
Mikić, Gizela 81, 88, 251, 280
Milivojević, Dragan 79, 93
Miller, Jim 514, 547
Mills, Jean 9, 25
Minkov, Miriam 185
Moguš, Milan 7, 26, 31, 93
Mohl, Adolf 103, 184
Moin, Victor 185
Montgomery, Keith 548, 558, 561, 563, 590
Montrul, Silvina 14, 26, 39, 41, 43–45, 68, 87, 93–94, 179–180, 184, 285, 289, 303, 314, 415, 438, 443, 471, 485
Moring, Tom 260, 281
Mösch, Matthias 239, 246
Mønnesland, Svein 72–73, 81, 93, 539, 547
Mrazović, Pavica 81, 94
Mufwene, Salikoko S. 207, 210
Muhvić-Dimanovski, Vesna 79, 94, 617, 623
Muljačić, Željko 416, 443
Musulin, Maša XI, 22, 128, 165, 198, 235–236, 243, 270, 273, 335, 337, 376–377, 462, 480–481, 510, 515–516, 531, 566, 569, 571, 573, 595, 617, 623

Muysken, Pieter 15–16, 25–26, 41, 52, 55, 61, 63, 86, 94, 217, 246, 395, 399, 457, 485, 566, 590
Myers-Scotton, Carol XI, 15, 23, 26, 29, 34, 38–39, 42, 50–53, 60, 64–66, 70, 75, 77, 91, 94, 137, 184, 187, 210–211, 233, 235, 237, 243, 245–246, 263–264, 281, 343–344, 358, 456, 462, 485, 510, 548, 585, 590, 604–606, 623, 627–631, 636–637, 639, 641–642, 647–648, 650–651, 656, 659

Nagy, Naomi 548
Nagy, Sabine 103, 184
Nejašmić, Ivica 9, 26, 219, 246
Neweklowsky, Gerhard 33, 87, 94, 104–105, 107, 163, 179, 184,186
Newlin-Łukowicz, Luiza 9, 26
Novak, Kristian 33, 94
Núñez Méndez, Eva 14, 26
Nyomárkay, István 33, 94

Olesch, Reinhold 565, 589
Orlović, Marija 80, 98
Otheguy, Ricardo 43, 94–95, 471, 485
O'Shannessy, Carmel 74, 95

Øverland, Orm 406, 443

Pahor, Milan 362, 399
Papahagi, Pericli N. 205, 211
Parovel, Paolo G. 361, 399
Pátrovics, Péter 161–162, 185
Pauwels, Anne 43, 49, 95, 459–460, 485, 497, 549
Pavešić, Slavko 313, 545
Pavičić, Josip 163, 185
Pavlinić, Andrina 81–82, 95 see also Pavlinić-Wolf, Andrina
Pavlinić-Wolf, Andrina 58, 80–81, 95 see also Pavlinić, Andrina
Pawischitz, Sabine 116, 185
Peña, Elizabeth D. 357
Piccoli, Giovanni, the following author:
Pires, Acrisio 41, 88, 96
Pereltsvaig, Asya 77, 95, 357–358
Perinić, Ana 205, 211

Perpiñán, Silvia 290–291, 314
Perta, Carmela 358
Pescarini, Diego 192–193, 211
Peša Matracki, Ivica 142, 185
Peti, Mirko 313, 545
Peti-Stantić, Anita 8, 25, 67, 95, 517, 548
Petrović, Bernadina 150, 186
Petrović, Ivana X, 1, 21, 46, 79, 95, 126, 128, 165, 170, 194, 198, 235–236, 243, 270, 273, 275–276, 393, 337, 340, 349, 353, 376–379, 385, 415, 419, 422, 447–448, 485, 516, 523, 531, 533, 566, 569, 580, 605, 617–618
Petrović, Velimir 33, 95–96
Piasevoli, Vesna X, 1, 19–20, 120, 122, 130, 137, 143, 147, 159, 165, 170, 175, 188, 194, 197–198, 235–236, 240, 243, 270, 273, 277, 319, 322, 324–325, 335, 337, 345, 349–353, 361, 363, 386, 390, 393, 399, 415, 462, 465, 471, 477, 480–481, 508, 515–516, 523, 531, 566, 569, 573, 580, 583, 605, 617–618, 656
Piccoli, Agostina 119, 181, 185, 205, 211
Piccoli, Giovanni 33, 88, 119, 181
Pires, Acrisio 41, 96
Piškorec, Velimir 33, 94
Pišković, Tanja 145, 150, 185
Podgorelec, Sonja 99
Polinsky, Maria 16, 26, 40, 42–45, 53, 68, 70, 74, 85, 87–88, 95–96, 179–180, 185, 289–290, 303, 315, 357, 359, 378–379, 393, 396–397, 399, 411, 415, 422, 438, 443, 471–473, 475, 482, 485, 543–544, 548, 656, 660
Poplack, Shana 51, 54, 96, 263–264, 281
Potowski, Kim 14, 26
Pranjković, Ivo 7, 25, 93, 163, 172, 185
Price, Charles 494, 548
Protassova, Ekaterina 185
Prpić, George Jure 8, 26, see also Prpić, Jure
Prpić Jure 406, 443 see also Prpić, George Jure
Putnam, Michael 41, 96
Rácz, Erika 110, 112, 115, 934, 127, 144–145, 148, 155–157, 162, 174, 185

Raecke, Jochen 65–66, 81, 96, 217, 246, 274, 281
Rasporich, Anthony, W. 449, 485
Récatas, Basile 188, 211
Resendiz, Maria D. 357
Rešetar, Milan VI, 33, 96, 109, 185
Riehl, Claudia Maria 264, 281
Ritter, Elizabeth 544, 546
Roca, Ana 13, 26
Romaine, Suzanne 162, 185, 515, 548
Romić, Daniel 69, 81, 90, 475, 484
Ronelle, Alexander 86, 483, 589
Ross, Malcolm 70, 96
Rothman, Jason 40–41, 44, 92, 96
Rott, Julian 217, 246
Rotter, Ivan 87, 107, 179, 185–186
Runje, Maja 81, 96
Runjić-Stoilova, Anita 416, 442
Rutkowski, Paweł 538, 548
Ryan, Camille 407, 443

Sakel, Jeanette 131, 175, 184
Salmons, Joe 512, 548 see also Salmons, Joseph
Salmons, Joseph 14, 25, 512, 546 see also Salmons, Joe
Samardžija, Marko 7, 25, 93
Sammartino, Anton100 33, 96, 110, 119, 185, 192, 194, 201, 211
Sankoff, David 263–264, 281
Sankoff, Gillian 514, 548
Sánchez, Liliana 41, 96
Sarhimaa, Anneli 246
Sarić, Daliborka 70, 97
Sasse, Hans-Jürgen 227, 232, 297
Savić, Jelena 415, 423, 439, 443
Savić, Svenka 295, 315
Schäfer, Florian 97, 533, 545
Schallert, Joseph 196, 211
Schatz, Henriette 566, 590
Schiffrin, Deborah 514, 548
Schmid, Monika 45, 96, 285, 289–291, 311, 315, 410, 443
Schmitt, Elena 53, 96, 627, 660
Schöler, Hermann 82, 93
Scholze, Lenka 124, 179, 181, 974

Schumann, John H. 223, 246
Schütze, Fritz 257, 281
Schwartz, Mila 179, 185
Scontras, Gregory 42, 45, 70, 74, 85, 96, 179, 185, 289–290, 315
Scotti, Giacomo 33, 96
Sebba, Mark 51, 96
Sedlaczek, Robert 256, 281
Sekulić, Ante 87, 180
Sekulić, Duško 79, 100
Seliger, Herbert 289, 315
Serratrice, Ludovica 415, 443, 471, 485
Seršić, Josip 251–253, 281
Sevinç, Yeşim 34, 50, 86
Sharwood-Smith, Michael 290, 315
Silić, Jos 97–98, 172, 185, 618, 623
Silva-Corvalán, Carmen 41, 43, 97, 471, 485
Sinnemaki, Kaius 440, 442
Sinovčić, Marko 595–597, 623
Skaaden, Hanne X, 19, 81, 97, 285, 289–292, 294–296, 302–304, 306, 308, 310–312, 315
Skelin Horvat, Anita XI, 1, 22, 128, 165, 198, 235–236, 243, 270, 273, 335, 337, 376–377, 462, 480–481, 510, 515–516, 531, 566, 569, 571, 573, 595, 617, 623
Skok, Petar 126, 185, 611, 623
Smith, Daniel 627, 660
Sobolev, Andrey 70, 97
Sočanac, Lelija 30, 97, 376, 386, 393–394, 399
Sohler, Karin 254, 281
Sokcsevits, Dénes 110, 112, 179
Sopta, Marin 221, 245, 451, 485
Sorace, Antonella 471, 485
Spicijarić Paškvan, Nina 33, 97
Spiliopoulou Åkermark, Sia 246
Sridhar, Kamal 52, 97
Sridhar, Shirakipur 52, 97
Stankovski, Miodrag 80, 97
Starčević, Anđel 60–61, 69–70, 79, 97, 448, 486, 540, 548
Stevanović, Mihajlo 198, 211
Stoffel, Hans-Peter XI, 2, 21–22, 26, 58, 60, 79, 97–98, 126, 128, 150, 190, 235–237, 243, 270, 273, 275–277, 335, 337, 349, 376, 378, 422, 430, 462, 465, 472, 480, 510, 515, 517, 523, 553–554, 558, 560–563, 565, 567, 570–572, 576–577, 579, 581, 583, 585, 589, 590–591, 605, 612, 615, 617, 650, 656
Stojanović, Ilija 80, 98, 217, 247
Stojak, Marina 253, 281
Stojić, Aneta 217, 247
Stolac, Diana III, IX-X, 1, 21, 80, 98, 126, 128, 151, 159, 165, 175, 197, 235–236, 243, 270, 273, 275, 335, 337, 349–351, 353, 376–377, 385–386, 390, 393, 405, 415, 462, 465, 471, 475, 480–481, 493, 499, 539–540, 548, 566, 569–570, 573, 575, 580, 583, 605, 612, 615, 617–618, 656
Stölting, Wilfried 59, 80, 98, 217, 247 see also Stölting-Richert, Wilfried
Stölting-Richert, Wilfried 80, 98 see also Stölting, Wilfried 99, 549
Strčić, Petar 361–362, 399
Striedter-Temps, Hildegard 30, 97
Sučić, Ivo 87, 105, 1008, 167, 179, 186 see also Szucsich, Ivo
Summers, Connie L. 357
Surdučki, Milan 57, 59, 63–64, 78, 98, 448, 487, 508, 548, 554, 567, 569, 571, 591
Sussex, Roland 580, 591
Svendsen, Bente 503, 547
Szilágyi, József 186
Szucsich, Ivo 87, 180 see al 99 Sučić, Ivo
Szucsich, Luka 140–141, 159–160, 186

Šabec, Nada 453, 487
Šakić, Vlado 221, 245
Šarić, Ljiljana 293–294, 307–308, 312, 315
Ščukanec, Aleksandra 992, 17–18, 97, 99, 101, 105, 107, 118, 121, 129, 133, 175, 186, 189, 197, 199–200, 202, 235, 241, 243, 251, 319–320, 335, 337, 376, 386, 430, 462, 480, 508, 516, 527, 529, 540, 566, 569, 617, 656
Šimičić, Lucija IX, 1, 18, 118, 121, 129, 133, 217, 228, 247, 320, 335
Šimundić, Mate 54, 98, 565, 591
Šimunović, Petar 565, 589, 591

Šipka, Danko 407, 409, 443
Škaljić, Abdulah 30, 98
Škara, Danica 79, 98
Škevin, Ivana 33, 98
Škvorc, Boris 63, 80, 99, 498, 549
Šojat, Antun 87, 179–180
Šojat, Ljerka 87, 180
Šporer, Željka 79, 100
Šprljan, Cristian 595–597, 624
Šutalo, Ilija 493, 495, 498–499, 549
Švob, Melita 82, 99

Tadmor, Uri 202, 211
Tamaskó, Eszter 110, 113–114, 186
Tannen, Deborah 53, 99
Tannenbaum, Michal 49, 99
Tarantini, Angela VII
Taylor, Bradley 202, 211
Taylor, Donald 601, 623
Thibault, Pierrette 548
Thomason, Sarah VI, 14–15, 26, 29, 33–38, 49, 51–52, 57, 66, 99, 187, 211, 455–456, 461, 464, 483, 487, 507, 549
Thüne, Eva-Maria 223, 245
Tkalčević, Mato 494, 498, 549
Toivanen, Reetta 246
Tomašević, Mijo 80, 97, 99
Tomelić-Ćurlin, Marijana 416, 422
Toribio, Almeida Jacqueline 237, 245
Tornow, Siegfried 160, 186
Tosco, Mauro 14, 25
Treffers-Daller, Jeanine 43, 54, 97, 99
Trlin, Andrew 553, 555, 557, 563, 590–591
Trubetzkoy, Nikolai S. 187, 202, 211
Trudgill, Peter 70, 99
Turk, Marija 30, 99, 516, 549
Türker, Emel 75, 99, 285, 315

Udier, Sanda Lucija 353, 359, 415, 443
Uldrijan, Ivan 408, 443

Vago, Robert M. 173, 183, 289, 315
Valdés, Guadalupe 40, 99
Valentić, Mirko 103, 186
van Buren, Paul 290, 315
Van Coetsem, Frans 36, 49, 99

van der Heijden, Hanneke 396, 398
Van Hell, Janet 627, 659
Van Hout, Roeland 395, 399
Vannebo, Kjell I. 289, 314
Vascotto, Patrizia 363, 399
Vellupillai, Viveka 74, 99
Veltman, Calvin 458, 487
Verschik, Anna 35, 55, 99
Vidmarović, Đuro 113, 186
Vidoeski, Božidar 194, 211
Vince, Zlatko 7, 26
Vlastelić, Anastazija 499, 540, 548
Vlasits, Josef 87, 179–180 *see also* Vlašić, Joško
Vlašić, Joško 87, 179, 186 *see also* Vlasits, Josef
Vranić, Silvana 416, 444
Vuk, Dora IX, 17, 101, 113–114, 123, 145, 155, 186, 189, 197, 199–200, 202, 235, 241, 243, 251, 319, 430, 527, 529, 540
Vuletić, Nikola 228, 247
Vulić, Sanja 87, 150, 179, 186

Wackernagel, Jakob 192, 415, 444
Wahlström, Max 199-100, 197, 211
Waldrauch, Harald 254, 281
Ward, Charles 58–59, 79, 99, 405, 444
Wasserscheidt, Philipp 160, 1001, 186
Weilguni, Werner 33, 99
Weinreich, Uriel 100, 35, 50, 99, 410, 413, 444
Wiley, Edward 314
Winford, Donald 15, 26, 36, 54, 57, 62–63, 99–100, 447, 487
Winland, Daphne N. 217, 247
Winter, Jo 497, 549
Woods, Anya 254, 281
Woolford, Ellen 51, 100
Wurzel, Wolfgang 523, 549

Xingjia Shen, Rachel 179

Yıldız, Cemal 88
Yılmaz, Gülsen 285, 289–290, 311, 314–315
Zečević, Vesna 313, 545
Zentella, Ana Celia 43, 94–95, 471, 485

Znika, Marija 87, 179–180, 186, 313, 545
Zubčić, Sanja 82, 100, 405, 444
Zvonarich, Stefan 87, 179–180

Žagar-Szentesi, Orsolya 30, 100
Žepić, Stanko 264, 281
Živković, Ilija 79, 100

Županović Filipin, Nada X, 19, 120, 122, 130, 137, 142–143, 159, 175, 185, 188, 194, 197, 235–236, 240, 243, 270, 277, 319, 326, 359, 386, 390, 393, 415, 462, 465, 471, 477, 508, 515, 523, 566, 569, 573, 580, 583, 656